POLITICS AND SOCIETY IN PROVINCIAL RUSSIA:
SARATOV, 1590-1917

Politics and Society in Provincial Russia: Saratov, 1590–1917

Edited by *Rex A. Wade and Scott J. Seregny*

Ohio State University Press

COLUMBUS

Library of Congress Cataloging-in-Publication Data

Politics and society in provincial Russia : Saratov, 1590–1917 /
edited by Rex A. Wade and Scott J. Seregny.
p.   cm.
Includes bibliographical references.
ISBN 0-8142-0494-5 (alk. paper)
1. Saratovskaia oblast (R.S.F.S.R.)—History. 2. Saratov
(R.S.F.S.R.)—History. I. Wade, Rex A. II. Seregny, Scott Joseph.
DK511.S3P65   1989
947'.85—dc20   89-36185
CIP

The paper in this book meets the guidelines for permanence and
durability of the Committee on Production Guidelines for Book
Longevity of the Council on Library Resources.

Printed in the U.S.A.

9 8 7 6 5 4 3 2 1

Contents

Illustrations

Preface

THIS BOOK had its origins in the individual research projects of the authors, each of whom was drawn to the study of Saratov by its rich history and source materials. Credit for the initial concept of the project belongs to Thomas Fallows, Timothy Mixter, and Donald Raleigh. The editors took up the project later and brought the participants together at a conference held in the summer of 1985 at Urbana, Illinois, funded by a grant from the National Endowment for the Humanities, and sponsored by the Center for Russian and East European Studies at the University of Illinois. Preparation of the manuscript for publication was supported by the National Endowment for the Humanities and the University of Hawaii Foundation. We wish to express our appreciation to each of these institutions for their support.

We also want to thank our colleagues in this endeavor, the contributors, for their cooperation, patience, and good humor. In the effort to make a more cohesive volume, we asked most of them to make changes in their original essays, which sometimes involved extensive new research and writing in order to bridge gaps. Their cheerful willingness to do so has made this volume a truly cooperative venture.

Many institutions and individuals have assisted the editors and the various authors; regretfully, they are too numerous to name. The editors would like, however, to give special thanks to Janet Agena for her cheerful and invaluable help throughout. They would also like to thank Alex Holzman of Ohio State University Press for his strong support and interest in Saratov.

All dates follow the Old Style calendar, which in the nineteenth century was twelve days and in the twentieth century thirteen days behind the Western calendar. Spelling is a simplified version of the Library of Congress transliteration system, but names and words with a common English spelling are used in the latter form (Soviet, Plehve, Alexander). In the text, soft-signs are omitted for all Russian terms except where they occur in the middle of personal names; strict transliteration is adhered to in the notes and bibliographical materials.

R.A.W. and S.J.S.

Map I. Districts and District Towns
Inset: Saratov Province within European Russia

SARATOV PROVINCE

Annenkovo •   KUZNETSK

Urleika •
Spassko–Aleksandrovskoe •
Plan •

Nikolaevka •   Lopatino •

Ershovka •

KHVALYNSK

Khovanshchina •

Bekovo •

SERDOBSK

PETROVSK

VOLSK

Makarovo •
Rtishchevo
Mikhailovka • Sestrenki •
Malinovka   Berezovka •
Teplovka •
Bulgakovka •

Krasnoiar •
Sokur •   Irinovka •
Sukhoi
Karbulak •

Trubetskoe •
Turki •   Arkadak •

Idolga •

ATKARSK

Volga R.

Romanovka •

Balanda •
Nikolaevskii
Gorodok •
SARATOV

BALASHOV •   Ivanovka 2 •

Pokrovskaia
Sloboda

Sinenkie •

Kazachka •

Samoilovka •
Medvedevka •
Mordovo •

Nizhnaia
Dobrinka •

Elan •
Verkhniaia
Dobrinka •

KAMYSHIN

Salamatino •

Volga R.

Olkhovka •
Kamennyi
Brod •

Dubovka •

TSARITSYN

Map 2. Villages and Railroads

1. Saratov as Russian History

Scott J. Seregny and Rex A. Wade

AT THE turn of the last century the British traveler Henry Norman emerged from his "large and verminous cabin" aboard a Russian steamship moving down the Volga River to survey the surrounding country from the deck. To Norman's right lay an "uninterrupted bluff worn steep by geologic time," dotted here and there by a village clinging to the mudcolored slope; this was Saratov Province. Soon the city of Saratov came into sight. "Its center is a mass of red brick buildings, and on each flank is a long suburb of wooden houses, tailing out at last to a fringe of poverty. High white churches with green roofs are dotted over the city, and all the wide main streets fall precipitously to the water's edge at a right angle, looking at a distance more like streams than roads." Norman commented on the busy river traffic, pronounced the city "quaint," and moved on.[1] Those travelers who did stop, however, noted that Saratov was a bustling provincial center, although few cared to inquire in depth about what human activity was occurring in its dusty streets and within its public and private structures, much less about life in the villages that lay beyond the bluff of the Volga's right bank.

Nearly a century later this task has been undertaken by a dozen scholars from across the globe. Independently, each noticed the vitality of Saratov, as well as the opportunity it presented to provide a fresh perspective on significant questions of Russian history. They have come together in this book to examine the social and political movements that developed in this Volga province and to explore how these can shed light on the broader trends of Russian history, especially the last half-century of the Old Regime.

The history of Russia has been studied almost exclusively from the perspective of its two capitals, Moscow and St. Petersburg, leavened only slightly by studies of some of Imperial Russia's national minority regions and a few works dealing with narrow time periods or specialized topics. Conspicuously absent are broad studies of the Great Russian regions. This is a curious omission, not only because it is the population group from these areas which formed the foundation of the modern Russian state (and of the contemporary Soviet Union), but because both supporters and opponents of the Old Regime realized that it was here that the battle for Russia's future would be waged and won. Indeed, it was control of this Russian heartland that provided the base from which the Bolsheviks would fight and win the Civil War. We need to know more about this vast Russian countryside and its numerous cities and regions. Detailed study of even one such province allows us to test whether interpretations based primarily on the two capitals hold for the Great Russian heartland and country as a whole. Indeed, may not study of the provinces offer new perspectives on and alter our understanding of developments in Moscow and St. Petersburg? The relationship between capital and province was, after all, a dynamic and interactive one. We believe that an in-depth study of a locality is an important way to grasp historical reality in all its complexity and thereby to test broad generalizations; for our understanding of the history of Russia and the Soviet Union, such an in-depth look at a Great Russian locality is both especially important—and long overdue.

Saratov seems a particularly fruitful choice for such a study. It was a predominantly Great Russian province (76.7 percent) but contained significant enclaves of Ukrainians and non-Slavic ethnic groups. Saratov was a major producer of grain and other foodstuffs but also boasted a dynamic urban sector. It shared the broad social, economic, and political features, problems, and development typical of the Russian Empire of this era. Although no place can be claimed to be absolutely representative of the entire country, Saratov City and Province, with their rich and varied social and political life, provide us with a reasonable microcosm of the issues and tensions facing Imperial and revolutionary Russia. Moreover, as there are unusually good source materials over a long period, Saratov appears to be a good subject for such a study.

Saratov was an important frontier area for two centuries, typifying the problems of state expansion, agricultural settlement, and developing commercial activity during the seventeenth and eighteenth centuries. Its open land and forest lured religious dissidents, conscripts, and serfs fleeing the exactions of the Russian state and social order. The Saratov region also attracted the state and its servitors, whose efforts to replicate Muscovite social and political institutions on the frontier were repeatedly challenged by regional forces, the most famous being the Razin and Pugachev revolts, both of which swept through Saratov. With Pugachev's dying gasp the state finally consolidated its hold over this Volga periphery; but tension between center and frontier continued into the nineteenth and early twentieth centuries. Close examination of Saratov well reflects the state's effort to maintain the bases of the Old Regime during its last half-century as well as the local forces which both threatened and supported them. This book focuses on the latter period, from the 1860s to 1917, when Saratov came of age and began to play a significant role in the life of the country, making it suitable both for study in its own right and as a basis for comparison with other regions. Nevertheless, its frontier history and recent integration into the empire left a deep imprint on the later Imperial period.

Serfdom, that fundamental matrix of social and political relationships in Imperial Russia, came late to Saratov. Hence, the peasantry's collective memory incorporated the pre-serfdom past, which contributed to the oft-noted rebellious nature of the local population and sharpened agrarian relations. Indeed, Saratov, or more precisely its northwestern districts *(uezdy),* represented the extreme southeastern extension of gentry landholding and serf economy in the Russian Empire, the "last *pomeshchik* advance post."[7] Beyond this advance, in the southeastern districts with their sandier, less fertile soil, state peasants, Volga Germans, and various small holders and settlers predominated, and serfdom was less developed. The large and middling estates of Saratov Province were concentrated in the northwestern districts of Atkarsk, Balashov, Serbobsk, and Saratov, with their rich black earth *(chernozem)* and dense population. Serfdom and the social relations typical of the older Central Agricultural Region were replicated here, affecting agrarian relations beyond the Emancipation of 1861 and into the twentieth century. The area came to include pockets of market-oriented estates using machinery, advanced crop rotations, and migrant wage labor, but was dominated by peasant subsistence agriculture and gentry estates utilizing peasant tools and work animals, traditional crop rotations, and labor procured through exploitative leasing and sharecropping arrangements.

Some historians have recently questioned the existence of an "agrarian crisis" in late-nineteenth-century Russia, but many of its elements appear to have been present in Saratov's northwest districts. Peasant land hunger was intense and social and economic tensions acute, a situation aggravated by often precarious climatic conditions that brought drought and poor harvests with tragic regularity. It was in Saratov Province, after all, that Governor P. A. Stolypin identified the roots of Russia's agrarian crisis and the volatility of the communal peasantry, and went on to develop a reform agenda that later, as prime minister, he attempted to implement on the national level.

Despite the importance of peasant and agrarian issues, Saratov also developed into a bustling commercial and industrial center (the most developed and urbanized of the Volga provinces), with all the attendant problems. In this respect Saratov stands as an excellent example of what was transpiring across Russia during the late Imperial period. By 1861 Saratov City was a provincial capital of 69,000 inhabitants on the verge of rapid transformation. As an already thriving commercial center on the Volga, it served as an entrepôt for the processing and transshipment of the grain and other produce of its rich hinterland. Indeed, in 1862 one observer predicted a rosy future for Saratov as a major trading and manufacturing center and as a crossroads between Russia's central provinces and Central Asia, the Urals, and Siberia beyond.[3]

Such promise was quickly realized. The advent of steam power revolutionized river transport, rendering obsolete an army of 300,000 Volga boat haulers and ushering in steamship lines like the "Caucasus" and "Mercury" which seemed to symbolize the dawning age of iron, speed, and technological transformation. The coming of the first major rail link with Moscow in 1871, the Riazan-Urals Line, quickened the pulse of provincial life. By the 1880s railway spurs linked Saratov City with its district towns and larger market villages, intensifying agricultural production (and exploitation of peasant labor on gentry estates) and giving rise to new occupational groups like railway workers and employees who, by the turn of the century, would play an active role in local politics and social movements. Coming on the heels of the emancipation of the serfs, these developments speeded Saratov's transformation into a significant industrial center, which on the eve of World War I contained 190 factories, mostly small ones involved in food processing but also metalworking plants and related manufacturing. Saratov's industrial workers grew, accordingly, to over 13,000 in the early 1900s and about 25,000 in

1916. The city's total population increased dramatically, reaching 137,000 in 1897 (thus ranking it among the eleven cities of European Russia over 100,000) and 242,000 on the eve of the war. Within the Volga region Saratov's growth rate was only surpassed by its junior city to the south, Tsaritsyn (the future Stalingrad; Volgograd) a boom town of 80,000 by World War I.[4]

At the same time, Saratov grew into a vibrant cultural center, a magnet for the best and brightest from the entire mid-Volga region. By the end of the nineteenth century it was frequently referred to as "Athens on the Volga." The city possessed a creditable museum named after the famous critic of Catherinian Russia, Alexander Radishchev, a native son from Kuznetsk District. The Radishchev Museum, among other things, "boasted an unusually enlightened [art] collection for the time," and Saratov "was the chief provincial art centre in Russia at this time [late nineteenth century] up to the 1920's."[5] Primary and secondary schools in the city exceeded one hundred on the eve of the Great War, and in 1909 Saratov finally received a university, established initially as a medical faculty. Twelve publishing houses operated in the city, and five daily newspapers reported on local and national events. In the 1890s there were forty-two bookstores, which placed it on a par with Riga (46), Kiev (38), and Kharkov (23); St. Petersburg had 142. For those who could take advantage of it, Saratov in the early twentieth century offered some of the urbanity, comfort, and cultural sophistication of the capital cities.[6] Culture was also beginning to penetrate the countryside. By 1900 the Saratov provincial zemstvo had begun an impressive program of rural modernization and expansion of health, education, and other services, all publicized in its *Saratovskaia zemskaia nedelia* (Saratov Zemstvo Weekly), which gained a national reputation.

Saratov's rapid growth also spawned a host of problems, as occurred in other areas of the empire undergoing rapid development in the last decades of the tsarist regime. Sprawling suburban slums, noted by Henry Norman, spilled into the ravines at the base of the adjacent Sokolov Hill, outstripping the city's antiquated water system. Residents choked amid the clouds of dust whipped up from Saratov's streets, only one-quarter of which were paved; travelers approaching the city from the Volga often commented on the yellow dust cloud hovering over the city. Sanitary conditions were poor, factories primitive and unsafe, and the mortality rate (forty-four per thousand inhabitants) substantially higher than that in cities of central Russia. The changes and attendant problems placed added burdens on much of the peasant population and created new strains and challenges in the expanding urban sector. Peasant and worker unrest combined in the years preceding and during the Revolution of 1905–07 to make Saratov one of the most volatile provinces in the empire and its peasant movement the most destructive, evoking memories of the Pugachev rebellion.

These sources of unrest stirred the imaginations of Saratov's well-organized and articulate radical intelligentsia. The city's radical political culture also drew inspiration from a tradition that included N. G. Chernyshevskii and major Populists of the 1870s. With its lively society and culture, Saratov was favored by political exiles denied residence in St. Petersburg and Moscow, and thus veterans of the Populist trials of the "50" and the "193," as well as student radicals of the 1880s, helped Saratov pass on earlier radical traditions to the next generation. Indeed, a short list of Saratov radicals reads like a "Who's Who" of the Russian revolutionary movement: Vera Figner, Mark Natanson, Georgii Plekhanov, Viktor Chernov, Ekaterina Breshko-Breshkovskaia, Aleksei Rykov, and the worker Semen Kanatchikov, among others.[7]

Saratov's politics reflected a dynamic interaction between center and periphery. Russia's dominant agrarian party, the Socialist Revolutionaries (SRs), for example, traced many of its intellectual and organizational roots to the mid-Volga, Saratov in particular. Not only was Saratov a party stronghold, but the experience of local activists in the Saratov countryside convinced SRs at the national level of the revolutionary potential of the peasantry and the need to exert greater efforts in the villages.[8] In 1905 the tactic of a general political strike was first tested in Saratov and on the Riazan-Urals Railway, which ran through the city, and then emulated elsewhere in Russia.[9] As elsewhere, local SRs and Social Democrats took advantage of the appearance of new professional groups spawned by Russia's social and economic development between the Great Reforms of the 1860s and World War I. The zemstvo "Third Element," in particular, played a crucial role in political and social mobilization in the provinces, providing a critical link between the elite political culture and a mass constituency in both town and countryside. Given the absence of a university at the time, Saratov's radical intellectual life was dominated by zemstvo professionals. Doctors, statisticians, teachers, and others plunged into the ideological debates between Marxists and Populists in the 1890s and often provided cadres for penetration of the countryside by revolutionary parties; indeed, a Ministry of Interior survey of 1902 revealed that Saratov had the highest number of radical zemstvo employees in all of Russia, surpassing even Moscow Province.[10] One can see similar patterns in many of the thirty-four provinces of European Russia with zemstvo institutions, but they are etched particularly sharply in Saratov.

Politics, high or low, were not monopolized by the radical left. Local gentry were active in Saratov politics and helped set the agenda for both liberal and conservative political movements at the national level. Saratov zemstvo gentry played a prominent role in the Liberation Movement of the early 1900s and, in their efforts to forge an alliance with the radical intelligentsia and gain peasant support, helped move the nascent Russian liberal movement leftward in 1905. Saratov provided some of the most articulate spokesmen for the national post-1905 gentry reaction; the conservative political alliance forged by Peter Stolypin after 1906, the "June Third System," originated here. Thus, in Saratov we see early reflections of the polarizations among gentry and intelligentsia that soon took concrete form on the floor of the State Duma and in the organization of national political parties after 1905, processes in which *Saratovtsy* played a major role.

All of the political conflicts of late Imperial Russia swirled through Saratov. Local leaders, often on the brink of national prominence, joined with exiles and visiting figures from the capitals to fight, sometimes first in Saratov, the battles that shaped radical, liberal, and conservative movements in Russia. This process continued until 1917, when local adherents of the national parties—Bolsheviks, Mensheviks, SRs, and Kadets—fought for control of the strategic city and province. Examination of Saratov's often volatile political scene calls into question the conventional view that national developments were simply echoed and replicated in the provinces. The relationship between capitals and provinces was symbiotic. Not only did political activists move in both directions between Saratov and the metropolis, but party programs, as well as official government policies, were frequently shaped and transmuted at the local level, sometimes occasioning revision of policy at the national level. Equally important, Saratov's politics provide insights into the nature of local leadership and the processes of political mobilization in the locales, both relatively unexplored aspects of Russia's history.

Saratov and its hinterland clearly offered much more of interest than a casual visitor like Henry Norman could ever have imagined. Just a few years later an official report commented on its role in the 1905 revolution:

The city [of Saratov] has long been liberal, serving as the center for revolution-aries of a large region, and during the era of the "liberation movement" it stood in the first rank. Revolutionary organizations gathered strength and came out openly. Within city and zemstvo institutions there were quite a few people of extreme views, not to speak of the so-called Third Element. Even among the gentry, representatives of extremism showed their true colors (for example, Count Nessel'rode). Nowhere else did the agrarian disturbances manifest such force as in Saratov province. The city of Saratov and Saratov province sent to the State Duma deputies of the most radical tendency, "Trudoviki" such an Anikin, Zhilkin, Bondarev, Semenov, etc. The local press, especially its extreme liberal wing, after publication of the law on freedom of the press exceeded the limits of all decency: lies, insinuation and provocation became its distinguishing traits.[11]

The city's unimposing streets and the province's myriad rural settle-ments (forty-five hundred by one estimate) were clearly the scenes of intense social and political conflicts, struggles that ultimately contributed to the fate of the tsarist order and the revolutionary solutions of 1917. As in the case of official analysts, it was the intensity of life in this Volga province that originally attracted the contributors to this book. This fact, however, should not obscure the typicality of Saratov and its value as a prism through which provincial Russia can be viewed and assessed in all its complexity.

Because of tense agrarian relations and a unique peasant mentality, the Saratov countryside was especially volatile in the period of the emancipa-tion of the serfs, and particularly during the revolutions of 1905–07 and 1917. The ghosts of Razin ànd Pugachev hovered over the landscape, evoked by folktales, topographical names like "Thieves' Field," and the recent arrival of serfdom. Despite its explosiveness, however, Saratov reflected broader patterns of peasant protest typical of the arc of black-earth provinces stretching from the Volga, through the Central Agri-cultural Region, into the Ukraine. While its working class was not the largest in provincial Russia, the rapid urban growth and social pressures engendered by rapid industrialization faithfully reflected the experience of millions of Russians who at the dawn of the twentieth century were coming to grips with a new world of risk and opportunity.

With its vibrant cultural life and deeply rooted political traditions,

8

Saratov Province was often ahead of sleepier provincial centers. For this reason the sharply etched political dynamics, alliances, conflicts, and tactics revealed there provide a valuable perspective on the more inchoate and less developed politics of provincial Russia as a whole. During the era of Great Reforms, for example, we can clearly trace in Saratov the growth of an educated "public," distinct from and increasingly critical of the state. In the 1870s, and again in the early twentieth century, attempts by the radical intelligentsia to mobilize the masses against the Old Regime were dramatically evident in Saratov's towns and villages. The liberal-radical alliance between zemstvo gentry and the Third Element which stood at the center of the anti-tsarist opposition at the turn of the century, and the Liberation Movement of 1905, seems particularly vital in Saratov. The social and political polarizations of 1917 stand out in sharp relief. No matter how clearly seen in Saratov, these patterns show up in other provinces in other Russian regions, and in this sense Saratov does mirror the broader processes of social and political mobilization in the last decades of tsarist Russia.

In Saratov one also sees something of the problems involved in governing Russia's provinces. Official efforts to analyze, control, and manage the social and political forces challenging the Old Regime were often more innovative, timely, or forceful in Saratov than elsewhere, but at the same time they helped to shape policies at the national level. In Saratov one can see vividly the effect of government efforts to contain an emerging "public" during the 1860s, or to thwart the demands of zemstvos or professionals for more autonomy at the turn of the century, as well as the resultant role official policies played in radicalizing provincial society. The cycle of mutual suspicion, repression, and radicalization that often seemed to characterize state-society relations in these decades stands out in Saratov; but one can also appreciate, and to some degree sympathize with, the dilemmas faced by loyal and essentially well-meaning bureaucrats who sought to advance Russian progress while upholding state authority. In short, in Saratov's history one can see unfolding the intense struggles that were waged over Russia's future and how these involved the millions of inhabitants of that sprawling empire.

2. From Frontier Outpost to Provincial Capital: Saratov, 1590–1860

James G. Hart

IN 1780 Catherine the Great designated Saratov as a new regional administrative center *(namestnichestvo)*.[1] Her action came abruptly only six years after Saratov and the entire district surrounding this Volga River town had suffered the violence and anarchy of Pugachev's rebellion and was part of the long-range effort of the empress to establish effective control over the unruly southern and eastern borderlands. This area midway between the middle and lower Volga regions was still very much a part of the turbulent, unsettled frontier, still subject to the whims of the wild and destructive cossacks who had claimed the Volga as their river. The new status bestowed upon Saratov was a symbol of the Russian state's determination to bring this vital area under firm control and transplant there Great Russian social, economic, and political institutions.

Catherine showed great foresight in choosing Saratov as her new center midway on the Volga between Kazan and Astrakhan, the two towns under whose jurisdiction Saratov had fallen in the previous two hundred years. In the course of the nineteenth century, Saratov would become not only a densely populated, thoroughly settled province, but the city would become the commercial anchor for the entire middle Volga region, a bustling metropolis controlling the movement of goods both of local origin and from distant sources for distribution throughout the empire.

The first Russian settlers in the middle and lower Volga regions manned dozens of fortress outposts built first along the great river itself, but also along the tributaries inland connecting the Volga to the Don, the

Sura, or the Oka. These provided a network of defense lines protecting Moscow from unknown forces "beyond the steppe." After Ivan IV defeated the Tatars of Kazan and Astrakhan in the middle of the sixteenth century, outposts were set up at Samara in 1586, Tsaritsyn in 1589, and at Saratov in 1590.[2] Saratov was originally located on the left (eastern) bank of the Volga, in what would later be Samara Province, opposite the yellowish cliffs on the western bank. Indeed, the name Saratov derived from the Tatar word for "yellow mountain" *(sara-tau)*. The establishment of these outposts secured the river route from Kazan to Astrakhan for Muscovite economic penetration and exploration toward Siberia, on the one hand, and toward the Caspian Sea and Persia or even Central Asia, on the other. For more than a century, however, these outposts in general remained poorly staffed and nearly inconsequential regulators of Volga River traffic. They represented a defense line rather than a jumping-off point.

Saratov's earliest garrison, with a fortress situated on the left bank, across the river and just north of the city's present location on the right bank, was substantial, numbering over fifteen hundred men. However, repeated assaults by cossack rebels during the Time of Troubles and a great fire in 1613 served to deplete its strength. In 1616 the state reconstructed the fortress on the left-bank site, but its garrison was only a third the size of the original.[3] A merchant from Moscow noted in 1623 that all the residents of Saratov lived behind the walls of the fortress, that there was no landholding in the countryside to the east, and that all supplies were imported, including grain.[4]

There is evidence, nevertheless, that as early as 1634 a primitive but distinct trade quarter *(posad)* existed in Saratov. A military census in that year showed that of the five hundred adult males in the garrison, eighty-three, or 16 percent, worked as craftsmen (shoemakers, bakers, carpenters, and so on) or as merchants for the military personnel. The census distinguished these "townsmen" from the servitors and suggested their origin to be from among the fugitive peasantry from central Muscovy. The Holstein traveler Adam Olearius passed Saratov in September 1636 and took note of the town's military character. But he also noted the many commercial ships plying the Volga waters with their cargoes belonging to the state or to wealthy monasteries.[5] The number of townsmen steadily increased over the next few decades, as peasants continued to flee from serfdom to the southeastern frontier, providing the nucleus for a much larger and more active "urban center" within the fortress outpost.

The earliest settlement on the right bank, or bluff side of the Volga, where the city eventually relocated, was similarly tentative and precarious but nonetheless indicative of the character of settlement that would evolve in the late eighteenth and nineteenth centuries. For example, there were several fishing operations conducted by monasteries on the Volga north of Saratov. Although the income derived from such activity was substantial, as is evident from archival records of the Makarev-Zheltovodskii and Trinity monasteries and the Patriarch's Office in Moscow, less than a hundred persons were involved in each operation. However, their very existence confirmed the importance of Saratov and helped to ensure its future growth.[6] To the west of the Volga, along the banks of the Sura, Khoper, and Medveditsa rivers, in what would become the northern districts *(uezdy)* of Saratov Province, existed settlements of non-Russian tribesmen, mainly Mordvinians, Chuvash, Cheremis, and Tatars. In the middle of the seventeenth century these still seminomadic peoples set up beekeeping and hunting preserves in the forests there, and their more or less Russified descendents would continue to live among the dominant Russian settlers, becoming incorporated along with them into serfdom in the eighteenth century.[7]

Through the seventeenth century, nonetheless, the Volga, especially from Simbirsk south to Astrakhan, might be described as still a cossack river. Russian freebooters and adventurers from the southwest, the Don River Cossacks, frequently harassed Volga River traffic and attacked the state's outposts throughout the region. Moreover, Kalmyk tribesmen to the east made frequent raids on frontier settlements, destroying Samara in 1639 and Saratov itself in 1643. Slightly less common but no less destructive were outbursts by Tatars and Bashkirs, again from the east.[8] Secure Russian settlement and development of the region was impossible for the time being. The state's response to these threats was uneven and generally unenthusiastic. Moscow was simply not yet strong enough to develop the region either by building new and larger fortresses or by mounting continuous campaigns against the various violators of the peace. The garrison at Saratov remained small, the soldiers underpaid and overworked. The ordinary servitor at Saratov endured an extremely difficult life. He received few provisions from Moscow 915 versts (606 miles) away, had to struggle to secure necessary supplies from the surrounding region, and also faced constant competition from the influx of fugitives from the central regions who demanded part of the meager sustenance available locally.[9]

If the state did not provide much assistance, it did what little it could to encourage the economic development of its frontier. In the 1650s Saratov residents were granted permission to operate their own fishing concerns and thus gain a share of the profits that had previously gone exclusively to monasteries, the Patriarch, or to the tsar's own coffers. The state granted its military servitors small plots of land to encourage self-sufficiency and thus reduce the pressure on the state's resources.[10] It is true that ultimately the state sided with the monasteries and rich merchants who complained about competition from enterprising servitors, but it is important also to note that, whether consciously or unconsciously, it was promoting the development of an independent, free-spirited, energetic local population on the frontier. This process persisted into the eighteenth century and became an important factor in the development of Saratov as a lively "urban center" on the lower Volga in the nineteenth century.

The relationship between Saratov's earliest military population and the cossacks and other rebellious or free-spirited groups was not always adversarial. The two mixed frequently on business and direct clashes were rare. Since raids most seriously affected only the property of rich merchants, the highest nobility, or the special agents of the tsar, the state's military servitors often proved ineffective defenders in particular incidents or even went over to the camp of "the enemy."[11] This close relationship between the town and the cossacks and the tenuousness of Moscow's hold were demonstrated when "the great cossack," Stepan (Stenka) Razin, made his appearance on the Volga in the summer of 1670, after three years of brigandage on the lower Volga and Caspian Sea. Most residents of Saratov were neither surprised nor fearful at his approach, not perceiving his cossacks as threatening invaders. Despite the contrary perceptions of the state's officials or the church, they saw Razin's cossacks as simply laying claim to "their Mother Volga" and the settlements along the way, a view many in Saratov could share.

Razin approached Saratov early on August 15, 1670, together with some six thousand Don Cossacks. He was assured by two or three Saratov residents, who had visited him in Tsaritsyn, that the town would surrender without a fight. And, as predicted, Saratov's residents, led by the head of the Bogoroditsa Monastery, came out in a procession bearing bread and salt to welcome the great cossack. The military servitors and the approximately five hundred *strel'tsy* (members of Muscovy's standing army of musketeers) in Saratov, as in Astrakhan, Chernyi Iar, Tsaritsyn, and later Samara, chose not to resist this action. Those residents who did not flee cooperated fully with Razin, the Don Cossacks, and rebellious nonmilitary residents of the town, becoming in essence cossacks themselves. In fact, the townsmen arrested the military governor themselves and brought him to Razin in chains. Razin ordered him executed.[12]

Razin placed fellow Don Cossacks Vasilii Fedorov and Grigorii Savelin in charge of the outpost and then departed with his huge army for bigger prizes, Samara and then Simbirsk. Fedorov and Savelin stayed in Saratov until the middle of September and then took a force consisting mainly of Saratov residents to Penza, a new fortress outpost located a hundred and twenty-five miles to the northwest on the Sura River.[13] Saratov, it appears, was left largely deserted. When Razin reappeared there for the second time in the middle of October, this time in flight after having been defeated on October 5 at Simbirsk, he received no support and had to continue on down the Volga to his home on the Don.[14] Later in October and in November, as its residents filtered back from campaigns with Razin's emissaries in the middle Volga region, Saratov resumed its revolt.[15] It was not until December that Prince K. O. Osipov was able to recapture the town and the state could appoint a new military governor.[16]

Moscow's hold, however, remained precarious. In May of 1671, even while Razin was awaiting execution in Moscow, another cossack, Fedor Sheludiak, threw the Volga into turmoil once again. Saratov's residents rose up, deposed their government, and murdered the metropolitan. Only in November of that year was Sheludiak captured and the revolt suppressed. That similar dangers persisted is evident from the dispatch sent by the new military governor in the summer of 1672. He claimed that Saratov was "defenseless" in the face of cossack and Tatar attacks and lamented that even though Astrakhan was secure, it only served to entice Saratov's strel'tsy to flee there.[17]

The magnitude of the social disturbance caused by Stenka Razin and the cossacks prompted the state to rebuild Saratov on a completely new foundation.[18] The clearest indication of this attitude was the decision to transfer the town to the right bank of the Volga, to a site nestled between the Sokolov and Tysyi hills and their wide ravines. In addition to giving the town greater security from occasional Kalmyk raids from the south-eastern steppe, the relocation had the further significance of putting the town, specifically its trade quarter, into easier contact with central Muscovy. The character of Saratov as a frontier outpost would change accordingly. For example, the predominant feature of the new town was to be a marketplace, constructed in 1674, next to which were to be situated the offices and homes of the military governor and other state representatives. To symbolize the permanence of this decision, construction of a stone cathedral was begun in 1681. A fortress wall was thrown up, but well beyond the center of town, and it was never regularly maintained. The soldiers' quarter, usually the predominant feature of all frontier outposts, was relegated to a location in the heavily forested hills beyond the Vorovskii ravine to the northwest. Clearly, Saratov was to be more than just a military outpost and the military governor would have more than just military responsibilities.[19]

Saratov's refoundation on the right bank put it directly on the "diplomatic route" from Moscow through Kazan to Astrakhan. It now became the terminus of the "southern defense route" from Moscow to Rostov, through Shatsk and Penza to the Volga.[20] In 1696 a new fortress called Petrovsk was built at a site sixty miles northwest of Saratov. Petrovsk was to become one of the major towns of northwestern Saratov Province and was one more link in the chain connecting Moscow to the Volga.[21] Saratov's growing permanence was underscored by the fact that by the mid-eighteenth century the defense line extended southward to the town of Tsaritsyn and was defended by a garrison of Don Cossacks.

With its new location and added security, Saratov was well placed for commercial expansion and quickly became known as a transfer point for a variety of goods being sent to central Muscovy. There was rapid construction of numerous storehouses, barns, warehouses, and the like to accommodate increasing commercial activity. Fish, salt, and Persian goods were among the main items passing through Saratov at the turn of the eighteenth century. Nogai and Kalmyk Tatars regularly drove cattle and horses through Saratov to markets farther west in the Central Agricultural Region at Novokhopersk, Tambov, and Shatsk. And with this increased activity, Saratov townsmen found the opportunity to conduct an annual "bargehaulers bazaar" beginning in 1698, which attracted thousands of traders from up and down the Volga.[22]

Saratov's dual identity as a budding trade center but still sparsely settled frontier outpost attracted thousands of settlers to the area beginning in the late seventeenth century. This diverse migration included fugitive Russian and Ukrainian peasants, runaway conscripts from Peter the Great's forced labor projects and wars, Mordvinian and Tatar tribesmen, cossacks, military servitors, and Old Believers. These people moved permanently to the city of Saratov itself and to the lands of Saratov Province west and north along the Medveditsa, Khoper, and Sura rivers.[23] The state encouraged this by allowing military servitors from the old Tambov-to-Simbirsk defense line, whose function as frontier guards was becoming less important, to obtain some of this rich land in exchange for a most informal pledge of service. This arrangement made the "homesteaders" *(odnodvortsy)*, as they were called, almost petty gentry.[24] Together with the various classes of peasantry coming to the region, who were landless but now free on the frontier, the homesteaders took a stake in the land, settled on it, put down roots, and began the permanent settlement of what was to become Saratov Province. This was largely an uncontrollable and nondirected settlement of empty lands.

In the second half of the eighteenth century, conscious state policy played a larger role in shaping the growth and social geography of Saratov. Two factors of special importance were the opening of salt mine operations at Lake Elton in the 1740s and the invitation made to German settlers to come to Saratov in the 1760s. In 1747, Saratov's military governor, in cooperation with the state's Salt Commission, decided to seize the benefits of exploiting Lake Elton, located 136 miles southeast of Saratov.[25] They began to recruit workers for the operation of extracting and hauling salt from the lake to the Volga whence it could be distributed throughout the empire. Scores of new warehouses and storehouses were built in Saratov itself, and thousands of Russian peasants from Voronezh Province and from points farther to the west and southwest in the Ukraine flocked to the province. These settled predominantly near Kamyshin on the Volga south of Saratov and from there as far west as Balashov.[26]

By 1754 over three million *pudy* (one *pud* equals approximately 36 pounds) of salt passed through Saratov annually. The Salt Commission set up a regional office in the town and became involved in the details of town administration. For example, the commission's five-member board organized the town's first fire brigade and undertook various other projects of urban planning such as widening streets, constructing new storehouses, and expanding the town's limits.[27] The trade quarter grew as well, further indicating Saratov's emergence as a significant trade center and its declining function as a frontier military outpost. In 1717 there were approximately 1,500 adult males in the trade quarter, and in 1752 there were 2,056, an increase of new traders large enough to prompt the old-line merchantry to complain to the Legislative Commission of 1767. A census in 1772 put the *total* population of Saratov's trade quarter at approximately six thousand.[28]

The second state-directed stimulus to permanent settlement in Saratov Province was Catherine's invitations to Germans and other foreigners to come to Russia. The German migration, which was well under way by 1766, introduced an extensive "Volga German" presence, which, as James Long shows later in this book, was to remain a distinct and major feature of this province. Some seven thousand families settled, mainly south of the town on the right bank and north of the town on the left bank.[29] Those on the right bank settled in what would become the Kamyshin, Saratov, Tsaritsyn, and Atkarsk districts of Saratov Province; those on the left bank were in Samara Province.

The first thousand families were granted 40,000 *desiatiny* (one *desiatina* equals approximately 2.7 acres) of land, an amount consistent with the grants made to the homesteaders earlier in the century. The land was held in common by the community, not to be bought or sold individually, but it was nonetheless an enticing incentive to permanent settlement and a successful measure for the continuing transformation of the region from wild frontier to an integral part of the Russian Empire. The state forced the German recruits to take up agriculture, despite the fact that a large number, perhaps a majority, of them were not accustomed to farming. Many refused to be listed in censuses as farmers, even though they had little choice as a group but to live off the land.[30] And, as could be expected, many attempted to get away from the land to pursue occupations in Saratov itself or in the several large villages in the region. A member of the Academy of Sciences toured the region in 1769 and reported that already colonists were present in surprisingly large numbers in the trade quarter of Saratov. As a result, the German settlers made an important contribution to the expanding commercial diversity of the town.[31]

In order to strengthen the Russian element on the Volga, Catherine also extended an invitation to state peasants and to Russian Old Believers, who had taken refuge in Poland, to return and settle in the middle Volga region. Although actual figures are sketchy, the invitation met with considerable success. The Russian schismatics joined the already extant Old Believer villages mainly east of the Volga and north of Saratov on the Irgiz River. The state peasants were settled on state lands throughout the region. Many of these newcomers brought with them the special skills necessary for the commercial development of the region. Among the native Russians coming to Saratov in the second half of the eighteenth century were market gardeners from Rostov, masons and plasterers from Iaroslavl, carpenters from Kostroma, and stonecutters from Olonets.[32]

But as important as this non-serf, non-noble, "miscellaneous class" settlement of Saratov Province was for the emergence of this area from the frontier and for its eventual transformation into an important trade center on the lower Volga, it was the mass influx of peasant migrants from the Great Russian and Ukrainian regions, and their settlement on privately held lands in the province, which defined the social and economic relationships of Saratov. Already in the middle of the eighteenth century, more than half the population of this region consisted of serfs and roughly half the land (especially to the west and northwest of Saratov itself) was owned by the nobility. This level of gentry predominance, which was comparable to that in long-settled regions of the empire, would continue to characterize Saratov Province until the Emancipation in 1861. The development of gentry agriculture and serfdom left a deep imprint on the social geography of the region. The "wild field" (*dikoe pole*), once a haven for refugee peasants, had now been pushed well south of Saratov and also beyond the Volga into the Samara steppe. In the region northwest of Saratov city, a region with rich black soil encompassing the future districts of Petrovsk, Atkarsk, and Balashov, plus Serdobsk and Saratov, an area of high population density, there were numerous gentry estates worked with servile labor. On the other hand, however, the southern and southeastern districts, with their sandier, less productive soil, contained fewer *pomeshchik* holdings and continued to be dominated by state peasants. This all points to an element of socioeconomic contrast worthy of attention as a factor in Saratov's later history.[33]

The proliferation of gentry estates was a result of the traditional practice, common up to the nineteenth century, of the regime rewarding its favorites and ensuring the loyalty of its aristocrats by making them enormous grants of land and serfs. The practice served the further purpose of encouraging the settlement of the wild frontier and led to the securing of these regions for the state. In the seventeenth and eighteenth centuries, the middle and lower Volga regions became available to the state. Thus the state began to recruit hundreds of noblemen, together with the thousands of state peasants, foreign settlers, non-Russian tribesmen, former military servitors, and the like, for the task of reclaiming the lands of the lower Volga from the frontier. The first wave of such grants of land in the future Saratov Province came in the 1690s and involved less than a hundred individual noble families. The Naryshkin family alone received seventy-nine grants totaling more than 20,000 desiatiny in the vicinity of Saratov.[34] The other grants were distinctly smaller, averaging by one estimate less than 500 desiatiny per aristocrat, with perhaps forty-five male serfs each.[35] But grants continued through the first half of the century, and by the 1760s surveyors for the Colonial Guardianship Office found that half the land available for settlement was already in the hands of the gentry.[36] Censuses conducted in the middle of the century found that of the 125,000 male peasants living in Saratov region, 58,000, or 46 percent, were serfs belonging to the gentry.[37]

But there was still plenty of land in Saratov available for settlement and for the state to award to its favorites, and it should come as no surprise that over the next century most of it went to the gentry rather than to the various classes of non-gentry settlers who had contributed to the emergence of the province in the mid-eighteenth century. In 1785, ten years after Pugachev's rebellion had devastated the region, Catherine the Great entertained petitions from scores of gentry for land there. By 1790 she had made grants to eight special aristocratic families totaling more than 10,000 desiatiny, the largest grant of 25,000 desiatiny going once again to the Naryshkins. Then, early in the reign of Catherine's grandson, Alexander I, another wave of grants took place. The practice continued through his reign and during the reign of his brother, Nicholas I, in the first half of the nineteenth century.

Various surveys show the effects of such grants. In the 1760s, 11 percent of all the land in Atkarsk District, directly west of the town of Saratov, belonged to the gentry. In 1803 the figure stood at 40 percent. By 1860 it had risen to 64 percent. In Kamyshin District, where the land had been traditionally reserved for non-gentry settlement, the gentry held 5 percent in the 1760s, 8 percent in 1803, and 14 percent in 1860.[38] And despite the fact that the number of serfs as a percentage of the entire peasant population of Saratov Province declined over the century between 1760 and 1860, as was the case throughout the empire, roughly 50 percent of all peasants in the province were owned by the gentry right up to the Emancipation.[39]

Thus, with respect to gentry landholding, Saratov Province was rapidly becoming like older, long-settled regions of the empire. The state was encroaching on the frontier in the person of the landholding nobleman and in the institution of serfdom. This development held particular poignancy for Saratov. Because of the proximity of the Volga and the steppe, Saratov's villagers, especially the non-Russians and Old Believers, were free-spirited and defiant of authority. On one hand, the frontier promised relief from socioeconomic oppression and a chance to start life anew; it was the stuff of dreams, the route to boundless freedom and adventure. But on the other hand, the frontier loomed as a threat; it was unknown, unpredictable, and dangerous. Although the Volga bore the trade that enriched not only the state but thousands of Russians both noble and non-noble, the river also abetted the transmission of cholera and typhoid epidemics. And for centuries the frontier, though physically great and economically abundant, was also the source of invasions, the open space across which surged fierce infidels "from beyond the steppe."

In the eighteenth century, the frontier's riches brought forth a new Saratov, a Saratov that would develop into the commercial anchor for the entire middle and lower Volga. But the frontier also threatened to sweep it all away in an orgy of the violence that had been a tradition since the Time of Troubles and the days of Stenka Razin. Pugachev's rebellion, which engulfed the region in the summer of 1774, demonstrated the double-edged meaning of the frontier for Saratov, a difficult lesson that did not fade even after Pugachev had passed and Saratov had become a provincial capital. What happened was essentially an explosion caused by the creation of a volatile mixture. Between 1750 and 1775, the overwhelmingly rural, agricultural, and by and large docile residents of Saratov were confronted by the intrusive, oppressive, and oftentimes violent agents of the state. The cataclysm occurred when something mysterious and powerful from the Volga was added to this mixture—the "court" and armed forces of "the cossack emperor," the "hero/antichrist," Emelian Pugachev. Like Razin before him, Pugachev sparked the interest and hopes of Saratov's villagers; but he also caused an eruption of mass fear, hatred, and violence, much of which was simply an expression of the peasants' resentment of recent intrusions.

Pugachev's invasion of the lower Volga region and his seizure of Saratov came at the very end of his year-long campaign, which had started out not far away at his home on the Don and had taken him a thousand miles eastward to the Urals, north to Kazan, and finally down the Volga to Tsaritsyn, where he was captured in September 1774.[40] The contrast with Stenka Razin's conquest a century earlier is instructive with respect to the changes in Saratov. While Saratov was one of the first towns to fall in Razin's campaign of 1670, it was one of the last conquests of Pugachev one hundred years later. There were other differences as well. Whereas Saratov's residents had been swept up in a sudden, wild *jacquerie* in 1670, they considered Pugachev a threat for a long time before the summer of 1774 and hesitated to join him until the very end, and then did so only for a short time, until the danger had passed. In 1670, Stenka Razin commandeered the whole lower Volga almost without a fight. In 1774, Pugachev brought a more violent and destructive rural and urban revolt to the area than had occurred earlier. This meant that Pugachev's rebellion was ominously more significant in the long run for the development of Saratov as a provincial capital than Razin's had been.

One sign of the progress Saratov had made toward becoming a provincial capital in the century between the two rebellions is evident in the preparations undertaken by its three main administrators to defend the town.[41] The military governor, Ivan Boshniak, the director of the Colonial Guardianship Office, I. I. Lodyzhenskii, and the empress's plenipotentiary representative on the Volga frontier, G. R. Derzhavin (the poet who would later play a major role in the development of the Russian literary language), met on July 24, 1774, in Saratov as soon as it became clear that Pugachev had decided to head south from Kazan rather than west toward Moscow. Derzhavin suggested a bold plan that took into consideration the changes Saratov had recently undergone. Because of the small size of the garrison, the absence of any military settlements, and the inadequacy of the town's fortifications, which had never been maintained by the trade-oriented settlers, Derzhavin judged that to await Pugachev's arrival and force him to lay siege to the town would be futile and in the end counterproductive. The defense could not possibly succeed and would likely lead only to a greater degree of destruction on the part of the plundering cossack horde. Instead, Derzhavin proposed to raise a large volunteer peasant army that he himself would lead into the field against Pugachev well before he reached Saratov—perhaps at Penza, or at worst Petrovsk. In the meantime, Saratov's residents, under the direction of the military governor and the director of the Colonial Guardianship Office, would construct a large earthen fortress in town near the banks of the Volga in which they would deposit as much of the riches and supplies of the town as they could. They would then take cover in the fortress themselves, leaving the rest of the town deserted. If Pugachev happened to defeat Derzhavin's force in the field and approach Saratov, it was hoped that, upon finding the town "open," he would either bypass it on his way to the Don or the steppe, or stop only momentarily to rest and gather supplies. The residents could then emerge from their hiding place to find their town spared the usual cossack plunder and most of their supplies and riches intact.

Derzhavin's plan had two flaws which betrayed his failure to appreciate the double-edged character of Saratov's development from frontier outpost to provincial capital. First, he grossly misjudged the loyalty of the rural population to the state and status quo and thus failed to predict their enticement by Pugachev's message. Consequently, his efforts to recruit an army of some fifteen hundred volunteers at the village of Malykovka, near Volsk, north of Saratov on the Volga, failed completely. In fact, the peasants of Malykovka and of the other northern districts of the province were among the earliest and most active supporters of the rebellion.[42] Pugachev's army moved swiftly through the region. After spending two days in Saransk, it approached and captured Penza on August 2. Before long it was upon Petrovsk, a mere sixty miles from Saratov. Derzhavin sent a small reconnaissance force of cossacks to Petrovsk, but upon hearing of Pugachev's success, and viewing the turmoil in the countryside, the force melted away. Its commander, a certain Major Gogol, returned to Saratov with the admonition: "Save yourselves!"[43]

The second miscalculation in Derzhavin's plan was in reference to the quality of leadership of the town's military governor, Ivan Boshniak. Derzhavin and Lodyzhenskii looked upon Saratov as a developing commercial center whose urban and rural inhabitants were not equipped for nor disposed toward fighting a pitched battle against an outside force and could best be protected by means of a strategic retreat, or even an orderly, disciplined and, of course, temporary surrender. But Ivan Boshniak, who had been military governor of Saratov since 1771, looked upon Saratov in a more traditional way. He saw the town as still a frontier outpost. In case of invasion, he would provide military leadership to guarantee the security of the region's rural and urban population and the state's interests. From the outset he disagreed with Derzhavin's strategy and seized upon any excuse to withhold his cooperation. On July 27, for example, after hearing that Pugachev's campaign had stalled in Saransk, Boshniak ordered Lodyzhenskii to halt construction of the earthen fortress in Saratov. Pugachev, he reasoned, would be intercepted by Field Marshal Mikhelson before he could get close to Saratov. In that case, the frantic preparations were unnecessary and indeed wasteful.[44]

Furthermore, on July 30, in defiance of protests from Derzhavin and Lodyzhenskii, Boshniak deployed 200 of the 750 soldiers in his garrison at the northwestern outskirts of the town, astride the Moscow Road, and had them begin refortifying the town's long-neglected fortress wall and towers. This action was a fatal mistake. First, as Derzhavin knew, Boshniak's advance force would be inadequate to stop Pugachev's army head-on. Second, and more important, since Boshniak's advance force was positioned beyond Moscow Gate to the west of Sokolov Hills, a key vantage point was surrendered to the rebel army. Pugachev would have the town, now defended by the remaining five hundred soldiers in the garrison, within easy artillery range, and he would possess an impregnable command post from which to direct an assault upon it. Perceiving the hopelessness of the situation, Derzhavin left Saratov just after midnight on August 6. Lodyzhenskii, in the meantime, had taken responsibility for loading crates of money from the state's treasury onto boats on the Volga. After having dispatched some fifty thousand rubles to Tsaritsyn, Lodyzhenskii also left Saratov.[45]

Just hours after Derzhavin and Lodyzhenskii had gone, Pugachev's army arrived at Sokolov Hills and Saratov lay prostrate before the "cossack emperor." At that point, several merchants met and decided to send a representative to Pugachev with an offer of surrender, hoping to spare the town the disaster of an attack. The military governor foiled this plan, however, by opening an artillery barrage on Pugachev's position. When the emissary from the merchants returned to town with a proclamation from Pugachev, Boshniak defiantly tore it into shreds. Pugachev had no choice but to attack.[46]

As Derzhavin had predicted, Boshniak's defense did not last long. Pugachev sent some three thousand rebels down from the hills after a brief artillery barrage. Boshniak's tiny garrison was no match for the invaders and all but sixty of the five hundred men soon joined the rebels. Then, when a separate rebel force attacked from the south through Tsaritsyn Gate, Boshniak and his lone loyal officer decided to make their way through the crowds to the Volga where they escaped by boat to Tsaritsyn. The battle for Saratov lasted perhaps two hours.[47]

Pugachev's rebels ran through the town rounding up as many "enemies" as they could find. By evening some eighty persons had been executed, most killed on the spot without ceremony as the result of mob fury. The orgy of violence that Derzhavin and Lodyzhenskii had feared resulted in massive destruction in the town, with scores of homes of merchants, administrators, and clergy looted and pillaged. As far as can be determined, the rebels came from the immediate countryside and were joined by prisoners from Saratov's jails and by about a hundred barge haulers, who swaggered into town bearing the riches they had gathered from boats fleeing down the Volga. At nightfall, Saratov's residents gathered in the town square and took an oath of allegiance to Pugachev as "Emperor Peter III."

Pugachev remained in Saratov for only two days. He ordered that a portion of the state's treasury and all of the grain in the many warehouses in town be distributed to the local population. He designated a certain local cossack, Ivan Ufimtsev, to be commandant of the town and named the man's sons lieutenants. Intending perhaps to set up a kind of ruling senate for the town, Pugachev ordered a magistrate to draw up a list of all leading local merchants. But of the hundred and fifty names on the list, only six could be found still in town. On August 9, Pugachev left Saratov, taking with him his vast army with their looted treasures and supplies.[48]

Disorder continued for weeks in the countryside surrounding Saratov. Priests who refused to pray for Pugachev were murdered. Nobles and their estate managers were captured and murdered. Rebel peasants seized vast quantities of supplies, livestock, and money, and plundered the property of the state and the gentry throughout the region. There is evidence that in some villages only the serfs took part in the violence, while the other peasants simply surrendered their property or even protected the gentry who had been kind to them. Nonetheless, the state's retribution in the rural areas was severe. Thousands of peasants were

24

rounded up and punished, and many perished in battles with government troops. And because the fields went untended, the area suffered a famine the following year.

The town of Saratov returned to normal more quickly than did the countryside. The state's commanders, Muffel and Mellin, recaptured Saratov without a struggle on August 11 and set up headquarters on Cathedral Square. It was there and in Sokolov Hills that the gibbets stood when Field Marshal Mikhelson arrived on August 14 to dispense justice. Despite a complaint filed by Derzhavin, Ivan Boshniak was given an award for his heroic defense of Saratov and was reappointed military governor, a position he held until his retirement in 1788 at the age of seventy-one.[49] In short, the state's victory over Pugachev seemed secure. This notion was powerfully reinforced in subsequent decades by the final integration of this Volga frontier province into the framework of the state's administration and also by the deep rooting of the socioeconomic structures—gentry landholding and serf economy—that had been long dominant in the Russian center.

Pugachev's rebellion, even more than Razin's, marked the crucial turning point in Saratov's administrative history. The early success of Pugachev's uprising brought the tsarist government to the realization that its bureaucratic control over the vast empire needed to be strengthened. Reform of local government and administrative reorganization thus followed.[50] In 1780 Catherine II ordered the creation of a new "provincial administrative unit" along the middle Volga. This *Saratovskoe namestnichestvo* encompassed all the lands around Saratov formerly assigned to the Kazan and Astrakhan territories, including Saratov itself. To consolidate these lands the government began to build six new district headquarters that joined the four towns already established in the area. Saratov now had the ten district centers it would possess until the Soviet period: Saratov, Kamyshin, Petrovsk, Tsaritsyn, Atkarsk, Balashov, Khvalynsk, Kuznetsk, Serdobsk, and Volsk. Emperor Paul tampered with his mother's scheme in the last year of the century, but in 1802 his son, Alexander I, named Saratov a *guberniia,* making it a full-fledged provincial capital. The consequent establishment of a regular bureaucracy in Saratov and its satellite towns seemed to validate the efforts and vision of both Boshniak and Derzhavin just as it helped to exorcise the ghost of Pugachev.

A rapid increase in gentry settlement likewise served to consolidate

Table 2.1. Peasant Population of Saratov, 1828

	Thousand Souls	Percent
Serfs	507	52.5
Monastery (ekonomicheskie) peasants	93	9
State peasants	68	7
German colonists	62	6
Odnodvortsy	52	5
Crown (udel) peasants	50	5
Tatars	37	4
Others	111	11.5
Total	980	100

SOURCE: L. N. Iurovskii, *Saratovskie votchiny.* (Saratov, 1923), p. 23.

the Saratov countryside. Between 1785 and 1820 the government distributed over one million desiatiny of fertile land to its favorites. Most of this went to very wealthy landowners already in Saratov, such as the Naryshkins, who were well connected with the center. There were smaller owners as well, many the descendants of the military servitors, the "homesteaders," who had migrated to the northwestern districts of the province as early as the late seventeenth century. On the eve of Emancipation, Saratov's landowners were divided into two groups: wealthy aristocrats each of whom owned more than a thousand male serfs, and the middling or smaller gentry, with an average of five hundred serfs each. The first group consisted of just ninety-one noblemen, only 4 percent of the gentry in the province; yet they owned 128,000 male serfs, or 40 percent of the provincial total. The second group consisted of nearly twenty-five hundred nobles, owning 140,000 male serfs.[51]

Gentry settlement and serfdom continued to be concentrated in the northern and western districts of the province: Kuznetsk, Serdobsk, Atkarsk, Khvalynsk, Balashov, Petrovsk, and in part of Saratov District.[52] As noted earlier, this was a result of soil conditions, settlement patterns, and population density. But the increase in the number of serfs in Saratov after the Pugachev rebellion is striking. Their numbers increased from 58,000 male souls in 1742–47 to 137,000 in 1781–87, and then to 310,000 in 1844.[53] Moreover, in contrast to trends across the empire, serfs in 1828 still represented the largest group of peasants in Saratov, and these were concentrated in the northwestern districts (see tables 2.1 and 2.2). In the southeast, peasants were bound to the state or crown and thus enjoyed relatively more autonomy than their privately

Table 2.2. Concentration of Serfdom in Saratov, 1828
(Thousand Souls)

	Serfs	Percent	Crown Peasants	Percent	State Peasants	Percent
Kuznetsk	44	98	0		1	2
Serdobsk	81	94	0		5	6
Atkarsk	78	94	2	3	3	3
Khvalynsk	39	93	2	6	1	1
Balashov	82	81	10	10	9	9
Petrovsk	70	81	1	1	16	18
Saratov	55	80	2	3	12	17
Volsk	44	66	19	28	4	6
Kamyshin	23	52	11	25	10	22
Tsaritsyn	4	28	2	17	8	55
Total	520	81	49	8	69	11

SOURCE: L. N. Iurovskii, *Saratovskie votchiny.* (Saratov, 1923), p. 52.

held brethren in the northwest. These regional contrasts became more pronounced in the decades leading up to the Emancipation.[54]

By the early nineteenth century, Saratov, a frontier outpost only a quarter-century before, had taken on the trappings of a typical Russian provincial capital and was firmly incorporated into the administrative framework of the empire. Saratov also serviced a rural hinterland that seemed to reflect faithfully the socioeconomic and cultural patterns developed in the Russian heartland. Moreover, it held out the promise of further commercial development, which indeed was soon realized. Still, early-nineteenth-century tranquility masked deeper social tensions that were rooted in Saratov's troubled past and would soon be exacerbated by the region's subsequent development. Urban growth would foster its own special problems and create new social types and new opponents to the tsarist state that eighteenth-century officials like Boshniak and Derzhavin could not have imagined. In the Saratov countryside, particularly in the northwestern districts, the advent of gentry culture and economy obscured the fact that serfdom was a recent arrival to Saratov and that collective memories of "freedom" and of Pugachev and Razin, as well as the constant proximity of the open steppe across the Volga, exercised a profound influence on peasant mentality, fostering a rebellious spirit that would characterize this province into the twentieth century. The state's victory in 1774 was not final. The ghost of Pugachev still hovered over the land.

3. Conspiracy and Circumstance in Saratov, 1859–1864

Alan Kimball

THE SARATOV regional staff officer of the Russian Imperial Corps of Gendarmes, Major Globa, was morally certain that conspiratorial evil-doing surrounded him and his provincial post. On March 12, 1862, he submitted a troubled report to General Alexander Potapov, his commanding officer in remote St. Petersburg. The source of all local evil-doing, he wrote, could be traced upward into the highest levels of provincial administration. Principal among the suspected miscreants were the director of the Saratov Crown Lands Allotment Administration, Nikolai Mordvinov, and the physician N. N. Minkevich, men who seemed to Globa to exhibit especially harmful moral inclinations. "These people frighten me with their malignant intentions. All the more so since both of them enjoy a particularly close relationship with the Governor of the province, Mr. Baranovskii." Moral instinct substituted for evidence as Globa continued his letter: "A moral feeling inspires me to think that they are contemplating something bad. With all my power I am trying to penetrate their secret, but up to this time I have not succeeded in attaining that goal."[1]

Globa looked upward in the hierarchy for signs of conspiracy rather than all around him at the circumstances of public life in Saratov. That was, after all, his job. His chiefs in St. Petersburg saw the matter in much the same way. Seeking to discover the causes of the "criminal acts" of rebellion which gripped the Russian Empire in 1862, they looked abroad, to the émigré community, and found Alexander Herzen, Nikolai Ogarev, and Mikhail Bakunin. They concluded that these demonic figures, with the journal *Kolokol* and other materials smuggled into the empire, were corrupting "inexperienced young minds."[2] The chief gendarme and head of the Third Section of His Majesty's own Chancery, Vasilii Dolgorukov, reported to the emperor that rebellion flowed from abroad and had no roots in Russian "native soil" (what he said literally was *narodnykh istochnikakh,* "popular sources").[3]

Globa in Saratov and his bosses in St. Petersburg found it difficult to see anything but treason and sedition in the new spirit of social activism that accompanied the early reform years of Alexander II. The larger and more active organizations of the epoch—Litfond, Chess Club, the Literacy Committee of the Free Economic Society, Sunday schools, for example—were officially approved and perfectly legal. Yet these vigorous enterprises, some of them new and some recently revitalized, threatened the state's sense of rate, extent, and magnitude of reform. These and other national organizations leapt suddenly to life and expanded widely into the provinces, to regional administrative centers, like Saratov. Sunday schools were found even in the countryside. The implications of independent social organizations of this sort were grave for an autocratic and unlimited state that had not yet extended its own bureaus so vigorously or so far.

Globa and many subsequent historians have been disinclined to look carefully at the full context of local social activism within which political opposition and revolutionary movements originated in the empire. Saratov provides an instructive provincial perspective on a process of national significance. The enthusiasm in society for reformist change *(pereustroistvo)* was excessive, it seemed. So also was the new critical spirit and openness *(glasnost)* expressed in the provincial journal *Saratovskiia gubernskiia vedomosti,* whose unofficial section was edited by Daniil Mordovtsev. The constant roar of peasant disorder in the surrounding countryside further confused and darkened Globa's sense of reality. Spontaneous "civilian" innovation finally had to be dealt with as evil and criminal conspiracy, even when the evidence did not always confirm moral instincts. While the state, centered in the metropolis, moved resolutely ahead with its extensive military, legal, administrative, and peasant reforms, it assumed a hostile attitude toward the emerging "public" *(publika, obshchestvo,* or *obshchestvennost),* possibly the one new element of national life most needed to insure the success of state reforms.

Unable to link forces with an awakened public, the state felt compelled to control or suppress it. Among the membership of social organizations there were thus those who concluded that the imperial state was the main obstacle to progress in their land. Some of these sought to turn the tide of peasant disorder against the state in order to force limitations on its otherwise unchecked authority in public life. Frustration among activists and among police accelerated the process of radicalization. The state had to "criminalize" the most threatening enterprises in order to crush or emasculate them; the more resolute social activists had to go under-ground to continue their pursuit of satisfactory political change. Indeed, the grand political design which bears the name Land and Liberty (*Zemlia i volia*) found its way to Saratov and other provincial centers largely as a result of the state's jealous and oppressive "social" policy. Conspiracy was a negligible force at first.

The fastest growing and by 1862 the largest social organization in Russia was the Society for Aid to Needy Writers and Scholars (*Obshchestvo dlia Posobiia nuzhdaiushchimsia literatoram i uchenym,* or Litfond), which had its executive committee in St. Petersburg. Some of the most prominent figures in Russian literature, journalism, scholarship, and public life counted themselves among the nearly eighty founding members: Ivan Turgenev, Konstantin Kavelin, Nikolai Nekrasov, Nikolai Serno-Solov'evich, and Pavel Annenkov. Saratov's most famous son, Nikolai Chernyshevskii, the political editor of the most exciting journal then being published in the empire, *Sovremennik,* was a founder. Litfond received large donations from the royal family. It published a mem-bership list that grew toward six hundred. Grigorii Blagosvetlov, editor of the other popular national journal, *Russkoe slovo,* was among the first to join Litfond. Blagosvetlov also counted himself a *Saratovets;* he had gradu-ated from the Saratov Theological Academy and maintained close ties through correspondence with fellow journalist Mordovtsev in Saratov.

As Litfond extended itself beyond the capital, in October 1860, one of Globa's prime suspects, Mordvinov, became Saratov regional Litfond commissioner. In the following year Evgenii Belov, a teacher in the Saratov Gymnasium and inspector of the Noble Girls' Institute, assumed that post as well.[4] Moreover, Governor Baranovskii, though not a Lit-fond member, supported its programs and carried on a correspondence with Aleksei Pleshcheev, the Moscow Litfond commissioner.[5]

In these years Litfond played an important role in the intellectual and cultural life of several provincial cities. It was a major vehicle for social self-expression of the type Globa so mistrusted. Litfond commissioners functioned in Ekaterinoslav, Grodno, Odessa, Taganrog, Tambov, Tver, and Vilno, as well as in Moscow and Saratov. Literary evenings, readings, lectures, stage plays, and even banquets at which major figures recited from their works, performed famous roles, or delivered talks came to be a regular feature of city life, and proved one of the most successful ways to raise money for social causes.[6]

Mordvinov and Belov, with the help of local circles and their salon, sponsored public lectures and other literary presentations in the name of Litfond. On November 25, 1861, they sponsored a literary evening to benefit students arrested during recent disturbances at St. Petersburg University. They were refused use of the hall in which the gentry assembly met but received permission to meet in the Commercial Club. Ivan Aksakov's "Brodiaga," Shchedrin's "Rasskaz pod"iachego" and "Nepriatnoe poseshchenie," and selections from Gogol and Lermontov were read. At the end, Dr. Minkevich, whose younger brother was among the students arrested in the capital, proposed a toast to the health of students. In his report, Globa portrayed the gathering as a political demonstration of solidarity with arrested student rebels. Globa emphasized the dangerous social diversity of organizers, drawing special attention to the two merchants who most actively supported the gathering. Globa did not have to spell out for his superiors the obvious threat to public order posed by this reckless mixing of the social estates.[7]

Literary evenings unexpectedly proved to be more than fund-raisers. These assemblies were raising a new force in Russia: a public. Everyone felt a great emotional energy which sprang not solely from the podium or out of the written words themselves but also from the hearts of an actively listening public.[8] Assembled citizens not only *got* the message, they *gave* it too. Pleshcheev touched a sensitive point in his correspondence with Governor Baranovskii when he emphasized how Litfond brought everyone together in a single enterprise, whatever their status, power, or wealth. Membership represented an esthetic and refined version of the French revolutionary idea of *citoyen*. Public assemblies were miniature exercises in *liberté, égalité et fraternité*.

That tradition was strong in Saratov even before Litfond. From the 1840s forward, the "unofficial" section of the provincial *vedomosti,* which Mordovtsev now edited, and the local gymnasium served as institutional anchors for active and varied social circles in the city. A further pattern had established itself, in which the provincial governor served as a patron of a new and reform-minded public. The exiled historian, N. I. Kostomarov, served in the governor's chancery and received privilege and protection, to the constant dismay of the local police commander.[9]

When in 1851–53 Chernyshevskii taught at the Saratov Gymnasium, he associated with these local circles. His boss, A. A. Meier, director of the Saratov Gymnasium, gained wide support in society for his strict housecleaning administration which brought an end to graft there. Meier was not always comfortable with his new teacher, but Chernyshevskii was allowed to introduce innovative pedagogical methods, based on mutual respect and freedom in the relationship between teacher and pupil. He established "Literary Conversations," in which students made public presentations of original work and received formal criticism. Some thought he expected too much of his students, but more than one of them published the results of their work. A large number of them remembered his emphasis on personal moral or ethical independence and self-sufficiency, and responsibility in a public setting.[10]

The close ties that Chernyshevskii forged with his students were maintained in subsequent years.[11] Some measure of spirit or inspiration from gymnasium days very likely accompanied those ex-students of Chernyshevskii to Kazan University, where they played a big role in student organizations. Several transferred to Moscow and established an important student organization, the Library of Kazan Students.[12]

In the late 1850s, Chernyshevskii on occasion returned home from the capital to see his parents. He also visited the Litfond commissioner Belov, his old associate on the faculty of the gymnasium. Belov was still an active member of a salon that now included Mordvinov, Dr. Minkevich, Mordovtsev and his wife, as well as L. G. Ernst, the principal at the Noble Girls' Institute; Auguste Klaus, German colonist and administrator; plus V. G. Varentsov, I. A. Gan, medical doctor S.F. Stefani, and Pavel Rovinskii. Altogether they represented a society of Russians, Poles, Ukrainians, German "colonists," men, women, rich and poor. They were daughters and sons of priests, poor gentry, merchants, *raznochintsy* (people of various ranks, déclassé), and middling folk. Among them were the sons of a cossack farmer (Mordovtsev), an aristocrat of ancient lineage (Rovinskii), and a powerful *chinovnik* grandee (Mordvinov).[13]

It seems unlikely that these people gathered to sing the "Marseillaise," but the very composition of the group seemed to intone that frightful hymn in Globa's ears. Such a salon was not illegal, nor was the literary evening; they were just unsettling. The actual projects of Saratov circles helped to define the network of shared interests among groups in the provinces and capital, and reinforced the bad impression that their mixed social composition made on Globa. When N. F. Fon-Kruze, a liberal and popular member of the national censorship committee, was removed from his post, Saratov writers and readers signed and submitted a public protest to authorities, following the lead of St. Petersburg and Moscow savants. Mordvinov astonished the establishment when he launched a campaign against the unbearable arbitrariness of A. D. Ignat'ev, governor of Saratov. Ignat'ev fought back in the probable confidence that no middle-level bureaucrat could unseat a provincial governor. Herzen's *Kolokol* and the St. Petersburg satirical journal *Iskra* helped to bring the light of glasnost to this unusual struggle against administrative and landowner abuse. Mordvinov's efforts were crowned with success when Baranovskii replaced Ignat'ev.[14]

Public life quickened on the eve of the Emancipation. Mordvinov joined a group of prominent Litfond founders and members on the vacation Isle of Wight just off the English coast in August 1860 to discuss the creation of something like a popular auxiliary to Litfond, a "Society for the Promotion of Literacy and Primary Education."[15] In April 1861, the venerable Imperial Free Economic Society brought unity to several similar enterprises when it formed its "Literacy Committee." The committee set out to found technical and agricultural schools, to publish textbooks and other reading materials for the *narod,* and to gather data on education throughout the empire. Within weeks the Literacy Committee had 170 members in thirty provinces, including Saratov.[16]

Sunday schools also appeared everywhere at this time and grew in the same natural way out of dispersed but very similar perceptions of social needs. Directly after Elizaveta Mordvinova returned with her husband to Saratov from the Isle of Wight, she joined with Sof'ia Tepliakova, Liudmila Moskvina, Iuliia Kondrat'eva, and Malvida Belova (Evgenii's wife) to found a Sunday school for girls. A. A. Meier, the director of the local gymnasium, oversaw the creation of another Sunday school.[17] Eventually three schools were established in the city of Saratov and an equal number in the province. Private initiative raced ahead of church and state and significantly augmented primary educational opportunities in the province.

A solid network of pedagogical associations formed across the empire. Schools required teachers, curricula, books, and other materials. In the absence of settled guidelines, volunteer societies worked on their own. In February 1861, the Ministry of Education approved regular meetings of a national executive committee and representatives from regional Sunday schools, in order to "assure unity of activities." Pavel Annenkov served as first chairman.[18] By the summer of 1862, Sunday schools were meeting in nearly every region with official approval and with the goal of providing free primary education for the poor.[19] The activities of the schools were to some degree coordinated and their social/political implications were reasonably clear to all, but they were not conspiratorial.

For Globa in Saratov, however, as for Potapov and Dolgorukov in the capital, these and other social endeavors were interpreted as conspiracies. The police urged officials to end all paternal indulgence of social freedom. Increasingly the police explained social vitality in terms of malignancy and alien infection. Globa's "moral instincts" reflected a growing insecurity in the relationship between state and society. Minister of Interior Peter Valuev was beginning to see things much as did the police.[20] On the basis of Globa's report on the literary evening in Saratov, Alexander II ordered an investigation of Mordvinov.

The fears of Globa and his superiors rested not only on their view that sedition was a foreign import and that social endeavors were conspiracy, but also on a dread that educated "society" might join and reinforce traditional peasant unrest. As the tempo of disorder in the countryside quickened, the state's fear and jealousy of anyone who sought to come between it and its narod deepened. As social activism flourished in the cities, popular discontent flared into disorder in the countryside. The state perceived the danger that these two processes might coalesce in a great uprising. Sunday schools provided a dangerous line of communication between civil society and the narod. The fear of a new Pugachev, this time a "student-Pugachev" was very real, even if the threat of such was largely illusory.

Beginning in 1859, Daniil Mordovtsev contributed to these fears when he introduced on the pages of *Saratovskiia gubernskiia vedomosti* extensive coverage of the harsh economic realities shared by urbanites and peasants alike. Mordovtsev's journal described the suffering not just of the dark masses, but of the local administrative and business "elite" as well. These columns, if they had not mortified Globa, might at least have helped him to understand the circumstances, rather than the conspiracies, that promoted self-help circles, cafeterias, free libraries, and other "positive" initiatives among Saratov chinovniki, raznochintsy, and students.[21]

Recalling the memory of another famous son of Saratov, Alexander Radishchev, Mordovtsev wrote of an eye-opening trip "From Saratov to Atkarsk and Return." Atkarsk lies sixty-six miles west of Saratov where the road to Tambov crosses the Medveditsa River, a tributary of the Don. Mordovtsev, like Radishchev in his "Journey from Saint Petersburg to Moscow," described a pitiful scene: architectural decrepitude, poverty, and illness. In the village of Elshanka he did not find Anton Goremyka ("the Wretch"). "I looked around and saw that there is not one Anton. The whole village is Antons: the children, the grandchildren, the great grandchildren of Anton. . . ."[22] In a time when most journalists employed the phrase "improvement in the conditions of life for the peasantry," Mordovtsev wrote in clear strokes: "Abolish the hated and destructive serfdom and we will straightway see how free working forces will overflow the whole land everywhere its necessity is recognized."[23]

But was serfdom all that Mordovtsev meant to imply, was serfdom all that his readers understood him to mean? Few thought the problem was limited to the servile relationship of agricultural laborer to aristocratic landowner. Serfdom was coupled in Mordovtsev's mind with systemic economic backwardness, absence of self rule through elected officials, absence of any control over assessment and expenditure of tax revenues, and absence of a legal and administrative system directly responsible to the people through national elections. Mordovtsev's attitude toward serfdom was of a piece with a widely shared general set of political, social, and economic attitudes. These ideas were hardly elaborate enough to be called an ideology, but they were just a bit too uniform and structured to be called only a "mentality." They represented a shared perspective on the era of reforms which, without conspiracy and even without clear and direct political challenge to the state, terrorized Globa and the police administration.

Certainly, Herzen and his *Kolokol* in London broadened political consciousness in Saratov; Chernyshevskii and his *Sovremennik* in St. Petersburg, though muted by the censor, did much the same. Individually, Blagosvetlov and his journal had a clearer and more direct influence on Mordovtsev than Herzen or Chernyshevskii; Mordovtsev and Blagosvetlov exchanged a fascinating professional correspondence. Mordovtsev's commitment to glasnost and pereustroistvo, what we might call his "perspective," stemmed from the same disgusting circumstances of national life that had shaped Herzen, Chernyshevskii, and Blagosvetlov themselves.

The state did not welcome anything like "shared perspectives" in society; it sought from society no ideas about what the people needed. It turned its back on the very gentry committees it itself had invited to design projects for reform. Increasingly it was coming to fear society—especially when that abstraction, "society," expressed itself as a "public" and took concrete organizational form in provincial gentry committees, peasant cooperatives, urban literacy societies, Sunday schools, salons, circles, literacy committees, and free-enterprise joint-stock companies, such as the steamboat lines that plied the Volga and connected Saratov with the wider world as never before. Society in these forms was more than an "untrustworthy" nuisance; it had become a dangerous competitor with easy access to an aroused agricultural population. In order to deal with it, the state had to search for conspiracy in what was essentially a natural, if unprecedented, outburst of social vitality.

The peasants of Saratov Province were no less quick than urban raznochintsy intellectuals to discover means, sometimes blunt, to promote or defend their interests. Even prior to emancipation, the temperance movement dramatically demonstrated that ability. The movement resulted from a state decision to increase the excise tax on alcoholic beverages.[24] Without any apparent central direction, peasant "temperance societies" or "brotherhoods" sprang up all over the empire. They appeared first in western provinces, but they arose at about the same time in Saratov, notably in Atkarsk, Balashov, and Serdobsk districts. Excise collections in Saratov over the previous four years had equaled just over 482,000 rubles; they were now to be trebled.[25] In response, elders assembled whole villages of adult males who took oaths and signed written pledges not to consume spirituous liquors. Sentries patroled entrances to taverns in Balashov to prevent the purchase of vodka or to bring offenders to justice before peasant judges.[26] The goal was not so much temperance as organized defense of defined economic interests.[27]

Faced with economic losses, the state intervened. In the name of public order and legality, it took measures to bring an end to temperance societies; as Herzen sarcastically put it, drunkenness had become a patriotic and Christian duty.[28] Peasants in Saratov and elsewhere still resisted. For example, in late June 1859, in the river town Volsk north of Saratov, three thousand villagers rioted, destroyed several drinking establishments, and seriously injured the town bailiff. Over the next few days disorders spread. Crowds of peasants appeared at taverns, broke windows, forced doors, and destroyed all spiritous liquors.[29] By summer there was less evidence of oaths, brotherhoods, and temperance; instead there were drunken mobs angry about deceptive and exploitative price hikes.

Alleged conspiracy, illegal assembly, and now disorder served as pretexts for state action. Dolgorukov reported to Alexander in the spring of 1860 that the movement in Saratov and elsewhere required suppression in response to "willful criminal acts of zealots of sobriety." The state reminded local authorities that they could not allow "the willful establishment by inhabitants of any sort of societies and written oaths, nor [could] they be allowed to take the law into their own hands."[30] Further reflection convinced Dolgorukov that the growth of temperance organizations had been far too rapid to be spontaneous. The chief gendarme, who did not drink peasant vodka himself, could not perceive anything of the natural causes for immediate and ubiquitous popular resistance to exploitative state fiscal policy. To his way of thinking, the temperance movement had to be a conspiracy. By 1860 the movement was suppressed, often by military means.[31] Of the 780 arrests nationwide connected with the crackdown on the temperance movement, 220, or nearly one-third, were made in Saratov Province.[32]

Much the same sense of individual and collective self-interest guided peasants in Saratov and other provinces in their rejection of the proclamation of February 1861 that putatively abolished serfdom. Disorders erupted on 120 Saratov gentry estates. The government responded with explanations that peasants could not accept, and then with brute force that peasants could resist only feebly.

The most extensive uprising took place on the Chetvertinskii estates located inland from Kamyshin, about halfway between Saratov and Tsaritsyn, straddling the Volga and Don watersheds. Prince V. I. Vasil'chikov was on his family's estate in nearby Balashov District and witnessed the uprising. He reported in a letter to Moscow associates in the Agricultural Society that the manifesto was pronounced with great and obscure pomp on the steppes, just as everywhere else in the empire, and that no one could get his hands on the actual statute which explained what emancipation really meant. "This has allowed everyone to interpret the manifesto in his own way. That's what started the whole brouhaha." Setting the stage for this explosive confusion, Prince Chetvertinskii, had "in a most exacting manner laid waste to 6000 souls in Kamyshin District. Many have been reduced to nothing. A few years previously they appealed to the local Governor [A. D. Ignat'ev], but that notable of the realm could not hear an appeal from muzhiks (although it is said that he could hear the sound of 12,000 silver rubles from Prince Chetvertinskii). . . ."[33]

Peasants immediately preceived the central notion of the pompous emancipation declaration: their freedom was put off for two years. In the absence of the actual statute, however, they refused to honor continuing *barshchina* (feudal labor dues) obligations. Local authorities tried on their own to get peasants to work, but with no luck. Then a chinovnik from the Guberniia administration, Rakhmaninov, arrived but did no more than repeat the old story: in addition to the manifesto, there is a specific statute in which everything is explained. Peasants asked to see the statute. Rakhmaninov, whom Vasil'chikov calls "the Guberniia goose," assured them that he wanted to show them the statute but had forgotten the keys to his baggage. "What a fool!" Vasil'chikov erupts. "Naturally no one wanted to listen to him any more."

Then came aide-de-camp L. Ia. Iankovskii, directly from the *tsar-batiushka,* Alexander II. He did not have the statute with him, nor could he explain anything. Peasants replied in terms of sly naiveté that some have mistaken for idealization of the emperor. Surely tsar-batiuska would not send them such an ineffective and ignorant aide-de-camp? They questioned whether Iankovskii might not be an impostor and demanded to see his identification papers. A lovely political moment, this, when the peasants through their village agents sought to confirm the credentials of the tsar's agent. Iankovskii showed his written orders and departed in a huff.[34]

Iankovskii had exhausted the limited repertoire of imperial measures for dealing peacefully with popular discontent—namely, bluff. He had no further recourse but to troops. Two battalions appeared, composed of 560 troops under his own command. They moved systematically from village to village. Vasil'chikov described the scene:

It is true that up to this time, so far as I could see, no whips had popped, but the aide[-de-camp] found other methods. To feed the troops, they slaughtered chickens, lambs and calves. Then if they [the peasants] did not go to work they slaughtered the cattle too. The peasants, who were destitute enough before this, were now finally and completely ruined. Is this the sort of thing these fools think will strengthen the authority of the government?[35]

Vasil'chikov should have known perfectly well that the imperial state did not depend on the good will of the toiling masses in the countryside, even though it did very directly depend on their toil. Two fears lay at the foundation of the state action: that the disorder might spread, and that it might result in the fields not being planted. Good will, unlike grain and taxes, was a luxury, not a necessity.

April 5 was the day of crucial confrontation. The notorious Governor Ignat'ev and the marshals of both provincial and district nobility accompanied Iankovskii and his troops. Peasants bore some firearms but mainly brandished the traditional rustic weaponry of discontent, staves and pitchforks. They vowed to die rather than consent to loss of their land or to false liberty. A powerful as well as dignified imperial force and an unruly but righteous mob confronted one another. Negotiations dragged on for three hours while Iankovskii deployed his troops in an encirclement. Soldiers surprised and captured leaders of the uprising and had them flogged. After requesting thirty minutes to talk things over, peasants reported that some still stubbornly refused to give in but the crowd would disperse.[36] Thus we observe tsarist social policy in the Saratov countryside during the year of Emancipation.

Resistance flared to new heights in 1862, inspired by the widely held and astonishingly plain assumption that the manifesto granted land and the liberty to work it.[37] Deterioration in living conditions further provoked disorder. Saratov justice of the peace A. N. Minkh described the decline in average income of Saratov peasants as going from approximately 60 to 45 rubles per year, in some places to only 30. Drunkenness reached new heights, and the dingy taverns, earlier the site of powerful peasant self-organization against the excise tax, were now the scene of frequent brawls and occasional murders. Many more than usual froze to death in the countryside. All the while, the peasant village assembly struggled unsuccessfully to cope with the situation.[38]

Troops were deployed in the Saratov countryside sixty-four times in the two and one-half years after Emancipation. Over this period Saratov exceeded all other provinces by a substantial margin, alone accounting for more than 10 percent of the 619 uprisings suppressed by military force in forty-one provinces throughout the empire.[39]

Conspiracy was not altogether absent from a scene as volatile as this, but conspiracy was mainly the product of events, and it took two forms. First, as we have seen, the intelligentsia and the peasants, independently of one another, began to organize themselves without seeking, or waiting for, formal state approval. Second, the intelligentsia opened communications with the narod, via proclamations, with an eye to connecting their own organizations with the energy or potential of popular discontent. A third possible form of conspiracy did not occur: the narod made no reciprocal motion toward the organizations of the intelligentsia.

Conspiracy from the metropolis appears first to have found its way to the Saratov periphery in Alexander Sleptsov's bags in the spring of 1862. Sleptsov's family had estates there, and Mordvinov's brother was one of Sleptsov's closest associates in St. Petersburg. Sleptsov traveled down the Volga, eventually to Saratov, as an agent of the Literacy Committee, but one who thought of that organization in the grandest historical terms.[40] He was in western Europe when the literacy project first got under way, and now he represented the Society for the Publication of Inexpensive Books for the People *(Obshchestvo dlia izdaniia deshevykh knig dlia naroda* or *Redaktsionnaia komiteta dlia izdaniia populiarnykh knig),* centered in St. Petersburg with Annenkov, A. F. Pogosskii, P. V. Pavlov, and other national leaders of the Sunday school movement at its head. The organization had ambitious plans to supply books and materials to the far-flung volunteer school system. The new endeavor promised employment for translators, writers, publishers, administrators, and other representatives of the nascent intelligentsia.[41] Sleptsov liked to think of the enterprise as a component of yet a grander concept, Land and Liberty, which he felt was already coming into organized existence.

Globa wrote his troubled letter to Potapov, in which he spoke of his moral certainties, at the time of Sleptsov's visit to Saratov. Curiously, Globa never mentions Sleptsov, in this letter or any other reports. Sleptsov conferred, by all accounts, with two separate Saratov circles. First, he met with fellow Litfond members and their associates, Mordvinov, Belov, and their circle. Second, he met with an earlier acquaintance from Kazan, Alexander Khristoforov. He might at this time have met other members of Khristoforov's circle of twenty or so university students. Many of these were participants in Sunday schools and maintained close ties with the teachers at the Saratov Gymnasium.[42]

Khristoforov's circle consisted mainly of young natives of Saratov who had earlier gone off to college in the big cities, Kazan, Moscow, and St. Petersburg. The bolder ones became involved there in organized defense of student rights and the liberal gains of the post-Crimean university. At the university they formed libraries and other student service organizations, met in regular assemblies of their own creation, and fought to protect the admissions and tuition policies that had recently opened higher education and access to service careers to people just like themselves, the raznochintsy intelligentsia. These advances, seemingly encouraged in the early years of Alexander II's reign, were all now in the process of being reversed.[43]

In various connections, most of these former students had been arrested and were now together in Saratov as gently exiled "untrustworthies." Returning them to their homes after arrest was thought to be a mild extension of their punishment. They were seasoned activists, or on the verge of becoming so; they had time on their hands and were concentrated in what was fast becoming a volatile location. One, Alexander Volkov, had received financial aid from Litfond. Some, like Viktor Umnov and Nikolai Peskov, took part in Professor Shchapov's demonstration in commemoration of the Bezdna massacre in Kazan Province, just up the river from Saratov.[44] Another, Dmitrii Karakozov, had done nothing yet to distinguish himself, but four years later he seriously altered the course of public life in Russia when he shot at, and missed, the emperor.

Sleptsov's appearance must have encouraged local activists, but Khristoforov received little of direct use from the visit. He wrote later that the "significance and purpose" of Sleptsov's visit was "not altogether clear to us."[45] Sleptsov certainly met also with Mordvinov and his associates.[46] But Sleptsov's grand scheme did not yet seem of any particular value to these provincial activists, whose momentum and direction were defined by local circumstances. Pavel Rovinskii, whom Sleptsov visited in Kazan, recalled later that there were at that time few members and even fewer agents of Sleptsov's grand organization in the provinces, "but there were many people who were intellectually sympathetic."[47] For his own part, Sleptsov was disturbed to find little more than isolated circles in Saratov and other provinces. These tended just to fade away, he said, never realizing "that circles with analogous objectives and goals, but of course with variations, existed side by side, often in one and the same city."[48]

Sleptsov perceived the similarities between circles like Khristoforov's and Mordvinov's but failed to see that they did work closely with one another and, in their own local way, were already in synchronization with national trends. They accepted and circulated many of the same proclamations and supported one another on local political issues. Over dinner at public restaurants, where agents eavesdropped, Mordvinov imprudently recommended that the Saratov gentry imitate the rebellious Tver gentry, thirteen of whom had just been arrested. The "Great Deeds," as the three formal papers of the Tver nobility were titled, were printed in Berlin and circulated illegally in Saratov and elsewhere that spring.

The demands of the Tver gentry were known to all literate Russians: that national credit policy address the plight of both landowner and serf; that temporary bondage be terminated and the peasant assume dominion over the land with full property rights, financed by the nation as a whole; that the financial system be placed under national control, courts be made open and independent of administration, and public scrutiny be introduced into all branches of state and social administration; that "harmful relations between classes" be abolished; and that an assembly of delegates elected by the whole nation be convoked.[49]

In addition to the Tver "deeds," Khristoforov and his associates showed a particular preference for three proclamations, "Officers!," "Zemskaia duma," and "What do the People Need?"[50] When the Volga entered spring breakup in 1862 and the season's first steamboats of the "Caucasus" and "Mercury" plied the river again, these and other pamphlets found their way to Saratov docks in sailors', junior officers', and stock-holders' bags. Their larger "shared perspective" is more remarkable than their internal differences.[51] Without exception, all assumed that the folk would need, perhaps even seek, the guidance of a learned, privileged leadership—people like Sleptsov, Khristoforov, Mordvinov, and Rovinskii.[52] Globa read the proclamations and looked about him with clear recognition. They seemed perfectly tailored to the local situation. Furthermore, differences between the Khristoforov and Mordvinov circles were negligible enough that Globa assumed the two were joint authors of the proclamations.[53]

Globa's fear that these printed pages represented real associations of intellectuals with the narod was not altogether outrageous; he just did not understand that proclamations actually functioned more as instruments of self-definition on the part of the intellectuals who wrote them and read them with earnest fascination. He was, of course, dead wrong in his certainty that Khristoforov and Mordvinov were joint authors. And neither group had more than the most remote relationship to the disorders in the countryside. But Globa was quite right to see in proclamations and in local groups a congruence of defined problems and projected solutions.

Saratov groups worked closely with one another on the local scene and in Sunday schools but not in the fields and villages with the mutinous peasantry. A characteristic action was the one taken jointly in the spring of 1862 in support of students in the gymnasium. The director had addressed an unresponsive student in excessively harsh words. Upperclassmen, after consulting with Khristoforov's circle, demanded that the director make a public apology. Students held meetings in the school which the director tried to break up. In one instance, a demonstrator ignored the director's instruction to leave a classroom. The director grabbed him by the arm as if to pull him through the door, at which point the student struck him in the face. The city was shocked when the story got around. One local wrote excitedly to Ivan Aksakov in Moscow describing the event and giving a particular flavor to the physical assault.

Now there's our liberalism for you, our high regard for the individual and law! You will say that this is the sort of thing that could happen at any time. Yes, such things happen all the time, but they do not always arise from this source. In this case one must adopt a different opinion. The specific source and the attitude of society toward the episode—these are the essence of the matter. Is it not significant, for example, that the question has arisen not about whether this fellow ought to be punished but about whether the director ought to be allowed to continue in his post? Yes such things are not unusual, not out of the ordinary, but now they are calling it an accomplishment and the perpetrator a hero, a *champion* of freedom and truth, a martyr for ideas.[54]

The episode was not over. When officials endeavored to gather testimony about the event, one of the Khristoforov circle refused to answer questions: "Your stupid laws are written by just such scoundrels as you. I refuse now and in the future to answer your stupid questions."[55] With the support of Khristoforov's and Mordvinov's groups, the students petitioned the regional board of education, located in Kazan. The director there, in turn, sought guidance from Minister of the Interior Valuev.

As a consequence, the director of the gymnasium was relieved of his duties and the aggressive student, who had been made a soldier in a punishment brigade, was freed.[56] The whole incident was a comedy of bad manners and behavioral excess, hardly on a par with the temperance movement or more recent peasant disorders; but the Khristoforov and Mordvinov circles could count it another victory of the public over incompetent officialdom. For Aksakov's Saratov correspondent, the whole edifice seemed to shake. Nor could Globa have been heartened by this development.

At about the same time another distressful episode shook the community. Emboldened by one or two drinks too many, Dr. Minkevich became boisterous at the crowded theater buffet when he overheard someone refer to "the monarch." "Monarch!" the bold medic pronounced for all to hear, "He'll learn about monarch when we set upon him with brooms."[57] It was not clear whether Minkevich meant with his broom to urge the tsar to greater speed, as one might a troika, or whether he meant to sweep the monarch out altogether. Given the choice of interpretations, the buffet crowd prudently headed for the exits.

Globa's persistence began to pay off, as events of this sort added spice to the bubbling caldron of popular uprising. Globa's fear of an alliance among the Mordvinovs, Khristoforovs, and pugnacious gymnasium students, on the one hand, and the people, on the other, found support among his superiors, even though such an alliance did not exist. As rural unrest mounted toward its most intense season in early 1862, Dolgorukov dispatched a special commission to Saratov, headed by imperial aide-de-camp N. V. Mezentsov. Mezentsov's reports in July alleged that Baranovskii's liberal governorship was the essential cause of unrest on the middle Volga. Mezentsov also named Mordvinov and several of the exiled students.[58]

Perhaps Mezentsov's most important observation, however, was that the evildoings in the city of Saratov were not spilling over into the countryside. Minister of the Interior Valuev nonetheless soon took steps to have Governor Baranovskii removed. The good Dr. Minkevich was exiled by administrative order to Kostroma.[59] Measures were also taken to scatter student exiles concentrated in the city. Khristoforov and some of his associates were sent away in November. Mordvinov was first transferred, then fired in 1865.[60]

Events in Saratov were replicated elsewhere in the empire, and most decisively in the capital. On May 31, 1862, when the embers of a great fire that threatened to destroy the center of the capital had not yet cooled, Globa's immediate chief, General Potapov, borrowed some of Globa's style for his own report to Dolgorukov. He averred that open war against the government had broken out, launched not just by "demagogues and socialists" but also by liberals, even by civilian and military servitors. Circumstances called for measures that were "lamentably" repressive. He recommended the suppression of the Sunday schools, the Free University, the popular libraries, the Chess Club, and the Student Section of Litfond. "In harmony with this, do not allow any new societies or enterprises under any name, except commercial and industrial enterprises."[61] The state acted on all Potapov's recommendations. By mid-June these organizations had been suppressed throughout the empire. Several individuals most active in the Sunday schools were arrested. *Sovremennik* and other journals were suspended. In July, Dmitrii Pisarev, Chernyshevskii, and Nikolai Serno-Solov'evich were arrested. By September, over one hundred writers, scholars, intellectuals, social activists, students, officers, and others were in prison, under arrest, or warranted for arrest.

The political situation had so deteriorated that the only possible substantial efforts toward social activism were in the radical underground. "Underground" and "secret" contradicted the "public" and publicity concepts so dear to activists up to this point, but the state had now cleared the horizon of significant legal organizations and opportunities. Land and Liberty emerged from this process. It was not the creation of an aggressive, coherent, and centralized revolutionary movement; instead, it was shaped under the heavy press of events, particularly in the aftermath of closures and arrests. In mid-June 1862, Rovinskii played a key role in organizing the most important affiliate in the Volga region, in Kazan.[62] The organization came into its own only toward the end of that year, the small, stamped-upon remains of a much larger and spontaneous epoch of social activism.

By then it was too late to connect with popular discontent except in Polish and Belorussian regions of the empire. And just up the Volga from Saratov, a far from glorious final episode in the brief history of Land and Liberty unfolded in 1863. The Kazan Conspiracy consisted of false manifestoes and other rebellious initiatives, directed less at meeting the economic and political needs of the Russian people than the military needs of the besieged Polish uprising. Rovinskii opposed the venture, as did most of the Volga activists, but plans nonetheless went forward. The Kazan Conspiracy was a backdoor attack launched to divert Russian troops from Polish independence fighters. The state swiftly and decisively crushed it.[63] Land and Liberty soon dissolved.

Public activism in Saratov flared up again weakly, but without any direct connection to Land and Liberty. Dr. Vetter chaired another literary evening, with the approval of the new governor, V. A. Shcherbatov. In the eyes of the state, Shcherbatov had served as marshal of the Saratov nobility with distinction throughout the deliberations on Emancipation. Other provinces had been more like Tver, troublesome and assertive. So when Baranovskii was replaced in October 1862, Shcherbatov was a natural choice. Globa, however, was quick to link the new governor, as he had the preceding one, with untrustworthy associates and vague threats to the regime.

The police were most upset with the doings of three or more new craft associations *(arteli, masterskie)* that appeared to be supported by Khristoforov and some of his earlier associates who had found their way back to Saratov by the summer of 1864. Khristoforov and his group now fashioned themselves as a commune, following a popular trend most visibly represented by the recent publication of Chernyshevskii's prison novel *What's to be Done?* With money and other support from Mordvinov's circle, Khristoforov's commune sought to provide "start-up" loans to several déclassé cabinetmakers, cobblers, and tailors in order to encourage them to form cooperative enterprises. They were guided by a publication which they had been busily translating, E. Pfeifer's *Assotsiatsii,* which recommends co-op practices as an antidote to proletarianization and revolutionary agitation.[64]

These were hardly seditious acts, although they might be said to have presented an unwelcome competition with merchant entrepreneurs who had the crafts in Saratov essentially under their authority. Of Khristoforov's several initiatives, however, apparently only the woodworking cooperative had any success. Without state approval, it set out on its own to submit bids for work. The gymnasium, possibly acting under the influence of sympathetic teachers there, contracted with the co-op for the handsome sum of 500 rubles to fabricate new windows. For another business, Antonina Inzhevskaia's seamstress shop, Khristoforov published advertising leaflets on an underground press. Inzhevskaia's shop was of no political importance except that, like the craft co-ops and the press, it also operated without state approval.

As investigations got under way, Governor Shcherbatov requested that the whole matter be dropped, as it was no serious threat to state security. This convinced the police that he was trying to protect the great number of local officials and other highly-placed persons who supported Khristoforov and his enterprises. Valuev did not heed Shcherbatov's request and in fact stepped up investigations. Khristoforov and other leading suspects were arrested and tried. No real evidence of specific crimes could be generated, but never mind. Again the state exercised its "administrative exile" option and sent Khristoforov to Arkhangelsk and others to lesser exile outposts.[65] The political crisis in Saratov was over.

Social discontent in the cities had reached high levels and was expressed in a wide variety of public organizations and enterprises that raced ahead of, or away from, governmental bureaus and programs. Social discontent in the countryside had similarly reached high levels and was more dramatically expressed in massive refusals to go along with governmental agents and programs, which required forceful suppression by the state. The parallel refusal of the state to support public initiatives and the failure of urban and rural groups to unite with one another in opposition to state social policies sealed the fate of social movements in Saratov and throughout the empire.[66] For this reason it can be said that Russia in the 1860s experienced a revolutionary "situation" but not a revolution, not even a coherent revolutionary conspiracy. The politics of the cities and the countryside represented an authentic crisis, but the crisis arose from circumstances, not from conspiracies.

Dolgorukov was wrong to seek alien sources of rebellion, but in a sense he was correct when he said that rebellion had no roots in the native soil or in native sources. Revolution did not flourish in the 1860s because it had not yet *sufficiently* rooted itself. For the first time in Russian history, modern revolution, of the sort that would eventually topple Dolgorukov's world, had sent up tender shoots and found nourishment in the countryside, in provincial cities, and in the capitals. But the season for growth was in the future. Although the time of small circles had passed, the time of national political organization had not yet come. When Dolgorukov said that the movement had no roots, what he meant was that he could easily uproot it.

Fearing all forms of social initiative, the state set its powerful and arbitrary police and administrative/judicial mechanisms in motion against a suspected underground conspiracy. It sent in troops against temperance societies and took administrative measures, like those of Mezentsov in Saratov, to clear the countryside and cities of their most vigorous social organizations. It freely employed administrative exile to crush and alter the lives of its bolder citizens, often on the basis of no more evidence than moral certainty. By these acts the state crippled the natural expression of social interests and actually contributed to an underground conspiracy. We might still call the military, legal, administrative, and peasant reforms of this era "great," but autocratic "social policy" was miserable.

Land and Liberty—conspiracy in general—was the consequence, not the cause, of the political crisis; but once it appeared on the scene it provided police, future activists, and historians alike with a menacing symbol of nationwide revolutionary organization. The struggles to exist of temperance brotherhoods, salons, circles, public lectures, Sunday schools, the Literary Fund, and scores of other public initiatives, and their defeat in Saratov and elsewhere, created the situation out of which Land and Liberty grew. Forgetting this, policemen and historians have too often stripped events of their lively spontaneity. And yet in the same stroke, as they searched for a simple structure, they have denied historical experience its subtle coherence. Perhaps the most enduring legacy of the 1860s was a civil society still hungering for independence but bitter and cynical about the possibility, under conditions of autocratic centralization, of their achieving what in that distant era they called "glasnost" and "pereustroistvo."

4. Populists, Workers, Peasants, and the Beginning of Worker Organization in Saratov

Pamela Sears McKinsey

SARATOV PROVINCE in 1877 was the site of curious events. Three blond St. Petersburg metalworkers wandered about the Saratov countryside that summer, searching unsuccessfully for a spot to practice a craft and form friendships with the local population. The peasants took them for the advance party of German settlers. Meanwhile, in the little village of Ershovka, Khvalynsk District, on the banks of the Volga, a few self-effacing Populists rented a smithy and lived there quietly for two months. However, after receiving telegrams, they disappeared in mid-July—so suddenly that they left behind their newspapers and the books *The Practical Shoeing of Horses* and *The Country Kitchen Garden*. In the fall of that year, in the outskirts of the city of Saratov, a St. Petersburg Populist with an increasing renown spoke outdoors to *Saratovtsy* and visitors on the topic: What is the value of strikes and protests?[1]

The development of a revolutionary workers' organization in Saratov is the central theme of this chapter. This process accelerated rapidly in the second half of the 1870s but had its roots in the preceding two decades. The attempt to propagandize the Saratov workers was not simply a result of the influence of visitors from St. Petersburg and Moscow, or of autonomous Saratov circles, but of an interaction between the two. One striking feature of this story is the role played by several city workers from St. Petersburg in stimulating the effort in the later 1870s.

The beginning of left-liberal agitation in Saratov may date to 1851–52, when N. G. Chernyshevskii, a native of the city, returned from St. Petersburg University to teach in a gymnasium. Although he soon quarreled with the bishop and in 1853 returned to St. Petersburg to begin his writing career for *Sovremennik* (The Contemporary), he had searching conversations with students, intellectuals, and gentry in Saratov. "Thanks to the influence of Chernyshevskii," there were a number of people in Saratov, even among bureaucrats, who considered themselves "liberals and even radicals."[2] These, as Alan Kimball (chap. 3) demonstrates, began to coalesce into a "public" by the early 1860s.

The Volga provinces became an important focus of attention for the intelligentsia of St. Petersburg and Moscow in the late 1850s and early 1860s. Folklorists collected songs and poems that proved the folk memories of Razin and Pugachev were still alive. The terms of the serf reform were ungenerous, and the 120 incidents of peasant unrest in Saratov province in 1861, of which 64 required military suppression, suggested that the Volga peasants' spirit of revolt was strong. Many people expected the peasantry to express its unhappiness by rising up, and some even went into the countryside to survey the mood.[3]

The group Land and Liberty of the early 1860s planned to target areas of discontent, setting up committees affiliated with the central St. Petersburg organization. With this in mind, one of the leaders, Alexander A. Sleptsov, in the summer of 1862 journeyed along the Volga, contacting young people in Saratov, among other cities.[4] In spring 1863, Polish students from St. Petersburg University in contact with Land and Liberty distributed a false manifesto in the Volga countryside, hoping against hope to create a diversion to relieve Russian military pressure on Poland. Several copies of the manifesto were distributed in Kuznetsk District.[5]

One of the earliest attempts in Russia to forge links with Saratov workers was Alexander Kh. Khristoforov's 1863 founding of producers' cooperative organizations. Khristoforov had taken part in student protests at the University of Kazan in 1861 and was in contact with Land and Liberty and the Polish students.[6] Officials in Kazan considered him a bad influence and exiled him to the city of Saratov. There Khristoforov and several friends convinced some joiners, shoemakers, and tailors to leave their masters and set up cooperative workshops, with the profits to be divided equally. To launch the workshops Khristoforov collected over a hundred rubles from some well-respected members of Saratov society. His associates included officials, teachers, doctors, gymnasium pupils, and the director of the Saratov gymnasium. The latter encouraged the joiners' cooperative by contracting with it to make window frames for the school building. Khristoforov preached the attractive message to the workers that, as all people are equal, it is wrong for a master to enrich himself at his employees' expense. He and his friends read to the workers excerpts from Proudhon on property, from Fourier on the situation of women, an item on religion, and extracts on cooperatives in England, France, and Germany.[7]

While Khristoforov claimed that he wanted to help the workers out of simple compassion, the investigating gendarme believed that he was undermining the bases of society by encouraging "communistic ideas," and that if disorders occurred, Khristoforov would assume command of the workers to no good end. The officer was particularly irate at the governor who tried to suppress the inquiry, saying, "I know that many in Saratov are sympathetic to this work of Khristoforov, and the inquiry should not be pursued so as to avoid irritating people of liberal tendency." Even the Saratov chief of police refused his assistance.[8]

This early attempt to organize workers in Saratov suggests that the Saratov intelligentsia participated in the progressive intellectual movements of Russia and even of Europe. Further, the moderate tone of the attempt attracted a wide cross-section of Saratov's society. As for Khristoforov, since no criminal activity could be proven against him, he was simply exiled from Saratov and later went abroad, where he became involved in publishing.

Khristoforov's message was not forgotten. In 1877, when G.V. Plekhanov was in Saratov, he discovered that "Khristoforov had become friends with many local workers. They long remembered him. In 1877 they told us *zemlevol'tsy* [members of Land and Liberty] that from the time that he lived in Saratov the spark of revolutionary thought which he had lit never went out in the local worker milieu. People who had not known him personally traced their intellectual genealogy to him."[9]

Saratov Province also nurtured extremists. Several years after Khristoforov's activity, the Saratov natives D.V. Karakozov and N.A. Ishutin joined with some of the students close to Khristoforov in making plans to free Khristoforov from exile. With the collapse of the Karakozov organization after his attempt on the tsar, widespread arrests occurred in Saratov, and the gymnasium and seminary were temporarily closed.[10]

The urban laboring population of the Volga provinces by 1870 was small. In the five provinces of Saratov (in 1871), Samara, Simbirsk, Penza, and Nizhnii Novgorod (in 1870) there were, all told, only fifty thousand people engaged in factories and workshops of whatever size; and over the next decade the total did not grow by more than eighteen thousand. Most of these worked in small concerns that processed food products, flour mills in particular.[11] Cottage trades proliferated. In the second half of the nineteenth century, the main cottage trades of Saratov Province were woodworking, including wagons and simple wooden furniture, wicker and bentwood furniture, wooden trunks, wooden dishes, and pipes; the forging of farm machines and tools (centered in the German colony "Lesnoi Karamysh");[12] preparing millstones; the working up of animal hides, including tanning, the work of furriers, and the shoe trade, done mostly by women; and finally, the working up of cotton, wool, and hemp, including the weaving of calico (done in the German colonies, especially in Kamyshin District, a trade which by the end of the century was valued at two million rubles yearly and employed seven thousand people, one-half of them women, weaving calico in their homes), rug weaving, and the hand-knitting of wool items by women and girls, rope making, and some sewing of peasant clothes and the making of felt items.[13]

But it was the archetypal farming peasant who attracted the Populists to Saratov. They allowed themselves to hope once again that the land of Razin and Pugachev would provide the peasant forces to topple the autocracy, if they could only be mobilized. Unfortunately for the Populists, peasant rebelliousness on the Volga was temporarily dormant; studies of peasant disturbances in Russia in the 1870s have found fewer instances for the whole decade than for the preceding six-year period.[14] However, the famine in Samara Province in 1873 encouraged revolutionary hopes that conditions were ripe for a peasant uprising on the Volga.

Furthermore, the mood in Saratov itself soon grew expectant. In the early 1870s people read the literature of moral obligation, were concerned with "being a useful member of society," while the works of Dobroliubov, Bervi-Flerovskii, and Chernyshevskii, and various journal articles on the worker question and associations circulated in the gymnasium.[15] The pupils got a taste of Petersburg radicalism in the spring of 1873, when the sister of one of them brought from St. Petersburg some underground literature published abroad; and a Petersburg propagandist visited briefly, forming acquaintances among the young people and disbursing literature.[16] The gymnasium pupil Stepan Shiriaev and his friends "greedily. . . attacked the 'forbidden fruit,' at once swallowed all there was, and went about as if in a fog, like madmen—so new was this, so unexpected, and at the same time, fascinating beyond expression."[17]

The person most responsible for introducing St. Petersburg radicalism to Saratov students and workers was Porfirii I. Voinaral'skii of Penza Province. The wealthy illegitimate son of a landowner, Voinaral'skii, in the autumn of 1872 during a visit to Moscow, found that his zemstvo-liberal ideas could not be sustained in debates with the students there. He went to St. Petersburg to experience the student movement at its center, renounced his moderate views, and began searching for a way to be useful to the revolution.[18]

In the winter and spring of 1874, many radical students developed plans to contact disaffected groups in Russia, hoping that these might serve as a spearhead to rebellion against the autocracy and existing social system—or, failing that, might at least provide shelter and funds for the propagandists. These groups included peasants stricken with drought and famine; robbers and thieves, as victims of the oppressive social system; non-Russian ethnic groups; religious nonconformists; and finally, the trans-Volga, because of its traditions of rebellion. At large gatherings students discussed the plans for the coming summer. Voinaral'skii committed himself and his fortune to setting up places for the propagandists to shelter all across the trans-Volga area, which, along with the Urals, was considered the ripest ground for propaganda.[19]

Voinaral'skii, in Moscow in April 1874, financed I. N. Myshkin's printing press and opened a shoemaking shop headed by an apprentice shoemaker and associate of the Petersburg Chaikovskyites, Iogan (Johan) Pel'konen. In mid-May he and Pel'konen moved the shoemaking shop to Saratov. The shop was to serve three purposes: as a place for binding the sheets printed in Myshkin's press, as a shelter for individuals returning from walking trips among the peasants, and as a place where radicals could "cultivate protesting natures" among the local student participants.[20] The radicals Dmitrii M. Rogachev, Sergei F. Kovalik, and their friends soon arrived. The shop attracted police notice; on the night of May 31, the place was raided and Pel'konen and several others arrested. But in mid-July Voinaral'skii, Rogachev, and others set up two new safe addresses in Saratov, and Voinaral'skii leased one floor of an inn to serve as a hangout; the password there was "the revolt and the Pretender." Voinaral'skii was also active in the cities of Samara and

Kazan; he dreamed of covering the whole trans-Volga with a network of safe houses for propagandists.[21]

By the end of May or early June, Voinaral'skii, Rogachev, and a Tambov associate, A.I. Faresov, had made friends with the local Saratov seminary and gymnasium pupils, some of whom attended Pel'konen's shoemaker's shop until it closed. Perhaps the most distinguished pupil was the former seminarist Fedor E. Geraklitov. Most of the circle survived the collapse of Pel'konen's workshop, and meetings with Rogachev and other propagandists continued. Two radicals reported in July that "in Saratov the causes are going well"; the seminarists were working, relations were established with four exiles, with several village teachers, and with city workers; and "the local indigenous forces are uniting in a real organization," composed of seminarists, gymnasium pupils, and village teachers; one added, "I made the acquaintance of carpenters and shoemakers; I read them a tale; the *narod* is suitable; in a few days the carpenters will disperse about the village in various provinces; we are giving [them] books."[22]

The "new push" given by the visiting propagandists provoked a widespread excitement unknown in the area since Khristoforov and the Karakozov arrests. Local officials were tolerant of the ferment: "Due to the patriarchal attitudes of the police large meetings took place" even in the city park and on the street, attracting both students and bureaucrats. The main result was the popularization among the Saratovtsy of the idea of revolution and the formation there of a socialist tradition,[23] one that, as Michael Melancon shows (chap. 5), would inspire the radicals of the 1890s. A Saratov native recalled, "The short visit of these agitators in the city remained vivid memories for those who knew them—and many knew them; there was no end to the tales about this period" in the local gatherings of friends during the following months. "In the gray and humdrum life of a provincial city with its narrow-minded milieu, at that time drowsy and completely lacking in ideas, these people flashed by like meteors, soaring in from a completely different world and revealing a glimmer of this different world." Only now had the Saratovtsy acquired a vista of "real life, of the struggle and the hope of humanity."[24]

Despite the arrests and the increasingly cautious local administration and school officials, the ferment was so strong that it continued on its own momentum after 1874. In 1875–76, the former Saratov seminarist and student of Moscow's Agricultural Academy, Fedor E. Geraklitov, began propagandizing among the city workers. In the fall of 1875, Geraklitov began working in a bookbinder's shop and rented a room from one group of small craftsmen to make their acquaintance, then moved to a second and a third. In each place he propagandized, and his worker friends, drawn from various trades, grew to number about forty. Soon he needed assistance, so he brought in gymnasium students who, along with himself, had been friends with Voinaral'skii and Dmitrii Rogachev the year before; these included P. S. Polivanov, Stepan G. Shiriaev, and, from a younger group, Peter Shiriaev, A.V. Kirkhner, and I. I. Mainov. Both these groups were Lavrovist, and *Vpered!* (Forward!) was their bible. Late in 1876 a Bakuninist group also formed. "Through the example and personal influence of Geraklitov," some of these people joined carpenters' workshops; one became a typesetter; another, an unskilled worker in the Plotnikov cast-iron foundry; and others took part in a joiner's workshop and a shoemaker's workshop. Toward the end of 1876 Geraklitov gathered about ten of these propagandists into a special group dedicated to organizing the trans-Volga city workers in anticipation of a future uprising. They planned to send several workers in the spring of 1877 to other Volga cities and the Urals to found circles there. They met weekly with a "rather sizable circle" of workers, read new publications aloud, sang revolutionary songs, and set up a library and a treasury with the goal of mutual aid.[25] Outstanding workers included an engraver, Pavel F. Riabov, "one of the most active and brave workers," and the fitter Fridrikh Ia. Nagel, both from the Plotnikov cast-iron foundry; and Ivan E. Bobylev, also a fitter, who in turn propagandized the workers of a railroad workshop. But in late January and February 1877, arrests decimated the group. Geraklitov escaped abroad.[26]

The radical movement in Saratov was well-rooted by the mid-1870s, thanks to the lively participation of the Saratovtsy and the periodic visits of activists from St. Petersburg. It was also characterized by the moderate tone of its leaders, which, coupled with the region's distance from the capital, helps to explain why so many members of local society were interested in socialism and encouraged toleration and discourse with the radicals. The leftist movement there was the broadest of any in all the Volga cities.

The Saratov countryside underwent a major invasion in the summer of 1877, not only by St. Petersburg Populists, but, curiously enough, also by workers from the capital. The background to this invasion deserves elucidation, especially the reason why urban laborers, a new ingredient, joined the Populists in the countryside and what attitudes they brought with them.

In the early 1870s Populists conceived the idea of the city workers as emissaries or intermediaries between the intelligentsia and the peasants. The Populists were always interested in the contributions that both urban labor and the peasantry, each acting in its own milieu, could make to the socialist cause. Soon they developed an inclination to take some city workers with them into the Russian countryside. They believed that these workers, often not many generations removed from peasants, could communicate with peasants more effectively than they, and so could explain socialism in terms a peasant could understand. Further, the craft skills of the workers might provide an economic base for their revolutionary colony in the countryside.

The theory was probably first applied in 1873 under the pressure of the events of the time. The members of the Chaikovskii circle, attempting to organize Petersburg workers, were impressed by the difficulty of maintaining the worker circles, especially among the semipeasant weavers and spinners. All too frequently these workers found propagandizing in their factories too difficult and preferred to try their hand at it in their own familiar corner of the countryside. Leonid Shishko, the Chaikovskyite who was in contact with one of these groups of workers that melted into the countryside, later wrote, "Like every strong organization, the [Chaikovskii] circle was inclined to hold on firmly to the work it had once begun, and had no desire to squander its energies on side issues, or to take a fancy to broader revolutionary plans." However, "concerning the workers, on precisely their part began to appear the tendency to abandon the factory and to go to the countryside for propaganda. All this could not help but have an effect upon the programmatic views of our circle, which were as yet just barely worked out." Thus "our first attempts at socialist propaganda, the first practical steps on the path to rapprochement with the worker masses, led us to this very conclusion: the most conscious city workers did not at the time sense around them the revolutionary influence of the factory situation, but did feel an attraction to the countryside."[27]

In response, the idea of the worker as a revolutionary emissary to the countryside was adopted. The revised Chaikovskyite views are set forth in Peter Kropotkin's program for the circle "Must we take up an examination of an ideal for a future order?" In November and December 1873, various leading Populists began to accompany their worker acquaintances into the countryside, and this development was an important contribution to the beginning of the "to the people" movement.[28]

But city workers were not all alike. While many unskilled and semi-peasant workers maintained their ties to a rural commune, many city-bred skilled workers did not. In the spring of 1877, when radical Petersburg Populists around Mark and Olga Natanson began their plans for rural settlements in Saratov Province and encouraged some skilled metalworkers of their acquaintance to accompany them, these "aristocrats" of the metalworking trades looked down their noses at the proposition. The skilled, rather well-paid workers of St. Petersburg felt a certain "pity verging on contempt" for the Russian peasantry and for the newly arrived workers from the countryside who still retained all the peasants' cultural as well as legal and economic disabilities.[29]

Legally, the peasant estate had remained subject to punishment by blows of a birch rod in the peasant volost courts, whereas the remaining estates, since 1863, had been freed from corporal punishment—an important difference between the urban worker who juridically was considered a petty bourgeois or guild craftsman, and the peasant and recently arrived worker from the countryside. The skilled city workers, such as those in the metalworking trade among whom the Populists propagandized, looked on corporal punishment as a violation of human dignity. Sometimes the workers showed Plekhanov newspaper articles on the flogging of peasants, and Plekhanov "often had difficulty deciding which agitated them more: the ferocity of the torturers or the passive submissiveness of the tortured."[30] Until 1885, juridical peasants were subject to the soul tax, and those who continued to hold land in the peasant commune were subject to redemption dues. The hereditary townsman escaped these tax burdens.

The newly arrived peasants' lack of saleable skills handicapped them in the urban labor market, where competition for the unskilled jobs kept wages low. In addition, as furloughed labor, they were at the mercy of their commune government for permission to go to the cities for work. The case of Ignatii Bachin is illustrative. Bachin, a metalworker propagandized by the Chaikovskii circle, had spent over a year in prison, and when released in the summer of 1876, since he was juridically a peasant, he was obliged to arrange a new passport for himself from the commune to which he was registered. Since he had fallen behind on the payment of taxes to his commune, the elders prescribed punishment by flogging with willow rods, a routine sentence in the peasant courts. But to Bachin the idea was extremely debasing, and he reacted so violently that the elders did not try to carry out their punishment.[31] Bachin left the village unmolested, though the incident made a deep impression on him and he came to hate the countryside with a passion.

Finally, city workers became culturally different from the peasants and newly arrived workers. The latter retained peasant habits and dress and only slowly relinquished calico shirts and long-skirted coats, "which the plant workers laughed at."[32] Alcohol consumption was noticeably higher among these unskilled workers than among skilled city workers. They "drank terribly," an observer noticed, in contrast to the skilled workers, most of whom had developed a sense of moderation in their drinking habits.[33] The newly arrived worker, earning only 20 to 25 rubles a month, could not afford private living quarters and had to share lodgings with others (often from the same area of the countryside, forming the homeland gathering, or *zemliachestvo*). One individual usually rented an apartment, and the other workers sublet sleeping space. In contrast, some skilled workers, such as the well-paid skilled metalworkers, who earned as much as 2 or 3 rubles a day, lived very well indeed.

Plekhanov later wrote that the skilled-worker milieu was distinguished by two striking features: its significant mental development and its surprisingly large number of physical requirements that no longer were considered only luxuries.[34] The radicals were struck by the fine accoutrements of the furnished rooms of two metalworker acquaintances, Dmitrii N. Smirnov and Semen K. Volkov. They spent money on books and subscribed to journals. They preferred a bottle of good wine to beer or vodka. They dressed very well, "like dandies." Such worker-aristocrats dressed incomparably better than students, and furthermore "were neater and cleaner." Usually each owned a good black suit and looked quite distinguished when dressed in it. The radical students were dismayed at the consumption patterns of these workers and attempted to preach asceticism to them to counteract this tendency to *embourgeoise* themselves, but with little effect.[35]

The cultural distinctiveness of the newly arrived peasants was underscored by their lack of education. Virtually all the skilled workers had managed to acquire some schooling, and many were fond of attending evening lectures on such subjects as astronomy and the natural sciences. Indeed, the socialist skilled workers judged the worth of a potential candidate by whether or not he went to evening classes; only such a person was worth recruiting. More than by strictly formal education, however, the city worker's cast of mind was molded by his city environment. The true urban workers had a certain level of urban culture; they were, in a sense, city slickers. "Smart and talkative, knowing how to stand up for themselves and relate critically to their surroundings, they were *city dwellers* in the best sense of the word." The peasantry and workers newly arrived from the countryside seemed naive, slow, and gullible to them.[36]

In time, even the unskilled worker-peasant gradually submitted to the influences of urban life. The longer he worked in the city the more fragile grew his ties to the countryside, until he no longer felt comfortable there. One such worker who had become interested in the "woman question" was horrified to discover that his parents had chosen a bride for him in the countryside. He refused to have anything to do with the proposed arrangement.[37]

In sum, workers with extended residence in the city, including many who were juridically peasant,[38] shared an image of the countryside as a place full of primitive, benighted, economically oppressed people with less than full human legal rights, and they tended to group with the peasantry those who were newly arrived from the village. The cultural gap was wide between the city and the countryside. In subsequent decades, these realities would continue to challenge urban radicals seeking a popular base in the Saratov countryside—and elsewhere.

When the radicals around Mark and Olga Natanson, nascent zemlevol'tsy, encouraged their skilled worker acquaintances to accompany them to the Saratov countryside, then, it was not surprising that most balked. One worker later told police that Natanson urged the workers to go to the countryside and help create an uprising, "but the workers did not agree." A little later he heard that "the workers wanted to break off with Natanson for pestering them with his proposals to carry out an uprising, but how this ended I do not know."[39] Another worker told a Lavrovist in the capital that the radicals were "putting pressure" on the workers to go to the countryside, "for which they are incapable." Instead, this skilled worker wondered why the radicals did not limit their proposals to the semipeasant laborers "who arrive in the summer (or winter) for several months to make earnings" and then return home; they were perhaps the sole useful means for propaganda in the villages, since any others would seem foreigners and objects of suspicion.[40] The antipathy of some of these skilled workers was all the greater because they were trying to create their own working-class organization at the time. They viewed the Populists' attempts to persuade some of their members to abandon St. Petersburg for the Saratov countryside as a personal insult to them, an attempt to undermine or corrupt their own efforts.[41]

A few workers, however, were persuaded by the Populists. Three of them, whom Plekhanov characterized as "experienced people who were sincerely dedicated to the Populist ideals and deeply imbued with Populist views,"[42] agreed to accompany the zemlevol'tsy into the Saratov countryside. One was a boiler-maker named Ivan Egorov. He was from the Milk-Drinker *(Molokane)* sect from Arkhangel Province. Osip Aptekman called him a "white Arkhangel bear." He liked to spend his evenings pouring over books. At one point he took up Herbert Spencer's *Foundations of Biology*. When Plekhanov advised him to give it up for something easier, he became angry and replied "What is this? Do you still think that we workers are total fools?"[43] It may be that the Populists thought Egorov especially promising for work in the Saratov countryside because of the great number of religious nonconformists in the area.

A second worker who accompanied the Populists was Ivan V. Arkhipov-Korsikov (or Korsakov). In 1877 he was twenty-one years old, a juridical petty bourgeois from Bezhets, Tver Province, and was employed as a fitter at the Makferson Works. He was of Karelian descent, of average height, thick-set, tow-headed, with a broad, open face and light blue eyes clear as a baby's. His temperament was buoyant, peaceful, and even, though somewhat inert. He had been a participant in the worker-radical organization "The Society of Friends" in 1876–77, until its collapse.[44]

Also accompanying the Populists was a metalworker named Nikolai, whose last name is not given (Plekhanov does not mention it and Aptekman confesses he has forgotten it and simply calls him "Nikolai the fitter.") Nikolai should have been able to set himself up in some village to practice his metalworking trade, the Populists estimated. But he was "an extremely high-strung person, with raw nerves, quite overstrained." His childhood and adolescent years, while he was in school, were full of deprivation, "of bitter wrongs and martyrdom," and he was scarred from beatings with birches. He was intelligent. In his bearing he made the impression "if not of a German, then in any case a student." He spoke rather well, and loved to scatter foreign words and bookish locutions throughout his speech.[45] Nikolai also loved to take part in theoretical arguments. He resolved all problems, from the simplest to the most complex, by a pat formula: "All this, you see, proceeds from an abnormal social order." Aptekman observed, "This for him was some sort of password, with the aid of which, as if he held a master key in his hands, he unlocked the most intricate courses of events of our time."[46]

The goal of the radical Populists in 1877 was to encourage the peasants to form local organizations, which in turn would serve as the "first steps in the preparation of an uprising."[47] Three areas were targeted because of their rebellious traditions: the Don, the Kuban, and the Volga—in particular, Nizhnii Novgorod Province (where a settlement had been formed the previous year); Samara Province, adopted as the favored site by the Chaikovskii circle (which since the end of 1876 had acted independently of Natanson's close associates); and Saratov Province, the area favored especially by Natanson's group, the nascent "Land and Liberty." Other loosely associated circles also went to the Volga. In all, over twenty people gathered in Saratov Province. This assortment was mixed: "some barely knew each other."[48]

Vasilii F. Troshchanskii, a close friend of Natanson's since the early 1870s, worked for the zemstvo board of Volsk District and provided others with jobs; he also established a secret central apartment for the zemlevol'tsy in Saratov City. Olga Natanson and Alexander Mikhailov arranged a central bureau and big apartment in the city to serve all the groups in the countryside, and Mikhailov drew up a master plan for covering the province with underground Populist settlements.[49] Further, a group associated with the Chaikovskii circle set up a blacksmithy in the village of Ershovka, Khvalynsk District, in May 1877.[50] Mikhailov was especially interested in the Old Believers. His great hope, a hope that several generations of radicals had expressed beginning in the early 1860s, was that the religious nonconformists would form a partnership with the revolutionaries against the government. Mikhailov settled with an Old Believer family on the edge of Saratov; in bed by nine, praying every morning, observing many fasts, he diligently studied their customs. He dressed as they did, learned to cite their texts, and eventually felt that he could perform their "10,000 Chinese ceremonies." He also took part in a disputation at a gathering of Old Believers and Orthodox. He then worked as a rural teacher in the Old Believer village of Sinenkie, Saratov District, until April 1878.[51]

Some of the Populists found work in the zemstvos as medical assistants and nurse-midwives, or as teachers. Other lucky ones worked for volost governments as village teachers or volost clerks. Still others set up workshops, and several planned to lease a small flour mill. However, many were unable to find work, despite spending days tramping Saratov District. These individuals, whose numbers increased with new waves of visitors, congregated in the city of Saratov at the big apartment on Kamyshinskaia Street.[52]

One of the Populists who could not find work in the countryside despite strenuous efforts was Georgii V. Plekhanov, the future "father of Russian Marxism." "He kept trying to go to the countryside 'to the narod.' But circumstances unluckily were against him, and all his attempts in this direction ended in failure," Aptekman remarked. Plekhanov tried very hard to find a zemstvo teaching job. Armed with an application and Mikhailov's gymnasium certificate as identification, he secured an interview with the Atkarsk school board. The priest on the board unnerved Plekhanov when he mistook him for the son of an acquaintance named Mikhailov, but Plekhanov bluffed his way through the meeting, and the priest interceded for him. However, the skeptical district police officer replied that the father could be a fine man and yet the son a propagandist, and he firmly voted against accepting Plekhanov, who was obliged to return to his work among the Saratov city workers and intelligentsia.[53]

Three others who found the countryside incompatible were the three blond metalworkers who had come from St. Petersburg to help the zemlevol'tsy. They, like Plekhanov, had to change their plans and turn to the city workers. The zemlevol'tsy had not intended to establish relations with the workers of the city of Saratov. After having failed to create a working-class demonstration on St. Petersburg's Kazan Square the previous year, the zemlevol'tsy wanted to work only among the peasants.[54] Olga Natanson explicitly refused to use some of her time in Saratov City to form relations with city workers, declaring that she intended to spend no more time there than necessary before transferring to the countryside; otherwise "it would be necessary to live [in

Saratov] a long time."[55] But when the three Petersburg metalworkers and Plekhanov failed to establish themselves in the countryside, they turned to the city of Saratov.

The three metalworkers were repelled by the primitive conditions and were unable to tolerate life in the villages. Aptekman writes: ". . . our workers shirked work in the countryside. This is a fact." However, upon reflection, "there was nothing astonishing in this" since the workers, Nikolai the fitter, Ivan Egorov, and Arkhipov-Korsikov, "were *plant* workers, receiving a relatively *good* salary and already accustomed to a certain degree to *cultured* surroundings." How could the Populists have expected the boiler-maker Egorov, who loved to tackle books such as Spencer's *Foundations of Biology,* to adjust to life in a Saratov village? he reflected in retrospect.[56] Arkhipov-Korsikov, "a calm cheerful type," was, in Aptekman's opinion, the best suited of the three for the countryside, perhaps because he bore the deprivations without complaint. But he had no idea of how to go about finding a job of some sort in the countryside, and he soon sank into lethargy. Nikolai the fitter "was deeply dedicated to the narod," remarked Aptekman, "and theoretically could have established himself in a village" working at his own metalworking trade. But unfortunately he was a high-strung, sensitive person, and despite his dedication to the Russian peasants, "it was beyond his strength to live with them, to live in the countryside." Aptekman does not explain just what aspects of rural peasant life agitated Nikolai so, but simply states that the countryside, with its "brutal, harsh reality," assaulted his carefully nurtured sense of human dignity. Perhaps he witnessed a flogging, or perhaps the accumulation of small deprivations, poor food, mud, and dirt affected him; perhaps he discovered that the peasants were quite unable to debate his favorite subjects with him. In any case, his nerves gave way, and he was driven clear out of the countryside. He escaped to Saratov; "Nikolai the fitter, in a word, was a man of the city and here was fully at home." In Saratov City "workers related to him with esteem, and listened to him willingly. From the very beginning there was no reason to send him to the countryside, except in the name of some point of our program." Thus, none of the worker Populists came to be situated in the countryside, and all the weight of this work had to be borne by the intelligentsia exclusively; "a gap appeared in our rural tactics from the very beginning."[57]

Plekhanov was surprised at the "alienation from the 'narod' of its city children. But the fact was obvious and we had to abandon the idea of drawing the workers into a particularly peasant business." The conclusion that Plekhanov drew is apt not only for these three workers but for the skilled city workers generally. "The Populist ideas prevailing in the milieu of the revolutionary intelligentsia naturally made an impression on the *views* of the workers also. But they were unable to remake their *habits* and thus the real city workers, i.e., the workers completely habituated to the conditions of city life . . . seemed unfit for the countryside. To merge with peasants was even more difficult for them than for the revolutionary 'intelligenty.' "[58]

Like Plekhanov, the three metalworkers abandoned the countryside for the city of Saratov, where some of Fedor Geraklitov's associates who had escaped arrest had begun to pull together a new worker organization. After the police broke up Geraklitov's worker organization at the beginning of 1877, most of the workers either dispersed from Saratov or lost their connection with the propagandists still at liberty and "sank into the mass," so the organization temporarily fell apart. However, several propagandists still at liberty, in particular I. I. Mainov and P. S. Polivanov, over the course of the summer began gathering workers whom Geraklitov had known; and others were newly attracted from a wide range of social classes, including, besides students and workers, women teachers, military cadets, and local bureaucrats. Meeting nightly, they debated the future order of society and read *Vpered!*, *The Clever Trick*, or other underground publications. Soon a new ingredient was introduced into the circle: some of the radicals temporarily in Saratov and the St. Petersburg workers.[59]

Mainov and Polivanov expended great efforts to revive the Saratov worker-Populist organization and felt rewarded when they succeeded. "The receptivity which the city workers displayed to socialist ideas" was incontestible proof to the propagandists of the truth of these ideas. "The world of the 'laboring and burdened'" had seemed so remote and was known only through books; but now a small portion of that world was revealed, and each propagandist "was able to see with his own eyes a particle of this narod and come into contact, if only in part, with its laboring life." And just as the books had said, that life was horrible; the workers labored twelve to fifteen hours a day in stifling plants and dusty workshops. In appearance also they were disheveled and covered with soot. Yet "they seemed, in fact, living people with a sensitive spirit, with an inextinguishable desire for the light, for freedom, for a dream of universal brotherhood." The propagandists successfully sought out two workers from Geraklitov's circle, a tailor, Vasilii K. Karpov, and a joiner, Anton Fedorych, who acted as links to the worker milieu. Two typesetters propagandized the previous year, named Egorov and Maslennikov, who were quite educated and distinguished by their convictions, as well as several other workers, were "found after long searches." Toward fall, as many as twenty young people were propagandizing in workshops and small plants. A socialist worker would make an effort to take part in the meetings of an unfamiliar workshop, arousing interest in social questions. On a subsequent visit he would bring a propagandist dressed simply, perhaps as a fitter, medical assistant, or clerk, recommending him as a friend.[60]

Mainov and Polivanov often visited workers together; Mainov would begin the conversations, drawing the workers out. Then Polivanov would burst out with a fiery speech, often incomprehensible to the workers but still attractive and stimulating in spirit. The workers "pardoned the intellectual quality of his speech for the sake of the strong and arousing feelings he evoked." "There in some basement with clouded windows, among the joiners' benches, the dust, the half-planed boards, in air penetrated with the smell of fresh shavings and damp wood, in front of listeners sometimes barefoot and beltless," the socialist felt he at last "was where his duty called [him], with laboring people in their own dark and underground world, from which he would show them the path to light and freedom."[61]

The Saratov propagandists had a strong Lavrovist inclination, believing that the narod was exploited because it lacked organization and information about remedies, and that the socialist intelligentsia's task was to provide it with fundamentals of organization. Opinion was so uniform that these issues were not even debated; resurrecting the worker's organization is what absorbed them.[62] But this unanimity ended with the appearance of the visiting radicals.

The Petersburg workers' preference for life in the city and Plekhanov's failure to find rural work induced the zemlevol'tsy to pay attention to the Saratov workers. While other zemlevol'tsy were in the countryside, Plekhanov remained in Saratov.[63] He entered the worker's circle "quite successfully," according to Aptekman. "The workers admired him, highly valued him, and were proud of him." Furthermore, "he had the ground beneath his feet in Saratov, and did not have to put himself out." His main helpers in propagandizing among the city workers were the three Petersburg metalworkers, who once in Saratov established relations with local laborers. The visitors were aided by a fourth Petersburg metalworker, Vasilii Ia. Savel'ev, who, under an assumed name, had been hiding in Saratov (along with the visiting radical N. P. Moshchenko) since spring because the police in Petersburg were actively looking for him; the two had already met the members of the worker circle. Furthermore, soon the zemlevol'tsy developed a rationale for this activity: it would be useful to provide the revolutionary organization with support from Saratov's worker population, because "when the Volga peasantry rose up, the Saratov craftsmen would prove useful."[64]

Who were the local workers attracted to the newly reformed organization? Plekhanov later wrote, "In Saratov factory-plant industry was poorly developed; the workers there were predominantly small craftsmen. . . ." There is no doubt that industry was poorly developed at that time. The total number of factories in the province by the end of the century reached only 858, employing 12,482 workers (though the value of the production was the highest, 37,910,000 rubles, for the five-province area also including Samara, Kazan, Simbirsk, and Astrakhan). Four hundred and sixty-nine of these factories, employing 4,645 workers, processed food, mostly milled flour, representing 66.1 percent of the value of the province's industrial production.[65] In the 1870s it was not surprising that the radicals' adherents were mostly craftsmen, not factory workers. The 1897 census of the city population, which may give some hint of the situation two decades earlier, lists the following jobs as the most common in the city of Saratov (excluding people in trade): domestic and day labor (13.7 percent of the total city population), preparation of clothes, the armed services, construction work, metalworking, cabbies and wagoners, working up food products, and woodworking, in descending order.[66]

Plekhanov was personally acquainted with the worker circles in Rostov, Saratov, Kiev, and Kharkov, and wrote: "In their composition they were much more diverse, more mixed than the Petersburg [ones]. Members joined who by education and by the high level of needs were not inferior to the Petersburg workers, yet along with them joined quite 'gray' [people], sometimes illiterate." It was not unusual to find small independent craftsmen predominant in these circles, and not journeymen but owners of shops. Plekhanov had not found such people among the socialist worker circles of Petersburg and "felt myself in a strange position when, as it happened, the revolutionary-employer advised me to be cautious around his *worker,* who was an *unreliable* person."[67]

Stepan Shiriaev wrote a letter to Peter Lavrov late in 1876 which provides more information on the propagandized Saratov workers. He proposed a question for discussion in *Vpered!:* what is the appropriate sort of literature for workers? He related that he "came to the awareness of the urgency" of the need to tailor the literature to their level of education as a result of his work among the Saratov laborers during 1876. He dismissed fairy tales, allegories, and proclamations out of hand; the worker wanted literature that provided "facts and more facts" on the social order against which he struggled. Further, the great majority of workers, who had "little access to the printed word,"[68] needed publications that were very short, simple, easily understood, immediate, and direct in form, and in content "touching on life in an obvious and clear way." A good example was the booklet exposing the burden of indirect taxes, *The Clever Trick.*

In contrast, a handful of workers had broader needs in literature. "These few persons of the *narod* by chance had the possibility of securing a broader intellectual development; a wide range of subjects is accessible to their understanding," and they had the leisure time to pursue knowledge. Shiriaev recommended developing literature for them in various areas of knowledge; for instance, for historical texts he recommended Khudiakov's *Ancient Russia* and various other popular histories. "We must do this for the serious though small circle of readers among our working people. Such literature can create a valuable type of social-revolutionary activist—people of the *narod* who are 'mighty in knowledge.' And this after all is the goal of our revolutionaries."[69]

In sum, the socialist workers of Saratov were predominantly craftsmen, often owners of their own shops, but also some metalworkers from small plants, such as the Plotnikov Works. Many of them craved better literature than was available, especially the handful of workers who had managed to acquire an education; perhaps these people included the well-educated typesetters whom Mainov mentions.

The visitors' message to the workers stood in striking contrast to the moderate educational work of the local propagandists.[70] It was difficult for the Lavrovist-minded, rather inexperienced Saratovtsy to take a stand in debates against Plekhanov and his cohorts. The central question debated was: what attitude did the common people have toward the different attempts of the radicals to incite them? For instance, would they greet favorably an appeal to strike or to hold a street demonstration? Under the onslaught of the radicals' views, local Lavrovism began to pale. It suddenly seemed that Lavrovism, which shunned such activities, had isolated itself from real life.[71]

At one meeting of workers and propagandists that took place in a ravine behind the crest of Sokolov Hill, Plekhanov took up the subjects that had been provoking the bitterest quarrels in the capitals: was serious education really necessary for the socialist, and what were the lower classes' reactions to the incitement of strikes and protests? The local propagandists had not touched on these themes among the Saratov workers because, first, it seemed that without knowledge one would not succeed at anything, including revolution, and second, they believed that no ground existed in Saratov to support agitation for strikes or protests (at that time it was still supposed that strikes were events initiated by action of the intelligentsia). Plekhanov approached these themes from a buntarist point of view. He called on his listeners not to be troubled by the sacrifices inevitable to the struggle, or by the failure of individual acts, but "to move forward tirelessly, protesting, revolting, infecting the inert mass with the example of one's 'seemingly fruitless' heroism." His speech "called out to young hearts like an invocatory bell, justifying his grandiose pseudonym, Nabatov."[72] The buntarist promotion of propaganda by the 'deed' began to subvert the local gradualism.

Events beyond Saratov in fall and winter of 1877–78 reinforced this inclination among the Saratovtsy: the widespread unhappiness with the outcome of the Russo-Turkish War, the trial of the propagandists of 1874, and the trial of the fifty (both of which involved defendants from Saratov), and Vera Zasulich's attempted assassination of General Trepov and trial. The stridency of the visitors combined with these events to impel the Saratov propagandists to militancy. It no longer seemed sufficient to promote socialist enlightenment among the workers (or even to practice the mild, nonthreatening agitation among the peasants that had been common). A new, more extremist period in the history of Saratov's radicals was developing. As the autumn waned, the worker-organizing activity became more conspiratorial to counteract police surveillance, and also intensified. One worker in particular was striking in his revolutionary enthusiasm and readiness for self-sacrifice: the typesetter Egorov (or "Zharkov").[73] He later accompanied Plekhanov to St. Petersburg to manage the radicals' press there.

On November 26, 1877, the police raided the apartment on Kamyshinskaia Street, and the city organization of the visitors collapsed.[74] However, the native Saratovtsy continued their worker organizing activity "in the former spirit," but with renewed attention to conspiratorial details and a new tendency toward activism. In the following year, Mainov, Polivanov, and Ponomarov attempted to organize several cooperatives among the city joiners, engravers in wood, and upholsterers in order to unite them for a struggle with two or three big furniture firms. Hundreds of workers and small craftsmen were dependent upon business provided by these companies, and unorganized, they were at the companies' mercy.[75] When Vera Figner arrived in Saratov in the spring of 1878, she found energetic propaganda being carried on among the Saratov city workers.[76]

Whereas Saratov Province had been the principal target of the zemlevol'tsy in 1877, the following spring the Populists of the Chaikovskii-circle "separatists" settled in the province. Vera N. Figner, Alexander I. Ivanchin-Pisarev, and others discovered a dozen or so remaining visitors from the previous year, and attempted to join them, but relations between the two radical Populist groups had never been smooth and the effort to merge fell through. However, the separatists, with the help of sympathetic zemstvo activists, managed to set themselves up in the countryside. Ivanchin-Pisarev worked as a clerk for the volost governments of Bulgakovka and then Baltai in Volsk District for almost two years, "defending the interests of the peasantry." Several others also worked as clerks. In Petrovsk District, Vera Figner worked as a medical assistant, and her sister Evgeniia as a teacher.[77] Though cautious about breaching their security, the group also had close relations with some liberal-radical bureaucrats and well-placed members of society in Saratov, as well as with the local radicals,[78] but apparently preferred to leave worker-organizing activity to the latter. When in the spring of 1879 one of the separatists in St. Petersburg, Alexander K. Solov'ev, fired at the tsar, the colony dissolved.

The years 1877–78 marked the height of the worker-organizing activity in Saratov. By the following year, as Mainov observed, "a whole period of Russian history inspired by Proudhon and Bakunin, expressed concretely by various attempts to establish rapport with the common people" came to a close. Solov'ev's shots and the ensuing debate over terrorist acts provoked many Saratovtsy to reevaluate their work. Interest in theory gave way to revolutionary struggle against the government, "whereas, earlier, theory and practice went together."[79]

Most of the Saratovsy refused at first to take sides between the People's Will and Black Repartition, holding that their differences had no significance in the provinces; participation in terrorist acts was left up to each individual. But eventually a filial branch of the People's Will was formed in Saratov. Though three of its members, Mainov, Polivanov, and A. P. Iuvenal'ev, attempted to carry on relations with city workers, labor organizing fell into decline. Workers long associated with the radicals could be bent toward the activism of the People's Will, but it was extremely difficult to acquire new adherents in the worker milieu, in part because of the increased vigilance of the police.[80]

In 1880 the circle began agitation that contributed to the difficulties. When a famine occurred in the area that winter, a senator came to inspect the situation. The local People's Will decided to try to mobilize a mass of unemployed workers to go to his hotel with a petition for the tsar for aid, expecting that a street brawl would develop between the mob and troops, and the petition would be accepted but ignored, thus producing "an irritated and revolutionized mass." Despite agitation in the bazaars and cheap restaurants, the circle was unable to bring off the demonstration. They blamed the failure on their inability to exert influence over the worker circles and on a lack of agitators.[81]

Once again struggling to improve relations with the city's workers, in 1881 five radicals were appointed a "Worker's Group"; in succession, three representatives of the Executive Committee of the People's Will came to help (L. M. Kogan-Bernshtein, M. E. Novitskii, and M. D. Raiko), and agitation continued among the Saratov workers up to the latter's arrest in August 1882. By that summer, arrests had decimated the core of the local branch of the People's Will. Thus ended the active role of "that circle of *Saratovtsy* who were attracted to the movement in the mid-seventies."[82]

In the following period new people emerged, and soon new tendencies developed. Some continuity with the earlier movements was retained, however, predominantly by radicals who had been on the periphery of the main organizations in Saratov. In the winter of 1880–81, the local branch of the People's Will helped to create several peripheral circles, whose members subsequently took part in the activity of revolutionary groups, not only in Saratov, but also St. Petersburg, Moscow, and Kazan.[83] In the first half of the 1880s, one of them, Peter Stepanov, also propagandized among religious dissenters.

In the 1880s faith in the imminence of a social revolution faded. Not only had the peasants not risen up in 1881 after the assassination of Alexander II, but the scantiness of the revolutionary forces induced many to remain in the city centers rather than disperse to the countryside. That aspect of the Populist revolutionary program which stressed the propaganda of city workers received emphasis. This predominant orientation initially owed little to Marx or to any perceived increase in the pace of industrialization; rather, it was a continuation of the earlier Populist appreciation of the value of city workers, now shorn of the heavy peasant emphasis that had somewhat disguised the Populists' interest in urban labor in the past.[84]

In 1883 a People's Will circle took shape in Saratov which lasted until 1887. It had a rather large membership, owned a press, and carried on propaganda among students and workers. Its membership included, besides newcomers, some peripheral radicals of the earlier period, including Peter Stepanov, Alexander L. Blek, and Ia. S. Sevast'ianov, who was active among the Saratov city workers.[85] Such local radicals, plus many returning exiles who settled there, formed the basis of the Saratov neo-Populist groups of the 1890s, including Mark Natanson's organization, the Party of People's Rights, and by their presence helped to create a bridge between the movements of the 1870s and the agitation that led to the formation of the Socialist Revolutionary party.[86]

Saratov in the second half of the nineteenth century was not isolated. Rather, it exemplified the dynamic relationship existing between St. Petersburg (and Moscow) and provincial centers of the empire, a theme covered in other chapters of this book. Saratov participated in the major intellectual and political movements, not only of Russia, but also of western Europe, albeit sometimes with a time lag of several years. Leading radicals came to and stimulated activities in Saratov, but also had their own thinking altered by what happened to them there; Plekhanov's experiences with Saratov's peasants and workers not only illustrate this interaction, but were important to his own evolution toward Marxism and thus the ideological orientation of future generations of Russian

radicals. Saratov not only highlights the intelligentsia's growing appreciation of worker organizing, and the first forays into that milieu, but also
the dynamics of this process, particularly from the workers' perspective.
In these tentative beginnings one can see the early appearance of a self-
assured worker cadre, which a generation later was to play a most visible
role in labor and socialist movements in Saratov and throughout the
empire.

5. Athens or Babylon? The Birth of the Socialist Revolutionary and Social Democratic Parties in Saratov, 1890–1905

Michael Melancon

THE ORIGINS of revolutionary parties in the Russian Empire's provincial towns and cities have attracted little attention from Western historians. Yet party leaders in the emigration and in the capitals rarely determined or controlled events in the localities. Activists on the spot, those of Saratov not least among them, often distorted or ignored directives from above, if there were any. Specific local requirements usually shaped local organizations and their activities. Only detailed study of provincial revolutionary movements can reveal the concrete realities of this phenomenon. However, one can assert that, although they received their first sparks from Moscow or St. Petersburg, neither the 1905 revolution nor those of 1917 could have reached the scale they did or, in 1917, achieved ultimate success without the enthusiastic participation of cities and provinces across the empire. Indeed, local revolutionary movements often ranged far ahead of those in the two capitals, where central leaders, beset with national responsibilities, often dared take only cautious steps.

This chapter undertakes to examine the origins and early activities of the two great Russian socialist parties—the Socialist Revolutionaries (SRs) and the Social Democrats (SDs)— in Saratov. But comparing SR and SD history in Saratov in this era is much like comparing apples and oranges. To the SRs, Saratov appeared a shining place, a center of great strength and influence or, as they called it, "Athens on the Volga," whereas the SDs often found it a place of frustration, a "Babylon."[1]

The real differences, of course, lie not in perceptions but in more substantial matters such as when and how their organizations arose, how large and effective they became, and what status they occupied in their respective national organizations. On the one hand, former members of the earlier Populist parties, such as the Land and Liberty, the People's Will, and the Party of People's Rights, abounded in the province, making it fertile soil for the growth of the Socialist Revolutionary party. Repeatedly in the 1890s and early 1900s, Saratov neo-Populist organizations and leaders not only exercised formidable local influence but played central roles in their national organizations. On the other hand, Marxism came quite late to Saratov, and Social Democratic circles and a committee developed even later. Despite Lenin's early description of Saratov as "one of the most powerful Social Democratic centers," the SD organization there grew only by fits and starts. Even so, by the onset of the 1905 revolution, the Saratov SDs had won impressive achievements. On the whole, however, the Athens-Babylon epithets do reflect the dichotomy of the two parties' early experiences in Saratov.

Socioeconomic conditions helped shape the character and timing of local revolutionary developments. By the 1890s Saratov City was a thriving administrative and commercial center. The large intelligentsia consisted of students and teachers; bureaucrats in city and zemstvo administration; and clerical employees of the Riazan-Urals Railroad offices. By 1890 Saratov also had 103 factories with 2,362 workers, and the province, including Tsaritsyn, had 775 such concerns with a total of 13,369 workers; augmented by handicraft workers, the province's industrial work force reached 19,069. A decade later the number of workers had more than doubled to 46,069, of which 13,280 worked in factories of Saratov City and District (*uezd*), and 8,000–9,000 of which were artisanal workers. The size of Saratov's factories was not impressive. In 1890 the largest ones—flour mills, tobacco firms, and the Nobel Plant—each employed from 100 to 150 workers; the machinery shops, bell factories, and metal forges employed under 100 workers each. By 1901, new larger enterprises had arrived; the Riazan-Urals Railroad workshops employed 3,190 workers; the Volzhskii Steel Foundry, 1,000; Gantke Nail and Wire Plant, 120; several iron foundries, 675; machinery plants, 600; the Bari Ship Builders, 400; print shops, 586; and flour mills, tobacco firms, and others employed an additional 7,789 workers.[2] Saratov finally had a genuine, if small, proletariat.

As elsewhere in Russia, factory conditions were poor. Workers engaged in an unsuccessful struggle to prevent real income from falling. To lower production costs, employers often reduced wages by indiscriminately fining workers. In the early 1900s, Saratov machinery shops had an 11.5 hour workday; flour mills, oil presses, and lumber yards, a 12 to 14 hour workday; and artisanal workers labored 16 to 17 hours a day. The depression of 1901 caused heavy layoffs that by 1904 approached 40 percent of the labor force. Massive unemployment and worsening work conditions ensued; cutbacks in break time and the cancellation of some holidays confronted those who kept their jobs. The recollection of one local worker about his plant, that "working conditions were those of hard labor in prison," aptly described factory life in Saratov.[3]

By a cruel twist of fate, the fertility of Saratov's black-earth lands led, by the end of the nineteenth century, to grave land shortages and endemic hunger among its peasant population, a circumstance other chapters in this book document very well. Perhaps even more than the industrial laborers, Saratov's peasantry could inspire revolutionary sentiment by their plight and contribute to a revolutionary movement by their actions.[4]

At first glance, then, Saratov's socioeconomic profile (a large exploited peasantry, a sizable intelligentsia, and a relatively weak proletariat) would appear to account for the early strength of the Populist-Socialist Revolutionary forces and the initial backwardness of the Marxist movement. However, further consideration suggests caution. Most neo-Populists in Saratov and elsewhere devoted their attention primarily to the intelligentsia and workers and only in the early 1900s rediscovered the peasants. The poverty of the province's peasantry does not therefore explain Populist strength during the 1890s. Furthermore, until the late 1890s in most areas of Russia, Social Democracy found support primarily from the intelligentsia and prospered in some places with as few workers as Saratov. It follows that the city's late industrial development does not entirely account for Marxism's relative weakness among the local intelligentsia and proletariat.

Neo-Populists, who would become the SRs, appeared on the scene first. The return of M. A. Natanson and his wife, V. I. Natanson, from Siberian exile in 1890 was the catalyst for the revival of the local revolutionary movement. Energetic as always, the Natansons organized a revolutionary circle that united Populists of various tendencies, including

A. L. Blek, N. D. Rossov, and the famous O. V. Aptekman. Prominent local citizens such as zemstvo doctor I. I. Molleson, city mayor N. P. Frolov, and city duma secretary A. V. Milashevskii provided close support.[5] These individuals, most of whom had long revolutionary experience and many of whom worked in zemstvo and city duma administration, created a chain of circles, groups, and organizations that reached directly to the Socialist Revolutionary party in Saratov in the early 1900s and played an instrumental role in the founding of the neo-Populist movement in Russia.

The Natanson circle's program aimed at a socialist-liberal alliance to achieve constitutional reform as a basis for overthrowing tsarism, a position the Party of People's Rights later adopted. For the moment, members focused their attention on the intelligentsia and workers, more or less to the exclusion of the peasantry. A former People's Will activist provided ties with the city's proletariat. N. S. Tiuchev organized self-educational circles among students and founded the Fine Arts Society, whose public functions served as a forum for the circle's agitation and fund-raising efforts and which played a powerful role in the city's life. Under Natanson's guidance the circle established ties with similar groups in other cities, including the Petersburg Group of the People's Will. Molleson, V. D. Chenykaev, and others performed local tasks, while a second contingent (Rossov, Aptekman, and so on) traveled to Tambov, St. Petersburg, Odessa, and Nizhnii Novgorod.[6]

During the summer of 1892, the Saratov circle arranged a national conference, which even N. K. Mikhailovskii attended. N. F. Annenskii agreed to publish a revolutionary newspaper for the new organization, which took the name Party of People's Rights *(Partiia Narodnogo Prava)*. Although the Natansons and other party leaders soon moved their headquarters to Orel, the Party of People's Rights held its first conference in Saratov during the summer of 1893. Local activist A. I. Bogdanovich had a hand in writing the party's manifesto, which received a favorable response from V. I. Lenin. When arrests broke up the party's national leadership in 1894, Saratov activists escaped unscathed and local circles under Rossov and P. A. Gorelin recruited new forces, distributed illegal literature, and for several years, in the words of a police agent, "spread the idea of . . . conspiracy and agitation among workers."

At the same time, a former People's Will activist, V. A. Balmashev, organized a separate circle, which took the hallowed title "Land and

Liberty" and which included A. A. Argunov, N. I. Ivanov-Okhlonin, and G. A. Gliko. With Argunov and Gliko's help, Ivanov-Okhlonin worked out a program that advocated both legal and illegal methods, including terror, and thus rejected the Party of People's Rights' plan of cooperating with liberals. Despite its title, the Land and Liberty circle held that propaganda among the peasants would only "interfere with the concentration of revolutionary forces at present," as a result of which work should proceed only with the proletariat and intelligentsia.[7]

In 1894 police raided the circles, but they had covered their conspiratorial tracks so cleverly that the authorities, lacking evidence, failed to press charges. Argunov and Ivanov-Okhlonin then formed a new circle, which between 1894 and 1896 had ties with the Petersburg Group of the People's Will. When the Petersburg Group, which had been migrating ever closer to the SDs, suffered heavy arrests in 1896, the Saratov circle decided to "go it alone" and created the famous Union of Socialist Revolutionaries, one of the progenitor groups of the Party of Socialist Revolutionaries (PSR).[8]

With the goal of refuting the growing SD tendency toward "economism" and "evolutionism," the Union of SRs reworked the program of the original People's Will. In theory the Union espoused terror, but in fact, it preoccupied itself with building a mass organization. It attempted to improve its ties with workers, agitated among students, issued revolutionary literature, and laid plans to publish a newspaper edited by A. V. Peshekhonov and V. A. Miakotin of the Populist legal journal *Russkoe bogatstvo* (Russian Wealth). "Work among the peasantry stood in second place," recalled Argunov.[9] The Saratov Union of SRs immediately established contacts with groups in Tambov, Moscow, Voronezh, Petersburg, and Kiev. But the Kiev Union of SRs (later the Southern Union, and later yet the Party of SRs) rejected certain aspects of the Saratov Union's program, especially the plank on terrorism, a circumstance which foreclosed the possibility of an early unified neo-Populist party.[10]

During 1897 the Union of SRs transferred its headquarters to Moscow, leaving behind a circle under the leadership of V. A. Balmashev (father of the famous terrorist Stepan Balmashev) and Ivanov-Okhlonin. During 1897 and 1898 the various Saratov circles had to choose between two competing Socialist Revolutionary groups, the Northern Union (Moscow) and the Southern Union (Kiev and Voronezh), each of which desired to be the kernel of a new national party. By 1898–99 the local circles had come together into two centers—the Balmashev group, which favored the Northern Union's program, and the Rakitnikov group, which leaned toward the Southern Union's rejection of terrorism. Of the two, the Rakitnikov position eventually won out.[11]

After the departure of Ivanov-Okhlonin in 1898, Balmashev, with the help of N. D. Stepanov and N. S. Aref'ev, formed his group, the New People's Will, which advocated terror and looked to workers as "the class most inclined to all propaganda against the existing government." The chief meeting place of the New People's Will, as it had been for the Union of SRs, was the "small, poor apartment" of the old Populist A. Cherniavskaia, enthusiastic member of both groups. In the course of 1897 and 1898, the Union of SRs and then the New People's Will succeeded in forging ties with Saratov workers, which later served as the basis for both SR and SD efforts in that milieu. Several intelligentsia-worker circles operated during this period. One, led by Irina Rakit-nikova and based in the railroad workshops, lasted six or seven months, after which, according to one witness, the workers grew dissatisfied with her leadership and stopped coming.

D. I. Maleev enjoyed greater success when he founded a popular free school for workers that offered both literacy and analysis of "the fateful questions of the day."[12] Thus the proletariat in Saratov received its first education under Populist auspices. Many of the individuals involved later became leaders of the Saratov SR and SD parties, and some achieved national prominence. A cross-section of the city's socialist elite, including future SR leaders N. and I. Rakitnikov, L. P. Bulanov, and M. B. Evreinov, and founding members of the city's first SD organizations, E. O. Zelenskii and P. A. Lebedev, attended an August 1898 memorial in honor of veteran Saratov Populist P. I. Voinaral'skii, an event which therefore symbolizes the founding of a modern revolutionary movement in Saratov.[13]

During this formative period, few activists showed much interest in the peasantry, a fact ruefully noted by the "Grandmother of the Russian Revolution," Ekaterina Breshko-Breshkovskaia, when she returned from Siberian exile in 1896 and began her travels around Russia to rebuild a revolutionary Populist party. She often visited the Volga provinces, especially Saratov, where before the turn of the century she made her headquarters. She found the region's peasantry "in an almost unbeliev-able state. The cows and horses were very small because of lack of pasturage. There were no fowls except chickens. The peasantry had stopped growing flax, because there was barely enough land for grain. The population had multiplied, and the patches of land owned by the peasants were too small. . . . The peasants could do nothing but go to the landlords or the kulaks. The peasants regarded the landlords and kulaks alike as enemies." Breshko decided that, after all, peasants were suitable targets for revolutionary agitation, but her efforts to promote the cause did not convince most Populists; similarly, when Chernov tried in 1898 to interest Rakitnikov and other local leaders in his peasant-oriented work in nearby Tambov Province, they turned a deaf ear.[14]

Nevertheless, Saratov's villages were already witnessing some activity. Rakitnikova recalled that the famine of 1891–92 caused a new "going to the people" among Petersburg youth. In this case, however, they found a ready welcome in the countryside from teachers, feldshers, clerks, and— miracle of miracles—even peasants. In some districts, the Third Element (zemstvo doctors, teachers, feldshers, and so on) had widespread ties with the peasants and regularly distributed well-printed revolutionary literature to them. When the outsiders arrived in Balashov District in the early 1890s, "they were in seventh heaven"; the zemstvo doctors Chenykaev and Shmelev, the peasant Feologov, the zemstvo teacher V. S. Aref'ev, and the feldsher M. N. Obukhova had already created a peasant-oriented revolutionary organization.[15]

The cases of Chenykaev and Aref'ev are of special interest. Aref'ev had been associated with the famous Astyrev circle in Moscow, which in 1890 had revived the long dormant idea of peasant agitation. Meanwhile, far out in the Balashov District of Saratov Province, Chenykaev had already begun working in the villages. Upon Aref'ev's return to his native Saratov in 1891, he and a Petersburg student, V. I. Iakubov, utilizing Chenykaev's ties, conducted direct agitation at village meetings *(skhodki),* to which Aref'ev, the son of a peasant, had an entrée. The success of the work in Balashov District led to a broadening of efforts. One detachment went to the village of Makarovo; another, including I. Al'tovskaia (later Rakitnikova), traveled to Serdobsk District; third and fourth groups went to Atkarsk and Petrovsk districts. All this activity quickly led to arrests that resulted in Aref'ev's exile to Nizhnii Novgorod and Iakubov's dramatic escape back to Petersburg. Despite the threat of arrest, between 1892 and 1895 the Chenykaev circle, which now included several feldshers as foot-soldiers, intensified its antigovernmental and antireligious agitation and even urged peasants not to pay taxes. Alerted by the constant stream of "suspicious" characters streaming in and out of Chenykaev's clinic at Turki (Balashov District), the police arrested the whole lot. For lack of evidence, Chenykaev escaped conviction, but several hapless feldshers received eighteen-month terms.[16]

The close call quieted Chenykaev's efforts for a year or two, but agitation among Saratov's peasants did not altogether cease. For example, during 1897 police arrested future Marxist A. A. Bogdanov, at the time a village teacher in Petrovsk District, for distributing peasant-oriented revolutionary literature, which he had received from local Populist circles. That same year Chenykaev used his influence as local zemstvo deputy to open and supervise a school in the village of Chirikova. To the chagrin of the police, he hired a staff of radicals, among them his sister-in-law, Obukhova, and two Aref'ev sisters. The peasants Ivanov and Svetitskii served as propagandists for what was in reality a revolutionary circle at the Chirikova zemstvo school. During 1898 and 1899 police again initiated proceedings against Chenykaev and his associates and investigated both the Turki clinic and the Chirikova school. Despite testimony from certain peasants that the doctor headed an active revolutionary circle, concrete evidence against the wily Chenykaev again proved elusive. After innumerable searches, arrests, and various judicial processes, one of the Aref'ev sisters and both peasant agitators were condemned to several years in exile, and even Chenykaev was to be sent out of the province for two years. In the event, his close ties with prominent zemstvo officials M. Orlov and N. L'vov prevented his exile or even the closing of the school, as a result of which he resumed subversive activities within a year or so.[17]

During the 1890s rural and urban Populist circles had struck deep roots in Saratov. By contrast, Marxism arrived late. While Social Democracy was flourishing in the rest of Russia during the mid- and late 1890s, SD organizations were slow to coalesce in this Volga province. Although some Soviet historians attempt to place the origins of a local Marxist movement in the 1880s, fitful and somewhat confused first efforts actually date from the late 1890s.[18] Sometime after his arrival in 1895, journalist V. S. Golubev was the first person in Saratov to speak regularly about Marxism. By 1896–97, a small group had begun to gather at the apartment of Golubev and his wife, E. P. Golubeva, where locals were at least exposed to Marxist literature. One of the group, M. M. Essen, recalled that there were "several Social Democrats in Saratov" by 1897, the same year that she, as a rather timid neophyte, began to lead a workers' circle from the railroad workshops. Essen may have taught the workers Marxism but, since Golubeva was still an ardent Populist, the political message at the Golubevs' was mixed. In any case, by the late 1890s, Golubev was the first to polemicize in a Marxist spirit against the ubiquitous Populists.[19]

The matrix out of which Social Democracy grew between 1897 and 1900 was an overlapping web of worker-intelligentsia circles (mostly in the railroad workshops), all of which at first had Populist ties. With the workshops' rapid expansion after 1895 and the founding of new metal plants after 1898, many workers, some with previous revolutionary and even SD experience, arrived from Petersburg, Tula, Ivanovo-Voznesensk, and Moscow. Simultaneously, several students formed the city's first Marxist intelligentsia contingent.[20] During 1898, a certain E. I. Zelenskii arrived in Saratov. A fiery speaker and talented organizer, Zelenskii galvanized several workers' circles into a group to which he explained both Marxist and Populist literature in terms that workers understood; at one meeting Zelenskii analyzed and praised the manifesto of the new Russian Social Democratic Workers' Party.[21]

After Zelenskii's arrest in January 1899, new leaders eventually expanded the circle and made contact with the Marxist student group. The new worker-student circle then issued a proclamation for May Day 1899 and signed it "From the Russian Social Democratic Workers' Party," marking it as the very first local SD document. Thereafter, the circle began to call itself the "Saratov Social Democratic Workers' Group." One of its leaders recalled that student-worker tensions existed but did not hinder the group's activities. During the summer of 1899, the worker and student SDs decided on the audacious step of publishing a workers' newspaper. The two issues of *Saratovskii rabochii* (Saratov Worker) were actually hefty brochures with articles written by the students and checked by the workers. The newspaper came to an abrupt halt in August 1899, when two provocateurs betrayed the entire membership of the SD group.[22]

Some Soviet commentators have lauded *Saratovskii rabochii* for not conforming to the "economism" (emphasis on economic over political goals) prevalent among SDs at the time; others have inflated the overall significance of Zelenskii, the Saratov SD group, and its newspaper. More cautious observers have noted that *Saratovskii rabochii*'s Marxism was untutored rather than "Leninist" or "economist"; the group was SD in name only; and its founder, Zelenskii, was hardly a Marxist at all.[23] Nonetheless, the episode marked a signal step in the development of Social Democracy in Saratov. Occurring simultaneously with an ephemeral conversion of local intelligentsia youth to Marxism (in 1899 all Saratov students considered themselves Marxists), the formation of the first Social Democratic group opened the door for some of its members to form a more advanced organization a little later.[24]

Although no other socialist organizations arose between 1899 and 1901, the atmosphere of these two years indelibly stamped its character on the Saratov revolutionary movement. Worker and student circles met together and incessantly debated about SD and SR theories and programs, a salutary process that laid the foundation for future informed choices. Soviet historian G. Malinin calls this a time of "storm and new beginnings." While flirting both with Marxism and the newly formed PSR, students took part in demonstrations and were arrested. Venerable Populists Golubeva and E. A. D'iakova converted to Marxism and played key roles in the early SD movement. Stepan Balmashev and A. Al'tovskii ran the full circuit from Populism to Marxism and back to the Socialist Revolutionaries. After leaving the Rakitnikov circle, the young student A. I. Rykov engaged in circle work as a Marxist. Soviet historians and SD memoirists have reluctantly admitted that the SRs had more followers, more circles, and enjoyed greater influence among workers. One activist intimately involved in Marxist circle work and in all SD groups from the late 1890s on reported that in the early 1900s his party's central task was not to win workers to one or another SD tendency but to wean them away from the SRs.[25]

Despite a natural competitive spirit, friendship and cooperation characterized relations between SDs and SRs. SR founder Argunov referred to the SDs as *"drugi-vragi"* (friendly foes) and, with striking similarity, E. V. Baramzin, a leading Leninist in Saratov, described the SRs as *"vragi-soiuzniki"* (enemy-allies).[26] In Saratov members of the two parties were friends more than foes.

In the absence of well-defined SR and SD organizations, "salons," "clubs," and "evenings" provided locales for revolutionaries to gather, dispute, theorize, propagandize, and sing revolutionary songs. The Fine Arts Society still served this purpose for liberals, SRs, and SDs of the intelligentsia, although workers attended rarely. Cherniavskaia's Populist salon and the rival Marxist one of Auntie Marseillaise (the former Populist D'iakova) were democratic: workers and the intelligentsia intermingled there. Auntie Marseillaise, who loved to bang on the piano while singing the worker anthem, became a sharp critic of Populism. Although D'iakova and Cherniavskaia rarely exchanged visits, virtually identical persons attended their rival salons and other similar gatherings.[27] Most students and workers still retained a politically unsophisticated point of view, and widespread adherence to one or the other party came somewhat later. Fierce debates broke out nevertheless, with Golubev and one or two others acting as Marxist tribunes against the more numerous SRs. At one event, the Marxists Al'tovskii and Rykov spoke about capitalist development in Russia, while all eagerly awaited the talk of Breshko-Breshkovskaia. In order to counteract the Marxist wave, during 1900 Breshko and Bulanov intensively propagandized local students and, despite a lively SD response, won back most of them, including Balmashev and Al'tovskii, both of whom played important roles in the PSR.[28]

Still, SDs and SRs remained close. When several factory workers, including the SD activist S. I. Kanatchikov, lost their jobs, they borrowed 100 rubles from the SR Zota Sazonov (brother of the terrorist Egor) to set up the furniture-making cooperative *Khoziain* (Master). This enterprise, which also served as a workers' club, produced furniture with marvelously clever hiding places for illegal documents. And when SR leader A. V. Panov moved to Saratov in 1900, he brought with him an extensive library with the largest collection of Marxist literature in town; SD, SR, and nonparty workers found his door always open and borrowed his books freely.[29] The atmosphere of cooperation, derived from constant contact, personal relationships of all kinds, and above all, outright need, helps to explain events in the Saratov underground for years to come.

Socialist cooperation in Saratov and elsewhere was rooted in a common revolutionary culture, originating in the 1890s and extending into the 1900s. Because the SDs had not yet mastered printing techniques, the agitational literature used by all Russian revolutionaries during the 1890s often originated either from People's Will groups in Petersburg and Kiev or from Populist organizations in the emigration. Like that of the Marxists, the Populist program for workers espoused a shorter workday, unions, government insurance, and so forth. Furthermore, between 1895 and 1897 Populists and proto-SRs, along with the SDs, helped to popularize May Day as a proletarian holiday. By the late 1890s, the socialist (SD and SR) programs for workers, often expressed in printed materials of Populist origin, had become part and parcel of proletarian consciousness.[30]

Revolutionary poems, stories, and songs also played a great role in the early socialist movement. According to two Soviet compilers of revolutionary songs, until well into the 1900s the songs used by both parties had originated in the Populist movement of the 1870s. By far the most popular song through 1905 and beyond was the "Russian Marseillaise" (or "Workers' Marseillaise"), which had a text by Lavrov set to the tune of the French revolutionary anthem. In the hopes of supplanting the Populist-oriented "Marseillaise," during 1903 the SDs in the Volga region introduced the "International"; since they too had joined the Socialist International, the SRs also included this tune in their songbooks.[31] The SDs of Saratov and elsewhere did not "spring from the head of Zeus fully armed" with a revolutionary culture but borrowed freely from the Populists, as a result of which SRs and SDs approached the masses with identical songs, poems, stories, and, as regards workers, very similar programs. Within the socialist movement, centripetal forces still overpowered centrifugal ones.

During 1901 Saratov entered a new phase of its revolutionary history. Crop failures sparked peasant unrest which did not subside until 1907, and massive factory layoffs caused the first significant strikes and demonstrations in Saratov labor history. Revolutionary circles, including a new SD group in the railroad workshops, became more active; in February and March of 1901, students, reputedly joined by some workers, marched in Saratov. The first tiny May Day demonstration took place in that year and, during June, individual SD and SR workers led the city's first strike.[32] By spring the lively mood in the city had convinced SD *intelligent* (member of the intelligentsia) P. Lebedev that the time was ripe to establish a local SD committee; Lebedev cautiously sounded out prominent SDs, who all responded favorably. Thus several SD *intelligenty* and the worker Kanatchikov founded the Saratov Committee of the Russian Social Democratic Workers's Party (RSDRP). The new committee set itself the tasks of printing its inaugural proclamation and of forging ties with workers. Having obtained print and a hectograph machine, the youthful SDs found that their printed sheets were illegible; likewise, their attempts to create a workers' circle at a local flour mill failed. Since the

84

committee had a majority of moderates, including N. Arkhangel'skaia (vocal defender of Kuskova's "Credo"), it tilted toward economism. Lebedev admitted that, once the committee had mastered printing techniques, its leaflets "had no clear political character" but were aimed at the needs of workers. "As soon as a dispute arose between workers and the owner at a plant, we issued a proclamation with workers' demands, widening this to broader concerns later"—a clear synopsis of SD economism.[33]

As the SD Committee struggled with its problems, several already existing SD workers' circles combined to form their own independent group, which locals informally called the "workers' committee" (*rabochii komitet*). The workers' committee even published an underground newspaper, *Rabochaia gazeta* (Workers' Gazette), and other agitational literature. The existence of parallel committees did not represent profound political disagreements; heavily influenced by a recent influx of economist-oriented workers from Petersburg, the workers' committee was also staunchly economist. *Rabochaia gazeta*, of which at least seven hectographed issues appeared during 1901, even disputed with *Iskra* (the central SD organ, at the time under Lenin's influence); the rambunctious workers rebuked the Leninist paper for its severe polemics against the Petersburg economist newspaper *Rabochaia mysl'* (Workers' Idea). Until 1902 the official "intelligentsia" committee and the workers' committee had no contact whatsoever and, even after they established communications, operated separately until at least 1904. At a time when such divisions had waned elsewhere, the existence of parallel committees in Saratov reflected a belated sharpening of worker-intelligentsia antagonisms.[34]

Paradoxically, the more or less regular arrival in Saratov of *Iskra* during 1901 sparked an even higher level of SD-SR cooperation than already existed. Lebedev recalled how SR leader Al'tovskii triumphantly showed him several *Iskra* issues and urged Saratov SDs to follow its example. During May of 1901, the local SRs who, in Lebedev's words, "entered the path of political agitation earlier than we did," issued a brochure urging all revolutionaries to reconcile their differences and to enter the political (as opposed to economic) struggle.[35] In this case at least, Leninism helped to bridge gaps. In January 1902 Stepan Balmashev reached an agreement with a number of SD and SR activists to create a joint organization specifically dedicated to propagandizing Saratov's numerous artisanal workers. The SR-SD group took the title "Saratov Socialist Artisanal Union" and, until its dissolution in June 1902, issued numerous leaflets, published two issues of a newspaper, and organized and led several sizable artisanal circles.[36]

During January 1902 another group of activists founded a second, more important joint SR-SD organization under the title "Saratov Unified Group of Social Democrats and Socialist Revolutionaries" (nicknamed the *"Ob"edinnenka"* or "Unity." The chief SD organizer was future Soviet statesman A. Rykov, who had become an ardent adherent of political struggle. Dismayed at the sway of economism over local SDs, Rykov, without the approval of the SD Committee, joined with the SR Al'tovskii to construct the Ob"edinnenka. During the preceding months, the SRs had conducted intense political agitation among workers. Their "revolutionary" spirit attracted conscious workers and also some SD activists, who had found SR newspapers more appealing (that is, more political) than SD ones. With *Iskra* as catalyst, the Ob"edinnenka arose out of a mutual admiration between SRs and Leninist SDs.[37] On a somewhat wider scale than the Artisanal Union, the Ob"edinnenka printed proclamations, published several issues of a newspaper, issued leaflets, and conducted heavy agitation in workers' circles.[38]

In spring of 1902, the SD Committee, the SR Committee, the Ob"edinnenka, and the Artisanal Union all issued leaflets for the upcoming May Day celebration and cooperated to organize a demonstration. On the day itself, a smallish corps of demonstrators, carrying banners with slogans against the government and in praise of local hero Stepan Balmashev (recent assassin of Interior Minister Sipiagin) marched along several streets in downtown Saratov until police attacked and dispersed the column and arrested sixty-two SDs and SRs, including Rykov, whom they beat severely. Within a few weeks the authorities had released most of the detainees but scheduled others for trial. Local SDs and SRs issued numerous proclamations before, during, and after the November 1902 trial, which the national party newspapers also covered in detail.[39]

This seemingly routine affair was in fact the baptism of fire for the Saratov revolutionary movement, after which nothing would ever be quite the same. Police repression increased drastically. After May Day the police carried out a wave of arrests and, fearing the worst, SD leader Lebedev fled to the Caucasus. On the eve of the November trial, the authorities conducted "the most massive [arrests] in memory," reported

Iskra. Locals called it "St. Bartholomew's Night"; cordons of police swept through the city picking up SD and SR leaders and activists. When those on trial for the May Day affair received lifetime Siberian exile the shock was complete.

The matter, however, went even further. Before the events of summer and fall of 1902, local police had handled revolutionaries lackadaisically. Memoirists recalled that during the 1899–1901 period of socialist "evenings" and "salons" the authorities often called in participants for questioning and almost inevitably released them without consequences. When police conducted searches for illegal materials, they were easily fooled. Some activists hid literature in obvious places, such as under tablecloths or beneath the chair cushions upon which the police sat as they carried out initial interrogations. Many activists hid materials in furniture made by the cooperative Khoziain. Agents provocateurs were few in number. Even when police arrested socialists, after a few weeks they usually released them under observation, as had happened with the entire 1899 SD group. Now everything changed; a plague of provocateurs descended on Saratov. Arrests often brought jail terms or exile. An arrested cabinetmaker revealed the secrets of Khoziain's furniture.[40] Life had hardened; conspiracy lost its light-hearted aspect.

To add to the problems, during the summer of 1902 Lenin published two articles in *Iskra* that condemned "the opportunistic practice of SD-SR unions."[41] What with already high tensions in Saratov, these articles set off bitter SR-SD disputes. The first article, which appeared in June, led to the disruption of the Artisanal Union. Although the SRs responded with a pointed critique of Lenin's new land program (outlined in the same June *Iskra* issue), Rykov still refused to contemplate breaking up the Ob"edinnenka. However, when the August issue of *Iskra* with Lenin's second article arrived, the SRs "declared anathema" on the SDs and issued a public appeal for all revolutionaries in Saratov to join the PSR. At first, the SDs in the Ob"edinnenka reacted by joining with the SRs to send a protest to *Iskra.*[42]

At this point the SD Committee, which had a new Iskrist orientation and had set itself the goal of unifying all SDs, stepped into the fray by ordering all SDs to leave the Ob"edinnenka; by September the joint organization's SDs and SRs had all gone back to their respective parties. Thus, from the SD side, Leninists had helped build the Ob"edinnenka and Leninists had broken it up. As one local SD wrote to *Iskra,* "a real battle is taking place between the SRs and the SDs."[43] In addition, the Saratov SRs finally set up their own committee, in response, thought SD Lebedev, to what his own party had recently done. Harsh disputes, reported in *Iskra* and the SR *Revoliutsionnaia Rossiia* (Revolutionary Russia), continued for at least a year over whether or not Balmashev had been an SR, whether SRs had played a role in the Artisanal Union, and whether any SRs had taken part in the May Day 1902 demonstration and court trial. The most acrimonious debate focused on Balmashev and the Artisanal Union. Apparently concerned that the SRs were capitalizing on worker sympathy for Balmashev's act and for him personally after his execution, the SDs decided to attack on all fronts. Although the two sides offered directly contradictory testimony on each issue, the SRs apparently refuted all charges.

Regardless, memoirists reported that once the first storm had blown over, the two parties resumed surprisingly good relations. As Lebedev put it, "in general we worked side by side *(bok-o-bok)* with the SRs in a rather friendly manner and sometimes carried out cooperative ventures with them." During the fall of 1902, in the midst of the worst squall, Baramzin, the leading Saratov Leninist, informed *Iskra* that few SDs, even among the Leninists, approved of the newspaper's August issue. Later he again warned that the harsh tone of *Iskra* ill fit the realities of revolutionary life in Saratov. Similarly, M. Liadov, a Saratov delegate to the Second Congress of the RSDRP, recalled that on meeting Lenin there he remarked that "in the opinion of the Saratov Committee, it would be better if *Iskra* did not attack the economists and the SRs so sharply."[44] New realities may have required that local socialists more clearly define their organizations, but cooperation, hallowed by tradition and fostered by need, continued.

After the turbulence of 1902, a rather uneasy calm, punctuated only by occasional student demonstrations, prevailed in Saratov City for the next two years. In 1904 Governor Stolypin noted that, despite the relative quiet, the intelligentsia remained extremely antigovernment. Worker unrest stayed at a low ebb, but in the villages disorders of a virtually revolutionary scale persisted almost unabated.[45] In this situation both parties continued activities of all types.

The years from 1901 to 1904 are especially interesting in regard to the Socialist Revolutionaries, as the local organization served as the chief center of the party inside Russia. Arrests in November–December 1902 and again in 1903 threatened this important function, but the organization always revived. At least one reputable source has claimed that the Saratov Committee fulfilled the role of Central Committee inside Russia until the First SR Congress in late 1905. Oddly enough, the formation of a Saratov committee in late summer of 1902 was almost an afterthought. Saratov's prominence in the national movement was a result both of local party strengths and national problems. During 1900 Argunov had launched the Moscow Union of SRs' new paper, *Revoliutsionnaia Rossiia*, with the goal of unifying all neo-Populists. In 1901 he made the last of several trips to Saratov to negotiate with the already formidable local leaders (the Rakitnikovs, Bulanov, Rossov, Al'tovskii, and Breshko-Breshkovskaia). Upon his return to Moscow, he received the news that the police had seized the press the SRs had set up in Tomsk to print their newspaper; much of the Moscow Union's personnel also soon fell prey to the police. Top party leaders P. Kraft, G. Gershuni, S. Klitchoglu, and others then sought the safe haven of the commodious Saratov organization, which included exalted personages such as city mayor Milashevskii.

The arrests of Bulanov and Milashevskii during the fall of 1902 and Al'tovskii's narrow escape from the city affected the SRs only slightly. In May 1903, the authorities incarcerated a majority of the committee, including Rakitnikov and Gershuni. "No center in Russia now existed," woefully commented Sletov. Even so, the depth of local party cadres enabled Rakitnikova and I. Starynkevich to reconstruct an organization that remained the center of the party inside Russia until, according to B. Nikolaevskii, late 1905.[46]

By late 1902, party work centered in two SR "clubs." The Central Committee of the PSR had commissioned the setting up of a club at Klitchoglu's place, where Kraft, Gershuni, and M. Mel'nikov concerned themselves with national affairs. For instance, Kraft and Mel'nikov set about planning the assassination of von Plehve, until Azef, who also visited from time to time, betrayed Klitchoglu. The apartment of old People's Will activist E. I. Averkieva was the site of the club where the local "generals" met. Here, under the supervision of Zota Sazonov, the locals directed workers' circles and maintained a hectograph machine for printing leaflets; Breshko-Breshkovskaia looked after peasant agitation.[47]

Although after 1901 Saratov SRs devoted enormous and successful attention to the village, they did not neglect the workers. Soviet historian Saar noted the existence of SR workers' circles alongside SD ones in the main factories and workshops between 1900 and 1904. During September 1902, the police broke up an extensive SR circle at the railroad workshops in Pokrovskaia Sloboda, across the Volga from Saratov. During 1903 and 1904, the Saratov SRs produced large quantities of worker-oriented literature, which the police often found in the possession of workers they arrested. By May 1903, the Saratov Committee had set up a "Union of Artisans and Workers," otherwise known as the SR Workers' Union *(Rabochii soiuz)*, which printed its own revolutionary materials. During July 1903, the Saratov Committee issued an enormously detailed "Program for studies in workers' circles," which was published in *Revoliutsionnaia Rossiia*.[48] In September 1903, the Saratov Committee issued a leaflet "To the workers of the Bering Plant," which called for the overthrow of "the tsar-despot and the cunning capitalists. Down with Autocracy! Long live Socialism!" To prevent a strike at the plant, police then arrested a number of SRs, including workers, and seized the committee's printing press. In January 1904, the SR Committee again issued a proclamation to workers at the Bering Plant and communicated to *Revoliutsionnaia Rossiia* a critique of the SD Committee's "economist" line. According to the SRs, the SDs advised workers to turn with their requests first to the factory owners, then to the labor exchange, and finally to the governor. The SRs instead recommended direct action in the form of strikes to obtain the rehiring of fired workers, one of the chief causes of the prolonged unrest among Bering workers. Sometime in 1904, several SR workers' circles united to form a "workers' committee," paralleling the still-existing SD workers' committee.[49] Along with intensified agitation among peasants and soldiers, by 1904 the Saratov SRs issued more worker-oriented proclamations than ever before.

Despite the successful efforts of Chenykaev and other activists in the villages, the central Populist and SR circles in Saratov showed minimal interest in the peasants until 1900. By 1900–01, however, even before the peasant uprisings of 1902–03, the winds of change had begun to blow. In the emigration, Chernov recruited several old Populists into his Agrarian-Socialist League, which had the primary goal of propagandizing the peasantry. By 1900, evidently prescient activists in various regions of Russia showed a heightened interest in peasants, and nowhere was this more the case than in Saratov. The testimony of Breshkovskaia and Rakitnikova suggests, indeed, that the Saratov organization played a vital role in this crucial nationwide phenomenon.[50]

Nothing having been written for peasants in over two decades, lack of appropriate literature was the chief stumbling block. The new agrarian activists partially filled the vacuum by smuggling Agrarian-Socialist League publications into Russia, but the newly formed PSR, which did not wholeheartedly embrace the peasant cause until mid-1902, found this a hazardous and expensive task. Undaunted, Breshkovskaia tilled the fertile Volga soil; during the first years of the new century, Saratovtsy such as the Rakitnikovs and Bulanov, plus outsiders like Kraft, joined Breshkovskaia to create a distinguished organization quite willing to focus its major energies on peasant matters. Saratov quickly became a fount of hectographed, mimeographed, and printed booklets, brochures, and leaflets for peasants. In mid-1901, local enthusiasts brought out a thick journal (sometimes incorrectly called a newspaper), *Krest'ianskoe delo* (Peasants' Cause), the five hundred mimeographed copies of which in no way filled the vast demand. Technical difficulties prevented the journal's continuation, but students, medical personnel, and teachers heeded the PSR's call and turned out huge quantities of peasant-oriented leaflets, which spread their way throughout the province and into the entire Volga, Urals, Ukrainian, and Caucasus regions.[51]

The young Saratov intelligentsia and the peasants themselves saw both the slick Agrarian League literature and the cruder local products "as manna from heaven," recalled Breshkovskaia. No doubt one of the crucial elements in Saratov's early and enthusiastic conversion to peasant-oriented work was the fact that the Chenykaev-Aref'ev circle of Balashov District and the Mariinskii Agricultural Institute of Niko-laevskii Gorodok (Saratov District) had already established ties with peasants. In 1899, M. Sokolov and several of his fellow students, some of whom were of peasant origin, formed a circle committed to rural work at the Mariinskii Institute. In 1901 the Mariinskii circle established a smithy-turner cooperative in Nikolaevskii Gorodok, which also provided ties with workers, some of whom became skilled agitators. By 1902 the Mariinskii circle, augmented by students from the nearby Kazanskii Agricultural High School, had sixty-six members.

After winning a reprieve from exile, Chenykaev now entered into the most radical phase of his long revolutionary career. During the late 1890s, his propagandists had restricted themselves to calls for political rights and had avoided the explosive land question. During 1901–02 his circle, which now consisted of roughly eighteen members including thirteen literate peasants, displayed no such restraint in agitating openly both for the overthrow of the tsar and for the seizure of land from the gentry. The circle inundated the villages of Balashov District with primarily SR literature obtained from the Mariinskii circle or directly from Saratov. At least thirty-five peasants of fourteen villages proved willing to collect and distribute materials. Simultaneously, the Mariinskii circle, also with the aid of numerous peasants, propagandized villages in Saratov, Serdobsk, Petrovsk, and Atkarsk districts. Activists printed materials in Saratov and then channeled them to the villages through the Mariinskii and Chenykaev circles, with peasants acting as agents and propagandists.[52]

When police broke up the Chenykaev circle once and for all (the Mariinskii circle escaped unscathed) in February 1902, disorders had already seized much of Balashov District.[53] By spring of 1902, all of Saratov Province and several Ukrainian provinces were experiencing the most alarming peasant uprising since the Pugachev revolt. Observers unanimously noted the special character of this peasant rebellion as compared to ones of the past. Especially notable was the role of books or, as peasants called them, *khoroshie knizhki* (good little books), some of which came from the Social Democrats, the Tolstoyans, and the liberals, but the vast majority of which were Socialist Revolutionary in origin.[54] Partially under the influence of these books, the peasants used different tactics than in the past. Of all the provinces in revolt during 1902, commentators have singled out Saratov as the place where peasants showed the greatest discipline and consciousness. In a few cases, peasants assaulted ill-reputed landowners; more often, but not indiscriminately, they used the "red rooster" (arson). A peasant delegation visited a certain priest suspected of police ties, after which he hurriedly complied with their invitation to leave the area; hired laborers methodically struck exploitative gentry and kulak employers; peasants demanded grain from public warehouses and, if refused, seized it; many villages grazed their livestock on gentry land; peasants approached offending landowners with requests for the redressing of wrongs.[55] In a reversal of the usual order of things, villagers from Makarovo in Balashov District thrashed a detachment of cossacks; thereafter the government sent out cossacks only in force. In 1902 alone, the authorities brought twenty-six major court cases against peasants of Balashov, Petrovsk, Saratov, Atkarsk, and Serdobsk districts.[56]

Despite active repression, the disorders in Saratov Province, as opposed to those in the Ukraine, hardly faltered in 1902, 1903, and 1904. In Balashov District, laborers continued to boycott kulaks and peasants put numerous gentry houses around Turki to the torch. During 1903 and 1904, villagers in other longtime centers of unrest, such as Trubetskoe (Balashov District), Spassko-Aleksandrovskoe (Petrovsk District), and several villages in Atkarsk District, employed similar methods. As one correspondent put it in May 1903, "agrarian terror is penetrating our province and more."[57] To quell the disorders, Governor Engelgardt and his replacement, Stolypin, dispatched ever larger cossack units.

Socialist Revolutionary agitation played a major role in the agrarian movement. In 1902 the PSR founded the SR Peasant Union, which had the goals of uniting at each level of the party organization all individuals engaged in peasant work; of recruiting new members; and of carrying out urgent, direct revolutionary agitation among peasants. The SR Peasant Unions of Kharkov and Saratov provinces were the first in Russia to function, and in Saratov eventually reached a grandiose scale. The Chenykaev circle did not revive, but the Mariinskii group continued its work. During 1903 the police exaggeratedly referred to the school as an "affiliate" of the PSR. In June and August 1903, the police arrested numerous persons in Balashov District, but to no avail. *Revoliutsionnaia Rossiia* reported an "unpleasant atmosphere" throughout the province during the winter of 1904, when police raided numerous villages and arrested peasants and teachers. During searches, the authorities confiscated large quantities of revolutionary literature and listed the titles in the indictments. The charges indicate that by 1904 Saratov peasants were being arrested for "membership in the PSR." Disquieted officials lamented that "this is the pass we have come to: peasants are messing in politics [*muzhiki politikoi zanimaiut'sia*]."[58] The SRs had laid a solid foundation for what was to come in 1905.

Nor did Saratov Social Democrats entirely neglect peasant agitation. Baramzin and other Saratov correspondents often complained to central party organs about the shortage of materials suitable for peasants. Finally, in 1902, when the SD Committee commanded growing resources, Lebedev and several others founded the SD Agrarian League. League members began to make the rounds of the villages and, with the help of some Mariinskii students, set up several circles. However, the status of agrarian work for most SDs can be judged by Lebedev's comment that the local SD Committee provided "not one kopeck" to the league. Having no SD literature, the league distributed SR materials, with certain deletions.[59]

Between 1901 and 1904, the SD organization underwent significant changes. Through early 1902, economism prevailed in both worker and intelligentsia committees and, in fact, received a big boost with the arrival of the powerful economist speaker P. P. Maslov. As yet Iskrist tendencies were extremely weak. In December 1900, V. Artsybushev brought copies of *Iskra* to Saratov, but few converts rallied to the cause. Activists from nearby Samara, where Lenin and Martov had built a solid Iskrist organization, including Lenin's brother, D. Ul'ianov, Artsybushev, and G. M. Krzhizhanovskii, planted the seeds for the growth of *Iskra*'s influence in Saratov. In January 1902, Krzhizhanovskii and other Iskrists organized the "Bureau of the Russian *Iskra* Organization" in Samara; soon thereafter the bureau sent Baramzin to Saratov, where, with Golubeva, he formed a tiny cell within the SD organization. Under the *nomme de guerre* "Embryon," Baramzin wrote to *Iskra* in London that during the spring of 1901 a favorable mood for Leninism existed in Saratov, which prompted a query from Krupskaia (Lenin's wife and secretary) as to Embryon's identity. Lebedev's recollection that the regular receipt of the Leninist paper "made a difference" supports the accuracy of Baramzin's report.[60]

After the virtual destruction of the SD Committee duing the 1902 May Day affair, the staff of the new committee—N. G. Smidovich, I. M. Liakhovetskii (Maiskii), Golubeva, Baramzin, Lebedev, et al.—was distinctly more Iskrist than the old one. In the midst of the September 1902 dispute with the SRs, Krzhizhanovskii reported to *Iskra* that Baramzin's influence in Saratov was "growing lately." Toward the end of the year, Krupskaia thanked Baramzin for the pleasant news he had sent about local affairs. Indeed, in December the Saratov Committee sent an open letter to *Iskra* , which proclaimed the Leninist paper its official organ and espoused the unification of all SD groups under *Iskra*'s leadership. Saratov delegates to the Second Congress of the RSDRP supported Lenin on most issues. During the fall of 1902 the Saratov Committee resolved to assign "propaganda and agitation among the local worker population the highest priority" and during the following months distributed thirty-two thousand copies of worker-oriented leaflets. The SD Committee, however, still controlled neither SD workers' circles nor the workers' committee, had only one worker as a member, and had not yet overcome the predominant SR influence among local workers.[61]

Nevertheless, until something went awry, the Saratov SDs were in the process of building a powerful organization with a Leninist tilt. Sometime after the new year (1903), contact with the outside world became sporadic. During the spring Lenin and Krupskaia repeatedly asked their Samara agents to "connect us with Babylon, connect us with Babylon!" When Baramzin finally wrote to *Iskra* in May, he complained that no SD literature was available. Various sources indicate that during the spring and summer of 1903 the SD Committee was compelled to distribute SR literature in the factories. *Iskra* complicated the crisis by failing to send anything for over seven months.[62]

Internal conflicts also began to torment the SDs. Some members of the organization formed a special group, *"Volia"* (Freedom), for the purpose of reviving the SR-SD joint committee. To make matters worse, huge arrests after May Day 1903 forced the SDs "to refrain from mass agitation in favor of internal organization." By September, *Iskra* reported that some Saratov SDs, incensed at the committee's inactivity, had formed separate groups; in addition to the left-wing Volia, a fractious Menshevik group had taken shape on the right.[63] Many new members from elsewhere—some Bolsheviks, some Mensheviks—had come into the Saratov organization. I. P. Gol'denberg, who was nominally a Bolshevik but quite moderate on most issues, dominated the Saratov Committee from the moment of his arrival during the fall of 1903. Other vocal SDs, such as Liakhovetskii-Maiskii, also took moderate stances, and influential local activists such as D. A. Topuridze and Essen were right-wing Mensheviks. Despite growing Menshevik influence, the committee voted in December 1903 to support the Bolshevik Central Committee against the Mensheviks and shortly thereafter proclaimed this in a second open letter to the newly Menshevized *Iskra*. Soviet historian Konovalov's judgment that the Saratov Committee "vacillated" at this time fits the existing evidence.[64] Deeply under the influence of the eloquent but moderate Gol'denberg, the committee worked a compromise between almost equal left and right wings that moved it firmly to the center.

Throughout late 1903 and all of 1904, the committee was out of touch with party leaders in western Europe and took progressively less clear positions. Unresolved Bolshevik versus Menshevik tensions underlay the malaise; the summer of 1904 witnessed the most acute clashes to date.

After failing to win a majority at a local party conference, the Mensheviks formed a faction, *"Svobodnoe slovo"* (Free Speech). Compounding the rupture was the continued existence of the independent workers' committee. In 1904 six propagandists were the SD Committee's sole link with workers' circles: SD workers listened to lecturers from the official committee but subordinated themselves in every way to the workers' committee.[65]

The SD Committee did not therefore attain its goal of unifying all SDs, a failure that did not prevent circle work from continuing and even prospering. Moderate SD Semenov, often a harsh critic of his own party's efforts, recalled that "serious work" among the proletariat began only in 1904.[66] Historians may exaggerate the extent to which the SDs eliminated SR influence in local factories, but the Saratov Marxists, by concentrating on one segment of the population, did finally become the leading element among workers; the existence of the workers' committee, which isolated workers from the squabbles within the SD Committee, actually contributed to this accomplishment. Thus, by the eve of the 1905 revolution both parties had established considerable organizations in both the city and province of Saratov and over a period of several years had carried out widespread propaganda among the mass elements of society.

In a sense, the 1905 revolution in Saratov began during the fall of 1904 with the onset of a series of political banquets. These banquets, it so happened, set off the famous nationwide Banquet Campaign, which played such a crucial role in fostering oppositionist sentiment thoughout Russia. As *Iskra* commented in wonderment: "in Saratov there now exists something unforeseen and inconceivable. Full freedom of meeting and speech now reigns."[67] Saratov zemstvo officials unwittingly precipitated this chain of events by arranging a banquet on November 5, 1904, in conjunction with the opening of a national zemstvo congress in Moscow. Speakers at this intelligentsia gathering maintained a parliamentary style of discourse while criticizing the government with unwonted openness. The affair proved so popular that two weeks later local jurists arranged a second formal banquet at a fine hotel, and "democracy" organized its alternative to take place simultaneously at a large tearoom, with tickets apportioned between SDs and SRs. At the boisterous democratic banquet of roughly a thousand workers and revolutionary activists, the SD and SR leaders, who had no experience in public speaking, made excruciatingly dull speeches; for all that, they boldly criticized the existing order and, in the words of one commentator, "outlined in abstract terms the basis for revolutionary change," thus going much further than their counterparts at the society affair.[68]

Surprisingly, as every lecture, musical or literary event, and social gathering now became an excuse for political speeches and debates, the authorities stood aside. Saratov liberals from the Union of Liberation quickly reached an agreement with SR and SD leaders to bring together "society" and "democracy" in a single joint affair on December 14. At this banquet of roughly a thousand persons from the entire spectrum of Saratov society, liberals called for universal suffrage and socialists intimated the need for more radical social and political changes. Although the event was a great success, the salutary accord among liberals and various socialists quickly began to break down. The Menshevik *Iskra* joyously greeted Saratov's liberal-socialist cooperation, whereas both Lenin and national SR leaders condemned it. Lenin's complaints did not stop the supposedly Bolshevik SD Committee from taking part in several well-attended public banquets in early January, the last (and by far the largest) of which, on January 8, 1905, brought the national banquet campaign to a close. Displeased with the circumlocutions even the socialists had used at the December 14 affair, most local SRs heeded their national leaders' directives not to attend the January banquets.[69]

In Saratov and environs, so-called people's banquets with SR and SD speakers continued long after the zemstvo banquet campaign; peasant banquets took place in Balashov District and in Pokrovskaia Sloboda, across the Volga from Saratov. After several orators spoke in an "unabashedly SR spirit" at a liberal-organized Saratov teachers' banquet, SRs and SDs plotted together to disrupt an upcoming fund-raising ball for needy Saratov students. When the affair opened on the evening of January 10, with an SR teacher presiding, some three hundred workers and peasants augmented the large crowd of students and teachers. When the stunning news of the Bloody Sunday massacre arrived, several SRs created a furor with impromptu speeches, after which a succession of SR and SD students and workers rose to call for a "general protest strike."[70] Thus the stage was set for the next scene of the 1905 revolution in Saratov.

The following day both the SR and SD committees voted for a general strike, issued proclamations with nearly identical political slogans, and conducted vigorous agitation to shut down the factories. As Bolshevik activist-historian Nevskii pointed out, evidently in reference to the zemstvo and people's banquet campaigns, the ground for a strike "had already long been prepared by the mood of zemstvo employees and workers."[71] On the evening of the eleventh, a meeting of about forty SD workers approved a strike. The next morning, several factories walked out on strike, followed quickly by the workshops of the Riazan-Urals Railroad. During that evening and the next day, print shops, schools, and various other institutions joined the movement; to everyone's surprise railroad clerks came out as well. As late as January 17, just as the strike began to lose momentum, the city's office clerks joined in. Some ten thousand Saratov workers ultimately left their workplaces, which, if not a general strike, sufficed to jeopardize the economic and civil life of the city. Governor Stolypin stressed in one report that Saratov faced a "revolutionary movement"; he summoned cossack reinforcements from the Urals and placed guards on the railway lines to ensure their arrival, with the result that the government never completely lost control of the city. So, although between January 12 and 17 the strike moved ever closer to a general one, after the seventeenth it began to dissipate, and by January 22 was history.[72]

Several factors account for these developments. Between January 10 and 12, both socialist parties backed the strike and agitated for it in virtually identical terms. By January 12, a wide variety of workers, including those from the railroads, Saratov's largest industrial employer, had struck; that evening a meeting at the railroad workshops, attended by representatives of various factories and city and zemstvo offices, elected deputies to a central strike committee, which then endorsed a SD-sponsored list of political demands, including the call for a general strike.[73]

How the strike committee was chosen is not clear, but, according to the SRs, it had one shortcoming: it had no SRs. As Soviet histories refer to the strike committee only elliptically, a perhaps biased analysis from *Revoliutsionnaia Rossiia* will have to serve as the basis of the following remarks. At the outset the SRs suggested to the SDs that, on the basis of past practice, the two parties coordinate the strike jointly, but they were refused on the ground that the SDs (still smarting from the SR pullout from the banquets?) "did not want to answer for the [SRs'] actions." The SDs then negotiated with liberals among city and zemstvo employees and railroad clerks to create a strike committee of SD-liberal persuasion (thus recapitulating the alignment of the recent banquets). To attract wider worker support, the SRs and SDs, operating separately, issued leaflets that supplemented the original political demands with economic ones, such as pay raises, the eight-hour day, and relief from fines.[74] In response to the growing threat, Stolypin mounted a counterattack. Police descended on strike meetings and arrested SD, SR, and liberal strike leaders. Cossacks menacingly patrolled strategic points in the city. The strike committee cautioned against open clashes and, in fact, there were none. The SRs, however, called for resistance and named a place and time for a mass meeting on the evening of the fifteenth, at which they hoped to proclaim an armed uprising. Forewarned, Stolypin sent troops to occupy the area in advance. On the following day, with tensions rising on all sides, the SD Committee, until then aligned with the moderate SD-liberal strike committee, appealed for a continuation of the strike and for an armed uprising, seconding the SR call of the previous day. That evening the best SD and SR orators, such as Gol'denberg and Knushevit-skii, delivered fiery speeches to a crowd of roughly two thousand gathered outside the city. Unanimity prevailed: the strike should continue at all costs until all workers' demands were met.[75]

On the seventeenth, just as the office clerks were joining the movement, the central strike committee, swayed by a sudden call from the SD Committee to end the political strike, announced that the "goals of the political strike were achieved" but that workers who continued an economic strike would receive full support. Stunned by the SD Committee's volte-face, the SRs issued a leaflet on the eighteenth that insisted on maintaining the general political strike. But factory meetings began to split, some voting to continue, others to call off the strike. In an adroit maneuver, railroad and factory administrators made economic concessions. With no unity among the socialists, the movement ran out of steam and the last strikers returned to work on January 22.[76]

The indignant SR's accusation that their exclusion from the strike leadership had hindered the progress of the strike was probably accurate; the record reveals that the broader the socialist consensus, the more effective the action. Still, in cooperating with liberal forces and in calling for an end to the political strike when they did, the SDs had logic on their side. The strike attained as threatening a dimension as it did precisely because a very broad spectrum of society (workers, students, city and zemstvo employees, and railroad clerks) became involved. Although political in inspiration, the strike had attracted most workers only after the socialists added economic clauses to their list of demands. Since the strike did not spread beyond the confines of Saratov and since no one had mastered the techniques of armed resistance, the political strike was doomed once managers made economic concessions. Then again, the SRs had a point when they noted with irony that the SDs had refused to cooperate with them but willingly blocked with liberals, thus allowing undue moderate influence in the strike leadership. Paradoxically, the white-collar employees in the strike guaranteed both its severity and its brevity. Soviet historians could shed light on the matter by commenting on whether or not it was the liberals who pressured the SDs to call off the political strike.

The SRs conceded that the SDs had stolen the show when they created a strike committee responsive primarily to themselves, but criticized— indeed ridiculed—the SD boast that they had "proclaimed and called off" the political strike.[77] The SRs (accurately) intimated that SD control over the workers was by no means absolute. When, for instance, the SDs and SRs formed an underground strike organization of railroad workers, the SRs soon took it over. The chief of railroad gendarmes blamed the strike primarily on SR agitators, who had called "for strikes against Russia's political and economic system." Jonathan Sanders, who has written a history of the January strike, notes that support for the SRs "outshone" that for the SDs.

Regardless, as Sanders and Henry Reichman argue, the Saratov strike, which did win economic concessions, served as a model for later strikes, including the famous October 1905 general railroad strike in Moscow.[78] When worker and middle-class elements joined together, their power was awesome, but, as both the January Saratov strike and the October national strike showed, this (socialist-liberal) alliance was fragile.

Unresolved tensions in Saratov almost led to a replay of the affair a few weeks later. On February 7 flour-mill workers, who had played no role during January, struck over economic problems. Since administrators at many plants had failed to fulfill the commitments that had ended the earlier strike, workers at various factories, joined a day or two later by railroad workers, telegraph workers, printers, and sawmill workers, also left their workplaces; the total reached ninety-five hundred at over ninety concerns. In the hope of widening the strike on the January model, the SR and SD committees and the SR Workers' Union issued leaflets with political and economic demands; in this case, neither students nor white-collar employees responded, and the strike remained entirely economic. The SD railroad worker Sokolov later claimed that workers demonstrated more purposefully and stubbornly in February than in January, a claim supported by reports of street clashes between workers and police during the second strike. As in January, administrators made economic concessions, which brought the strike to a close by February 22.[79] Although technically a success, the February strike, perhaps because of its lack of a political agenda and its narrow social scope, has lapsed into obscurity.

After the turbulent fall and winter, the spring of 1905 was anticlimactic. Heavy arrests had damaged both parties, especially the SDs. During the late winter and spring, the SR Committee and its Workers' Union continued to issue proclamations to workers, peasants, soldiers, and citizens, as, on a smaller scale, did the SDs, with little distinguishing the contents of the two parties' publications.[80] The SRs became preoccupied with their rapidly expanding network of rural groups, while the SDs argued over Menshevik and Bolshevik maneuverings at the national level.

Soviet historians evaluate this period as one of renewed "vacillation" for the SD organization. SD activist N. M. Druzhinin recalled that although the SD Committee operated during 1904 and much of 1905 under the leadership of nominal Bolsheviks (Gol'denberg and V. Obukhov), Mensheviks such as Topuridze, Liakhovetskii, and several others wielded increasing influence. With the approval of local and national Mensheviks, the SD Committee had cooperated with liberals during the banquet and strike campaigns. During the spring of 1905, when the issue of the Third Social Democratic Congress exploded on the national SD scene, Saratov SDs failed to take a firm position; Liadov, whom the Bolshevik Bureau had sent to the Volga area to summon support for the congress, wrote that "the Saratov organization wavered badly." Only after sharp clashes with local Mensheviks did Liadov win very qualified support for the Bolshevik congress. In addition, the SD Committee had still not solved the problem of regularly producing printed materials, nor had it broadened its base to include more workers, prompting Lenin's complaint that if "the Saratov Committee had only one worker, it was because the Saratov Committee did not know how to select appropriate workers."[81]

Under these conditions local SDs confronted a gradual revival of strike activity during late spring and a definite outburst of antigovernment sentiment by May Day. Before May 1, the SR and SD committees and the SR Workers' Union all issued very similar leaflets with economic and political slogans and calls for a general strike.[82] On the eve of the holiday, SDs and SRs each held preparatory meetings aimed at arranging mass demonstrations the next day outside the city. According to SR sources, several SD workers came to the SR meeting to invite them to the SD gathering, a request the SRs did not take seriously because of the hostility the SDs had shown in January. In the morning, the two meetings, of roughly 250 persons each, took place as scheduled. After further negotiations, the parties summoned a joint meeting for 5 P.M. outside the city. Roughly nine hundred persons arrived to find the trees and bushes around the meeting place hung with SR and SD proclamations and placards; orators of both parties called for a political strike, but verbal sparring between the SDs and SRs marred the event. Nevertheless, the next day the strike broke out, followed by further joint mass meetings. As in January, however, the SDs suddenly proclaimed the political strike "over," its goals allegedly having been achieved. In this case, economic strikes continued and printers eventually won the eight-hour day and wage increases; other workers remained on strike for weeks without attaining anything whatsoever. The SRs reiterated their amazement at the unilateral SD action, which had again broken the unanimity of the strike.[83]

During the summer of 1905, both parties became involved in organizing labor unions. Early in the summer, local activists founded the All-Russian Railroad Union's Saratov filial. The membership defeated an SD resolution to supplant the national union's Socialist Revolutionary-oriented program with a Social Democratic one. Interestingly, almost a third of the railroad clerks voted for the resolution, while the railroad workers ignored the SD alternative. In a surprising turnabout of normal SD attitudes, local Mensheviks then adopted a highly sectarian stance on union–party relations by proclaiming it better to have no unions at all than non-SD ones, and persuaded the SD Committee to define the unions as subordinate "party organizations"; local Bolsheviks rejected this view, so closely associated with Leninism elsewhere. In the course of the summer, SDs organized partisan unions of printers, office clerks, and railroad clerks and evidently dominated metalworkers', tailors', and carpenters' unions. With much fanfare, the SRs responded by forming their own unions. Meanwhile, national Menshevik and Bolshevik leaders took the Saratov SDs to task on this issue and local activists complained that the sectarian union policy did not suit the city's basically nonaligned proletariat. By October, the SDs had modified their union policy, after which the SDs and SRs cooperated in creating nonpartisan labor unions.[84]

Although the SR Committee retained a stable leadership into the fall, various factors wrought considerable changes in the makeup of the SD Committee. Most importantly, the central Bolshevik organization co-opted Gol'denberg, who therefore left Saratov in August. The new committee of six persons had a stronger Bolshevik orientation than the previous one, and the party organization as a whole evolved greatly during the summer and early fall. Each city district now had its responsible leader under whom operated a group of organizers for each factory or establishment who had direct contact with workers and activists in the factories. By late summer the committee had created an armed detachment *(druzhina)* and a special agrarian group. SD organizations had also arisen in Balashov, Nikolaevskii Gorodok, and several other towns of the province. Still, intelligenty dominated the SD organization, which continued to operate on a joint Menshevik-Bolshevik basis, despite Lenin's criticisms on both scores.[85]

The SR Committee maintained its contacts with workers through its expanding Workers' Union, which took on the task of organizing and propagandizing district and factory cells and which issued a series of leaflets. The committee members themselves devoted most of their efforts to the organization and agitation of peasants. Coming into the fall, the two parties squabbled over some issues, such as union organization, and agreed on others; both, for example, advocated a boycott of the Bulygin Duma elections and issued calls for an armed uprising. Perhaps because of the SRs' central role in the turbulent peasant movement, in early October the authorities held the Rakitnikovs, G. Ul'ianov, and several other party leaders for interrogation, whereas for the moment they did not disturb the SDs.[86]

In Saratov the news of the October national general railroad strike released revolutionary and oppositionist pressures that led to events somewhat different from but no less turbulent than those in other cities.[87] The fateful telegram from Moscow arrived in the Saratov offices of the Riazan-Urals Railroad at 2 P.M., October 9. The railroad clerks, many of whom belonged to the railroad union, struck immediately and arranged a mass meeting to which they invited SR and SD representatives. The meeting proclaimed a general political strike, vowed not to return to work until the election of a State Duma, and elected a railroad strike committee that included several liberals, SDs, and SRs. The following day the railroad workshops, depots, metalworking plants, and other concerns joined the strike, and several SRs and Bolsheviks harangued a series of mass meetings. The Okhranka reported, "thus did the revolutionary organizations take the leadership of the strike into their hands."

Thereafter, socialist agitators continued to make inflammatory speeches at strike meetings, which followed one upon the other; the SR and SD parties collected money and arms and created a joint armed detachment. At noon on the twelfth, Liakhovetskii (Maiskii) chaired a huge meeting, which, after listening to several agitators, passed resolutions that called for the destruction of the police and the autocracy and the construction of a democratic republic. That evening over ten thousand persons gathered on the premises of the city duma; the mayor and the duma toyed with the idea of turning over all city funds to the revolutionary movement but finally decided against such a rash action. After speeches from the SRs M. M. Borisovskii and Iosifov and the Bolshevik A. A. Bogdanov, the crowd elected a central strike committee, including the SRs Gusev and Iosifov, the Bolsheviks Dr. Uzemblo and Kal'manovich, the Menshevik Topuridze, and several liberals. Thereafter, the central strike committee took over the management of strike meetings, which continued one after another.

Despite pressure from the police to crack down, the city authorities, wishing to avoid exacerbating antigovernment feelings, at first made very few arrests. By October 14, however, the authorities abandoned this tactic and dispatched police and troops to prospective meeting places, where they methodically arrested strike leaders. Within a day or two, the strike began to falter, shops reopened, and some factories returned to work. A major turning point came when, in the midst of the police crackdown, the liberals abandoned the strike. Nevertheless, at SR and SD urging, the railroad workshops voted to continue the strike no matter what and resolved to arm the civilian population, to demand the expropriation of land without compensation, and to put the strike leadership on a purely socialist conspiratorial basis.

On the evening of the eighteenth, in the face of heavily intensified repression, huge crowds gathered at Theater Square to hear the speeches of the Menshevik Liakhovetskii and the SR Nadezhdin. Rumors then circulated that "Jews" had caused "disorders" at the Theater Square; on the nineteenth, Blackhundred mobs attacked a crowd of five thousand, who had gathered to hear the increasingly brazen revolutionary speeches of SD and SR orators. This set off a brief skirmish with the SR-SD druzhina, led by the SR D. P. Serguchev, in which the Blackhundreds, with the help of cossack units, dispersed the lightly armed detachment. That evening and the following morning, police and army patrols in the streets failed to intervene as mobs carried out a vicious pogrom against the Jewish population. To prevent further mass meetings, on October 20 the authorities deployed a large cossack force at Theater Square; some individuals fired shots at the cossacks and someone even threw a bomb, all of which resulted in especially heavy arrests. After October 21 military reinforcements arrived in Saratov, and offices and factories gradually reopened. Although tensions remained high and the minister of the interior noted widespread revolutionary propaganda in the Saratov garrison and a high level of peasant unrest in the villages, for the balance of October and all of November the city witnessed no further demonstrations.

Saratov was unusual in that workers had as yet elected no soviet, although Moscow, too, despite its very active revolutionary movement in October and November, elected its soviet quite late.[88] At the urging of national SD leaders, the Saratov SD Committee issued a proclamation on November 30 calling for a workers' soviet by no later than December 7. When the soviet met on the appointed day, its forty deputies from the railroad workshops and other industrial concerns were of SD, SR, and nonpartisan alignment. The makeup of the executive committee—four SDs and three SRs—may reflect the party proportions in the soviet; Bolshevik A. A. Petrov, a turner in the railroad workshops, became chairman. An alliance of SR, Menshevik, and nonparty deputies defeated a Bolshevik-sponsored resolution to have the soviet adopt the SD platform; the soviet then approved an SR-sponsored resolution stating that "the soviet of workers' deputies should be the only guide of the revolutionary parties of the proletariat in the struggle with the government and should not adopt the platform of any one party."

The day after its formation, the soviet heard of the renewed general strike in Petersburg, Moscow, and on numerous railroad lines. Local depot and workshop employees immediately left their jobs; on the ninth, the executive committee of the soviet assumed leadership of the railroad strike, which it wished to extend. For some reason, however, the soviet delayed calling out the rest of the city's workers and thus gave the police an opportunity to arrest many of the railroad strike leaders. Under pressure from workers, especially printers, the soviet resolved on December 11 to proclaim a general strike for December 13. The SR and SD committees went even further by calling for an armed uprising, the seizure of government buildings, and for soldiers in the garrisons to join the rebellion. On the evening of the twelfth, the government lashed out at the parties with massive raids and arrested numerous SDs and SRs. Police dispersed worker and soviet meetings and arrested any soviet deputies they could find.

Nevertheless, the strike intensified. On December 14, the SDs issued a leaflet that called for Saratov to imitate the armed resistance in Moscow: "To battle, comrades." General Maksimov, commander of the local garrison, reported that "several thousand striking workers from the factories, printing plants and railroads are moving through the city. Today there was an attempt to attack the jail houses. . . . Arrests continue." On the fifteenth, the soviet summoned a large demonstration for noon the next day at Institute Square. The large crowd that gathered elected a Bolshevik to preside over the meeting and, under the protection of the socialist armed detachment, listened to impassioned SR and SD speeches. When the cossacks inevitably attacked, they at first met with lively resistance, but the lightly armed detachment quickly suffered eight dead and twenty-four heavily wounded, of whom seven died later. Police now made sweeps through the streets, rounding up hundreds; the soviet's next meeting, scheduled for December 17, could not take place because its membership was sitting in jail. Between December 19 and 28, striking plants gradually returned to work. In Saratov, as in other Russian cities, military force suppressed a numerically powerful but poorly armed revolutionary movement. Hope for revolution gradually faded.

Saratov's peasantry, which had entered into conflict with the existing order in 1902, remained in the fray through 1905 and beyond. The Saratov SDs were quite aware of the special quality of unrest in the villages and, by 1905, intensified their efforts at peasant propaganda and organization. Encouraged by the recent formation of SD groups in several district towns, in August the Saratov Committee founded the so-called Agrarian Group, which had greater resources at their disposal than the SD Agrarian League of 1902–03. Unfortunately, some Soviet historians have extrapolated this incremental increase in SD peasant activism into SD (or even Bolshevik) hegemony in the 1905 Saratov peasant movement.[89]

Operating largely under its own impetus, the peasant movement found most of its organizational support and leadership from the Socialist Revolutionaries, as one would expect. Several years later Rakitnikov recalled that in early 1905 the Saratov SR Committee—first of all the Russian committees—sent organizers to survey the province. To their astonishment, they discovered groups sympathetic to the SR program in almost all district towns and "in a quantity of villages"; it only remained to help them form local committees and link them with the party organization. By spring, the SRs could count over 150 village groups. "The map of the province," recalled Rakitnikov, "on which had been marked all these groups, acted upon our comrades both in Russia and in the emigration as a great revelation." Consequently, by summer of 1905 the party's local budget increased from roughly 100 rubles per month to 1,000–2,000 per month, collected largely from Saratov's radical intelligentsia and channeled into the town and village groups for the purchase of literature and arms, for which there was a huge demand.[90]

In April 1905, Governor Stolypin sent a report to the Ministry of the Interior that confirmed Rakitnikov's picture: provincial land captains making their rounds of their districts during March (just as the SR organizers made the same trek) observed "tendencies toward a new mobilization and intensified distribution of revolutionary proclamations in the villages" of Balashov, Saratov, Petrovsk, Atkarsk, and Serdobsk districts. Besides such "underground" activities, land captains noted that "medical and pedagogical personnel" were conducting "bold and open agitation." In another report, Stolypin specified SRs Chenykaev and Feologov in Balashov District, certain persons in Atkarsk District, and personnel from the Mariinskii Institute in Saratov District as being involved in the conduct of "revolutionary propaganda." The governor claimed, however, that for the moment open peasant disorders were rare.[91]

During the summer, police reported that Third Element zemstvo employees were deeply implicated in the widespread distribution of both

SD and SR literature, which was having a great impact, especially on the peasant youth. Beginning in May 1905, the SR Peasant Union involved itself in the organization of local affiliates of the nonpartisan All-Russian Peasant Union. The SR Peasant Union, in the person of G. K. Ul'ianov, the Rakitnikovs, N. N. Chernenkov, and E. A. Serebriakov, printed and distributed the resolutions of the first All-Russian Peasant Union meeting in the province. By early June, the Saratov Peasant Union went into operation with the SRs S. V. Anikin, Ul'ianov, A. A. Minin, and Chernenkov as leaders. Police noted that, although the Peasant Union was officially autonomous, it worked out its program conjointly with the SR Committee. After a mid-August conference of activists, SRs further intensified efforts to expand the network of Peasant Union committees. In his capacity as member of the Russian Academy of Sciences, PSR Central Committee member V. G. Tan-Bogoraz implemented this strategy during extended travels around the province.[92]

The activities of Ul'ianov (future member of the First Duma), in particular, impressed the police as threatening. As a former teacher who had suffered for his political convictions, Ul'ianov exercised immense authority among the province's teachers. Through his connections, he "spread . . . great quantities of illegal literature; monitored the organization of village circles; [and] supplied direct links with local SR committees." During the early fall, police commented on SR activities both in spreading rural propaganda and in organizing Peasant Union groups and specified the Rakitnikovs, Ul'ianov, Aref'ev, Nadezhdin, and others. The party enjoyed great success in enlisting village teachers, volost clerks, feldshers, and midwives. Ul'ianov saw to it that peasant activists were escorted into Saratov City for meetings and indoctrination. As before, Nikolaevskii Gorodok and Balashov, each with SR and SD groups, served as centers of subversion.[93]

By December 1905, twelve persons, including the SRs Chumaevskii, Borisovskii, Feologov, and the intrepid Chenykaev, comprised the leadership of Saratov's Peasant Union. At the initiative of the PSR, the Peasant Union opened its congress on December 18 across the Volga from Saratov. When some delegates raised the possibility of merging the nonpartisan Peasant Union with the SR Peasant Union, the conference rejected this path in favor of maintaining the independent status of the Peasant Union, on which basis the congress elected six SRs and six SDs to the union's provincial committee. Nonetheless, the Peasant Union remained firmly under the sway of the PSR. Chairman of the congress had been Chenykaev; SR delegates composed its "Manifesto to the armed forces and all people," which, among other radical measures, espoused the creation of armed peasant brotherhoods and exhorted soldiers not to obey government orders; the published manifesto carried the signatures of the Peasant Union and the SR Committee.[94] Both directly through its party organizations and indirectly through the Peasant Union, the PSR remained predominant, both organizationally and ideologically, in the Saratov peasant movement. SDs also played a growing role, the nature and limits of which will be clearer after an examination of the province's 1905 peasant uprising.

If the first months of the year witnessed few open peasant demonstrations, by May the Ministry of the Interior reported "serious peasant disorders" in Atkarsk, Balashov, Petrovsk, and Saratov districts, all long associated with unrest and revolutionary activity. The episodes now included fires, strikes of agricultural laborers, seizures of grain, and attacks on police stations, the last of which provided arms for party and Peasant Union druzhiny. From this time forward until the end of the year, the scale of such actions increased, with October marking the highest peak. Monetary losses in Saratov Province from agrarian disorders (some 9,500,000 rubles) constituted one-third of such losses for the empire and more than double those of the next highest province.[95]

The rapid growth of peasant-oriented revolutionary committees of the Peasant Union, the SRs, and the SDs occurred in precisely the above-mentioned districts, and both arose out of and further inflamed the peasantry's truculent, sometimes violent, mood. The SRs, with help from the Peasant Union, attempted to focus the chaotic impulses of the peasantry by organizing armed brotherhoods, usually at the village level. Brotherhoods in Atkarsk District began to function in late summer; most came into being in October, especially after the arrival of the October Manifesto. (Several members of brotherhoods in Atkarsk and Saratov districts left memoirs recounting the histories of their respective brotherhoods.) SR and SD agitators and organizers often attempted to induce the brotherhoods to attack government outposts and jails and establish revolutionary order in their respective villages and districts. The peasants' relationship with party organizers was sometimes uneasy, sometimes cordial. When the brotherhoods clashed with reinforced cossack and infantry units in October and November, many suffered arrest; others survived for a year or two.

In most of the districts, the SRs, more or less unchallenged, provided the leadership of the peasant movement. However, in Nikolaevskii Gorodok, the site of the Mariinskii Institute, the SDs actually challenged SR leadership. Here the SD Agrarian League had established an SD circle in 1903; by 1905 this circle had made contacts with peasants of Saratov District and in nearby parts of Atkarsk. Even some peasants in Nikolaevskii Gorodok considered themselves to be SDs. Under the auspices of this group, the Saratov SD Committee's newly founded Agrarian Group made its main effort to influence the province's peasantry. In Nikolaevskii Gorodok itself, the SDs sponsored and played a great role in the armed druzhina. During the October unrest, SDs, SRs, anarchists, and nonparty activists created a revolutionary committee to take control of the area, with the SDs having the largest and most influential contingent. At the same time, SDs in Nikolaevskii Gorodok and one or two other areas where they had groups sponsored peasant "congresses." Memoirists reported that in these instances, although SRs might attend, their speeches were often spurned; likewise, at the more numerous SR-sponsored peasant congresses, SDs wielded little clout. In an analysis that rings true, the SR Studentsov recalled that SD delegates to peasant congresses were often not well known and, when leaders were elected, usually found themselves bypassed in favor of SRs.[96]

The SDs' peasant program clearly hampered the party's efforts. For most of the year, the Saratov SDs adhered to the planks of the Second Congress's agrarian program, which called for agitation on "cutoffs" (land taken from the peasants at Emancipation) and for "nationalization" of the land—neither of which issues aroused the interest of peasants. Lenin's new thinking, reflected in the Third Congress's call for an alliance of workers and peasants, did not receive support from the Saratov Committee until October 1905—rather late to have any effect. The few peasant-oriented proclamations issued by the Saratov SDs reveal all too clearly their isolation from peasant life. Saratov SD literature patronized the peasants by extolling urban workers as models ("learn from the workers") and by overstridently advising them to follow "to the letter" the instructions of the SDs, who "alone knew the correct path." Such rhetoric met a cold response from the peasants. The Saratov SD Committee's relatively unpopular program for work in the villages (which SD national leaders accurately praised as the most sophisticated and effective in the whole party) limited the role the local organization could play among the Saratov peasantry. Except for the area around Nikolaevskii Gorodok, the SRs could claim credit for leading the province's remarkable 1905 peasant movement.[97]

Several important themes of Russia's revolutionary history around the turn of the century were worked out in an interesting and revealing manner in Saratov. For various reasons—having partly to do with the nature of the local intelligentsia, partly with the socioeconomic structure of the city and province, and perhaps also owing to fortuitous circumstances—in the 1890s Saratov became a major center of neo-Populism and, in the first years of the new century, the new Party of Socialist Revolutionaries. Marxism arrived late, developed slowly, and, at first, had its chief impact upon the student intelligentsia; during the last couple of years before, and during 1905, it also became influential among the workers. One may surmise that had Saratov possessed a university, with its accompanying influx and outflow of university students, so many of whom fell under the spell of Marxism in the 1890s, Social Democracy would have enjoyed an earlier and greater influence locally, as occurred in university towns like Kazan, which had an even smaller proletariat than Saratov.

With the awesome rise of Saratov's peasant movement in 1902, the Socialist Revolutionaries, who had solid ties to all branches of the intelligentsia, were able to capitalize on their advantages to construct an organization that even Social Democratic memoirists often conceded to have been much superior to their own. This organization was not based solely on the intelligentsia and peasantry but also on the workers, with whom Populist groups had first forged ties in earlier decades. A contingent of Marxist intellectuals, many only recently converted from Populism, also made contact with the city's workers, some of whom had become SDs before arriving in Saratov during the industrial boom of the late 1890s. From this connection arose the SD organization which between 1900 and 1905, despite problems in controlling independently operating SD workers' circles, advanced slowly in size and influence until it had supplanted the SRs as the predominant party among workers. But SD influence in the factories and workshops never became exclusive; nor did the SRs eschew worker propaganda and organization. Although, on the basis of their new prominence, the SDs took a certain leadership role in the 1905 revolutionary movement in Saratov City, the SRs still had a significant following among workers, the deepest and widest ties among the intelligentsia, and, despite belated SD efforts among the peasantry, overwhelming sway in the villages. A fair judgment might be that the SRs remained predominant in the province, while yielding to some degree to the SDs in the city.

Perhaps the real story of the Saratov revolutionary movement concerns the relationship between the SDs and the SRs, as well as between the two branches of Social Democracy. Despite squabbling between Mensheviks and Bolsheviks, the two remained in the same joint SD organization, a phenomenon more common in Russian provincial cities, even quite large ones, than is commonly realized. The realities of life and work in such places prevented the luxury of allowing polemics to determine organization. The very same realities guaranteed that the SDs and SRs, even after occasional squabbles, would remain close. In the late 1890s and early 1900s, when the parties in Saratov were still inchoate, little separated one from the other. This was reflected by joint organizations as late as 1902. After memorable altercations during 1902, the two parties drew their lines more distinctly, but more often than not continued to work together. Despite renewed hostilities in early 1905, the record of summer and fall reveals that interparty struggles faded virtually in inverse proportion to the intensification of the revolutionary situation. The period October through December of 1905 shows close coordination of actions, with only rare evidence of partisan maneuvering. The commentaries of memoirists such as the SD Druzhinin and the SR Studentsov, police reports, and Soviet historians, all draw attention to the left block that operated in every phase of revolutionary activity in Saratov during the fall of 1905. As Studentsov put it, "SRs and SDs helped one another."[98] In Saratov, as in many other places, revolutionaries of various tendencies were friendly enemies.

Remarkable, too, is the extent to which, between 1890 and 1905, revolutionaries managed to propagandize extensive portions of the province's population—from intelligentsia, to workers, to peasants; the resulting radicalization spoke poorly for the potential of solving Saratov's (and Russia's) daunting problems with merely reformist policies and did not bode well for the survival prospects of the Old Regime. By the end of 1905, events in "Athens-Babylon" already foreshadowed Russia's fate a few years later.

6. Zemstvo Rabbits, Antichrists, and Revolutionaries: Rural Teachers in Saratov Province, 1890–1907

Scott J. Seregny

TWO IMAGES of the rural teacher confront the historian of late Imperial Russia. The first is of the "zemstvo rabbit," timid, vulnerable, and oblivious to wider professional concerns or to the burning social and political issues that preoccupied educated society. This type is characterized by material insecurity, low status, and subordinate administrative position, as well as by meager formal education aggravated by cultural deprivation on the job. Above all, these teachers suffered from isolation—isolation from educated society and the culture of urban Russia, isolation from their professional colleagues, and finally isolation within the peasant community, where teachers were often viewed as outsiders. This image is firmly anchored in zemstvo and other materials, including those from Saratov, which yield a collective profile of the profession over a long period, and it has been reinforced by recent scholarly studies.[1]

The second image of the rural teacher in Russia is quite different and derives mainly from official sources: the teacher as inveterate Populist agitator. Beginning with the "To the People" movement of the 1870s, the regime targeted teachers as a potential link between revolutionary groups in the cities and the peasantry. Indeed, Minister of the Interior V. K. Plehve claimed in 1903 that the humble rural teacher posed a major threat to the social order.[2] And as Pamela McKinsey has shown for the 1870s, and Michael Melancon for the 1890s, one can indeed find evidence for such a link in the Saratov countryside.

"Zemstvo rabbits," revolutionaries—both types existed. The fact that there is evidence for both suggests that reality was far more complex. Indeed, as generalizations that would offer a textured and dynamic picture of social and political relations in the village or of the development of professions in Russia, both of these paradigms are seriously flawed. Plehve's view owes much to the policeman's preoccupation with security and the search for non-peasant radicals as an explanation of rural unrest. The kind of pallid and static social history derived from zemstvo statistics and selected memoirs offers a distorted picture of continuity while reinforcing the supposed immutable nature of teachers' status and rural social relations. Neither accounts for the transforming effects that periods of revolutionary change such as 1905 had on these relations, and neither takes into account the existence of a dynamic teachers' movement.

The period from 1895 to 1905 saw an unprecedented upsurge of professional and political activism among rural teachers, profoundly shaped by their changing relations with state, society, and peasantry. Given the sharply etched political and social conflicts in the province, Saratov provides a good view of these dynamics, particularly teachers' shifting relations with government, local elites, and *narod*. In terms of numbers and proximity to the village, rural teachers in Saratov, as elsewhere, were the most important component of the zemstvo Third Element and can thus provide insight into the evolving role of new professions in rural Russia and the changing relationship of the peasantry to the outside world, as well as into political mobilization in Russia's provinces at the turn of the century. Indeed, in Saratov one is struck not by the unremitting isolation of rural teachers (and peasantry) but by the degree to which teachers stood near the center of those competing and conflicting forces that were wrestling for Russia's soul and future.

The 1890s marked a critical juncture in the history of Russian education. Before this decade few zemstvos evidenced any sustained commitment to public education, and Saratov was no exception. The devastating famine (1891) and cholera (1892–93), however, exposed the backwardness of rural Russia in dramatic terms and lent a special urgency to the task of educating the "dark masses."[3] Zemstvo men and educators concurred that schooling was the bedrock for rural modernization and the success of other zemstvo endeavors. As P. N. Davydov, a Khvalynsk gentry marshal, recalled, the cholera riots of 1892 and peasant disregard of zemstvo sanitary instructions stemmed directly and tragically from peasant ignorance.

During the next decade, some zemstvo men endorsed schools as a means to spread agricultural skills; still others, to help integrate peasant society into the dominant culture and rear a generation of literate, responsible citizens.[4] Whatever the prescription, a consensus that schooling should be a national priority took shape in the aftermath of 1891–92. Zemstvos in Saratov and elsewhere launched an impressive campaign to extend the school network. The Balashov zemstvo led the way, followed by the Saratov provincial zemstvo, which saw its task as spurring on the traditionally lethargic district bodies.[5] Funding for primary education increased dramatically. In the twenty-six years before 1892, the Saratov zemstvo had allocated on average 12,000 rubles per year for schools; during the decade 1893–1904 this increased to 36,000. One hundred and eight schools were opened during this period (with 527 zemstvo schools in 1903), and zemstvos assumed costs previously borne directly by rural communes. For the first time, the zemstvo initiated adult education programs.[6]

Tied to this campaign was a flurry of efforts to galvanize the torpid and neglected teaching profession, then in a state of crisis measured in plummeting educational qualifications, low morale, and headlong flight by male teachers into the new state liquor monopoly.[7] Piecemeal improvements were made in salary levels,[8] but the most significant developments came in the areas of teachers' association and access to cultural amenities. These addressed the most debilitating aspects of their existence—isolation and cultural deprivation—and played an important role in uniting teachers and shaping a professional ethos.

Access to reading material in isolated rural settlements was a pressing problem for teachers, practically and psychologically. The Saratov zemstvo was among the first in Russia to subsidize the teachers' purchases of books and periodicals (from 1901), pointing out that only some of the younger teachers without family obligations could devote a portion of their modest budgets to such outlays.[9] Zemstvos also helped to establish professional organizations. In 1898 a teachers' mutual aid society was established in Balashov District, followed in 1900 by a provincial organization. Funded by the zemstvo and destined to play a pivotal role in the teachers' movement, the Saratov Teachers' Society during its first year attracted 383 "active" members (teachers and former teachers, mostly from rural schools), as well as 93 "associates" (zemstvo deputies and others involved in the education drive). The officially approved statute restricted the society's activity to material assistance, above all, maintenance of a hostel in the city for teachers' children attending secondary schools.[10] Members became increasingly dissatisfied with these limitations, expecting the society to address a wider range of professional concerns. Despite these drawbacks, the teachers' society offered teachers an important point of contact with elements of educated society and with their fellows. Like the legal associations that supported an emerging "public" in Saratov during the 1860s (see chap. 3), the Saratov Teachers' Society and kindred organizations aided the political mobilization of local society around the turn of the century. In particular, it gave substance to the very important left-liberal alliance between Third Element and zemstvo gentry that was beginning to transform the province's political life.[11]

Summer refresher courses for teachers played a similar role. These had not been held since the 1870s because of zemstvo apathy and official concern that such gatherings might be exploited by radicals to recruit teachers as rural propagandists. The courses were resurrected after 1895. Zemstvos saw them as a means to raise and standardize qualifications and enhance morale. Happily, the government was willing to accord a measure of toleration to teachers' association during this period. The Saratov zemstvo took advantage of this climate. The inaugural courses of 1897 were a major event, replete with luminaries from Saratov society. Teachers heard lectures on pedagogy and, in a novel departure, the more experienced of them delivered reports dealing with questions of teachers' status. This marked the first foray into public life of future leaders of the teachers' movement such as Stepan V. Anikin. Teachers also visited the Radishchev Museum and other cultural attractions offered by "Athens on the Volga." The experiment was a huge success and the zemstvo continued to sponsor courses annually during 1898–1901, with increased teacher attendance. The Balashov and Kamyshin zemstvos also organized summer courses.[12]

The content of the courses soon became a source of controversy. Initially, they dealt chiefly with teaching methods. Teachers argued that such emphasis was misplaced, since most auditors had a good grasp of methodology. Instead there was strong support for "general education subjects" (history, literature, psychology, and so on) which would help teachers supplement meager formal educations and provide cultural replenishment. The Saratov zemstvo was one of the first to introduce such subjects into the curriculum, inviting lecturers of national repute.[13] Conservatives protested this shift, asserting that the zemstvo was not a tourist bureau allowing teachers to "gaze at the wonders of Saratov." At the zemstvo assembly of 1900, P. A. Krivskii, the grand old man of the Saratov zemstvo right, questioned just how much education was appropriate for the masses and the teacher's role as an "agent of enlightenment" in the village: "And what is so surprising if our teachers, having heard such lectures [on psychology], disperse to their villages and begin to preach that we do not have souls, but only an [empty] cavity, that immortality and life beyond the grave is all nonsense. They will deprive the peasant of his last faith, take from him the last comfort . . . this is unforgivable and cannot be tolerated." The majority was not swayed.[14] The expanded courses corresponded to the wider role that many zemstvo men were projecting for the teacher within the peasant community. As the primary agent of a rural cultural revolution, the teacher would have to respond to a variety of peasant queries, particularly as adult education programs expanded, and to achieve a position of authority. Accordingly, their intellectual horizons had to be broadened.

Teachers, especially those who aspired to "public activism," concurred. The zemstvo conducted a survey of participants in the Saratov courses, which from 1899 included lectures on natural science, ethnography, Russian literature, hygiene, and psychology. Of 225 responses concerning the value of such subjects, 214 (95 percent) gave unqualified support. On this basis the zemstvo planned further to expand the program for 1902–03.

Many respondents to the survey also cited the invaluable opportunity the courses gave teachers to gather and exchange experiences with their comrades. As one participant replied, "the courses raised the energy of teachers through contact with their fellows and reinvigorated them after a long winter of solitary labor." Another remarked that "those who live in town cannot comprehend what these courses mean to us, residents of backwaters." Others pointed out that the courses instilled a consciousness of teachers' ideological ties with "society," the "zemstvo's mission," and "zemstvo people." The crucial issue of contact with educated society was stressed repeatedly. One teacher wrote: "I see great value in large gatherings of teachers and in the sympathy shown by zemstvo activists and educators toward school and teacher. Seeing such a multitude of people who have sacrificed themselves for the good of the school, seeing the concern of zemstvo men, the teacher is renewed and departs for his village reinstilled." Another agreed: "Only since 1897 has the teacher of Saratov province looked upon himself as a personality who possesses a tie with the government and zemstvo, and only since then has he understood that the enlightened sector of Russia is concerned about him, and this fact has contributed mightily to an uplifting of his spirit."[15] The impact of these gatherings on the profession was substantial. Recorded impressions of teachers who attended the summer courses leave little doubt that the experience worked a sea-change in teachers' consciousness: renewed commitment to teaching, solidarity and militant embracing of the mission to transform peasant society, and a vital sense of being connected with the vibrant cultural and political life of Saratov.

Two other experiments, district teachers' congresses and zemstvo school commissions with teacher participation, also aided the professional mobilization of teachers. In 1899 the Ministry of Education lifted a twenty-year ban on district teachers' congresses. Although school officials exercised tight control over the proceedings, this was still a major departure. Unlike summer courses, where most teachers were passive auditors, the congresses would elicit active discussion of professional concerns and accord teachers a modest degree of input into school management. The congress in Balashov (1902) was typical. The Balashov zemstvo, a liberal stronghold active in education, lodged its petition in 1900. Ministry officials removed from the program important issues such as adult education projects and the problem of frequent teacher transfers. Nevertheless, discussion at the Balashov congress was wide-ranging and substantive. One hundred and twenty-two teachers attended and explained, among other things, why parents habitually pulled their children out of school before the end of the term (by early May they were needed to work in the fields). Teachers made concrete suggestions to remedy the problem: amend the schedule in zemstvo schools and grant graduates the same privileges bestowed by ministry schools (shortened military terms and immunity from corporal punishment). As Balashov teachers pointed out, peasants were eminently practical, evaluating schooling in terms of direct dividends; as soon as children acquired the rudiments of reading and writing they would be removed unless other inducements could be devised. The zemstvo then implemented various teacher recommendations.[16]

Another initiative, modeled on existing practice in zemstvo medicine and taken in response to appeals voiced by teachers at summer courses, was taken by the Saratov district zemstvo in 1901: involving teachers' representatives as nonvoting members of the zemstvo's school commission. Twenty teachers were invited to discuss "questions of the internal life of the school" along with nine zemstvo deputies and the state school inspector. One of the first in the country, the Saratov experiment was hailed in the national press as a "step forward" in the relationship between Third Element and zemstvo men.[17] Even a cursory reading of the commission's record shows that teachers made solid contributions on many issues: peasant receptivity to the zemstvo's adult education programs; curricula; techniques used to spark peasant interest in Sunday public readings; the effect of labor demands on school attendance, and so on. In many cases the opinions of teachers were accepted by the zemstvo men, and the Saratov school commission continued to meet in subsequent years with increased teacher representation. Indeed, its work was sufficiently valuable that it survived the post-1905 zemstvo reaction against activist teachers.[18]

The cumulative effect of these developments was the internalization by teachers of a new professional ethos as optimistic, self-confident cultural activists. That this identity was rapidly politicized there is little doubt, due largely to the government's ambivalent and vacillating policy. On the one hand, the state had made a limited commitment to education, though given its industrialization priorities it was unable to allocate adequate funds. At the same time the state was concerned with security, namely, the potential threat schooling and the teacher posed to the traditional social order: peasant monarchism, deference, and religiosity. Thus its approach to the profession had always been restrictive and often repressive: inspectors wielded considerable police powers; professional and even intimate social gatherings of teachers had at various times been banned; rural teachers were not allowed to read materials cleared by censors for the general urban population; mutual aid societies were hampered by official regulations; teachers' courses and congresses were subject to a haphazard and often arbitrary petitioning process.

Moreover, given the inherent tension in official policy, its approach was often inconsistent. When in the wake of agrarian disorders in 1902 in

Kharkov, Poltava, and Saratov, official attitudes tilted toward preoccupation with security, the promising developments of recent years were stifled. Teachers' congresses were not held in Saratov Province after 1902; more significantly, the Saratov zemstvo, despite repeated petitions, was unable to organize summer courses after 1901.[19] The years 1902–04 throughout Russia saw steady erosion of legal means for professional association, part of a futile attempt to quarantine the countryside from mounting political opposition in the cities. Teachers came to perceive the state as now perpetuating their isolation and cultural deprivation and, in light of rising expectations and solidarity, the result for many of them was a high level of frustration, which took form in political opposition.

Recently awakened "zemstvo rabbits" thus became receptive to the arguments of liberal and radical opponents of the regime, and some Saratov teachers were drawn into the evolving alliance between zemstvo liberals and Third Element radicals. Their increasing politicization found expression in both legal associations and revolutionary politics. Both the Saratov and Balashov teachers' societies sent delegates to a national congress of mutual aid societies in Moscow reluctantly sanctioned by the government over the 1902–03 holidays. The mood was surprisingly oppositional; Saratov delegates S. V. Anikin, G. K. Ul'ianov, and S. I. Akramovskii delivered blistering attacks on official policy on education and the profession.[20] Echoes soon reverberated locally in both societies, where teachers called for more autonomy: the rights to police their own profession through "courts of honor" and to nominate candidates to new teaching posts, and greater involvement in zemstvo policymaking. Symptomatic of a new militancy, society members voiced open criticism of the police functions of their superiors, the school inspectors.[21]

There is also ample evidence that the revolutionary parties, particularly the Socialist Revolutionaries, were gaining recruits among rural teachers at this time. Along with the zemstvo liberal A. D. Iumatov, three SRs and one Marxist were elected as officers of the Saratov Teachers' Society at its May 1903 assembly.[22] Police reported that teachers and other Third Element personnel comprised the backbone of the SR party's rural cadres, while in his annual report for 1902 the governor pointed out that it was mainly male teachers who engaged in agitation, since they were most dissatisfied with "economic insecurity and the fact that they find themselves abandoned in isolated, uncultured rural settlements."[23]

Here he recognized the connection between political opposition and professional status. SR interest in rural teachers was underscored by the formation in 1903 of a party Union of Teachers. The party's central committee noted the potential of teachers as propagandists, since many were of peasant origin and could easily "find the road to the peasant mind and heart." Even a teacher of non-peasant background, as the "lone representative of the intelligentsia in the village," could exert a "sustained influence on peasant affairs, on the decisions of village assemblies, on peasant conflicts with officials, priests and landowners." "All of this compels us to pay special attention to teachers with the aim of making them conscious propagandists."[24]

What were the prospects? To answer this question we must examine the teacher's position in the countryside. Within the rural community the teacher was an "outsider," legally, socially, and culturally. He or she lacked the right to participate in communal affairs or, as Balashov teachers noted at their 1902 congress, even attend rural assemblies as passive observers without permission of the village elder.[25] Hence there was strong support among teachers for reform of local institutions, particularly for a "small zemstvo unit" that would enfranchise all rural residents. Men of peasant origin, it is true, comprised a large contingent of male teachers (in 1901 nearly half of the 275 men in Saratov's zemstvo schools). Nevertheless, the salient characteristic of the profession was feminization, steady in most provinces since the 1890s, and the result of low salaries and relative opportunity. In 1901, 406 women taught in Saratov's zemstvo schools, and in all rural schools (including those directly under the Ministry and German confessional schools), the female contingent was 56.2 percent in 1898, 59.6 percent in 1901, and 83.0 percent by World War I.[26] Few of these came from a peasant background, reflecting the low priority placed on girls' schooling (19 percent of schoolchildren in 1903 were girls, and these had lower graduation rates than boys); rather the largest component came from the clerical estate. Moreover, women tended to be younger than their male colleagues (23.3 percent versus 6.2 percent under the age of twenty), overwhelmingly unmarried, and with shorter tenure, due to attrition because of marriage and the fact that many had entered the profession during the recent drive.[27]

Overall, women tended to be better prepared in terms of formal qualifications, a higher percentage of them having "complete secondary" educations (including the modest diocesan schools); but contemporaries questioned their ability to exert "authority" within the partriarchal commune. N. N. Lozanov, based on his experience in Saratov District as a school inspector, noted that peasants generally preferred male teachers, as was evident from communal petitions to open new schools. According to Lozanov, women had less success in conducting adult education programs and, "aside from this, peasants do not go to women teachers for advice on the puzzling questions of rural life; and she does not attend the village assembly when questions of school upkeep are discussed. All of this can be accomplished by a man, on condition that he serves in one school for a long time and adapts to local conditions."[28] In a world that paid deference to age and the male sex, increasing numbers of teachers were young, unmarried, and female.

Turnover, as Lozanov implied, had a negative effect on the teacher's position. Longevity in a given locale, crucial to acquiring a measure of influence, was the exception, not the rule. Flight from the profession (to other occupations, continued education, or marriage), as well as the rapid expansion of the school network after 1895, contributed to rapid turnover. Frequent transfers and dismissals aggravated the problem; during the school year 1900–01, 23.4 percent of personnel in Saratov were transferred. In many cases these moves reflected teachers seeking better conditions, but nearly a third were initiated by inspectors and school boards, which by statute handled transfers and dismissals with little input from zemstvo and community, and no appeal from teachers. As a result, many rural teachers had been employed for a short time: in Saratov Province 53.7 percent of men and 62.4 percent of women in 1901 had been teaching three years or less.[29]

Evidence from Atkarsk indicates that turnover accelerated in the period 1900–05 and that arbitrary decisions by school officials played a large role. As we shall see, this was connected with heightened official surveillance (*nadzor*) over the Third Element and increased social polarization in the countryside in the wake of the 1902 peasant disorders. Numerous accounts testify that petty conflicts with rural officials or anonymous denunciations sufficed to trigger such actions. As a zemstvo man from Atkarsk put it, "it is enough for the teacher to be at odds with some local bigwig for the latter to obtain the teacher's removal."[30] That ministry officials usually followed the path of least resistance in instances of conflicts between teachers and *volost* clerks, land captains, and clerics—by transferring the teacher—was admitted in 1905 by a Ministry of Education commission.[31] This phenomenon speaks volumes about the low professional status of teachers and surely affected their position within the community. Teachers lacked firm roots in the locale, and it was difficult for them to shed the "outsider's" image. In this respect, the teacher was at a disadvantage compared to his common antagonist, the village priest.[32]

Moreover, as an occupation, teaching did not automatically command prestige. Peasant attitudes toward education were still ambivalent, and the older generation suspected teachers of being carriers of an alien, secular culture. Intellectual labor was not held in high regard. In addition, teachers' dependence on the commune for fuel and other necessities often bred contempt and resentment among peasants who felt that zemstvo taxes, which supported schools, fell disproportionately on their shoulders. Excessive dependence on communal officials was a common complaint voiced at teachers' meetings, and zemstvos gradually moved to alleviate the situation by directly assuming such expenditures.[33] Moreover, as the most visible agent of zemstvo policy, Saratov peasants often held the teacher responsible for unpopular zemstvo decisions, for example, a maximum enrollment of eighty pupils per teacher.[34] Peasants also had a keen nose for power relations in the Russian countryside, and the teachers' extremely subordinate administrative position did nothing to enchance their authority. No doubt, teachers themselves sometimes perpetuated the social distance separating intelligentsia from narod. Their comments attest to a hypercritical attitude toward village mores, *grubost,* in the eyes of teachers.[35] Teachers universally cited the "coarse" conditions of rural life as one of the most debilitating aspects of their lot.

All of the above would seem to have militated against teachers gaining authority and the status of "notables" in the village.[36] There were countervailing factors, however. Surveys of rural opinion in Saratov evidenced growing acceptance of the value of schooling.[37] A survey conducted by the Saratov provincial zemstvo in early 1905 suggested that if peasants were dissatisfied with the zemstvo school this was often because the course of instruction was too limited (three years), with high rates of recidivism. As part of the same study, 328 "correspondents" (peasants, teachers, rural officials) were asked to comment on the population's attitude toward the rural intelligentsia. In only 34 cases were peasants' attitudes toward teachers and medical personnel described as positively hostile: this compared favorably with the negative ratings attached to peasant relations with land captains (88), communal officials (118), and local police (126). Animosity toward teachers was ascribed to the factors cited above, as well as to the general observation that peasant ignorance made it difficult for benighted villagers to discern friend from foe. Nevertheless, to use Teodor Shanin's typology, it was clear that peasants viewed teachers as "stranger-outsiders," culturally alien but benign, in contrast to those who wielded coercive power, the "plenipotentiary-outsiders."[38]

In sum, there was considerable tension inherent in teacher-community relations and ambiguity in the teacher's status in the village. Nowhere is this tension as strikingly manifest as in Saratov Province before and during the Revolution of 1905, when teachers' fortunes underwent abrupt shifts, reflecting the impact of local and national events upon politics and social relations in the village. Saratov demonstrated the dire consequences of the intelligentsia's estrangement from the narod, but also the potential of teachers and others to influence peasant affairs. Because of this potential teachers were swept up in the gathering political storms and conflicts in Saratov Province after the turn of the century.

One important conflict was between the Orthodox church and secular forces. Tension between church and zemstvo, clerics and teachers, heated up before 1905, particularly in Saratov. At one level this stemmed from recent zemstvo efforts in popular education, which seemingly competed with church-run schools. In 1901, after heated debate, the provincial zemstvo voted to cut off subsidies to "literacy schools" managed by the Holy Synod.[39] With the sudden expansion of zemstvo schools, teachers seemed to be competing with the village priest for the hearts and minds of the population. Conflict between clerics and teachers as rival "authorities" within the community appears to have been endemic. More prosaic tensions within the school reinforced the rivalry. Teachers complained that priests were not fulfilling their obligation to teach religious classes (zakon bozhii), forcing teachers to assume these duties without pay, as ministry catalogs reckoned this a compulsory subject in which pupils would be examined upon graduation.[40] By 1905 activist teachers were calling for complete secularization of the curriculum.

Official suspicions overlay and reinforced conflicts with the church. The year 1902, as Michael Melancon notes, marked an important watershed in Saratov's politics and in official analyses of unrest, and to a degree this was true of Russia as a whole. Suddenly officials in Saratov confronted an increasingly vocal liberal movement in the zemstvos as well as in Social Democratic and Socialist Revolutionary organizations which, among others, had a strong base of support among Saratov's radical Third Element. A police report of 1902 contained a list of one hundred doctors, statisticians, and other zemstvo employees under police surveillance, which constituted 10 percent of zemstvo personnel, the highest in Russia.[41] At the same time, local officials were faced with serious peasant unrest in 1902, which continued on into 1903 and 1904. The prospect that the urban opposition might forge closer ties with Saratov's restive villages through the medium of teachers was a chilling one. The uncovering of the revolutionary circle around Doctor V. D. Chenykaev and the appearance of SR pamphlets in the countryside suggested that the first links in this chain had been forged. The radical Moscow congress of teachers' societies at the end of 1902, where *Saratovtsy* played such a vocal role, only confirmed the dire possibilities. Hence officials in Saratov needed no special prompting when Plehve's assessment of the rural teacher as a special security risk was relayed to the provinces. They moved to isolate teachers: first, as already noted, by cutting short the recent upsurge of professional gatherings; and second, through intensified inspector and police supervision of teachers in the village. Indeed, respondents to the zemstvo's survey of 1905 cited the post-1902 *nadzor* as a factor in strained teacher-peasant relations: "All the same, in the village the teacher is not his own person . . . because the stifling atmosphere of police spying does not permit any [outsider] to enter into close relations with the narod. If one begins to converse with peasants about the weather the police try to find out what the conversation was all about."[42]

The result of clerical hostility and intensified official vigilance was a spate of denunciations and dismissals of teachers in Saratov Province during the 1903–04 school year. In Balashov District more than twenty teachers were fired, the result of anonymous charges of seditious and irreligious behavior and conflicts with the local inspector, Prakhov. Recent agrarian disorders in Balashov fostered a climate in which teacher "sedition" appeared plausible and Plehve's warnings were apparently realized. A purge of teaching personnel followed in Saratov District in early 1904, when clergy mounted a campaign against teachers. Governor Stolypin pressured the chairman of the zemstvo board, Prince Ukhtomskii, to dismiss M. D. Kuvshinov, head of the zemstvo's education department, who had been responsible for recruiting "seditious" teachers. Eight teachers were arrested and others dismissed (mostly professional activists involved in the zemstvo's school commission).[43]

In one denunciation the priest in Lokh (Saratov District) claimed that M. M. Borisovskii taught atheism and disrespect for autocracy. Borisovskii, who was of urban lower-class background *(meshchanin)*, had been teaching for eighteen years, had represented the Saratov Teachers' Society at the Moscow Congress, and had been one of the most articulate teachers' representatives on the district zemstvo's school commission. The local school inspector judged Borisovskii to be one of the best teachers in the district, but the police charged him with belonging to the Socialist Revolutionary party and organizing a revolutionary peasant group under the guise of an agricultural artel. The latter claim is difficult to substantiate, although in Petrovsk District S. V. Anikin, a teacher of adult courses, was also arrested and subsequently admitted that he had utilized his post to organize "peasant brotherhoods" of the PSR.[44]

It is not surprising that these "pogroms" of teachers occurred in Balashov and Saratov: both had been the scenes of especially concerted activity by zemstvos in popular education, fierce competition between zemstvo and church schools, and professional mobilization of teachers. Kuvshinov, for example, had been a strong opponent of zemstvo subsidies to church schools and in the villages had lobbied in favor of zemstvo schools. One source asserts that the 1903–04 campaign in Saratov District had been planned in advance at a meeting of clergy in the city, and all agree that conflicts between priests and teachers played a central role in the purges.[45]

With the onset of the 1905 revolution, supporters of the old order moved even more vigorously to turn popular sentiment against the rural intelligentsia. Nowhere was this agitation more evident and its apparent effects on the population more ominous than in Saratov in late 1904 to early 1905, when clerics, abetted by local authorities, orchestrated a campaign against the Third Element aimed at neutralizing their secular rivals and appealing to peasant monarchism and patriotism in the face of military setbacks in the war with Japan and mounting opposition in urban Russia. Teachers were identified with both "internal sedition" and with Russia's external foes. (A common theme was that the opposition intelligentsia was subsidized by Japan and England; 18 million rubles was a frequently cited price tag for this act of treason.) Teachers were branded from the pulpit as "Japanese agents," "enemies of the father-land," "blasphemers," and "minions of the Antichrist."[46]

Priests in Kuznetsk and other districts inveighed against the sacrilegious behavior of teachers, and peasant communes responded by compiling decisions demanding that the culprits be dismissed. Heeding the warnings of their pastors that secular schools had a depraving influence on the younger generation, undermining respect for their elders (and even lead-ing to "revolt and mob law"), peasants in scattered locales demanded closure of zemstvo schools. Some teachers reported sharp drops in atten-dance, as parents pulled their morally endangered children out of school. In one village rumors circulated that the local teacher was part of a plot to acquire peasant blood needed to imprint the "stamp of the Antichrist."[47]

The zemstvo's experimental "repeater courses" for adolescents and adults, in particular, fell under a cloud of popular suspicion. Designed to combat recidivism among primary school graduates and supplement the three-year program, the repeater courses had been initiated by the pro-vincial zemstvo in three districts in 1902–03. Touring teachers, all men with considerable experience, offered these classes, each in two or three central villages in a given district. So successful was the endeavor that the zemstvo funded courses in eight districts for 1904–05, where they were targeted by clerics and local officials who charged that they were being used for political propaganda. Serious conflicts arose in at least five districts, and in early April 1905 the zemstvo felt compelled to suspend them throughout Saratov Province.[48]

Indeed, clerical agitation against rural *intelligenty* in Saratov assumed, according to the zemstvo, a "systematic" character, and was led by the reactionary archbishop of Saratov, Germogen, whose pastoral letters to the faithful were an open invitation to attack teachers, medical personnel, and other "seditious persons." Reports suggested that such agitation was strongly supported by rural police. In some places there were threats of violence, and teachers, doctors, and medical assistants were forced to abandon their posts. In the large village of Elan, Atkarsk (pop. 18,000), a drunken mob was incited to loot the zemstvo school and was reported to have boasted that "for the murder of the teacher they would receive only thanks from the authorities and would have to answer for it less than for killing a frog." Peasant suspicion in Elan had been cultivated by local clergy.[49]

Anti-intelligentsia agitation in Saratov became so widespread that the zemstvo threatened termination of all services and appealed to the Ministry of the Interior, the Holy Synod, and Governor Stolypin to help restore order and rein in the police; ominously, the zemstvo predicted that if the current agitation were permitted to go on unchecked into an anticipated period of cholera, provincial authorities would have an uncontrollable situation on their hands. In March the zemstvo itself issued an emergency circular to volost offices urging rural officials to combat the campaign of calumny against the intelligentsia conducted by "dark forces."[50] Medical personnel reacted more forcefully, finally initiating the Balashov doctors' strike, described by Thomas Fallows (chap. 8). As for Stolypin, he ordered his land captains and police to explain to the population that teachers and other Third Element personnel were "state servants" and therefore agitation against them was a criminal act. Pledging that the "peaceful activity" of rural intelligenty would be protected by the authorities, he assured the zemstvo that Germogen had promised that all subsequent efforts of his clergy would be directed toward instilling "peace and love" among the masses. At the same time, Stolypin warned that "both the clergy and civil authorities were obliged to explain to the population the criminality of revolutionary brochures and appeals which in recent time have been distributed in great quantities in the villages." Pointedly, he called on teachers to join this effort.[51]

What teachers labeled a rural "Blackhundred" movement was not confined to Saratov during this period. However, in Saratov it was more focused and seemingly well coordinated, reflecting the acute polarization of politics and social relations in this Volga province, where a recent upsurge in zemstvo and teacher activism was hotly contested by conservative forces that had also been mobilized in response to the agrarian distrubances in 1902–03. The fact that radical teachers like Anikin played prominent roles in the Banquet Campaign in Saratov in late 1904 and early 1905, and even arranged for peasants to attend political meetings in the city, further inflamed conservative suspicions. Clearly, the ignorance of the Saratov countryside was an underlying factor in the pervasiveness of the anti-intelligentsia campaign. In terms of ratio of inhabitants to schools, Saratov ranked thirtieth among the thirty-four zemstvo provinces (4,023:1); more than one thousand villages (49.1 percent), many with more than a hundred households, lacked any school whatsoever; and literacy rates, based on the 1898 military draft, were not especially high (54.6 percent).[52] Whatever the causes, the experience had a profound impact on teachers, their perceptions of rural politics, and their own role in the revolutionary events of 1905. Attacks by clerics and officials had the effect of politicizing many "zemstvo rabbits" by demonstrating that the mounting contest between opposition and Old Regime was no longer confined to cities and elites but had spilled over into the countryside, where it would have a profound effect on teachers' personal and professional fates.

The first reaction by teachers to the rural "Blackhundreds" came in early March 1905 at a "noisy" assembly of the Balashov Teachers' Society, where teachers castigated local clergy and the school inspector. As the largest legal teachers' association in the province, however, the Saratov Teachers' Society became the natural focus for teachers' professional and political concerns in 1905. Membership had grown steadily since incorporation in 1900 and, as its debates make clear, many teachers had arrived at the conclusion that educational reform and improvement in teachers' status were contingent on the autocracy's demise. The society adopted a constitutionalist resolution in November 1904 as part of the nationwide banquet campaign.[53]

The Saratov Teachers' Society's radicalization was also reflected in a new, more aggressive leadership elected in 1903 in the aftermath of the Moscow congress. The liberal head of the zemstvo board, A. D. Iumatov, served as chairman. The moving spirits, however, were activists like Stepan Anikin and Grigorii Ul'ianov who, as former teachers, still claimed full, "active" membership in the society and, as teachers dismissed for their "convictions," enjoyed considerable prestige as martyrs among their fellows. Both were Socialist Revolutionaries and of peasant origin. According to police reports, Ul'ianov, as secretary of the society, maintained extensive contacts with rural teachers. In this capacity he supplied them with illegal literature and monitored the party's network of rural organizations. With the aid of sympathetic liberals, dismissed teachers like Borisovskii and Ul'ianov had found refuge in zemstvo and municipal employment and continued to be active in the society, as did the roving teachers of repeater courses.[54] This radical contingent, as official reports attest, held sway over the mass of young recent recruits to the profession. Only the older teachers with families were immune to attempts to steer the society onto a radical course, since they were primarily interested in its mundane functions of emergency aid and subsidies for teachers' children studying in secondary institutions in the city.[55]

Conditions were ripe for an explosion in the Saratov Teachers' Society when its membership assembled on May 29, 1905. The tsar's decree of February 18, 1905, had granted corporate bodies (including professional societies and peasant communes) the right to discuss political reforms. This lent a stamp of quasi-official approval to the efforts of radical teachers in Saratov and elsewhere to mobilize the rank-and-file for political activity in the countryside. Stolypin cited precisely this fact, and the inadequacy of the Saratov garrison, as justification for not prohibiting the meeting. The sessions lasted three days and according to all accounts were stormy, attended by 300 to 350 persons: at least 200 teachers (mostly from rural schools), plus Third Element people and others.[56] Routine business was quickly dispensed with and discussion centered around reports made by Ul'ianov, D. Kh. Sobel'ev, and Anikin. These dealt with adherence to the All-Russian Union of Teachers recently organized in Moscow and St. Petersburg, with educational and political reform, and with the role of teachers in the Liberation Movement.[57]

Anikin's address dominated the proceedings. The membership agreed with his proposal that schooling should be universal, compulsory, free, and based on a ladder system with easy access to secondary and higher institutions. Moderates objected to his plea that religious teaching be removed completely from the curriculum, but the majority were swayed by V. S. Dokunin, who taught in Ol'shansk (Balashov) and argued that religious classes were the source of perpetual conflicts with clergy. Here Saratov teachers were more radical than many of their fellows who met in other provinces that spring, but given recent attacks by the church their decision is understandable. In light of recent events, there was considerable opposition to Anikin's proposal that the school system be decentralized and management functions transferred to peasant communes. Given the "stagnation" and "ignorance" of sectors of the rural population, particularly the communal administration, the assembly deemed Anikin's plan premature.

The society accepted resolutions calling for a constitution, civil rights, a people's militia in place of the regular army, and self-determination for minorities. Finally Anikin, supported by repeater course teachers Vede niapin and Nikolaev, called for expropriation and nationalization of all private lands. Their proposal passed. Acceptance of this resolution by the

Saratov society would seem to reflect SR influence and clearly placed Saratov teachers on the left of the Russian teachers' movement, as demonstrated by meetings of other mutual aid societies that spring, as well as the platform adopted by the national Teachers' Union. And yet it also presaged a general shift among activist teachers during the coming months, culminating in teacher participation in the peasant union movement and the election campaign to the First Duma.[58]

The Saratov teachers also leveled sharp cirticism at school officials, some of whom were present at the assembly as "permanent" members, as mandated by the society's statute. Teachers denounced inspectors as police spies (specific instances were recounted) and the meeting voted unanimously to exclude the provincial school director, A. P. Karpov, as well as inspectors Lozanov, Kulikov, and Prakhov from membership. Archbishop Germogen, who was not present, suffered the same fate.[59] After the assembly had adjourned, Stolypin secured the society's closure for one year. But, according to the local police chief, the damage had been done, as at the end of the session teachers "quite openly remarked that after such discussions they would act dishonorably if they did not begin strenuous propaganda among the narod." In this frame of mind, he warned, some two hundred teachers dispersed to their villages.[60]

According to Anikin, most members of the Saratov society adhered to the semilegal All-Russian Teachers' Union, which aimed to bring the Liberation Movement to the peasantry through a campaign of political enlightenment and organization. By year's end, nearly four hundred teachers in Saratov Province, or one-third of those in zemstvo and other primary schools under the Ministry of Education, had adhered to the union.[61] A cluster of factors impelled rural teachers toward political activism in 1905. The experience of the past decade had taught that basic political change and resolution of teachers' professional demands were intertwined. Recent conflicts in the village had raised the issue of peasant monarchism: that the autocracy might appeal to a loyal narod against the urban-based opposition and its allies in the village. Activist teachers, especially, saw an urgent need to seek support among the "conscious" elements of the peasantry against the "dark forces" perceived to be behind the recent agitation against rural intelligenty. Teachers' professional aspirations and their position (even survival) in the village seemed to dictate that they take a political stand.

Liberal zemstvo men shared similar concerns, particularly that peasant activism might be wholly destructive and indiscriminate: spontaneous violence directed, not only against gentry property and officialdom, but against "culture" (schools and clinics) and the intelligentsia, often lumped together in the peasant mind with privileged "gentlefolk." Painfully conscious of their own lack of vital ties with the narod, some Saratov zemstvo men sought to enlist teachers in support of moderate, reformist solutions in the countryside. Such efforts reached a high point in the spring and summer of 1905, representing the culmination of a decade-long alliance between liberal zemstvo activists and the radical Third Element forged in the crucible of Russia's education drive. In Balashov, police noted that the chairman of the zemstvo board, K. B. Veselovskii, under the guise of a "conference on popular libraries" (May 18), sponsored a political meeting of seventy teachers. Backed by activist teachers Dokunin, Vinokurov, and Vedeniapin, he urged his audience to spread propaganda among the peasantry, promising that the zemstvo would rally to their defense in case of retaliation by the authorities (in fact, officials alleged that Veselovskii, who also chaired the Balashov Teachers' Society, threatened to dismiss teachers who failed to heed his appeal).[62] Other zemstvos voted funds to aid teachers in subscriptions during 1905. This had been a key professional issue for some time, but the decisions of 1905 (in Petrovsk, Tsaritsyn, and Saratov) no doubt reflected concern that teachers be prepared to undertake political enlightenment. Even in backward Khvalynsk, a conference of zemstvo men and teachers recommended that teachers be furnished with periodical literature, not pedagogical fare but journals such as *Russkoe bogatstvo, Mir bozhii,* and *Obrazovanie* that commented on current issues and events.[63]

Encouragement from their zemstvo patrons was not a negligible factor in the mobilization of teachers, although it should be noted that even when they were so inclined, zemstvos had few means to appeal dismissals. More liberal zemstvos could continue to issue salaries to teachers suffering reprisals, but this became increasingly unlikely by late 1905, given a zemstvo fiscal crisis (caused by poor harvests and nonpayment of taxes) and a rightward shift among zemstvo deputies.[64] A more decisive role in sparking teacher activism was played by peasant demand.

The year 1905 registered unprecendented peasant interest in national affairs, measured in high levels of subscriptions to newspapers and interest in the press. Fueled by thirst for news from the front, interest was sustained by tumultuous domestic events: Bloody Sunday, workers' strikes, and news of agrarian disturbances deluged the village. Such events demanded interpretation, arcane political concepts (many derived from foreign sources) demanded explication, and in many instances the printed word required literate decoders. Not surprisingly, peasants turned to literate villagers, clerics, and often teachers for assistance in deciphering imperial decrees or the August 6 manifesto announcing the Bulygin Duma.[65] The government's hesitant attempts to provide an outlet for rural grievances and, it was hoped, to tap a reservoir of peasant loyalty, also stimulated peasant interest in broader issues. The decree of February 18 granted peasant communes the right of direct appeal to the tsar, an alluring prospect for Russia's peasantry, which generated sixty thousand addresses during the spring. Above all, these petitions addressed economic issues, especially land hunger; yet they also echoed the wider political demands of educated society: democratization of education, civil freedoms, an end to the war, controls over police and officials, reform of local self-government, and even a constitution.[66]

Rural teachers and other Third Element personnel in Saratov, as elsewhere, played a visible role in this petition campaign. Official decrees seemed to provide a legal basis for political enlightenment and there was considerable demand from peasants that teachers provide such services—for example, that they explain what a "constitution" was and what benefits the population might derive from it. Teachers commonly drafted petitions at the request of communes, and many came to accept political education as a natural extension of their professional role. In an open letter, a group of teachers from Dubovka (a large settlement of 16,521 with ten schools in Tsaritsyn District) proclaimed that, "as the most important intelligent force in the countryside" teachers' primary function now was to "articulate both their own needs and those of the narod in current discussions of state reforms."[67]

Governor Stolypin and other officials were quick to blame the Third Element for peasant political statements. Such analysis may have provided them comfort, but it did not accurately reflect reality. Not only does Timothy Mixter demonstrate that Saratov peasants were interested in broader political issues in 1905, but official claims that rural intelligenty somehow hoodwinked or pressured peasants into signing such documents are belied by what we know of teacher-peasant relations. Nevertheless, Stolypin, ever alert to Third Element influence in the village, warned zemstvo employees against participating in the petition campaign, charging that, under the influence of persons "completely alien to the commune," peasants in Saratov were adopting resolutions inimical to private landownership and the Fundamental Laws of the Empire.[68] A number of teachers were dismissed, according to the local Teachers' Union, on direct orders of the "Hooligan-Governor of Saratov," for their involvement in the compilation of peasant addresses. Already in March, peasants in Ivanovka 2 (Balashov) adopted a petition in favor of political reform and nationalization of land; copies were mimeographed at the provincial zemstvo board and then circulated throughout the province. In connection with this episode, Stolypin demanded the dismissals of the manager of the Balashov zemstvo's education section, as well as of A. A. Shchipakin and two others who taught in the local advanced ministry school, reputed to be the best in the province. All were members of the Teachers' Union which, with community support, had some success in boycotting their posts at the start of the 1905–06 school year.[69]

To summarize, a number of factors facilitated the political mobilization of teachers in 1905: their own professional aspirations, promptings from liberal zemstvo patrons, and peasant demand. The logical outcome of this process of political enlightenment was political organization, most notably the formation of peasant unions.[70] As yet little studied, the peasant union movement succeeded, in a remarkably short time, in organizing tens of thousands of peasants around a program that included radical land reform (expropriation of gentry lands) as well as reform of education, local government, and constitutional transformation. Aside from its program, the tactics of the peasant union appealed to teachers, who distrusted spontaneous peasant activism as an elemental jacquerie that might sweep all "culture" away along with the landlords' estates. The peasant unions promised to steer the peasant movement into peaceful channels supportive of the broader goals of the intelligentsia. This became doubly urgent after the promulgation of the October Manifesto, when teachers faced official repression and a sharp shift to the right on the part of their zemstvo employers. Even in Saratov, where under SR influence and in response to heavy-handed pacification by government troops, local peasant unions adopted a militant stance (organized land seizures and armed self-defense), teachers and other rural intelligenty supported the unions as part of a "conscious," organized peasant movement.[71] The Teachers' Union endorsed the peasant unions, and information from local peasant unions and village meetings in autumn 1905, as well as arrests and trials of union agitators, indicates that rural teachers played a prominent role.[72]

It seems clear that in many cases teacher-peasant relations improved during the course of 1905 (this was the conclusion of a teachers' assembly in Saratov at the end of the year).[73] There is little evidence of popular hostility against rural intelligenty during autumn 1905, in contrast to other regions and despite a renewed campaign waged by Archbishop Germogen and his subordinates, particularly during the election campaign for the First Duma.[74] Teachers' influence in the village seems never to have been stronger, as they identified closely with popular demands (above all, support for radical agrarian reform) while impressing upon a rural constituency the close connection between social and political reforms.

Nowhere is the close relationship between teachers and peasants more apparent than in the elections to the duma in Saratov Province. Despite the fact that the electoral law barred most rural teachers (women and men not from the peasant estate), a good number of teacher candidates were put forward by the peasantry. In Petrovsk District four of seven electors from the peasant curia were teachers (or, more accurately, "former" teachers who had suffered reprisals for political agitation and peasant union organization). Three of ten deputies sent to St. Petersburg from Saratov Province, including Anikin and Ul'ianov, were teachers of peasant origin.[75] Peasants selected such rural intelligenty for several reasons: many were of peasant origin and knew the village firsthand; they possessed the literacy and political savvy to defend peasant interests in competition with other groups (for example, gentry) in a national forum. Most important, and this stands out in teachers' statements at various congresses during this period, teachers were perceived by peasants as having the latter's interests at heart. Intelligenty who in the course of 1905 or earlier had demonstrated their support for popular interests, often at considerable personal risk, would not again betray them.

The year 1905 stands as a high watermark in political activism among teachers in Saratov and elsewhere and their influence within the villages. Propelled by their own professional interests and pressure from below, many of these "zemstvo rabbits" enlisted as vocal opponents of the autocracy, immersed themselves in rural politics, and achieved a measure of "notability" in local affairs. Most of these gains, however, appear to have been quite rapidly erased.

The government, once it reasserted control in late 1905, cast a suspicious eye upon activist teachers and other intelligenty. Agrarian disturbances flared up in November–December 1905 (272 estates were damaged in Saratov Province), and officials tended to construe all political efforts, even simple discussion of the tsar's own manifestoes, as incitement to agrarian riot.[76] The result was a massive purge (dismissals, arrests) of teachers in 1906–07. Saratov was among the heaviest hit provinces. According to Ministry of Education figures, seventy-one teachers lost their jobs in Saratov as a result of "anti-government activity" during the 1905 revolution, a figure higher than for most provinces, and certainly incomplete. Most of those purged were men, some with long records of teaching in the countryside (in one case, twenty-seven years).[77]

Given their isolation in the village, administrative subordination, and weak organizational networks, teachers were particularly vulnerable to these and other attacks after 1905. In many cases, peasants tried to shield "our" teachers. When the teacher and peasant union activist N. M. Podgornov returned from prison to the village of Plan (Kuznetsk District) in August 1906, villagers greeted him with: "Don't worry, we will feed you, and if the authorities don't permit you in the school we will rent a peasant hut and you will teach there."[78] But the absence of community control over schools undercut such efforts, and the rightward shift among their zemstvo employers meant that little support came from this quarter. In fact, some local zemstvos threatened to dismiss those who continued political activity or adhered to the Teachers' Union. In addition, support for teachers' professional activities dried up; the Saratov provincial zemstvo in early 1906 cut off its subsidy to the teachers' society, depriving forty-three teachers' children of city lodgings. Teachers' professional organization was dealt a shattering blow: not only was the Teachers' Union proscribed, but summer courses would not be again held in Saratov until 1911, and the modest mutual-aid societies would only begin to recover on the eve of World War I.[79] By all accounts such repression cowed and demoralized the profession. Moreover, feminization, a natural process accelerated by the purge, tended to dampen teachers' activism during the reaction while undermining their authority in the village. In 1917 rural teachers generally exerted little influence in the village, in rather sharp contrast to 1905.

Once again, teachers had become "zemstvo rabbits." But the post-1905 tragedy should not overshadow the rise of professional and public activism among Russian teachers that culminated in the 1905 revolution, nor obscure what this experience tells us about professional mobilization in Imperial Russia and about social relations in the Russian countryside. For one thing, the status of rural teachers was not immutable. In modern, literate societies, where the overriding and often sole function of school-teachers is the instruction of children, the profession's status is generally low. As a sociologist notes, low status inevitably accrues to "teachers in primary schools to which *everyone goes* to learn *what everyone knows.*"[80] Prerevolutionary Russia was not such a society. Indeed, the basic issues of peasant schooling and rural modernization were still unresolved and, moreover, held a central place in the struggle between educated society and autocracy. In this context, teachers occupied, at least potentially, a strategic position. Plehve realized this fact, as did opposition groups. How teachers would respond to these challenges depended, first of all, on how they perceived their role in society. This perception, as well as concrete opportunities for action, were shaped to a large extent by external forces: state, society, and peasantry. The teacher's status and potential were quite fluid, and neither stereotype—the "zemstvo rabbit" or the "revolutionary activist"—can adequately convey the dynamics and complexities of the situation.

Saratov illustrates quite well the upsurge of teacher activism in the wake of the great famine of the early 1890s, particularly the powerful influence that zemstvo activists and the revolutionary intelligentsia exerted on teachers and other rural intelligenty. The patron-client relationship that developed between zemstvo liberals and teachers, in particular, was instrumental in the development of corporate activity and the forging of a professional ethos emphasizing broad public-spiritedness. The pervasive radical culture of Saratov helped to sharpen and politicize this new identity. Teacher radicalization in 1905, however, would have been unlikely if not for the ambivalent and often repressive policies emanating from St. Petersburg and implemented by officials in Saratov. Ultimately, official policy toward education and the teacher was misguided. Not only did the regime fail to enlist teachers as enthusiastic champions of the political order (Prussian schoolmasters and French teachers under the Third Republic come to mind), but the Russian autocracy, jealous of professional autonomy and often oblivious to teachers' basic needs, turned some of the most dedicated among them into vocal opponents. In tsarist Russia professionalization quite naturally generated political disaffection. By 1905 an unprecedented number of teachers had come to see involvement in the Liberation Movement as a natural response to professional problems.

The radicalization of Russian teachers thus had its roots in their own professional struggle. Examination of Saratov Province shows how teachers' professional mobilization also became intertwined with, and was reinforced by, broader social and political conflicts among officials, clergy, and other conservatives on the one hand, and zemstvo liberals, Third Element radicals, and revolutionaries on the other. These conflicts were often sharper and often appeared earlier in Saratov, but nonetheless faithfully reflected national developments. The same is true of teachers' changing relations with the peasantry.

The period around 1905 saw dramatic changes in teachers' status within the village, nowhere more than in Saratov. Pressures internal to the profession combined with those from educated society to push teachers beyond the narrow confines of the village school into the uncharted waters of public activism and rural politics. Here the shoals of police vigilance and the eddies of popular suspicion were especially treacherous; witness the anti-intelligentsia campaign in Saratov Province which cast rural teachers in the role of "antichrists." But this proved short-lived, as teachers were often compelled by local peasant communities to play a mediating role between the village and wider society, whether as political educators or as popular tribunes in the peasant unions and duma. Herein lies the tragedy of the Russian teachers' movement of 1905 and its repression at the hands of the government. In a society where the links between the popular masses, on the one hand, and state and society, on the other, were so tenuous, the neutralization of potential mediating (and moderating) forces in the countryside—like teachers—in the long run proved to be destabilizing.

7. The Volga Germans of Saratov Province between Reform and Revolution, 1861–1905

James W. Long

FOR OVER a century, the foreign settlers who immigrated to the Lower Volga in the 1760s led a unique existence based on autonomy and special government patronage. Beginning in the 1860s, all this changed when Emperor Alexander II initiated a broad program of reforms intended to modernize Russia, significantly transforming the lives of the Volga Germans by abolishing many of their privileges and integrating them into Russian administration. It was then that the zemstvos intruded upon the Germans' local autonomy and isolation. The zemstvos gradually extended their financial assistance and personnel to promote health, education, and welfare in the colonies. In 1871 the Saratov Office for the Guardianship of Foreign Settlers was abolished. Although not always responsive, this special office had at least received the colonists' petitions and presented them to the central authorities in St. Petersburg. After 1871 the Volga Germans found themselves under the same paternalistic administration imposed upon all other peasant elements. In 1874 the Russian government began to implement universal military conscription, which introduced the democratic concept that all classes were obliged to serve—including the Saratov Volga Germans. Thus the colonists became ordinary rural proprietors by the last decades of the nineteenth century and were subject to the same obligations as all other rural dwellers. The nature and impact of these reforms on the Saratov Volga Germans will be the focus of this chapter.

The Volga Germans experienced rapid population increases throughout their history. The original settlers had numbered only about 25,000, most of whom came from the small western German principalities; but by 1858 their numbers had increased eightfold, reaching 205,161, according to the tenth revision. In that year, more than 114,000 lived in fifty-seven settlements in Saratov Province, with the remainder living in the trans-Volga steppe of Samara Province. In 1858 the foreign settlers comprised 8 percent of the province's population. This growth represented natural increase inasmuch as immigration to the Lower Volga had ceased by the 1780s. The average size of the colonies had grown to over 2,100 inhabitants, with the three largest colonies having over 5,000; a dozen colonies had fewer than 1,000 residents. Similarly, colonist households were quite large, the average family consisting of eleven members.[1]

The 1897 census again revealed a remarkable increase in the Saratov colonies. Population had grown by 45 percent, reaching 163,661. Since no new colonies had been founded in Saratov after the 1850s, the size of the settlements had noticeably changed, transforming many of the former colonies into large towns. On the eve of World War I, the average size of the colonies had reached over 4,200, with the four largest communities now having over 11,000 residents.[2]

The actual pattern of settlement looked like a patchwork quilt, with the German colonies interspersed among state peasant and Crown peasant settlements inhabited by Russians and Ukrainians. The tsarist government's efforts to establish an orderly and uniform settlement of the foreign colonies had failed as a result of outsiders' illegal seizures of colony allotment lands, already existing settlements located on choice lands, which forced the colonies to scatter, and the whims of the original colonists themselves, who sometimes refused to homestead in their designated areas. State peasants poured into Saratov between 1790 and 1840, separating the original forty-four colonies from the thirteen "daughter" colonies established after 1840 in southern Kamyshin District to relieve the colonies' population pressures. Of the fifty-seven colonies, all but seven lay on the rolling, less fertile, and rock-strewn terrain of southeastern Saratov Province where there were few gentry estates, south of the city of Saratov and north of the town of Kamyshin in Kamyshin District. Three colonies were founded in Saratov District and lay approximately thirty miles northwest of Saratov and sixty miles north of the next closest colony. Four other colonies lay southwest of Saratov and became a part of Atkarsk District, an area of large gentry estates. Unlike their brethren who settled on the left bank, or "meadow side," of the

Volga River in what came to be Samara Province, most of the Saratov Province or "mountain side" colonists, as they were popularly called, never saw the Volga, as they lived anywhere from twenty to forty miles from it; the tsarist government had earlier allotted most of the land adjoining the Volga between Saratov and Kamyshin to Crown peasants.

While the Volga Germans overwhelmingly remained rural settlers, a very small number (less than 2 percent) resided in towns. The government granted the first colonists some land just outside the town of Saratov, known as the "German settlement," which by 1820 had become a part of the town itself. By 1860, over a thousand Germans lived in Saratov, working as artisans, merchants, and domestics.[3] The other town that attracted a sizeable number of colonists was Kamyshin, which had over five hundred Volga Germans; interestingly, over half of them were women serving as domestics.

The first Alexandrian reform to affect the Volga Germans significantly was the reform of local government. The 1864 zemstvo legislation broke the administrative isolation and segregation of the colonies by summoning the entire population of a district to direct its own local affairs. The 1866 establishment of zemstvos in Saratov fostered a community identity drawn along geographic or territorial lines rather than an ethnic identity. It provided colonists with opportunities for civic participation and cooperation outside the colony. The exemplary progressive record of the Kamyshin zemstvo, one of the few "peasant" zemstvos controlled by a partnership of foreign settlers and state peasants, is impressive, particularly in its willingness to spend large amounts of money for such essential services as education, health, and agricultural know-how. In 1895 the official provincial newspaper, *Saratovskiia gubernskiia vedomosti,* publicly praised it as the most active and effective zemstvo in all of Saratov in addressing the needs of the rural peasantry.[4] It allocated three times as much to primary education as other district zemstvos and was in the vanguard in Russia in employing agronomists as disseminators and promoters of enlightened agricultural practices. Zemstvo policies contributed to the narrowing of the historical differences among state peasants, colonists, and serfs, and to the training of a large Third Element cadre that encouraged reform and peasant enlightenment, especially during the Liberation Movement of 1905.[5]

In 1867, following on the heels of the emancipation of serfs and state peasants, the government charged the Ministry of State Domains with the drafting of regulations to implement land and administrative reforms for all colonies in Russia, with the ultimate goal of "complete amalgamation of the colonists with the peasantry in all areas: social position, administration and government."[6] After review and approval by the State Council and Alexander II, the regulations proposed by the ministry became law on June 4, 1871.

From the vantage point of modern state-building, the law could be viewed as a progressive measure placing all peasants within a uniform administrative and legal framework. To the colonists, however, who now became "settler proprietors," it was a retrograde act because the new system had serious shortcomings.[7] The law abolished the Saratov Office for the Guardianship of Foreign Settlers, which had administered the colonies and reported directly to the Ministry of State Domains, and placed the colonies under the provincial and district administrative structure.

Despite colonist criticisms of the Saratov Office, it was a much more adequately staffed, enlightened, and efficient institution than the Saratov provincial administration.[8] Close supervision and regular inspections of the colonies had resulted in a fairly honest, accessible, and open government in the colonies themselves. Progressive officials, some of them former colonists with knowledge of their problems, had established two teacher-training schools for the colonies, promoted fire protection and insurance, created savings and loan banks, and ably defended colonists' interests before the Ministry of State Domains—to name only a few of their accomplishments. Saratov provincial administration, on the other hand, had long been notorious for corruption and incompetence. Konstantin Popov, who worked most of his life in Saratov provincial government, confirmed the widespread deficiencies of provincial administration while also praising a few well-run agencies, including the Saratov Office: "Here served the best bureaucrats and everything was kept clean and neat, and the bureaucrats, for that time, received good salaries and incomes."[9]

The 1871 legislation changed, but did not radically transform, the structure of village and *volost* government in the Volga colonies. Excluding the three northernmost colonies, each remained segregated within its own volost, not consolidated with noncolonies. Internal government changed. It already had become nearly impossible to get enough heads of households to convene village and volost assemblies; now these two institutions were made representative rather than directly participatory organs. Henceforth, colonists could elect one household head per ten households to represent them in the village commune, and one per twenty-five households to represent them at the volost level. The power of the commune, however, remained; it continued to be responsible for the strict discharge of fiscal, land, and communal obligations.

Russification had a more profound impact on colony government, for the 1871 law also stipulated that all decisions and official correspondence of the village and volost assemblies, as well as of the volost courts, had to be written in Russian. Now, instead of the Saratov Office bureaucrat speaking the language of the colony officials, the latter were directed to learn and speak the language of the Russian provincial officials. Facility in Russian became a prerequisite for colony officials, fostering a new type of colonist official who was bilingual in Russian and the Volga German dialect, and for some time these officials carried both German and Russian titles.

The 1871 land arrangements followed those set forth in the statutes of 1861 and 1866, which established land norms and regulations for serfs and state peasants.[10] The colonists simply retained their existing land allotments, provided they did not exceed the established norm of fifteen *desiatiny* per male colonist. Confirmation of each settlement's holdings was in the form of the *vladennaia zapis'*—literally, "possessional record"—which contained the number of settlers in the community, land under its possession, forests, amount of land rent to be paid, and a description of the boundaries. As the term clearly implied, only land possession was conferred upon the colonists, who felt, like the Russian peasants, that they should have received free and clear title to the land. The only new assessment was a collection to support the newly created local peasant administrative organs.

During the spring of 1872, the land arbitrators, who went around the colonies and granted the possessional records, found all but four colonies to have the prescribed allotments.[11] The land-short colonies of Pobochnoe, Sevastianovka, Golyi Karamysh, and Gololobovka requested additional allotments in Saratov Province; the government denied these requests but permitted families to settle on state lands in Samara Province, granted to the Volga colonists in the 1840s. Overall, however, the former colonists, like the state peasants, would have to redeem their lands over a forty-nine-year period; yet both groups received land on more favorable terms than the former serfs, who often lost their forests and common lands.

The statute of June 4, 1871, contained a noteworthy clause not found in the serf and state peasant emancipation legislation. Article 9 explicitly granted the colonists a ten-year grace period to decide whether they wished to abandon their holdings and leave Russia. Those who renounced Russian citizenship and emigrated were not held responsible for any of the capital loaned to the original colonists; however, all private and public debts had to be paid. Although the land arbitrators informed the colonists of the right to emigrate, the colonists did not respond. By the end of 1872, provincial authorities reported that none of the colonists had availed themselves of the privilege to emigrate; however, they did report that many communes were encouraging families to resettle in Samara instead by granting 80 rubles to every resettled male.[12] Only after 1874 and the introduction of military conscription would a few colonists find emigration an attractive alternative.

Between 1871 and 1889, government authority over the colonies grew much weaker and ineffective. The fact that the land arbitrators, who implemented the new land reform and supervised the colonies between 1871 and 1874, were chosen from the ranks of former Saratov Office bureaucrats facilitated a smooth transition. However, between 1874 and 1889, supervision of colonist and peasant affairs was taken over by an understaffed and alien three-member district committee *(uezdnoe po krestianskim delam prisutstvie)*, consisting of the district police chief, the district marshal of the nobility, and a member selected by the provincial zemstvo assembly. A small staff and too many rural settlements to supervise resulted in a notable decline in law and order in the colonies. These committees simply could not satisfactorily supervise the administration of justice, maintenance of law and order, and collection of taxes in the former colonies.

In an effort to reform and remedy rural affairs, particularly peasant officials' mismanagement and abuse of power, the government in 1889 abolished the district committees and introduced the land captains, or *Landhauptleute*.[13] Despite the government's intentions, many Volga Germans came to resent deeply the intrusion of land captains into their affairs. While many of their actions probably were well-intentioned and directed mainly toward the largest colonies, particularly the volost seats, the land captains' interference in village and volost affairs both alienated and angered the colonists. The land captain, in effect, became the chief judge and magistrate of a rural area, exercising broad powers over the colonists and their elected village and volost elders, including the right to impose disciplinary punishments. He remained completely independent of the Volga Germans, being confirmed in office by the minister of the interior and subordinate to the provincial governor, although the latter provided little supervision. Moreover, some were indifferent or blind to what was happening in the German colonies; being Russian, they could more easily comprehend the workings of the Russian settlements under their jurisdiction. As a result, in the early 1890s, several Volga German volost elders "fled" (*sbezhali*) the arbitrary actions of the meddlesome land captains by resigning from their administrative offices and seeking elective positions in the zemstvos, where they could more effectively influence rural life.[14]

The Saratov colonists had markedly different experiences with land captains because they formed parts of three different land captain constituencies. The southern colonies of Kamyshin District apparently received the most beneficent direction. Their first land captain was a jurist particularly well liked by the colonists for his fair enforcement of tax assessments and collections, and who was given credit for largely eliminating the illegal pocketing of surplus tax monies by the village elders and clerks. He also preserved badly exploited colony forests by curbing overcutting and requiring reforestation. In 1910, another land captain received commendation for his efforts in promoting better farming methods and land use in the colonies.[15]

The colonists of northern Kamyshin District, in contrast, endured over twenty years of the vindictive and corrupt rule of Mikhail Khristoforovich Gotovitskii, who had his office and a residence in the colony of Lesnoi Karamysh until April 1917, when the colonists expelled and publicly denounced him. His "crimes" against the colonists included tampering with the volost assemblies by refusing to confirm the elected candidates and by fining and even jailing volost assembly members for refusing to pass his resolutions; pocketing fines of village and volost officials—in one case alone, over 500 rubles which should have gone to the volost treasury; appointing unauthorized persons to the local school examination commissions (which examined students and awarded graduation certificates); imposing his decisions on volost courts; and inequitably assessing fiscal and military obligations on the colonies.[16] Under

Gotovitskii, village and volost self-government became a sham, because the officials of these units had become totally dependent upon him. As a result, few colonists wished to fill these posts or even bothered to participate in the village assembly unless threatened, knowing that its decisions might be overruled.

The three colonies of Iagodnaia Poliana volost in Saratov District also suffered under arbitrary and ruthless land captains. In 1904 the colony assemblies were stripped of control of the leasehold enterprises located on their lands; the land captain, in connivance with the volost elder, usurped the right to determine the lease terms and lessees, particularly of the lucrative water-powered mills, which in the past had been strictly controlled by the village assemblies.[17] In 1906 the colonists complained of the callousness of the land captain who, despite two consecutive crop failures that caused acute destitution in many Volga German households, rigorously exacted payment of all taxes, including arrears; instead of showing leniency and compassion, the land captain seized the livestock and personal property of defaulted colonists and sold the goods in Petrovsk, the nearest town.[18]

The unwelcome intrusion of the land captains and other bureaucrats concerned and frustrated the Volga Germans, not so much because of their tyrannical behavior, but primarily because of their great numbers and prerogatives, which made local government much more complex, confusing, and time-consuming. What is often designated as the autonomy and self-government of the pre-1860s colonies could be more accurately described as an absence of central authority because of the tsarist state's inability to extend its influence down to the local level. But by the 1890s many more appointed officials, often Russians and outsiders, had appeared on the local scene, including the land and police captains and the school and tax inspectors, all of whom played a greater role in the affairs of the colonists. These officials also reported to three different ministries and sometimes feuded over jurisdictional rights. Increasingly, village decisions and functions required the review, approval, or supervision of some government official. Gradually the role of village and volost elders changed from one of representing and administering the local affairs and concerns of the colonists to one of executing bureaucratic requirements for which the Russian higher authorities held them accountable. Most of their time was consumed in disseminating and implementing government decrees, preparing the necessary government reports, keeping the village tax, court, and business records, and enforcing payment of taxes. A frequent complaint of the colonists was the paralysis of colony government, caused by the unwillingness or inability of colony officials to do anything without the approval of the appropriate government official. In 1906, colonist Jacob Dietz publicly expressed this frustration with bureaucracy: "The fate of our German colonists serves as a graphic example of how our all-encompassing bureaucratic system can lead to such poverty, ignorance, and intellectual decay."[19]

Despite the administrative and bureaucratic problems, the most emotional, sensitive, and divisive issue in the colonies from the 1860s until 1905 unquestionably revolved around the changes taking place in the colony church or parish schools, the so-called *Kirchenschulen*. Strong sentiment within the colonies to reform the church schools first appeared in the 1860s, almost two decades before the imperial government began its assault on them. The reformers, chiefly colony officials and settlers engaged in trade, attributed the colonists' backwardness to the overcrowded, niggardly financed, and inadequately supported schools.[20] Blame for this predicament had to be shared by the clergy, who narrowly stressed religious education and rote learning; by the communes, which established a short school year and abused and overworked the teachers; and by parents, who placed the family's economic and work needs above school attendance and education. These abortive efforts to improve the church schools led to the rapid spread of private cooperative and zemstvo schools in the colonies in the 1860s and 1870s.[21]

The government struck its first serious blow against the colony church schools on May 2, 1881, when the Ministry of Public Education assumed supervision of them and ordered that a course in Russian language be offered in every school. Thus the Kirchenschulen became a part of the public education system of Saratov and subject to the appropriate secular authorities. The clergy lost their place of preeminence to the public-school inspectors and were limited to the supervision of the religious and moral instruction in the schools. Through a government directive of September 24, 1891, empowering the public-school inspectors to appoint and dismiss teachers, the parish schools came effectively under Russian government administration.[22] The directive also decreed the rigorous and expeditious enforcement of Russian language instruction stipulated in the 1881 law. Finally, on February 24, 1897, the State Council directed the minister of public education to begin the strict implementation of the program making Russian the primary language of instruction in the colony church schools, permitting only religious instruction in the native tongue.[23]

The intrusion of secular authorities and Russification into the Kirchenschulen deeply disturbed and confused the colonists, because tampering with the schools raised many serious religious and social issues. The emphasis in the Kirchenschulen was on morality, not learning, which was attested to by the fact that schooling ended once a child was confirmed. The reform of the church schools threatened to undermine the capacity of the colonists to transmit the Volga German dialect, customs, and traditions to their children, because the more Russianized and secular the schools became, the less effectively they functioned as transmitters of Volga German ethnicity. The church schools' emphasis on religion and traditional values fostered continuity and tied the pupils to the colony, inasmuch as schooling got one into the church and therefore into full membership in the village community; the more Russianized and secular an education a colonist received, the greater likelihood that he would leave, because rarely could an educated colonist find suitable employment in the colony. A reduction in religious instruction to make time for other, secular subjects threatened to corrupt beliefs, contribute to a decline in knowledge of basic doctrine and tenets, and ultimately place in jeopardy one's hope for salvation. The changes also threatened to undermine the position and influence of the pastor, the highest authority in the village. The introduction of a secularly educated teacher *(Lehrer)* to replace the barely literate but religiously indoctrinated schoolmaster *(Schulmeister)* challenged the pastor's intellectual hold over the colonists. Literacy threatened to undermine the traditional order of the community because it would bring more people into the mainstream of society and political life. The emergence of a better-educated and Russian-speaking youth could pose a leadership challenge to their elders.

To make matters worse, the tsarist government badly bungled the implementation of the educational reforms, producing disastrous educational and political results and even losing the support of that segment of colonists which had previously advocated school reform. Scarce financial resources and an overambitious program led the government to impose the new program of mandatory Russian language and secular instruction on the existing colony parish schools, a program for which they were not designed and could not fulfill. Russification, not reform, prevailed inasmuch as the only major change was the addition of a Russian-speaking teacher. Overcrowding and poor facilities remained serious problems. Overzealous school inspectors sometimes expelled qualified Volga German teachers to appoint Russians. Many colonists, like Peter Sinner, felt betrayed: "This would have been good [school reform] if they [school inspectors] had not begun to propagate Russification policies, expelling the German teachers and appointing Russians, against the will of the master of the school—the people."[24] Some of the new teachers were barely more literate than the teachers they replaced. The inspectors threatened and cajoled teachers to devote more time to teaching Russian at the expense of other subjects. In 1898 the Kamyshin zemstvo reported that Russian-language instruction was "extremely bad" and that "the local population was dissatisfied with the inspectors and the extremely low level of education possessed by the inspector-appointed teachers."[25]

Besides education, the Russian government launched an assault in 1874 on the Volga Germans' century-old exemption from military service. Catherine II's July 22, 1763, manifesto had exempted the colonists from military service, a privilege also retained by the nobility and merchants. General Dmitrii Miliutin's introduction of universal military conscription removed the burden of military service from the lower classes and extended it to every able-bodied male irrespective of class. The 1874 law established a six-year term of active service and a nine-year term in the reserves while also excluding draft-age colonists from the 1871 ten-year right-to-emigrate provision; in 1888 the government reduced active duty to four years but extended the reserve obligation to eighteen. After the Russo-Japanese War, the term of active service was reduced to three years.

The colonists' exemption from military service had come under government scrutiny and public criticism as early as the 1850s. In 1852, when granting Prussian Mennonites permission to settle in Samara Province, the imperial government declared that new foreign settlers would receive only a twenty-year exemption from military service. In 1860 the first public expression attacking the Volga Germans' freedom from military service appeared in a St. Petersburg newspaper article by Alexander Leopol'dov, who concluded the Volga colonists should be conscripted or, barring that, made to pay for their continued military exemption to aid

Russia in rebuilding its defeated army. Interestingly, a writer sympathetic to the colonists challenged many of Leopol'dov's arguments but agreed that subjects of a state should bear public duties equally without exemptions.[26]

Despite their initial fears and concerns, the Volga Germans obediently but resignedly accepted military conscription. Unlike the Mennonites, the Volga Germans never objected to the draft on religious grounds. Visitors to the colonies noted strong antipathy to conscription, but instead of protest and resistance they encountered public acquiescence.[27] The Saratov Province colonies had five draft centers; all except one included both Russian and German settlements. On November 12, 1874, the first draft lottery occurred in the colony of Linevo Ozero in the presence of the provincial governor, M. N. Galkin-Vraskii, and an imperial observer, Major-General V. A. Rodionov. After the Orthodox clergy had blessed the Russian peasants in the public square, the draft-age colonists retired to the Lutheran church for religious services. The minister's sermon, based on Romans, chapter 12, stressed the theme of obedience, duty, and service, and exhorted all those present to fulfill their duties if conscripted.

After the service, the young men gathered in the schoolhouse for the lottery. The first order of business was reading and verifying the eligibility list; though given the opportunity to raise questions and challenge eligibility, the Germans raised none, while three Russians appealed. The authorities declared 275 men eligible: 115 Russians and 160 Germans, with the center responsible for supplying 58 recruits. After a fifteen-minute break, the lottery began, each young man drawing his lottery number out of a drum placed in front of a mirror and a picture of Emperor Alexander II. The drawing did not end until nine that evening. The following morning the draft authorities announced the names of the draftees, which included thirty-seven Germans and twenty-one Russians, who were instructed to report for active duty on December 20 at Kamyshin. Draft authorities reported that the lotteries at the other four centers had proceeded as quickly and efficiently as the first one at Linevo Ozero.[28] Although the departure of the first recruits was a sad and emotional experience, the Volga Germans contributed without resistance.

The 1874 conscription act unexpectedly fostered the Russification of the young male colonists, serving as the most powerful stimulus for them to learn Russian. "Especially it [learning Russian] began to penetrate with the introduction of military service."[29] The first non-Russian-speaking Volga German recruits had such difficult military service that some colonists sent their younger sons to live in good Russian homes in neighboring settlements to learn the language. A better solution was found by establishing Russian-language schools, private cooperative and zemstvo, in the colonies. Invariably, those colonists who had become fluent in Russian were the ex-soldiers, who had been forced to function in a completely Russian environment. As one Volga German readily admitted about the "Russianized" Volga German soldiers: "But those boys served in the army and they took a lot of Russian. They were good in the Russian."[30] Likewise, the former soldiers became strong advocates for Russian-language instruction in the schools, arguing convincingly how much more difficult military service was for the non-Russian speaker. Often, in fact, it would be the ex-soldier who convinced his father to train his younger brothers in Russian.

The Volga German soldier returned to his settlement transformed, a "real" man with enhanced social stature. Although sometimes the brunt of jokes, overall the veterans enjoyed the respect and admiration of the villagers. The soldier symbolized strength and courage because he had endured the harsh military regimen. He also represented independence and self-sufficiency, having lived alone in an alien and unknown world. The veteran had a store of exciting and fascinating tales to tell about life in the outside world, and the years of military discipline and cleanliness even physically marked off the soldier from the unkempt nonmilitary village youth. Veterans assumed increasing leadership and authority in the community. As one colonist said, "At the community meetings they [former soldiers] shoved the elders and those who had not served into the background."[31]

There yet remains to be explained the common refrain that the Volga Germans fled Russia to escape military conscription. In fact, there was little emigration from the Volga colonies in the 1870s. The Saratov provincial zemstvo reported that only a few families, between 450 and 500, or about 2 percent of the Volga German population, emigrated between 1874 and 1881.[32] While it is true that the 1874 law initiated the first limited emigration, conscription soon ceased to be the primary motive for it. An author familiar with this early emigration stated that "with the lapse of years the colonists on the Wolga [*sic*] had come to look upon conscription as a matter of course, and letters relating the hardships in the New World had given military service the appearance of a lesser evil."[33] In 1877 an avowed critic of the Volga Germans admitted that only a few colonists had emigrated or planned to emigrate, and that their acceptance of the draft was commendable: "But the indifference and undisguised tranquility of the Germans, who appeared for the drawing of the first draft lottery numbers at the end of 1874 . . . forces us to repudiate our conjecture which was so unfavorable to the Germans."[34]

The data from Saratov indicate that between 1874 and 1917 the Volga Germans supplied one out of every ten to twelve conscripts each year. The 1874 draft lottery enrolled 303 Volga Germans, amounting to 22 percent of the eligible German males. Thus, annually, about one out of five draft-eligible, twenty-one-year-old male colonists entered the Russian army. By the eve of World War I, approximately 20,000 Volga Germans living in Saratov had served in the Russian army.[35]

Mobilization of reservists, not conscription, drove more Volga Germans from Russia. The call-up of reservists during the Russo-Japanese War triggered an exodus of Volga Germans, which has been confusedly and erroneously described as an attempt to avoid conscription. The war suddenly and drastically interrupted the tranquil life of the colonists, who since 1878 had experienced a quarter-century of peace. Until 1904 the Volga German reservists had never been activated; the conscript dutifully completed active service and then returned to civilian life, having no further contact with the military. The 1904–05 mobilization weighed heavily on the colonists, causing many of them to fear and suspect future mobilizations, and may even help to explain the recurring rumors of war that swept the colonies between 1906 and 1914.

Beginning in 1904, many Volga German reservists—men between the ages of twenty-five and forty-three, some of whom had been discharged as far back as 1886—decided to emigrate illegally rather than face being reactivated to fight in some distant war of no concern to them. These emigrants were not the single, twenty-one-year-old conscripts, but older men, now married, many with families, and some acting as sole heads of households. It could even happen that a father was mobilized while his healthy, nondrafted sons had no obligations. Thus, the mobilization of reservists for the Russo-Japanese War involved thousands of colonists (about 20 to 25 percent of male villagers), while the annual conscription only affected about five hundred young men with no family obligations. In fact, most of those Volga Germans who fled Russia for military reasons were veterans who feared being recalled to active duty.[36]

The mobilization of reservists by provinces and districts was done in a very inequitable manner; only selected provinces had their reserves activated, Saratov being one of them. In 1904, six of the ten Saratov districts, including Saratov and Atkarsk (where colonists lived), received mobilization orders, whereas Kamyshin District reservists faced mobilization in 1905. Yet peasants in neighboring districts and adjacent provinces were not mobilized! Likewise, male villagers who had never been drafted were not called up because the trained reserve was not exhausted. Thus some colonies and colonists were more adversely affected than others. The authorities of Grechinnaia Luka, in Atkarsk District, complained that all colonial reservists had been recalled, including its blacksmiths. Reports from Iagodnaia Poliana, in Saratov District, stated that mobilized reservists' families had been disastrously affected: "Some of the families could not even sow, but had to lease out their allotments." Zemstvos reported that the war had greatly excited the colonists, who feared the loss of sons, brothers, and fathers and the attendant economic hardships caused by a shortage of male labor.[37]

There is no better evidence of the unpopularity of the Russo-Japanese War among the Volga Germans than that contained in the recollections of some of their descendants in America. While most colonists knew little Russian history aside from having heard of "Kaiser" Nicholas and the Romanovs, comments, anecdotes, and stories about the Russo-Japanese War abounded. The crooked General Kuropatkin mismanaged the army, lost the war, caused the soldiers unspeakable hardships, and even allegedly betrayed his army for the favors of a Japanese woman.[38] Soldiers did not receive the proper clothing and food, often being forced to live unsheltered and to eat dog meat, which caused terrible swelling and pain. The bodies of soldiers killed in action were never returned home but instead were interred in the wilds of Siberia without a proper religious service. The colonists learned of these things mainly from letters received from the front, although officials also reported a noticeable increase in newspaper reading and discussion of the war. Consequently, as one former colonist stated, it was no wonder that many colonists preferred to go to America rather than to Manchuria.[39]

The long pent-up and deeply felt resentment of the Volga Germans finally erupted during the revolutionary days of 1905, when the foreign settlers joined the broad-based Liberation Movement that swept Saratov. However, volost and colony authorities directed their energies chiefly toward the reform of local government by requesting greater autonomy and reduced bureaucracy; there were no popular outcries for political autonomy, constitutional monarchy, a national zemstvo organization, or any other political bodies. Zemstvo elements, primarily the teachers, sought a radical reordering of education to enhance popular enlightenment. Moreover, the colonists adopted nonrevolutionary means to achieve their goals, which contrasted strikingly with the anarchic outbreaks of arson, pillage, and land seizures being committed by former serfs with small allotments. The massive agrarian disturbances so characteristic of Saratov were in fact generally concentrated in the former serf and large-gentry estate strongholds of the northwestern districts. The economic crises and exploitative arrangements, which Timothy Mixter (chap. 9) reveals exacerbated peasant-gentry relations, were largely absent in the southeastern districts, inhabited overwhelmingly by former state peasants and colonists. Accordingly, while the northwestern tinderbox burst into flame on gentry estates in the summer and autumn of 1905, the southeast remained quiescent.

Within the southeastern districts there was no violence directed against the Volga Germans, which attests to the comparable socioeconomic conditions of the colonists and neighboring Russian and Ukrainian peasantry and the generally good relations between the two communities. In Saratov, the sizes of the landholdings of the colonists closely approximated those of the former state peasants but significantly exceeded those of former serfs. The size of individual male allotments in 1886 in Kamyshin District, where 80 percent of them resided, fell between those of the state peasants and serfs: 8.9 desiatin for state peasants, 8.2 for colonists, and 3.9 for ex-serfs. A province-wide survey taken over a decade later revealed similar results (7.9 for state peasants, 6.1 for colonists, and 3.4 for former serfs), but it noted the sharper decrease in the colonist allotments. Another comparative indicator is the size of landholdings per household. Here things appear to place the large-family colonists in a better light as landholders, while also revealing that notable extremes existed among the colonists themselves, with about 10 percent of the households having less than 10 desiatin allotments while 7 percent had allotments triple that size. The allotments of these two groups seem enormous when compared to the 7 desiatin the former serf households of the province averaged in 1877, which had shrunk to just a little over 5 desiatin by 1905.[40]

Finally, the development of a flourishing cottage industry *(kustar* or

Table 7.1. Desiatin per Household

	1877	1905
Saratov District		
State peasants	17.4	11.7
Colonists	12.5	9.3
Atkarsk District		
State peasants	20.4	14.3
Colonists	23.4	19.3
Kamyshin District		
State peasants	22.8	15.6
Colonists	29.9	19.7

SOURCE: Saratovskoe gubernskoe zemstvo, *Materialy dlia otsenki zemel' Saratovskoi Gubernii* (Saratov, 1905), 1.

Hausindustrie) in the Saratov colonies alleviated the pressures on land and provided a mixed economy not completely dependent upon grain cultivation. The putting-out system for weaving cotton cloth became the largest and most important domestic industry in the Volga German settlements, concentrated almost exclusively in the colonies of Kamyshin District. The production of simple, agricultural machinery was another well-developed cottage industry in the colonies. Besides providing a supplemental source of income, often crucial during famine years, cottage industries also relieved the acuteness of the land problem, because many families leased out all or part of their land allotments to other households. A 1903 zemstvo survey of the Volga German colonies with cottage industries concluded that there was less poverty and socioeconomic stratification than was found in neighboring volosts with a purely farming population.[41] Therefore, agrarian relations in the southeast were much less severe than those of the northwestern districts.

Although the turbulent months following the senseless Bloody Sunday massacre elicited no mass Volga German uprising on the scale of that of the former serfs residing in the northwestern districts of the province, the lapse of governmental authority allowed unparalleled scattered acts of defiance and protest in the colonies to occur. While it is difficult to generalize, most acts were directed not against the few neighboring private estates but against depressed economic conditions and local officialdom. The only major reported violence broke out in the Samara Province port colony of Rovnoe, erupting over low wages and scarce jobs. In May 1905, the spring thaw set in and it was time to move the winter-stored grain. Hearing of the growing strike movement in Russia, the local workers, who hauled grain from the granaries to docked barges and most of whom were Volga Germans, protested their low wages by going out on strike and forcing the grain merchants to grant wage increases. The sudden appearance of large numbers of poor, distressed, nonlocal, seasonal workers threatened to destroy the strikers' recent wage agreement. The press reported that "the German haulers feared the outside workers as competitors for their jobs, and as soon as the nonlocal workers appeared on the river bank the Germans drove them away."[42] Unfortunately, several of the nonlocals did not manage to escape and were badly beaten. As the local authorities were unable to control the belligerent Rovnoe dockworkers, the government finally dispatched a seventy-soldier detachment to quell the disturbances and restore order.

In response to the decree of February 18, 1905, granting communes the right to appeal directly to the tsar, several colonies petitioned for local autonomy and the reform of the colony assembly as a classless one in which all male residents could vote and participate, instead of only the heads of the farming households.[43] Heretofore, all other village adults, such as grown-up sons, clergy, teachers, artisans, merchants, and any noncolonist, such as a Russian merchant or trader residing in the colony, had remained totally excluded from local government. Therefore, vital issues affecting agriculture, education, and the welfare of the colonists were discussed and resolved by the eldest, often more backward and traditional-minded of the farming colonists. The Volga Germans also asked that local village government be given control of the police, who were despised for their dishonesty, idleness, drunkenness, and failure to preserve order. The euphoria of the revolutionary events even emboldened colonists to make public denunciations of the land captains in the press:

They [land captains] transformed elected village and volost elders into policemen, who, upon the orders of the land captain, arrested their own voters and put them in jail, where they themselves also were put upon the order of the land captain.

They made pastors and priests into bureaucrats, who, being rewarded with decorations and awards, had to betray the confidences and beliefs of their parishioners.

They made teachers purveyors of their Russification ideas and inculcated in pupils the ideas of meekness and submissiveness.[44]

There soon followed petitions for a classless volost government and court, which would end the political segregation and second-class citizenship of all peasant rural dwellers, into which category the colonists fell after the 1871 reforms. Until 1917 the volost, as a territorial-administrative subdivision of the district, remained an organization of the peasant class; landed proprietors, urban residents, and all other nonpeasant elements remained free and apart from volost government. Likewise, volost courts handled disputes and litigation only between peasants, and decisions were resolved on the basis of custom and tradition, not law. Illiterate judges often presided in these courts. The government ignored the colonists' petitions, thus perpetuating paternalistic administration as well as the paralysis and powerlessness of colony government.

The anti-intelligentsia campaign discussed by Scott Seregny (chap. 6) penetrated the colonies as well. The general strike begun in early October 1905, which paralyzed the government and brought the Russian Empire to a standstill, prompted a marked increase in Volga German defiance and protest directed chiefly against the government's irksome Russification policies. Ironically, the object of the colonists' wrath was not the land captains or local police but the Russian-language teachers, or "Russifiers," as the Volga Germans often called them, many of whom were Volga Germans themselves. Generally speaking, by this time most colony schools had at least two teachers, one a Volga German and the other a Russian. The issue of Russification was also often connected to that of secularization. As colonists lamented, "The school has stopped fulfilling its purpose. . . . Now the Russian teachers read the children various fables and fairy tales about mice, birds, and monkeys, rather than from the Bible."[45] This last statement also reveals the tension between church and zemstvo, clerics and teachers, which pervaded the Saratov countryside in 1905. By the end of October, twenty-eight communities in Saratov had voted to expel the Russian-language teachers from their schools.[46] Some teachers narrowly escaped bodily harm, while others were locked out of their lodgings and schools. None received salaries. In one school, pupils, at the instigation of their pastor and parents, threw down their Russian books, screamed that they would not study Russian, and fled from the classroom. In other colonies, public furor became so explosive that officials closed schools for fear that enraged colonists would destroy them. Many teachers who remained on the job carried weapons in self-defense.

While there was no apparent organization or effective leadership of the growing unrest within the colonies, as no peasant or teacher unions propagandized there, for the first time Volga German zemstvo elements and youth appear to have wielded considerable influence, and in some settlements challenged the more conservative leadership of the elders. For example, in five Samara Province settlements soldiers returning from Manchuria and young teachers agitated in the village assemblies for nonpayment of taxes, which they claimed had been set too high by the land captain. In the colony of Kazitskoe, the police reported that young males, many of them ex-soldiers, and the poor disrupted the communal assembly and refused to pay taxes. In Rovnoe students attempted to take over the teacher-training academy.[47] Although radicalization of the teachers is evident, notably in their letter-writing campaigns in the local press urging political activism, they lacked the Socialist Revolutionary political indoctrination and organization more readily apparent in the northwestern settlements of the province.

The issuance of the October Manifesto by Emperor Nicholas II, granting the basic civil liberties of freedom from arrest, freedom of opinion, the press, assembly, and association, and promising the creation of a State Duma, elicited a wild outburst of enthusiasm and resulted in a gradual ebbing of colonist agitation. The Volga Germans greeted the October Manifesto with much hope and expectation, believing it to be the start of a new order. Very quickly they began to utilize the newly granted civil and political liberties to express their views and promote their goals. As a result, their grievances began to take on more clearly distinct form and various elements began to perceive the need for political action and organization. Although the post-1905 period is very important to the study of the Volga Germans, space does not allow for a full discussion of it here.[48] Suffice it to say that they vigorously engaged in political debate in the State Duma elections, quickly adopted a policy of cooperation with the local peasantry, rejected initiatives for a pan-German political alignment, allied themselves with the radical Trudoviki elements that dominated Saratov, and even elected one of their own people to sit in the First Duma.

In sum, the imperial government's post-1860 modernization efforts wrought many, often unforeseen, changes on the Volga Germans. Overall, tsarist officials remained pleased with and impressed by the colonists' acceptance of their new status and their strong sense of duty to their adopted motherland. Legally, socially, and economically, the colonists became ordinary rural proprietors and citizens of the Russian Empire, subject to the same obligations as all other rural dwellers. The Volga German settlements experienced an erosion of autonomy and self-government and a movement toward bureaucratic administration and integration. Bureaucrats assumed greater control over village and volost life and officials, but they did not improve greatly the operations of local government. The demise of self-government contributed to colonist apathy and indifference. The government's efforts to acculturate or assimilate the Volga Germans through Russification of their schools generated the greatest colonist vehemence, enmity, and resistance, inasmuch as these policies ultimately threatened to destroy their way of life. Ironically, it was the army, not the school, which served as the chief instrument of Russification. Though not intended as such, military conscription acted as a much more effective tool than school reform because the Volga Germans took on not just a Russian uniform but also the language. However, the colonists did not challenge the imposition of military conscription in 1874. Parents, elders, and religious authorities enjoined young men to fulfill their military duties if drafted. Mobilization of reservists, not conscription, caused the colonists the most alarm. As Russian subjects, they had loyally served in the tsar's army; but activation of reservists for an unpopular war sorely tested that loyalty. Yet even then, most of the Volga German reservists returned to the ranks and served loyally. Only the revolutionary events of 1905 allowed full expression and public airing of their essentially noneconomic grievances. Good colony-controlled schools and responsive, classless local government remained the paramount issues for Volga Germans, while national and economic issues were of secondary importance.

8. Governor Stolypin and the Revolution of 1905 in Saratov

Thomas Fallows

PRIME MINISTER P. A. Stolypin brought to the tsarist government a new dynamism in facing Russia's political and social problems on the eve of its demise. He is most famous for his peasant land reforms, his relatively flexible approach to handling adversaries in the State Duma, and his willingness to use violence to suppress revolution where necessary (witness the "Stolypin necktie"). Yet where did he develop this approach? Clearly what he had experienced in the provinces affected his activity as a national politician from 1906 to 1911.[1]

Stolypin's provincial experience had two phases: first, his work in Polish-dominated western provinces (as district gentry marshal [1889–97], and provincial gentry marshal [1897–1902] in Kovno Province; then as governor in Grodno Province [1902–03]); and second, his years as governor of Russian-dominated Saratov Province (1903–06). His experience in the western provinces certainly was important in stimulating his interest in agrarian modernization and the dissolution of the commune; but, on balance, Saratov provided the more decisive framework for his later political life in St. Petersburg.

The governor's Saratov experience was unique in several ways. Compared to the western provinces, Saratov's was a more typical example of Russian local administration. It also gave him his first exposure to a politically active provincial gentry and urban society (through the zemstvo and city *duma*). Furthermore, the Saratov experience immediately preceded Stolypin's arrival in St. Petersburg in 1906, and his reaction as governor to the revolutionary events on the Volga helped to determine the style and orientation of his national leadership. From his intimate observation of the 1905 revolution, Stolypin gained an acute awareness of the weaknesses in the social and administrative order in the provinces and grew more certain of the need for reform.

The purpose of this chapter is twofold: to set forth the basic events and themes of the Revolution of 1905 in Saratov and to understand the evolution of Stolypin's outlook and actions in the context of this experience. Saratov was one of Russia's most radicalized areas in 1905, yet there are few historical studies of the region in that turbulent year. I seek to fill important gaps in Stolypin's biography and the history of Russian provincial politics.

In this Volga province Stolypin found an entirely new environment shaped by Saratov's well-developed political culture. As Michael Melancon makes clear (chap. 5), Saratov had prototypes of the Socialist Revolutionary and Social Democratic parties already in the 1890s. Within educated society there were several activists who would become prominent in the Liberation Movement, and a liberal faction had arisen in the zemstvo at the turn of the century. Industrial disturbances broke out in Tsaritsyn, Saratov, and elsewhere as early as 1899. In 1902 peasant unrest erupted in Balashov, Petrovsk, Serdobsk, and elsewhere in the form of a wave of arson nearly matching the intensity of the better-known disturbances of Kharkov and Poltava in the same year. Urban disorders and incidents of "hooliganism" in 1903 only added to the sense of an alarming threat to the existing order in the province.

Saratov had an unusually strong tradition of cooperation between liberal representatives of the educated public and their more radical counterparts among the intelligentsia and the *narod*. This fact became significant in 1905, when liberals from the zemstvo and city duma played a direct role in the revolution, at first encouraging it and then suffering its consequences. Before the Banquet Campaign, the SRs and SDs worked underground, surfacing only in sporadic incidents (such as in the demonstrations of May 1902). Throughout the early 1900s this liberal-radical tradition in Saratov expressed itself in the dynamic ties (both positive and negative) between zemstvo deputies and their employees, between the gentry landowners and urban property-owners of the zemstvo Second Element and the more "democratic" representatives of the Third Element. This liberal-radical interaction provided an aspect of provincial politics that Stolypin had not seen in Kovno and Grodno.

Before the outbreak of the Russo-Japanese War, the governor's main confrontation with the Saratov public centered precisely around the zemstvo leaders and the Third Element. In his pre-1905 encounters with gentry zemstvo leaders, Stolypin revealed a number of traits that would become characteristic of his behavior during and after the revolution: a tendency to personalize his involvement in politics, meeting directly with opposition leaders; an understanding of the need for economic reform in the countryside to combat the threat of rural propaganda; and a willingness to upset traditional gentry-dominated rule in local administration in order to strengthen the state order (e.g., his endorsement in late 1903 of increased peasant suffrage in order to promote the emergence of a "serious and hard-working zemstvo colleague").[2]

When war broke out with Japan in January 1904, the governor devoted his thoughts to organizing Saratov's contribution to the war effort. While helping military authorities to coordinate the requisitioning of troops and supplies, he became aware of a weakness in provincial administration that he was to see increasingly over the next two years—the difficulty of creating a unified command because of the conflicting powers of local representatives of one ministry or another.[3] Despite these war concerns, Stolypin managed to leave Saratov in late August of 1904 to vacation at his family estate in Kolnoberzhe (Kovno) and then in Vienna.[4]

The fact that Stolypin could abandon his province for a family vacation introduces an interesting paradox about his personality and attitude toward state service. Below we shall see examples of his outlook as a "servitor of the state" (*gosudarstvennyi sluzhitel'*) who placed the interests of the state above the desires of the landed nobility. Yet Stolypin was a landed nobleman himself, and some of his actions also reveal an attitude akin to that of a landed *barin* with primary allegiance to his land, home estate, and personal life. The governor's 1904 return voyage to Kolnoberzhe might not seem noteworthy, as the Russo-Japanese War did not make any extraordinary demands on Saratov politics and society, but his departure again in the middle of the Revolution of 1905 certainly shows a set of priorities different from purely statist concerns. In late summer of that year, after he had survived the worst moments of the Balashov doctors' strike in July 1905, Stolypin once again dropped everything in Saratov and left for his family estate in Kovno; as we shall see below, he returned from this vacation to find Saratov literally in the midst of street fighting following the announcement of the October Manifesto.[5]

When the Stolypin family returned to Saratov in October 1904, they found the mood in the city troubling and the situation in the countryside even worse. As Timothy Mixter shows (chap. 9), war demands placed a heavy burden on the Saratov peasant economy. The requisitioning of men and work animals left peasants with a decline in the amount of sown land and rendered the village economy increasingly vulnerable to the risk of a bad harvest (such as occurred the following year).[6] Although the local public initially greeted the war with a burst of patriotic enthusiasm, by the early summer the mood began increasingly to turn against the war effort, as was reflected in the renewed attacks by the provincial zemstvo on the government and its bureaucratic restrictions.[7] By October, an atmosphere of confrontation had developed between the public and the authorities which was manifest even at concerts and balls.[8]

THE BANQUET CAMPAIGN (WINTER 1904–05)

The revolutionary process in Saratov could well be summarized by focusing on three critical moments: (1) the Banquet Campaign and the radical agitation around the time of Bloody Sunday (October 1904 to January 1905); (2) the growing conflict between the Third Element and right-wing elements (summer 1905); (3) the intensification of unrest and violence in both the towns and villages of Saratov, which led to the formation of more ideologically oriented political parties in the pre-Duma electoral campaign (autumn 1905 to spring 1906).

Troubles began in the fall of 1904 with the preparations for the Banquet Campaign, a series of thinly disguised political meetings organized by the Union of Liberation. Saratov (compared to provinces other than Moscow and St. Petersburg) displayed an unusually high involvement in the national agitation of late 1904, due both to the region's tradition of radical Populism and to the presence of a large number of exiled leftists, as well as to the fact that many leaders of the Union of Liberation happened to come from this province (and Balashov District, in particular) and thus were able to organize on a local level what they had been planning for the country as a whole. They included Nikolai L'vov (gentry leader and founder of the Union of Liberation, prominent nationally in the zemstvo constitutionalist movement), S. A. Kotliarevskii (zemstvo deputy from Balashov District and also a University of Moscow professor), M. N. Orlov (gentry marshal of Balashov District), S. A. Unkovskii (formerly the gentry marshal, now a zemstvo deputy from Balashov), and A. M. Maslennikov (a lawyer, a zemstvo deputy from Saratov District and also a member of the Saratov city duma).[9] It is no coincidence that Balashov was almost the first location in Russia where a "banquet" meeting was organized, on October 14.[10]

While L'vov and others were off in St. Petersburg working for a constitution, their liberal allies back in Saratov were encountering a phenomenon that was to become increasingly important in shaping local politics: the presence of the crowd. Radicals and workers in Saratov challenged zemstvo leaders for the right to lead society and the narod. At first this challenge was not very clear because of the frequent collaboration between constitutionalists and socialists in late 1904 and the first part of 1905, but it became increasingly apparent thereafter.

The intermingling of liberals and radicals and of diverse social types was an implicit goal of the Banquet Campaign but was rarely practiced in Russia to the degree shown in Saratov. Even within the radical camp a spirit of compromise prevailed: the SDs and SRs often worked together in 1904–05, and within the local SD organization the Bolsheviks and Mensheviks avoided factionalism in favor of unity.[11] Until the centrifugal forces of revolution separated the constitutionalists from the socialists in the fall of 1905, the various groups generally cooperated.

This spirit of liberal-radical collaboration in Saratov was best illustrated by the scene at the Saratov railway station, where a crowd of zemstvo employees under the encouragement of SR leaders applauded zemstvo liberals leaving to attend the November Zemstvo Congress. From November 1904 to early January 1905, the province witnessed a whole series of large public meetings in Saratov hotels, attended by upward of a thousand people, "extremely diverse members of society." At these meetings held from late November 1904 to early January 1905, the same spokesmen addressed the audience and the same actions were taken: telegrams to St. Petersburg appealing for wide-ranging civil liberties, political amnesty, and a democratically elected Constituent Assembly.[12]

The Banquet Campaign marked the first foray into mass politics by the liberal and radical activists who would ultimately become the respective leaders of the local Kadet and the SR and SD parties. The liberals drew their leadership from the zemstvo gentry landowners and urban professionals active in the city duma: Count A. D. Nessel'rode (one of the richest landowners in the province), A. D. Iumatov (gentry landowner of more moderate means, chairman of the provincial zemstvo board), and the lawyers A. M. Maslennikov, A. A. Tokarskii, and V. N. Poliak. The SR spokesmen came primarily from the Third Element (many were teachers such as Stepan V. Anikin and M. A. Gor'kov, but there were also zemstvo statisticians such as N. D. Rossov), as well as journalists such as A. A. Gerasimov (editor of *Saratovskii dnevnik*). The latter profession was similarly well represented among the SD leaders, for example, D. A. Topuridze, I. M. Liakhovetskii, and I. P. Gol'denburg.

The open discourse between liberals and the broader population was clearly demonstrated at the meeting of the provincial zemstvo assembly, held January 9–11, 1905. This conference proved to be one of the most leftist zemstvo meetings in Russia at the time, for it was the first provincial zemstvo (along with those of Tver and Vladimir) to come out openly in favor of a four-tail democratic suffrage.[13] Yet most remarkable about the event were not the resolutions adopted but rather the deputies' responses to the presence of a crowd. Thanks to the preliminary campaigning by liberals and radicals alike, the public of Saratov was anxiously awaiting this meeting to see what the reply would be to the tsar's tepid promises stated in his decree of December 12; large groups of townspeople, teachers, students, and workers ("essentially a revolutionary crowd," in the words of Stolypin) were present at the zemstvo assembly meeting.

Zemstvo provincial board chairman Iumatov took the floor and read four petitions, each signed by a broad mass of representatives of the public, each one encouraging the zemstvo to take decisive action to spearhead the campaign for reform. Swayed by these popular appeals, the assembly voted its support for the constitutionalist plank of the St. Petersburg All-Zemstvo Congress and then added its own appeal for four-tail universal suffrage and the workers' right to strike.[14]

The presence of a large audience at the session deepened among the liberals a sense of openness toward the narod, which grew out of their image of themselves as enlightened public activists who could share the thoughts of the lower classes and act on behalf of their interests. Many Saratov liberal *zemtsy* displayed confidence in their position within society, brazenly feeling that in the presence of popular agitation they would still remain on top and that their liberal goals would not be jeopardized by an outbreak of social violence. At the January 8 banquet prior to the opening of the assembly, one zemstvo deputy (probably Maslennikov, who spoke about recent strikes in St. Petersburg and Baku) was heard by the police to say that a workers' strike could only benefit the cause of the zemstvo, for it would strengthen the position of liberals vis-à-vis the state.[15] Then, at the assembly session, Maslennikov claimed the righteousness of his cause "because the blood of the narod that flows in my veins tells me what to do." Count Nessel'rode called on his colleagues to "take to the streets" with the use of propaganda, arguing that the constitutionalist cause could spread with as much success outside the zemstvo as it had within:[16]

They say that "the street" is unthinkable, but if the [zemstvo] telegram [to the government] doesn't get through, then I think it's time to take to the streets, where many people could accompany us to the governor. In Saratov there are many scholarly and cultural societies, and if they all gathered with us at the same time and went to the governor with the same demands, that would be the voice of society. . . . There's no reason for us to be afraid of horrible words. There are many horrible words, such as "propaganda." If we say that word here, why don't we go further and distribute our decision among the wide circle of local residents? At first in the assembly we had only a few supporters, but then our numbers quickly grew. It follows that we should expect the same thing among the population. Rather than sending the telegram we should get involved in propaganda.

Throughout the course of the following year, the Saratov zemstvo constitutionalists would have to confront the naiveté of their position that they could "take to the streets" alongside the population and not be swept aside by the flood of revolution. That process was now under way. News of the slaughter of workers in St. Petersburg on Bloody Sunday (January 9) reached the province on January 11, and the following day Saratov was to see its first major eruption of worker unrest. Beginning in mid-December, a radical group in Saratov led by the SRs Anikin, Gerasimov, and Chumaevskii, and the SDs Gol'denburg and Liakhovetskii, had begun to press its own campaign for worker and peasant action. These efforts were concentrated on two centers of industrial radicalism, the workers and employees of the Riazan-Urals Railway and the workers of the "Bering" iron and steel factory.[17]

The day the news of Bloody Sunday reached Saratov, the local SR and SD committees called for a strike, beginning on January 12, which led to a violent confrontation on the fifteenth between cossacks and an estimated three thousand workers (some armed). While the radical group met outside of town and was about to be attacked by cossacks, a group of liberal deputies from the provincial zemstvo and city duma came to Governor Stolypin's office, to request him not to use violence against the workers and to offer to negotiate as intermediaries between the workers and the police. A deputy from the duma told him that "the government would not be weakened if workers walked around on the streets singing revolutionary songs." Stolypin refused the liberals' request, and that evening the crowd was dispersed when two army battalions finally arrived from Penza. Meanwhile, the strike along the Riazan-Urals Railway came to an end on January 19 after management partially conceded to the workers' economic demands.[18]

The disturbances of January 12–19 represent the peak of unrest in Saratov in this first phase of the revolution. Despite the industrial unrest, the spirit of cooperation between liberals and radicals still held, as zemstvo constitutionalists appeared together with SR and SD orators at such occasions as the February 19 banquet in commemoration of the anniversary of the 1861 serf emancipation[19] and the March 17 demonstration following a lecture by zemstvo doctors on cholera epidemics.[20] In the coming months the liberals' willingness to support their radical allies would further be put to the test.

What were the actions and thoughts of Governor Stolypin during this first wave of revolution in Saratov? As the banquet campaign first developed in late 1904, his attention focused on the need to strengthen his police powers. At the outbreak of the January strike, Stolypin received the first of many threats against his life. In his correspondence with St. Petersburg, he frequently noted that the local police force was too understaffed to prevent radical gatherings. He became increasingly critical of the local military authorities for their failure to cooperate with him;[21] in the absence of outside military support, he learned to assert himself in the face of a popular disturbance, counting the number of policemen he needed in order to preserve order, intervening directly in the instance of a revolt, and forcefully reacting to any sign of protest.

At this stage of the revolution Stolypin displayed a rather strong concern for the observance of proper legal norms, complaining about state regulations that prevented him from making arrests and upholding a sense of legalism in his communications with the public. He also restrained himself from repressing the opposition in this period for fear of creating martyrs and more hardened underground radical organizations.[22] Yet he also showed a conventional policeman's orientation in his explanation for the troubles, which he blamed on outside agitators. In the governor's mind, the zemstvo Third Element and similar members of the provincial intelligentsia were primarily responsible for conveying radical propaganda to the peasants and workers. He argued his case to St. Petersburg by citing the example of the industrial center of Tsaritsyn, with its strong working class but weak presence of revolutionary elements, as a result of which workers pressed demands only on economic matters. After the January strike, Stolypin promised to wage a stubborn struggle against the "revolutionary elements" in the province and showed little mercy toward noblemen who were caught up in the Banquet Campaign: he recommended to the tsar that Count Nessel'rode be stripped of his aristocratic status, to which the tsar wholeheartedly agreed.[23]

At the same time, the governor continued to practice his special method of using "personal contacts and conversations" with liberal society (he termed it "pressure on influential personages") in his attempt to control the constitutionalist movement. He did this on several occasions, summoning the gentry marshal or any other dignitary responsible for cooperating with the opposition and admonishing him for his failure to prevent discussion of national political issues. On one occasion in early December, he even called to his office three intellectuals whom he considered most active in conducting agitation among the workers, in an attempt to reason with them.[24] From late November until mid-December, the governor engaged in a series of private debates and encounters with Mayor Nemirovskii and the city duma, one of which led to Nemirovskii's physical collapse.[25]

Finally, one should also note a further development in Stolypin's views on the economic needs of workers and peasants. While he continued to attribute the unrest to radical propagandists, he also displayed sensitivity to the depressed economic conditions in the factories and villages of Saratov. As social unrest became more widespread in the course of the year, the governor came to see more and more clearly the way in which poverty and rootlessness provided fertile ground for the radicals. In part, the governor's awareness of the problems of the narod stemmed from a traditional sense of the need for the administration's paternal care for the population (popechitel'stvo, a feeling of social obligation shared by many officials in the Ministry of Internal Affairs).[26] But, in addition, Stolypin had a far-sighted understanding (similar to that underlying the labor policy of MVD official Zubatov) that social problems had to be addressed before political stability could truly be achieved. Stolypin argued that "the tremendous majority of workers cannot be labelled an anti-government element. . . . Thus it is entirely possible for the government to battle successfully against revolutionaries for influence over the workers, through active efforts by the government to improve the economic conditions of their daily life."[27]

The governor was moving toward an understanding of the economic reform program that he was later to launch from St. Petersburg. He still had not yet focused his attention on the problem of the peasant commune, but already he could see that the peasants were potentially more dangerous to the regime than the workers (due to their greater susceptibility to propaganda). He also showed an early appreciation for the fragility of the left-radical alliance in Saratov and an awareness that moderate members of the public could be brought to side with the government against the revolutionaries. The governor argued in early 1905 that "it is a matter of state wisdom to put an end to the confusion (*sputannost'*) reigning among public circles and to direct into a peaceful channel of legal and creative work the dominant desire within the public to participate in deciding upon all-state matters."[28]

STORM OVER THE THIRD ELEMENT
(SPRING–SUMMER 1905)

By the spring of 1905 the initial turmoil had cooled down somewhat, and the center of controversy shifted from city to countryside, where the key actors were the doctors, teachers, veterinarians, and other zemstvo/town employees. Of particular concern was the activity of the radical Third Element in Balashov and Petrovsk districts. The events surrounding the Balashov doctors' strike in the summer of 1905 dramatically revealed the growing tensions among Stolypin, the public, and the revolutionary movement. The radical activity of the Petrovsk zemstvo Economic Council marked the peak in the development of the liberal-radical alliance in Saratov politics and sparked the first successful resistance, by conservative members of the Saratov public, to the leftward drift. Both incidents aroused nationwide attention, and Stolypin's role in handling the Balashov affair helped to create an image for the governor in St.

Petersburg as a state official who could remain cool while dealing with an increasingly polarized and violent society.

Of all instances in 1905 of work stoppage by zemstvo employees in Russia, the Balashov doctors' strike was certainly the largest, best publicized, and most dramatic clash between the Third Element and the local administration.[29] Several developments provided the background for the summer strike. The shortage of medical personnel in the district, a result of the military call-up for the war, placed increased stress on the remaining staff and made zemstvo leaders less willing to sanction a work stoppage in the face of a cholera threat in the lower Volga; as of April 1905, more than one-third of the thirty medical posts in the districts were vacant.[30] Second, the continuing involvement of zemstvo employees in radical activity in the first half of 1905 aroused hostility among more conservative elements of society as well as among the police. The most glaring demonstration of Third Element radicalism in the first half of 1905 was the raucous May 29–31 meeting of the Teachers' Union (attended also by the liberals Maslennikov and Iumatov), where, as Scott Seregny shows (chap. 6), a wide variety of revolutionary demands were passed.[31] Medical employees were also engaged in radical agitation in the spring of 1905, which led Stolypin to force the removal of six doctors and assistants.[32]

The final blow suffered by the Balashov doctors prior to their strike was the so-called "black agitation" organized against the Third Element by local priests and policemen, orchestrated, according to Third Element spokesmen, by the archbishop of Saratov, Germogen. As early as February of 1905, medical employees throughout the province began to complain that the police and clergy were spreading rumors that zemstvo specialists had been bribed by the Japanese and the English to ruin the Russian war effort. Teachers in the Atkarsk village of Elan were nearly killed by rioting peasants in early March, and physicians attempting to lecture peasants about precautions against cholera were severely beaten in several villages.[33] On two occasions (February 24 and March 19) the provincial zemstvo protested against this "black agitation" to Stolypin and warned him of the possibility of a Third Element strike if measures were not taken to curb the violence inflicted on zemstvo employees.[34]

The crisis came to a head in early June, when a crowd of peasants in a Balashov village beat to unconsciousness A. K. Men'shov, a schoolteacher accused of conducting antistate propaganda. Policemen took Him to a local jail and left him there, without treatment, for seven days before he was accidentally discovered by two doctors. Outraged by this cruelty, twenty-two representatives of the Union of Medical Personnel of Balashov District sent a notice to the district zemstvo declaring that they would go on strike as of July 15 if conditions were not improved.[35]

The liberals did not make a strong response to this challenge. Zemstvo deputies in both the Balashov district assembly and the Saratov provincial assembly sympathized with the physicians, but their faith in legality and in the zemstvo's responsibility to serve the population prevented them from condoning a strike. At an extraordinary session of the Balashov zemstvo on June 12, the deputies adopted a firmly leftist position with regard to national politics; but instead of supporting the doctors' demands, they called on the Medical Union to abandon the strike plan, at least until the threat of cholera had passed.[36] Stolypin firmly refused to concede to the doctors' demands, and threatened to arrest any doctor who failed to work after July 15. Meanwhile, new doctors were requested from St. Petersburg. This is how things stood as the July 15 deadline passed.

The indecisiveness of the zemstvo liberals in resolving the Third Element crisis became particularly striking at the July 15–17 extraordinary session of the provincial assembly, for the liberal deputies held total control of the meeting but did little to help their employees. In an extremely tense meeting, socialists from the audience twice interrupted debates when they rose to collect donations for revolutionary committees of the Socialist Revolutionary and Social Democratic parties and for a fund called "for a popular uprising." Count Nessel'rode publicly contributed 30 rubles to the SD committee. L'vov and other liberals assumed an aggressive stance on the field of national events, endorsing the rejection by the July Zemstvo-Town Congress of the government's recently proposed constitutional reform (the so-called Bulygin Duma). Yet with regard to the Balashov strike threat, the provincial zemstvo took only one action (occurring one day after the July 15 deadline): it requested that the Medical Union reconsider its strike plan until a more appropriate time could be found.[37] The day after this meeting, a local newspaper criticized the Balashov liberals for failing to defend their staff at a critical moment; in the words of the newspaper, the Balashov zemstvo deputies had begun a process of "involuntary self-destruction."[38]

The growing tension became explosive in the next few days. Stolypin went out to Balashov to inspect the scene on July 18, and as he passed the village of Turki (home of the exiled physician Chenykaev and some of his followers), a terrorist shot at the governor but missed. Two days later, L'vov, Veselovskii, and other Balashov liberals met with the medical staff to try to prevent the strike. While zemstvo leaders sat in the library of the executive board, a group of about forty radicals held an evening gathering of their own in an adjoining office; L'vov and Veselovskii heard the loud singing of revolutionary songs coming from the other meeting, and later discovered that the portrait of the tsar hanging in that office had been removed. Townspeople also reported hearing voices from the zemstvo building shout: "Down with the Autocracy!" and "Beat the Police!"

The following day an angry crowd assembled outside of Balashov's Central Hotel, where the doctors (and L'vov) were staying. After the crowd physically attacked one doctor, the panic-stricken doctors inside the hotel ran upstairs to L'vov's room begging for protection. After the prominent landowner admitted them to his room, he was pelted by bricks thrown by the crowd as he stood on his hotel balcony. Just as the townspeople rushed past the gates and began pounding on the hotel door, Stolypin happened to arrive at the scene with a squadron of cossacks. Shortly thereafter, the governor sent word to the hotel promising protection to any doctor who wished to leave and set up a protective corridor of cossacks to separate the departing doctors from the angry crowd of peasants and townspeople, estimated by the police to number around two thousand. "Not a hair on your heads will be harmed," the governor reassured them.

But Stolypin's control over the cossacks was not as strong as he thought. As the doctors exited from the hotel, suddenly the protective wall collapsed: as the cossacks stepped back and allowed the crowd to stone the physicians, some of them even joined in the attack. L'vov was struck in the head, back, and shoulder by flying debris. Stolypin himself was wounded on the arm. After the doctors managed to escape alive to the railway station, the crowd turned to attack the houses of various local public activists, destroying the apartments of two merchants who served in the zemstvo. Meanwhile, cossacks led some of the doctors off to the Balashov jail, where they endured still another round of beatings.[39]

The Balashov pogrom of July 21 became the central issue in Saratov politics for the next two and a half months, until the October general strike. Now the entire staff of the Balashov District Executive Board went out on strike, and another terrorist in Turki shot at Stolypin. On August

1–2, the Saratov Medical Union held a congress where it called upon "all members of the zemstvo to arm themselves" and asked the zemstvo assembly to allocate funds to purchase weapons. Meanwhile, Tsar Nicholas II added to the controversy by sending a telegram to the townspeople of Balashov thanking them for their "patriotism" (participants in the pogrom had carried portraits of the tsar) and for punishing the rebels. By the end of the month, the issue had shifted to the question of punishment for the July 21 incident. After Iumatov demanded an investigation to determine whether or not the police had assisted in the beatings, Stolypin on August 25 ordered the arrest of thirty-six Balashov physicians and medical assistants for their participation in the radical gathering the evening before the pogrom (the order also called for the arrest of twenty-two peasants and townspeople for disturbing the peace).[40]

Stolypin's order only hardened the anger of the physicians, for it placed under arrest more doctors than pogromists and issued harsher sentences for the radicals. At a meeting on September 5–6, members of the Saratov Medical Union agreed unanimously to stage a collective resignation in all districts if the August 25 order ever went into effect. (In the end this tactic worked, for Stolypin never implemented his order.) The union also published an "Open Letter to Governor Stolypin," in which the doctors denounced, among others, "the hypocrite N. N. L'vov" for believing the governor's lies.

Now Saratov liberals finally began to react. On September 5 a congress of chairmen of district zemstvo boards sent a telegram to St. Petersburg protesting the unfairness of the governor's actions. On September 15 the Saratov district zemstvo called for a repeal of Stolypin's order of August 25, while the Saratov duma followed suit with a similar appeal on September 21. Finally, on September 22–24, the provincial zemstvo assembly took up the Balashov matter, resolving to appeal to St. Petersburg for a repeal of Stolypin's order, to request a senate investigation into the pogrom, to express sympathy for the victims, yet also to appeal to the physicians to abandon their strike. During the debate, Unkovskii exclaimed that "Stolypin is ultimately leading us to revolution" and called for the governor's dismissal. In early October, Iumatov spoke in St. Petersburg with the new police chief, Trepov, requesting that the state overrule Stolypin's order. Trepov refused this request and instead sent thirty-five army doctors to Saratov as scabs to break the strike.[41]

However much they may have wished to gain the trust of the doctors, the liberals could not convince the Medical Union to call off the strike. Only a few weeks after the union had issued the pamphlet describing L'vov as a hypocrite, a crowd of about two hundred radical doctors attended an illegal gathering organized by both the SRs and SDs on September 22 (coinciding with the opening of the extraordinary provincial zemstvo assembly meeting), where they denounced the zemtsy for "shamefully" failing to uphold their duty as popular representatives by defending the strike.[42] The Balashov strike was destined to continue in this way throughout the fall, and traces of it persisted into the spring of 1909.

In the meantime, the Third Element became the center of controversy in Petrovsk. Whereas the Balashov strike was essentially a defensive response to the "black agitation," the Third Element controversy in Petrovsk represented an offensive move on the part of radical zemstvo employees. In early March 1905, the zemstvo's Economic Council discussed the problem of peasant poverty. Agronomists raised the issue of peasant land shortage, emphasizing the inability of peasants to pay taxes, while zemstvo liberals stressed the need to take advantage of the civil liberties granted in the tsar's decree of February 18 and to discuss the land problem more extensively with local peasants. The Petrovsk zemstvo assembly endorsed this idea at an extraordinary session of March 6–7, instructing the Economic Council to hold meetings with peasants in order to find out more about their needs and prevent the growth of "black agitation" against doctors and other employees.[43]

The organization of educational sessions among the peasantry on a variety of reform issues was pursued by many zemstvo liberals throughout Russia during the summer of 1905, a period of the zemstvo movement's greatest flirtation with the left. The Petrovsk liberals were only practicing a local version of a broader nationwide tendency. Carrying out the task assigned by the assembly, the district board chairman, K. Ermolaev, convened on June 24 a large gathering of zemstvo employees and peasants to discuss economic problems; nearly two hundred peasants attended. Soon after the Economic Council began its discussions, a radical element led by the SR Stepan Anikin and other zemstvo employees came forward and dominated the debate.[44] Ermolaev, Iumatov, and other zemstvo liberals who were present later claimed that they felt uncomfortable with the political direction of the discussion but were pleased to see peasants actively participating in meetings organized by the zemstvo. By the end of the session the radicals had led the peasants to issue an unprecedented statement on local economic affairs, a sharply radical appeal for the organization of a Peasant Union and the seizure of all land from private landowners for redistribution to peasants on the basis of need.[45]

Despite the radical content of the Economic Council proposals, Ermolaev and his zemstvo staff began to print leaflets containing the Economic Council's resolution (all carrying the seal of the local zemstvo board and signed by Ermolaev) and to distribute them in the villages of Petrovsk District. Local authorities and landlords naturally took alarm at these actions by an elected zemstvo official. On July 21 Petrovsk police brought Ermolaev and the board secretary into headquarters for questioning. Shortly thereafter, zemstvo conservatives staged a coup by organizing an unannounced session of the zemstvo assembly (arranged with Stolypin's assistance), where the liberals were poorly represented.[46]

The August 4-12 meeting of the Petrovsk District zemstvo assembly marked the turning of the tide, when the provincial right-wing forces began to organize against the revolutionary movement. In one of the angriest zemstvo assembly sessions in Saratov during this entire period, the dominant family of the right-wing Petrovsk party (the Kropotovs) led a group of twelve conservative deputies to censure the executive board for its action. In reaction, the zemstvo left of Petrovsk (led by the Ermolaev and the Iumatov brothers) resigned from the board, allowing the Kropotov party to place in power a new slate of zemstvo officials. In protest against the conservatives' coup, a large group of Petrovsk physicians, veterinarians, agronomists, and other employees resigned from their zemstvo positions.[47]

The Balashov and Petrovsk incidents provide an appropriate background for understanding the development of Stolypin's thoughts in the summer of 1905. On July 2 he took his standard personal approach to the growing controversy in Balashov by writing to the local zemstvo board chairman, K. B. Veselovskii, affirming his affection and respect for the zemstvo. The letter clearly articulated Stolypin's idea of his role in Saratov society: the governor is the man charged by the emperor to stand above all private interests of the province and preserve the peace and safety of society as a whole.[48] However, by the end of the summer, as the Balashov doctors' strike became more irreconcilable, Stolypin appeared to be losing his patience with the liberals: on September 7, in a memo to St. Petersburg, he denounced L'vov and other zemstvo liberals for siding with the doctors and concluded that "under these circumstances it is unacceptable to be weak in the presence of the doctors, [for] the only authority capable of exercising any order anymore is the administration."[49]

The Economic Council scandal in Petrovsk helped to sharpen Stolypin's analysis of social and economic problems. In a new report to St. Petersburg, he cited the growing threat of unrest in the village—forty instances of arson had already taken place in the countryside since mid-June. The governor assigned troops to protect the estates of prominent landowners, such as those of Prince L'vov (!) and Prince Viazemskii, but these efforts did not prevent peasants from stealing rye from the estates of others. Once again, Stolypin blamed radical propagandists above all and depicted the majority of peasants as conservative victims of the agitators.[50] He strongly hinted at the existence of a "tsar myth" mentality among the peasants, according to which peasants were concerned that the governor was hiding a special rescript from the tsar promising to give back the land parcels "cut off" from the peasants in the 1861 settlement. He attributed this vulnerability to propaganda in part to their living conditions, "for the *darstvenniki* are in a terrible economic plight in many areas:"[51] "The narod cannot wait for long. What is necessary is not promises but the immediate formation of a state land fund and an allocation of it to those most in need of land, divided up in accordance with the initiative and will of the Tsar. This land issue is now being exploited by everyone—the zemstvo, the economic councils, the revolutionaries." Stolypin prophetically added a sense of urgency, for, in his words, the situation would only get worse by the early autumn after the harvest was in.

Stolypin's battle with the Third Element led him to rely increasingly on one of his few political allies in the province, the conservative landowners. He came to see the need for a counteroffensive by public leaders on the right in order to challenge the Third Element on the left. The village was unstable and threatened by the propagandists, and police efforts against the radicals would remain frustrated so long as the liberal activists (who in his opinion were under the sway of the Third Element) continued to dominate the zemstvo. Stolypin needed outside support, which he found in the conservative landed gentry.

The incident of the Petrovsk Economic Council gave him a chance to test this strategy. It is no coincidence that the critical moment in the Petrovsk affair occurred in early August, when Stolypin (with questionable legality) authorized the conservatives to hold an improvised meeting of the assembly, where the surprised and poorly organized liberals were badly outvoted. Over the next few months he came increasingly to require the support of Olsuf'ev, Uvarov, the Pavlovs, the Kropotovs, and other gentry conservatives, and already by July of 1905 he had clearly formulated ideas on strategy: "In the future one is reduced to expect the formation of a landed party, rooted in the nation, which contrary to the theoreticians might counteract and neutralize what is harmful in the Third Element."[52]

One additional effect of the summer disturbances in Stolypin's political circumstances was that his handling of the Balashov crisis publicized in St. Petersburg his ability to deal with unrest. In his July report on the Petrovsk Economic Council, the governor asked permission to come to the capital and discuss provincial problems with the current minister of the interior, Bulygin. By the time he arrived in St. Petersburg in late September, he had already acquired a reputation as a strong governor who (as in the Balashov pogrom) could confront revolutionaries while preventing any deaths.[53] The tumult of the summer of 1905 enabled Stolypin to take an important step on the road to becoming prime minister.

URBAN RIOTS, PEASANT UNREST, AND THE NEW POLITICS (LATE 1905–06)

Stolypin's final period in Saratov proved to be the most difficult six months he ever faced in his provincial training. After spending another late summer vacation in Kolnoberzhe, he returned to Saratov on October 20, 1905, to find the province already inflamed by revolt. In these last months before his final departure from Saratov on April 22, 1906, to assume new responsibilities in the capital, he witnessed a new and increasingly polarized phase in the development of provincial politics.

As we have already seen, the liberal-leftist alliance was traditionally stronger in Saratov than in most other provinces: in the late summer and fall of 1905, the old alliance of the Liberation Movement held together longer in Saratov than nationally. Elsewhere in European Russia, the liberals were drifting away from the left by August/September as a result of the division caused by the government's announcement of the so-called Bulygin Duma (the public activists and zemstvo liberals decided to accept it, the radicals did not). In Saratov, however, the liberals preserved their oppositionist spirit, albeit with a change in membership: gentry liberals were put on the defensive both on their estates and in the zemstvo assemblies, and leadership of the oppositionist public in Saratov now passed to the lawyers, teachers, journalists, physicians, clerks, and other representatives of the new liberalism.

The national October General Strike began in Saratov on the ninth, when the local employees of the Riazin-Urals Railway received first news of railway strikes in Moscow. The purpose of the Saratov strike was a joint SR-SD effort to protest the restricted suffrage of the Bulygin Duma. On October 10, railway employees went off to the main factories and offices of the provincial and district zemstvo board and of the town duma, as well as to pharmacies, to find supporters. Two days later the strike became violent, as a crowd of about three thousand people (mostly workers) encountered ten mounted cossacks, whom they roughed up. A fresh detachment arrived later that day and seized 185 people for questioning, then held thirty-three agitators without formal charges. That night another crowd of about three thousand heard SD and SR orators from the railway strike committee call for armed resistance to bring about the collapse of tsarism.[54]

The events of the evening of October 12 show once again the effect of the crowd, as liberals were compelled to take a more aggressive stance than they probably would have desired. During a late-night session of the city duma, a group of railway-worker spokesmen entered to announce that the police were beating the people held in jail. City Mayor Nemirovskii closed the duma meeting and led a delegation to the police to investigate. Next, the duma petitioned the acting governor (Vice-Governor Knol', acting in the absence of Stolypin) to release the detained thirty-three, and then requested the Interior Ministry to remove the cossacks from the province. In reply Knol' announced the release of only twenty-three of the total of thirty-three detainees, arresting the remaining ten. Dissatisfied, the Saratov radicals returned to the duma halls and formed a "Central Strike Committee" (also called the "Provisional Revolutionary Government") to support the strike until those arrested were released. Included on this committee were not only the railway leaders from the socialist parties but also future Kadets (the lawyers Maslennikov, Tokarskii, Kal'manovich, and Poliak, as well as the physician Uzemblo and a future Octobrist, Mayor Nemirovskii).[55]

The next day, October 13, the Central Strike Committee planned a mass rally in front of the city duma building and train station. The same SR and SD figures who had organized the initial railway strike called now for an armed attack on the jail to free the ten comrades. That evening a hundred-man brigade composed of railway workers marched on the jail but were driven away by the police. Now, however, Vice-Governor Knol' began to reinforce his police patrols and banned all public meetings. He also seized control of the building of the provincial zemstvo to prevent private meetings of the Third Element. Peace was restored and shops were reopened on October 14 and 15. Then, on the following two days, October 16 and 17, railway workers were allowed to hold a large gathering at the train station, thanks to the intervention of the liberal director of the Riazan-Urals Railway, D. P. Kandaurov. Once again the same scene was repeated: radical spokesmen from the railway union called on their comrades to continue the strike until the government was overthrown.

Publication of the October Manifesto (news of which arrived in Saratov on October 18) produced two days of heightened unrest, culminating in a right-wing pogrom. To prepare for an uprising, the organizers planned a secret meeting on a Volga steamship scheduled to leave Saratov on the evening of the eighteenth. Through informants the police heard of the proposed secret cruise and arrested 122 people on board the steamer as it was about to depart. That same evening large crowds attending another session of the duma demanded that Mayor Nemirovskii and the deputies visit the bazaars to persuade shopkeepers to join the strike. The duma representatives refused, claiming that such action would only provoke violence between the cossacks and the revolutionary public.[56] Nevertheless, the Saratov liberals stood relatively close to their radical counterparts. Mayor Nemirovskii sent a telegram from the city duma to Count Witte in St. Petersburg appealing for release of all political prisoners, and after a gathering of socialists and democrats at Theatre Square that same day he joined a group of liberals from the zemstvo and city duma who presented an identical appeal to Knol'. The vice-governor gave in, and with the arrested radical leaders now released from jail, the revolutionary movement enjoyed a brief period of freedom of action. On October 19 socialist spokesmen exhorted large gatherings, again at Theatre Square, to denounce the tsar and demand his over-throw.[57]

Violence quickly followed. The leftist demonstrations and Knol''s concessions outraged the lower-middle-class trading population of the city. The night of the nineteenth the crowd attacked the synagogue and the house of the rabbi, and the following day they further terrorized the Jewish section of the town by looting stores and burning homes. Mean-while, radical disturbances continued. Leaders from the railway union shot at troops surrounding the office of the Riazan-Urals Administration. That afternoon at Theatre Square, a terrorist threw a bomb from a hotel at a group of cossacks, wounding one and provoking a new pogrom directed against the town's intellectuals. Order was not finally restored until Governor Stolypin (who had arrived in town only that morning) himself intervened, directing troops throughout the day. A final tally of the victims of the October 19–20 pogrom showed 9 dead, 110 wounded (50 gravely), 168 shops and apartments looted, 11 homes burned and 52 people arrested for looting. Among the apartments burned were those of two prominent liberal lawyers, Tokarskii and Kal'manovich.[58]

Meanwhile, in the villages the news of the October Manifesto had an even more devastating impact. As Timothy Mixter shows (chap. 9), the Saratov village endured increased stress in mid-1905 due to a bad harvest, increasingly tight terms of labor rent (otrabotka), and shortages caused by military demands. Added to these economic concerns was the effect of radical propaganda. Over the previous decade Saratov had developed several centers of rural propaganda where semieducated peasants with contacts in the city or in the railroad could meet with other peasants and pass on radical literature.[59] The pattern of unrest in this peak period of rural rebellion (late October to early November, provoked by the news of the October Manifesto) generally followed the network of villages either adjacent to these rural centers of propaganda or close to railway stations in Saratov where railway workers were able to spread the word.

The village revolt of late 1905 had a tremendous effect on Saratov politics, striking terror into the hearts of local landowners. Saratov led the nation in landed property damage during this period. All gentry landowners felt an indirect challenge from the wave of unrest, but some felt the threat personally. The immediate victims tended to be not a random sample of landowners but, rather, a more select group with some common characteristics: they tended to be noble landowners with 1,000 *desiatiny* or more; the attacked estates tended to have been among those most committed to agricultural progress and most involved in the new, more market-oriented land-rent policies; and the centers of unrest were located in Balashov, Petrovsk, and Atkarsk districts.[60] The zemstvo liberals were particularly well represented in these categories, and the list of victimized landowners in Saratov reads like a Who's Who of Saratov gentry liberalism. Nikolai L'vov was attacked twice in late October, while Mikhail Orlov, Konstantin Veselovskii, Nikolai Iumatov, A. V. Sumarokov, and all three Ermolaev brothers suffered one attack apiece in the last months of 1905. By contrast, the only victimized property owned by a conservative figure in Saratov politics was the Serdobsk estate of the widow of P. A. Krivskii, the gentry marshal very active in agricultural innovation, who died in 1904. No conservative nobleman belonging to the Saratov zemstvo in 1905 suffered an attack on his estate in this period.[61]

The peasant disturbances provoked a partial liquidation of gentry estates, as landowners rushed to the Peasant Land Bank to auction their properties. Once again the rural center of intensity was in the northwest part of the province. The noblemen most interested in selling their land were concentrated in a few districts: Atkarsk (114,000 desiatiny sold), Serdobsk (87,000), Saratov (66,000), Petrovsk (47,000), and Balashov (43,000). Among the frightened landowners were several who had been liberal activists in the earlier Banquet Campaign, such as Nessel'rode and two Ermolaev brothers (M. S. and K. S.), who sold off the bulk of their estates.[62]

Just as order was beginning to be reestablished in the village following the violence of late October and November, new troubles arose in the city of Saratov in December. Following the example of the St. Petersburg Soviet, in late November the Saratov socialist parties decided to form a local soviet and campaigned for popular participation in elections to do so.

Finally, on December 8, the Saratov Council of Workers' Deputies held its first meeting.[63] News of the outbreak of the Moscow Armed Uprising reached Saratov in the second week of December. According to the Saratov police, rumors were flying in worker and intellectual circles that the revolutionary forces in Moscow had gained the upper hand; crowds began to gather on the night of December 15 in the city of Saratov and headed toward the prison, where their efforts to free jailed comrades were thwarted by cossacks. The next day, a crowd of over two thousand people gathered outside of town and then marched on the jail, where they encountered a contingent of cossacks and two infantry companies. Workers exchanged shots with the police forces in two assaults but in the end were beaten back. The final toll following the December 16 shoot-out included seven dead and nineteen wounded.[64] The following day most of the SD leadership were captured at a gathering of the Saratov Soviet.[65] The local SR leadership, in turn, fell victim to another wave of arrests in late December and early January, as police brought in people accused of working on behalf of the Peasant Union after the union members held a local congress on December 18.

Significantly, in these last days of revolutionary resistance in late 1905, the leftist parties still cooperated closely with each other: both SRs and SDs served as members of the local committee of the Peasant Union, and both parties were equally involved in the armed shoot-out of December 16.[66] Between December 10 and 21, police in Saratov captured seven leaders of the Peasant Union, including several people with ties to the zemstvo (the arrested figures included the chairman of the Atkarsk zemstvo board, Lapitskii, and the Atkarsk zemstvo statistician Obukhov). The zemstvo landowner and physician Vladimir Chenykaev returned from exile to serve as chairman at the December 18 Peasant Union congress in Saratov but then was captured by the police in early 1906. Thus, the final months of 1905 represent the peak of organized resistance by SRs and SDs in this phase of the revolution. By early 1906, police arrests as well as growing factional infighting were to weaken severely the strength of the revolutionaries. It was only now, while the SDs were forced into a retreat, that the Bolshevik-Menshevik division became significant for radical circles in the province.[67]

To complete this survey of Saratov politics before Governor Stolypin departed for St. Petersburg, we should note one final development of late 1905–early 1906: the structure of political groupings within educated society was changing as public leaders reacted to the new pressures being placed on them. The rural violence of late 1905 caused the gentry landowners of the zemstvo constitutionalist movement to recede into the background, while the leadership of progressive liberalism passed to the urban and rural professionals who came to be associated with the provincial Kadets. The leaders of the Kadet party as it emerged in the early months of 1906 included a few zemstvo liberals of the old type (such as L'vov, who was soon to abandon the party because of its land program, which he considered too leftist); but by and large the new dominant figures were lawyers, journalists, physicians, veterinarians, and employees of the zemstvo and railroad, as well as some industrialists and duma deputies.[68]

This tendency toward increased ideological polarization accelerated under the stimulus of the spring 1906 elections to the State Duma, which forced the remaining public leaders to engage in an unusually open political discourse with workers, peasants, and townspeople.[69] The land question and popular rights were debated in ideological terms more explicitly than ever before; the process of preparing for the Duma elections catalysed the establishment of new political parties formed along more modern, organized lines. The polarizing tendencies of the moment were clearly expressed by Count Uvarov at an Octobrist meeting in March 1906, when he remarked that "there are only two parties in Russia now, the left and the right, those for the tsar and against."[70]

The confrontational tone of local politics increased significantly in this last phase of Stolypin's governorship. The day before news of the October Manifesto arrived in the province, the deputies of the provincial zemstvo and Saratov city duma met on October 17 in a rare joint session to petition St. Petersburg with a restrained appeal for land reform and the creation of a State Duma.[71] But then the news of the October Manifesto and the spectacle of the Saratov pogrom of October 19–20 combined to force a shift in the public's political mood, one so sudden that even Stolypin remarked on it in a note to St. Petersburg: "Even all the extreme zemstvo and city circles recognize the new dangers, and have begun to express their full confidence and solidarity with me, and request that I take energetic measures [to restore order]. The change in their mood is striking."[72]

Now the right wing began to coalesce into a more organized and ideologically articulated party supported by conservative elements among the gentry landowners, provincial administration, and the church. As was the case with Alexander Guchkov in Moscow, in Saratov the return from the Manchurian front in late 1905 of Count Dmitrii Olsuf'ev served as a catalyst. Having endured the horrors of war and Japanese captivity, Olsuf'ev was a source of patriotic inspiration for the resurgent conservatives. He could argue persuasively to a biased audience that zemstvo liberals bore responsibility for Russia's defeat. It was also widely believed that Olsuf'ev's considerable fortune helped to finance the new right-wing efforts. He joined the right-wing leaders who had remained in Saratov in 1905—Uvarov, Grimm, the brothers Pavlov (A. A. and N. A.) and Oznobishin (S. N. and V. N.)—in forming the "Party of Legal Order" in December 1905, which grew into the "Right Bloc" in January 1906 and then into the Octobrist coalition in March–April of the same year.[73]

These same Saratov noble landowners were also present among the highly disciplined "group of thirty-four deputies" who totally demolished the liberal party at the regular session of the provincial zemstvo assembly (January 22 to February 7, 1906). Iumatov and other members of the existing executive board were denounced for their "illegal" representation of Saratov at the 1904–05 zemstvo national congresses. The conservatives also formally prohibited strikes by zemstvo employees, eliminated over 50,000 rubles from the provincial budget, and closed down the *Saratov Zemstvo Weekly* edited by the liberal Golubev. The Sanitary Department, headed by the prominent physician N. I. Teziakov, and many other zemstvo services similarly fell victim to this right-wing purge, whose main purpose was to cut off funding for those liberal-inspired services which had provided jobs for the radical Third Element.[74] (Similar conservative zemstvo attacks on the Third Element were taking place throughout European Russia in late 1905–early 1906.) As a sign of how extreme the rural fear had become, a few weeks later the provincial gentry society, deliberating on how to spend a 250,000-ruble windfall in insurance coverage from property damage, decided on March 10 to spend the money on hiring guards to protect estates and forests.[75]

The elections to the Duma provided the liberals and radicals with the opportunity to make a counterattack against the new conservative forces. The Saratov Kadet party was formed in the winter of 1905–06 and included such figures as the lawyers A. M. Maslennikov, A. A. Tokarskii, V. N. Poliak, and B. A. Arapov, the journalist P. A. Argunov, the railway official A. A. Dobrovol'skii (Riazan-Urals Railway), and the Ministry of Agriculture official I. I. Gil'denberg. In preelection meetings with large popular audiences, Kadet spokesmen debated publicly with SR and SD representatives on the great issues of the day. In the end the Kadets made a strong showing but were still much smaller than the main force in the elections, the radical "Union of Laborers" (*Soiuz Trudiashchikhsia,* also known as the "Union of Employees"). The latter party was formed in Saratov late during the Duma campaign, in April 1906, in response to successful compaigning by the Kadets in the city. It was composed mostly of SRs plus a few Bolsheviks and Mensheviks who disagreed with their respective parties' decision to boycott the Duma elections. Once in St. Petersburg as Duma deputies, these Saratov members of the Union of Laborers played a key role in organizing the national Trudovik group.

The Saratov electoral campaign reveals once again the liberal-radical alliance, appearing now in the form of Kadet–SR cooperation in elections on both the city and provincial levels. The party alignment here was such that local reporters wrote only about a left and a right, ignoring any fine distinctions between Octobrists and their more right-wing allies or between Kadets and their radical allies. In the first round, for Saratov city delegates (March 23), the Kadet-dominated leftist group won by a landslide, beating the Octobrist-right coalition by a vote of 23,844 to 5,990. Then, in the district elections of April 6–7 (following the SR-dominated peasant elections on the *volost* level), the leftist coalition again took the upper hand, electing 102 delegates over the 35 Octobrist-right delegates. (Conservatives like Olsuf'ev recognized that they had no chance and conducted their own "boycott" of the district elections.) Finally, the left commanded the majority of votes at the provincial round of elections on April 14, selecting eight SRs and two Kadets. The radicals clearly dominated the coalition, for in the deputy-by-deputy round of balloting the first five seats had already gone to SRs (including Anikin, Zhilkin, and Ul'ianov) before the Kadets L'vov and Kotliarevskii were elected along with three other SRs. (A third Kadet, Tokarskii, was also elected as the deputy from the city of Saratov.) Two days before, on April 12, the right wing had secured its own presence in St. Petersburg when the provincial zemstvo elected Olsuf'ev as its deputy to the State Council.[76]

Meanwhile, what effect did these events have on Governor Stolypin? For one thing, the threat of revolution was now drawing closer to him personally. Following the assassination attempts in Balashov District in the summer of 1905, he faced a terrorist attack in his home in November. A high-ranking military official, Adjutant General Sakharov (sent to the province to oversee repressive activities in the village) was shot dead at the governor's mansion in Saratov by a woman named Bitsenko. As a reflection of how wide the gulf had grown between the liberal public and the administration, a few days after Sakharov's assassination a few public activists sent an appeal to Stolypin requesting Bitsenko's release, while the zemstvo deputy/lawyer Maslennikov sent flowers to her jail cell.[77]

In the midst of these attacks on state power the governor's thoughts increasingly focused on the use of police measures to restore order, and Stolypin's old musings about "personal contacts and conversations" with the public were heard no longer. He became a sharp critic of the military for failing to send him adequate troops in time. Now liberal society no longer occupied a major place in his thoughts, for the activists had either been devastated by the rural revolt and gone over to the conservative party, or had joined the Kadets in siding with the revolution. In his mind the issues had boiled down to a confrontation between the forces of violence and order, and Stolypin was determined to reassert state authority as he traveled from village to village.[78]

Shortly after the first wave of peasant unrest had died down (there was to be another in the spring–summer of 1906), Stolypin in early 1906 devoted his attention to the underlying weakness of the regime. He identified this as the unstable rural society aroused by the land question. He arrived at the first clear articulation of his future land reform in writing his annual "Report to the Tsar" (officially covering the year 1904). The governor began his argument by describing the poverty of the Saratov peasantry and its dependence on weather for the success or failure of a harvest. He then explained how this economic backwardness was the result of a negative mentality created by the village commune. Here, his experiences in Kovno and Grodno were crucial in allowing him to prove that it was indeed possible to change peasant habits and attitudes. Since the only force contrary to that of the commune was private property, Stolypin felt that small property-owners were necessary as bastions of support for the state. At present the only peasant property-owners were kulaks, who were frowned upon by Stolypin, so a new type of private property-owner would have to be created, a "work-loving farmer" (trudoliubovimyi zemlerob). Stolypin added that such steps were drastically necessary in a region of peasant poverty such as Saratov.[79] In a later interview with a Saratov journalist, as prime minister, Stolypin summarized the effect of his Saratov experience on his own thinking, which prompted him to utter his famous statement about the long-term survivability of the tsarist regime:

The shortcomings of administrative authority in the districts became familiar to me personally when I served as governor of Saratov during the disturbances of 1905–06. I doubt that anyone could say in good conscience that there is nothing in the existing structure of the district administration that needs changing. . . . The main item on the agenda is to strengthen the lower-class population *(nizy)*. The entire force of the country is within them! The roots of the state will be healthy and strong, and the words of the Russian Government will carry a new weight in Europe and in the whole world. . . . Give the state twenty years of peace, both domestically and externally, and you will not find the Russia of today.[80]

It is important to understand the perspective from which the governor viewed his future program. Even though he was a wealthy landowner of noble birth, Stolypin saw himself in the end as a state servitor, an official dedicated to strengthening the state in the most practical way possible. Therefore, although he clearly sided with the landed gentry during the peasant disturbances of late 1905 and worked with Olsuf'ev, Uvarov, and other noble members of the "Right Bloc" in the electoral campaign in the spring of 1906, one should not conclude from this (as did the conservative gentry, which explained their disillusionment of 1907–11) that Stolypin's prime motive was to support gentry rule in the countryside. Rather, he was using his available resources in order to serve his ultimate goal: the strengthening of the state. Only by understanding this perspective can one realize why Stolypin later pursued local administrative reforms that came to threaten cherished gentry institutions. The governor's daughter recalls his comments on this issue at the end of 1905, when a liberal landowner asked him to rush troops to his estate to put down an uprising. Stolypin's refusal to do so highlights his reasons for disagreeing with the landed nobility in future years:

Father firmly decided not to send military detachments into the countryside, for he understood well that as long as provincial authority was able to carry out its responsibilities calmly, the revolution could not triumph. . . . Father felt that the main task was to protect the entire state administrative apparatus, that this was the only thing that could save Russia. The estates are not so numerous, and the pogroms against them cannot continue for long. "The strength of Russia does not lie in large-scale agriculture," said father. "The large estates have outlived their time. The owners of the unprofitable ones have already begun to sell them to the Peasant Bank. The support for Russia lies not in them but in the tsar."[81]

Four days after he departed on April 22 for his assignment in St. Petersburg, Stolypin was declared the new minister of internal affairs; in July he became prime minister. His "training" in Saratov made a heavy impression upon the last phase of his career, for it not only gave him a more clearly refined set of social and economic reforms but also provided him with a network of political figures whom he had previously encountered in Saratov: Olsuf'ev in the State Council; Uvarov, Pavlov, and Oznobishin, who participated in the national gentry conferences; and adversaries in the Duma ranging from the Kadets L'vov, Kotliarevskii, and Tokarskii, to the Trudovik SRs Anikin, Ul'ianov, and Litvinov.

The purpose of this chapter has been to trace two themes of 1905: first, the unusually oppositionist stance taken by many liberals in Saratov who were so committed to reform that they were willing to cooperate with radicals for the support of the lower classes; and second, the evolution of Stolypin's political education as he lived through a challenging period in a difficult province before arriving at the national level of politics. Neither one of these stories can be told in isolation, for Stolypin and political figures in Saratov had a very strong reciprocal influence.

One may conclude from the above that Saratov politics in 1905 presents both a reflection and an unusual development (or, in the provinces, an extreme case) of the liberal-radical alliance seen throughout Russia in the period. On the one hand, Saratov reformists in both the zemstvo and city duma took a daringly oppositionist stance in 1905. Liberals were willing to lobby with the governor to prevent his use of repression against workers in January, to distribute oppositionist literature in the villages in July, and to join strike committees and appeal for the release of political prisoners in October. By appealing so openly for reform, they demonstrated a confidence in their position in local society, a faith that they could tamper with the status quo and not run the risk of provoking a social conflagration that would destroy themselves as well as the tsarist regime. Their resolve to challenge the government was based in part on a fear of growing peasant unrest, felt increasingly since 1902, which led them to do and say things that may seem naive in hindsight. Nevertheless, zemstvo liberals deserve credit for their vision and willingness to cooperate with the left for the progressive cause. In large measure they owed this unusual attitude to the political circumstances of Saratov, an environment that encouraged this alliance of diverse political groups.

On the other hand, the radical parties of Saratov were also unusual in their relatively open attitude toward politics, as was shown both by the Bolshevik and Menshevik cooperation and SR-SD joint efforts throughout 1905. The liberal-radical alliance was based on reciprocal ties, for the leftists depended on their "society" friends in the zemstvo and duma for economic protection and moral support in the same way that the liberals needed these democratic employees for their ties to the narod.

The *tenacity* of this spirit of center-left cooperation is a striking feature of the Revolution of 1905 in Saratov. At the beginning of this story, the province was one of the leading provincial areas of the Banquet Campaign, and these liberal-radical ties remained strong throughout 1905. It was characteristic of local affairs that the Kadets and the SRs joined in a coalition for the Duma elections, and even in late 1906 the local Kadets proclaimed their dedication to a working alliance with the radicals as a "bloc of illegal organizations."[82]

In his Saratov years Stolypin refined his ability to challenge his adversaries face-to-face, be they the "popular" rioters of Saratov during the pogrom of October 20, the rioting townspeople in Balashov of July 21, or the zemstvo and duma leaders encountered during the Banquet Campaign. The Saratov years clearly provided a major foundation for Stolypin's distrust of the Kadets. His experiences in 1903–06 taught him the propensity of the liberals to submit to the influence of the radical Third Element. The liberals did not renounce the revolution, he reasoned, and from this weakness of the public arose the anarchy of 1905. Hence, to prevent new attacks on the regime, he sought out public leaders who could be trusted to stand on the side of order. From his 1905 experience he came easily to develop a very different attitude toward the Octobrists than he had toward the Kadets.

Stolypin's feelings toward social unrest operated on two levels. He unflinchingly applied military force to suppress disturbances, and in fact showed that repression could succeed, that it was possible for him to prevail over the revolutionary movement. Yet he was also aware of the underlying issues that gave rise to the revolutionary threat. Generally, the newly emerging Stolypin program could be summarized under three themes: (1) the need to use police power to restore order, with its emphasis directed against radicals; (2) the recognition that mass unrest arose from structural economic and social problems, so that once peace was restored the regime should pursue fundamental reforms; and (3) the understanding that the government was dependent upon the creation of a new political regime through an alliance with the landed gentry and public moderates with whom he could use his "personal contacts and conversations" in order to achieve those reforms.

Stolypin saw himself as a government servitor standing above the special interests of any particular social group. He became especially sensitive to the need for land reform under the unusual pressure of unrest in Saratov in 1905. He perceived the peasant problem from the point of view of the state, and similarly, his attitude toward the landed gentry embodied that same perspective. He was closely allied to other landowners in the province and came to find the conservative gentry as his main social ally in his war against the revolution. Yet his vision emphasized the need to protect the interests of the state as a whole, an approach which would also lead him to contemplate reforms that threatened traditional gentry-dominated institutions. Altogether, the Saratov years helped the governor develop into an unusually dynamic statesman for the tsarist regime prior to its demise.

9. Peasant Collective Action in Saratov Province, 1902–1906

Timothy R. Mixter

"IN POLITICAL development Saratov Province proceeds in advance of all peasant Russia." Such was the opinion of one of the most astute observers of peasant life at the turn of the century.[1] Others also commented on the way the peasants of Saratov Province stood out among the rural inhabitants of the Volga region. One wrote:

So, for example, at the same time that the migrant laborer from Penza Province has the appearance of a downtrodden, dejected, emaciated, and tired man, the Saratov Province migrant worker, on the contrary, carries the look of a city worker, of a jaded, bold optimist; while the first looks impoverished in appearance and dress, the second looks prosperous, with a sense of his own dignity, in a costume that attempts to mimic urban styles.[2]

Given such comments, it should not be surprising that peasant collective action in Saratov during the period 1902–06 was in several ways unique or that it exhibited, in a more pronounced fashion, patterns discernible elsewhere. Significant waves of unrest often began in the province earlier than they appeared in other parts of the country, especially in the winter of 1902, the winter and fall of 1905, and May 1906. Property damage resulting from agrarian protest there reached 9,550,320 rubles—more than double that in any other Great Russian province in 1905.[3] Saratov peasants also showed a propensity to adopt new forms of collective action, such as combined rent and labor strikes as well as mass boycotts. They proved more willing to confront the state and its officials than in other provinces and were more likely to coordinate action between villages than in any other region, with the possible exception of the Right Bank Ukraine and the Baltic provinces.[4] Representatives from Saratov villages played important leadership roles at the national level, invariably propounding views that were staunchly on the left of the peasant political spectrum. They participated actively in the Peasant Union and their organization for the provincial elections to the First State Duma became the prototype for peasant organization within that body, namely, the Trudovik Group. The number of village declarations sent to the government and to Duma deputies was higher than elsewhere. Finally, through their protest, Saratov peasants within a few years of the revolution forced the sale to them of a greater amount of land than was the case in other provinces of European Russia. Why and how did such a peasant movement come to the fore in Saratov Province in particular?

The attempt to answer this question will start with an elaboration of seven key factors that promoted peasant collective action in the province, proceeding from more indirect to immediate causes and focusing on 1902–04, followed by a survey of the peasant movement in Saratov in 1905–06. The seven factors are: (1) the historical, demographic, and environmental evolution of specific localities; (2) the intrusion of state officials and state policies with regard to such issues as emancipation, the Peasant Land Bank, taxes, railway construction, army conscription, zemstvo employees, and so on; (3) the impingement of local, national, and international markets upon the peasantry and the farming practices of private landowners; (4) the cohesion of peasant communities, which helped the peasantry to mobilize in defense of its interests; (5) the existence of a peasant culture, quite free from outside hegemony, that perpetuated other ways of seeing, memories of long-hostile relationships with private landowners, and collectively agreed-upon concepts of moral rights, obligations, and norms, which in times of crisis tended to give priority to local community welfare over individual profit; (6) the penetration of the outside world into the village by means of railroad lines, newspapers, education, wars, and groups such as the Third Element, zemstvo activists, and outside radicals—all at times carrying revolutionary ideologies with them; (7) opportunities and tactical mobility provided by the polarization of political and social life at the local and national levels as well as by peasant creation and perpetuation of relatively independent social spaces and institutions.

Historical, Demographic, and Environmental Factors. The historical, demographic, and ecological evolution of Saratov Province certainly played an important role in the mobilization of peasant collective action. The province had a turbulent history; the marches of Stepan Razin and

Emelian Pugachev and the resultant village uprisings lived on in peasant folklore. Serfdom had come to the area mainly in the eighteenth century and the peasantry could thus more easily recall and preserve memories of freedom and land being solely under the control of their forefathers, which partially explains the fact that even in the first half of the nineteenth century peasants in Saratov Province engaged in collective action more than in most other regions. Troops were called into the Saratov countryside far more times (sixty-two) in 1861–63 than elsewhere to quell protests against state emancipation policies and the intransigence of local gentry landowners. All this activity attracted to the area a large contingent of radicals and political exiles with dreams of fomenting further revolt.[5]

The half-century before 1905 saw a burgeoning demographic problem. The rural population of Saratov Province grew from 1,476,700 in 1858 to 2,096,200 in 1897, while the number of peasant households increased by 64.4 percent between 1877 and 1905. The population density at the turn of the century equaled 47 persons (38 peasants) per square mile in contrast to 33.5 for European Russia as a whole. The problem was especially acute in large villages surrounded by vast estates in Petrovsk, Serdobsk, as well as the northern and eastern parts of Balashov, Atkarsk, and Saratov districts, which were among the most restive locales in 1905–06. In Balashov, for instance, the population rose 52 percent between 1858 and 1901, while peasant landholding expanded only by 17 percent.[6]

The demographic problem was exacerbated by an ecological one. Because of the relative absence of water in this largely steppeland province and the need to locate villages near its sources, communities were quite large and widely scattered (Saratov villages averaged 422 persons in 1897, in contrast to barely over 300 in the Central Black Earth region and Left Bank Ukraine). This circumstance forced many peasants to walk long distances to get to their fields, losing much work time in the process. If large villages surrounded by estates were spread out on the banks of rivers in an elongated fashion, the distance to fields was even greater, making manuring almost not worth the effort.[7]

The relatively large size of Saratov villages contributed to peasant rebellion. Not only were peasants in large villages more likely to feel constricted by the lack of sufficient good land close by, they also often had a greater degree of tactical mobility and space, enabling them to mobilize in defense of their interests. Large villages could support a greater number of cultural institutions and meeting places in which ideas and contacts with the outside world could be nurtured and exchanged. Peasants in such communities had more ties with educated artisans, more possibilities for employment independent of the control of local agrarian elites, and more exposure to conflicting political viewpoints such as those articulated in disputes between the rural intelligentsia and priests. Such places after 1903 were also more likely to have cossack and police guard units, which invariably antagonized the local population, fostering various forms of contention. It is not surprising that all the thirty-nine villages with histories of repeated unrest between 1890 and 1906 had populations of over 700 persons, even though the average size of villages in the province was 422. Indeed, the list of particularly restive villages included seventeen with populations of over 2,000, and fourteen of between 1,000 and 2,000. Stolypin, for one, believed that most of the disturbances occurred in larger villages.[8]

Peasant land problems and anger at the state and the nobility often increased after Emancipation. The nobility generally gave the peasantry as little land as possible, kept the best land, and retained almost all forests, meadows, and property with water on it, thus maintaining a monopoly on resources that forced the peasantry to work for them at low rates. Private landowners also interstripped their land with peasant arable and drew boundary lines practically on the back walls of peasant huts. Alternative sources of income from livestock raising, wood pruning, hunting, and fishing were curtailed, and peasants had to bargain with the nobility for transit permission so that they could farm their own strips or rent more land. Frequent immediate causes of peasant collective action in the period 1902–06 were disputes over access rights, the distance away of land offered for rent when better-quality land was available closer to the village, and extortionist gentry labor policies according to which peasants were able to procure small plots of rented land only if they accepted work at rates well below market level.[9]

The Intrusion of State Officials and Policies. It appears that government policies had greater impact on agrarian relations in Saratov Province than in other regions. The most obvious example was the emancipation of the serfs itself. For instance, as a result of land "cut off" (*otrezki*) in that process, the Saratov peasantry soon after 1861 no longer had free access to some 1,621,323 acres—42.6 percent of the land—they had utilized before this date. The percentage cut off was greater than in any other province of European Russia and was to become a prime source of contention.[10] Particularly hard-pressed were the *darstvenniki,* who took the so-called ¼ allotments on which they did not have to pay redemption dues (therefore *dar* = "gift"). Darstvenniki made up approximately one-third of former serfs in the province, and by 1906–07 were 16.92 percent of the male peasant population. The province with the next highest figures was Ekaterinoslav, with 9.24 percent. Beginning in the 1870s, Saratov darstvenniki became caught in a squeeze, as rent and sale prices for land began to soar with the coming of the railroad and the steady rise of the peasant population. The darstvenniki became increasingly locked into an exploitative rent relationship with private landowners that led to mounting tension, especially in a number of restive large villages.[11]

Saratov peasants were also more extensively ensnared in a relationship with the Peasant Land Bank than villagers elsewhere. Through this state institution Saratov peasants bought 1,215,360 acres of land between 1883 and January 1, 1901, considerably more than in any other province. In such restive villages as Irinovka, contention over payment schedules and bank regulations led to protests against the state in the 1902–06 period. Heavy state, zemstvo, and commune taxes also provoked tax boycotts in several villages from the 1890s on.[12]

State sponsorship of railroads also affected agrarian relations. Where the railroad appeared, rent prices tended to go up considerably, as nearby private landowners often chose to lease out less land and farm more. Loss of access to land customarily rented to them was, for peasants, a serious violation of the moral economy and led to much agrarian unrest after the turn of the century. At the same time that they disrupted agrarian patterns, railroads helped peasants to mobilize and brought in outside information, and occasionally agitators. It is perhaps no accident that large villages lying along major transportation routes were often the hubs around which peasant rebellion occurred in 1902–06. The impact of railroads was clearest in the fall of 1905, when peasant unrest was sparked by the railroad strike and broke out first along railway lines. Agitators hopped from village to village by train. So, however, did the repressive forces, which were frequently billeted near railway stations and whose behavior time and again angered local citizens, leading to new protests.[13]

The Russo-Japanese War, which entailed economic hardship for many families, was a further source of discontent. In the four mobilizations of 1904, the five districts where peasant unrest was to be most intensive— Balashov, Petrovsk, Atkarsk, Serdobsk, and Saratov—provided 82.7 percent of the reservists called up, even though they consisted of only one-half of the districts of the province. The call-up was also higher in Saratov than in most of the other provinces, a discrepancy which peasants in overrepresented areas noted with resentment. Hard-pressed wives of soldiers became angry and besieged *volost* and zemstvo offices demanding promised subsidies, which were late in coming due to the unexpectedly high conscription rate in the province. In response to this debacle, demobilized soldiers thrust themselves into leadership roles when the agrarian movement of 1905–06 broke out and used their newly acquired literacy and knowledge of organization to good effect.[14]

Finally, the state helped peasants to mobilize through zemstvo employment of Third Element doctors, teachers, statisticians, and so on. Vera Figner and Sof'ia Perovskaia had served as zemstvo employees in the 1870s, and the cholera epidemic of 1892–93 brought a new contingent of radicals to the province, including I. I. Rakitnikova (Al'tovskaia), the brothers Plaksin, and K. M. Takhtarev. By 1902, Saratov Province boasted 1,002 zemstvo employees, ranking it sixth out of thirty-four provinces, while the percentage of employees under police suspicion for being radical was 10 percent in 1902—higher than in any other province. Such zemstvo positions as correspondent for the *Saratov Zemstvo Weekly*, statistician, insurance agent, and teacher in the rotating repeater courses entailed much travel between villages, which facilitated the dissemination of radical ideas. The impact of zemstvo employees and the large number of political exiles is well described by Michael Melancon and Scott Seregny (chaps. 5, 6).[15]

The Impingement of the Market. Some recent historiography has suggested that there was no agrarian crisis in Russia at the turn of the century and has justly claimed that peasant living standards for Russia as a whole were probably slowly improving. However, in an arc of provinces stretching from northwestern Saratov and Samara provinces in the east, through southeastern Tambov, the middle districts of Voronezh, southern Kursk and Chernigov provinces, northern sections of Kharkov, Ekaterinoslav, and Kherson provinces, and finally into Poltava, Kiev, and Podolia provinces, an agrarian crisis does seem to have been developing, especially in large villages that were surrounded by vast, privately owned estates. In this area the penetration of the market for labor, land, rent, and grain was spasmodic and evinced a peculiar pattern interlacing what Soviet historians have called the "remnants of feudalism" and new features of "developing capitalism." Here, unlike areas farther to the south, population density was high enough to keep wages low and rents high, but the soil was still rich enough and the growing season sufficiently long to allow large-scale commercial agriculture for the expanding market in grain, sugar beets, and other crops to be profitable for the landed elite. In such transitional areas, the peasantry suffered the worst of both worlds—low wages, little land to rent, and what there was, tendered only at high rates. Caught in such a bind, peasants in many large villages in the arc of provinces became restive during the period 1902–06.[16]

These problems were especially intense in the northwestern corner of Saratov Province—Serdobsk, Petrovsk, Balashov, northeastern Atkarsk, and much of Saratov District that lay away from the Volga. In these locales, estates were often of vast size and the percentage of privately owned land greater than in most other areas of Russia.

Because the return on rye, the predominant crop planted, was less than on wheat, and because of unfavorable railroad tariffs and the greater distance away of the main export ports and agricultural machine depots, Saratov grain growers felt at a competitive disadvantage in comparison to commercial farmers in the wheat belt of New Russia and the Kuban Oblast. Faced with relatively intractable marketing expenses and lower potential income, estate owners in the northwestern districts of Saratov compensated by introducing inexpensive improvements, holding down labor costs, and generating income through the leasing out of land. This amalgam of practices may have at times been traditional and/or exploitative, but it was not backward. It represented a rational response to the market on the part of increasingly entrepreneurial members of the landed elite, who because of the configuration of rich soil, high rents, and low wages prevailing in the transitional arc had more options than farmers elsewhere. By playing the grain, labor, and rent markets against each other, they combined "progressive" practices with coercive labor and rent policies designed to cut expenses and generate increased income. Saratov landowners practiced deceptive bargaining techniques in hiring markets and, behind Marshal of the Nobility P. A. Krivskii, led the national fight for repressive labor legislation in the 1880s and 1890s. They commonly hired peasants in the winter for future harvest work for less than they would have to pay the following summer by finding out which villagers were in tax arrears and short of the resources needed to make it through the winter. Finally, in return for rented land, which many peasants needed to ensure an adequate supply of food, they gained peasant labor for rates that were effectively below the price they would have had to pay in the hiring markets—an arrangement known as *otrabotka*.[17]

Gentry responses to the market also affected leasing arrangements in ways inimical to peasants' economic interests and sense of justice. While in European Russia the amount of land rented (without pasture) only equaled 19 percent of the land peasants had bought and held in allotment, in Balashov, Serdobsk, Petrovsk, Atkarsk, and Saratov districts about one-third of the total land peasants sowed was leased. Thus negotiations with private landowners concerning rent were more frequent and important for peasant well-being here than in other regions. When wheat prices went up after 1897, and private landowners reduced the amount of land they rented out in order to take advantage of the more favorable grain market by farming more of their land, peasants were angered to find that there was less land available to lease and that rent prices increased.[18]

Desperate after such poor harvest years as 1901, and in general lacking money and sufficient food, many peasants had little choice but to enter into these unequal agreements. In general, it was the large and middle-sized gentry estates in the northwestern districts that not only rented out less land to the peasantry but exacted very harsh terms for what they did choose to lease. The gentry estates here were the main sites of peasant disturbances in 1902–06. Contention over rising rents and labor practices, especially in the large villages surrounded by the vast estates in the northwestern districts, was a major factor in the peasant-perceived agrarian crisis in Saratov.[19]

Village Cohesion. Peasant communities in Saratov exhibited good internal cohesion, which was a prerequisite for successful collective action in 1902–06. This cohesion was sustained by several factors. There is statistical evidence that communal repartitioning to prevent stratification increased in Saratov Province after the 1880s, as population pressure began to strain resources. Repartitions may also have signaled that an egalitarian political and economic ethos pervaded these settlements. They occurred especially in the large and/or darstvennik villages, which were also the ones that engaged in repeated collective action most frequently in the 1902–06 period. Collective responsibility, communal renting of land, customary law, charivaris, perpetuation of a largely oral culture, family cyclical mobility, mutual aid, courting and other cultural rituals, the use of hinge men to deal with outsiders, and control by the communal assembly of the major economic, legal, and welfare resources and institutions—all contributed to ensure the relative cohesion of peasant communities. These practices reinforced the moral economy of kinship, reciprocal ties, and community subsistence instead of fostering market relations and stratification. Even when these mechanisms broke down and peasants began squabbling among themselves, communities still tended to come together when they had to confront outsiders and the authorities. Although the poor and middle peasants were the most apt to protest, in the majority of cases Saratov villages engaged in collective action as a whole during the period 1902–06, whether they engaged in strikes, wrote declarations to the Duma, or attacked and destroyed estates. Attacks on estates in 1905–06 were frequently planned at village assemblies, and villages often closed ranks to prevent punishment of leaders.[20]

Intervillage strife appears to have been more prevalent than contention within settlements. Villages fought over the buying and renting of land. Conflict resulted when strikebreaking occurred or when villages claimed a monopoly on local employment to the detriment of migrant laborers or peasants from settlements lying farther away from a local estate. Not all conflict was economic, however, and large "conscious"[21] villages at times scorned more politically backward ones. One such political dispute began when peasants from Krasnoiar beat up a teacher from Romanovka who, while passing through Krasnoiar on his bicycle, offered up some chance remark about the Russo-Japanese War. In response, peasants from several neighboring "conscious" villages imposed a boycott on Krasnoiar, refusing peasants from there all sorts of services, including the right to water horses or grind grain at a nearby mill. They also refused to visit or greet *Krasnoiartsy*.[22]

The large size of estates and relatively high rates of gentry absenteeism also facilitated communal cohesion, since these impaired the ability of the landed elite to develop strong paternalistic ties to the peasantry that might have molded peasant behavior. Local police and clergy were often more under peasant sway than vice versa, and villagers were adept at subverting outside attempts at reform to their own ends. While the expansion of the market and the intrusion of state policies and officials, such as the land captain, did serve to impair the ability of traditional mechanisms used to protect peasant communities, they were not strong enough to destroy them. Peasant communities survived intact and remained angry enough to mobilize against outside forces that threatened their existence.

Peasant Culture and Other Ways of Seeing. A distinctive peasant culture and way of seeing the world, and especially a perception of moral norms being transgressed, rather than poverty and economic deprivation per se, tended to spur protest and collective action in 1902–06. The most common violations of the peasantry's view of the moral economy were: (1) gentry disregard of peasant landownership claims; (2) increasingly strict landowner definition of what constituted private property, as well as refusal to continue to rent out land and engage in customary paternalistic practices; (3) outright deception on the part of the employers, or interference of outsiders in the hiring markets.

Landownership claims were an intractable source of conflict; the peasant leader Stepan Anikin stated that "village children are most sensitive to two things: village fires and stories about plots of land that once 'were ours.'"[23] Two of the most remarkable traits of Saratov peasants were the obstinacy with which they pursued sophisticated methods of trying to win back land which they believed the gentry had stolen from them, and their readiness to use new ideas to reaffirm traditional peasant perceptions and goals—including new, revolutionary forms of collective protest. In fact, in 1902–06, it was often the larger villages enmeshed in the market, not the most isolated hamlets, which purposely reaffirmed traditional values, culture, and forms of collective action, at the same time willingly buttressing them with new ideas, cultural institutions, and forms of collective action. In this period peasants did not necessarily view the old and the new as contradictory. Thus, the conscious village of Ivanovka 2 could use such new words as *capitalist* in its declarations but at the same time chose traditional religious terminology to express thoughts that were on the verge of being socialistic.[24]

Saratov peasants also proved more than ready to defend their claims in the bastion of elite culture, the law courts, where a premium was placed on written documents. For instance, in the middle of 1907 in Balashov District, there were 3,523 undecided suits recorded in the gentry affairs chancery concerning boundary disputes with peasants, and in Kamyshin District, 1,105.[25] Peasants thus often resorted to legal means to solve disputes. Only after the long, drawn-out court process failed to satisfy what they believed to be moral claims did the frustrated peasantry resort to other forms of collective action.

Such a process was at work in the large village of Khovanshchina. In 1902 peasants from this village remembered that in the distant past they had had more land, but they could not prove it. They elected representatives and charged them with finding the necessary documents. And, mirabile dictu, after some hard detective work, these amateur historians unearthed in the Moscow Land Court some sort of map and extracts from documents which they claimed fully proved the right of the peasants to the land. The triumphant return of the deputies with the "proof" stirred up all the peasants. In order to nip the ferment in the bud, the local police officer seized the box with the documents in it and hid it in a gooseberry bush outside the house of an auxiliary policeman. When the local peasants found out what had happened, they stormed the volost office, beat the police officer and volost elder, and eventually found the priceless map and papers that had cost them so much time and money to find. Troops and the governor, though, soon arrived, and after severe conflicts in which women and children led the resistance to arrests, fifteen people were hauled away to prison. In such a way, traditional protest revolving around the concept of a moral economy could be transformed into hatred of the government. Khovanshchina became a hotbed of activism in 1905, with a pro-active strike movement replacing the 1902 defensive justification of a moral economy. Thus revolutionary events and the further intrusion of the state they entailed transformed the repertoire of collective action. Peasants, far from being conservative, showed themselves capable of quick and flexible adjustments, given the opportunity. Cases of contention over landownership were to continue to fuel protest in 1905–06.[26]

A second type of violation of moral norms as perceived by the peasantry—aggressive landowner assertion of property rights and refusal to continue traditional leasing and paternalistic practices—was largely behind the wave of arson that engulfed the districts of Balashov, Serdobsk, and Petrovsk in 1902 and 1903; the wave began in February 1902, well before the more famous Poltava-Kharkov revolts. These grievances motivated the attacks on state grain warehouses and the barns of General Ustinov in Bekovo, because the authorities and the general proved to be tardy or unwilling to fulfill their customary moral duty to distribute grain in a time of need following the poor harvest of 1901.[27] Similar actions were widespread.

The rural elite also violated peasant moral norms as it felt growing pressure to adjust to changing political and economic circumstances, including shifts in the market for grain. Prior indulgence of peasant encroachments, such as marginal cattle grazing or hay mowing on gentry land, declined and a new mode of thinking began to emerge, just as it had in England during the crisis period of 1790–1832. Actions that had earlier been ignored or had over the years become de facto customary rights—at least in peasant eyes—were at times redefined at the turn of the century by state officials, the gentry, and other farmers as crimes against the sanctity of private property and evidence of "class struggle." Furthermore, when they could get away with it, private landowners at this time began to force peasants in some areas to engage more heavily in the money economy by charging money rents for previously customary-use rights such as pruning wood in the landowner's forest or grazing livestock on the stubble after his harvest had been gathered, by placing cash surcharges on natural rents, by pervasive levying of fines on workers, by demanding that rent be paid in advance of the harvest, and in other ways. Peasants deemed such changes violations of the moral economy. When they protested, they felt that they were *upholding* customary rights, not breaking the law. They saw nobles, individual kulak renters, and police as revolutionary lawbreakers who had redefined traditional usages as crimes and abandoned flexible paternalistic welfare arrangements and dependent relations for impersonal monetary gain and a new concern for the strict boundaries of private property and social space.[28]

Peasant anger at such changing practices was most apparent in cases involving the leasing of land. As grain prices began to rise after 1897, landowners, particularly in the northwestern districts, started farming more of their land themselves and renting out less to the peasantry. In 1900–01 alone, they removed some 1,350,000 acres from circulation.[29] Changed rent practices were the main reason for peasant protests in 1902 and 1903, especially on large estates with a high percentage of demesne land. Those landowners who no longer rented out to peasants in the neighboring village were almost certain to be targets during the wave of arson, illegal pasturage, and other acts that occurred between 1902 and 1906.[30] Kulaks and merchants who were able to outbid local commune members in the tight land market and who also had no paternalistic traditions were subjected to particularly severe reprisals. When a kulak leased out land immediately behind the homes of Urleika peasants to villagers living several miles away, members of the victimized commune burned the kulak's property three times and sent him anonymous threatening letters. When he went even further and began to define as his private property paths customarily used to drive Urleika livestock to water, he was shot at and lost his left eye. In Trubetskoe, peasants even tried to drive one woman landowner away by fashioning a makeshift cannon out of a pipe and lofting a volley through the bedroom window of her mansion.[31]

The third way in which peasants tried to assert their version of morality was in the hiring markets for agricultural laborers. Well before the beginning of the twentieth century they had organized strikes by refusing to leave the market until the employers had consented to their idea of a "just" price. Occasionally, in such places as Arkadak and Khvalynsk, laborers sought to ensure that employers in the future would adopt peasant definitions of moral behavior and ways of seeing: they beat up those who had lied to or cheated them in the past if the latter perchance appeared in the hiring market, and they protested police interference in bargaining. Worker violence within this social space was not wanton, but invariably occurred only in response to the perceived immoral behavior of employers and outsiders.[32]

The stories of plots of land that once "were ours" and other beliefs about economic morality were part of a largely oral, traditional peasant culture that, in John Berger's words, kept alive "another way of telling and seeing"—in essence, another view of history that claimed events did not have to turn out as they had. The counterparts of such storytelling were songs about Stepan Razin, unwritten customary law and the public mocking of the charivari set against written state statutes, the labor principle as opposed to elite concepts of private property, as well as peasant-manufactured rumors, dissembling, purposive failure to understand, and reinterpretations of documents that gave villagers hope and led them to rebel even in the face of the depressing information handed down from church pulpits and through government edicts.[33] Still, peasant culture was not unchanging, as the following discussion makes clear.

The Influence of Outsiders and the World Beyond the Village. Assessment of the relative influence of non-peasants and outside events on the mobilization of Saratov peasants for collective action is extremely complex. Although some historians have implicitly tended to portray the interaction between peasants and outsiders as a one-way street, peasants were not just passive in their relationship with the outside world. Indeed, they often actively sought out information and contacted non-peasants rather than waiting for the latter to come to them. Public library periodical rooms in the city of Saratov were said to be full of peasants who read only the progressive press, and *muzhiki* who lived near railroad lines were known to besiege trains for the latest newspapers.[34] While some villages sent representatives to the city to look for "intelligent people," more "backward" villages sometimes dispatched one or more of their members to search in neighboring hamlets for *studenty,* as peasant radicals were known.[35]

Saratov itself had been an active center for progressive newspapers since the early 1880s, and it appears likely that the progressive cultural and political atmosphere of the city of Saratov—unusual for provincial Russia—had an important influence on the politics and perceptions of those who lived in the rural hinterland.[36] The alacrity with which Saratov peasants engaged in collective action in response to the Poltava-Kharkov revolts in 1902, the general railroad strike in 1905—well before the October Manifesto which most peasants elsewhere waited for—and the ministerial declaration to the Duma on May 13, 1906, all suggest that Saratov peasants were well-attuned to the outside world as a result of their own efforts. Given the repressive forces they were subject to, knowledge of real opportunities, as reflected in newspaper reports of splits among authorities and within society, was often as essential a prerequisite for the mobilization of peasants for collective action as was peasant reinterpretation of tradition.

The three main groups of outsiders that influenced peasants were liberal zemstvo activists, the Third Element, and members of the radical parties. As we shall see, liberal zemstvo activists had an important role in assisting peasant mobilization in the spring and summer of 1905. The lines separating peasants, the Third Element, and members of radical parties were more blurred. Party members and zemstvo employees often came from peasant backgrounds and perhaps should not be considered outsiders at all. Still, because of their professional skills, Third Element people were active in founding many of the new cultural spaces in the village—reading rooms, cooperatives, temperance societies, and so on.

During 1905 they were concerned to protect the village cultural institutions they had done so much to promote and in many cases tried to restrain their communities from engaging in some of the more violent forms of collective action.

The influence of the radical parties was usually mediated through village leaders, often Third Element employees, who had different agendas. Direct contact with villagers was rare. According to Anikin, even in Saratov where it was better organized than elsewhere the SR intelligentsia had strong interaction with only 30 of the 210 large peasant settlements in Saratov District, and 21 of 280 in Petrovsk. The number of peasant brotherhoods in the province, usually containing eight to twelve people, according to one observer was about two hundred in the summer of 1905; but if Anikin is correct, this number may be too high.[37] Still, it would be unwise to conclude that the revolutionary parties had no influence at all. There is much to suggest that their influence was considerable and at times even crucial. Revolutionary party members were known to be active and at times assumed leadership in villages which either were repeatedly involved in collective action in the period 1902–06 or participated in the initial outbreaks of the peasant movement. Only for a few of the thirty-nine most active villages is it difficult to show the presence of revolutionary ties.

The SRs clearly had an important impact on the outbreak of disorders in Balashov District near Turki in 1902, and even though contagion more than direct contact was responsible for most of the estate destruction in the fall of 1905, the initial outbreaks in Atkarsk, Saratov, Serdobsk, and Petrovsk districts involved the participation of SR or SD agitators. Outsiders also helped to spark the strike wave that began in May 1906 in Berezovka, Atkarsk District. Revolutionary agitators, in particular, provided peasants with models of organization, a new language, and in some cases new tactics. They helped peasants to compose declarations, petitions, and instructions, and they circulated prototypes of these documents. They explained non-land issues and current political discourse, especially foreign-based words like "regime" and "corporation." They weaned some peasants from their beliefs in the tsar and religion and translated such traditional peasant concepts of customary law as the labor principle—God-created land to those who work it—to accord with political platforms calling for the socialization of the land.[38]

The biggest effect of the radical parties, though, may have been in the area of tactics. The peasant revolt in 1902–03 and early 1905 was mostly defensive, a reaction to state and gentry impingement on resources, and peasants resorted mainly to arson. To a large extent, the radical parties stressed more proactive tactics, such as land encroachments and invasions, as well as the ousting of local authorities and the use of boycotts and strikes. Over time, villagers increasingly adopted the use of these tactics, particularly as they saw the need for better organization and outside advice after the severe repression of late 1905. These new methods of protest showed the Saratov peasantry to be far from conservative. On the contrary, given the opportunity, they quickly and flexibly employed new strategies that went beyond the defense of old customs and challenged existing social relationships and state policy in a potentially revolutionary way. One observer, at least, believed that the revolutionary parties, despite being decimated by arrest, had more influence on the peasantry after October 1905. The shift in peasant tactics to strikes and boycotts in 1906 seems to corroborate this analysis, at least in part.[39]

Opportunity: Splits in the Elite and the Creation of Independent Spaces. Several historians, including John Bushnell, have recently stressed the importance of opportunity in the generation of peasant and soldier protest, noting in particular the fluctuating state of repressive forces, the impact of splits in the elite, and the crisis of authority faced by the tsarist bureaucracy, as first the Liberation Movement of 1902–04, then the urban revolution of 1905, and finally the State Duma of 1906 challenged it in successive waves. All these factors were important in promoting peasant unrest in Saratov Province. Bushnell has also stressed peasant dependence on outside authority, but while that was often important in the past and even in 1905–06, it ignores the desires of many peasants in certain large villages of Saratov Province to create independent social spaces, "declare themselves," and take responsibility for their political actions.[40]

Among the most important elite cleavages at the local level was that between Saratov gentry conservatives and gentry liberals. They split into something close to two political parties, differing on a number of issues, such as summer courses for teachers, agricultural labor laws, zemstvo suffrage reform, and the degree of power to be given Third Element professionals. This split in the elite allowed peasants to find allies and challenge authority more easily. Zemstvo liberal protection of the Third Element and active promotion of peasant interests in the summer of 1905 were important factors in spurring peasants to mobilize. Yet the relationship was reciprocal, with peasants to some extent *causing* splits and opportunity: the agrarian revolt of 1902 in Saratov, as well as in Poltava and Kharkov provinces, was one of the key factors that caused certain nobles to move leftward, seeking a way to bridge the social gulf in the hope of warding off revolution through reform. Liberals and nobles such as N. N. L'vov and S. A. Kotliarevskii were to play prominent roles in the Liberation Movement. Similarly, the conservative All-Russian Union of Landowners and the United Nobility had leaderships with a significant Saratov tinge, also partly the result of the strong peasant movement there in early 1905.[41] These divisions found an even more meaningful reflection in conflicts at the village level. Splits within the village between priests, on the one hand, and teachers, village clerks, and peasant leaders, on the other, were often the crucial factor in the mobilization of a particular village, as Scott Seregny details (chap. 6).

Opportunity, though, was not just a result of shifting splits in the ranks of non-peasants at the national and local levels, factors that predominate in the analyses of most historians who discuss the issue. Opportunity and tactical mobility were also created within the village by peasants themselves. They were the products not only of the cohesion of the commune and the economic position of the middle peasantry, as some historians mention, but they also resulted from the creation of social spaces that often allowed an independent peasant culture to flourish, free from elite hegemony. In Saratov Province, these spaces included a few large villages (which sometimes had a wide influence on surrounding hinterlands); hiring markets; peasant parks; forest meeting grounds; and village associations such as choirs, cooperatives, temperance societies, reading rooms, and so on. Here peasants could learn through outside contacts, break their reliance on kulaks and non-peasants, gain confidence in their own abilities, preserve their culture and distinctive ways of seeing, practice the mobilization of resources, assert their dignity, "declare themselves," and strive for social equality. While contagion played a definite role in the origins of peasant unrest, *individual* village collective action and the beginning of waves of protest in an area usually took place in locales where such social spaces existed. In these spaces, peasants could respond to opportunities created at the national level or to their own realistic or unrealistic hopes.[42]

Because they placed great emphasis on "book culture" as well as on literacy, and were more likely to scorn those who drank excessively or put too much stock in religious rituals, it was most often the village "youth" who set up the new institutional spaces, particularly in large villages where they could be supported. Such efforts could even lead to battles over space that had political overtones. In Irinovka, despite the attempt of the village priest to derail the effort, village youths bought forty-eight rubles worth of books and established a library, using the proceeds earned from renting and farming as an artel five acres of sunflowers. In another village, when youths found out that a priest had helped organize a Blackhundred fire brigade and was trying to incite it to attack their newly found cultural space, an agricultural society, they tarred the cleric's gate. Elsewhere there were reports of the poor controlling parts of certain villages and even demanding the splitting of a village or commune into two, "black" and "red," since a schism in basic attitudes had become unbridgeable.[43] In Ivanovka 2, where perhaps the most "conscious" peasants in Saratov Province lived, the establishment of a new credit cooperative led to the ousting of a local kulak usurer, who in revenge became a police spy. Here, too, the youth constructed a large park of which they were immensely proud. In a reversal of the frequent city practice of excluding the lower classes from certain spaces, the peasants christened their glade "a peasant park." In a manner reminiscent of a traditional charivari, these youth, or a specially formed guard, hooted and chased away non-peasants, particularly cossacks and police, if they tried to enter the park. The space was even maintained despite the pressure of the local priest and his family, who allegedly incited others to vandalize the park. The youths threatened to break a rib of each of the perpetrators for every sapling destroyed.[44]

An integral part of the process of change was an assertion of dignity and self-confidence. Among their demands, agricultural workers called for polite treatment and even separate living quarters for single and married workers, defending this latter request by saying that the employer himself had averred that "it is necessary to respect humanity." In another instance one Saratov gentry woman recounted that peasants would not yield the road as they had done in the past whenever a member of the upper classes approached in a carriage. Such actions proliferated after the turn of the century and bore witness to a new overt assertion of peasant self-dignity, so necessary to the manufacture of collective action and challenge to authority. Young peasants in particular exhibited a strong sense of their own dignity and desire for equality with other classes; observers remarked on the growth of a sense of identity and dignity reminiscent of that cultivated by gentry and intelligentsia youth who had protested against authority in the 1860s.[45]

PEASANT COLLECTIVE ACTION IN 1905

Peasant collective action, scattered throughout 1902–04, escalated dramatically in 1905. According to V. M. Gokhlerner, there were approximately eighty-five cases of peasant collective action between January and May 1905. The level of unrest grew over time and was higher than in most other provinces during the period, with many of the early cases attributable to long-running land disputes. The preferred form of peasant action in the first half of the year was arson, and numerous estates were virtually destroyed by burning. Other forms included unauthorized cutting of timber, illegal pasturage, plundering of grain stores and barns, and attacks on local authorities.[46] Although these acts were typical of all villages in this period, the dramatic events at Ivanovka 2 (Balashov District) best illustrate the social polarization and politicization of the village, the assertion of dignity, the new vehicles of protest, peasant cohesion, and other features of peasant development discussed in the previous pages. In Ivanovka 2, most of the inhabitants were reasonably well-off, owning an average of 17.6 acres per male adult peasant. Among the cultural spaces forged by the peasantry and crucial to the mobilization of protest were a reading room, a teahouse, a public park, a cooperative, and a five-class school. Magic lantern shows were frequently held. Speakers at the village assembly were even provided with a lectern. Peasants in Ivanovka 2 prided themselves on being politically conscious. According to one source, little heavy drinking occurred in the community and parents rarely beat their children. The *Ivanovtsy* had been active in 1902, and in late 1904 and early 1905 they joined the Banquet Campaign, organizing three such festive evenings. On January 17, 1905, they issued a declaration in which they proclaimed that they would not pay taxes and at the same time fired local village officials, replacing them with their own elected people. On February 19, the anniversary of the Emancipation, they organized a village demonstration replete with red flags and the singing of revolutionary songs.[47]

The most noteworthy act of the Ivanovka 2 peasants, though, was their compilation of the first important peasant political declaration in Russia, a response to the tsar's February 18 decree, which invited the public to submit petitions for political reform. The declaration was written by a twenty-year-old volost clerk by the name of L. Bychenkov and was ratified on March 29, 1905, by 156 of the 230 homeowners. In it, the peasants strongly objected to people who had seized the land and lived by the labor of others. Land was God's and belonged to everyone. The Ivanovtsy stressed other issues as well, particularly education and cultural backwardness. They charged that the authorities, including the priests, kept books from them, substituted parish schools that taught useless Old Church Slavonic, and chased away teachers whom the peasants had come to respect. "We have intellect and it is necessary not to obscure it but develop it in order to know what and how things happen in the world and why." Ivanovtsy also complained about high taxes and called for freedom of speech and press and an end to the law on strengthened security. They denounced the Russo-Japanese War and demanded the summoning of elected popular representatives who would state their needs truly and begin the restructuring of the state which the February 18 decree had promised.[48] The declaration boldly put forward the peasant viewpoint; no longer did privileged society have to guess who its adversaries were by deciphering anonymous letters or interpreting the message of yet another "red rooster" consuming yet another hayrick in the dead of night.

Governor Stolypin responded with alacrity to the challenge. He arrived in the village on April 29 and proclaimed himself tsar of the province, with the power to reduce Ivanovka 2 to dust. He demanded to know who had written the declaration and ordered the peasants to fall on their knees and beg forgiveness. No one moved until Bychenkov courageously accepted responsibility. Stolypin did not believe the young clerk, probably because the governor continued to have a mania for seeing the influence of revolutionaries everywhere and did not believe the peasantry capable of a declaration of such literary and political sophistication, even though Bychenkov wrote out a facsimile of it at Stolypin's command without access to the original. The governor locked the peasants in a building for two hours and harangued them, after issuing the threat that anyone who chose to speak back to him would suffer dire consequences. He finally left, and as part of his usual routine demanded within twenty-four hours the compilation of a new, submissive declaration which, in essence, he could use to cloak himself in legality in case there were charges that he had trampled on the peasants' right to petition the tsar. Twenty persons were arrested.[49]

Stolypin's actions failed to pacify Ivanovka 2. The peasants refused to reconsider the old declaration. Villagers pitched in to help the families of those arrested and sent money to the prisoners. When the latter returned home they became instant heroes. Parades of carts and horses decorated with red ribbons and green leaves ushered them into the village. Youth choirs sang the Peasant Marseillaise instead of traditional folk songs. Banquets without vodka were held even though it was the height of work season. May 1 was also celebrated by up to twenty "illuminations" (cases of arson) and a few street demonstrations in the area around Ivanovka 2 and Turki. Despite police repression, the villagers of Ivanovka 2 were to remain intransigent throughout 1905 and 1906. In the summer, partially as the result of a harvest failure, the peasants with great unanimity refused to pay rent, carted away grain from the fields of private land-owners, and pastured their sheep without authorization. They also cut back on emoluments given to priests and sent threatening letters to the police.[50]

The "parades," celebrations, banquets, and anointing of new heroes, the language of the declarations, the youth choirs, and even the hint of emerging socialist culture all suggest the formation of a new conscious-ness that drew on or transformed aspects of peasant tradition and jettisoned others. The cultural spaces they had created in their settle-ments promoted the mobilization of protest. Peasants in places like Ivanovka 2, in fact, proudly declared themselves members of the "con-scious" party and showed more interest in drawing inspiration from new peasant heroes than from a traditional naive faith in the tsar.[51]

The Ivanovka 2 declaration had influence far beyond the village. It was printed and circulated across Saratov Province, to many parts of Russia, and it even reached the émigré press. It was not the only one in the province, and the peasants of Saratov Province compiled more declarations in the spring and summer of 1905 than were compiled in most other regions. Invariably, the first demand of these declarations was the transfer of all land to those who worked it, according to the amount of land each could work by his own labor. This was one of the major tenets of the peasant moral economy. A second major demand was for educa-tion, and another was for equality before the law and an end to *soslovie* privileges. Other frequent demands included the convocation of a Constituent Assembly, freedom of speech and press, an end to the war, and abolition of indirect taxes. For instance, the peasants of Petrovka, in their declaration of June 24, 1905, complained that "We are withering away without learning like grass in a forest without light." Now, however, "comes a new time; to live without literacy and learning is shameful and no longer possible." They demanded access to all books, not just those written "for us on purpose." They also exhibited a firm sense of self-worth when they wrote: "The fields of distant and alien Manchuria are inundated with the blood of our fathers and brothers; why for us is there one set of laws, one set of judges and for other *sosloviia* different sets? There is no justice in such systems. We are also people and we demand that there be one law for all, merciful and fair, and that the authorities for their improper activities answer before an open and public court."[52]

Disturbing as these were—Governor Stolypin in July prohibited further attempts to compile such declarations—even more upsetting to authorities was the coming together of radical Third Element activists and peasants in meetings such as the Petrovsk District zemstvo economic council meeting on June 24, 1905. Despite the fact that it was held in the middle of harvest season, many peasants attended the meeting, where they accepted resolutions worked out by Stepan Anikin and other radicals. These, quite radical for the time, included a demand for the abolition of private property, since land was a gift from God. It was to be redistributed according to those who worked it (the issue of compensation was left purposely vague). The resolution also supported a progressive tax system, an end to censorship, and the convocation of a Constituent Assembly elected by all the people, regardless of sex, religious faith, education, or language. Local militias were to replace a standing army. Finally, those present declared themselves founders of the Petrovsk District Peasant Union and asserted their desire to work to carry out the resolutions and to inform the population of them. The provincial zemstvo also endorsed the peasant unions as a means to dampen class hostility and avert "civil war."[53]

The distribution of the Ivanovka 2 and the Petrovsk Economic Council resolutions and the support of some liberal zemstvo men seems to have spurred some villages to action in the summer of 1905. Stolypin's repression of the declaration campaign did likewise, proving the argument of the radical parties that hopes that peaceful tactics would bring about fundamental change were just so many "soap bubbles." If these actions were insufficiently persuasive, poor harvests in 1905 (60 percent of the average harvest and one-fourth of that collected in 1904) helped to transform peasant protest from a defensive to an offensive posture, as villages began not just to protect their own traditional resources but to seize those of others. In general, peasants felt they had little alternative but to seek fodder for their livestock either by encroaching on the pastureland of private-estate owners or seizing grain, green sunflowers, or hay. Peasants picked their targets carefully, though, and for the most part refused to act against those estate owners who were still willing to engage in any form of paternalistic welfare. When the police proved unable to suppress the summer encroachments, peasants became emboldened enough by autumn of 1905 to extend these activities farther through direct attacks at the heart of estates—the houses and barns of the landed elite.[54] According to Gokhlerner's figures, in the months of May–September there were 260 cases of peasant collective action; fifty villages were the sites of more than one instance. Arson was still the most frequent form of protest, but encroachments best characterized the movement in summer.[55]

Along with such collective actions, the peasants in the summer of 1905 demonstrated a new self-confidence and a new political orientation. They were anxious to make themselves heard; in Irinovka they asserted that "it is necessary . . . to declare that *we are here,* that we hate the old system and are prepared to struggle for a new one—in some manner to make ourselves known to the government and the revolutionaries." Some suggested terrorist acts, but a majority, encouraged by the rural intelligentsia, decided that a mass agricultural strike would suit their purposes better. Within a short time they had organized a work stoppage. When thirteen people were arrested, this action served to win over most of the village to the cause, since all were indignant that anyone should be deemed a criminal for asking for a raise in pay.[56] Besides strikes, encroachments, and arson, Saratov peasants in the spring and summer of 1905 demanded that nobles sell grain at a just price; challenged, replaced, or beat village officials and police; cut back on emoluments to the clergy or burned their grain; organized demonstrations; and held meetings with agitators in forests and ravines. In one or two cases villagers beat up estate managers. Wives of soldiers protested at zemstvo boards about delays in receiving their subsidies, and peasant women attempted to thwart many arrests by marching up to cossack horses in a prearranged tactic, usually with babies in their arms (some not their own). Commune members signed resolutions demanding that land only be rented to whole communities and not to individuals.[57]

As a result of all this activity, Stolypin spent almost the entire summer riding from village to village in an effort to contain the spreading unrest. On July 18, 1905, when he was traveling between the restive villages of Mikhailovka and Turki in Balashov District, two shots rang out from the bushes, barely missing the governor. Nevertheless he persisted, and by September six hundred peasants had been given prison terms for their role in agrarian disturbances in the first half of the year; in the village of Medvedevka alone, seventy persons had been carted away. And the massive destruction of estates in the fall had not yet even begun![58]

In autumn 1905 pillaging and burning of estates increased dramatically. Two hundred and seventy-two estates were plundered, set fire to, and virtually destroyed in Saratov Province that fall, and about three hundred were to meet such a fate in the course of 1905. These represented 31.3 percent of the 772 estates destroyed in European Russia, six times more than the average number of estates decimated in other provinces. Whether a *pomeshchik* was liberal or conservative seems to have made little difference to peasants. Nor did the social class of landowners; during the October–December period, the estates of most large private landowners—whether gentry, merchant, or kulak—were attacked. Although the peasants vented their anger by destroying the property of private landowners, they almost completely refrained from violence against the person of an estate owner. In this sense they were much less violent than the punitive expeditions, sent to suppress the collective action, which beat and killed numerous peasants. Peasants tended to resort to personal violence only when they met with forcible resistance, and they were most likely to use it against non-gentry renters or recent buyers who were from outside the local area, as they were deemed to have immorally taken away local resources.[59]

The actual destruction of estates in most instances was preplanned and not a sudden and spontaneous act. The villagers listened to peasant agitators from their own and other communes, elected people to serve in the armed detachments that were to lead the attacks on the estates, determined ways to procure new weapons, and discussed the best method of spreading protest elsewhere. Even the flags, songs, and dress many peasants adopted seemed to reflect a pride in the very fact that they had adopted new tactics. Interestingly, the most popular slogans— "Struggle for Freedom" and "Freedom or Death"—evinced a primary concern less about the land than about politics and a desire for a change in the social structure. Songs sung as the marchers left the village were invariably revolutionary. They often adopted resolutions justifying their actions in advance and offering rational moral arguments for their actions rather than manipulating the symbols of outside power. Some declared that peasants were taking back land that had belonged to their ancestors or that their economic status was deteriorating thanks to immoral landowner practices. Some of the resolutions were outright political, criticizing the current government, urging its overthrow, or demanding that legal estates be abolished and officials and police boycotted or replaced. Legitimate authority was now explicitly declared to reside in new institutions: land was to be provisionally divided up equally until the spring, when the Duma or a Constituent Assembly could meet. Other resolutions challenged the traditional political, economic, and social system at the local level. Peasants resolved to get rid of priests, elect new village officials, appoint estate managers, lower rent prices, end otrabotka, and force estates to rent out land to rich and poor peasants alike or to the commune as a whole rather than to individual peasants.[60]

Given the threat of starvation and the tardiness with which the government adopted relief measures, it is hardly surprising that grain was the most popular item confiscated when peasants attacked estates. The task of hauling away grain was one of mammoth proportions. In some instances two and a half days were needed to haul it all away. In one case, five hundred carts were used, while in another it took twenty hours for sixty wagons to take away 342 tons of grain. Though there were cases of peasants hauling away gilded pieces of furniture and fancy dresses, such pilfering was more the exception than the rule. The main purpose was culture-smashing. Boys and girls would run around a house breaking windows in with sticks. Parquet floors, Bohemian crystal, mirrors, glass sideboards and wardrobes, porcelain, Japanese miniatures, marble statues, foreign artwork—anything that smacked of superfluous Western culture collected by noblemen at peasant expense while village children were growing up undernourished—these objects bore the brunt of peasant anger and were often smashed to smithereens. Belokurov, a peasant leader, was amazed at the extent to which peasants would go to vent their ire: "For example, one peasant, holding in his hands a heavy stick, pounded it, with all his strength, into some piled up storm windows, endangering the eyes of those surrounding [him], since from his blows fragments flew in all directions. It was impossible to stop him; he was filled with a thirst for revenge against his eternal oppressors and was conscious of nothing else."[61]

Peasants burned estate buildings less out of a desire for vengeance than for rational tactical considerations, which later proved largely correct. They wanted literally to smoke out the landed magnates so that they could not easily return and might even consider selling out, especially as insurance claims increasingly went unpaid. They also hoped that land prices might fall and that there would be no place to house troops. If soldiers had to lodge in village huts, it was thought, they could be more easily won over to the peasant cause. Finally, given the paucity of rifles and other arms in the village, arson was one of the few weapons available to the peasants.[62]

The influence of the revolutionary parties, non-peasant intelligentsia, and outside events on peasant collective action in the fall of 1905 was extremely complex. For one thing, unlike in other provinces, the railroad strike was more important than the October Manifesto for the instigation of protest in Saratov; rural unrest occurred first along the railroad lines and at railroad grain storage depots in many places.[63] Outside agitators often played a role, and collective action frequently broke out first in places where the influence of outside revolutionaries and supravillage forces can be discerned. Their role, and its relation to longstanding grievances, is well demonstrated by events in the largely Mordvinian village of Sukhoi Karbulak in Saratov District. It had a long history of land disputes, and in the 1890s peasants there and in neighboring villages even took the incredible step of petitioning the king of Denmark, begging him to make his son-in-law, Alexander III, recognize their claims. When this peaceful means of appeal failed, they engaged in arson, sabotaged dams, pastured livestock on the disputed land, besieged the governor's house in Saratov, and even marched on the courthouse during trials. When part of the land was sold, they refused to let the outsiders work it.

However, the initial spark for estate plunder and burning in the autumn of 1905 in Sukhoi Karbulak seems to have been the arrival of two SR agitators, who told the peasants that now was the time to chase the pomeshchiki from their estates. Similarly, at Nikolaevskii Gorodok the arrival of two SD agitators, along with news of the October general strike, seems to have sparked events there that led to the establishment of a virtual mini-republic. The ousting of local officials, the establishment of virtual mini-republics in such places as Balanda and Ol'khovka, and attacks on some forty-five state liquor stores, often the only symbol of the state in the village, tended to occur in large villages where peasants had had connections with one of the radical parties or the Peasant Union. Nevertheless, peasant leaders who in the past had had close ties with radicals such as those in the darstvennik village of Irinovka, not far from Saratov, reported that they had had no contact with non-peasant party agitators between August and October and were moved to act and "declare themselves," not because of the assistance of outside radicals, but in protest against the latters' condescension and indifference. In most places, apparently, outside agitators played no discernible role in disturbances.[64]

Saratov village actions attracted outside notice and influenced national events. One such was the particularly harrowing incident that occurred in the relatively poor village of Malinovka, Serdobsk District, of which a procurator wrote, "As to the horror done, it scarcely has an equal in the entire history of Russian justice." Here, one neighborhood in the village fell under the sway of a former soldier, Sinev, who began to struggle with the local priest for cultural supremacy over the village and allegedly called the tsar a "bloodsucker." Some of Sinev's followers organized an attack on the estate of a local landowner. In the village the priest's house was burned, and although it is unclear who was responsible, it allowed the Blackhundred element to round up support in neighboring villages using bribe money and gave rise to rumors that orthodox churches were being defiled. Soon a lynch party was formed, thanks in part to the tacit or active support of members of the clergy, the police, and the land captain. Forty-two "conscious" peasants were sought out in premeditated fashion and systematically murdered one at a time over the course of five days. Some were beaten and then stabbed in the eyes or chest with pitchforks. Others had either their ears or nose chopped off before they were killed; sometimes they were shot in the mouth. Five or six of those killed were from villages other than Malinovka. No one was punished for these murders.[65]

The Malinovka incident attracted national attention, which exaggerated and distorted events and had an important influence on the debate at the national congress of the Peasant Union meeting in Moscow on November 6–10. The mostly SR-leaning Saratov delegates found themselves castigated for the province's violence. They were desperate to get the congress to take a firm stand because, unlike in much of the rest of Russia, the agrarian movement in their province had already erupted in all its fury and the delegates wanted immediate support in order to neutralize the punitive expeditions being launched at the beginning of November. However, the *Saratovtsy* soon found themselves isolated on the left wing of the congress, unable to convince others, on the one hand, of the urgency of the situation in the province and, on the other, that contrary to press reports few if any landowners had been killed and bulls had not been carved up in churches. Therefore their appeal for congress support for an armed uprising was defeated: 30 opposed, 15 for, and 12 supportive of the tactic only as a last resort. The majority backed the more peaceful tactics of a general strike and boycotts. The Saratov delegates in the end were only able to salvage a resolution that gave pride of place to Saratov peasants in the events of the fall; one of the sentences of the final declaration said that all the years of gentry and state oppression had only led to "an uprising of the peasants of Saratov Province and disturbances in twenty-three other provinces."[66]

As might be expected, the resolutions of the Saratov provincial Peasant Union meeting in December were much more radical than those of the national congress. Delegates, including many non-peasants, voted to end private property in land by a count of 50 to 1 and resolved 49 to 2 to transfer without compensation all land fairly to the working people, who were not to be allowed to employ wage labor. The resolution called for the election of all officials by universal equal and secret suffrage. The most radical section urged peasants to arm themselves, first, for protection against government terrorism and, second, to guarantee the convocation of a Constituent Assembly. Soldiers returning from Manchuria were to be encouraged to free arrested peasants and to set up temporary governments. Villagers were urged to compile declarations exhorting soldiers to refuse to fight the people or face boycotts upon return home from service.[67] This resolution took place too late in the year to have much effect on the nature of direct peasant collective action in the province in 1905, since most of it had occurred in October and early November. Nor was the Peasant Union boycott of the Duma heeded. Still, the December congress's emphasis on the use of combined rent and labor strikes to shut down estate operations and its call for a boycott of taxes, conscription, the liquor monopoly, and officials currently having jurisdiction over villagers were important for determining the types of tactics that peasants would choose in 1906.

The government responded vigorously to the peasant actions. Although armed force had been used earlier, often led by Governor Stolypin himself, its use gained momentum after the November 3 arrival of a large expeditionary detachment commanded by General Sakharov. This and other government forces made little attempt to distinguish between the guilty and the innocent. If those singled out as examples denied their guilt, they were handed over to cossacks who beat them mercilessly, pulling out hair and cutting off bits of flesh. Beatings were the norm because prisons were overcrowded and the authorities felt such punishment was the best way to reestablish a sense of inferiority among the peasants. Invariably villagers were also made to cart back grain they had taken from local estates. As a final indignity, to cloak the actions of the authorities in a veil of legality, peasants were often forced against their wills to compile resolutions that accused fellow villagers of crimes and exiled them to Siberia. Such acts freed police from having to gather evidence and prove their case in court. Cossacks, and less often soldiers, also stole property and committed a number of rapes.[68]

Terrorists, mainly SRs, tried to strike back and to raise peasant morale by assassinations. In late November, General Sakharov received what he thought was a woman landowner in his office. She handed him a petition and, as the general finished reading what one report claims was actually an SR death sentence, she fired four shots point-blank at him, killing him. The Saratov Peasant Union at its December Congress hailed the heroism of this SR activist, Bitsenko, and demanded her release from prison. Vice Governor Knol' was the target in March of 1906; while Stolypin was the intended victim of five such attempts in 1905 and early 1906. However, the threats on his family's lives and attempts on his own did not deter him from marching in full dress uniform into one village after another, and sometimes won him grudging respect. Stolypin was even able to cow revolutionaries by his quick thinking under pressure. In one village, while he was haranguing peasants who had illegally felled some timber, he noticed a man approaching somewhat awkwardly. At the last instant, Stolypin threw the stranger his cloak and ordered him to hold it. The latter, completely nonplussed, succumbed to his ingrained instincts and did as he was told, failing to wield the ax that he had tucked under his coat. As Stolypin finished his speech, the man, who turned out to be a member of an SR brotherhood, was led away to prison.[69]

The conservative Saratov nobility, which helped found the national "Union of Landowners" and provided leaders for the "United Nobility," exhibited a new organizational strength in various ways too. First, several conservative nobles took over the provincial zemstvo assembly and board and then purged the Third Element and cut back on social programs. Second, they supported efforts to organize right-wing activity in the village. While the Blackhundreds were never very strong in rural Saratov Province, their presence was evident even in such restive large villages as Turki, Samoilovka, Lopatino, and Urleika. The third way in which convervatives, and for that matter most nobles owning medium or large estates, exhibited their power was to hire estate guards, including cossacks. By the end of 1905, most estates resembled armed camps. Landowners traveled around protected by cossack retinues. Guards were ordered to shoot at anything that moved on estates at night. The forces of reaction mobilized various other means of action as well. Police detachments were stationed in larger villages, a move that further radicalized peasants. Peasants were beaten, exiled, sometimes killed. Others languished in prison, and families faced economic disaster. Authorities also cracked down on those manifestations of popular culture, such as night-courting, which had often served as covers for radical activity, but this only further alienated the villagers, since it politicized even more the spheres of everyday life. Peasants, though, often struck back. Various boycotts of police took place in larger villages, village women presented the authorities with their children's toy guns when weapon searches were made, and hunger strikes occasionally were engaged in by peasants in prison. By 1906 many estate guards and cossacks had begun to sympathize with peasants, and the job of land captain became so unpopular that of seventy vacancies for the post in 1906, only nineteen candidates could be found to fill the position.[70]

PROVINCIAL ELECTIONS AND THE DUMA

Despite the repressive measures of the winter of 1905–06, the peasantry steadfastly stuck to their views of their rights and showed new flexibility in striving to achieve them, as is well reflected in the elections to the first State Duma in early 1906. They ignored the calls of the SDs, SRs, and Peasant Union for a boycott and sought to elect delegates who would press their point of view. They resisted not only the boycott calls of the left but also the attempts from the right to influence the elections. Persistent and clumsy efforts by authorities to control elections served to harden peasant resolve to elect their own spokesmen, as did claims by outsiders to represent peasant interests; peasant delegates to an electoral meeting contrasted the dress of the Kadets with their own and derided the liberal party's conception of justice, especially on the issue of compensation for land expropriation, calling it "gentlemen's fairness." One village delegate illustrated the peasant perspective. Facetiously apologizing for speaking *po-muzhitskii,* he counterposed the peasant concept of land as belonging to those who worked it to elite conceptions of private property and condemned the land cut-offs at the time of Emancipation as robbery—a violation of the moral economy.[71]

However, the peasants looked to spokesmen rather than insisting on electing only peasants. Many of the chosen delegates had nonagricultural jobs, although most, including the five elected from the volosts to the Duma, had a good knowledge of farming or worked the land part-time. Among those elected delegates at the volost level whose occupation can be determined were six teachers, eight volost elders, four zemstvo deputies, two shopkeepers, two volost or village clerks, two paramedics, as well as a lawyer, volost judge, sexton, village elder, trader, liquor-store clerk, and railroad administrator. Several of those elected had prison records or were currently in jail. Peasants believed that a stint behind bars indicated a commitment to the cause. In many of the volosts dominated by large "conscious" villages such as Balanda, Khovanshchina, Sinenkie, Annenkovo, and Sokur, the candidates chosen were young, between twenty and thirty years old. Of the five delegates elected at volost assemblies who eventually made it to the Duma, three were between thirty-four and thirty-seven and the other two were in their early forties. Literacy, education, knowledge of the outside world, and ability to articulate and firmly uphold peasant interests were usually the most important characteristics peasant electors looked for. The sway of traditional patriarchal power seems to have been in decline in Saratov villages. The overall composition of the delegates suggests that peasants actively supported the rural intelligentsia and by 1906 had seen through the anti-intelligentsia propaganda of early 1905.[72]

Saratov peasants in a number of ways showed more sophistication in their election tactics than peasants from other provinces. In Kamyshin, Atkarsk, Petrovsk, and probably other districts they held preelection meetings which eventually assured that all the delegates from the volost assemblies sent to the provincial election meeting held positions to the left of the Kadets. To a large extent, the credit for these preelection meetings, including three or four held before the April 15, 1906, provincial elections, belonged to Stepan Anikin. Through articles written in the Menshevik-leaning newspaper *Privolzhskii krai* and his own short-lived peasant-oriented *Golos derevni,* he called for the formation of a union of laboring people and helped to formulate a platform on which future instructions to Duma deputies were modeled. He wanted the peasants to merge with the Union of Laboring People *(Soiuz Trudiashchikhsia),* a sort of Union of Unions in the city of Saratov. The Saratov Union of Laboring People was the prototype for the later Trudovik Group in the State Duma, which was to a great degree led by Saratov deputies Zhilkin, Anikin, Ul'ianov, and Bondarev. It was yet another way in which local events in Saratov Province were to affect national ones. Saratov peasants also showed sophistication by reaching an understanding with the Kadets on an election strategy even though they distrusted the liberals. Learning from mistakes peasants had made in early elections in other provinces, peasant electors allowed two liberals to win but ensured themselves eight of the ten local Duma seats, guaranteeing that the Saratov delegation was the most radical sent to the national assembly.[73]

The input of the Saratov villagers did not end with the elections. Saratov peasants, especially those in large, restive villages, sent numerous petitions, instructions, and resolutions to their representatives and the Duma—more than any other province. The question of the representativeness of the resolutions with regard to peasant attitudes is a complex one, but by and large these documents seem to be authentic expressions of the will of the village. If the desire to proclaim their existence was evident in decisions to launch strikes and hold peasant congresses in 1905, in 1906 peasants were putting such sentiments in their declarations. As one such document phrased it, "We, the peasants from Nikolaevka, presenting ourselves as a fragment of Russia's population, cannot remain apathetic onlookers of all that took place around us, because it is painful and distressing to hear about those bloody horrors that are occurring in all parts of Russia and also because, given the existing system of administration, our life has become insufferable, difficult, degraded, and devoid of rights."[74]

According to one survey, of 77 Saratov declarations sent to the Duma deputies, there were 46 demands for land, 42 political demands, 28 calls for amnesty, and 26 expressions of support for Duma deputies. Among the other demands made were abolition of the death penalty, an end to martial law, elimination of the State Council, free elementary school education, equal access to higher education, freedom of speech, assembly, and press, the end of *sosloviia,* elimination of the office of land captain, abolition of the gendarmes, local control of the police, formation of local militia to replace the army, introduction of the volost zemstvo, accountability of officials and judges to public supervision, more agronomic help, elimination of indirect taxes, implementation of a progressive tax, and separation of church and state. Peasants also showed concern about supravillage issues now and then, including demands for better treatment of soldiers, an eight-hour work day, and the vote for women.[75]

It appears that peasants often viewed the Duma deputies as an alternative authority. They asked deputies for advice, protection against cossacks and estate guards, or help against an unjust court or prison system. Land Settlement Commissions were boycotted because peasants claimed that only the Duma deputies had the right to decide the land issue. The Duma deputies became popular heroes. Postcard photographs of them surpassed even religious icons and portraits of the tsar in popularity in the city of Saratov.[76] Many Saratov peasants were obviously following the Duma debates closely; they snapped up newspapers when they arrived by train, quoted deputies' speeches, and in their telegrams and resolves noted specific dates of deputies' resolutions and state responses. The Duma deputies' battle with the bureaucracy, like that of teacher versus priest at the local level, also forced peasants to take sides and articulate positions. Alternative ways of seeing gained legitimacy, and the willingness of Duma deputies to stand up for their vision of progress encouraged peasants to do the same. The split at the national level, caused in large part by peasant votes in the Duma elections, also suggested to peasants that their opportunity to act might yield results.

As time passed in the spring of 1906, however, Saratov peasants began to show less and less faith in parliamentary solutions to their problems. Peasant declarations soon began to complain about the lack of resolve in solving the land and other issues. Even more striking was their quick reaction to the government declaration of May 13 reaffirming the inviolability of private property. A journalist in Serdobsk District wrote that the peasants saw it as a rejection of village expectations, "and the village, for its part, already has begun to react: the district burns." In Saratov Province more than elsewhere, the May 13 declaration seems to have been the breaking point for the most "conscious" peasants, and they reacted with alacrity. The government was discredited, and there was an immediate upsurge in peasant unrest. Overall, the declaration had a greater impact than the June 20 communiqué which termed compulsory expropriation "inadmissable" or than the dissolution of the Duma on July 8–9.[77]

PEASANT COLLECTIVE ACTION IN 1906

After a lull from late December through mid-March of 1906, collective action accelerated, reaching a peak in mid-May through July. In addition to existing sources of unrest, two new ingredients added to peasant frustration. The first was the May 13 ministerial rejection of the Duma's agrarian program, which dashed peasant hopes for a peaceful resolution of their grievances through the Duma. The second factor was the threat and actuality of starvation. The poor harvest of 1905 was virtually identical with yields registered in the famine year of 1891, and hence reserves were very small. The harvest of 1906 promised to be even lower, and so it proved to be; the yield of rye in 1906 in Saratov Province was 19 percent of the average harvest in the period 1899–1904, and not more than 10 percent in Balashov, Atkarsk, Saratov, and Volsk districts.[78]

Unrest continued to be greatest in 1906 in the same five districts as before, with Atkarsk (132), Saratov (110), Serdobsk (106), Balashov (54), and Petrovsk (41) accounting for 443 of the 535 cases, and with the thirty-nine large villages still centers of revolutionary activity. Tactics, however, shifted once again, reflecting peasants' ability to respond flexibly to changing circumstances and opportunities. The fierce repression of late 1905, the continuing presence of large numbers of cossacks and estate guards, the arrest of both rural party agitators and many of the most "conscious" peasants, and increased activity of conservative forces meant that Saratov peasants faced a more formidable opposition than peasants in other provinces. In many instances they saw that direct attacks on estates, as carried out in fall 1905, would now be suicidal. Arson continued to account for the largest number of incidents, but in 1906 relatively peaceful strikes and boycotts, which were less likely to provoke repressive measures, began to increase relative to arson and pillaging of estates. With the increase in strikes, moreover, the number of participants in the agrarian movement of 1906 may have been larger than in 1905, when cases of arson were often carried out anonymously by individuals or small groups.[79]

Given the pressures and repressive forces they now faced, Saratov peasants in 1906 increasingly recognized the need for united action among villages, and even the need to support the demands of migrant laborers. In many cases, four or five villages struck together, while there were several instances in which ten or more communities supported the same demands. Strikes were usually organized through the communal assembly and the resolutions sometimes taken by messengers to other villages to get them to compile similar documents. Peasants threatened those who refused to join the strikes with arson, fines, boycotts, and confiscation of tools or allotment land and warned that those who stood apart would be kept off lists for seeds and food relief. The coordination of strike activity in Saratov, particularly among villages, was perhaps the strongest in European Russia, with the possible exception of the Right-Bank Ukraine and Baltic areas.[80]

The flexibility and sophistication of Saratov peasants was also manifest in combined rent and labor strikes, at times aimed at driving the gentry to lease or sell off their entire estates. Such tactics struck at the ability of landowners to play the rent market against the labor and grain markets, switching to whichever was more advantageous at any particular time. Strike resolutions usually called for lowering of lease rates. Occasionally they also proposed that land be rented closer to the village or be of better quality and that payment should not have to precede the removal of crops from the fields. Sometimes peasants demanded the abolition of otrabotka, and a few communes resolved that only the entire commune should be permitted to lease land, which seemingly reflected a desire for social leveling.[81]

Agricultural worker strikes mainly focused on higher wages, although quite often other issues were raised. Peasant laborers wanted such things as better food, shorter hours, overtime pay, more reliable medical help, abolition of piecework and fines, removal of estate guards, replacement of certain stewards, and so on. Prevention of deceptive hiring and pay practices was an issue reflected in demands for control over hiring markets, for daily settling of accounts, and similar measures. Some strikers demanded polite treatment, which may have expressed a desire for a change in traditional social relations; and some strove to replace local officials.[82]

Although few of the rent or labor strike statements included overtly political demands, that did not mean peasants were apolitical. They knew that landowners could or would do little by themselves to satisfy peasant demands. Therefore, many of the most conscious villages involved in strikes in the period from late May to July sent declarations full of radical political demands to their Duma deputies in May and June.[83]

The most remarkable event in all of rural Saratov in 1906, and one that can stand as an illustration of the strike activity, occurred in the hiring market of Arkadak, which from at least as far back as the early 1880s had been the scene of many protests. The darstvennik village of Arkadak was the hub of a 32,400-acre estate belonging to Prince L. D. Viazemskii, who, like other Saratov landowners, employed both progressive agricultural practices and retrogressive hiring actions. From a distinguished aristocratic family with close ties to the court, State Council member Viazemskii tried to replicate some of the most up-to-date methods he had experimented with during his stewardship of the tsar's properties. He organized a well-integrated agricultural system. Timber from his forests was used to fuel a distillery that produced vodka from potatoes harvested from ever-expanding acreage. In turn, even the distillery waste was made use of as feed for livestock. Scientific management of his estate operations, which proved economically efficient, was not, however, matched by a socially progressive policy of labor and peasant relations. Viazemskii purposely rented the peasants only enough land to support them at bare subsistence level, in the hope of ensuring a potential labor force nearby at little cost and forcing it to work for him.[84]

Restive throughout 1905, by spring of 1906 the Arkadak peasants were ready to act. In April they asked the estate manager to exchange the far fields normally leased to them for ones closer to the village, and to lower the price of rent; he was unwilling to give a definitive answer to the request. By mid-June, a significant number of migrant laborers (probably around six hundred) and a slightly smaller number of local laborers had arrived in the Arkadak hiring market. The local day-laborers chose this moment to start a strike by ensuring that no one went into the fields. The usual pattern of the communal assembly running the strike was eschewed and the innovative step of electing a strike committee was taken. The voters included villagers from Arkadak and several surrounding villages. Migrants apparently also had some say in the committee's composition. As was often the case in rural collective action, a local cobbler, Grigorii Savich, was a principal organizer and chairman of the election assembly. An urban worker appears to have played an important role as well. The strike committee fashioned a rostrum from an old crate for medicines, and numerous speeches were given, sometimes ending with the strikers shouting in unison, "Land!" Besides the rent demands were others concerning wages and working conditions, the primary one being for 40 rubles' pay per 10.8 acres harvested.[85]

Disillusioned by the lack of results in the Duma, the *Arkadaktsy* decided to act on their own, as the strike committee staged a de facto coup d'état by taking over the functions of a local government, an action that eventually brought the governor to Arkadak for a confrontation. The committee kept law and order, closed down the state liquor store, prohibited local bootleggers from operating, banned gambling on pitch-and-toss games, and even dispensed justice, sentencing two workers who had stolen cucumbers from Viazemskii's garden to sweep out the barracks that housed migrant laborers. The relief station for migrant workers was used as a facility through which the strike committee could organize the feeding and maintenance of its adherents. Beyond this, the committee began a relatively successful drive to support migrant laborers. This effort netted money, as well as grain and millet for the preparation of food. Peasants in the vicinity of the gentry magnate Naryshkin's estate even demanded and won the free maintenance of migrant laborers from Penza Province directly on the estate for the duration of the strike. When the collections appeared to be insufficient to support the growing numbers of migrant laborers, the strike committee sent home those workers who lived nearby for as long as the strike lasted so that they could be supported without exhausting the committee's resources.[86]

From Arkadak the strike eventually spread to encompass forty-three or more communes, including such earlier restive villages as Makarovo, Sestrenki, Trubetskoe, and Ivanovka 2 (which, along with Kazachka, served as a second strike center). Even Krasnoiar joined in, the Black-hundred village boycotted by its neighbors in 1905. Villages fifty miles away refused to send strikebreakers when Viazemskii's stewards tried to recruit them. Other social elements supported the protest, and the Arkadak events served to polarize practically all of local society. The laborers at Viazemskii's vodka distillery joined the strike, while railroad employees in the vicinity also stopped work. The physician Berdichevskii and the three main Saratov newspapers supported the strike. Viazemskii accused the Balashov police captain of showing "open sympathy" with the strikers, who in the opinion of the captain were waging a "peaceful struggle of labor with capital." Even the prince's estate guards proved restive and were unwilling to beat the peasants into submission as they had the year before.[87]

As the strike unfolded, Prince Viazemskii was pushed into an increasingly desperate position. The peasants had wisely struck at both his rent and labor options simultaneously. Local society was largely arrayed against him. The police and cossacks offered lukewarm support at best. Provocateurs and planted vodka failed to produce results. Some other employers had even begun to compromise with striking peasants. As a result, Viazemskii at first raised his wage offers but then withdrew them and in the end refused to yield. He seems, perhaps rightly, to have seen more at stake than wage and rent prices and to have been very alarmed by some of the strike committee's demands, such as the right to limit work hours, oversee harvest measurement, eliminate piecework, and ensure committee sanction before any workers could be hired or fired. Besides such demands, which teetered on the edge of a sort of primitive workers' control, the committee had virtually wrested control over local affairs from the prince's hands; this last was most graphically seen in a symbolic battle over space, when the committee insisted that the prince's son come to the strike headquarters to negotiate rather than their coming to him.[88]

Whatever the actual case, Viazemskii clearly saw Arkadak as being in "the hands of revolutionaries" and viewed the struggle as one of control over local resources. Sensing the broader issues, he wrote to his son: "I would sooner reconcile myself to the loss of all my rye than accept the laws of some base committee, whose days are numbered."[89] Indeed, his vast resources, of which the rye crop was a minor part, allowed him to take a firm stand.

Viazemskii's prestige and personal ties also proved to be formidable weapons. He induced the new governor, Tatishchev, to come and put down the strike by force. The latter reopened the liquor store in Arkadak, halted the collection of strike funds, and made arrests. These actions eventually brought an end to the strike after more than two weeks. Workers had been able to force employers to come up somewhat from their initial wage offers, but the police interference, the desperate straits of the migrant laborers, and the poor harvest all militated against peasants realizing their dreams.[90]

Besides strikes, another prominent feature of the 1906 agrarian movement in Saratov Province was the number of boycotts and protests leveled at priests, police, and state authorities that usually took place in large villages with histories of unrest. These took many forms. As noted by Gerasimenko (chap. 10), boycotts of the land settlement commissions were widespread, especially in the five most restive districts. Tax boycotts were also frequent. In some instances, the boycott action was applied against military conscription, but in most cases the recruits did show up after staging demonstrations replete with revolutionary songs (which sometimes brought support from other people as well).[91]

Peasants also used boycotts to challenge the authority of the clergy, who according to some observers were in many cases more reactionary in Saratov Province than elsewhere. Given the political views of many Saratov peasants, the comparatively high level of the flight of priests and community exiling of clerics from the province should not be surprising. Peasants in such traditionally restive villages as Makarovo, Teplovka, Malaia Dmitrievka, and Kamennyi Brod actually drove priests from their village. In the case of Salamatino, this was the final act in a long series of actions taken against the clergy, landowners, and the state that included strikes, radical declarations to the Duma, arson, illegal pasturage, invasion and division of gentry land, refusals to billet soldiers, attempts to prevent arrests, and cutback of support given to the clergy. Elsewhere peasants resorted to less drastic measures in challenging the authority of priests by refusing to allow them into their homes, cutting back on emoluments and perquisites such as wood allotments, taking away land, and burning grain. Villagers also protected members of the rural intelligentsia from local authorities and from attacks by priests and the reactionary Bishop Germogen.[92]

By the end of July 1906, with the dissolution of the Duma and the onset of fierce repression, the agrarian movement in the province began to die out, only reviving in a few places in 1907. What had the peasants gained? Land, for one thing. Despite repressions, some peasants did reap partial success from their collective action. To some extent violence worked. Because of it, especially estate destruction, the number of estates and land sold in Saratov in 1906 and 1907 was much larger than in most other provinces. Between November 1, 1905, and January 1, 1907, 503 estates with an area of 1,908,900 acres were sold to the Peasant Land Bank. The vast majority of these estates were located in the five most restive districts.[93] Although these sales were extensive, not all peasants benefited equally. According to one author, it was often not the very rich or very poor peasants who got use of this new land, but middle peasants, whom their fellow villagers dubbed the "new pomeshchiki."[94] The landless poor and darstvenniki not only often did not benefit from land sales, they also gained little from the abolition of redemption dues on land. However, the rent and wage strikes of 1906 led, at least temporarily, to better conditions. Rent prices fell between 2 and 3 rubles per desiatina in the five most restive districts between 1904 and 1906. A survey of some of the wage strikes indicates that in fifteen out of twenty-three cases in which results were recorded, the workers' demands were satisfied. According to another report, wages in Saratov Province in 1906 were slightly above the average for the years 1902–04. This slight increase suggests that the strikes were quite successful if the extremely poor harvest of 1906, which lessened demand for labor, is kept in mind.[95]

Despite the relative peasant success, most reports concerning the Saratov countryside suggest that all the major social groups, including peasants, the gentry, and estate guards, were disgruntled with their fate after 1905–06. Many felt insecure, dissatisfied, fearful of the future. Peasants felt that they had not achieved their goals and resented the repressive measures used against them; many families had members in jail or exile. Those who had gained land felt their position to be precarious. The gentry moved about surrounded by guards.

The measure of goodwill toward gentry landowners that had sometimes been evident in the autumn of 1905 had dissipated. Then, some landowners had actually been warned to take their families away, as an attack was imminent; this no longer happened. The fierce repression at the end of 1905 and the continued presence of estate guards and cossacks served to increase peasant anger toward the landed elite. Growing peasant hostility was apparent to one observer, who noted that now there were more cases of manor house windows being smashed or gentry dogs being poisoned, particularly after the Duma had been prorogued and the strike wave had crested, leaving peasants frustrated but too scared to attempt overt collective action.[96] The estrangement between the peasantry and the landed elite was to last until 1917, when the gentry to a large extent were routed out of their nests once and for all.

The agrarian movement of 1902–06 in Saratov Province was arguably the most intense in all Russia. There the movement was dominated not by economic strata within the village, but by the larger villages acting cohesively, particularly in the northwestern districts. Not only were these villages confronted most dramatically by changing economic relations with large surrounding estates, perceived locally as violations of moral norms, but they possessed local institutions and cultural spaces that facilitated defense of their perceived rights. Peasants in the larger villages were also better connected to towns, had more ongoing contact with outsiders, and in the short period from 1902 to 1906 seem to have overcome village parochialism to a greater extent than other peasants. Moreover, Saratov's vibrant urban political culture played a role in stimulating villages to action; contacts with radicals, for example, were often crucial to the initial outbreak of disturbances. The large villages were more likely to be exposed to national conflicts articulated at the local level, as when priests and Third Element or peasant youth battled for cultural supremacy or when repressive forces intervened, often making the situation worse by their harassment of peasants and politicization of everyday life and culture. Saratov Province, more than elsewhere, was the scene of a sophisticated but often raucous debate among persons ably representing all segments of the political spectrum; peasants, as well as other social groups, were forced to clarify where they stood. This experience, and that gained during frequent rent negotiations, lawsuits, and contacts with state officials involved with conscription, the Peasant Land Bank, tax collection, and food loans, helped to spawn a more politically aware peasantry and leaders whose skills were honed enough to function adeptly at the local, and occasionally national, level in an assertive and confident manner.

Therefore it is hardly surprising that Saratov's large villages were not solely concerned with the land question but raised broader issues of political reform and the fundamental democratization of local institutions and social relations. More than other villages in 1905–06, they ousted local officials, established mini-republics, boycotted taxes, priests, and police, attacked state liquor stores, combined rent and labor strikes, compiled political declarations, demanded educational equality, linked villages in collective actions, resisted arrests, supported the families of prisoners, and celebrated new holidays and heroes. What is striking about the Saratov agrarian movement is the tactical flexibility it displayed; protest that began as a traditional defense of a moral economy could quickly evolve into acts aimed at local political control and a revolution in social relations. In the process, traditional peasant culture was often both built upon and partially transformed. Indeed, the events that made up the rich 1902–06 tableau of life in rural Saratov Province call into question the traditional view of peasant conservatism and unchanging village culture.

The ability of Saratov peasants to form alliances with other groups demonstrates much the same flexibility. Because of formidable opposition from the gentry, Bishop Germogen and the clergy, as well as Governor Stolypin, local peasants understood the absolute necessity for allies— hence their support for the Third Element and their temporary alliances with zemstvo liberals in the summer of 1905 and with Kadets in the Duma elections. Indeed, 1906 may well have been the high point of peasant ties to outsiders and concern over the outcome of national political and social conflicts. As the 1906 Arkadak strike suggests, Saratov society began to polarize after this point. In 1917, peasants won a relatively easy victory that required few allies, and then they retreated more fully than ever before from contact with city and state until confronted a decade later with the cataclysm of renewed state intrusion in the form of collectivization.

Leaders of the Trudovik Group in the First Duma: *left to right,* A. F. Alyadin (Simbirsk Province), I. V. Zhilkin (Saratov), and S. V. Anikin (Saratov). Reprinted from *American Monthly Review of Reviews* 35 (April 1907): 493.

Religious procession led by Archbishop Germogen and marking the opening of Saratov University on December 6, 1909 (note the police holding back the crowds). Reprinted from *Niva,* no. 1 (1910): 17.

View of Saratov from Sokolov Hill. Engraving made on the occasion of the 300th anniversary of the city's founding. Reprinted from *Niva*, no. 19 (1891): 433.

Rural teachers and lower medical personnel (feldshers and midwives), most likely in the Saratov countryside. Reprinted from William E. Walling, *Russia's Message: The People Against the Czar* (New York, 1917), opposite p. 190.

The Second Men's Gymnasium (secondary school), located in Saratov's commercial district. Courtesy Library of Congress.

Saratov City Public Library (note the electric tramway). Courtesy Library of Congress.

Moscow Street, Saratov's main thoroughfare, with Stock Exchange on the right. Courtesy Library of Congress.

Cathedral of the Intercession of the Blessed Virgin, with general view of city. Courtesy Library of Congress.

The First Men's Gymnasium (secondary school). Courtesy Library of Congress.

10. The Stolypin Agrarian Reforms in Saratov Province

Grigorii Alekseevich Gerasimenko

PRIME MINISTER P. A. Stolypin's agrarian reforms occupy a prominent place in Soviet historiography on the period of imperialism. Historians have written extensively about the state apparatus's promotion of tsarism's new policies, the Peasant Land Bank's role in implementing the reform, peasant resettlement, the influence of land reorganization on landownership and land tenure, and the reforms' results.[1] These very considerations have also attracted the attention of researchers interested in the reforms' implementation in individual provinces and regions.[2] In regard to Saratov Province, for example, M. Ia. Kosenko's candidate dissertation ("Stolypin's Agrarian Reforms in Saratov Province," 1950) and 1956 article "From the History of the Introduction of the Stolypin Agrarian Reform in Saratov Province" have analyzed this problem.[3] While tapping the scholarly literature on this topic, I attempt in this chapter to trace the history of the reforms in Saratov Province and to shed light on those questions least illuminated in existing historical writing—namely, the attitude of the various strata of the village population toward the land reorganization and the role that reform played in exacerbating the [class] struggle in the countryside.

As is well known, after the Emancipation of 1861 the tsarist government based its relations with the peasantry on the firm convictions that the village commune *(obshchina)* was a conservative institution and that the members of the commune represented a popular and reliable support for the monarchy. During the second half of the nineteenth century, tsarism protected the commune with all means at its disposal. All legislation from this period designated for the countryside had a definite purpose: to preserve the commune and village administration as it was, and thereby to keep the peasants under government influence.

At the same time, however, major economic developments in agriculture undermined communal ways, increasingly affected public opinion, and eventually influenced the policies of tsarism itself. With the growth of capitalism, differentiation among the peasantry and the disintegration and breakup of the village commune intensified. More and more often, and on the most varied pretexts, the impoverished peasants' allotments fell into the hands of well-to-do peasants; less and less frequently, village assemblies tried to reallot communal lands. Agriculture, like industry, conformed to the general laws of economic development and slowly but surely shed the old feudal-serf ways.

The retention of old customs retarded the development of agriculture and banefully influenced the entire economy. At the turn of the century a series of disastrous harvests befell the country (1897, 1898, 1901), directly resulting in mass famine. The peasantry's unenviable economic and political condition aggravated the crisis in the country at large and enhanced the likelihood that revolutionary outbursts would occur. In 1901–02, a wave of peasant disturbances swept through Kharkov, Poltava, and Chernigov provinces. Although tsarism suppressed these disorders with comparative ease, they nevertheless played an important role in the fate of the commune. During the unrest, new features of rural life and the considerable revolutionary potential of the peasantry were manifest. The communal peasants destroyed the estates of gentry landowners, seized their belongings, and clashed with police, gendarmes, and troops. The lower link in the village administration not only failed to restrain the peasant movement but in fact often introduced order and organization into it, thereby giving it massive striking force.

The growth of capitalism and revolutionary disturbances in the villages compelled the tsar to reexamine the government's policies toward the commune and peasantry in general. On the eve of the Revolution of 1905, the government carried out preparatory work in this direction. The decisive step, however, was taken with the publication of the decree of November 9, 1906. According to V. I. Lenin, the edict was part of the "progressive capitalist development of Russia"[4] but represented the so-called Prussian path that was to cause much agony for the toiling peasantry. The new agrarian reform was conceived as a means to save the monarchical system and its basis—gentry landownership. In determining the class nature of the reform, Lenin wrote that Stolypin's bold demarche "remolds and adapts the old landowning system to capitalist relationships—but wholly in the interests of the landlords and at the price of the utter ruin of the peasant masses."[5]

The idea behind the decree was expressed in its first section, "On the Rights of Peasants to Consolidate and Withdraw from Communal Land." Peasants were now permitted to request the village assemblies to consolidate their scattered strips, confirm them by deed as personal property, and withdraw from the commune.[6] It was this statute that enabled tsarism to break up the commune and separate from it those elements of the rural population that the government needed most. It strove to propagate private ownership in place of communally held land thus expanding the stratum of landowners to fortify the autocracy—"to lay," as Stolypin put it, "that foundation on which the reorganized Russian governmental structure will be erected."[7] Private landownership was to strengthen the rural bourgeoisie, not at the expense of the redistribution of privately owned, especially gentry land, but at the expense of the peasant's allotment lands.

The decree formally granted all peasants the equal right to withdraw from the commune and consolidate their scattered strips into one contiguous area; however, in actuality the government patronized the better-off peasants and, among them, those who had the means to enhance their economic independence. "The government has realized," wrote Lenin, "that the peasant masses are against it and it is trying to find allies among the rich peasants."[8] All government institutions and central and local administrative bodies supported the "separators," especially the most prosperous ones. Moreover, they did this quite openly, showing obvious sympathy to this stratum of the village population. Those remaining in the commune, the *obshchiniki,* and that element among them against whom the decree was directed, understood the pro-kulak nature of the Stolypin reform. The edict evoked considerable interest among the peasantry, who found out about it through various means—from representatives of the authorities who addressed village assemblies, from worker or student agitators, from newspapers, and so on. Explanations of the decree were varied but more often than not led to similar results: village assemblies would voice the view of the majority, who reacted negatively to the new tsarist policies.

Opposition in the countryside found expression as early as the reform's organizational stage, when land settlement commissions *(zemleu-stroitel'nye komissii)* were being formed. As is well known, land commissions began to be set up following the decree of March 4, 1906. Organization of the commissions really did not get under way until the fall of 1906, however, and only after credits were allocated and staff for these institutions were assigned. Besides gentry landowners, administrative officials, and zemstvo agents, the decree of March 4, 1906, also gave peasants the right to elect three representatives to each district *(uezd)* commission. They were selected by casting lots from among those candidates nominated at canton *(volost)* meetings.

The reforms did not benefit the majority of peasants, who scorned the organization of the land settlement commissions. They ignored meetings called to nominate representatives to the commissions, boycotted elections, and refused to discuss the matter at volost assemblies. On October 8, 1906, the newspaper *Birzhevye vedomosti* (The Stock Exchange Gazette) noted that "the [village] assemblies resolved to return [to the authorities] documents issued concerning the land commissions."[9] Reports that peasants refused to take part in the creation of the commissions flowed in from all districts in Saratov Province. In Kamyshin District only sixteen of twenty-six volosts named candidates; in Atkarsk ten volosts boycotted the elections altogether, while candidates already chosen in eight volosts refused to elect representatives to the commission; as a result, twenty-four representatives turned up at the district congress instead of forty-two.[10] Only eighteen peasant deputies attended the Petrovsk District congress of candidates (there were thirty volosts in the district at the time), and they refused to participate in the congress, declaring that only the State Duma could resolve the land question.[11] The peasantry's opposition to the government's agrarian program was strongest in Balashov, Serdobsk, and several other districts. For example, 80 percent of the volosts in Balashov District, 70 percent in Serdobsk, 60 percent in Kamyshin, and 50 percent in Saratov, refused to name their representatives.[12]

Peasant opposition to the organization of land settlement commissions slowed down their actual formation. During 1906 commissions began functioning in only 184 districts[13] in the entire country and in six of ten districts in Saratov Province.[14] Even official documents such as the "Survey of the Activities of Land Regulation Commissions During the First Year of Their Existence," admitted that "the peasants' unsympathetic attitude toward the commissions" affected the rate at which they were being created.[15]

In January 1907 Stolypin ordered governors to intensify efforts to organize land commissions.[16] Afterward, pressure from the authorities on the peasants increased. In many locales new elections were scheduled, but even this did not yield the desired results. For example, the land captain twice convened an assembly in Rybushanskaia volost of Saratov District, but the peasants nevertheless refused to select representatives to the district commission.[17] Events took a similar turn in several other places. Thus, peasants in the village of Makarovo in Balashov District refused to collaborate with the land commission on the pretext that the State Duma was already studying the agrarian problem. In the village of Balanda, an assembly of communal peasants convened for the second time unanimously declared that they were not bound to organize land settlement commissions and that it was necessary to wait and see what the State Duma had to say about the matter.[18]

The authorities broke the peasants' resistance in various ways: in some instances they resorted to direct force; in others they falsified the elections themselves. In a circular issued to governors, Stolypin admitted that crude violations of order were occurring in selecting peasants to the land commissions.[19] The actions of the authorities in Saratov Province did not differ at all from those taking place at the time in many other provinces. Even though eighty-five volosts refused to elect their representatives, Saratov's Governor Tatishchev announced to local authorities that "the peasants' rejection of the land commissions does not represent a legal obstacle to starting up the operations of these institutions."[20] In accordance with this instruction, during the summer of 1907 commissions were formed in the four remaining districts and a provincial land settlement commission began its work.[21] On the whole, the creation of commissions continued throughout the country for several more years. According to S. M. Sidel'nikov, 198 district land commissions convened in 1907, 18 in 1908, and 22 in 1909.[22] But the matter did not end there, and the process of forming them continued to take place in 1910, 1911, and in 1912.[23] In September 1911 the *Sankt-Peterburgskie vedomosti* (St. Petersburg Gazette) reported that to date some 434 district land commissions were in operation in the country.[24] In March 1913 that same paper informed readers that in 47 provinces of European Russia there was a total of 510 commissions—47 provincial ones and 463 at the district level.[25] As we have seen, it was difficult for the government to create the apparatus necessary to carry out the reforms. One of the major obstacles the authorities encountered in organizing land commissions was the majority of peasants' strong opposition to tsarism's agrarian policies and their boycott of the institutions in question.

After promulgating the decree of November 9, 1906, and organizing land commissions, the government launched a spirited campaign to publicize the new principles of village life. Central and local organs of the government, semiofficial political and public institutions and organizations, newspapers and periodicals all took part in it. The major agitational and propaganda efforts urged the communal peasants to have their scattered strips confirmed by deed as private property during the first stage of the reform, to consolidate their strips into one contiguous area, and, finally, to go on *khutor* and *otrub.** Brochures and posters were issued and exhibits were organized expounding these themes. Model private farms were set up. Tours were arranged from the Russian provinces to those, mainly in the western region, where conditions were more favorable for establishing private individual farms. Enormous efforts were expended to popularize new methods of farm management. The government spent hundreds of thousands of rubles on advertising the khutor and otrub farms and explaining their advantages over communal land tenure.

Much of what was done in the country was also carried out in Saratov Province. In particular, on August 27, 1908, Saratov Governor Tatishchev petitioned the committee on land settlement regulations to release fifteen thousand rubles to organize model farms. The committee granted the governor's request.[26] From the beginning of the Stolypin reforms the government sought to involve the zemstvos in land reorganization, and not without success. In the fall of 1908, the Saratov District zemstvo board at its own expense sent a group of peasants to Volynsk Province "to familiarize themselves with managing khutor farms."[27]

As mentioned above, the majority of peasants were negatively disposed toward the new agrarian policies. Despite opposition in the countryside, groups of the rural population were nevertheless found who

Otrub and *khutor.* A consolidated holding cultivated by a peasant family that still lived in the village was an *otrub.* The ideal envisaged by the Stolypin reform was the *khutor,* a consolidated farm upon which a peasant family actually lived. (Translator's note.)

wished to take advantage of the decree with the help of land settlement officials *(zemleustroiteli)*. The strong, economically solvent households turned out to be the cutting edge of the Stolypin land reforms. It was this group that the government had gambled on, and it was with their interests in mind that the decree of November 9, 1906, was drafted and enacted. Preferable conditions were created for the better-off households, and land officials, the administrative apparatus, and police and gendarmes were on their side. It was this stratum of the peasantry that proved to be most interested in destroying the village commune, liquidating allotment land tenure, and propagating private landownership. "There's been enough dividing up of the land into bits and pieces, and cutting off a mere thirty strips," they tried to convince the communal peasants. "The land doesn't belong to man, but to the proprietor. Let he who can improve the land, own it, and let he who can't go to work for a landlord or for a factory in Petersburg."[28]

Withdrawal from the commune onto consolidated farms without sufficient resources soon led to failure and financial ruin. In opting for private land tenure, the peasant had to weigh all of his assets thoroughly. According to I. V. Chernyshev, setting up an individual household on a new plot of land cost from 300 to 800 rubles, whereas the government allocated no more than 150 rubles in such circumstances.[29] Moreover, if in the process a homeowner struck a deal with the Peasant Land Bank— and this took place fairly often—he had to keep in mind that he would have to pay off his debts quickly. In a word, only that stratum of the peasantry that had more land than the average communal allotment and sufficient capital for setting up a household in a new location could benefit from the November 9 decree.

Nevertheless, not all of those who withdrew from the commune were rich peasants: from the very first days of the reform the poor began to leave the commune as well. Following the Emancipation of 1861, a certain portion of the communal peasants, as a result of the growth of capitalism, had migrated to the cities, turned to handicraft production or transportation work, but maintained their right to an allotment. The decree of November 9 gave them the opportunity to break decisively with the commune, have their allotment confirmed by deed as private property, sell it, and thereby free themselves from the land altogether. The desire of the less-well-off peasants to consolidate their allotments into private property with the single aim of selling them was frequently written and talked about at the time. Newspaper columns were literally packed with such reports that came from the most diverse regions of Russia. "Some two years ago," wrote the newspaper *Staryi Vladimirets* (The Old Vladimirian), "peasants engaged in handicraft production . . . showed little interest in their allotment land. Now the heads of these peasant households, who had lived elsewhere, demand they be granted the allotment due them and do so only in order to sell the land to others, sometimes even to complete strangers."[30] The newspaper *Volzhskoe slovo* (The Volga Word) in the summer of 1908 published a note from Nikolaevsk District, Samara Province: "Peasants in our village, Krivoluche-Ivanovka," it said, "are beginning to withdraw from the commune. Many of them are doing so with the aim of selling their land and migrating to Siberia."[31] A few days later *Volzhskoe slovo* published a report from Balakovo. "Local kulaks and those from neighboring villages are eagerly buying up land from local peasants who have left the commune. The appetites of some of these buying up the land are so insatiable that they are trying to talk the other peasants into withdrawing from the commune. The poor, starvng peasant, won over by the kulak's promise to buy his land for a good price, is hurrying to grab his share."[32]

Since the poorer elements who left the commune abandoned the countryside, the village population now invariably consisted of those well-off peasants who had withdrawn from the commune and those who had remained in it. Thus it was between these that a struggle over land settlement unfolded. The selfish aims and intentions of the better-off householders who had withdrawn from the commune dissatisfied and aroused the enmity of those peasants compelled to farm on allotment lands. As a rule, the consolidation of allotments into private property deprived the peasants of the best lands, often made access to reservoirs and pastures more difficult, noticeably exacerbated the condition of the communal peasants, and caused endless clashes and conflicts in the villages. "The desire to receive a consolidated holding (otrub)," wrote *Novoe vremia* (New Times), "directly arouses a storm of indignation in village society."[33] A land captain from Petrovsk District reported to the Saratov governor that "hostility exists between communal peasants and those who had withdrawn from the commune" in almost all of the villages in his region. According to the land captain, this occurred because land surveyors normally gave the best lands to those who had separated.[34]

The village assemblies' refusal to accept applications for withdrawal from the commune became one of the most widespread forms of peasant opposition to the reform. "If there is such a law," peasants said, "then let them manage by themselves without a decision from the village community."[35] Peasants expressed such opinions at assemblies in many villages and volosts in an overwhelming majority of provinces in Russia, including Saratov. In February 1907, already during the first season of land reorganization, a communal assembly in the village of Idolga in Saratov District denied the request of some villagers to consolidate their allotments and withdraw from the commune.[36] In accordance with the law, in those cases in which village assemblies refused peasants their apportionment, the land captain was to make a ruling within a month from the date the application was submitted. For the most part, he did so in the separators' favor. The land captain's ruling, usually announced at village meetings, made matters even worse. The communal peasants could see for themselves that the authorities favored the withdrawers, and this deepened the rift in the villages and pitted the interests of the commune members against the consolidators even more. Communal peasants in the same village of Idolga declared after the land captain supported the withdrawers, "Let them break away, but the land's going to bear them nothing but weeds."[37]

The village assemblies' negative rulings against consolidating land into private property and withdrawing from the commune protected the interests of those who remained in the commune and saved allotment lands from being purloined by kulaks and better-off peasants. More than anything else, such opposition to the reform reflected the toiling peasantry's dissatisfaction with the agrarian policies of tsarism and corresponded closely to the scale and depth of opposition in the villages. The disagreement of the village assemblies with the intention of part of the peasantry to withdraw from the commune was the disagreement of the majority of the rural population with the Stolypin land reorganization as a whole. The collective refusal of village assemblies of those who wished to abandon the commune was the most easily understood and, of particular importance during the heat of the Stolypin reaction, comparatively safest form of peasant opposition to the reform. It is precisely for this reason that it was so widely practiced.

An especially large number of applications were rejected in Saratov Province, where in some districts and volosts almost all requests to withdraw from the commune were turned down. In Elshanskaia volost in Saratov District, village assemblies rejected all applications during 1910–13. Village assemblies discussing requests for withdrawal tended to reach a standard decision: to "deny consolidation of land into private property" whenever "withdrawal from the commune upsets land tenure."[38] An exceptionally high percentage of rejected petitions were registered in Serdobsk (99 percent), Khvalynsk and Kuznetsk (up to 97 percent), Balashov (96 percent), Kamyshin, Tsaritsyn, and Volsk districts (94 percent).[39] On the whole, in Saratov Province only 9,498 heads of households, or 7 percent, received permission to break away from the commune, of a total of 131,777 who had expressed a desire to do so.[40] According to a correspondent from *Rus'* (Russia), these 7 percent of peasant homesteads that received the consent of their fellow villagers, "did so as the result of the 'assistance' and 'dilligence' of zemstvo officials."[41] I. V. Mozzhukhin, who observed the carrying out of the reform at the time, maintained that assemblies which granted permission for withdrawal often did so under pressure from the authorities. He wrote, "To receive the needed majority of votes it is necessary to resort to extreme measures up to and including summoning the police." At times the authorities used measures of an altogether different nature to compel the village assembly to grant requests for withdrawal. The same Mozzhukhin told of one such measure when members of an assembly who had voted against the would-be "Stolypin peasants" were threatened with losing the land they rented from the Peasant Bank. In other cases, "they threatened" the elders of those unyielding villages "with all possible official repressions for neglect in land tenure regulations." All of this, in the words of the author, gave rise to "the most embittered conflict of interests.[42]

In such circumstances even the authorities' most determined efforts sometimes failed to lead to the desired results. Even after rejections prompted appeals to the land captains by the would-be Stolypin peasants, the communal peasants continued to pressure their fellow villagers. "If you manage to get land without our consent," the peasants would say in such circumstance, "you'd better keep in mind that we're not going to let you live in peace."[43] There were thousands of heads of households who, under pressure from the communal peasants, changed their mind about withdrawing from the commune. For example, in Perm Province 2,361 heads of households, or 11.2 percent of all those who submitted applications, later withdrew them; in Voronezh, 7,075 or 6 percent; in Kazan, 8,389; in Nizhnii Novgorod, 3,790, or 6 percent, and so on.[44] There were many cases in Saratov Province as well. Of the 131,777 heads of households who were having their petitions for withdrawal considered, 5,898 eventually reconsidered under pressure from the communal peasants.[45]

The authorities overcame opposition in the countryside by the most diverse methods and devices. In time, however, administrative and police coercion became the most important means of implementing the reform—that is, open force with regard to the communal peasants. In conflicts between communal peasants and the separators, peasants who had declared their intention to withdraw from the commune more often than not received support from the state apparatus, and the majority of them eventually achieved their goal. Withdrawals from the commune were particularly high during the first years of the reform. Between 1906–09 in Saratov Province, 50,262 households broke away from the commune, or 52 percent of all such incidents that took place while the reform was in force.[46]

The process of consolidating possessions into private property and withdrawing from the commune did not meet with success in all districts of Saratov Province. The agrarian reform was implemented most intensively in Atkarsk, Balashov, Kamyshin, Petrovsk, Saratov, and Serdobsk districts. Here the level of market relations was more developed, social differentiation among the peasantry was more advanced, and land settlement officials carried out their work more zealously. The number of separators lagged significantly behind in the remaining districts (Volsk, Kuznetsk, Khvalynsk, and Tsaritsyn).[47] Land hunger was more acute in these districts, there were more national minorities, and capitalist relations were less developed.

The main difficulty the new Stolypin agrarian reform encountered in Saratov Province, however, as in other Russian provinces, was the dissatisfaction and opposition in the villages of the majority of peasants to land reorganization. The most frequent forms of opposition were the following: communal peasants voiced antigovernment sentiments at assemblies convened to discuss the decree of November 9, 1906; they insulted members of the land commissions; they ignored decisions reached by the commissions; they complained about land settlement officials and representatives of the authorities at all levels, right up to the tsar himself and his wife and mother; they refused to give money, people, horses, carts, and materials necessary for surveying the land; they interfered in all sorts of ways with attempts by the land regulators and their assistants to prepare themselves for field work; they hampered surveyors by insulting them verbally, trampling their measuring lines, knocking over surveying compasses and surveying rods, shoving and physically abusing the surveyors and their helpers. When the authorities succeeded in delimiting consolidated plots, peasants pulled out and destroyed landmarks, filled in the furrows delimiting the fields, and continued to plow the lands as in the past without taking into account the new borders.

Often the peasants influenced those representatives of the village and volost administrations who worked together with the land settlement officials. At routine elections, peasants relieved them of their duties, selecting instead proponents of the commune; frightened them with various punishments, including burning them out; insulted them and members of their families; damaged their holdings, and so on. The communal peasants applied equal pressure on their fellow villagers who assisted the surveyors: they threatened them and made good their threats, burning down houses in which the land regulators were accommodated. There were instances in which peasants stole and destroyed materials used by surveyors in marking land, plans for land redivision, and measuring equipment. Authorities were unable to record all such cases and report them at each level. As a wide variety of archival materials confirm, peasants in Saratov Province employed all of these means to fight land settlement officials.[48]

Several conflicts over land settlement attained impressive levels. In particular, on September 18, 1909, in the village of Bulgakovo in Volsk District, they began to allot land for otrub. "At the site where this was going on," read the report sent to the Department of Police, "was a crowd of peasants from Bulgakovo who opposed the land reform . . . numbering about two hundred persons and led by the village elder. They demanded that the work stop." The next day police arrived in the village, arrested the most active communal peasants, and locked them up in detention quarters. The peasants sounded the alarm and tried to free those arrested, but the police repelled the assault and dispersed the crowd.[49] The dissatisfaction of the peasant majority with the land reorganization was the basis of an enormous front the peasants formed against the Stolypin land reform. To be sure, open battle was not being waged at all points on the front; much of what occurred in the villages never came to the authorities' attention. During the height of the reaction following the Revolution of 1905, the masses' weariness and despair only infrequently took the form of outright demonstrations.

Peasants carried out an especially widespread and diverse struggle against their fellow villagers who sought to turn the reforms to their own advantage. Although the authorities could send at will rural police, soldiers, or cossacks to protect the surveyors at work, they were unable to post a police guard over each separator. Moreover, the communal peasants and those who declared their desire to break from the commune or who had already done so lived side by side; their homes, gardens, allotments, and fields were located in close proximity to each other. This permitted the communal peasants to pressure the Stolypin peasants relentlessly, and to do so without evidence or witnesses. One governor reported to the Department of the Police that "the forms of the peasants' hostility toward the better-off heads of household are virtually unlimited."[50] The broad scope of the peasants pressure on the separators ranged from hostile glances to arson and murder.

In several places the peasantry's struggle against the Stolypin peasants took unbelievably odd forms. For example, in the village of Saklovbash in Ufa Province, peasants prevented the consolidators from burying their dead in the village cemetery. Peasants exerted moral and physical pressure on those who withdrew from the commune and on members of their families, damaged and destroyed farm buildings and property, and maimed livestock and poultry; they threatened to burn out the Stolypin peasants and quite often made good their threats. Children of those who had taken advantage of the Stolypin legislation were not admitted to schools; their young people were not allowed to marry in the church; they were prevented from using roads, wells, rivers, lakes, and ponds; their livestock were driven from the common herd; they were deprived of their share of income from lands, forests, and reservoirs purchased by the commune, and so on. Peasants especially often damaged the crops and hayfields of the separators. A communal peasant, riding past a field belonging to a Stolypin peasant, would make a point to trespass upon it, even if with a single wheel. Damage to crops, in the true sense of the word, assumed massive proportions. And all of this, to one degree or another, occurred during the implementation of the Stolypin reforms in Saratov Province.[51]

Saratov Governor A. A. Shirinskii-Shakhmatov was correct when he wrote to Stolypin, "In many parts of Saratov Province the communal peasants' behavior toward those who embraced the new forms of land-tenure was truly hostile."[52] Here is how a land captain from one of the regions of Petrovsk District characterized the situation in the countryside: "Relations between peasants in the village of Kutino in Malo-Serdobskaia volost who consolidated their allotments into private property and exchanged it for a contiguous plot, and those remaining in the commune, are extremely strained. First, the communal peasants do not want to allot them land; second, they intimidate them with all sorts of lies, as a result of which landholding in the community is in total stagnation. Moreover," continued the land captain, "I believe it not without interest to report that the communal peasants consider all explanations in regard to land settlement to be boring, and they refuse to listen to them."[53] It is not surprising that, in view of the communal peasants' relentless and universal hostility and hatred of those who had withdrawn, comparatively large-scale clashes broke out that attracted the attention of the authorities and aroused public opinion. The conflict in the village of Khanenevka in Lipovskaia volost in Saratov District was exactly of this nature. As a result of this event, widely discussed in the papers, local authorities conducted a lively correspondence with officials in the Ministry of Internal Affairs.

Relations between the communal and Stolypin peasants in this volost were extremely hostile because surveyors drew up landmarks for consolidated holdings that favored the latter and noticeably worsened the situation of those remaining in the commune. The peasants reckoned in particular with a peasant on otrub named Seregin, who had bought up several allotments of the best village lands totaling 45 desiatiny. In the spring of 1911, Seregin decided to set up an independent household on his plot and began constructing a home and farm buildings. The peasants warned Seregin several times to stop building and return his land to the communal holdings, but he ignored them. On May 28 the communal peasants for the umpteenth time began destroying the homes of the *otrubshchiki* and throwing rocks through windows. Then someone cried, "Let's go burn out Seregin!" and the crowd set out for his farm, located about a mile from Khanenevka.[54] They stacked up brushwood against the buildings and set it on fire. Seregin jumped through a window, pulled out his children and part of his property, and began to put out the fire.

The peasants, however, started shooting handguns at him and forced him to flee.[55] For such actions the authorities brought eleven peasants to trial.[56]

A short while later, in the village of Grigorevka in Saratov District, communal peasants set fire to the buildings of three peasants who had gone on otrub because surveyors had allotted them plots from the best communal lands. Rumors circulated in the village that through their actions the peasants hoped to force those who had left the commune to reject the otrub form of farming. Six peasants from this village were sentenced to various terms of imprisonment.[57]

Such conditions made it increasingly difficult to expedite land settlement, and an ever greater part of the work load fell on the surveyors, their assistants, and those responsible for the reform. Some officials began to doubt the undertaking and spoke of the hopelessness of the changes and of the fatigue and apathy of those introducing the reforms. Member of the State Senate Chaplin, who under directives from Stolypin visited eighteen provinces to inspect local conditions, reported: "One can already observe among the government agents involved in land settlement signs of despair, caused by the hopelessness of their efforts and recognition of the impossibility of involving the masses in the ever-growing work which, in the final analysis, breeds apathy and inertia."[58]

Stolypin may have banked on carrying out the reform over twenty years, but the less optimistic head of the Chief Administration of Land Settlement and Agriculture,* A. V. Krivoshein, hoped for forty. He reported to Nicholas II on the results of the first five years of land settlement: "if land reorganization in European Russia continues at the present rate, we can expect to complete the reorganization of all peasant lands in the course of thirty or forty years."[59]

As early as 1911, Lenin maintained that Stolypin's agrarian policy had failed. In his article "Stolypin and Revolution," published in October 1911, he wrote: "After the revolution the landowner monarchy of Nicholas II sought support in the counterrevolutionary sentiments of the bourgeoisie and in a bourgeois agrarian policy put into effect by these very same landowners. The failure of these attempts, which even the Kadets, even the Octobrists can no longer doubt, is the failure of the *last* policy *possible* for tsarism." And further: "Stolypin's policy ended in failure."[60]

*In 1905, the Ministry of Agriculture was renamed the *Glavnoe upravlenie zemleustroistva i zemledeliia*. (Translator's note.)

This is exactly what happened in Saratov Province, where the period of more or less intensive withdrawal from the commune drew to an end by 1912. Ninety percent of all local withdrawals took place between 1906 and 1912, when 87,467 heads of households consolidated their land into private holdings and withdrew from the collective fold. In the remaining years of the reform, only 9,762 household heads took advantage of the legislation.[61]

During the ten years the reform lasted, diametrically opposed groups of communal peasants appeared in the countryside as a result of economic relations. On the one hand were the enterprising, independent, well-off peasants for whom the regulation of the commune was burdensome and unnecessary; on the other hand were the poorer, more unfortunate, increasingly destitute peasants, many of whom lived permanently away from the villages in cities or in workers' settlements. The decree of November 9 drove the latter group to break completely with the land. Namely, these two strata of the population took advantage of the legislation and withdrew from the commune, with the one difference that the poor abandoned the countryside altogether while the kulaks, securing extra allotments for themselves and buying up the land of the poor, became economically more powerful and influential. Taking advantage of the aspirations of these two sections of the population, the government managed to move land settlement from a standstill and in some provinces actually achieved considerable success. In Saratov Province, for example, 25 percent of all peasant households secured their land into private holdings and withdrew from the commune.[62]

At the same time, however, this success marked the beginning of the end of Stolypin's agrarian policy. The results were insignificant when compared with the gigantic volume of work that needed to be done across the entire country. Moreover, the number of withdrawals from the commune by 1910 had fallen sharply and continued to decline in the remaining years in which the reform was in force. In 1907, nationally, 48,271 households withdrew; in 1908, 508,344; in 1909, 579,409. But by 1910 the number had declined to 342,245; by 1911, to 145,567; and by 1912, to 122,314. During the entire 1906–12 period, 2,747,850 households, or 17 percent of all peasant households, withdrew from the commune in the forty-seven provinces affected by the legislation.[63]

As we have seen, the peasants resisted the administrative and police pressures of the state machinery and prevented the breakup of the commune. Further, before long a noticeable countertrend made itself felt—Stolypin peasants were beginning to ask how they might return to the commune. In February 1909 the newspaper *Russkoe znamia* (Russian Banner) wrote: "Recently many newspapers have reported cases in which peasants who have withdrawn from the commune are seeking to return to it. Such incidents are becoming more and more frequent."[64] As the author suggested, the main reason for the separators' return to the commune was pressure from communal peasants. To the question of what had induced those who had withdrawn to take such a step, peasants replied:

"We thought, let's withdraw, things'll get better. In fact, they turned out worse."

"Why?"

"It's too hard to live. The village community is hostile because we withdrew."

"And in reality," concluded the author, "fellow villagers act with hostility or coolness toward the independent-minded peasant who caused them so many difficulties."[65] Reports that separators were trying to return to the commune came in from the Volga region, the western, central, and several other Russian provinces.[66] On October 12, 1911, the newspaper *Rech'* (Speech) informed readers that peasants in Otradnen-skaia volost in Tsaritsyn District "who fell under the spell of the land commissions' promises and who had agreed to go on *otrub* . . . are now submitting requests to return to the commune and former means of land tenure." Reporting to the governor in June 1913 on the slow carrying out of the reform in his district, a land captain from Petrovsk also called attention to this phenomenon. "Throughout the period in which the law was in force," he wrote, "in Kutino only twenty heads of households have improved their allotments, and many of them have already announced that they are returning once again to the commune, even though they will be deprived of land altogether during reallocation." According to the land captain, "this can be explained by the fact that many communal peasants are relentlessly hostile to those who had withdrawn from the commune and intimidate them."[67]

Peasants continued to oppose tsarism's agrarian policy during World War I. Reports of conflicts over land in 1914–16 came in from Volynsk, Kharkov, Moscow, Vitebsk, Podolsk, and from Saratov and other provinces.[68] Reacting to such developments, the government issued Circular

No. 31 on April 29, 1915, which had major repercussions in the country. Minister of Agriculture Krivoshein ordered a stop put to all cases in which the communal peasants and those who wished to leave the commune could not reach an agreement.[69] In the practical work of land settlement, concerns predominated that were carried out despite the will of the village assembly. For this reason Circular No. 31 undermined the agrarian reform. The number of land surveyors had fallen sharply already by the fall of 1915, and in 1916 land settlement broke off altogether, even though conflicts in the village continued that year. Probably, this battle was directed at liquidating the consequences of Stolypin's agrarian reform: communal peasants strove to force the Stolypin peasants to return their holdings to the allotment fields and rejoin the commune.

Such was the dialectic of events that accompanied the implementation of Stolypin's reform. The entire purpose of the reform had been to destroy the commune, to divide up allotment land, to promote private ownership of land, and thereby to expand the stratum of well-off peasants. Stolypin's basic principle had been to separate the most enterprising, independent peasants from the commune and to merge their social position with that of the landlords.

Owing to an array of political, economic, and financial measures implemented by the tsarist government over the course of ten years, the prosperous village elements had the opportunity to abandon the commune at any time and secure their economic position at the expense of restraining those remaining in the commune even more. A significant part of the peasantry failed to take advantage of this opportunity. In all of Russia only 2,008,432 households withdrew from the commune. Moreover, in accordance with the decree of July 14, 1910, 469,792 households consolidated their land in those villages in which land reallocation had not been carried out for a long while. Thus, during the period in which the Stolypin reform was in force, 2,478,224 heads of households, or 22 percent of all peasant households in the country, withdrew from the commune.[70] The rate of separation was even higher in Saratov Province, where it reached 27.2 percent.[71]

But not all those who availed themselves of the opportunity were prosperous peasants: the village poor withdrew as well. This does not contradict the notion that the Stolypin reform was carried out in the interests of the economically prosperous peasants. The village poor consolidated their allotments into private possession in order to sell them and sever all contact with the land.* The prosperous peasants who withdrew from the commune had sufficient land, sowing area, draft animals, and agricultural inventory to strengthen their farms and grow rich. According to the compilations of M. Ia. Kosenko, in Saratov Province 44,166 households that had withdrawn, or 52.5 percent of the total, had at their disposal 776,378 desiatiny of land, an average of 17.5 desiatiny per household.[72] At the same time, 22,924 heads of households, or 24 percent of those who had withdrawn, sold their strips.[73] The well-off peasants purchased this land at favorably low prices. In Tsaritsyn District, for example, the poor sold their allotments for 25 rubles per desiatina; in Atkarsk, 40 rubles; in Serdobsk, from 15 to 66 rubles, when the market rate averaged 100 rubles per desiatina.[74] The Stolypin reform improved the situation of prosperous peasants at the expense of the complete ruin of the village poor. In the final analysis, the withdrawal from the commune of a significant percentage of enterprising, independent households caused the further impoverishment of the commune and a certain leveling of its members. The correlation of forces within the commune gradually turned to the benefit of the poor and middle elements of the peasantry.

The Stolypin reform strained relations between the communal peasants and those who had withdrawn to the breaking point. Both were in a state of constant war against each other. "One sets off for the field, and the other follows him with an axe," said officials in the Ministry of Internal Affairs, characterizing the situation in the countryside in regard to the Stolypin land settlement.[75] Such were the socioeconomic results of the legislation.

Apart from this, the reform had significant political consequences. Those who had broken from the commune lost the right to vote at village assemblies. The most serious loss for them was the right to elect and to be elected to volost and village administrative organs. Tsarism wanted agrarian reorganization to strengthen the well-off peasants economically, and it succeeded in doing so to some degree. However, the political status of the separators was weakened, for the communal peasants simply drove them away from village assemblies. As one volost clerk observed, as a

*Approximately 34 percent of those households in Saratov Province which withdrew from the commune sold their allotments. About 6 percent of the local peasants who left the commune, roughly twice the national average, established the ideal khutor-like farms. (Translator's note.)

result of the new changes in the countryside, "the communal peasants remove the rich peasants from the village meetings by the scruff of the neck."[76] From the province it was reported that "the Stolypin peasants are no longer permitted at village meetings, even though these heads of households virtually remain in the same standing in society as before."[77]

Here we must face a sociopolitical paradox, where resolving one complex problem gives rise to several new and equally serious ones. The relationship between communal peasants and those who had withdrawn was similar in all provinces in which the reform was carried out, including Saratov. The communal peasants not only deprived the separators of the right to vote at village assemblies but also lavished hatred on volost leaders, elders, clerks, and other civil servants who supported the consolidators. The communal peasants applied typical methods of pressure against them, especially arson. Peasants in the village of Staroe Demkino in Petrovsk District set fire to barns storing grain belonging to volost elder E. B. Novikov.[78] Peasants torched the farm buildings of the village elder in Tatarskaia Pokaevka in Savkinskaia volost of the same district in July 1909 and on October 18 and 25, 1910.[79] Twice the property of the elder of Planskaia volost in Kuznetsk District was burned down.[80]

In several cases peasants resorted to extreme measures. In April 1908 the head of the constabulary in Saratov District reported that in the village of Idolga in Shirokinskaia volost an attempt was made on the life of the elder, A. N. Kozhevnikov, because he had promoted the new land regulations to the peasants too diligently.[81] During discussion of the land reorganization in the village of Krasavka in Atkarsk District, peasants beat the village elder mercilessly.[82] Assemblies also removed from office those who had withdrawn from the commune. For example, in the village of Eremikh in Balashov District, peasants illegally dismissed the clerk appointed by the land captain.[83] A village meeting in Kazanla in Volsk District resolved "to dismiss the village foreman, Trofim Belov, who had withdrawn from the commune in accordance with the law of November 9, and in his place to appoint another peasant who had remained in the commune, Konstantin Anikin." The same assembly removed an official, A. F. Al'shev, for the sympathy and support he had rendered to the Stolypin peasants.[84] In electing volost and village officials, rural assemblies favored the communal peasants.

This tendency intensified after the February Revolution. In several places consolidators tried to organize their own administrative units and elect administrative organs distinct from those of the communal peasants. In particular, otrubshchiki in the village of Verkhniaia Dobrinka in Kamyshin District in the spring of 1917, when their relations with the communal peasants had reached a breaking point, resolved with the sanction of the provincial commissar to set up their own governing body and elect a village elder. The volost executive committee, however, comprised of communal peasants, arrested the elder, took away his official seal, and dispersed the village administration. The district commissar tried to defend the otrubshchiki. He ordered the communal peasants to release the elder, return his seal to him, and interfere no more in the otrubshchiki's organization; but this was not to be. As was reported from Verkhniaia Dobrinka, "the volost committee is returning neither the seal nor the insignia, ignoring the authorities' orders."[85]

On May 11 the newspaper *Saratovskii vestnik* (Saratov Herald), in an article on events in Khvalynsk entitled "What Is Going On in the District," reported that "the independent peasants virtually never take part in the elections."[86] The paper *Saratovskii listok* (Saratov Sheet) published a letter from otrubshchiki in the village of Sokur, which noted: "The otrubshchiki, after all, are not hooligans, yet the peasants from Sokur consider us enemies: they prevent us from taking part in elections and deny us the right to vote."[87] The same newspaper published an unusually interesting letter written by otrubshchiki from Elshanskaia volost in Volsk District: "It's as if we otrubshchiki are not really citizens, for we are deprived of political and civil rights."[88] Otrubshchiki from Tersinskaia volost in Atkarsk District wrote to the paper *Zemlia i volia* (Land and Liberty) that because they had removed their holdings "we clash with the communal peasants at each meeting and hate each other more than the Germans."[89]

Frequently, the weakening of the political influence of the well-off segment of the village population was discussed at congresses of landowners, where complaints from the gentry rose in a single chorus with those of the peasant consolidators. On May 19, 1917, at the Saratov Province Congress of Landowners, Prince Vasil'chikov, landowner Sokolov, and the otrub peasant Gusev all spoke from the same rostrum. Moreover, Gusev announced: "Since March 1 our life, that of the petty proprietor, has changed beyond recognition. We tremble and cautiously watch from behind the gate. I own only 12 desiatiny, but they destroyed the meadow, damaged the forestland, and took away the last prisoner of war. Where can you turn for help? Not the the village committee."[90] The committee, elected by the communal peasants, would not render him any assistance.

This thought was even more clearly expressed at a congress of land-owners of Saratov District. According to a newspaper article that published speeches of the congress's participants: "Both the gentry-land-owners and the peasant-otrubshchiki are united in their indignation over the actions of the communal peasants and village and volost committees. The otrubshchiki maintain that the communal peasants don't let them organize themselves . . . and restrict them in all sorts of ways. . . . The communal peasants or these same volost committees always turn out to be right. Who belongs to them? The very same communal peasants. They don't let us otrubshchiki assemble and they threaten us with arrest. Who is making these threats? The proletarians, who don't have a thing but who are ready for just about anything. But the otrubshchiki are not in the slightest degree well-off. This is how they have turned against us."[91]

Finally, we shall turn to Deputy Minister of Agriculture N. I. Rakit-nikov, one of the most prominent Socialist Revolutionaries. Addressing the First All-Russian Peasant Congress, he said: "Peasants relate to the otrubshchiki with extreme enmity. If a peasant had gone on otrub, even if he were a Socialist Revolutionary, it would be such a blot on his character that he would not be chosen for any office."[92] The same was reported by the Provisional Committee of the State Duma's Department of Provincial Affairs. "Otrubshchiki and petty proprietors with 30 to 50 desiatiny of land are not elected to the volost executive committees and their interests remain unrepresented."[93]

As we have seen, one of the main unforeseen consequences of the Stolypin reform was the fact that in 1917 it greatly assisted the poor and middle peasants to predominate in volost and village committees. This circumstance imparted particular poignancy and dynamism to events in the countryside during the Revolution of 1917. A far from complete enumeration of all that occurred in the countryside in 1917 includes: thousands of peasant disturbances; a colossal and difficult-to-assess array of methods for struggling against gentry landowners and the village bourgeoisie; the working out of entirely new legal norms; and the gradual elucidation of the aims and tasks of the class struggle. And, to a significant degree, these developments were due to the predominance in volost and village committees of the revolutionary and democratic forces of the rural population.

11. The Impact of World War I on Saratov and Its Revolutionary Movement

Donald J. Raleigh

WORLD WAR I shook all of Russian society to its foundations and put the autocratic system to a severe test which it did not pass. It redefined and aggravated serious grievances and issues—discussed earlier in this book—that had been manifest for over a generation. The war contributed to the outbreak of revolution and strongly influenced its outcome. It realigned politics, including the liberal-radical alliance that had been such an important feature of Saratov politics earlier, and made a Bolshevik revolution (and civil war) much more likely. To illuminate the impact of the war on Saratov province, I shall examine the demographic changes brought about by the conflict and the repercussions these had on working conditions. I shall also survey the extent to which the war interrupted the rhythm of change in the countryside and analyze the revolutionary movement during the war and on the eve of the Revolution of 1917. The latter task necessitates a digression into the fate of the local revolutionary movement following the defeat of the Revolution of 1905–1907. The reader should bear in mind that the history of the radical movement between 1907 and 1917 is the least studied and most poorly documented of all periods dealt with in this book.

The extraordinary population dislocation caused by World War I had a profound impact on the populations of Saratov and of the district towns, and on the course of the local revolution. Roughly one-third of the city's working class was drafted (a complex system granted exemptions according to one's family conditions). Moreover, as a center of noncombat military activity, Saratov belonged to the Kazan Military District, one

Table 11.1. Populations and Strength of Garrisons in District Towns,
Saratov Province, 1917

Town	Population	Size of Garrison or Regiment Number*
Atkarsk	12,500	9,000
Balashov	17,400	135th and 145th
Kamyshin	24,800	?
Khvalynsk	19,300	None
Kuznetsk	29,500	147th and 148th
Petrovsk	19,800	134th and 145th
Serdobsk	10,100	161st
Tsaritsyn	134,683	93d, 143d, and 155th
Volsk	36,000	150th and 245th

SOURCES: A. F. Milozorov, *Sel'skokhoziaistvennye raiony Saratovskoi gubernii* (Saratov, 1924), p. 18; I. Romanov and N. Sokolov, *Ocherk istorii revoliutsii 1917 goda v Tsaritsyne (Stalingrad)* (Saratov, 1930), p. 6; A. I. Razgon, "O sostave sovetov Nizhnego Povolzh'ia v marte-aprele 1917 g.," in *Sovety i soiuz rabochego klassa i krest' ianstva v Oktiabr'skoi revoliutsii* (Moscow, 1964), p. 93; M. Frenkin, *Zakhvat vlasti bol'shevikami v Rossii i rol' tylovykh garnizonov armii: Podgotovka i provedenie Oktiabr'skogo miatezha, 1917–1918 gg.* (Jerusalem, 1982), p. 16.

of the largest war machines in the country. All of the district centers within Saratov Province housed garrisons except Khvalynsk. As table 11.1 shows, in some instances the garrisons were larger than the towns themselves, and in all instances local soldiers played a major role in local politics in 1917.

The Great War altered Saratov's ethnic makeup. When the Central Powers threatened Russia's western borders, the government evacuated entire defense-related industries, including their Latvian and Polish workers, to safer locales such as the Volga. In July 1915, for instance, all of Riga's factories were evacuated (and the population of the city fell from 500,000 to 200,000). By the fall of 1917, more than twenty thousand Poles, an additional six thousand Polish Jews, and thousands of Latvians had been evacuated to Saratov Province. Arriving from areas with a greater history of labor unrest than Saratov had, the evacuated Latvian and Polish workers proved more militant than their local counterparts, especially those evacuated from Revel and employed at the Zhest metalworks, which became the largest factory in the city, and those from Riga at the Titanik factory and Russian-Baltic plant. Although most prisoners of war were accommodated on farms in the rural areas, some were housed in the town of Saratov. An unknown number of Hungarian prisoners of war forged links with the Saratov revolutionary underground.[1] Thousands of students from the western provinces and Jews from the pale also ended up along the Volga. After only one year of war, 113,667 refugees had settled in Saratov Province. According to a city duma report, in 1916, fifty to seventy-five thousand displaced people dwelt in Saratov. Cramped together in inferior housing, the refugees had an unsettling impact on the city. Epidemics broke out frequently. Town authorities had to cope not only with a housing shortage and health problems but also with increasingly erratic food supplies, poor sanitation, and increased levels of crime and hooliganism. Finally, as in the rest of the empire, war conditions brought about a decline in the birth rate, eroded family structure and limited cohabitation. The number of illegitimate births shot up, accompanied by widespread public concern over the growing incidence of venereal disease.[2]

Because of the fluid nature of the population during the war, statistics on Saratov's population on the eve of 1917 must be used cautiously. Estimates range between 204,000 to roughly 250,000 inhabitants. Refugees, transferred workers, students, and soldiers in the garrison, however, tend to be excluded from these figures. Their inclusion would put the population of the greater metropolitan area in 1917 closer to 300,000. If one takes into account that this figure included 25–75,000 refugees, 60–70,000 soldiers, thousands of evacuated Latvian and Polish workers, Jews, and peasants from the countryside, and then recalls that one-third of the indigenous industrial proletariat and at least that number of unskilled workers had been drafted, one can conclude that, at a conservative estimate, one-third of the city's population in 1917 had not been there before the war!

The city's social makeup during the war is as difficult to assess as Saratov's fluctuating population. As part of a national operation, the Saratov city duma conducted a local census in early 1916 in order to ensure better handling of food supplies. Census takers divided the town's population into five defined social categories that are much more revealing than the old-fashioned government classification by legal estates (*soslovie*). As table 11.2 indicates, the 1916 classifications were: (1) workers—factory workers, artisans, unskilled workers, domestic and industrial servants, and others; (2) *sluzhashchie* and officials—salaried employ-

Table 11.2. Population of Saratov, 1916 (By Sex and Social Class)

	Males		Females		Both Sexes	
Class	Number	Percent	Number	Percent	Number	Percent
Working class	56,533	53.6	66,509	52.5	123,042	53.0
Professional middle class	17,136	16.2	18,883	15.0	36,019	15.5
Commercial middle class	9,688	9.1	13,191	10.5	22,879	9.8
Students boarding in Saratov	5,190	4.9	3,718	3.0	8,908	3.8
Refugees and others	17,128	16.2	24,039	19.0	41,167	17.9
All classes	105,675	100.0	126,340	100.0	232,015	100.0

SOURCE: I. N. Kokshaiskii, *Predvaritel'nye dannye perepisi naseleniia goroda Saratova i ego prigorodov* (Saratov, 1916), p. 15.

ees, white-collar workers in commercial and industrial enterprises, government officials, people of free professions (military officers, clergy, teachers, lawyers, doctors, and so on); (3) merchants and factory owners, including those owning businesses or those living on income from rented dwellings, capitalists; (4) students in secondary or higher educational institutions, living independently in the city without their parents (a transient group); and (5) those not belonging to any category, mainly refugees without specified employment.

According to the 1916 census, Saratov's population was 232,015. The compiler of the published proceedings informed readers, however, that the city's real size was larger because the figures excluded the majority of troops who lived in barracks and those recuperating in military hospitals. Slightly more than half of the population belonged to the working class. The compilers of the census suggested that this group was actually larger, too, because the statistics left out some workers who rented dwellings and small shops, tailors who took in work at home, and others who lived in special housing facilities. Since one-third of the population had not yet reached the age of fifteen, it can be assumed that, of the 123,042 members of the working class, about 80,000 were adults and thus part of the labor force.[3] Yet other sources note that only a portion of these workers— about 25,000—could be classified as "industrial proletariat" employed in approximately 150 factories in town. The city housed twenty-three metal-processing and machine-building plants employing about 4,000 workers, seventeen wood-processing enterprises, eleven butter creameries and vegetable oil presses, eight flour mills, and numerous brick, leather, chemical, textile, and tobacco factories. The flour mills employed about 1,500 workers; the butter creameries about 560; the Zhest factory from

Riga about 2,000; the Gantke metalworks, approximately 650; and the Bering factory, 450. There also were an estimated 2,000 railroad workers in Saratov, 400 transportation workers hired by the Belgian-owned tram company, 1,100 workers employed in print works, and about 1,000 tobacco plant workers. The ten brick factories employed approximately 1,000 workers; the three leather plants, 260; the sawmills, 440; and the ship-construction yard, 400. The remaining part of the population classified as working-class by the 1916 census included large numbers of artisan workers, domestics, dock hands, and other unskilled types. Once again, the true impact of the war can be seen in the fact that refugees made up the second largest social group in town. What can be called Saratov's middle-class—merchants, factory owners, "flour kings," professionals, and the large number of office workers—constituted one-fourth of Saratov's population on the eve of 1917.

The economic strains of war affected workers' political consciousness to a large extent. What direct impact did the war have on working conditions in Saratov? As suggested earlier in this book, the economic situation of the Saratov working class differed little from that of workers elsewhere in provincial Russian towns. Because the local economy was tied to agriculture, the bulk of the working class remained an unstable urban element that maintained ties with the countryside. The legacy of social subordination and a low cultural level in the villages carried over into the cities and shaped relations between employers and workers. For most of the nineteenth century the government had denied workers the right to strike or organize, and this had all but guaranteed that economic protests could easily turn political. Ignoring the existence of a labor problem, the tsarist regime had favored a patriarchal relationship between employer and workers.[4]

Long hours, low wages, neglect of basic sanitation, and an accident rate higher than the national norm had characterized working conditions for Saratov's industrial workers. Skilled metalworkers, whose earnings topped national averages, received the best wages locally and enjoyed the highest standard of living. Unskilled workers, including women and adolescents, engaged in food-processing industries and the like, usually earned less than workers elsewhere. The whistle blast that signaled the end of the workday sent most unskilled workers home to a shack or factory barrack in the town's ravines or on the slopes surrounding the city, which also gave shelter to an estimated 4,000 tramps and beggars.

Smallpox, scarlet fever, diphtheria, dysentery, cholera, plague, and vene-real disease were an inevitable part of the lives of workers living in these slums. So was alcohol.[5]

The economic situation of Saratov's working class did not change dramatically after 1905. A 1911 factory inspector's report providing infor-mation on conditions at Saratov enterprises suggests a crude dichotomy in living and working conditions between skilled and unskilled laborers, which was in no way unusual for work conditions in Russia at the time. Admitting that factory owners had a clear advantage over workers in terms of employment, the inspector adopted an almost relentlessly criti-cal tone in his report. He censured all food-processing industries for widespread filth and lack of sanitation measures and found fault with the poor diet, medical care, and factory housing available to workers. Ad-monishing the city administration to do more to look after workers' health, the report recommended that factories be placed under constant sanitary inspection and proposed the implementation of a program through which the workers themselves, after proper training in sanita-tion and hygiene, would participate in future inspections.[6]

If any improvements in work conditions came about after 1911, the impact of the war negated them. The workers' movement after June 1914 indicates that workers were concerned over the rising cost of living, lack of housing (exacerbated by the flood of refugees), low wages, breakdown in transportation and restrictions on their modest trade-union activities. The war led to a reduction in real wages, except for a brief period at the end of 1915 and then only for workers in defense-related enterprises. During the first months of hostilities overall output in Saratov fell off. At one point, production at the Bering factory had plunged 80 percent. After the organization of the Saratov War Industries Committee in 1915, set up to assume responsibilities for military supplies, this negative trend temporarily reversed itself. Measures that initially revived food and light industries were adopted during the war, and they resulted in the diversifi-cation of local industry and an upsurge in war-related production, es-pecially after the evacuation of factories from the Baltic provinces to Saratov. This wartime production, however, did not alter the predomi-nantly agricultural character of the Volga region.[7] According to the report of the Saratov Labor Exchange, an institution concerned with the problem of unemployment and job placement, the war at first increased unemployment among certain categories of unskilled workers because many light industries curtailed or even shut down production, whereas it increased demand for skilled labor to staff the defense industries.[8] Skilled workers and unskilled female laborers employed as domestics had the easiest time getting placed, while some salaried workers, such as office workers, bookkeepers, and sales clerks, had the greatest difficulty. The influx of refugees into Saratov after August 1915 complicated the tasks of the Labor exchange, which now sought to broaden its activities to aid the more than three thousand refugees who had registered with it during the five-month period before January 1916. As the war progressed, lack of fuel, raw materials, and inefficient transport caused many enterprises to reduce their output or close down. Unemployment became still more of a problem. Unfortunately, the limited sources do not allow an assessment of the impact of the war on the large number of artisans in the province. It would seem, though, that military conscription, inflation, and shortages hurt some cottage industries but stimulated others involved in the production of war materials.

Data on living conditions reported in the 1916 census corroborate the unenviable situation of Saratov's working people and the burden the war placed upon them. Other social groups—even the refugees—ate better than local workers, whose diet was high in starchy products and contained little meat, fish, eggs, or sugar. Workers also made do with less kerosene, soap, and other necessities. The compiler of the census cautioned that the working class had misunderstood the purpose of the questioning and the proposed ration-card system. Believing that the size of subsequent rations would reflect earlier consumption levels, workers had actually tended to exaggerate their access to desirable food items.[9]

War also interrupted the social transformation of the countryside. Emigration from Saratov to Siberia and other areas, which had helped to relieve local overpopulation in the rural areas since the 1890s, stopped altogether. The Stolypin agrarian reforms, as Grigorii Gerasimenko shows, came to an abrupt end and new life was breathed into the village commune. Military conscription, moreover, changed the population profile in the villages, vastly altering the ratio between men and women. Before the war there had been 102.5 women per 100 men in the countryside; in 1916 there were 121.8 women per 100 men. By 1917, 47.3 percent of the province's male population of laboring age (eighteen to fifty-nine) had been put into uniform,[10] a figure slightly above the national average. Requisitioning and conscription had likewise reduced the number of available draft animals in the villages.

The economic consequences of war for the countryside are difficult to assess because the war affected the economically diverse province in a variety of ways, making generalization problematic (to say nothing of the nature of the sources). Here we must differentiate between the highly commercialized cultivation of the large estates and the more primitive peasant economy. As the war unfolded, the gentry land-owners were less able to cultivate large tracts of land so the total area under cultivation was reduced sharply. After one year of war, the amount of land sown by all private landowners decreased 8.3 percent. The gentry landowners, who had relied on cheap farm labor, now found that the colossal channeling of peasants into the war effort had led to a rise in the cost of hired hands. Initially, the availability of prisoners of war offset this difficulty, but as the war continued the cost of hired hands gradually rose, according to one source, by as much as 100 percent and more.[11] Moreover, peasants resented the gentry's access to prisoners of war, in part because it kept the cost of hired hands from inflating to the peasants' advantage. When the peasant movement broke out in the spring of 1917, Saratov peasants first sought to deprive the landowners of their advantage in the marketplace, especially in regard to their cheap use of war prisoners.

Not all peasants conscripted into the army had been engaged in farmwork before the war; nonetheless, military conscription resulted in a lack of work hands in many locales. Women, children, old men, and prisoners of war helped to make up for the loss of male laborers,[12] and as a result the area under cultivation by peasants decreased only 1.6 percent during the first year of war. Virtually everywhere in the province local peasant economies produced less, even if only by a small percentage, except for the southernmost districts that had experienced several years of high yields. Still, it must be remembered that the war disrupted grain exports and transport, isolating Russia from the world market. It upset the equilibrium of trade and money turnover. And it set in motion a process that ultimately resulted in the peasantry's recession from the country's economic structure. Changes in the state of the market and consumption patterns, and prohibition, which promoted the brewing of moonshine (*samogon*), had increased the disposable income of some peas-ant families, but the long-term consequences of the shifting market forces must be considered. Russia was still able to feed itself, but the country was breaking apart into local, autonomous economic units.

On the eve of revolution the population of Saratov Province consisted of 2,702,000 rural and 673,371 urban dwellers. Roughly 5 percent of the 405,495 peasant households lacked land altogether, and another 15 percent, classified as *besposevnye* (without sowing area), had but a marginal amount of land. Each year of war brought greater strain to the countryside, complicating relations with the towns and foreshadowing food supply problems that were to become acute in 1917 and afterward. Although the evidence is somewhat contradictory, it appears that the economic status of the poorer or less stable rural elements who hired themselves out to gentry landowners or richer peasants (a stratum whose size is unknown) declined seriously. One source puts their decline in real wages at 25 to 30 percent between 1915 and 1917.[13] The total area of land under cultivation decreased steadily, as did the availability of manufactured items for rural consumption. Small peasant households often had to reduce the area they sowed because of labor shortages within the family. By mid-1917, 30.7 percent of all households lacked male laborers.[14] Prices for Russian wheat had skyrocketed by 50 percent, and this was after a good harvest and when virtually no grain was being exported! These considerations must be borne in mind in order to comprehend fully the sweep of the peasant movement during 1917, which above all else was aimed at eliminating what was seen as an unfair distribution of wealth.

The Great War magnified dissatisfaction with the government at many levels of Russian society but perhaps had its major impact on the revolutionary movement. The war resuscitated the liberal-radical alliance alluded to earlier in this book, yet at the same time it forced a split among the radical groups that was to prove far more important than the factional bickering which had been so much a part of "émigré" politics and which found only muted resonance in provincial Russia. As the war progressed and further exacerbated economic problems, the Russian radical movement showed serious signs of strain over whether or not Russia's war effort should be supported. This question caused controversy within the revolutionary parties, driving the more moderate elements into a deeper alliance with the liberals and separating out the more radical elements who would later accept the efficacy of revolutionary change in 1917.

The status of the revolutionary movement at the outbreak of war bore the telltale marks of the government's efforts to suppress revolution following the defeat of the Revolution of 1905. In Saratov Province waves of arrests and police infiltration had already begun to check revolutionary activities in December 1905. By mid-summer 1906, authorities had shut down the Social Democrat newspaper edited by Bolshevik P. A. Lebedev and other radical publications. Police agents permeated all of the revolutionary parties, and their active memberships declined. In June 1907, P. A. Stolypin, now prime minister, drastically changed the duma electoral laws, effectively disenfranchising masses of people, to create a docile legislature. The "system of the third of June" abruptly curbed revolutionary activity and drove antigovernment groups underground once again. By 1908–09, most activists carried out their party work in isolation, without regular ties with their party centers or skeleton organizations.

Police repression, fear, loss of leaders, and widespread demoralization slowed the growth of trade unions and dampened workers' willingness and ability to strike. Employer opposition and government repression also circumscribed the union movement, a circumstance that in the long run may have weakened workers' inclinations to trust reformist strategies, inducing them instead to militant revolutionary ones.[15] The government's basically hostile attitude toward workers' organizations is reflected in the fate of trade unionism in Saratov. Thirty-two trade unions had been registered in the province in 1906; by 1909 there were only seven.[16] Strike activity dropped off precipitously as well.[17]

Determined police crackdowns turned the national revolutionary leadership's attention once again to heated debates over appropriate strategies. Despite the formal reunification of Russia's Social Democrats in the spring of 1906, the leaders of both factions continued to maneuver for hegemony. As before 1905, factionalism and personality clashes consumed émigré energies, with the result that there again rose rival centers, rival newspapers, and rival conferences, few of which could claim to be representative of Russian social democracy. Even the main factions were now riven by subfactions.[18] Similar problems plagued the Socialist Revolutionary party.

But the situation in Saratov was different. Local conditions, as well as the personal inclinations of prominent homegrown revolutionaries, continued to shape the behavior of Saratov revolutionaries. Factionalism was unpopular within working-class circles, while the renewed factionalism abroad merely complicated relations between local groups and émigré centers. Take the example of the Saratov SD committee. In 1906, ignoring the party's call to boycott all electoral activities, it responded to working-class pressure from the Bering and Gantke plants and from railroad workers by participating in the election campaign to the First Duma.[19] Ironically, after the dismissal of the Second Duma and change in the electoral law in 1907, the SD party leaders, including Lenin, supported participation in elections to the Third Duma. But sentiment at the local level now favored boycotting, and local Social Democrats carried resolutions denouncing the duma elections. In 1908 the Saratov committee demanded the recall of the Social Democratic deputies from the Third Duma, which suggests that Bolshevik sentiments, albeit "recallist" ones, ran high locally. Saratov-born G. I. Lomov (Oppokov), who had directed the workers' armed guard in Saratov in 1905, may have been partially responsible for the Saratov SDs' position. A Bolshevik recallist active in the Moscow and St. Petersburg committees, Lomov often traveled to his hometown on behalf of recallism.[20]

Disappointed by the poor results of their political involvement and demoralized by ubiquitous police spies, many workers abandoned revolution. In describing a strike at the cotton-padding factory, a revolutionary named Ezhov, who arrived in Saratov in 1907, noted that among the Riazan peasants working there strike sentiments appealed only to young workers who made economic demands. The older, married workers with children protested against the strike, fearing reprisals and loss of their jobs.[21] As Ralph C. Elwood has demonstrated for the Ukraine, both the arrest or emigration of much of the revolutionary leadership and the tendency of the radical intelligentsia to abandon the cause at this time led to an increase in proletarian influence in the underground Saratov SD organization. By mid-1907 workers were running the local skeletal organization and those in the province's district centers.[22] Another wave of arrests in 1909 destroyed all coordinated committee work. Cells (*iacheiki*) and small study circles now predominated, as before 1905. One participant recalled that by 1909 party work consisted merely of discussing SD duma activity, and that this situation continued until 1912.[23] Although sources do not permit a discussion of local populism during this time, bits and pieces of evidence suggest that a similar fate befell Saratov SRs.

Despite the autocracy's efforts to contain the radical movement, several indicators suggest that the revolutionary camp was beginning to recover—modestly, that is—already in 1910. A second industrialization spurt took place in 1909–10, which contributed to a rise in working-class activism. Members of the local underground distributed émigré newspapers that managed to make their way to the banks of the Volga, and occasionally hectographed non-factional leaflets and proclamations. Lenin's sisters, Anna and Maria, moved to Saratov in late 1910 with Anna's husband, M. T. Elizarov. Maria, the Saratov police purportedly observed, was the "central figure among local Bolsheviks."[24] Another prominent revolutionary active in Saratov at this time was Alexander Konstantinovich Voronskii, a member of the party since 1904. Voronskii would attend the Prague Conference in 1912, and in 1917 he became chairman of the Odessa Soviet. He is best known, however, for editing the foremost literary journal in Soviet Russia following the revolution.[25]

Voronskii's fictionalized "autobiography" contains an interesting glimpse of party work in Saratov in 1910. He, Lenin's sister Maria, and Stanislav Krzizanovski formed a district Bolshevik group that by December had set up three separate circles. One circle comprised workers from the "scrap-iron factory" (probably Gantke); another comprised railroad workers and artisans; and the third was composed entirely of local high-school students. In all, some thirty people were involved. Voronskii's literary-historical work paints colorful portraits of Lenin's family; of the puritanical, sober Krzizanovski; of the supercilious radical youth; and of the workers, whom Voronskii romanticizes. In making a snide assessment of the students' "ostentatious display of self-importance," he argues that theory for theory's sake did not interest workers: "The essentially important thing for them was the human significance of a theory. They formulated their 'ideal' in accordance with man's nature; we, on the other hand, forced man's nature to conform to our 'ideal.'"[26]

At the same time, the Populist and SD intelligentsia were involving themselves in legal literary activities. It is important to note that Bolshevism and Menshevism still mattered little where practical issues were concerned. The popular Saratov Menshevik D. A. Topuridze collaborated with Lenin's sisters in publishing a newspaper, *Privolzhskaia gazeta* (The Volga-Region Newspaper), which in Aesopian but popular language sought to spread news on conditions among Saratov workers. (The local Okhranka soon arrested Anna for her work in putting out the paper.) The Bolshevik S. K. Minin arrived in Tsaritsyn at the same time, where, in support of Lenin's new call in favor of legal party work, he involved himself in publishing a journal and attacking those—Mensheviks, Bolsheviks, and SRs—who wished to liquidate all legal activities and return to the underground. I. V. Mgeladze (Vardin), who in 1917 became a prominent Saratov Bolshevik leader and a proponent of merger with the Mensheviks, arrived in Volsk in 1910, where he published a newspaper for two years, together with two SRs.[27] Before long, the Saratov governor reported to the capital that local Social Democrats had resurrected their committee. In fact, Saratov was one of twenty local party organizations represented at the Prague Conference in 1912 where, according to most writers, Bolshevism and Menshevism became two distinct parties. Although émigré leaders returning to Russia after the split at the Prague Conference of 1912 introduced a new wave of factionalism at the local level, Saratov SDs petitioned the Bolsheviks' *Pravda* (Truth) and the Menshevik liquidators' *Luch* (Ray [of light]) to end their bickering.[28]

A renewed strike movement also suggests that political activity was recovering. During 1911 Saratov railroad workers, lumberyard workers, dockhands, and tailors went out on strike and tried to organize an illegal May Day celebration. The following April government troops gunned down more than 150 unarmed striking workers in the Siberian Lena goldfields, an event that prompted sympathy strikes throughout the country, including Saratov, where the Bering workers and others struck. Weeks later, Saratov SDs sponsored a May Day strike in which an estimated two thousand workers from twenty-four factories participated. The next year an estimated ten thousand lumberyard workers struck in Tsaritsyn. Moreover, local revolutionary activists now infiltrated legal channels such as trade unions, consumer societies, and medical funds (*bol'nichnye kassy*). Laws issued in June 1912, permitting the creation of workers' funds to aid victims of illness and accident, led to a proliferation of mutual aid societies. By the summer of 1914, workers had set up fifteen medical funds in Saratov.[29] Saratov revolutionaries of all persuasions also entered cultural and educational clubs where, as in other endeavors, they collaborated with local liberals.

It must be repeated that sources shedding light on the period between 1907 and 1917 are fewer and less reliable than those illuminating earlier events in the history of the Saratov revolutionary movement. Few sources even acknowledge the activities of the Socialist Revolutionaries, and most exaggerate the importance of local Bolshevism. It seems probable that the fortunes of the other revolutionary parties in this era paralleled those of Saratov Social Democracy. Mensheviks remained active throughout the period and were even in the majority in some Volga-area SD organizations. Owing to the local SR committee's advocacy of terrorism, police repression against SRs may have been especially fierce after 1907. As Michael Melancon has argued, however, local Populists carried on more extensive activities after 1907 than is generally thought, and continued to carry on work among workers as before, even among Saratov's and Tsaritsyn's skilled metalworkers. A collection of police documents on Saratov's metalworkers' union, for example, reveals how influential SRs were among Volga-area metalworkers at this time.[30] By 1912, local SR activists could also boast broad involvement in legal operations, particularly in the cooperative movement.

Further, legal liberal parties became increasingly critical of the government at roughly the same time that revolutionaries were expanding their activities. Nationally, a surge of interest in municipal affairs and local politics had taken hold by 1909. In Saratov, middle-class "progressives," "the party of the Third Element and the free professions," had triumphed in local politics.[31]

A few other incidents, centered at the new university founded in Saratov in 1909, likewise indicate that antigovernment feelings had mounted. In the winter of 1910–11, university students, faculty, and professional groups in Saratov took part in illegal ceremonies marking the death of Lev Tolstoy, who had fallen out of favor with the government and the church during his later years. The government rightly interpreted the flood of emotion unleashed by Tolstoy's death as a rebuke of its policies. Demanding that a portrait of him be hung in the university library, student demonstrators faced strong reprisals from the authorities, who drafted the students.[32] Saratov society also denounced the government's shooting of workers in 1912. In a report to the Ministry of the Interior, the Saratov governor noted a move to the left of zemstvo organs and a revitalization of the Third Element.[33] Together with the revolutionaries, Saratov liberals intensified their activities within various clubs and educational societies as well as in the people's university movement. On the eve of the Great War, society's dissatisfaction was once again serving as the basis for a rising tide of political activism. As Elwood so aptly put it, the war, neither postponing revolution nor causing it, "merely served to define and to intensify grievances felt since the beginning of the century."[34]

In view of the vicissitudes in the history of the revolutionary movement during the so-called years of reaction, it is not surprising that the outbreak of war presented the radical movement with new dilemmas and opportunities. The world war destroyed the unity of world socialism; most socialists reacted to the outbreak of hostilities along national lines. Confusion was exacerbated in Russia by Lenin's advocacy of his own country's defeat. In Saratov and other Volga cities, arrests on the eve of the war once again debilitated party groups of all persuasions. S. K. Kukushkin, for example, was arrested in July while preparing a Volga-area SD conference. During the first months of war, Saratov revolutionaries had no ties whatsoever to their party centers, a situation not uncommon in the country as a whole.[35] Deep uncertainty over how to relate to the war held sway especially within local Bolshevik ranks. V. P. Antonov (Antonov-Saratovskii), who became one of Saratov's most influential Bolsheviks in 1917, is a case in point. Despite claims that he adopted an internationalist, Leninist position from the start, other, more convincing evidence shows that he supported the defensist (Menshevik) position until mid-1915.[36]

The events of 1917 would suggest that antiwar factions emerged in all of the local revolutionary party organizations before 1917. Available sources, however, permit discussion only of the fortunes of the local Social Democrats. Information trickling into Saratov from elsewhere eventually broke down defensist attitudes among local Bolsheviks. The government unwittingly helped speed this process by continuing to send political exiles, mainly revolutionaries, to Saratov. The local government complained in 1915 that more than one hundred exiles had already registered in Saratov, and about five hundred in Tsaritsyn.[37] Among these were V. P. Nogin, M. S. Ol'minskii, S. I. Mitskevich, Miliutin, V. A. Radus-Zenkovich, Iu. K. Milonov, and Vasil'ev-Iuzhin—an impressive contingent of activists who had closer contact with the émigré center and who by spring 1915 had linked up with local SDs such as Antonov and P. A. Lebedev. Ol'minskii, who brought to Saratov copies of Lenin's "The War and Social Democracy," published in the émigré *Sotsial-Demokrat* (Social Democrat), recreated ties with the center through Moscow contacts. Eight months had thus passed after the outbreak of war before Saratov Bolsheviks had become acquainted with the position of their Central Committee.[38]

It took a strong conviction to advocate Lenin's position on the war, because the Russian public, like that in other countries, had backed its country's entry into the hostilities. After the Russian victory at Przemysl in March 1915, a massive demonstration, supported even by some of Saratov's more "conscious" workers, celebrated Russia's military triumph. The Union of Michael the Archangel, led by local landlords, mobilized support for the war, and although its successes were negligible among skilled workers, it made inroads among the "ignorant lower-middle classes on the outskirts of the city." The Blackhundreds opened a cafeteria-club for workers and "spread slander" against Saratov Germans, Jews, and revolutionaries. Rumors of an anti-German pogrom spread throughout the province and the Blackhundreds purportedly threatened local radicals with violence.[39]

Not everyone, to be sure, had met the declaration of war with enthusiasm. Antiwar disturbances had broken out at induction centers in Volsk and Tsaritsyn; peasant disturbances had flared up in some districts in the countryside.[40] In Saratov itself, workers at the Gantke plant had responded to the declaration of war by going out on strike. The head of the Saratov police reported to his superiors that the tranquility of local workers should not be taken for granted. "The novelty of the attitudes evoked by the war, interpreted as a growth in patriotic feeling, will pass," he predicted, "and the old mood, capable of turning into open rebellion, will replace it at the first appropriate moment."[41]

Working-class attitudes toward the war are admittedly difficult to assess, but evidence shows that sympathetic feelings in Saratov gradually cooled. As we have seen, the government relocated more radically disposed Latvian and Polish workers to Saratov. At about the same time, the maimed and wounded began arriving for treatment in the Saratov garrison's war hospital. Further, bread-and-butter issues shaped the attitudes of the indigenous work force toward the war. Only those establishments filling war orders now operated at full capacity. The number of workers at cement and lumber-processing plants, at flour mills, print shops, and even metalworks decreased. By 1915, despite some pay increases, wages already failed to match the rising costs of consumer and food items. In August and November 1914, workers demanding higher wages struck in Tsaritsyn. The strike movement broadened in 1915, when workers from the Bering plant, Gantke plant, Iakovlev printworks, and Medvedev lumberyards went out on strike.

Growing economic unrest among the Saratov proletariat helped to revive activities among the revolutionary intelligentsia. Government-created guardianships or trusteeships (*popechitel'stva*), cooperatives, various educational organizations, and clubs continued to be the main legal institutions open to socialists. The war necessitated an increase in the scope of these institutions, especially after refugees and evacuees poured into Saratov. Antonov, moreover, promoted the opening of a labor exchange to deal with growing unemployment. Socialists similarly infiltrated cooperatives, clubs, and institutions set up to assist displaced persons.[42] The most important center for radical activity at this time was the club *Maiak* (Lighthouse), which had opened in 1912. Such adult educational organizations in Russia resembled the Verdandi, Chautauqua, and Sillon movements in Sweden, the United States, and France. Initially Maiak had served as a meeting place for the liberal intelligentsia, but once war had broken out more revolutionary types, including Bolshevik exiles who arrived in 1915, began to congregate there. During the war Kerensky, now a deputy to the Fourth Duma elected from Saratov, frequently visited the town, where he addressed gatherings at Maiak. In May 1915, Saratov Bolsheviks decided to concentrate their efforts there to attract working-class support rather than continue agitational work with student circles. It was at the same time that Ol'minskii and Nogin showed up in Saratov with copies of *Sotsial-Demokrat*. Antonov claimed that, by late spring 1915, Maiak and the Saratov committee of the RSDRP (still, apparently, united) had become synonymous and that working-class membership had swelled.[43]

Growing working-class unrest, a replenished Social Democratic group, and the establishment of ties with party circles in Petrograd, Moscow, Baku, and Astrakhan encouraged Saratov SDs to publish a newspaper in the summer of 1915. Despite the claims of Soviet writers, the circumstances surrounding publication of a paper revealed the myriad of opinions within local Social Democracy and the extent to which differing attitudes on the war began to break down the traditional camaraderie of local socialists. Ol'minskii, Mitskevich, and Antonov, who was making rapid progress in his intellectual journey to Bolshevism, had to contend with a large group of SD *intelligenty*, both local and from the outside, who insisted on an editorial board free from party control. What was at stake was their desire to avoid a formal split in the mixed Bolshevik-Menshevik group and to keep factionalism to a minimum so as not to alienate workers. Such prominent figures as Nogin and Lebedev remained critical of their party's stance on the war and did not wish to drive away their Menshevik comrades from Samara, who participated in the preliminary discussions to start up a publication. However, in the process of reaching a consensus on critical issues it became clear that the Bolsheviks held the upper hand, for it was decided to opt for a "party" paper. Articles appearing in the first issues of *Nasha gazeta* (Our Paper)[44] criticized the election of workers' groups to War Industries Committees (the Bolshevik position). Outvoted on this issue, the Mensheviks withdrew from the newspaper's editorial board, returned to Samara, and put out a defensist paper.

In all, ten issues of *Nasha gazeta* went to press between August 8 and October 20, 1915. By the time the police shut it down, the number of copies printed had increased from two to ten thousand (the leading Saratov dailies had circulations of six thousand copies).[45] The paper provides valuable insights into labor conditions in Saratov, devoting extensive coverage to medical funds and management's purported threats to take advantage of wartime conditions to counter workers' demands for improved wages. Workers complained of arbitrary fine systems, niggardly pay, the hiring of prisoners of war for low wages, and constant threats from their bosses to hire refugees, prisoners of war, or women if workers dared voice their discontent.[46] Monitoring *Nasha gazeta*'s contents and impact upon the labor movement, the Okhranka maintained that the paper "from the very first issue obviously aimed at inciting the workers not only against the government, but in general against the propertied classes as well."[47] Police confiscated two of the ten issues and censors purged others of provocative writing. Local industrialists, who complained that the paper encouraged strikes, pressured the police to increase its surveillance. On October 15, local courts closed down *Nasha gazeta* and ordered the arrest of several of its editors.[48]

The publication of *Nasha gazeta* had paralleled a resurgence in strike activity; yet the paper's role in stimulating this revival of the workers' movement is difficult to gauge. The growth of a strike movement in Saratov seems to have been part of a national phenomenon brought about by unpopular governmental policies and a worsening economic situation. In the summer of 1915, for instance, troops shot at striking workers in Ivanovo-Voznesensk, and on September 3 the government dismissed the State Duma. The local workers' movement had already revived on its own initiative by 1915, just as it had in Petrograd, and may have actually encouraged the SD intelligentsia to organize a party committee and publish a paper. More strikes had broken out in 1915 in Saratov than during any other year between 1912 and 1916. The May Day strike of 1915 shut down almost all large plants and factories.[49]

Nevertheless, the local strike movement intensified during the period when *Nasha gazeta* was being published. Tailors, bakers, printers, and workers at the Kostemolnyi plant went out first, but the movement soon spread to oil-press, lumberyard, and other workers.[50] Increasing strike activity reflected the growing financial burden the war had placed on the Saratov working class—a point *Nasha gazeta* repeatedly emphasized. Each month of hostilities brought greater economic difficulties to Saratov workers. The government scrapped decrees regulating work hours and limiting female, adolescent, and child labor. Prices of food and manufactured items shot up 40 percent by 1916, making many products unattainable for the wage-earner. The cost of such commodities as sugar and kerosene inflated 100 to 200 percent. Long queues became commonplace in the city. Victimized by the priorities of war and threatened with being sent to the front, workers looked increasingly to the revolutionary underground for direction. By September 1915, concomitant with the publication of *Nasha gazeta,* the strike movement had acquired new intensity, and by November inspectors reported a political strike.[51] Moreover, Saratov workers boycotted the War Industries Committee, thus revealing the influence *Nasha gazeta* and Bolshevik sentiments may have had over them.[52]

The revival of revolutionary activities in the second half of 1915 must also be viewed as part of a broader concern within Saratov society over the government's bungling of the war cause. Shortly after the publication of *Nasha gazeta,* Kerensky visited Saratov, where he organized a meeting of local representatives of all major liberal and radical groups. If Antonov's account of this gathering is to be trusted, the various individuals exhibited enormous camaraderie and shared the sentiment that revolution would shortly break out.[53] An additional factor in the intensification of antigovernment feelings at this time was the arrival in Saratov of evacuated students from Kiev University and from that city's commercial institute and higher educational courses for women. Local revolutionaries noted that the evacuated students helped to fill the need for political instructors and propagandists, and that the Kievan students were more radical than local ones. The police concurred.[54]

About the same time that Kerensky convened the meeting of the opposition parties, a demonstration took place in Saratov to commemorate the death of V. B. Lomtatidze, a Menshevik member of the Second Duma. Later that week, the police questioned Antonov, Lebedev, and several others responsible for it. A sharp rise in the price of flour a few weeks later prompted railroad workers and others to strike. Local SDs issued appeals and printed leaflets articulating the workers' demands. Within days the authorities had arrested Antonov, Lebedev, and Lomov.[55]

More arrests in early 1916 all but destroyed coordinated efforts within the revolutionary underground. Plans to conduct a May Day celebration under the slogans "Down with the War," "The Eight-Hour Workday," and "One Hundred Percent Pay Increases" were foiled by the police, who arrested all the revolutionaries they could find, dealing a crippling blow to Maiak and the radical movement in general.[56] When the Bolshevik T. V. Sapronov arrived in Saratov in June 1916, he found the party organization in shambles. Another recent newcomer to Saratov, A. Martsinovskii, reported dishearteningly that many workers still expressed patriotic sentiments and were unaware of the existence of trade unions.[57] Party cells existing earlier at most factories had broken down. As before, however, party members who were still free met at Maiak, and there Sapronov and Martsinovksii made their first contacts in Saratov, despite the fact that the Okhranka was methodically observing all activities on the premises.[58]

As was often the case in the history of Saratov Social Democracy, the arrival of outside activists such as Sapronov and Martsinovskii strengthened the underground. But the greatest initiative came from the SD workers Plaksin, Ignat, Bukin, Gulbis, Vorobev, and others, who formed the "Initiative Group," which for the next seven months tried to restore ties via medical funds with metalworkers, carpenters and lumberyard workers, Latvian workers, railroad workers, and tailors. The Initiative Group also attempted with little success to revive ties with SD committees in other Volga cities.[59] Lacking theoreticians, people able to deliver lectures, to write proclamations and the like, the Initiative Group failed to organize an actual SD committee. Members of the local Bolshevik intelligentsia still in town now shied away from contact with workers, while some workers viewed the underground with suspicion or hostility. Not surprisingly, the Initiative Group cooperated with other elements of the opposition. It joined the illegal political Red Cross—an organization

of intellectuals, mainly Mensheviks and Kadets, to aid political prisoners—and linked up with the Bund (the General Union of Jewish
Workers, an organization allied with the Mensheviks).[60] But attempts to
interest Bolshevik intellectuals such as Miliutin, Mitskevich, or Vasil'ev-
Iuzhin in practical work failed.

By January 1917 the economic and social strains of two and a half years
of war had created widespread anxieties among the townspeople. Saratov
newspapers documented these concerns, both the minor ones and those
of a graver nature. Even the minor complaints and apprehensions were
directly tied to the war. City officials discussed the construction of a
much needed bridge across the Volga, but the project had to be scrapped
owing to more pressing wartime needs. Irate citizens complained of
rampant hooliganism, while local medical funds at factories campaigned
for the opening of a new clinic. Even more seriously, the growing
incidences of draft evasion and desertion caused city officials to crack
down on those trying to elude military service. Health inspectors, meanwhile, had to cope with mange and typhus epidemics. After reporting
that half of the city's public baths should be closed because of unsanitary
conditions, the sanitation commission nevertheless grudgingly kept them
open. Saratov simply lacked other facilities. Supply problems, ironically,
also bred discontent in this food-producing province. Real and anticipated shortages of food items had locked the city administration and
food supply committee to heated debate over the introduction of a
rationing system for bread and other products. The city duma and other
public groups appealed to the government to convoke the State Duma,
the only institution "powerful enough to deal with the food crisis."[61]

City officials expressed hope that rationing would end speculation,
making it easier to handle projected decreases in available grain supplies
in February and March. Authorities reluctantly agreed to a system,
scheduled to begin in April. Yet rumors concerning the upcoming rationing had already increased speculation, and higher bread prices heightened discontent. Long lines at bread shops now were common. Meat
became a luxury. The city exhausted its tea reserves.[62] This grim situation, common to the district towns as well, is also reflected in the pages of
the official publication of the Union of Towns, whose reports indicate
that local authorities were even compelled to requisition food supplies in
transit to other provinces in order to stave off hunger.[63] This practice
would become much more common during 1917 and during the civil war.

Food deficits coincided with an energy and transport crisis that caused factories to close. Those industries forced to convert to electrical energy overburdened the city's few electricity power stations. To compensate, the public and private sectors reduced their lighting of public buildings and shop windows. Lack of coal gravely threatened the Riazan-Urals railroad line, which reduced its services, thereby further complicating the food supply issue. The city's labor exchange reported that unemployment in 1916 was twice as high as during 1915. The closing down of more factories in early 1917 made matters worse. In addition, the 8,060 refugees in Saratov sorely needed clothing and food at a time when the city expected the imminent arrival of a group of Rumanian evacuees.[64] In a private letter, Saratov governor S. D. Tverskoi wrote:

> What's going on? Eleven years haven't gone by since 1905. Yet once again we see the same people, hear the same words on the one hand, and see the same paralysis on the part of the authorities on the other. Once again, zemstvo activists from the nobility are taking up politics in the provinces. Once again, there are stinging resolutions against the hated government. And what will come of all this? In the future the unlettered muzhik once again will have his say and have his way. The situation is utterly distressing.[65]

Although the pressing problems and discontent linked with the war contributed immensely to a rising critical sentiment within Saratov society, the broad legacy of the past quarter-century determined political relationships that emerged in Saratov after the autocratic regime had been swept away. Since 1905, if not before, the mixed record of reform and reaction had engendered much hostility toward the government. The resulting vitality of progressive and leftist forces, more than anything else, shaped the political alignment after February 1917. Patterns of behavior and relationships among and within political groups, which had formed back in the early days of political activism at the turn of the century and later survived in the underground after 1907, were to cast a heavy shadow over 1917. At the same time, however, these relationships would become complicated and strained over how the various components of the liberal-radical alliance related to the war.

12. The Revolution of 1917 and the Establishment of Soviet Power in Saratov

Donald J. Raleigh

THE REVOLUTION of 1917 in Saratov should not be viewed as a distant echo of events in Petrograd, but rather as a distinctive parochial revolution, unfolding as a unique interaction between local structural conditions and larger events and issues. The cumulative success over the past generations of the revolutionary and liberal "bourgeois" parties, which had politicized society and weakened the autocracy through their implacable criticism of the regime, helps to explain society's reaction to the end of the tsarist system. Moreover, the vitality of a socialist political culture in the towns and surrounding areas became manifest. Given the opportunity to function legally, and owing part of their success to the unusual circumstances caused by the war, the revolutionary parties soon surpassed the liberal elements that had seemed so influential under different conditions. While the liberal parties represented the major challenge to socialist forces in Saratov, the Kadets' mass base remained restricted. How the radical wing of Russian socialism triumphed over the more moderate socialists who commanded such broad support in the spring of 1917 is the subject of this chapter.

On the morning of March 1, 1917, Saratov Governor S. D. Tverskoi received word of revolutionary developments in Petrograd. Sharing the information with a select group of confidants, he tried unsuccessfully to keep it from the town population, even from the city duma. News leaked out about unusual events in the capital, however, and duma leaders resolved to convene an evening meeting, to which representatives from the War Industries Committee, university administration, City Cooperative Board, garrison command, and other social organizations were invited. Revolutionary activists gathering that day at the workers' club, Maiak, elected the Bolsheviks M. I. Vasil'ev (Vasil'ev-Iuzhin), V. P. Miliutin, and a tailor named Stepanov to represent them at the evening duma meeting. That night the enlarged city duma met, discussed the events in Petrograd, but failed to take any decisive action. Two factions emerged at this meeting: the majority advocated a wait-and-see policy until more concrete information was received from the capital; the minority favored establishing a committee to direct the local power transfer should one be necessary.

On March 2, newspaper editors and other officials ignored Tverskoi's orders and began to disseminate information arriving by cable from Petrograd. Throughout the day professional groups met to discuss an appropriate course of action. Sources do not permit a confident reconstruction of the events leading up to it, but revolutionary activists visited Saratov's largest industrial enterprises and urged workers to elect representatives to a soviet. When the duma met that evening, it faced the direct pressure of a workers' soviet meeting at the same time in the basement of the city duma building. As in Petrograd, the formation of a soviet swayed the duma to take decisive measures. While the duma was locked in heated debate, deputies to the workers' council chose an executive committee comprising four Bolsheviks, three Mensheviks, and one Socialist Revolutionary. The Bolshevik Miliutin was named chairman of the Soviet, and Vasil'ev (a Bolshevik) and I. A. Skvortsov (a Menshevik worker from the Bering factory) were appointed vice chairmen.

Another factor contributing to the duma's formation of an executive body that evening was the unexpected appearance of soldiers from the Third Machine-Gun Regiment, who demanded the arrest of Tverskoi and other members of the old regime. Fearing independent actions on the part of the Soviet or armed soldiers, the duma created a Public Executive Committee (*Obshchestvennyi ispolnitel'nyi komitet*) empowered to serve as an impartial government and to work with the army "for a decisive victory over the enemy." The Public Executive Committee (PEC) included six representatives from the duma, three from the city's lawyers, one from the zemstvo, one from the cooperatives, and five from the Soviet. A lawyer and former State Duma deputy, the Kadet A. A. Tokarskii, was appointed chairman of the PEC, and the Popular Socialist N. I. Semenov, active in the War Industries Committee, was named provincial commissar, as governors were now called. The first meeting of the PEC ended on an ominous note: while the committee was being formed, crowds of soldiers and workers arrested more than three hundred tsarist officials, including Tverskoi, gendarmes, members of the Blackhundreds, and hated officers. Ignoring all appeals from the PEC and from their officers, the sixty-thousand-strong Saratov garrison formed a temporary and then a "permanent military committee."[1]

From Saratov the revolution spread to the district towns and from there to the countryside, inaugurating direct participation in politics by the heretofore disenfranchised Russian masses. At the district level the political transition generally took place before directives came from Petrograd; between March 4 and 8 newly elected executive committees and soviets had replaced the old administrations in all of the province's district centers. Broadly speaking, the social structure of these towns affected the response to the revolution. For the most part, the populations were involved in trade and handicraft activities and there were few industrial workers. Populism, and to a lesser extent liberalism, represented the most significant political currents among the intelligentsia. Occasionally one comes across an isolated Social Democrat, but such activists exhibited few partisan sentiments at this time. Factors such as the record of progressive elements locally before 1917 and proximity to Saratov or Tsaritsyn or to major railroad arteries also shaped the way the revolution unfolded at the district level. Yet in virtually every instance the army emerged as the truly decisive element in shifting the balance of forces against the old administrations. All of the district centers except for remote Khvalynsk housed garrisons that often were more populous than the towns themselves. Without exception, garrison troops, at times joined by workers, arrested the old tsarist police, gendarmes, unpopular garrison commanders, and officers.[2]

The villages likewise expressed few regrets over the collapse of the old order. Displaying the same penchant for independent initiative as the urban population, peasants elected their own volost executive committees to work toward what the revolution had signified to them: an end to the exploitative system of rents and the transfer of land to those who tilled it. On March 19 the Provisional Government recognized the legitimacy of the volost executive committees, transferring to them the responsibilities of the old volost administrations until the zemstvos were reelected along democratic lines.[3]

The February Revolution had dealt a death blow to centralized state power; all power relationships soon would become completely voluntary. The Public Executive Committee, for example, decided crucial issues on the spot, taking local conditions into account when considering directives from the center. Moreover, unlike the situation in Petrograd where, with the exception of A. F. Kerensky, Soviet leaders did not join the government, the organs of the Provisional Government at the local level contained heavy representation from soviets and other popular bodies from the beginning. As a result, in dealing with the most pressing problems—the need to maintain order, reorganize the old police force, alleviate food shortages, liquidate vestiges of the tsarist regime, democratize the city duma and zemstvo—the PEC began to yield to pressures from the garrison and Soviet.

The Saratov garrison elected a Military Committee on March 5, which served as the most authoritative organ in the barracks until the committee merged with the Soviet on June 1. In forming the committee, comprised of forty officers and eighty rank-and-file soldiers, independent initiative ruled once again. On March 6, the commander of the Kazan Military District called for the establishment of military committees in all garrisons in Saratov Province. The circular reached local garrisons on March 10–11, after they had already elected committees. Run by a nine-member presidium, the Saratov Military Committee (MC) contained a large number of junior officers—mostly of SR and Popular Socialist persuasion—promoted during the war. As one of its first measures, the MC issued a mandate to regulate the garrison and restore order. At the same time the Petrograd Soviet's Order No. 1, intended for the Petrograd district only, inspired the creation of democratically elected soldier committees at the company, battery, detachment, and regiment levels throughout the Saratov garrison and in other garrisons in the province.[4]

Within a week of the formation of the Saratov Soviet, 60 percent of the city's industrial enterprises had elected deputies to it. Throughout March the Soviet was almost in constant session, creating numerous committees and generating considerable political power. It consisted of a Workers' and a Soldiers' Section; *intelligenty* and professionals predominated in the Workers' Section, and SRs and other populists in the Soldiers' Section. By May the Soviet had increased in size to 532 members—322 workers and 210 soldiers. As was often the case in provincial Russia, one's length of service in the underground and overall prestige commanded more respect than one's party affiliation immediately after February. Despite the small number of Bolsheviks in town, they occupied six of nine seats on the Presidium, primarily because of the party's success in organizing workers during the war and because some well-known and widely respected leaders, such as Miliutin and Vasil'ev, were on hand. An analysis of the leadership of soviets from the Volga and Ural regions shows that seasoned revolutionaries controlled soviets in the entire area. Slightly more than half of the delegates to a regional conference of soviets held in Saratov were members of the intelligentsia, and approximately two-thirds of the remaining workers' delegates came from the metal-processing industry. The majority of delegates were SDs, with the Mensheviks in a slight majority. The policies of the Petrograd Soviet on all major issues of the day found universal approval.[5]

During the spring of 1917 an unusual paradox came to characterize revolutionary politics locally. The February revolution had atomized political power. Nonetheless, as March progressed the Soviet came to muster more power and prestige than even the most optimistic revolutionary could have expected a few weeks before; it consolidated its influence at the expense of the Public Executive Committee and city duma and became for many workers and soldiers the most legitimate power in the city. It was this emerging legitimacy of the Soviet in the eyes of the masses that gradually established an effective political medium for Bolshevik and left socialist aspirations. The Saratov Soviet wielded considerable political power, not only because it had organized the previously disenfranchised and supported their basic demands, but also because it played a major role in reorganizing the police force, regulating food supplies, and fighting to democratize the city duma.

Meanwhile, other political organs grew weaker. The duma in effect played no political role whatsoever until it was compelled by the Soviet to submit to general democratic elections in July. At the same time, structural changes and growing partisan attitudes weakened the PEC. At the end of May it selected a five-member collegium representing the five most important political parties to replace the provincial commissar, who had resigned. The Bolsheviks' refusal to join the body marked the end of their willingness to cooperate with the bourgeoisie and the beginning of their as yet restrained advocacy of an all-socialist government. Moreover, with the exception of the one Kadet deputy, the new leaders of the PEC also sat on the Soviet's Executive Committee; soon the

Provincial Public Executive Committee merely functioned as an extension of the Soviet. Newspapers document the committee's failure to meet regularly and the apathy of its members. The liberal paper *Saratovskii vestnik* (Saratov Herald) concluded that "as of late, power not only in the city but throughout the province has actually passed to the Soviet of Workers' and Soldiers' Deputies since the [Public] Executive Committee has not met for three weeks."[6] This extraordinary situation was not unique to Saratov but was common throughout European Russia, the Baltic, and Siberia, where in some extreme cases soviets actually set up local organs of the Provisional Government.[7]

Although class and social tensions were manifest in Saratov in March, they were overshadowed at first by a high degree of revolutionary camaraderie such as had long colored relationships among Saratov socialists and between socialists and liberals (see, for example, Thomas S. Fallows's chapter for a discussion of the liberal-radical alliance in 1903–05). The Petrograd Soviet's acceptance of revolutionary defensism and its conditional support for the Provisional Government struck a responsive chord in Saratov, where prominent socialist leaders also adopted moderate views on burning issues of the day. Local Bolsheviks stood close to other socialists on most tactical matters. During March and afterward, however, as the political parties formulated clearer positions on the key questions of the continuation of the war and support for the government, cooperation among socialists broke down and greater energies were expended in organizing party committees.

Saratov SRs launched a party newspaper, *Zemlia i volia* (Land and Liberty), as early as March 12. N. I. Rakitnikov, a prominent national figure, chaired the district zemstvo and headed the local SR organization, which soon attracted more popular support at this time than any other political party, particularly in the garrison, where the SRs boasted more than a thousand members in April. Social Democrats in many provincial towns entered joint party committees in the period following the February revolution; among Saratov Bolsheviks prominent intelligenty initially advocated formation of a joint Social Democratic organization but came into conflict with worker activists from the Initiative Group created in 1916. Consequently, a separate Bolshevik organization was formed, which started up a party paper on March 23, *Sotsial-Demokrat* (The Social Democrat). Miliutin chaired the local committee that coopted into its ranks V. P. Antonov (Antonov-Saratovskii) and P. A. Lebedev, who had just returned from exile. A few days after the first issue of the Bolshevik paper hit the streets, the Mensheviks began issuing their own paper, *Proletarii Povolzh'ia* (The Proletariat of the Volga Region). D. A. Topuridze, a popular figure in the Saratov underground, chaired the Menshevik committee. He and other Mensheviks had adopted an internationalist position on the war and favored the cause of union. Indeed, well into April elements within the local Bolshevik and Menshevik organizations continued to push for a national congress, as in 1905, to unify the two factions of social democracy. For the most part, the working class expressed consternation at the party bickering and theoretical squabbles they often failed to understand.

As a merger between the SD factions grew less likely in late spring, however, the Bolsheviks set up a citywide organization that was strong in the so-called factory and railroad districts but weak in the garrison and riverfront districts. Large numbers of refugees, prisoners of war, and relocated Latvians and Poles joined the organization. The Latvians represented an important pro-Bolshevik component within the local working class, especially after a national Latvian congress in May passed hardcore Bolshevik resolutions. A four hundred-member Bolshevik Military Organization surfaced in the garrison, but its leaders maintained few ties with the local party organization and often acted in concert with the Menshevik Military Organization: both advocated union and even printed identical political appeals.[8]

Perhaps more than anything else, Lenin's return to Petrograd in April destroyed the unity among Russian socialists. Calling for an end to the war, an end of support for the Provisional Government, and a transfer of power to the soviets, Lenin's theses at first shocked local comrades who questioned their validity, but the Miliukov Affair and the collapse of the Provisional Government added force to his arguments. At a city conference held on April 19–20, Saratov Bolsheviks accepted Lenin's proposals and backed the idea of a merger with all SD groups that rejected "civil peace" and supported class war. This decision shattered hopes for unification and resulted in the formation of an SR–Menshevik bloc within the Saratov Soviet. The April crisis also complicated political issues both at the national and local levels. Riots and looting broke out when the Miliukov Note was made public.[9] Passionate debates took place at party meetings and Soviet plenums as to whether or not the socialists should participate in the First Coalition Government created on May 6. Even though many moderates feared that joining the government would compromise their own party programs, they nevertheless endorsed the decisions of their central committees. The debate shifted to the Soviet plenum, which carried a resolution supporting the new government by a vote of 153 in favor, 76 opposed, and 11 abstentions.[10]

Apart from their disagreements over the First Coalition Government, relations among Saratov socialists became strained over the question of the war. The Soviet accepted the Petrograd Soviet's call for a speedy end to the conflict "on the basis of peace without annexations, contributions, and with the concession to each nation of the right of self determination," but found itself cajoling local troops to go to the front for the June offensive. The Bolsheviks' increasingly critical stance toward continuation of the war and their rejection of the First Coalition Government began to break down nonpartisan attitudes. After elections to the Soviet in May and its merger with the Military Committee on June 1, however, moderates came to dominate the Soviet, and the Bolshevik position within it weakened: the new executive committee chosen in late June on a proportional basis included thirteen SRs, nine Bolsheviks, and eight Mensheviks.[11] As the illusion of socialist unity shattered, the Bolsheviks withdrew from the bloc formed with the other socialist parties for elections to the city duma, slated for early July. Consequently, the election campaign took place in an atmosphere of increased tension in which political forces remained in flux.[12] Because of their commitment to coalition with the "bourgeoisie," the SRs and Mensheviks now sought to make the government's local bodies work too. But what they did not foresee was that the class-oriented Soviet would continue to muster more authority than a democratically elected duma, and that Saratov's working class and soldiers were beginning to listen more attentively to Bolshevik slogans.

In the spring of 1917 socialist jargon had split society into two antithetical groups: "the democracy," broadly defined as all political and social forces to the left of the Kadets, and *tsenzovoe obshchestvo,* or census society, as the propertied elements were called. The Kadets were the most politically viable alternative to the socialist parties and the least discredited element within census society. As elsewhere, most members of the party tended to be professional people—lawyers, teachers, civil servants, doctors, and office workers. During the war years the liberals had become increasingly critical of the government's poor image and inept handling of the war; since they had participated legally in local and national politics before 1917, they had acquired a firm foothold in the Saratov PEC. Advocating the postponement of fundamental reform until after the war, the party now sought to curb the revolutionary tide unleashed in the country at large. The Kadet tactical program, which opposed a return to monarchism, favored the enfranchisement of women, supported the Provisional Government, and called for a constituent assembly based on free elections. It also advocated "the continuation of the war to a victorious end," a tactic that ultimately determined the party's fate both at the national level and in Saratov. After the April crisis, which tarnished Miliukov's and the party's reputation, many provincial Kadet organizations abandoned their quest for mass support and instead found new allies with other forces of "law and order." According to William G. Rosenberg, the historian of the Kadets, the enrollment in the party of large numbers of Octobrists, Nationalists, and other "prerevolutionary parties" facilitated the party's shift to the right.

Which groups composed the democracy and how did they respond to the unprecedented freedoms ushered in by the February revolution? Even a partial answer to this question adds a needed perspective to our understanding of revolutionary processes outside Petrograd and Moscow.

First of all, the democracy included the urban workers. Although elements within the heterogeneous Saratov working class responded differently to the post-February situation, economic issues shaped working-class politics and attitudes the most. Saratov workers directed their first offensive in the economic realm at achieving the eight-hour workday. As economic life deteriorated in Saratov in the late spring, workers demanded higher wages, limits on night work and child labor, improvements in medical care, and job security. Economic breakdown, exacerbated by runaway inflation and a transportation crisis, increased unemployment; layoffs in April and May resulted in strikes. Apart from the Soviet, workers turned to their factory committees and trade unions to solve labor disputes. By May, eighty-five factory committees and sixteen unions had been set up in Saratov. Partisan attitudes developed earliest among metalworkers, railroad workers, evacuated Latvian and Polish workers, and later among local workers in the tobacco factories, lumberyards, and oil presses. The Titanik factory transferred from the Baltic was the first to demand an end to the war. In April and May, some Saratov workers issued resolutions expressing lack of faith in the Provisional Government and opposition to government-floated war bonds, and even called for workers' control over industry to prevent arbitrary behavior on the part of bosses. By summer the local industrial workers' sustained suspicion and mistrust of factory managers paralleled a hardening of class lines toward the Provisional Government and political power in general. Ironically, the growing dissatisfaction with the coalition government and antiwar sentiment corresponded with the consolidation of moderate socialists within local political institutions.[13]

The second major component of the democracy was the garrison soldiers. The attitudes and behavior of soldiers had also changed markedly by the summer of 1917, and this placed a strain on relations between soldiers and civilians. In late April, army battalions gathered to see off troops departing for the front; six weeks later the same units refused to take part in the June offensive. What caused this change of attitude? After February the common soldier was mainly concerned with preventing a return to the former command structure and a resumption of war on a major scale. Moreover, morale and discipline problems abounded. Substandard housing, infectious disease epidemics, the new concepts of discipline, bleak news from the front, rumors of desertion, and the influence of the *frontoviki,* soldiers recuperating in military hospitals, affected attitudes. The demands of Ukrainians, Poles, Tatars, Jews, Armenians, and Lithuanians for the formation of national units also bred discontent. Not only did the young draftees show growing recalcitrance, but also the "over-fortys," twenty thousand of whom had been furloughed to local villages for planting and haymaking. But it was the Miliukov Note and the formation of a coalition government that radicalized soldiers' attitudes the most. For one thing, the new government sought to restore discipline (the death penalty was reinstated) and ready troops for the offensive. A local branch of the Union of Army and Naval Officers as well as an array of party-backed organizations and educational societies (mainly SR) emerged. Shooting actually broke out in early June during a roundup of deserters, which resulted in more than a thousand arrests.[14] However, the moderate socialists' support of the government and the June offensive proved costly: it compelled many among the rank and file to listen to what the Bolsheviks had to say.

The peasantry made up the third major element of the democracy.

What is striking about their behavior at this time is their complete disregard for the Provisional Government's successive agrarian programs. Despite the strong pressure to hold off the land settlement until the Constituent Assembly, peasants throughout the Volga region proceeded to introduce their own land reform. There was no one to stop them. By May most volost committees, which were in the hands of the peasants, served as the vehicle through which the Russian muzhik fought for more land. At the end of April the government had called for election of land committees (to slow down the agrarian movement), but they merely complicated the question of power in the rural areas; by summer peasants controlled the lower-level and volost committees alike.

The impulse on the part of the Volga-area peasantry toward implementing land reform before the Constituent Assembly exposed the gap separating rural activists from the leaders in towns and cities. The peasant movement had engulfed all ten districts by June, reaching the highest levels in the fertile, interior districts of Atkarsk, Balashov, Serdobsk, and Petrovsk. Peasants interfered in and restricted the estate owners' advantage in market relationships, set favorable rent terms, seized pastureland and hayfields, and removed prisoners of war. In June they seized forestland and meadowland. As Gerasimenko's chapter suggests, their animosities were aimed not only at the landlords but also at those who had withdrawn from the commune. Denied a voice in village affairs, some Stolypin peasants returned to the commune while others joined local branches of the Landowners' Union. At this time deserters from the army played a negligible role in radicalizing the villages, but the more than twenty thousand over-fortys on furlough contributed to the peasant movement, as did a handful of Left SR agitators sent from the Kronstadt Soviet.[15]

How did the democracy in the district towns of Saratov Province respond to the new freedoms ushered in by the revolution? Despite the different pace of political life in the district centers of the province, local soviets or executive committees led by socialists had amassed considerable power by early summer. Although soviets had not been formed in the district towns during the 1905 revolution, they were elected in most district centers by the end of March 1917. This suggests the extent to which socialist ideas and propaganda had made inroads into the backwoods of Russia. It will be recalled that soviets of soldiers' deputies usually appeared first, and they in turn assisted in the election of workers' soviets. As was the case with soviets in the cities, most district soviets had nonpartisan memberships, but populist parties, especially the SRs, dominated local politics as they had since 1905. Toward summer a few soviets became involved in disputes with the old dumas or commanding officers. More often than not the dumas lacked the authority to deal with everyday concerns, which instead had fallen under the jurisdiction of soviets and executive committees. Elsewhere the dumas had to submit to reelection along democratic lines, as was the case in Khvalynsk. In Nikolaevsk, just across the Volga (in Samara Province but to be annexed to Saratov during the Civil War), the Soviet of Peasant, Worker, and Soldier Deputies declared itself the "highest political authority in the district" on June 2, dismissed the district commissar appointed by the Provisional Government, and replaced him with a people's executive committee selected by the soviet and headed by the Bolshevik V. I. Ermoshchenko.[16]

The situation that developed in Kuznetsk serves as a revealing case study of politics in the district towns at this time. Here the Executive Committee of Popular Authority, in which the "democratic elements" and SR party were entrenched, eclipsed the authority of the town duma and district zemstvo. Elected to the committee were the town mayor, a local factory owner, a liberal lawyer and zemstvo activist, an office worker, and a revolutionary named F. Bobylev (probably an SR at this time), who chaired the committee. The local executive committee co-opted peasant representatives into its membership and introduced its own land reform. Ignoring the national government and the Saratov PEC altogether, the Kuznetsk Executive Committee confiscated land from the gentry, set rent prices, divided forestland and meadows. It then set up volost and village land committees "without the slightest regard for the national government or provincial center." For good reasons, news-papers began calling the district the Kuznetsk "republic." The local executive committee democratized the duma and zemstvo, permitted private sale of grain, and forbade its export outside the district. In sum, it took whatever steps it deemed necessary to stave off anarchy and eco-nomic disruption.[17]

In reviewing the political changes ushered in by the February revolu-tion it appears that freedom had created an environment in which various social groups began to work toward their own diverse goals. By summer the unanimous revolution had yielded to political crisis and social polarization. Democratic elements had fought to democratize those institutions which had been the domain of Russia's privileged society; yet at the same time the formerly disenfranchised established their own class organs that mobilized the most authority: factory committees, soviets, soldier committees, volost and village executive committees. All of these bodies tried to establish some means of supervision over factory administrations, officers, or estate owners. The practices of the popular institutions had little in common with Western notions of representative political democracy, which the common people probably viewed with suspicion if they understood it at all. Social polarization also complicated the dilemma of Russia's moderate socialists, who entered the government in May. Many local SR and Menshevik leaders had correctly feared that joining with the middle class would compromise their party programs and beliefs. This was particularly true of the SRs who were so influential in Saratov Province. While the fate of some SRs became linked to that of the coalition government, others more directly involved at the lower levels with the peasantry undertook to carry out programs advocated by the party since before 1905. The more moderate leaders of the party were hard put to deal with "our Bolsheviks," as they called their impatient comrades. By early summer, workers and soldiers tended to ignore their own organizations when they advised restraint. Ironically, the impulse toward localism after February, followed by an emerging organizational malaise, contributed to a breakdown of the state apparatus and of law and order in general. As the year progressed, the atomization of political power underscored the need for a return to a state of normality and to an administrative order that would make things work again. This was why extremist solutions to the question of political power presented themselves in Russia after the halcyon days of revolution had passed. The other alternatives simply had not worked.

In July and August, local and national political attitudes underwent profound changes owing to the abortive July uprising in Petrograd associated with the Bolsheviks and the Kornilov affair at the end of August. The government's assault on the radical left after the July Days compounded the problem of political power at the local level, exacerbated relations between moderate socialists and the Bolsheviks, and gave a false sense of confidence to rightist elements who believed that only a conservative restoration could save Russia from anarchy, military defeat, and social dissolution. The ensuing attempt by Commander in Chief Lavr Kornilov to march on Petrograd and disband the Soviet benefitted the Bolsheviks greatly. The fight against surrogate Kornilovs at the local level gave a sense of urgency to the call for Soviet power that struck an increasingly responsive chord among broad elements of the population.

When news of the Petrograd uprising became known in Saratov during the first week of July, lower-level Bolshevik party members and evacuated soldiers defied bans on street demonstrations and held illegal political meetings. Despite the cautious reaction to the Petrograd events on the part of most Saratov Bolshevik leaders, local pro-Bolshevik manifestations distressed the moderates, who took the position that even if the Bolsheviks were not shown to have instigated the uprising "their agitation and demogogic tactics definitely shaped it."[18] As in Petrograd, the July Days caused the Bolsheviks to suffer temporary setbacks. Charges against Bolsheviks multiplied. According to P. A. Lebedev, it was unsafe for party activists to appear in the streets;[19] the Bolshevik newspaper could not find a publisher between July 23 and August 27. Further, elections to the city duma in the midst of the crisis gave the SR-Menshevik-Bund bloc 64.2 percent of the popular vote and 73 of 113 seats in the duma. Coming in second place, the Bolsheviks captured 12 percent of the vote and 13 seats in the duma. The third-place Kadets also won 13 seats.[20]

In view of fears evoked by the July Days and their strong showing in the duma elections, the moderate socialists strove to revive the authority of the city duma. An examination of the duma's efforts to govern in the summer of 1917 reveals how close Russia had come to civil war and also the enormity of the administrative crisis facing the country at large. The duma met infrequently and had trouble gathering a quorum. A mutual suspicion of Bolshevik tactics was sometimes the only issue upon which the moderate socialists and liberals could agree.[21] The duma accomplished virtually nothing at this time, while the Public Executive Committee remained an extension of the Soviet, which continued to command broad authority in Saratov. This should not obscure the fact that workers and soldiers were growing indifferent to the Soviet, too, probably because the advances of the revolution were coming to a stop owing to the deteriorating economic situation. Erratic food supplies, lack of raw materials, and transportation difficulties reduced production in Saratov during the summer and shut down flour mills, butter creameries, and the Russian-Baltic plant. As unemployment increased, workers resorted to the strike, occasionally ignoring their trade unions.[22] Moreover, the summer crisis marked the beginning of the erosion of SR influence in the garrison. The three thousand *frontoviki* in Saratov refused to depart for the front and contaminated other troops with their seditious behavior. Armed cossacks were brought to Saratov to force soldiers to leave, arrest the more militant, and crack down on desertion.[23] Efforts to restore discipline and improve the fighting capacity of the army intensified nationally and locally, as death battalions, shock brigades, and "Kerensky battalions" tried to counterbalance the impact of evacuated soldiers. All of these efforts amounted to very little.

In the district towns the soviets had emerged as sovereign organs, and this saved them in the summer. Yet even here the July Days had triggered minor disturbances in several district centers as a result of which the radical left and even more moderate Mensheviks temporarily came under fire. The most unusual developments unfolded in Tsaritsyn, popularly known as Russia's "Chicago," owing to its rapid industrial expansion in the decade after 1905. With a population of 134,000, Tsaritsyn had a larger percentage of industrial workers than other cities in the Lower and Middle Volga regions. It was not a typical *uezd* town. The local soviet, led by the Bolshevik militant S. K. Minin, commanded unusual prestige in the eyes of the city's large industrial work force and numerous frontoviki in the twenty thousand-strong garrison. Economic disruption and a concentration of Left SRs also helped to make Tsaritsyn one of the most radical centers in the country. When the local soviet carried a resolution to transfer power to the soviets and the Bolsheviks won the largest number of votes in duma elections in early July, the Provisional Government and Saratov Soviet decided to intervene militarily. They sent a force under Colonel Korvin-Krukovskii of the cadet (junker) school in Saratov, which quickly introduced martial law. The duma election results were abrogated, censorship was introduced, and a right-wing newspaper was allowed to resume publication, which called upon the townspeople to disband the soviet.[24]

Korvin-Krukovskii's military dictatorship heightened suspicions in Saratov that conservative elements were planning to seize the reins of government. As rumors of a right-wing coup circulated throughout the country in the wake of the Moscow State Conference, held August 12–14 to legitimize Kerensky's Second Coalition Government, the Bolsheviks and other elements of the left showed signs of recovery (even at their lowest ebb the Bolsheviks controlled the Central Bureau of Trade Unions and the Organizational Bureau of Factory Committees). Local workers now struck to protest the opening of the Moscow Conference, while Bolshevik resolutions began to attract more votes than the size of the party faction in the Soviet would warrant. As Kornilov marched on Petrograd, the All-Russian Central Executive Committee requested the Saratov Soviet "with all of its resources to help Tsaritsyn organize resistance to Ataman Kaledin," whose forces were moving up the Volga to support Kornilov. The Soviet declared a state of emergency in Saratov and demanded Korvin-Krukovskii's immediate departure from Tsaritsyn. On August 28 and 29, local soldiers and workers demonstrated in the streets of Saratov, carrying banners inscribed with "Down with Kornilov!" and "Long live Kerensky!" Proceeding to the town jail, they freed Tsaritsyn's Minin and other political prisoners.[25]

Kornilov's revolt posed the question of whether the Soviet should support Kerensky's government and led to a struggle between the city duma and the Soviet over which institution had the legitimate right to organize a "committee for the struggle against counterrevolution." The Soviet won this battle, but despite the passions aroused in establishing the committee, it met only once before disbanding; the Soviet again functioned as the leading administrative organ in Saratov. On August 31, a Soviet plenum carried a Bolshevik resolution on political power by a vote of 188 to 178. The resolution called for creation of a workers' armed guard and prompt convening of a Second Congress of Soviets. It also contained a veiled call for a transfer of power to the soviets, which was not unique to the Volga area; in the beginning of September, 126 provincial soviets demanded Soviet power.[26]

Fueling partisan politics in Saratov, the Kornilov affair poisoned relations between census society and the democracy and also between radical and moderate socialists. On September 6 the population began electing new deputies to the Soviet, and the entire presidium of the Soldiers' Section resigned after soldiers passed a vote of no confidence in it. Concomitantly, the Soviet reconfirmed the Bolshevik resolution on power passed earlier, and workers reacted to what they perceived as the threat of counterrevolution by setting up Red Guard units (see the following chapter by Rex A. Wade). The Soviet election gave the Bolsheviks a majority and marked a stunning reversal in the Military Section.

The Bolsheviks now had 320 deputies in the Soviet, the SRs, 103, and the Mensheviks, 76. As Lebedev put it, the Kornilov affair "with one stroke won back for us the sympathies of the masses." Antonov said it "electrified" the population.[27]

There was no easy, or perhaps peaceful, solution to Russia's political crisis after the Kornilov affair. A Bolshevik majority in the Soviet did not resolve the political impasse facing Saratov but compounded it. The situation in the provinces came to bear upon Lenin who, citing local affairs to add punch to his own arguments, called for a transfer of power to the soviets. Reacting to the popular mood, leftist elements among the SRs and Mensheviks joined with the Bolsheviks in urging the exclusion of the propertied elements from the new government. The moderate socialists, fearing civil war and even greater social tension, continued to shore up the coalition with the bourgeoisie, in spite of their concern over the bourgeoisie's involvement with Kornilov.

The economic situation during the late summer and early fall goes far to explain the burgeoning militancy of the local working class and soldiers and shows the degree to which a new set of revolutionary processes, reflected in the rising visibility of extremist groups, now determined political outcomes. Russia was breaking up into local economic units and officials at each administrative level were taking measures to ward off local hunger first. As the agrarian movement gained momentum, the food crisis worsened in Saratov. The shortages threatened to shut down still more flour mills and vegetable-oil presses. Rightwing agitation as well as anarchist activity reached new heights. Apart from food shortages, a swollen crime rate, speculation, and extremist agitation, typhoid fever and venereal disease epidemics broke out. The strike movement became more important than at any other time during the year. In September and October more than twenty strikes broke out in Saratov, involving more than two thousand workers.[28] Further, no authority could control the soldiers, who emerged from the Kornilov affair radicalized but not as stalwart Bolsheviks. As October approached, the city in a practical sense found itself at the soldiers' mercy. Confiscating public buildings, they began moving into town to avoid another winter in the delapidated barracks. Local newspapers linked the alarming crime rate to those "in soldiers' garb." Reports in the official publication of the Kazan Military District reveal that the situation was common throughout the province and Volga region.[29]

The Kornilov movement had the same jarring effect on the rest of the province. The Bolshevik- and Left SR–controlled Tsaritsyn Soviet resumed its normal functions and even considered declaring Soviet power locally. Although events were less excessive in the district towns, local groups feared that Kornilov had posed a real threat to the revolution and questioned the coalition with the middle classes. Even though the post-Kornilov climate was one of great ambiguity characterized by a lack of decisive authority at the local level, conditions had been created that contributed to a leftist victory in Saratov in October.[30]

Moreover, the Kornilov affair had taken place as the peasant movement was about to enter its most radical phase. In late summer the rural revolution converged with the urban one, as the Russian army disintegrated. Having seized land and repudiated rental agreements during planting season, the peasants now turned to taking equipment and livestock, felling trees, and mowing grass for haymaking. By September, when the harvest was in, the number of confiscations of estates and the use of force shot up markedly. As the proceedings of the Second Peasant Congress of Saratov Province, which opened in Saratov on September 10, reveal, self-demobilized armed soldiers and outside agitators pushed the situation to the left. The mood in the villages had become more militant than that of the urban-based populist party committees. Delegates spoke of the ubiquitous clashes between rich and poor, and of the election of peasant soviets. Despite real hostility to the Bolsheviks, the delegates passed Left SR resolutions that were virtually identical to Bolshevik ones. The congress adopted the SR land program and voiced its opposition to further coalition with the bourgeoisie. In the following weeks a more emboldened peasant movement broke out in Serdobsk District and spread from there into Balashov and Atkarsk, all of which had been centers of rural radicalism in 1905 (see Timothy Mixter's chapter).[31] The headlines of Saratov's middle-class *Saratovskii vestnik* flashed: "Russia experiences complete anarchy and demoralization."[32]

The most striking thing about the October revolution was that everyone expected it. Local and national socialist newspapers discussed Russia's political future at length, particularly the virtues and drawbacks of continued coalition with the bourgeoisie. As political debates shifted from Soviet plenums to factory and garrison meetings, moderate socialist leaders revealed their fear of the anarchistic temperaments of the masses that had been brutalized by poverty, ignorance, and years of suffering from the war. The lawlessness of everyday life and the readiness with which the people seemed to fall victim to opportunistic slogans of the more radical left merely reinforced their conviction that Russia was not ready for social revolution. In effect, the masses appeared to be behaving exactly as the moderates had feared: irresponsibly.

It soon became apparent that the majority of soviets along the Middle and Lower Volga backed the formation of an all-socialist government in conjunction with the Second Congress of Soviets. The Bolshevik Central Committee dispatched emissaries to the provinces to canvass the local mood before it voted on October 10 to put an armed uprising on the agenda; on October 8 Miliutin arrived from Petrograd to discuss the upcoming Second Congress with the local Bolshevik committee; a representative from the Moscow committee did the same in nearby Syzran, Simbirsk, and Kazan. On October 14–15 Saratov hosted a regional congress of soviets, which was one of many local meetings held in preparation for the Second Congress. The forty delegates included eight Mensheviks, one Menshevik "sympathizer," four SRs, eight Left SRs, and nineteen Bolsheviks. Commenting on reports from the locales given at the local congress, the Mensheviks' *Proletarii Povolzh'ia* reported that "all of the accounts were monotonous. All told of the ecstasy over the new majorities in the soviets, over the Bolshevik majorities." By a vote of 28 (Bolsheviks and Left SRs) to 12, the delegates endorsed a call for Soviet power, after which the twelve moderates withdrew in protest.[33]

During the next ten days tensions between the Bolsheviks and moderate socialists mounted in Saratov, hamstringing what little authority remained in the city. The Bolsheviks, who politically stood for Soviet power and an end to the war, competed against the moderate socialists and liberals. In terms of national politics, the contest revolved around support for the imminent Second Congress of Soviets (the Bolsheviks and left-wing factions of the other socialist parties) or for the Constituent Assembly (moderate socialists, liberals, some conservatives). On October 7 a Soviet plenum adopted a resolution expressing mistrust of the new government that Kerensky had formed a few days before. When he threatened to order a punitive expedition to Saratov, "several regiments endorsed the resolution of the Soviet, announcing that in the event that punitive forces were sent, the soldiers would answer with bayonets and bullets."[34] On October 11 the Saratov Soviet carried a defiant resolution affirming that it would no longer subordinate itself to the Provisional Government.[35] When the SRs withdrew from all executive organs of the Soviet a few days later, the Soviet Executive Committee approved a "defensive plan" to be implemented in the event an armed uprising broke out in Saratov. The local Bolshevik committee turned to Petrograd for news and directives but, as Antonov lamented, "there weren't any."

As the opening day of the Second Congress of Soviets drew close, reports circulated that "shady individuals" were planning to burn down Saratov. On October 24 talk spread that Provincial Commissar Topuridze had received a telegram about the outbreak of disorders in Petrograd. Another telegram on the twenty-fifth told of the beginning of an armed uprising in Petrograd. Local telegraph workers, who were Menshevik in their political orientation, shared the news with co-workers in other towns and called for a strike should the Bolsheviks make a move. In the meanwhile, Topuridze met with leaders of the moderate socialist parties and representatives of the duma, zemstvo, and food-supply organs, who agreed to keep information on the uprising from the populace as long as possible and to try to obtain assistance from cossack divisions stationed nearby. That evening a convocation of socialist party leaders broke up following a bitter exchange. Afterward, the duma, about an hour before the Second Congress opened in Petrograd, resolved to form a "committee to save the revolution."[36]

On the morning of October 26, both the Bolsheviks and the moderate socialists began to ready themselves for a possible showdown. Yet simultaneously they stalled for time: the Bolsheviks waited for directives from their Central Committee; the moderates pinned their hopes on a speedy rescue by cossack forces. While the Bolsheviks agitated in factories and barracks (where they tried to persuade the soldiers to obey only orders of the Soviet), the moderate socialists took advantage of the lack of Bolshevik cadres within the officer corps. In fact, a group of officers including Bolsheviks appeared before the Soviet's Executive Committee with a proposal to form a special nonpartisan military committee to govern Saratov that would not be subordinate to either the Soviet or the duma.

When the Soviet convened that evening the Bolsheviks reported on events in the capital and the proposal to form a nonparty military committee. Delegates rejected the candidacy of SR officers nominated to the committee, however, and SR officers and leading Bolshevik military leaders withdrew from the Soviet in protest, making the Bolshevik

Committee apprehensive over the nature of its support within the officer corps. Then Menshevik leaders announced that troops loyal to Kerensky had suppressed the Bolshevik uprising. After Antonov's emotional response denying this allegation, the plenum resolved that the Bureau of the Executive Committee would take responsibility for defending the city.[37] The Executive Committee formed a Military Revolutionary Committee and drafted a general appeal to the population to announce that the latter had assumed power on behalf of the Soviet. The Executive Committee then issued a decree on land (of local provenance) that was based on the SR land policy. Finally, it declared that Lebedev would replace Topuridze as provincial commissar, appointed emissaries to assume the responsibilities of former district commissars, and designated a military officer to direct operations in case of an attack on the Soviet.[38]

Townspeople who took to the streets on the morning of October 27 must have been confused by the contradictory signals bombarding them, for while the Soviet was taking the above actions, the duma declared itself "the only organ of power in the city and province." It now appealed to all able-bodied persons to appear at the duma building, and about three thousand people did so, including leaders of the moderate socialist parties, duma members, cadets from the officer training school, officials, office workers, seminary students, shop owners, and young students. Both sides took preparatory measures in the event that an armed struggle broke out. As the likelihood of bloodshed increased, however, the duma forces began to thin.

On October 28 the Soviet decided to force a showdown and ordered some three thousand Red Guardsmen and artillerymen to surround the duma. The Executive Committee began a round of negotiations with those inside, but shots rang out before any agreement could be reached. Efforts to resume talks after the duma supporters circulated rumors that Kerensky had taken Petrograd amounted to nothing. Shooting continued all night, as rain "poured from buckets" on the Soviet's forces that had taken the offensive. When the duma agreed to capitulate in the morning, there were several dead and wounded on each side. Vasil'ev expressed surprise that so few were still inside the duma building. He found mostly cadets and high school, commercial school, and seminary students but only a handful of duma deputies and leaders of the moderate socialists. "Neither Minin nor Didenko [leading SRs] turned up among the ar rested," wrote Vasil'ev, "and it seems that the first who tried to hide was the former provincial commissar, Topuridze."[39] And for good reason. As the defeated were led away to the governor's house where they were to be detained, a hostile crowd, some ten thousand-strong, pressed around them, demanding that they be shot or thrown into the Volga. One young cossack officer remembered how a crowd of angry women "threw themselves upon us, scratching our faces with their dirty hands. Murderers! [they yelled]." Another group of soldiers approached with machine guns, prepared to gun down the cadets. Both sides maintained that Vasil'ev's direct intervention and the responsible behavior of some Red Guard units saved the defeated duma forces from mob justice.[40]

The Saratov Soviet's victory over the duma gave rise to a rash of opposition to what the defeated parties saw as Bolshevik usurpation of the longed-for Constituent Assembly. The possibility of direct cossack intervention bolstered the anti-Soviet opposition, while news of conflict within the Bolshevik top leadership kept hopes burning locally that Soviet power would collapse. Anti-Bolshevik groups called upon the townspeople "to protest against the Bolsheviks' crude use of force." The city bureaucracy and government officials lashed out against the Bolsheviks; the Saratov Doctors' Union refused to treat Bolshevik patients; officers abandoned their units in the garrison; city employees went out on strike. In fact, a strike by telegraph and postal workers cut off Saratov from Petrograd for almost two months. Muffled communications, unreliable news, and false hopes guaranteed the circulation of a host of rumors that also left their mark upon local developments. Sustained opposition to the new regime, a lack of directives from Petrograd or contradictory ones, and an even more frightful level of lawlessness characterized the first months of Soviet power in Saratov.[41]

Nevertheless, the rupture of the SR party and the entrance of the Left SRs into the new government, the Council of People's Commissars, contributed immensely to strengthening the Bolsheviks' hand in the provinces. The local Left SRs' entry to the Executive Committee on December 3 helped to turn the tide in their favor and undermined the moderate SRs' confused efforts to end Bolshevik rule. Although united in their antagonism toward the Bolsheviks, the moderate socialists and Kadets simply lacked a broader base for cooperation; SR and Menshevik leaders who challenged the Bolsheviks relied on the armed support of cossacks and junkers who, for the most part, stood in a different political camp altogether. Moreover, the moderates now proved willing to break with the bourgeoisie if certain conditions were met. When the Soviet invited city employees and clerks to a meeting on November 21, an estimated ten thousand people held a counterdemonstration inspired by the SRs to condemn one-party rule and to demand freedom of speech and the press. Emphasizing the legitimacy of the upcoming Constituent Assembly, the meeting called for the creation of a new national government that *excluded the bourgeoisie.*[42]

As the storm clouds of civil war moved closer to Saratov, the Soviet, responding to lower-level pressures, adopted a more militant attitude toward its opposition. Apart from slamming shut the doors of the city duma at the end of November, it sequestered local banks, extended the duties of worker control groups, organized workers who had not taken part in unions earlier, took over the railroads, created a new militia, and assumed responsibility for the town's economic survival. The more power it wielded, the more impassioned the voices of opposition became. "Down with the autocracy of Lenin and Trotsky!" was answered with a decision by the Soviet in early December to shut down the non-Bolshevik press.

During the second week of November the people of Russia elected deputies to the Constituent Assembly, which had become the rallying point of all those opposed to Bolshevism. All indications suggest that the normal aspects of the campaigning outweighed the abnormalities. Within the city of Saratov, civilians cast 47,522 votes and the garrison, 12,660 votes. The Bolsheviks captured the most support of any single party, polling 22,712 votes, or 37.7 percent of the total. The Kadets came in second, with 11,971 votes, or 19.9 percent. Since July both Bolshevik and Kadet support had roughly doubled, while the SRs and Mensheviks lost almost 25,000 votes to both left and right. According to *Saratovskii vestnik,* 15,000 voters switched from the SR-Menshevik block to the Bolsheviks, while 10,000 former socialists moved into the bourgeois camp. Consideration of the garrison vote makes the nature of Bolshevik strength stand out more clearly: the Bolsheviks won 70.6 percent of the 12,660 votes cast by soldiers.

In Tsaritsyn, the other large city in the province, the results were similar to those in Saratov and followed class lines. The collapse of the political center in Saratov and Tsaritsyn thus paralleled developments in Petrograd and Moscow, where the Kadets also polled more votes than

Table 12.1. Number and Percentage of Votes Cast for Delegates
to Constituent Assembly in City of Saratov (Including Garrison),
November 1917, by Party

Ballot Number and Party	Votes	Percent
1. Kadet	11,971	19.9
2. Menshevik	4,100	6.8
3. Union of Ukrainian and Tatar SR Peasant Organizations	1,097	1.8
4. Old Believers	1,003	1.6
5. Orthodox People's	1,924	3.2
6. Union of Landowners	1,764	2.9
7. Volga German	1,280	2.1
8. Popular Socialist	2,920	4.9
9. Society for Faith and Order	2,589	4.3
10. Bolshevik	22,712	37.7
11. Peasants of Petrovsk uezd and Mordvinians	116	0.2
12. Socialist Revolutionary	8,698	14.5
All parties	60,174	99.9

SOURCE: *Saratovskii vestnik*, no. 247 (November 17, 1917): 3.

the SRs. Bolshevik strongholds—the cities—had likewise become centers of the Bolsheviks' class enemies. Although election results for the remaining districts of Saratov Province are incomplete, it seems that soldiers sustained bolshevism in the district towns in what was an indifferent or even hostile environment. In Serdobsk, where the Bolsheviks polled 33 percent of the garrison vote, Left SRs played an exceptionally important role that guaranteed a comparatively early consolidation of Soviet power. Left SRs also boasted a strong organization in Balashov. In Volsk, however, which in 1918 emerged as the center of an anti-Bolshevik uprising, the Bolsheviks appear to have mustered little enthusiasm. At the district level, the same strengthening of the political extremes at the expense of the center was fairly common, but not to the same degree as in Saratov or Tsaritsyn.

Across most of the country, ethnically Russian rural communities voted heavily for the SRs. The formal split within the party's ranks came shortly after the elections, and the peasants thus cast ballots for a party that was organizationally defunct. It is impossible to say how they would have voted had the elections been postponed and the peasants had had the option of voting for Left SRs. It must be remembered that many had

Table 12.2. Number and Percentage of Valid Votes Cast for Delegates
to Constituent Assembly in Saratov Province,
November 1917, by Party

Ballot Number and Party	Votes	Percent
1. Kadet	22,226	2.5
2. Menshevik	15,152	1.4
3. Union of Ukrainian and Tatar SR		
Peasant Organizations	53,445	4.9
4. Old Believers	13,956	1.3
5. Orthodox People's	17,414	1.6
6. Union of Landowners	13,804	1.3
7. Volga German	50,025	4.6
8. Popular Socialist	10,243	0.9
9. Society for Faith and Order	6,600	0.6
10. Bolshevik	261,308	24.0
11. Peasants of Petrovsk uezd and Mordvinians	6,379	0.6
12. Socialist Revolutionary	612,094	56.3
All parties	1,082,646	100.0

SOURCE: *Saratovskaia zemskaia nedelia*, no. 1 (February 5 [18], 1918): 17.

not yet heard of the October events, or of the Second Congress of Soviets'
endorsement of Lenin's land decree. Still, the national pattern held true
for Saratov, where the SRs won 56 percent of the votes cast in the
province, and the second-place Bolsheviks, 24 percent. Combined, the
two parties won 80 percent of the votes, and the Kadets a mere 2.5
percent, capturing a paltry 27,226 votes out of a total of over one
million.[43] The Saratov election results reinforce Oliver H. Radkey's
conclusions about voter behavior in the country at large.

The process of recognition of the new political order began in the
district towns at the end of October, when the Saratov and Tsaritsyn
soviets assumed power, and ended in January 1918, when soviets in the
last remaining district centers consolidated their positions. In Khvalynsk
and Petrovsk, armed clashes between the local soviets and their opponents broke out. In Balashov, Atkarsk, Volsk, Serdobsk, and Kuznetsk,
groups opposed to the Bolsheviks resisted Soviet power but did not
resort to violence. Usually moderate SRs and Kadets, ensconced in local
dumas or zemstvos, struggled most stubbornly against Bolshevik activists. The presence of cossack divisions in Balashov, Rtishchevo, Balanda,
and Elan also cooled the fervor of revolutionaries in these areas.

The recognition of Soviet power in the countryside is more difficult to summarize. It will be recalled that on the eve of the October revolution total disarray and anarchy had undermined any semblance of normality in the countryside. In this chaotic environment news of the consolidation of Soviet power in Saratov spread unevenly. Ties between Saratov and the district towns and volost centers had been broken or interrupted; misinformation abounded. In most places district and volost zemstvos reacted negatively to reports that the Provisional Government had fallen. As Bolshevik agitators from Saratov and Petrograd sought to enlighten the peasants in regard to the Saratov Soviet's Land Decree, SRs entrenched in the zemstvos agitated on behalf of elections to the Constituent Assembly. The more remote villages often learned of the revolution only after the elections had ended.

Above all, it was the peasant-soldier that played the leading role in establishing Soviet power in the countryside. Despite prevailing anti-Bolshevik feelings in the villages, the Saratov Soviet's Land Decree, plus the flood of self-demobilized soldiers back into the rural areas, enabled the Soviet to neutralize the peasantry and shift the balance of forces in favor of the new regime, even in those remote regions where anti-Bolshevik feelings remained spirited. Soviet power was nominally recognized in all ten districts in Saratov Province by January 1918, usually in conjunction with resolutions passed at local peasant congresses. Nevertheless, that power rested on a shaky foundation which often had to be bolstered by armed force or intimidation.[44]

Those SRs who had not sided with the Bolsheviks in October put up a stubborn fight to respond to the mass mood and to retain their support in the countryside. Ironically, on the same day that shooting had broken out in Saratov between the forces of the Soviet and city duma, the Provincial Land Committee, zemstvo board, and Peasant Soviet had finally agreed to call for the speedy transfer of all land to land committees. A Peasant Soviet that had emerged as the focal point of SR activities then issued stinging denunciations of Soviet power and demanded the creation of an all-socialist government excluding the liberals and Bolsheviks. However, Lenin's Land Decree eventually undermined the appeal of the Saratov Peasant Soviet, and with its neutralization the moderate SRs lost the villages. Outside activists from Petrograd also facilitated the acceptance of the new regime in Saratov Province. Further, on November 12 the Saratov Soviet resolved, on the advice of the Petrograd Soviet, to send to their home villages more than three hundred soldier-agitators from the garrison. The Soviet commissioned them to elect representatives to a provincial peasant congress slated to open on November 30, and to coax their fellow villagers to sell grain to food-supply organs. Almost half of the 192 surviving reports submitted by these agents reveal hostility toward the Bolsheviks; some villages even refused to send delegates to the peasant congress.[45]

SR leaders tried to undermine the impact of the Bolshevik agitators by calling their own provincial peasant congress a week before the one planned by the Saratov Soviet. Two days before it convened, though, the local SR organization carried by a slim margin a left-wing SR resolution. Committed to cooperating with the Bolsheviks in order to escape the political impasse and avoid civil war, the Left SRs now offered their own plan for conciliation, which undermined the Right SRs' upcoming peasant congress. The Left SR resolution welcomed the creation of an all-socialist ministry under the auspices of the All-Russian Executive Committees of the Petrograd Soviet and national Peasant Soviet. It encouraged prompt conclusion of a peace settlement and the transfer of land to land committees. Urging the convocation of the Constituent Assembly in late November, the resolution demanded the reestablishment of all political liberties and an end to civil war.[46]

Thus, when the peasant congress called by the Saratov Peasant Soviet opened on November 23, dissent within SR ranks guaranteed its failure. Instead, the Third Peasant Congress of Saratov Province, which met on November 30, approved Lenin's land decree and dismissed the Peasant Soviet. The congress elected a new peasant soviet that voted to merge with the Saratov Soviet. Throughout the proceedings the Left SRs supported Bolshevik resolutions but spoke out against the Saratov Soviet's closing of the city duma. The Third Peasant Congress's adoption of Bolshevik resolutions contributed singularly to the consolidation of Soviet power in Saratov Province. Returning to their home villages, peasant delegates spearheaded the election of soviets and the calling of district peasant congresses. In December, district peasant congresses in Balashov and Atkarsk ratified the proceedings of the Saratov congress. In January, peasant congresses in Kamyshin, Petrovsk, Serdobsk, Volsk, and Kuznetsk districts recognized Soviet Power.

Unfortunately, no clear answer emerges from the contradictory sources as to how representative the Third Peasant Congress was. More than half of the volosts had sent deputies (105), whereas sixty-five refused to do so and ten were unable to, for a variety of technical reasons.[47] Judging from the politicized rhetoric of the conference, conflict in the villages, as evinced in the high incidence of clashes between communal and Stolypin peasants, facilitated recognition of Soviet power. Again and again, sources show that the younger peasants who had served in the army voiced Left SR or Bolshevik sentiments. Undoubtedly, the true extent of the use of force and intimidation at this impassioned time will never be known.

Soviet power, then, became recognized in much of Saratov Province during the brief coalition between Bolsheviks and Left SRs both at the national level and locally, and can be seen in the steady growth in the number of soviets. Most soviets were formed in January and February 1918; and this corresponds closely with the situation throughout European Russia.[48]

This examination of Saratov suggests that the conflicts and conditions that brought about the revolution were by no means confined to the urban capitals. The tsarist political system, with all of its shortcomings, had provided rich soil for the growth of a local opposition movement. The autocracy had alienated much of the professional middle class. It had failed to satisfy the peasants' land hunger. It had hampered workers' attempts to mollify the social ills of industrialization and the arbitrariness of authority relations in the workplace. Then came war. The socioeconomic disequilibrium and extraordinary movement of people caused by it, and the government's suspicion of public initiative during it, furthered discontent, exacerbating antigovernment feelings even within official circles.

Dealing a death blow to the centralized state structure, the February revolution had swept away all of the barriers that had kept the Russian masses out of the country's political life; afterward, an array of other considerations led to October. The moderate socialists' theoretical conceptualization of the revolution as bourgeois-democratic undermined their party programs after February: in Saratov it caused them to abandon the legitimacy of the popular organs set up in 1917; and it eventually led to a rupture between party leaders and the rank and file who came to share the Bolsheviks' call for an all-soviet government. Although riddled with compromises, setbacks, and confusion, the Bolshevik party offered the most consistently plebian program to the Russian people and rode to power at the top of self-legitimized popular organs—soviets, factory committees, trade unions, Red Guard detachments, and soldier committees. In Saratov, as in Petrograd, Moscow, and Baku, the Bolshevik platform of land, peace, and bread, and the slogan "All Power to the Soviets," increasingly appealed to common people, whose expectations often soared to unreasonable levels as their economic situation deteriorated. The Bolsheviks' tactical flexibility and militant class interpretation of Russian political life (in the inclusive, Russian sense of the upper classes, *verkhi,* pitted against the lower elements, *nizy*) proved successful in a fluid setting characterized by economic ruin, growing anarchism, and a tottering structure of voluntary authority relationships. The October revolution in Saratov was not so much a Bolshevik revolution as a triumph of all radical groups that had broken decisively with those elements supporting further coalition with the bourgeoisie—Bolsheviks, Left SRs, SR Maximalists, Menshevik Internationalists, anarchists, and so on.

Recognition of soviet power in Saratov had marked a major realignment in political forces. Despite their unbending opposition to the new order, the local Bolsheviks could galvanize into action on their behalf the working class and for the moment benefitted from the heady, evanescent mood in the garrison. Behind Bolshevik leaders stood a mass of followers willing to defend those who promised land, peace, and bread. In stark contrast, the fissiparous tendencies so endemic to Russian radicalism and social thought crippled the potential power of the Bolsheviks' contenders. Riven by factionalism and weakened by indecisive leadership, the opposition parties were unable to present a united front. Even SR, Menshevik, and Kadet leaders writing from abroad years later admitted that they had lost the people. Their cries to rally behind the Constituent Assembly, as well as intensified solicitude lavished on the peasants, and the Mensheviks' and SRs' articulated readiness to end coalition with the bourgeoisie, fell on deaf ears.

Nevertheless, the acceptance of the new political order in the province would seem to have been inconceivable without the ubiquitous presence of the soldier masses and the fortuitous formation of a Left SR party that entered the Lenin government. It was not for nothing that the Bolsheviks' enemies began to call them "the party of the rear garrisons." In virtually every district town, and in the villages too, radicalized soldiers often proved the decisive factor in the recognition of Soviet power. From the district centers emissaries went into the villages and neutralized the peasantry by appealing to their great leveling instincts. The role played by the Left SRs should also be emphasized, even though sources do not permit an assessment of how large a following the more radical wing of Russian populism actually had at this time. Strong in those districts with the most volatile peasant movement, the Left SRs accepted the October revolution, thereby giving legitimacy and authority to the Bolsheviks at a critical moment. As a Left SR named Ezhov reasoned: "If the Constituent Assembly supports coalition, the Left SRs will not support the assembly. When they say all power to the Constituent Assembly and down with the Bolsheviks, they mean power to the Right SRs and Mensheviks and a struggle against the soviets."[49]

Even though the loci of power and the main transportation and communication networks had fallen into the Bolsheviks' hands, it was a tottering Soviet regime that saw the beginning of 1918. The considerable opposition to the new order constantly reminded Bolshevik leaders of the still unresolved nature of their political power. While some Saratov Bolsheviks moved in an increasingly militant way toward one-party rule, others lamented the collapse of revolutionary solidarity and feared the early signs of civil war. Sponsored by Saratov SRs, a December 31 demonstration on behalf of the upcoming Constituent Assembly turned into street disorders and bloodshed, which prompted the declaration of martial law in Saratov. After the government had closed down the assembly when it convened in Petrograd a few weeks later, city dumas in Saratov, Khvalynsk, Volsk, Balashov, and Serdobsk cabled their protests to Petrograd. For the most part, though, the population of Saratov reacted apathetically to the news of the shutting down of the ephemeral Constituent Assembly. Few probably realized that Russia would face an even more tortured period in years ahead.

13. The Saratov Red Guards

Rex A. Wade

SARATOV'S LONG history of turbulence and the broad trends sweeping Russia in 1917 came together in the formation of volunteer armed bands, especially what would come to be termed the Red Guards. One of the most striking characteristics of the Russian Revolution was the overwhelming urge of the populace, now freed from political control and censorship, to form organizations and associations of all kinds—political, social, cultural, educational, economic. Among the most important, most widespread, and most enduring of these were the volunteer workers' armed bands. Called by a variety of names—Workers' Militia, Workers' Guards, Fighting *Druzhina* (detachment), and Red Guards—they played a significant role in the course of the revolution in Saratov and across Russia. Moreover, it is perhaps not accidental nor dependent entirely on events of 1917 that the Red Guards were better developed in Saratov than in most provincial cities during 1917, given the long tradition of social-political violence in the area, stretching from Razin to the Revolution of 1905.

During 1905 organized armed bands developed both in the countryside and in the city of Saratov, although they were usually short-lived. Both the SR and SD parties organized *druzhiny* in late summer, and then merged them into a single unit during the October strike. The railway workers in Saratov organized a hundred-man brigade in October (the railway workers were to have the largest Red Guards detachment—seven hundred men—in Saratov in 1917). Several lives were lost in fighting between workers and soldiers in December 1905.[1] Thus a tradition of resorting to arms and even formation of armed bands existed in Saratov before 1917, and that tradition flowed easily into the new enthusiasm for voluntary organizations, including armed workers' bands, which appeared across Russia in 1917.

News of the February revolution in Petrograd reached Saratov early on March 1. An effort by Governor S. D. Tverskoi to hold up release of the information only delayed it for a few hours. A Saratov Soviet was founded the evening of March 2, in a small, dusty, dimly lit room hung with old portraits of the tsars in the basement of the city duma building. The Soviet action was followed quickly the same evening by the formation of a Public Executive Committee, including Soviet representatives, which declared itself the new city government. Quickly the old tsarist officials and institutions were replaced by new ones drawn from liberal society and the revolutionary parties. The garrison troops also declared their support for the revolution, which was quickly secured.[2]

Volunteer armed bands, especially of workers, emerged in Saratov simultaneously with the revolution. The workers quickly armed themselves and undertook to disarm and arrest police and other government officials, quite aside from any directives or lack thereof from the Soviet or other authorities. During the night of March 1–2 and continuing through the second, a spontaneous arming of workers and creation of detachments took place. At first these were self-defense oriented, but from late on the second, together with students and soldiers, they took more aggressive action in disarming police, freeing political prisoners, and arresting officials. It is indicative of how popular action outstripped nominal leaders that while the new Public Executive Committee during the early morning hours of March 3 was debating whether to arrest former government officials and police, the issue was in fact preempted by spontaneous popular action; some arrested officials were even being shut up in one part of the duma building while the debate was going on in another part. These included Governor Tverskoi, who was arrested about 5:00 A.M. Indeed, although public safety and securing the revolution were concerns of both the Public Executive Committee and the Soviet, neither seems to have given much attention initially to forming armed militias or doing anything with those that emerged spontaneously.[3]

The formation of militias among the workers continued from March 3 onward. At the large Titanik Metalworking Factory a general meeting on the night of March 2–3 authorized a workers' militia on the ground that the creation of "a strong, durable people's militia, well trained," was one of the most important steps to be taken in solving the country's problems. A general meeting at the Saratov railroad shops (Riazan-Ural line) on March 3 decided to form a militia and opened enrollment; six days later a list of members was sent to the Soviet. E. D. Rumiantsev, drawing on archives in Saratov, cites numerous examples of meetings at factories during the period March 2–4 at which, among other matters such as election of representatives to the Soviet, a militia was formed or authorized. At the large Zhest Metalworking Factory the factory committee authorized a militia on March 3. At the Saratov railway depot and station 109 men signed up for a militia on March 4; and the same day 54 of 124 workers at the Merkurii Factory joined the militia. The initial thrust to arm and organize continued; the Saratov *Izvestiia* reported several factory meetings during the first fortnight of the revolution that passed resolutions including a call for workers to form a militia or arm themselves. Between three and five hundred workers is the best estimate of the number of organized armed worker militiamen for the first week. This growth, it is worth stressing, took place with little or no help or guidance from the Soviet or the Public Executive Committee.[4]

The rapid organization of armed bands indicates that there was a sense of consciousness among the workers that the revolution needed to be defended and suggests the beginning of the social polarization that would increase as 1917 progressed. Although the sense of a need for arms seems not to have been as urgent as in Petrograd or even some other provincial cities, a worker consciousness on the issue was present. This manifested itself in the reaction to efforts on the part of the new city officials to establish a "city militia" to replace the old police force. The Public Executive Committee saw this as a fairly conventional police force of the Western type, concerned primarily with public safety and shorn of the political and other odious features of the old tsarist police. The workers, however, proved reluctant to accept that concept and were especially resistant to surrendering their arms. This conflict was played out in a low key at first—the euphoria that followed the collapse of the old regime glossed over many tensions—but became sharper later and led to the formation of the Red Guards.

While in the long run the workers were the most important volunteer armed bands, two other sources of significant armed force surfaced in the March days. One was the university and other higher-education students. They played an important role in armed bands during the first days, their numbers being about the same as the workers' militias in the first week of March.[5] Student involvement in armed bands soon declined, however, ceasing to be important after mid-March. Soldiers of the garrison provided the other source of spontaneous armed force. Although in Saratov, unlike Petrograd, the revolution did not involve a revolt of the soldiers and hence such an immediate and complete breakdown of traditional military relationships, soldiers did participate in the disturbances and helped patrol the streets and secure the revolution. During the night of March 2–3 soldiers arrested unpopular officers, and some participated in the arrest of police and in a march to the duma building. That same night, about the same time as the Workers' Soviet was formed, the soldiers elected a Military Committee. Reflecting the nature of the revolution in Saratov, they provided for extensive officer involvement: one-third of the representatives were to be officers, elected separately from the soldiers. The Military Committee became the primary directing force for the soldiers and, dominated by SR-oriented officers, provided some soldiers for patrol duty in the city.[6] Although on March 6 the Saratov Soviet was transformed into a Soviet of Workers' and Soldiers' Deputies, the Military Committee retained a separate existence and was the dominant force in the garrison until late spring; in June it merged into the soldiers' section of the Soviet. Although the soldiers remained a force in city affairs, they quickly ceased to play a role in the militias, even to the extent they did in Petrograd and some other cities.

The Soviet tended to waver on the issue of armed bands, especially among the workers. Emotionally they supported the idea of arming the workers, and arming all the people or workers had been a common plank in socialist party platforms, yet they also desired the restoration of public order. The initial Soviet approach reflected this. On March 6 the Soviet adopted "Regulations on the Militia of the Saratov Soviet of Workers' Deputies," proposed by V. K. Medvedev. This provided for a two-part militia drawn from the workers. One part was a militia for defense of the city and maintainance of general public order in place of the former police. The other part was a "militia *druzhina*" for safeguarding the factories. The worker militiamen were to be registered and approved by the factory committees. Duty lasted for two weeks, so apparently the Soviet envisioned a steady turnover that would, among other things, give a large number of workers experience with arms. The militia for defense of the factories would be set up by the factory committee and headed by a commander chosen by it.[7] The Soviet leaders, however, were also working with the Public Executive Committee and soon gave it priority in establishing a city militia. Expectations of a prominent worker role quickly evaporated. On March 10 the committee's appointed militia commander, A. A. Minkh, reported that a militia was being set up based on officers and soldiers wounded in the war and unable to resume regular military duties. The question of the role of workers' militia continued to be an issue, however, and was discussed at Public Executive Committee meetings. The rules for the city militia, ultimately adopted on March 24, provided for only twenty worker-militiamen in each district within the city, although with special status. They were allowed to choose their own senior militiaman and have a voice in their assignments with pay when on duty, which would be part-time. Thus they retained ties to the factory and had their own separate existence but were subordinated to city militia officials. The official transfer of authority over the militias to city officials took place between March 11 and 15, with Medvedev giving up his position as commander of a separate Soviet-sponsored workers' militia on March 14.[8]

There was some worker opposition to these developments, but it was fairly weak and certainly ineffective. There were factory resolutions opposing the arrangement and demanding that the workers be armed, such as at Zhest Factory on March 18. A meeting at the Titanik Factory resolved to organize a factory militia, but whether this was in protest against the city militia or merely the formation of a factory guard militia as provided for by the earlier Soviet regulations and implicit in the Public Executive Committee regulations is not clear from the brief newspaper report. However, it does appear that some factories turned toward advocating factory militias under the supervision of the factory committee and officially limited to factory security functions. The railway workers set up such a factory militia on March 15—that is, after the new provisions for the city militia had gone into effect. There was some opposition inside the soviet also. As early as March 3, one comrade Kaplan, a Menshevik, insisted that the militia must be composed of workers and argued—unsuccessfully—against cooperation with the Public Executive Committee and against including soldiers, students, and others in the militia. On a different level, the *Oblast* (Regional) Congress of Soviets meeting in Saratov on March 22 called for a transfer of the organization of the militia to the Soviet, but nothing came of this.[9]

By the second half of March the initiative passed to the Public Executive Committee and worker interest dropped off, with the workers' militia becoming inactive at most factories. Moreover, worker participation in the city militia dropped sharply: from 400 to 500 in March to 120 by April 1, to 35 by May 1, to 20 by July 22, to 9 on September 1.[10] Initially, such a slackening of worker interest reflected a general lessening of interest in the militia once the revolution was over, a development that occurred elsewhere as well. The rapid emergence of the socialist political leaders as the dominant political figures, and their control of the city government, seemed to signal this completion. A similar falling off of interest, it should be noted, affected other newly created organizations after the excitement of "February" subsided. However, one cannot ignore that this also reflected a shift in emphasis; workers who remained interested in such activities refocused their energies on more political and purely worker, Red Guard-type organizations rather than on general public bodies such as the city militia.

During the late spring and early summer the party alliances and political power in Saratov settled into a pattern similar to that of most Russian cities. The same moderate socialist versus Bolshevik split occurred, and a Menshevik-SR alliance emerged. In the case of Saratov, the Bolsheviks had been unusually strong in March, being the largest party in the Soviet and providing its chairman and many of its most prominent individual leaders. New elections between May 25 and June 1, however, reversed that situation. The Bolsheviks remained the largest single party in the Workers' Section, a point worth noting because the Bolsheviks were the only party to give the Red Guards much support, but they had only small representation in the newly formed Soldiers' Section. The SR-Menshevik bloc took control of the Soviet and, after elections in July, of the city duma.[11] Officially this Menshevik-SR leadership recognized the city government—first the Public Executive Committee and then the city duma—and the Provincial Commissar of the Provisional Government as the legitimate political authorities in Saratov, their own position being that of spokesmen for "the democracy" and watchdogs, even though they were the *real* power in Saratov. There was, then, a reflection of the *dvoevlastie* in Petrograd but with the very important difference that in Saratov the government was much more clearly controlled and run by the same socialist leaders who led the Soviet, whereas in the Provisional Government the socialist leaders of the Petrograd Soviet were influential but did not clearly control it. This political situation lasted until the end of August, until the aftermath of the Kornilov revolt, with the result that

Soviet and duma both were uninterested in, if not hostile to, the workers' militias.

Interest in armed workers' bands was not completely abandoned in the late spring and summer, however, for an undercurrent kept alive the notion of a workers' militia, or at least of arming the workers. The socialist party leaders raised the question from time to time, if only in a general way. An editorial in the Saratov *Izvestiia* on March 19, when general responsibility for and control of the militia were being turned over to the Public Executive Committee, stressed the general Social Democratic theories of arming the people. It pointed out that the minimum program of the party demanded replacing the standing army by a general arming of all the people. This demand was put in rather broad terms, acknowledging that it was not expected to be fulfilled immediately. The editorial was more a statement of general position, a justification for workers having arms, than a call for any real organization. An article in the Saratov Bolshevik newspaper, *Sotsial-Demokrat,* on May 21 was not much more explicit. Reacting to a speech of the city militia commander, Dmitrii Chegodaev, against the idea of a union being formed by militiamen, it repeated the doctrinal position of arming all the people and stressed the need for general militia training of the entire population. The Bolshevik paper reiterated the same ideas in an editorial of June 2 written in response to a Victor Chernov speech in Petrograd against the idea of arming all the people, but in this instance the writer did go a little further and called for the immediate arming of the workers of the main cities as the first step toward the general arming of all the people. Again, however, it did not propose any specific steps.

At least some workers retained a more active interest in the formation of their own armed bands. The reasons are not hard to find when one looks at their general situation in the spring and summer of 1917, and especially at the economic milieu. The euphoria of February, with its high expectations, quickly evaporated under the impact of harsh economic reality, giving way to frustration and hostility. As early as April, layoffs began because of supply shortages. Although metalworking and other plants were affected, the greatest problem was caused by the slowdown of grain shipments from the countryside. This caused layoffs in the flour mills and some other plants processing agricultural products, which despite the impact of war production still constituted a vital section of the local economy. Moreover, it gave rise to the threat of food shortages: in June rationing cards were distributed for bread, and rations were reduced on August 1. The specter of hunger hovered over the city and exacerbated tensions. Moreover, strikes—mainly over wages, but also over other issues such as length of the workday, medical facilities, night work—became serious by May and grew in significance as the summer progressed. The economic problems gave rise to crimes such as theft and muggings, and resultant vigilante measures. Both had a disquieting effect on the public. In addition to economic problems, political issues came more to the fore in worker resolutions and hence, one assumes, in their worries about the future. In May and June, resolutions against the government and the war began to appear, coupled with calls for the transfer of all power to the soviets. These increased steadily thereafter. Hostility to the propertied elements, especially in the persons of factory and mill owners and managers, became more pronounced and open.

Given all the above, it is hardly surprising that worker interest in maintaining separate, independent militia or druzhiny continued and grew. These were established at factories, usually under the direction and authority of the factory committees. Some of them developed out of the workers' militias formed in March which had survived after the Public Executive Committee took over the city militia; others derived from the special factory militias provided when the city militia was set up; still others were newly created in response to worker concerns and were quite unrelated to the militia laws. All were concerned primarily with protecting the factories and worker interests in them. Generally they demanded and got work-rate pay while serving, although in the summer—as elsewhere—an effort was made by the owners to drop this obligation and even to get rid of the entire factory militia. Most of those which survived were poorly armed, although the workers' militias of the railroad shops, Levkovich Tobacco, and Zhest factories were better outfitted than most.[12] Resolutions from factories on the workers' militia are scarce for this period but do surface. At the Titanik Factory in early May, a general meeting decided that the organization of a strong workers' druzhina was essential not only for it but for all factories, that these men must be paid at least work-rate by the management, and that this sentiment must be expressed to the Soviet. A notable characteristic of this factory, one of the largest, was that it had been evacuated from Riga with its work force and hence most of the workers were Latvians, not local. Interest in forming an armed force during this period also came from another factory evacuated from Latvia, the huge Zhest Factory. There, on June 15, a general workers' meeting discussed the question of a Red Guard, the first printed use of the term in Saratov. The meeting decided to work on one holiday to earn the financial means to support a Red Guard. Both factories passed resolutions against the Provisional Government during the same period—Titanik on May 12 and Zhest on May 19.[13] Both Zhest and Titanik factories had relatively large and well-organized druzhiny throughout 1917.

The organizational work at the factories in the summer underscores one of the characteristics of the Saratov Red Guard. Although they were mostly factory-based in all cities, and although factory committees played an important role everywhere, in Saratov the factory committees seem to have been especially important in organizing guards. This feature may explain why the activity of the Saratov armed workers' bands was so strongly directed toward local factory concerns in the summer and fall of 1917, much more so than in Petrograd. In Saratov there was an especially close bond between factory committee and workers' militia or Red Guard unit.

Armed workers' detachments, then, continued to exist in Saratov during the spring and early summer, even though quite small and weak. Their survival was due to local, factory-level organization and the determination of small groups of workers despite Soviet and city indifference or even hostility. For example, in Saratov as elsewhere there was an effort to get the workers and others to turn in their arms in the aftermath of the July Days in Petrograd. This was endorsed by the Soviet Executive Committee and specifically mentioned past and present militiamen.[14] There is no indication that the effort was any less unsuccessful in Saratov than elsewhere. Still, it would be a grave mistake to overestimate the size or strength of these armed workers' groups. Their overall condition was well summed up by a report at the provincial congress of soviets in May: "Saratov workers' militia—affairs disorganized. Factory militia is weak, affairs not right."[15]

In Saratov, as in many other places, the revolt of General Kornilov, news of which arrived on the night of August 27–28, sharpened political antagonisms and stimulated the organization of workers' militia, druzhiny, and Red Guard units. The Saratov case is a little deceptive because of a curiously delayed effect. The Saratov Soviet did not immediately form a "committee to save the revolution" and call for forming armed worker bands, a common response elsewhere. Instead the socialist leaders engaged in a protracted dispute, lasting from August 28 to 31, over whether to organize the anti-Kornilov effort via the Soviet or the duma, both of which they controlled. Not until August 31 did the Soviet, in the first Bolshevik-sponsored political resolution carried in the Soviet plenum since spring, include in a list of measures to counter Kornilov, "first of all to arm all workers to form factory druzhiny."[16] That it took three days to include such a reference suggests that the Soviet leaders, including perhaps the Bolsheviks, did not feel that there was great urgency to form workers' armed detachments. One reason may well have been that Saratov did not face an identifiable and immediate Kornilov military threat. The Saratov Soviet did receive a call from the Tsaritsyn Soviet for help against a possible move by General A. M. Kaledin and his cossacks in support of Kornilov, and on August 30 it agreed to send such help. In contrast, in Tsaritsyn, which was closer to Kaledin's troops, a Red Guard was set up quickly. What did occur in these days, however, was a sorting out of political allegiances, clarifying and deepening the moderate versus radical socialist distinction and setting the stage for the Bolshevik takeover of the Soviet in September.

The workers themselves at first did not seem to respond much more energetically than the Soviet, although a long-range trend toward arming did in fact begin. Although the railroad shop workers on August 30 passed a resolution on Kornilov in which they demanded the immediate arming of all the workers in a factory militia,[17] there is no evidence of other activity toward forming Red Guards in the August 28–31 period, not even other resolutions. The Saratov workers did not hastily form new Red Guard units, beef up existing armed bands, or search frantically for arms, as they did in many cities at this time. There were anti-Kornilov demonstrations by workers and soldiers, and some jailed political prisoners (mostly Bolsheviks from July) were forcibly freed. However, the main effect was to accelerate a shift that had begun in early August.

August had seen increased evidence of worker frustration and hardening of class lines, the result both of their own deteriorating economic conditions and renewed political activity by the conservatives. The Kornilov affair confirmed their fears of a counterrevolution. A new anger arose in September, and with it the conviction that they needed arms both for protection and to advance their economic and political interests.

The angry mood of Saratov workers was underscored by the railroad workers, who joined the national railroad strike of September 26–27 but refused to end it along with the rest of the country, ignoring the orders of *Vikzhel* (All-Russian Executive Committee of Railroad Workers). Strikes and layoffs fueled discontent: in September a newly formed union of flour-mill owners announced their intent to dismiss fifteen hundred workers on October 1. Moreover, the threat of hunger hovered over the city: in October it was without grain for one or two days on several occasions. The widespread peasant disorders in the area could not help but affect the mood of Saratov, both for its food implications and because of the close ties many workers still had to the villages. Agitation by extremists—both anarchists and Blackhundreds seem to have been vocal in Saratov—added to the uncertainty, as rumors of potential pogroms and criminal gangs circulated. Demands by garrison soldiers that they be moved from their inadequate barracks before winter and quartered in already scarce civilian housing caused new uncertainties. In all, the political and social situation was tense and, for workers, there was the overriding reality that their standard of living had visibly declined and that their presumed new political power had neither prevented that decline nor guaranteed them protection against counterrevolution and physical danger.

The situation was ripe, then, for the formation of armed workers' bands, and they came quickly in September and October. Four hundred workers of the Bushkov Factory on September 2 passed a resolution demanding the arming of all the workers and the formation of a factory militia. On September 6 the Zhest Factory workers discussed the question of organizing a fighting druzhina, demanded the arming of all the workers, and assigned 3,000 rubles for purchase of arms. On the seventh the Zhest Factory committee reported to the Soviet that it had created a detachment of 150 men and requested aid in obtaining arms. After hearing a report of their Soviet deputy, the workers of the Levkovich Tobacco Factory decided on September 9 to organize a Red Guard. A Red Guard was formed at this time also at the Bering Factory which, according to its organizer, numbered three hundred, but that number probably was not reached until later, closer to the October revolution. Red Guard detachments were formed at other factories during the late September to October period, including also some organized by trade unions, such as one of dock hands and river transport workers, which had about a hundred members. In some instances factory management still tried to prevent guard formation, such as at the Saratov State Stables, but were unsuccessful when faced with pressure from the workers or Soviet.[18]

The most important of all these druzhiny was the one formed at the Saratov railway shops. Workers' militia and druzhiny had existed there since the time of the February revolution. The Bolsheviks captured the railroad shops' "local executive committee" on August 30, and thereafter Ivan Erasov, the new chairman recently returned from exile, devoted a great deal of energy to building a well-trained Red Guard. According to the Menshevik newspaper, *Proletarii Povolzh'ia,* a Red Guard was formed there in mid-September which undertook training in the use of arms under the direction of instructors with military experience. The growth of the Red Guard received a boost at the October 3 general meeting of workers at the shops, when speakers stressing the guard's importance encouraged enrollment and a new commander, A. A. Fedorov, was elected. Considerable effort was made to obtain competent instructors. The two most important ones seem to have been V. N. Krasichkov and Dmitri Serov, the former a soldier recently returned from the front who was assigned to this task by the Bolshevik party organization in Saratov. Extensive training was necessary because many workers had never before handled rifles. The railroad Red Guard also took up the guarding of railway stores and strategic positions, alongside or instead of the soldiers previously assigned those tasks. The detachment grew from about a hundred in late September to above seven hundred by the time of the October revolution.[19]

Exact figures for the total size of the Red Guards during this period are not available, but several credible estimates exist. Two different contemporary sources cite six hundred by the first of October. We know that the size grew rapidly during October, a sevenfold increase at the railroad shops being especially spectacular. V. K. Medvedev gives a figure of two thousand for October 25 and E. D. Rumiantsev estimates about twenty-six hundred for October.[20] Allowing for considerable enrollment during October 25–27, after first news of the revolution in Petrograd, we can reasonably estimate a figure of well over two thousand on the eve of the revolution, swelling to about three thousand by time of the armed confrontation on October 28–29.

The Red Guard and radical political leaders also turned to better organizing the emerging Red Guard. On September 7 the Soviet approved regulations for a workers' druzhina. They provided for a druzhina of workers and employees, completely subordinate to the Soviet, which would choose the commander (the terms *druzhina* and *Red Guard* were used interchangeably during the discussion). Enrollment would be at the factory based on the recommendation of the factory committee, trade union, workers' medical fund office, or party committee, with training to be provided by instructors named by the military section of the Soviet. The resolution also provided for a Soviet commission to oversee organization of the druzhiny.[21] Increased Soviet support for organizing the Red Guard came in late September as a result of the reelection of Soviet deputies and subsequent reorganization of the Soviet leadership. When the elections were completed and the new Soviet was able to hold its first meeting on September 21, it had a clear Bolshevik majority: 320 of a total of 533 seats. These figures show a dramatic upsurge of Bolshevik support, especially among the soldiers. The Bolshevik triumph was registered in the new Executive Committee where the Bolshevik leaders now took over the top positions: V. P. Antonov-Saratovskii as chairman, M. I. Vasil'ev-Iuzhin and P. A. Lebedev as assistant chairmen along with a lone SR, Lieutenant Pontriagin.[22] The Red Guards could now expect more support from the Soviet.

By the end of September, when Lebedev made a new report to the Soviet, the organization of druzhiny and Red Guards had progressed to the point where a central staff was in existence and operating. This staff consisted of three representatives from the Soviet, one each from the factory committee and trade union organizations, and commanders of druzhina. The chairman at first was Lebedev, but because of his heavy work load this task was passed to Ivan Erasov. Both were Bolsheviks. The assistant chairman was an SR officer, Plemiannikov, whose military training was deemed valuable and who later became the city Red Guard commander for a time. It was this Red Guard staff which organized a test of readiness of the guardsmen that fired the enthusiasm of the latter and upset other elements in the city. One day in late September, after the workers had gone home from work, the warning signal at the railway works was sounded. Within thirty to forty-five minutes one hundred armed and two hundred unarmed railwaymen gathered and then proceeded to the Soviet, where they found workers from other factories and additional railwaymen. Despite being told that it was only a test of their readiness, the excited workers staged an armed parade through the city.[23]

One of the main problems of the Saratov Red Guard was obtaining adequate arms. They complained regularly of a shortage; the Zhest Factory committee reported that they had a druzhina of 150 but they could increase it to a thousand if they had enough weapons.[24] Repeated efforts in September to get arms from the soldiers via the military section of the Soviet were not very successful; the soldiers cited their own shortage of arms.[25] In all, it would appear that at the end of September, the various druzhiny were fairly poorly equipped compared to those elsewhere, although we have virtually no solid information on how many rifles and other arms they actually had. Calculation of arms available is made more difficult by the tendency of guardsmen always to stress the inadequacy of what they had, and indeed they always *felt* poorly armed no matter how many they possessed, while concealing information on how many arms they had from those to whom they were appealing. A few hundred rifles, held since February or obtained in one way or another since then, would probably be a reasonable figure.

Given the shortage of arms and their failure to obtain more via the military section, the Soviet leaders in October had to look elsewhere. On October 2 the Executive Committee of the Soviet sent a letter to the Moscow Soviet asking it to provide a thousand rifles and revolvers, for which they were willing to pay if necessary. The request was unsuccessful. On October 12 the Saratov Bolshevik committee sent A. I. Anan'ev to the Bolshevik Central Committee in Petrograd with a request that they help him obtain arms for the Saratov Red Guard, but he returned to Saratov only on October 30, after the revolution there. Ironically, at the same time that the Saratov Soviet was attempting unsuccessfully to obtain weapons elsewhere they were being besieged with requests not only from factories within the city but from other cities along the Volga which, in their own search for arms, appealed to Saratov as a provincial center.[26]

If most Red Guard units lacked adequate arms, and the Soviet could not get them, local initiative worked at least for the railway workers. Shortly before the October revolution they managed to heist from two wagons in the railway yards enough arms to outfit their druzhina. V. K. Medvedev mentions that at the time of the revolution the railwaymen had seven hundred rifles plus two artillery pieces hidden away.[27] As other sources indicate there were seven hundred Red Guardsmen there at the time of the revolution, it can be assumed that each member was armed. Overall, it appears that on the eve of the revolution arms were unevenly distributed among the Saratov Red Guard detachments and that there were not nearly enough for all the guardsmen in the city.

Political tensions in Saratov strained toward the breaking point as October wore on. The national debate over a transfer of all power to the Soviets at the upcoming second All-Russian Congress of Soviets and the possibility of a Bolshevik seizure of power had its local version in Saratov, with all the uncertainties and insecurities those questions involved. Two actions by the Mensheviks and SRs heightened the political crisis: their effort to revive the city duma, which they still controlled, as a locus of political authority after their defeat in the Soviet in September; and the decision of the SRs on October 18 to withdraw from the work of the Soviet's executive organs. Further controversy was stirred by decrees of the Soviet Executive Committee on October 20 designed to insure control over key functions such as food distribution, as well as steps taken to prepare it to deal with any disorders in the city. Although these Soviet measures appear to have been defensive rather than offensive, they further unsettled the political atmosphere and, added to the rumors and discussions of a major political upheaval in Petrograd, aggravated the tensions caused by the various economic and social problems we have discussed.

Word of the Bolshevik revolution in Petrograd first reached Saratov early on Wednesday morning, October 25, shortly after midnight, in the form of a telegram to D. A. Topuridze, the local commissar of the Provisional Government and a Menshevik.[28] October 25 and the first part of October 26 were relatively quiet, as both sides tried to assess the situation and pull together their support, while the Bolsheviks maneuvered to get a Soviet resolution of "all power to the Soviets." After an unsuccessful effort to persuade the local Bolsheviks to disassociate themselves from their Petrograd brethren—the Bolsheviks instead affirmed their support of the central leaders, even though they were hazy as to just what was happening—the Mensheviks and SR leaders organized a "Committee to Save the Revolution" based on the duma the afternoon of the twenty-fifth. The stage was thus set for an armed struggle for power in Saratov.

On October 26 the Bolshevik leaders increased efforts to get the Soviet to assume power. Their efforts were threatened by a group of socialist officers in the Soviet military section, including both SRs and Bolsheviks, who attempted to set up a compromise, "neutral" leadership to keep order and protect the revolution. This also failed, however, when the Soviet plenum met that evening and gave thunderous support for seizure of power under the slogan "All Power to the Soviets." After the Mensheviks and SRs walked out, the Bolsheviks were left in unchallenged control of a Soviet meeting completely filled with advocates for seizing power. During the early morning hours of October 27 (the meeting ran all night), the Executive Committee undertook to implement their declaration of power, among other measures announcing the replacement of provincial commissar Topuridze by the Bolshevik P. A. Lebedev, ordering the seizure by armed force of the post and telegraph, the closing down of anti-Soviet newspapers, and the issuing of a decree on land distribution.

On the twenty-seventh both sides moved to consolidate their armed support. Both the Soviet and the duma committee issued proclamations asserting their sole authority in the city. The duma called for volunteers to come to its aid and undertook to build up an armed force of military cadets, officers, and volunteers at the duma building. The same morning D. A. Topuridze telegraphed to cossack detachments in the area asking them to proceed to Saratov to aid the duma, but they never arrived. The Bolsheviks also moved that morning to organize their own armed support. Word had been sent to the factories on the twenty-sixth—by whom it is not clear—to start mobilizing their druzhiny and Red Guard. During the morning of the twenty-seventh a conference of Red Guards was held, with A. A. Fedorov named as commander of all the Red Guards in the city. The same morning the Soviet named Captain P. K. Shcherbakov commander of the garrison in an effort to assert control there. Curiously enough, according to Vasil'ev-Iuzhin, Shcherbakov was not known to the Bolshevik leaders but was accepted on the recommendation of Bolshevik soldiers. Finding a new "Bolshevik" to name as commander had become necessary after the leading Bolshevik officer in the garrison disgraced himself by joining the would-be "neutral committee." Following Shcherbakov's appointment, a "military council" composed of Shcherbakov, Vasil'ev-Iuzhin, and Antonov-Saratovskii was set up. They spent the afternoon and evening securing the support of the troops, especially the large artillery component, which wavered for some time before coming to full support of the Soviet. The scurry of armed men on both sides alerted the citizens to the prospect of fighting in the streets.

On the morning of October 28 the two sides faced off at last when the Soviet ordered that the duma building, which by then had been well barricaded, be surrounded. This took considerable time but was accomplished by 4:00 P.M. by a force of about three thousand soldiers and Red Guards. Neither side, however, wanted to start firing. The outnumbered duma defenders, surrounded and their hope of cossack help fading, sent a deputation to the Soviet to negotiate terms of surrender. At 6:00 P.M. the Soviet, in turn, sent representatives into the duma building to complete the surrender arrangements. Hardly had the Soviet group left the duma building after completing the negotiations, however, when firing broke out. Most Soviet histories, not surprisingly, claim that it was begun by military cadet supporters of the duma manning a machine gun in a nearby church belfry, and that Soviet supporters simply responded. However, Lebedev, who was in the midst of it, states that no one knows who fired first or why. Despite a freezing rain, shooting continued during the long cold night, joined by sporadic artillery fire from batteries that had taken up position on a hill overlooking the duma building. Finally, at about 6:00 A.M. on the twenty-ninth, the duma supporters capitulated. At 8:00, Vasil'ev-Iuzhin led out the duma defenders and, faced with threats of summary action from the soldiers, turned them over to the Red Guard for protection and convoy to Soviet headquarters, the guardsmen being considered better disciplined and more inclined to obey orders to protect the prisoners. Miraculously, the night of firing, including artillery bombardment, had led to only minor casualties: one killed and eight wounded on the duma side; two killed and ten wounded on the Soviet side. The barricades were quickly dismantled, especially the part composed of boxes of quinces, the hungry besiegers literally eating the barricades away. The Bolsheviks now held control of Saratov.

How important were the Saratov workers' druzhiny, militias, and Red Guards in the October revolution? This is very difficult to estimate. The various armed workers' forces gathered at the factories on October 26 and 27, where they were supplemented by new recruits and sent off to the duma or other points. Representative is the account of one guardsman that at the shoe factory where he worked the workers began to arm and organize themselves on the twenty-sixth. At the gate of the factory was a small shoemaker's cabin in which stood a blond artilleryman handing out arms and quick instructions on how to use them. They then proceeded to the leatherworkers' union and from there to the Soviet Executive Committee building to await their orders.[29] The gradual unfolding of events from the twenty-fifth to the twenty-eighth allowed the workers considerable time to organize and respond to the events. One is struck by the fact that neither contemporary records nor later Soviet historians cite a call from the Soviet or one of its bodies to the workers to arm themselves. Indeed, among the points in an appeal of the Soviet Executive Committee to the population on the morning of the twenty-seventh was one calling on the workers to remain at their jobs unless summoned by the Soviet.[30] This would suggest that the workers were acting by their own volition as they learned of events, or else that the decision of somebody—the military council, Red Guard staff, whoever—to summon them was made off the record and orally expressed. In a city with a relatively small worker population—about twenty-five to thirty thousand industrial workers—that could readily be done, especially as events unfolded over some days. It would seem, in any case, that the workers responded with a considerable amount of self-initiative. By the morning of the twenty-seventh, large numbers had converged on the headquarters of the Soviet Executive Committee.

These Red Guards played several roles in the October revolution in Saratov. Some of them remained at the factories, where they served both to guard the premises and as reserves. Some were sent to seize control of various important points—banks, telephone, post, others. They also disarmed the city militiamen (police). Their most dramatic function was in the siege of the duma building. Although troops were sent first to fulfill the task of surrounding the building, Red Guard units were also sent as the twenty-eighth wore on. They played an active role in the firing that continued through the freezing rain of the night of October 28–29.[31] Despite their relative unfamiliarity with arms, they apparently held their positions with determination. Lebedev relates that at the outbreak of firing on the evening of the twenty-eighth he suddenly found himself standing alone in the street, the soldiers having disappeared somewhere. He hurried to a nearby building and found shelter with a Red Guard detachment that had remained there under fire, returning the fire themselves.[32] P. K. Shcherbakov, a military man and the new Bolshevik commander of the garrison, later stated that "it is necessary to say that the Red Guard in the days of Great October 1917 had a great influence on the morale of the troops of the Saratov garrison."[33] His comments suggest that the workers' detachments played an important role as a morale-building and stiffening influence in the siege, as they did in the Petrograd events. Moreover, their numbers were probably a factor of considerable importance as well. There were about three thousand active Red Guards by the twenty-eighth. Some, of course, were on guard duty at factories or elsewhere, but that would still leave a large number available for action in the siege. Although we do not have precise figures, it appears that roughly half or more of the besieging force of about three thousand men were Red Guards. In other words, the armed workers turned out in force, in contrast to the garrison, where only a thousand to fifteen hundred of the nearly seventy thousand soldiers participated in the siege. If, as some sources suggest, the Red Guards were particularly determined and disciplined in contrast to the soldiers, then their role in deciding the outcome of events would be rather great indeed, and relatively greater than that of their counterparts in Petrograd.

14. Retrospect

Allan K. Wildman

THE INTENT and essential value of this undertaking have been to stimulate fresh thinking about Russian history by focusing on how it was played out in one of the representative areas of the vast empire. The results, I think, have more than justified the guiding conceptions of the organizers and the hard work of the contributors. My role, since I have not conducted primary research on the Saratov region, is to reflect on the portrait of Saratov drawn here and to speculate on what it tells us about this critical period in Russia's development. Thus, what follows makes no pretense at special knowledge of the region but rather attempts to apply my own understanding of the main themes and issues in Russian history to the findings of the other contributors. My efforts, I hope, will throw into relief how Saratov relates to the larger picture of Russian history and at the same time tie together into a coherent whole the rich empirical material presented here in this book.

Although it is true that every region or locale is unique and that diversities of development and experience should be appreciated, this alone would not justify regional history. It would take centuries of assiduous research to do justice to every part of Russia, and I doubt that the interest of even an informed readership could be sustained. Far more important is the fact that a regional focus lends an element of concreteness to important interrelationships that cannot be easily ascertained on a national scale; it is like switching from the tenth to the fiftieth power on a microscope, and injects into historical study some of the excitement that Galileo must have felt when he first observed the rings of Saturn and the mountains on the moon.

History is ultimately the science of the concrete, and if we are unable to establish historical connections and relationships in the particular, it casts doubt upon our venerated generalizations and assumptions. I am sure the considerations that have impelled this group of scholars toward regional concentration are the same that have moved others of us toward the selection of a particular social group at a particular point in time—in my case, soldiers in 1917. Both are ways of slicing history cross-sectionally to uncover its primal matrix and motive forces. In so doing we discover many unsuspected new truths and achieve more precise understandings of old ones.

But the history of a nation is not simply replicated in its various parts: far from it, national history is a composite of different processes taking place in various locales in various strata whose dynamics and interaction must be established. Regional history overthrows the prejudice that what the state decrees, or what is initiated in the metropolitan center, automatically ramifies to the periphery. Not only are many impulses lost or transformed in transmission, it is also a two-way street; and what occurs in the periphery, such as peasant disturbances or the migration of upwardly or outwardly mobile elements to the center, greatly affects the overall shape of things. Natives of the provinces on one occasion or another return to them, bringing back their accumulated experience; channels of reciprocal communication and influence become established, so that whatever occurs in either arena affects the other. Countless examples of this emerge in these chapters, so that we are far better able to conceptualize these relationships than if we held rigidly to the metropolitan perspective. It is the vocation of regional studies to capture the realities of this reciprocity, and it seems to me that this cardinal but seldom recognized axiom alone justifies the approach of this book.

One further point on the merits of regional history. Though these chapters cover mainly the modern period, they bring out the layered character of historical experience: something of each successive period stamps itself on subsequent ones. In the character and special personality of a region like Saratov we can see how these traces of the past reflect the major stages of the expansion of the Russian state and society, but in the concrete way that its particular geographical location and accumulated experience impart. And what do we see in this collection of studies of the deposits of time that lend to Saratov as a city, as a region, and as a society a particular stamp?

We see, first, the ancient riparian tradition of one of Russia's great waterways, then the tradition of the steppe, then of the frontier, the refuge for Russia's fugitive and outcast elements. And last, we see the late intrusion into the area of the Russian state, which took the form first of fortified outposts, then of bringing in *odnodvortsy* (single household settlers) and *sluzhilye liudi* (servicemen of various grades), then of inviting in settler communities such as the Germans and Old Believers, and, finally, of granting huge tracts of land to *pomeshchiki* and Catherinian grandees, who were encouraged to transplant their serfs and their way of life into this area. Under the umbrella of the administrative town of Saratov also emerged a *posad* population based on commerce across and down the Volga, so well described by James Hart. Saratov, both the town and the province, seems to have been the focal point where all of these disparate elements came together and impinged on each other while remaining very imperfectly amalgamated. The riparian tradition, of course, is the most ancient: the Swedish Rus' passed down this way; the Bulgars, the Khozars, and finally the Mongols came up this way; plunderers and traders plied Saratov's waters many centuries before Stenka Razin. One is tempted to speculate that Saratov might well have been the site of the encampment of the Rus' whom the Arab Ibn Fadlan observed on the banks of the Volga in the ninth century, with their enormous collection of booty.

In some sense, Saratov long preserved the aspect of an encampment and so appeared even to our English traveler of the late nineteenth century. It was from the beginning an improvised place, never finished, never adequately fortified, always oriented toward the business to be transacted on the waterfront, as significant for the goods and people passing through it as for what actually took place there. It had no ancient roots or identity like Kazan or Astrakhan; no exotic barbarians ever ruled there. When finally settled it was as an outpost, an administrative center for the territory, an arbitrary creation of the state, rather than of the population who lived there. The people who came in as settlers, of which James Long's Volga Germans are a notable example, came because the state wanted them there, wanted the area to be populated and held. The fugitive elements moved downstream or to the Left Bank and blended in with the world of cossacks and non-Russian peoples.

In other words, Saratov was not a true city or even a town in the Western sense until very late in its history. It was not a magnet, a mecca, or a melting pot even long after it had become a commercial center. The various population groups led very compartmentalized existences; outsiders came to transact their business and departed. The traders, quite powerless in the local establishment, were far more concerned with what took place in the locales their goods were moving to or from. When the crises of the Stenka Razin and Pugachev rebellions took place, it is clear that the posad population felt no great stake in the presence of the state and sought to make its own peace with the rebels. Nevertheless, the state reasserted itself, successfully carried out its mission, and created satellite district towns according to the model of Catherine's statute on provinces; and under its aegis the transplanted pomeshchik society took root and throve in Saratov's black soil.

What sort of society takes shape in these circumstances? For the pomeshchiki it is a good society—their agriculture flourishes with the benefit of serf labor, they are socially secure and comfortable, they take on the veneer of Western-educated culture, they send their children to good schools, they enjoy each other's company. Far from being a collection of Gogolian scoundrels and misfits, they appear here to be generous in spirit, open, serious about affairs, willing to receive outsiders in their midst— even those of other social classes so long as they fit into the milieu—in other words, the very opposite of narrow-minded provincial bigots. The touchstone of acceptability seems to be whether the newcomers share their commitment to public values, their *obshchestvennost'.* They are even capable of coopting into their midst the bureaucrats and officials of high rank that represent the state (but not apparently the police officials, who remain suspect). Insofar as they have a center, a gathering place, it is the city of Saratov—their children go to school there, it is where the zemstvo annually assembles, it is their residence in the harsh winter months, it is where one meets important people and receives visitors, where serious ideas are discussed, where culture is formed. The same would be true to a lesser extent of the district towns. Yet the pomeshchiki are not an urban or urbanized class. They do not amalgamate or mix with the town popula- tion—they have nothing to do with the business conducted on the wharves or in the counting houses, nor with the floating population of barge haulers, Tatars, Mordvinians, itinerant craftsmen, and peasant day la- borers. Most of their "public" concerns have to do with the needs of agriculture and their peasants. There are railroads and steamships, food-processing plants and a few small metal shops yielding a small but growing working class, but so far they represent just one more isolated enclave. They have not yet begun to reshape the structure of society, nor do they to any significant extent until the end of the century. It is pomeshchik society and those who are drawn into it who set the tone and acquire a public identity and sense of responsibility in the region.

However, we must note the obverse side of this development. The members of this society could afford to be generous because they enjoyed their comforts at the expense of peasant society. Under serfdom, of course, they had at their disposal a large pool of unfree labor that yielded a comfortable income and a secure position; but even after the Emancipation their circumstances did not change drastically. These well-meaning, liberal gentry made sure that they were adequately provided for in the Emancipation terms, that they continued to control most of the land, including the lion's share of the meadows, ponds, and woodlands, so that the peasants would continue to be dependent on them for additional rents and access to key resources. In effect, as Timothy Mixter describes, feudal practices persisted in the new era, despite the increase in money exchange, in the system of sharecropping, *otrabotka* (rent payments in workdays), and labor contracts, which carried over in thinly disguised form the former relationships of dependency. As time went on, the peasants felt the effects of this dependency ever more acutely, as the population increase put pressure on the fixed allotments.

What strikes one most about this elite society in the post-Emancipation period as it emerges from the studies of McKinsey and Kimball is its high degree of culture and public spirit. They feel themselves to be progressive; they are keenly aware of what is going on in the capital and the nation as a whole; they want to be a part of it, to contribute to it, to demonstrate their own worthiness to do so. They read newspapers and journals, they ply each visitor from the capital for information, they refuse to be left out. What is also noteworthy is that certain members of local society outgrow it and move to the capital to become part of the national scene. For some the object may be an advancement in *chin* (official rank); for others, the quest for the company of prominent people or the exercise of a new profession—all the way to a Chernyshevskii, whose intellect finds inadequate scope, develops a sense of mission, and seeks a wider audience for his message. Such persons come back to Saratov to visit but not to live. But the local *Saratovtsy* are very aware of their sons and daughters who have departed, keep track of their careers, and seek out their company when they return for a visit. Thus channels of influence and communication are established that link Saratov to the national scene. We do not see the more retrograde types of landowners, the hard-bitten foes of emancipation. They are undoubtedly there and a few references are made to them, but obviously they have been forced into the background by the more articulate, progressive elements and have little status. As for officialdom, we do not see much of the stereotyped *chinovnik*—the literal-minded, unimaginative slave of routine who is insensitive to the real needs of people. On the contrary, we see more enlightened types like Baranovskii and Mordvinov, who easily blend in with and contribute to the self-consciousness of local society. (An exception is the local police chief, who is alarmed at all this hustle and bustle and even reports on the extracurricular activities of his immediate superiors.)

Alan Kimball's chapter gives us a very sharp profile of the institutions and platforms through which this society shaped its basic values and commitments, its sense of public responsibility, or obshchestvennost. Unlike in the 1830s and 1840s, it was not so much a question of ideas and worldview as a definition of one's arena of activity, a self-justification through deeds and associations. Collectively, these groups created a consciousness that they were the public, had the capacity and desire to make things happen, were obligated to make the government see this, and since they didn't, to create the possibility anyway, as that was their mission and calling. Within the bosom of this progressive society it was perfectly possible for individuals and groups of more radical persuasion, even conspiracies, to crystallize and find protection. Their radicalism, in other words, did not exclude them—at least until their activities became very serious, as for example at the time of Karakozov's assassination attempt, or again in 1881.

One might ask why this enlightened gentry was so permissive, as obviously they would have had the most to lose should the radicals' vision of a just society come to fruition. Though they were materially secure, they were not so secure morally that they did not sense the injustice of their own position, that they were not attuned to the sufferings of the people. There was a Lavrovian overlay to their public consciousness, a sense that they owed a debt, that it was wrong to enjoy the benefits of culture at the people's expense. Therefore one had not only to find one's own niche in public activity, one could not allow other individuals to suffer for trying to live out their commitments. Therefore, at some risk to themselves, they were willing to protect and abet the activities of the more radical youth, viewing them as little more than misguided, but also learning from them and imbibing some of their radicalism and love of the people.

At the same time, this liberal society shared with the radical intelligentsia a feeling of alienation from the state, though it was the state that upheld their privileged position. Where did this sentiment come from, one might ask? Though it bears further exploration, I interpret it to a certain extent as a result of the Emancipation. Though the government had flattered the gentry by allowing them to form local committees, to draw up projects and petitions, to send deputies to the Main Committee in St. Petersburg, in the final analysis the government dictated the settlement and ignored the advice the gentry offered. In general, the state showed no sincere interest in drawing in the representatives of society to frame the real business of government, and the zemstvos were quite obviously a consolation prize for the "sacrifices" they had had to make in the Emancipation. Rebuffed in its desire to "crown the edifice" with a national zemstvo, liberal society developed a determination to exploit such freedom as they did enjoy to extend the arena even farther, to force the bureaucracy and unenlightened officialdom to make way for the real people. (Kimball has convinced me that, at least in this period, the term *narod* was inclusive of *obshchestvo,* not exclusive, at least in the minds of the liberal elements of society.) The result was the creation of a peculiar alliance of the liberal and radical elements that lasted very long—certainly until 1905 and in some respects until 1917. True, the alliance was less visible in the 1880s, or at least we have not been given a picture of it; but there is no question that a powerful, many-sided revival in the 1890s flourished until 1905.

The alliance flourished between the zemstvo men and the Third Element or, more precisely, Scott Seregny's teachers. The zemstvo boards promoted and encouraged their evolving sense of professionalism, trying to provide them with more resources, protect them from the intimidation of ministry officials, and so forth. Often they were unaware of harboring committed revolutionaries among their employees, and even when they became aware they continued to protect them. They might not have known when they hired a young man fresh out of the St. Petersburg Veterinary Institute that he was a Social Democrat and was conducting surreptitious propaganda among local workers, but even when they found out it did not alarm them; they could appreciate that he was acting out his "convictions." Often the zemstvo bureaus became a channel of communication for revolutionaries: Lenin's *Iskra,* for example, used the local zemstvo address for letter drops.

After 1905 there was an abrupt termination of this relationship. As Tom Fallows suggests, the liberal zemstvo men moved to the city and abandoned their erstwhile activities, while the Third Element was left to its own devices, subject to the persecutory activity of both the government and the new breed of more conservative zemstvo board men. But the liberal elements did keep their own networks alive, during the war resumed public activity, and after the February revolution of 1917 reemerged as active in politics. Donald Raleigh's study of 1917 illustrates that the old coalition in altered form was again revived in Saratov in the Public Executive Committee and the Soviet. It was the same symbiotic relationship with the roles reversed. The Soviet elements were now in charge and assumed responsibility for the management of affairs, but with the easy cooperation of local liberals. Unlike in the capital, in Saratov and doubtless in many local situations there was far less polarization and far more cooperation than one would suspect, and undoubtedly this was grounded in the connections and traditions of former times.

From the first to the very last, one characteristic of this milieu in all its various guises was a devotion to or a profound identification with the people, however defined, but certainly comprising the peasant masses. At the very minimum this took the form of a Populist-tainted liberalism; but it could take other forms, such as Slavophilism in the 1880s, Tolstoyanism in the 1890s, service to the people through the agency of the Third Element, a politically democratic shade in the Liberation Movement, a Lavrovian bent as Kulturtraeger among the people—all the various shades of revolutionary Populism which took on final form as the Socialist Revolutionary party. Saratov was obviously the homeland, indeed the heartland of this type of Populism. Here such ideas burgeoned in the salons and circles of the 1860s and 1870s; here most of the experiments with the various formulas took place; here the traditions were preserved through hard times, revived and flourished in the 1890s; and, indeed, from 1900 to 1905, to a certain extent, worked and were deemed vindicated in practice.

One could say that for decades this outlook, this gravitation toward the people, remained an article of faith, a hope for the future, a longing for fulfillment, with little compensation in the form of concrete results. One can understand how offended and defensive the Populists were in reacting in the 1890s to the assault of the Marxists, who could point to the remarkable successes of the working-class movement in contrast to the passivity and backwardness of the peasantry. Then, shortly after the turn of the century, the results of their labors started to pour in, vindicating the historical tradition. In some ways what occurred in Saratov leading up to and including the Revolution of 1905 was the Populist pipedream come true, satisfying every variety of Populism and Populist-tinted liberalism. There was indeed, in the fall of 1905, a great uprising of the people against their oppressors and an incipient Black Repartition. For the first time, the zemstvo activists, such as Scott Seregny's teachers, were listened to by the people; they helped draw up petitions and collaborated in organizing local peasant unions, and for the first time durable relationships between them were established. In the electoral process and the Duma experience peasants became an active part of a national undertaking, compensation for the liberal tradition in Populism that occasionally expressed itself in Populist programs calling for a *zemskii sobor* to proclaim a regime of political liberty, most recently in Natanson's Party of the People's Rights. The casualty in the 1905 experience was, of course, the liberal gentry, many of whom were at this time cured of their idealization of the narod. Remarkably, however, others of them did not completely forsake their convictions, but simply awaited more favorable times to resume their work. Whatever its vicissitudes, the durability, diversity, and recoverability of this Populist component of Saratov society, while not unique in Russia's provinces, was surely brought there to the highest level of development.

This entire cultural phenomenon, however, reflected premodern, predominately rural social relationships, the product of that selfsame pomeshchik-peasant society. We have as yet seen very little of any transformation that could be distinguished as urban-industrial-modern. The latter was very late in coming to Saratov, and when it did, in the form of railroads and steamships, it was still a sideshow, an enclave, not yet significantly reshaping the economic and institutional substructures. There was a small industrial working class, and, as Pamela McKinsey informs us, the Populists were active among them; but as yet they represented just one more isolated enclave of the population, not yet creating anything on the order of a specific working-class subculture or identity. It was not until the turn of the century, long after it had been visible in the two capitals, that the latter took shape and forced the local society to acknowledge that it had a "working-class problem." There had indeed for some time been a middle-class commercial bourgeoisie busily engaged in various economic activities, but so far we have heard very little about it. Its representatives seem to have avoided the public limelight, nor do we see them having much political influence in the local establishment. Perhaps new research would reveal more activity than we are presently aware of in zemstvo politics, in client relationships with the local bureaucracy, or in a higher degree of social acceptance, but certainly such a bourgeoisie did not dominate or set the tone of the cultivated society we have been describing.

At the turn of the century, the urban-industrial elements suddenly made an impact as the industrialization of the 1890s finally reached Saratov, and even more so, Tsaritsyn, in the form of a much larger working class, more railroads and railroad shops, more machine shops, foundries, and other infrastructural industries. Along with it came the characteristic phenomena of worker unrest, strikes, Social Democratic agitation, discussions of Marxism and economic development, and a new wave of constitutionalism in the zemstvo movement that reflected the larger specific weight of the professional, university-educated element. Much of this activity was directly imported from the more advanced centers in the form of exiled skilled workers from St. Petersburg, mobile printers and artisans, returned sons and daughters of Saratov who had been active in politics elsewhere and had passed through the cycle of arrest, exile, and reeducation. Many of them were Social Democrats and individuals with urban professional skills—engineers, doctors, lawyers, economists, and the like. Many were also very young and were committed to the revolutionary movement. By 1905 Saratov was fully caught up, fully involved in the dramatic chain of events from Bloody Sunday to the October Manifesto, reflecting all the various forms of urban revolutionary politics, from strikes and demonstrations to various types of political organization. Saratov was no longer a provincial backwater absorbed in its rural environment.

All this does not contradict that vivid picture painted for us by Michael Melancon of the intermingling of Populist and Social Democratic intelligentsia, just as it would not contradict the absorption of the new professional element into the zemstvo milieu. It is merely a question of timing. It was very characteristic of the early Russian Marxists to separate from older Populist circles while maintaining relationships and reciprocal influence, and only with the heavy debates over Marxist theory and the first major strikes of the mid-decade did the two revolutionary streams become sharply polarized. Saratov, as a provincial, non-university town, simply registered the same general trends at a later date—or perhaps never to the same degree, given the unique extent of tolerance in educated society that we have observed. I would accept the general proposition that the revolutionary ethos among radical *intelligenty* was a more determinative factor than the two ideological perspectives. Russia's Marxists, beginning with Plekhanov and expressing themselves in the manifesto of the Russian Social Democratic party in 1898, always acknowledged their debt to and origins in the revolutionary movement of the 1870s and treated their Populist counterparts as comrades to be converted, who were only temporarily suffering from theoretical errors. Marxism in nineteenth-century Russia was in some respects a bridge to modern Russia, but in many others it carried with it the freight of Russia's mainstream traditions. (Melancon must have felt vindicated by McKinsey's description of Populist propaganda among the workers of the 1870s.) Only the advent of urban industrial relationships in all their fullness and complexity could overcome this legacy.

The year 1905 was for all of Russia a watershed between the patriarchal past and the modern future, but for Saratov it had a very special meaning: its idyllic dream of an epic transformation of rural Russia into a Utopian future was dashed by the cruel chain of events that took place from the October Manifesto to the closing of the Second Duma. The cap was put on liberal-Populist hopes by the law of June 3, 1907, which brought to an end that long tradition of the "union of all vital forces" whereby the liberal and revolutionary elements lent each other a certain degree of moral reenforcement. Suddenly the protective umbrella of liberal society was no longer present in the form of safe houses, monetary contributions, or legal counsel. The revolutionaries became a hounded, isolated element in the grim years of reaction, being forced to go deep underground, abroad, or to become embourgeoised. Educated Russian society was changing, in some respects becoming modernized and urbanized, and Saratov was changing with it.

The broader social-structural changes after 1905 are far more complex than the political. With the so-called Stolypin reforms, the government actively intervened to transform the countryside and to alter permanently the social arrangements that undergirded the hopes of the liberal-revolutionary alliance. It sought to do away with the commune, break up the solidarity of the countryside, and create a class of prosperous farmers; to siphon off the restless, unviable elements to the towns, where they could become an unalloyed working class, a pool of submissive labor for aggressive capitalism—in other words, to lay the social foundations for a modern and, it was fondly hoped, less disruptive social order. The vision was clear if self-contradictory, but on what the reforms actually accomplished the jury is still out. Grigorii Gerasimenko's work affords us one kind of insight, in that he points out that there actually was a struggle within the villages between the communal majority and the separators, proving that the majority of the peasants resented this intrusion, as is expressed in the 7 percent figure of those few communes which actually confirmed separations. Those who did withdraw despite all obstacles were clearly branded as outcasts. But of those who did separate, how many did so simply for the sake of selling out completely in order to realize the modest value of their allotment land? Clearly quite a few, though the exact number still eludes us; but that, in and of itself, is not incompatible with the goal of separating urban and rural Russia. For many of the separators it was the completion of a process they had been undergoing anyway: many migrant workers had already struck roots in the cities, transplanted their families, and taken on new occupations, but had held on to their parcels because they yielded modest rental income or represented a fallback. The basic question, of course, is whether a process had been launched that was creating its own momentum, so that in, say, twenty or thirty years one could reckon that the agrarian order would have been at once more productive, less overcrowded, and more stable. I would suggest that the more information we have, the less optimistic the forecast becomes, and I am not aware of any new evidence that would contradict this view. Obviously more research is called for.

What does become clear is that by 1917 the potential for violent agrarian revolution was still present and in fact took place on a massive scale. The rupture in the authority structure in the countryside occurred not in October or even July, but as early as March, when all legal restraints immediately collapsed and the peasants took charge of their own fate. The Provisional Government from the outset was in the position of having to reestablish control even to determine what had transpired in the countryside, and it had to do so by force. When, in the summer months, it tried to bring food prices under control (and to curb spontaneous confiscations), the peasants reacted violently. Paradoxically, at the outset the peasants identified strongly with the new revolutionary government and were anxious to collaborate so long as peasant interests were not infringed. For them that implied that the land was theirs to dispose of and they would brook no interference. They were willing to temporize on redividing the land, as first the war had to be ended and the soldiers had to return. When patriotic appeals were made to supply grain for the front, many responded positively, even carting grain directly there. But their logic dictated that, if the needs of the front were para-mount, why should pomeshchik land lie idle or be worked gratis by war prisoners when the peasants themselves would be more than glad to do the same. Hence the inclination to organize sowings on private lands, to fix ridiculously low rents, to drive off or redistribute war-prisoner labor, and so on—all without reference to and in violation of government circulars and directives. When it became clear that the government was determined to impose price controls and to reverse decisions on land disposition, the peasants could only conclude that the rich classes were still in control and that henceforward only direct unilateral action was appropriate. This is what led in the summer months to the massive seizures and violence augmented by soldier-deserters who were finished with the war. Even their own SR leaders urged the peasants to wait for the Constituent Assembly; only the Bolsheviks encouraged them to follow their own instincts.

What, then, does this all mean? Had agrarian Russia triumphed over the urban-educated? Are we to understand the October revolution as the long-sought-after Black Repartition? Not quite. Bolshevik advocacy of immediate redistribution was merely a matter of political tactics to secure the success of the Soviet revolution. In fact, the Bolsheviks also were committed modernizers. When in power, the first problem they had to solve was how to feed the towns. Their natural constituency was the working class, whose interests above all had to be served. One can see in the events in Saratov an instructive example. The Bolsheviks did not wish their power to rest on the fast-fading peasant garrison but on the Red Guards, as Rex Wade has pointed out. They were happy to have the Latvians as an additional element to secure the urban-based revolution. Their dilemma was that the working class also was fast melting away under the pressure of the economic crisis, as they left the towns in droves simply to survive. Without the anchor of organized committed workers, it became increasingly difficult to maintain the integrity of the Soviet structure, and increasingly the Bolsheviks were obliged to resort to improvised measures based on force, armed requisition teams, and so forth. To the extent that they resorted to compulsion they also alienated the peasantry, and by mid-1918 they found themselves in confrontation with rural Russia. In fact, they faced the same dilemma that the Provisional Government had faced and were even less capable of resolving it. In other words, the titanic struggle between rural and urban Russia, between traditional and modern, continued into the Soviet period and was not resolved until far in the future. But that is the subject for some future conference and publication.

In retrospect, what have we learned from these studies of the motive forces of Russian history and of the part played in it by a province like Saratov? Should we equate our findings with the national trends or sharply differentiate them? Clearly both, or rather we should accent the unique blend of both. Saratov was certainly a representative part of the rural peasant-pomeshchik Black Earth Russia that figures so importantly in the national history from Razin and Pugachev to the revolutions of 1905 and 1917. The peculiar Populist-liberal ideology and public consciousness of Saratov's zemstvo-based social elite would certainly be shared by the comparable strata in other provinces, in a band from Penza and Tambov in the northeast to Chernigov and Poltava in the southwest, just as the revolutionary Populist traditions were rooted there. However, the long list of prominent national figures with roots in Saratov and the magnet-like attraction of Populist revolutionaries to the region set it apart as the hub or pivot of this socio-political culture.

Why should Saratov have become that sort of focal point? Again our examination of its history reveals the reasons. It was not just the oppressive system of serfdom that gave rise to rebellious and transformationist instincts (I eschew the more esoteric terms *millenarian* and *chiliastic*), but Saratov's contiguity with the fortified border zone between the Russian state and the *dikoe pole* ("wild steppe"), the world of fugitives, cossack freebooters, Tatar raiders, river pirates, and with the commercial networks that extended far into the latter zone. Geographically and historically, Saratov was the nexus of the fortified *Sech* (its eastern terminus) and the Mother of Rivers. Here the cossack freebooter and river pirate Razin and the Russian state vied for the soul of the much-oppressed serf-peasant. The revolutionary Populists were attracted to the region precisely because of these associations and fondly hoped that the narod remembered. It may seem a paradox that Saratov "society" or obshchestvo, which was clearly a scion of the state-transplanted pomeshchik society of the center, should forge a system of values and outlook that allied itself to the enemies of the state, the peasant *buntary* and the Populist revolutionaries. In that sense, however, Saratov was a laboratory replication of the overall problem the autocratic Russian state faced in trying to cement the loyalty of its client classes while denying them autonomy and public identity. That ambivalent relationship fostered in the zemstvo elite a certain negative disposition or alienation from the state and guilt feelings over the unjust social relationships in which they were enmeshed. Thus, they developed a public consciousness that legitimized their strivings and, despite the obvious contradictions, allowed them to confront the state with defined alternatives for the nation as a whole. Their values, their social commitments, their public activities alone harmonized the interests of "society" (*obshchestvo*) with the needs of the peasant narod. This kind of public consciousness could only flourish where rural, premodern social relations still obtained—it could not strike root in the more cosmopolitan capital (at least not without moral reenforcement from the provinces); nor in the central industrial region around Moscow, where the erstwhile serf-entrepreneur element was forging a culture of its own; nor in the northern industrial provinces like Tver and Iaroslavl, where an entirely different sort of zemstvo liberalism with strong urban-professional ties evolved.

Saratov's relative backwardness and socioeconomic isolation tended to prolong the life of Populism into the twentieth century and to water down considerably the "modern" ideology of Marxism. Yet the fact that the city of Saratov was the most commercialized of the Volga cities between Kazan and Astrakhan (though, as Raleigh has pointed out, Tsaritsyn was rapidly coming up), guaranteed that the modern-urban trends would eventually take root there and force an adjustment upon the cultivated social elite. Hence, Saratov after the turn of the century was bound to become a major ideological battleground between Marxists and zemstvo constitutionalists, on the one hand, and agrarian liberals and Populist revolutionaries, on the other.

In other words, as time progressed Saratov came more and more to embody all the conflicts being fought out in the national arena and found it more and more difficult to sustain the peculiar set of values that marshaled an idealized traditional, premodern Russia against the assault of urban-modern trends. Peasant *buntarstvo* was still a powerful reality in Saratov in 1917, but by then so was Marxist, working-class and middle-class, urban Russia. Thus, Saratov, though only one small part of the immensely diverse regional landscape of prerevolutionary Russia, was nevertheless a very strategic part, whose history throws into bold relief many of the national trends, yet yields a most fascinating identity of its own. It was, in Michael Melancon's felicitous formulation, both Athens and Babylon, the mecca of the peculiarly Russian Populist-liberal amalgam yet the opening wedge of modernizing forces into the region. Whatever circumstances led to its selection for a scholarly conference and book, Saratov was not at all a bad choice.

Notes

Chapter 1

1   Henry Norman, *All the Russias* (London, 1902), pp. 166–68.

2   L. N. Iurovskii, *Saratovskie votchiny: statistikoekonomicheskie ocherki i materialy iz istorii krupnogo zemlevladeniia i krepostnogo khoziaistva v kontse XVII i v nachale XIX stoletiia* (Saratov, 1923), p. 4.

3   *Volga ot Tveri do Astrakhani* (St. Petersburg, 1862), pp. 337–43.

4   *Rossiia: polnoe geograficheskoe opisanie nashego otechestva*, ed. V. P. Semenov-Tian'-Shanskii, 19 vols. (St. Petersburg, 1899–1913) 6:254–58, 288–92; *Istoriia Saratovskogo kraia, 1590–1917*, ed. V. A. Osipov et al. (Saratov, 1964), pp. 54–60.

5   Camilla Gray, *The Great Experiment: 1863–1911* (New York, 1962), p. 51.

6   S. A. Koroleva, *Povolzh'e*, is vol. 2 of *Velikaia Rossiia, geograficheskie, etnograficheskie i kul'turno-bytovye ocherki sovremennoi Rossii*, ed. A. N. Anuchin (Moscow, n.d.) pp. 104–07; Jeffrey Brooks, *When Russia Learned to Read* (Princeton, 1985), p. 110.

7   G. Ul'ianov, "Vospominaniia o M. A. Natansone," *Katorga i ssylka*, no. 4 (89), 1932, pp. 62–63; Reginald E. Zelnik, ed. and trans., *A Radical Worker in Tsarist Russia: The Autobiography of Semen Ivanovich Kanatchikov* (Stanford, Calif., 1986), pt. 4.

8   Maureen Perrie, *The Agrarian Policy of the Russian Socialist-Revolutionary Party from Its Origins through the Revolution of 1905–1907* (Cambridge, Eng., and New York, 1976), pp. 34–41.

9   Henry Reichman, *Railwaymen and Revolution: Russia, 1905* (Berkeley, Calif., 1987), chap. 5; Jonathan Sanders, "Lessons from the Periphery: Saratov, January 1905," *Slavic Review* 46, no. 2 (Summer 1987): 229–44.

10 N. M. Pirumova, *Zemskaia intelligentsiia i ee rol' v obshchestvennoi bor'be do nachala XX v.* (Moscow, 1986), pp. 193–94.

11 Tsentral'nyi Gosudarstvennyi Istoricheskii Arkhiv SSSR (Leningrad), fond 733, opis' 166 (1906), delo 827, list 11.

CHAPTER 2

1   Robert E. Jones, "Urban Planning and the Development of Provincial Towns in Russia, 1762–1796," in J. G. Garrard, ed., *The Eighteenth Century in Russia* (Oxford, 1973); and Jones, *The Emancipation of the Russian Nobility, 1762–1785* (Princeton, N.J., 1973), chap. 6. See also L. N. Iurovskii, *Saratovskie votchiny* (Saratov, 1923), p. 219; Saratovskii statisticheskii komitet, *Saratovskii sbornik: Materialy dlia izucheniia Saratovskoi gubernii* (Saratov, 1881).

2   The best survey of the early history of Saratov and Saratov Province is T. M. Akimova and A. M. Ardabatskaia, *Ocherki istorii Saratova, XVII– XVIII vv.* (Saratov, 1940). See also A. A. Geraklitov, *Istoriia Saratovskogo kraia v XVI–XVIII vv.* (Saratov, 1923), and A. F. Leopol'dov, "'Letopis': Saratovskaia guberniia so vremeni prisoedineniia k Rossiiu do 1821 g.'," *Zhurnal ministerstva vnutrennykh del* 39, nos. 2–4 (1841).

3   *Rossiia: polnoe geograficheskoe opisanie nashego otechestva*, ed. V. P. Semenov-Tian'-Shanskii, 19 vols. (St. Petersburg, 1899–1913), 6:474–75.

4   Akimova and Ardabatskaia, p. 11.

5   Pavel Smirnov, "Okladnaia rospis' piatiny po gorodu Saratovu 1634 g.," *Trudy Saratovskoi uchenoi arkhivnoi komissii* 33 (1916): vii–viii. See Samuel H. Baron, ed. and trans., *The Travels of Olearius in Seventeenth Century Russia* (Stanford, Calif., 1967), pp. 314–15.

6   Akimova and Ardabatskaia, pp. 14, 18; *Rossiia*, p. 475. See also S. I. Kedrov, "Bibliografiia," *Izvestiia obshchestva arkheologii, istorii, i etnografii pri Kazanskom universitete* 11, no. 3 (1893): 300–314, which is a review of F. F. Chekalin, *Saratovskoe povolzh'e s drevneishikh vremen do kontsa XVIII v.* (Saratov, 1892).

7   Akimova and Ardabatskaia, p. 19.

8   Ibid., p. 20; Baron, ed., *Travels of Olearius*, p. 315.

9   Akimova and Ardabatskaia, p. 26.

10 Ibid., pp. 22–23. See also E. N. Kusheva, "Saratov v pervoi polovine XVIII v.," in *Problemy sotsial'no-ekonomicheskoi istorii russkogo goroda: vtoraia polovina XVIII veka* (Moscow, 1967), p. 47.

11 Akimova relates the case of a cossack ataman who in 1650 was freed from the Saratov jail after the town's population interceded on his behalf (see Akimova and Ardabatskaia, p. 25). For examples of cossack expeditions on the Volga in the years immediately preceding Razin's rebellion, see E. A. Shvetsova, comp., *Krest'ianskaia voina pod predvoditel'stvom Stepana Razina: sbornik dokumentov*, 4 vols. (Moscow, 1954–76) 1: nos. 40, 53, 54, 60, 106, 120, 152; 2, pt. 1: no. 22. See Shvetsova for all documents on Razin's rebellion.

12 Shvetsova, 2.1: nos. 12, 19, 22, 32.

13 Ibid., nos. 137, 268, 311, 338. Razin's brother Frol'ka campaigned on the right bank as far west as the Khoper and Medveditsa rivers. For his testimony, see Shvetsova, 3: no. 81.

14 Shvetsova, 2.1: nos. 192, 311.

15 Rumors persisted in the middle Volga region for several months that Razin was gathering a new force at Saratov and preparing for a campaign that would take him to Penza and Shatsk and presumably on to Moscow. Shvetsova, 2.1: nos. 270, 338.

16 Shvetsova, 2.1: nos. 357, 378.

17 Ibid., 3: no. 176. On Sheludiak's rebellion, see 3: nos. 78, 126, 132, 143, 166, 168, and others.

18 On December 3, 1674, Moscow was informed that sixteen rebels from Saratov were sent into exile at Ustiugov. The list showed the involvement of six townsmen, eight *strel'tsy,* one soldier attached to a fishing operation, and one fugitive serf. Their families joined them in exile. Shvetsova, 3: no. 275.

19 Akimova and Ardabatskaia, p. 46; Geraklitov, *Istoriia, pp.*pp. 265–66; Kedrov, p. 313; Leopol'dov, no. 2, p. 261; Kusheva, pp. 27–28. In 1678, a total of 227 adult males lived in the trade quarter.

20 Akimova and Ardabatskaia, p. 41.

21 Peter the Great visited Petrovsk on his name day, June 28, 1698, on his way to a campaign at Azov. Petrovsk, like Saratov, was attached to Azov for administrative purposes in 1708. Later, Saratov would be assigned to Astrakhan (1717) and to Kazan (1764) before becoming a regional administrative center in its own right in 1780. See *Rossiia,* p. 470; Geraklitov, *Istoriia,* pp. 306–10; Akimova, p. 46; and Iurovskii, p. 219.

22 Geraklitov, *Istoriia,* pp. 266–68; Akimova and Ardabatskaia, pp. 41–46.

23 On the Old Believers in Saratov Province, see N. S. Sokolov, *Raskol v Saratovskom krae* (Saratov, 1888). A special cossack settlement was created at Dubovka, located thirty-one miles north of Tsaritsyn, in 1732. See *Volga ot Tveri do Astrakhani* (St. Petersburg, 1862), p. 347. See also Iurovskii, pp. 10–14, 20–22. On the proposed Volga–Don Canal project, which would begin at Kamyshin (called Dmitrievsk from 1710 to 1780), see Leopol'dov, no. 3, p. 413. See also *Rossiia,* pp. 505–506, Akimova and Ardabatskaia, pp. 41–48, and Geraklitov, *Istoriia,* pp. 269–350.

24 On the *odnodvortsy,* see N. K. Tkacheva, "Iz istorii odnodvortsev v XVIII v.," in *Ezhegodnik po agrarnoi istorii vostochnoi evropy 1968 g.* (Leningrad, 1972), pp. 133–41; and Thomas Esper, "The Odnodvortsy and the Russian Nobility," *Slavonic and East European Review* 45, no. 1 (January 1967): 124–34.

25 Geraklitov, *Istoriia,* pp. 362–69; and his articles: "Ocherki iz zhizni i byta

Eltonskikh solianykh lomshchikov i vozchikov poloviny XVIII v.," *Trudy Saratovskoi uchenoi arkhivnoi komissii* [hereafter Trudy SUAK] 26 (1910): 62; and "Uchrezhdenie v Saratove solianogo komissarstva (1747 g.)," *Trudy SUAK* 28 (1911): 1–7.

26 A very rough estimate of the degree of demographic change taking place can be gathered from Iurovskii's figures. He estimates that between 94,000 and 125,000 male peasants lived in the Saratov region in the 1740s. By the 1780s, the number had increased to 243,000 (see pp. 18 and 22). The number of settled places in the region increased from 342 in the 1720s to 634 in the 1740s (see p. 13). Both Kamyshin and Balashov became local administrative centers when Saratov was designated as a *namestni-chestvo* in 1780.

27 Geraklitov, *Istoriia,* pp. 356–57, and his article "Melochi iz proshlogo Saratovskogo kraia: k istorii Saratovskikh pozharov 1754 i 1757 gg.," *Trudy SUAK* 28 (1911): 1–19.

28 Geraklitov, *Istoriia,* pp. 356–62; Kusheva, pp. 26–51; Iu. R. Klokman, *Sotsial'no-ekonomicheskaia istoriia russkogo goroda: vtoraia polovina XVIII veka* (Moscow, 1967), pp. 285–89.

29 Geraklitov, *Istoriia,* pp.369–74; G. G. Pisarevskii, "Iz istorii inostrannoi kolonizatsii v Rossii v XVIII v.," *Zapiski Moskovskogo arkheologicheskogo instituta* 5 (1909): 182–204; Roger P. Bartlett, *Human Capital: The Settlement of Foreigners in Russia, 1762–1804* (Cambridge, Eng., 1979); Fred C. Koch, *The Volga Germans in Russia and the Americas from 1763 to the Present* (University Park, Pa., 1977); Hattie P. Williams, *The Czar's Germans, With Particular Reference to the Volga Germans* (Denver, 1975).

30 Bartlett, p. 98.

31 Ibid., p. 105. Occupations listed by Academician Falk include: saddle-makers, painters, engravers, goldsmiths, sculptors, hatmakers, weavers, and gunsmiths.

32 See ibid., pp. 35–36, 39–40, 48, 71, 95, 113, 125–26, 138; and N. S. Sokolov, *Raskol v Saratovskom krae.*

33 This contrast was pointed out in an unpublished paper by Thomas Fallows, entitled "Saratov as Local History," read at an NEH-sponsored symposium on Saratov held in July of 1985 at the University of Illinois.

34 Iurovskii, pp. 28–29.

35 Ibid., pp. 8–9, 29.

36 Ibid., p. 36.

37 Ibid., pp. 18, 22.

38 Ibid., p. 48.

39 Ibid., pp. 18, 22.

40 For the history of Pugachev's rebellion, see V. V. Mavrodin et al., eds.,

Krest'ianskaia voina v Rossii v 1773–75 gg., 3 vols. (Moscow-Leningrad, 1961–70); John T. Alexander, *Emperor of the Cossacks: Pugachev and the Frontier Jacquerie of 1773–75* (Lawrence, Kan., 1973); Paul Avrich, *Russian Rebels, 1600–1800* (New York, 1972; 1975); A. S. Pushkin, *The History of Pugachev*, trans. Earl Sampson (Ann Arbor, Mich., 1983).

41 The best account of Pugachev's rebellion in Saratov region is Ia. K. Grot, "Epizod iz Pugachevshchiny," *Drevnaia i novaia Rossiia* (Moscow) 3, no. 1 (1877): 229–48. See also Akimova and Ardabatskaia, pp. 93–94.

42 This region had long been settled by Old Believers. Pushkin says that Pugachev had visited Malykovka in 1772 but did not attempt to raise a rebellion at that time. See N. F. Khovanskii, "Pugachev i pugache-vshchina v selakh i derevniakh Saratovskoi gubernii," *Trudy SUAK* 29 (1912): 149–55.

43 A. P. Pronshtein, ed., *Don i Nizhnee Povolzh'e v period krest'ianskoi voiny 1773–75 gg.* (Rostov-on-Don, 1961) no. 26. See also Akimova and Ardabatskaia, p. 97.

44 Grot, pp. 233–34; Akimova and Ardabatskaia, p. 95.

45 Grot, pp. 238–39; Akimova and Ardabatskaia, p. 96. About 25,000 rubles arrived at Tsaritsyn by August 11. Another 15,000 rubles, loaded on a flour boat, were seized by the rebels en route. Approximately 25,000 rubles remained in town at the time of Pugachev's assault.

46 Grot, p. 240; Akimova and Ardabatskaia, p. 97.

47 Grot, p. 241; Akimova and Ardabatskaia, p. 98. According to the account of battalion commander I. Sapozhnikov, Boshniak stood and fought until the very end, even seeing to the raising of town banners in the face of the onslaught. See Pronshtein, ed.

48 Khovanskii, pp. 151–54.

49 Ibid., pp. 149–50.

50 See n. 1, above, and the recent book by John P. LeDonne, *Ruling Russia: Politics and Administration in the Age of Absolutism 1762–1796* (Princeton, N.J., 1984).

51 Iurovskii, p. 52. The statistics for Saratov compare favorably with the situation in the central regions of the empire, where some 6 percent of the wealthiest gentry owned over half the land at the time of the Emancipation. See L. P. Minarik, *Ekonomicheskaia kharakteristika krupneishikh zemel'nykh sobstvennikov Rossii kontsa XIX–nachala XX vv.* (Moscow, 1971), p. 76.

52 Iurovskii, pp. 236–37.

53 See the description in "Saratovskaia guberniia," *Entsiklopedicheskii slovar'*, ed. F. A. Brokgauz and I. A. Efron, 82 vols. (St. Petersburg, 1890–1904), 28:403–11. A factor in the growth of settlement in the northwestern

districts was the fertile soil there. Indeed, the richest soil (*chernozem*) in the entire province was to be found between the Khoper and Medveditsa rivers, west of Saratov. The farther east and south one traveled, the sandier the soil became. In Tsaritsyn nearly 30 percent of the soil was wasteland. The average rainfall also varied. In the northwest, the climate was wetter and the land more forested, but in the southeast the soil was drier and less vegetated. By the end of the nineteenth century, this geographic division was reflected in the different types of economic activities in the districts. In the north and west, peasants grew rye, barley, and oats; in the south and east, they grew wheat and fruit, and grazed sheep and cattle on the open steppe. See also Iurovskii, p. 22.

54 These two tables originally appeared in Thomas Fallows, "Saratov as Local History," an unpublished paper. Fallows cites Iurovskii, pp. 23 and 52.

CHAPTER 3

1 I. V. Porokh, *Istoriia v cheloveke: N. A. Mordvinov—deiatel' obshchestvennogo dvizheniia v Rossii 40–80 godov XIX v.* (Saratov, 1971), p. 73.

2 TsGIA, f. 1275, op. 1, ed. khr. 41, p. 4 ob. Ironically, many historians of Russian revolutionary movements see things in much the same way, asserting that political opposition was consciously conspiratorial and was coordinated by the revolutionary organization Land and Liberty under Chernyshevskii's direction and Herzen's inspiration. In the Third Section, as in scholarly opinion, political activists and movements in the 1860s are treated according to their relationship to a presumed revolutionary executive center. For a review of the historiography on this question, see Alan Kimball, "Revolutionary Situation in Russia (1859–1862)," *Modern Encyclopedia of Russian and Soviet History* (1983), 31: 54–57.

3 TsGAOR, f. 109, op. 85, ed. khr. 28, pp. 405–06 ob.

4 ORGPB, f. 438, nos. 1–11, passim.

5 N. K. Piksanov and O. V. Tsekhnovitser, eds., *Shestidesiatie gody: Materialy po istorii literatury i obshchestvennomu dvizheniiu* (Moscow and Leningrad, 1940), pp. 457–59. On Mordvinov's and Pleshcheev's earlier organizational association with the Petrashevtsy, see Alan Kimball, "Who Were the Petrashevtsy?" *Mentalities/Mentalités* 5, no. 2 (1988): 1–12.

6 F. A. Litvina, *Literaturnye vechera epokhi padeniia krepostnogo prava: Iz istorii obshchestvennogo dvizheniia i kul'turnoi zhizni Rossii*, Avtoreferat dissertatsii na soiskanie uchenoi stepeni kandidata istoricheskikh nauk (Kazan,

1970); and *Ocherki istorii narodov Povolzh'ia i Priuralia,* vols. 2/3 (Kazan, 1969), pp. 130–33.

7   The director of the Saratov gymnasium, A. A. Meier, sent to Litfond contributions gathered among *chinovniki* (state servitors, bureaucrats) and teachers in the city (ORGPB, f. 438, no. 9, pp. 184–184 ob.); Porokh, pp. 51–52, 72, reports the other local solicitations. Interestingly, Litfond records do not confirm that all the money collected made its way out of Saratov. Certain amounts appear to have been held back to finance local projects.

8   "Smes'," *Russkoe slovo,* no. 2 (1860): 75–76; V. N. Sazhin, "Literaturnyi fond v gody revoliutsionnoi situatsii," in *Epokha Chernyshevskogo: Revoliutsionnaia situatsiia v Rossii v 1859–1861 gg.* (Moscow, 1978), p. 156.

9   N. I. Kostomarov, *Avtobiografiia . . .* (Moscow, 1922), pp. 210–58.

10 Adol'f Demchenko, *N. G. Chernyshevskii,* (Saratov, 1978), pp. 225–33.

11 L. F. Panteleev, *Vospominaniia* (Moscow, 1958), p. 464; and M. V. Nechkina, *Vstrecha dvukh pokolenii (Iz istorii russkogo revoliutsionnogo dvizheniia kontsa 50-kh—nachala 60-kh godov XIX veka.) Sbornik statei* (Moscow, 1980), pp. 297–300.

12 E. G. Bushkanets, *Ucheniki N. G. Chernyshevskogo po gimnazii v osvoboditel'nom dvizhenii vtoroi poloviny 1850-kh—nachala 1860-kh gg.* (Kazan, 1963).

13 G. N. Vul'fson, *Raznochinno-demokraticheskoe dvizhenie v Povolzh'e i na Urale v gody pervoi revoliutsionnoi situatsii* (Kazan, 1974), p. 154 [hereafter Vul'fson (1974)]; and N. N. Novikova, *Revoliutsionery 1861 g. ("Velikoruss" i ego komitet v revoliutsionnoi bor'be 1861 g.)* (Moscow, 1968), pp. 244–45. Belov and Mordovtsev were on the mailing list to receive copies of the proclamation "Velikoruss" (Novikova, p. 333).

14 Porokh, pp. 54–70.

15 V. A. Chernykh, "Zemlevolets Aleksandr Mordvinov (Iz arkhivnykh razyskanii)," in *Osvoboditel'noe dvizhenie v Rossii* (1973), 3:42–43. Ivan Turgenev led discussions on the Isle of Wight. The young social activist and bureaucrat Alexander Sleptsov participated as discussions continued on the Continent. Another associate of the Wight discussions, Pavel Annenkov, brought Sleptsov into Litfond that fall, at the time Mordvinov became Saratov commissioner. I. S. Turgenev, *Sobranie sochinenii v dvenadtsati tomakh* (Moscow-Leningrad, 1958), 11:444–51; P. V. Annenkov, *Literaturnye vospominaniia* (Moscow, 1983), pp. 439–45; and M. K. Lemke, *Ocherki osvoboditel'nago dvizheniia "shestidesiatykh godov" po neizdannym dokumentam s portretami* (St. Petersburg, 1908), pp. 293–305 [hereafter *OOD*]; Vul'fson (1974), pp. 198–203; A. P. Shchapov,

Sochineniia, vol. 2 (1908), p. 554; Ia. I. Linkov, "Voskresnye shkoly i russkoe revoliutsionnoe dvizhenie 1860-kh godov," *Istoricheskii arkhiv*, no. 6 (1956): 178.

16 TsGIA, f. 92, op. 3, no. 1; D. D. Protopopov, *Istoriia Sankt-Peterburgskago Komiteta gramotnosti, sostoiavshago pri Imperatorskom Vol'nom Ekonomicheskom obshchestve (1861–1895)* (St. Petersburg, 1898).

17 *Vek*, no. 7 (January 15, 1861); Porokh, p. 61.

18 Vladimir V. Stasov, *Nadezhda Vasil'evna Stasova: vospominaniia i ocherki* (St. Petersburg, 1899), p. 107. Organizationally, Sunday schools were associated with the various literacy committees and with the goal of national enlightenment which Litfond set for itself. Iu. N. Korotkov, "U istokov pervoi 'Zemli i Voli' (neopublikovannaia stranitsa iz tetradi A. A. Sleptsova)," *Istoricheskie zapiski* 79 (1966): 192–94.

19 *OOD*, p. 416. See also Reginald E. Zelnik, *Labor and Society in Tsarist Russia: The Factory Workers of St. Petersburg, 1855–1870* (Stanford, Calif., 1971).

20 TsGIA, f. 1275, op. 1, ed. khr. 41, pp. 49–78, "O voskresnykh shkolakh i o deistviiakh Sledstvennoi komissii Vysochaishe uchrezhdennoi dlia izsled. deistvii lits zavedyvavshikh nekotorymi shkolami v SPb-e," September 11, 1862.

21 *Saratovskiia gubernskiia vedomosti*, no. 14 (April 4, 1859), p. 89; see also V. Mokshantsev, "Neskol'ko slov ob uluchshenii byta sluzhashchikh i ob ustroistve zashtatnykh chinovnikov," *Saratovskiia gubernskiia vedomosti*, no. 18 (May 5, 1862), pp. 195–96; "Mestnye izvestiia," *Saratovskiia gubernskiia vedomosti*, no. 13 (March 26, 1860), p. 115; and A. Bertal', "Neskol'ko slov po povodu literaturnogo vechera v pol'zu Saratovskoi tiuremnoi shkoly," *Saratovskiia gubernskiia vedomosti*, no. 47 (November 25, 1861), p. 370. See P. A. Gan, *O nastoiashchem byte meshchan Saratovskoi gubernii* (St. Petersburg, 1860); and Vul'fson (1974), pp. 80–89, 99.

22 "Ot Saratova do Atkarska i obratno," *Saratovskiia gubernskiia vedomosti*, no. 26 (June 27, 1859); Vul'fson (1974), pp. 185–86.

23 *Saratovskiia gubernskiia vedomosti*, no. 43 (Oct. 24, 1859); Vul'fson (1974), p. 187.

24 V. A. Fedorov, "Krest'ianskoe trezvennoe dvizhenie 1858–1860 gg.," in *Revoliutsionnaia situatsiia v Rossii v 1859–1861 gg.* [hereafter *RSR*] (1962), 2:110.

25 Kniaz' Mikhail Golitsyn, "Rasprostranenie trezvosti," *Moskovskiia vedomosti: gazeta politicheskaia i literaturnaia*, no. 76 (March 29, 1859): 567.

26 *Revoliutsionnaia situatsiia v Rossii v seredine XIX veka: Kollektivnaia monografiia* (Moscow, 1978), p. 135.

27 G. Lur'e, "Piteinye bunty 1859 g. i P. P. Lin'kov-Kochkin," *Zven'ia*, vols. 3–4 (1934); P. M. Poteten'kin, *Krest'ianskie volneniia v Saratovskoi gubernii v*

1861–1863 gg. (Saratov, 1940), pp. 20–21; and *Revoliutsionnaia situatsiia v Rossii v seredine XIX veka*, pp. 135–38.

28 *Kolokol: Pribavochnye listy k "Poliarnoi zvezde,"* no. 44 (June 1, 1859): 364–65.

29 "Pokrovitel'stvo Saratovskago nachal'stva otkupnym prodelkam," *Pod sud!* 8 (September 1, 1860): 73–76.

30 TsGAOR, f. 109, op. 85, ed. khr. 24, pp. 195–96.

31 Ibid., pp. 75–76.

32 Fedorov, p. 123.

33 I. A. Zhelvakova, "Saratovskii pomeshchik o khode reformy 19 fevralia 1861 g.," in *RSR* (1965), 4:451.

34 Ibid., p. 452.

35 Ibid.

36 *Krest'ianskoe dvizhenie v Rossii v 1857–mae 1861 gg.: Sbornik dokumentov*, ed. S. B. Okun' and K. V. Sivkov [hereafter *KDR*] (Moscow, 1963), p. 552.

37 Ironically, peasant protest against forced allotment of inadequate land rocked the Vasil'chikov estates. In January 1862, peasants submitted eloquent and well-inscribed appeals to Grand Prince Konstantin Nikolaevich. Globa helped to put down the protest. Gregory L. Freeze, ed., *From Supplication to Revolution: A Documentary Social History of Imperial Russia* (Oxford, 1988), pp. 170–72.

38 A. N. Minkh, *Iz zapisok mirovago posrednika: 1861–1866* (Saratov, 1911), pp. 14–18.

39 P. A. Zaionchkovskii, *Provedenie v zhizn' krest'ianskoi reformy 1861 g.* (Moscow, 1958), pp. 132–33.

40 V. A. Chernykh, "Pis'mo A. A. Sleptsova A. S. Korsakovu ot 21 maia 1861 g.," *RSR* 4 (1965): 420–25; and B. P. Koz'min, "Iz perepiski russkikh revoliutsionnykh emigrantov," *Literaturnoe nasledstvo*, nos. 41/42 (1941): 49–50.

41 TsGAOR, f. 95, op. 1, ed. khr. 214, pp. 20–26 ob., and 40–43.

42 Porokh, pp. 75–77.

43 T. G. Snytko, "Studencheskoe dvizhenie v russkikh universitetakh v nachale 60-kh godov i vosstanie 1863 g.," in *Vosstanie 1863 g. i russko-pol'skie revoliutsionnye sviazi 60-kh godov: Sbornik statei i materialov*, ed. V. D. Koroliuka and I. S. Miller (Moscow, 1960), pp. 176–322. See also Alan Kimball, "Student Interests and Student Politics: Kazan University before the Crisis of 1862," *Acta Slavica Iaponica* 4 (Sapporo, Japan, 1988): 1–15.

44 See Daniel Field, *Rebels in the Name of the Tsar* (Boston, 1976).

45 Porokh, p. 77.

46 Ibid., p. 80.

47 *RSR* 4 (1965): 428.

48 A. A. Sleptsov, "Vospominaniia A. A. Sleptsova," ed. S. A. Reiser, in *N. G. Chernyshevskii: stat'i, issledovaniia i materialy* (1962), 3:270.

49 *Blagorodnye deistviia tverskago dvorianstva:* I. *Postanovlenie tverskago dvorianskago sobraniia {February 1, 1862}*; II. *Adres tverskago dvorianstva {1861}*; III. *Polozhen'e mirovykh posrednikov tverskoi gubernii {December 12, 1861}* (Berlin, [1862]). See also Terence Emmons, *The Russian Landed Gentry and the Peasant Emancipation of 1861* (Cambridge, Eng., 1968), esp. p. 350.

50 "Officers!" emphasized the unwillingness of the state to carry out fundamental reforms and its thoughtless recourse to violence in its dealings with the people, which left the nation no choice but revolutionary resistance (*Kolokol*, no. 133 [May 15, 1862]: 1080–1081). The proclamation concluded with a political platform essentially like that of the Tver gentry. *Zemskaia duma* (*National Legislature*) appeared first in St. Petersburg among members of the Chess Club: *Kolokol*, no. 139 (July 15, 1862): 1153; V. Ia. Iakovlev, ed. *Materialy dlia istorii revoliutsionnago dvizheniia v Rossii v 60-kh gg.* Prilozhenie no. 2 to *Gosudarstvennyia prestupleniia v Rossii*, and vol. 5 of *Russkaia istoricheskaia biblioteka* (Paris, 1905), pp. 49–50. Both Mordvinov's and Khristoforov's groups took *Zemskaia duma* to represent their outlook. It set a bold and specific schedule for the convocation of a national assembly in early September 1862. It did not call precisely for a revolutionary uprising but expressed the hope that a unified and purposive citizenry might create an organization with a strong network across the whole land, overwhelm the state by sheer force of preponderance, and replace it with a Zemskaia duma. "What Do the People Need?" came to be what Sleptsov called the "political platform" of Land and Liberty. Ogarev had written the proclamation in London and published it in *Kolokol* the previous summer. *Kolokol*, no. 102 (July 1, 1961): appendix, pp. 1–4; N. P. Ogarev, *Izbrannye sotsial'no-politicheskie i filosoficheskie proizvedeniia* 1 (1952): 527–36.

51 Without exception, they all culminate in the expectation of a great national assembly based on democratic representation. Chernyshevskii perhaps authored the text of "Salute to Privately Owned Peasants," which described the future democratic and representational form of government in terms thought appropriate for a Russian peasant reader: "Now here's just what real freedom is on this earth: The narod is everyone's leader and every official is obedient to the *mir* [that is, the ministries are responsible to a popular assembly]. Courts are just, and courts treat everyone the same, and no one dares treat the muzhik improperly. The passport does not exist, nor does the poll tax. Military conscription does not exist. Now that's freedom like freedom really is. If it's not like this, then it means there is no freedom, it's all just deceptive talk." (N. G.

Chernyshevskii, *Polnoe sobranie sochinenii,* 16:946–53; William F. Woehrlin, *Chernyshevsky: The Man and the Journalist* [Cambridge, Mass., 1971], p. 276.) Volga activists Ivan Umnov and Pavel Rovinskii later paraphrased "Salute . . ." in their proclamation "Long Have They Crushed You, Brothers." Volga circles circulated Umnov and Rovinskii's text after November 1862. ("Dolga davili vas, brattsii," in A. I. Herzen, *Polnoe sobranie sochinenii i pisem,* ed. M. K. Lemke, 15:546–48.) Tver gentry asked the tsar to convoke a national assembly. The other pamphlets assume that the tsar will not do that; the people will have to rise up and make it happen. "Zemskaia duma" suggests that a well-organized public demand might make the transition relatively peaceful, and "What Do the People Need?" cautions against senseless violence and also favors communal land ownership; none of the others is as explicit or detailed on this point.

52 "Salute to Privately Owned Peasants" echoed the self-conscious claim to leadership, characteristic of the proclamations: "And when you are all agreed, then the call will come for all to begin together. We will see when the time comes and will announce it. You know we have our men everywhere, and news comes to us about the people and what they do. Thus we see that all is not yet prepared. But when all is ready, we will also see that. Then the declaration will be made that the time has arrived for the Russian people to begin the good undertaking, everywhere and at one time, because then everywhere the people will be prepared and in agreement, and one place will not lag behind another. Then it will be easy to win freedom. But until that time, prepare for the undertaking, but do not let on that preparations are going on among you." Chernyshevskii, *Polnoe sobranie sochinenii,* 16:946–53.

53 Porokh, pp. 94–95.
54 Ibid., pp. 84–85.
55 *Vosstanie 1863 goda: Materialy i dokumenty; russko-pol'skie revoliutsionnye sviazi,* subtitled "Powstanie styczniowe: Wspopraca rewolucyjna Polsko-Rosyjska" (Moscow, 1963), 2:292 [hereafter V63].
56 Porokh, pp. 86–87.
57 *V63,* 2:293.
58 Ibid., p. 292.
59 Porokh, pp. 91–97.
60 V. N. Shablin, "Iz istorii obshchestvennogo dvizheniia v Saratove v nachale 60-kh godov XIX v. (Gimnazicheskie volneniia v Saratove v 1862–1863 gg.)," in *Nekotorye voprosy otechestvennoi i vseobshchei istorii,* pp. 60–70, ed. V. M. Gokhlerner (Saratov, 1971). See also V. A. Sushitskii, "Iz istorii revoliutsionnoi deiatel'nosti A. Kh. Khristoforova v Saratove (organizatsiia rabochikh tovarishchestv)," *Katorga i ssylka* no. 6 (13) (1924): 84–94.

61 *Delo Chernyshevskogo: sbornik dokumentov* (Saratov, 1968), p. 139.

62 G. N. Vul'fson, "Soratnik N. G. Chernyshevskogo P. A. Rovinskii i Kazanskoe otdelenie 'Zemli i voli,'" *RSR* 8:134–47.

63 V. R. Leikina-Svirskaia, "'Kazanskii zagovor' 1863 g.," *RSR* 1: 423–49; V. A. D'iakov and I. S. Miller, *Revoliutsionnoe dvizhenie v russkoi armii i vosstanie 1863 g.* (Moscow, 1964); and V. A. D'iakov, D. V. Koroliuk, and I. S. Miller, eds., *Russko-pol'skie revoliutsionnye sviazi 60-kh godov i vosstanie 1863 goda: Sbornik statei i materialov* (Moscow, 1962).

64 See E. Pfeifer, *Assotsiatsii: Nastoiashchee polozhenie rabochego sosloviia i chem ono dolzhno byt'*, later translated and published by M. A. Antonovich (St. Petersburg, 1866). See also ["L. M."], *Arteli rabochikh dlia osnovaniia fabrik ili masterskikh (Assotsiatsii)* (St. Petersburg, 1862).

65 G. I. Ionova, "Revoliutsionnaia agitatsiia sredi rabochikh v nachale 1860-kh godov," *RSR* 1 (1960): 360–79 (a résumé of the case file, "O privlechenii k otvetstvennosti b. studenta Kazanskogo universiteta A. Khristoforova, b. gimnazista P. Nikolaeva i dr. za rasprostranenie kommunisticheskikh idei v Saratovskoi gub.," TsGIA, f. 1282, op. 1, 1864 g., d. 223.

66 Zaionchkovskii (*Provedenie*, p. 134) felt that the "agitation" of aristocrats, *raznochintsy*, and *chinovniki* did help to promote rebellion in the countryside. But for the whole empire over the three years 1861–63, he found in the files of the Third Section only sixty-one individuals who had "gone to the people," none of whose actions could be linked to an organization.

CHAPTER 4

1 O. V. Aptekman, *Obshchestvo "Zemlia i Volia" v 1870-kh godakh* (Moscow, 1924), pp. 255–56; "Zakliuchenie prokurora Peterburgskoi sudebnoi palaty, Fuksa, po delu 'Obshchestvo druzei' ot 10 dekabria 1877," *Istoriko-revoliutsionnyi sbornik* 3 (1926): 75, 102; Saratovets [I. I. Mainov], "Saratovskii semidesiatnik: Iz vospominanii," *Minuvshie gody* (1908), nos. 1, 3, 4; no. 3, p. 182.

2 N. Volkov [I. I. Mainov], "Iz zhizni saratovskikh kruzhkov," *Byloe*, no. 4 (May 1903): 3. Mainov's memoirs are summarized in D'ova (first name unknown), *Revoliutsionnye kruzhki v Saratove* (Saratov, 1906).

3 Other promising areas of the country included the North, where, it was hoped, memories of the *veche* had been retained; the volatile mining population of the Urals; the cossack organizations; the Central Industrial region (perhaps because of its factory population); and the nationalist regions of the Ukraine and Lithuania. L. F. Panteleev, *Vospominaniia* (Moscow, 1958), p. 292.

4   Ibid., pp. 316, 327.

5   Here some of the peasantry were taken in by the manifesto and believed that the tsar was sending the proclamations directly to them to avoid the officials and landowners. But police measures contained the unrest. A. Ershov, "Kazanskii zagovor 1863 g.," *Golos minuvshago,* 1913, nos. 6 and 7; no. 6, p. 228.

6   Panteleev, p. 327; V. A Sushitskii, "Iz istorii revoliutsionnoi deiatel'nosti A. Kh. Khristoforova v Saratove," *Katorga i ssylka,* 1924, no. 6(13)(1924): 86, 89.

7   V. A. Sushitskii, "Iz istorii revoliutsionnoi deiatel'nosti A. Kh. Khristoforova v Saratove," pp. 88, 93.

8   Ibid., pp. 89, 91.

9   G. V. Plekhanov, "Russkii rabochii v revoliutsionnom dvizhenii (Po lichnym vospominaniiam)," *Sochineniia* (Moscow, 1928), 3:196n.

10 Volkov, pp. 2–3.

11 V. N. Ginev, *Narodnicheskoe dvizhenie v srednem povolzh'e* (Moscow-Leningrad, 1966), pp. 11–12. Compare with Moscow Province, which alone had 135,000 workers (ibid.).

12 See Fred V. Carstensen, *American Enterprise in Foreign Markets: Studies of Singer and International Harvester in Imperial Russia* (Chapel Hill, N.C., 1984), pp. 119–20, 253–54 nn. 2, 3, on the German colonies' production of farm machines.

13 This summary of cottage trades is drawn from *Rossiia: polnoe geograficheskoe opisanie nashego otechestva,* ed. V. P. Semenov-Tian'-Shanskii, 19 vols. (St. Petersburg, 1899–1913), 6:246–53. This source gives the districts and volosts where the crafts were practiced.

14 In the period 1864–69, 389 cases of Russian peasant protest have been identified, but only 254 cases for the succeeding decade (Ginev, pp. 19–21). For the period of 1875–79, in the whole of Kazan, Nizhnii Novgorod, Penza, and Saratov provinces, P. A. Zaionchkovskii found only eleven disturbances. (*Krizis samoderzhaviia na rubezhe 1870–1880 godov* (Moscow, 1964), pp. 480–81; cited in Ginev, p. 21).

15 "Avtobiograficheskaia zapiska Stepana Shiriaeva," *Krasnyi arkhiv* 7 (1924): 75.

16 Ibid. The propagandist is not identified.

17 "Dva pis'ma S. G. Shiriaeva k redaktoru 'Vpered'," *Byloe,* no. 4 (1903): 22.

18 M. F. Frolenko, *Sobranie sochinenii* (Moscow, 1930), pp. 217–18.

19 Bazilevskii [V. Ia. Vasilev], ed., *Gosudarstvennyia prestupleniia v Rossii v XIX veke,* 3 vols. (Paris, [1903–05]), 3:151, 202. B. S. Itenberg and S. S. Volk, eds., *Revoliutsionnoe narodnichestvo semidesiatykh godov XIX veka: Sbornik dokumentov,* 2 vols. (Moscow, 1964–65), 1:317.

20 Itenberg and Volk, 1:318; Bazilevskii, pp. 4–5, 146–48, 167–68.

21 Itenberg and Volk, 1:315. Bazilevskii, pp. 166, 170, 199–200; Starik [S. F. Kovalik], "Dvizhenie revoliutsionnogo narodnichestva po bol'shemu protsessu (193-kh)," *Byloe* (1906), nos. 10, 11, 12; no. 11, pp. 46–47.

22 Voinaral'skii was arrested in Samara on July 24, and Rogachev, one of the letter writers, became a Volga bargehauler. (Volkov, p. 5; Starik, no. 10, p. 29; Bazilevskii, pp. 168–70, 198–99; Itenberg and Volk, 1:315–17, 467; O. V. Aptekman, "Dmitrii Rogachev; 'Ispoved' k druz'iam' i pis'ma k rodnym," *Byloe,* no. 26 (1924): 75–76.

23 Volkov, p. 4.

24 Saratovets, pp. 255–56.

25 Letter of Peter Shiriaev to his brother Stepan, quoted in Ginev, p. 133.

26 Ibid., p. 134; Volkov, pp. 5–7. Geraklitov returned shortly afterward and was arrested but escaped. He died of tuberculosis at a friend's Crimean estate in 1878. Stepan Shiriaev later became a member of The People's Will.

27 Leonid E. Shishko, "K kharakteristike dvizheniia nachala 70-kh godov (Iz lichnykh vospominanii)," *Russkoe bogatstvo,* no. 10 (1906): 76–77.

28 Pamela Sears McKinsey, "From City Workers to Peasantry: The Beginning of the Russian Movement 'to the People,'" *Slavic Review* 38, no. 4 (December 1979): 629–49. See, on Kropotkin's program, Itenberg and Volk, 1:102–103. The Chaikovskii circle at this very time also had the example of the Dolgushin circle before it. Shishko and others were undoubtedly aware that the Dolgushin circle in the summer of 1873 had encamped in the countryside outside Moscow with a worker in tow. It seems at least possible the Dolgushin circle also believed that workers had a special rapport with peasants, though the literature on the circle does not state this, for example, A. A. Kunkl', *Dolgushintsy* (Moscow, 1931).

29 Plekhanov, p. 135.

30 Ibid., pp. 135–36.

31 Bachin's reply was in this vein, as paraphrased by Plekhanov: "You are out of your minds. Just try to touch me and I will burn down the whole village, and you will not have heads on your shoulders; I will personally knock them off. You will be sorry that you meddled with me." Ibid., pp. 136–37.

32 Ibid.

33 Itenberg and Volk, 1:53.

34 Plekhanov, p. 133.

35 Ibid., pp. 132–34. This and other kinds of disagreements could cause friction between the radicals and the workers; this subject is explored in more depth in Pamela Sears McKinsey, "An Uneasy Friendship: Con-

flicts between Russian Workers and Organizers at an Early Period of Industrialization," unpublished paper delivered at the meeting of the American Historical Association, New York, December 1985.

36 Plekhanov, pp. 134, 138–39 (emphasis in original). A common term of slander among the urban workers was "country bumpkin." In 1875, when the workers of the Munitions Works on Vasil'evskii Island were discussing the outbreak of rebellion in Herzegovina, a young worker mistakenly thought that "the defender of Herzegovina" referred to a steadfast lover championing his lady "Herzegovina." Such a slip was unforgivable; he was called "countrywoman" and henceforth was labeled "the gray one" (ibid., p. 135).

37 Ibid., p. 137; and see p. 144.

38 In the metalworking field, for example, the Petersburg census of 1869 found that (by my count) 54 percent of the 15,402 hired metalworkers were juridically peasant. *Sanktpeterburg po perepisi 10 dekabria 1869 goda* (St. Petersburg, 1875), 3:98–101. Suburban workers were not captured by the census.

39 "Zakliuchenie prokurora," pp. 104–105.

40 Boris Sapir, ed., *Vpered! 1873–1877: Materialy iz arkhiva V. N. Smirnova* (Dordrecht, Netherlands, 1970), 2:521.

41 This early background to the organization eventually to be known as the "Northern Russian Worker's Union" has been set forth in Pamela Sears McKinsey, "The Kazan Square Demonstration and the Conflict between Russian Workers and *Intelligenty,*" *Slavic Review* 44, no. 1 (Spring 1985): 83–103.

42 Plekhanov, p. 136.

43 Ibid., p. 143; Aptekman, *Obshchestvo,* p. 265.

44 Aptekman, *Obshchestvo,* pp. 265–66.

45 This remark suggests a possible candidate: Nikolai I. Pavlikov, a participant in the Kazan Square demonstration of 1876 and a member of the Society of Friends. However, at the time he worked as a lathe operator, not a fitter, at Makferson. In 1917 he wrote to Plekhanov, "Your former pupil of the Baltic [Works] Sunday School writes this to you—or perhaps, as you remember it, the Makferson Works in Galernyi Gavan'; the last lecture that you gave was about *enfuzoriiakh* [*sic*; apparently the word he was seeking was "evolution"]. I just now see you when you were at the blackboard—this was in the evening—[You] explained to us about *enfuzoriiakh* and in conclusion said that everything we see could not be created by means of a magic word in the course of six days, but rather all this was created gradually" (*Zven'ia: Sbornik materialov i dokumentov po istorii literatury, iskusstva i obshchestvennoi mysli XIX veka* [Moscow-Leningrad,

1934], 3–4:733, 736). However, fondness for exotic or foreign words was a rather common trait among the skilled and literate workers, and this identification of Pavlikov as "Nikolai the fitter" is only a suggestion. There is also an individual identified as "Nikolai the gas-fitter," also a Makferson employee, who was fired from his job in the spring of 1877, and whom the radicals made efforts to help economically. "Zakliuchenie prokurora," p. 90.

46 Aptekman, *Obshchestvo,* pp. 265–66. In the same year, the blacksmith Vasilii Griaznov accompanied the other major group of Populists, the Chaikovskyite separatists, to Samara Province.

47 Anna Pribyleva-Korba, *Aleksandr D. Mikhailov* (Leningrad-Moscow, 1925), p. 10.

48 Ibid., p. 48. Mikhailov's words.

49 Aptekman, *Obshchestvo,* pp. 269–70.

50 "Zakliuchenie prokurora," pp. 75–76, 102. This settlement lasted only until mid-July.

51 Pribyleva-Korba, pp. 30–31, 49, 64.

52 Aptekman, *Obshchestvo,* pp. 261, 268.

53 Ibid., 219, 263–64.

54 McKinsey, "Kazan Square," pp. 101–103.

55 "Zakliuchenie prokurora," pp. 75, 101–102.

56 Aptekman, *Obshchestvo,* p. 265. Emphasis in original.

57 Ibid, p. 266.

58 Plekhanov, pp. 136, 134. Emphasis in original.

59 Volkov, pp. 7–8.

60 Saratovets, no. 1, p. 267.

61 Ibid., pp. 267–68.

62 Ibid., pp. 265–66.

63 Using the pseudonym "Nabatov" (from *nabat,* the tocsin), he roomed with a friend of Polivanov's and soon expressed a desire to join the workers' circle. Plekhanov's reputation as the orator at the Kazan Square demonstration in St. Petersburg the previous year, and the obvious esteem in which the other visitors held him, gave him a certain aura in the eyes of the Saratovtsy. Ibid., no. 3, pp. 180–82.

64 Aptekman, *Obshchestvo,* pp. 264, 219; Plekhanov, pp. 136, 189–90; Saratovets, no. 3, pp. 180–81.

65 See *Rossiia,* pp. 254–63, for all the main branches of industry in Saratov Province.

66 Tsentral'nyi statisticheskii komitet, *Pervaia vseobshchaia perepis' naseleniia Rossiiskoi Imperii, 1897 g.,* vol. 38: *Saratovskaia guberniia* (St. Petersburg, 1904), pp. 148–49.

67 Plekhanov, p. 194. Emphasis in original. A worker from St. Petersburg, Vasilii Ia. Savel'ev, joked with a tailor friend of his in Saratov, "Yes, indeed, you yourself are an exploiter since two workers labor for you." The tailor, confused, could only reply: "Well, what's to be done, brother? I myself am not happy that such [social] conditions exist now, but one must live. When the revolution comes, then I won't be an exploiter [any more]" (ibid.).

68 The census of 1897, which may give a hint of the literacy level two decades earlier in the century, found that of a Saratov City population of 137,147, slightly more than half of whom were male, the literacy rate for males was 57.5 percent, and for females, 38.3 percent (extracted from the figures given in Tsentral'nyi statisticheskii komitet, *Pervaia vseobshchaia perepis'*, pp. 14–15). Undoubtedly the requirement was little more than the ability to write one's name.

The census suggests, reasonably enough, that city illiteracy was highest among the migrants from the countryside (juridical peasants, 36,036 males and 31,908 females, made up 49.4 percent of the city's population in 1897). The survey of literacy for the province as a whole found only 34.6 percent of the males literate, and only 13.5 percent of the females. The degree of migration from the countryside at that time is suggested by the fact that, of the "juridical peasants, cossacks and foreign settlers" in the city (virtually all of whom were juridical peasants), only 18.7 percent of the males and 30 percent of the females had been born in Saratov District (ibid., pp. 2, 35).

69 "Dva pis'ma," pp. 24–28.

70 Saratovets, no. 3, pp. 181–82.

71 Volkov, p. 10.

72 Saratovets, no. 3, pp. 182–83.

73 Volkov, p. 10.

74 Most escaped, including Plekhanov; of those arrested, many were soon released. Gradually people began drifting away from the countryside. Aptekman asks why a new central department was not set up to continue the coordination of the countryside settlements. The Saratov experiment failed, he concludes, not simply because of police repression, which was only a mild, reproachful tap. Lack of money and an inability to preserve secrecy severely handicapped them, and internal quarrels of no apparent significance demoralized them. As Aptekman summarized: "We had no tenacity and discipline." And events in St. Petersburg seemed too exciting to follow at a distance. (Aptekman, *Obshchestvo,* pp. 269–72; Saratovets, no. 3, p. 183.)

75 Volkov, p. 12. As far as I have been able to determine, the endeavor did not result in a strike.

76 Vera N. Figner, *Vospominaniia* (Moscow, 1964), 1:159.
77 Ibid., pp. 156–58; A. I. Ivanchin-Pisarev, *Khozhdenie v narod* (Moscow-Leningrad, 1929), pp. 416–19. Itenberg and Volk, 2:394.
78 Saratovets, pp. 189–94; Itenberg and Volk, 2:92.
79 Volkov, pp. 11, 14.
80 Ibid., pp. 14–16.
81 Ibid., pp. 17–18.
82 Ibid., pp. 17–20.
83 Ibid., p. 19. These individuals included the brothers P. S. and S. S. Stepanov, A. L. Blek, A. S. Chumaevskii, Moiseev, Zaroastrova, and Teselkin.
84 Indeed, even Social Democrats, "subjectively" speaking, "drew the theoretical theses of their views in part from the experience" of the Populists; in this aspect, the SD movement "was already wholly and completely prepared, in part from German and Polish literature, towards the end of the 1870s (the circumstance is frequently forgotten, but many of the first S.D. groups even called themselves *neo-narodovol'skie*)." V. Akimov, quoted in St. Nechetnyi [Stepan Sletov], "Ocherki po istorii P. S.-R.," *Sotsialist-Revoliutsioner,* no. 4 (1912): 35.
85 V. V. Shirokova, *Partiia "Narodnogo prava"* (Saratov, 1972), p. 18 n. 4, pp. 33–36.
86 Ibid., pp. 33–37, 138–68; Nechetnyi, pp. 36–44.

CHAPTER 5

1 A. A. Argunov, "Iz proshlogo partii Sotsialistov—Revoliutsionerov," *Byloe,* no. 10 (1907): 103; G. A. Malinin, *Sviazhite nas s "Vavilonom!": Iz istorii rasprostraneniia proizvedenii V. I. Lenina v Saratovskoi gubernii* (Saratov, 1973).
2 G. F. Khodakov, *Ocherki istorii Saratovskoi organizatsii KPSS* (Saratov, 1968), pp. 36–37; G. Saar, "Vozniknovenie Saratovskoi organizatsii RSDRP," *Proletarskaia revoliutsiia* [hereafter *PR*], nos. 6–7 (77–78) (1928): 265–69; *Istoriia Saratovskogo kraia, 1590–1917,* ed. V. A. Osipov et al. (Saratov, 1964), pp. 97–125.
3 G. F. Khodakov, pp. 20, 36; *Vestnik Sar. gubk. RKP(b),* no. 6 (1923): 70.
4 "Iz istorii krest'ianskogo dvizheniia nakanune i v period pervoi russkoi revoliutsii, *Voprosy istorii,* no. 7 (1957): 105; *Istoriia Saratovskogo kraia,* pp. 84–95; V. B. Ostrovskii, ed., *Lenin i Saratovskii krai: sbornik dokumentov i materialov* (Saratov, 1975), pp. 27–67, 81–89; G. F. Khodakov, 8–13.
5 Others involved in the circle were P. and S. Stepanov, V. Khar'kovtsev, and D. Maleev. Varvara I. Natanson was Mark Natanson's second wife; by this time, his first wife Olga may have perished in Siberia. V. V.

Shirokova, *Ocherki istorii obshchestvennogo dvizheniia v Saratovskoi gubernii v poreformennyi period* (Saratov, 1976), pp. 58–59; A. I. Spiridovich, *Partiia sotsialistov-revoliutsionerov i eia predshestvenniki, 1886–1916* (Moscow, 1918), p. 34; I. Rakitnikova, "Revoliutsionnaia molodezh' 90-kh godov na rabote v derevne," in *Narodovol'tsy 80-kh i 90-kh godov,* 2 vols. (Moscow, 1929) 2:176–77.

6 Spiridovich, *Partiia,* pp. 34–35; Rakitnikova, "Revoliutsionnaia molodezh'," p. 177; Shirokova, *Ocherki istorii,* pp. 59–64; O. V. Aptekman, "Partiia Narodnogo prava," *Byloe,* no. 7 (1907): 188; Argunov, "Iz proshlogo," p. 103.

7 Shirokova, *Ocherki istorii,* pp. 64–66; Spiridovich, *Partiia,* p. 34; V. I. Lenin, *Polnoe sobranie sochinenii,* 5th ed., 49 vols. (Moscow, 1958–64) 1:345–46; *Letuchie listki izdavaemye fondom vol'noi russkoi pressy v Londone* [hereafter *LL*], no. 41 (December 9, 1897); Saar, "Vozniknovenie," pp. 271, 281; S. N. Sletov, *K istorii vozniknoveniia partii sotsialisto-revoliutsionerov* (Petrograd, 1917), pp. 32, 49–51; Argunov, "Iz proshlogo," p. 103.

8 Shirokova, *Ocherki istorii,* p. 69; Saar, "Vozniknovenie," p. 271; *LL,* no. 6 (May 26, 1894): 6.

9 Argunov, "Iz proshlogo," p. 104; Manfred Hildermeier, *Sotsialrevolutionare Partei Russlands: Agrarsozializmus und Modernisierung im Zarenreich (1900–1914)* (Cologne, Vienna, 1978), pp. 38–39.

10 Argunov, "Iz proshlogo," p. 105.

11 Ibid., pp. 104–107; Shirokova, *Ocherki istorii,* p. 69; Hildermeier, p. 37; Spiridovich, *Partiia,* pp. 49, 70–71; Sletov, pp. 41–48, 78–79, 80–81.

12 Maleev's circle endured until at least 1900 (Shirokova, *Ocherki istorii,* p. 70); T. Akimova and V. K. Arkhangel'skaia, *Revoliutsionnye pesni v Saratovskom Povolzh'e* (Saratov, 1967), p. 96; Sletov, p. 45; Malinin, p. 11; G. Lushnikov, "Vospominaniia o vozniknovenii v Saratove sots.-demokraticheskoi rabochei gruppy 1896–1899 gg.," *Kommunisticheskii put',* no. 10(35) (1923): 169–75; Saar, "Vozniknovenie," p. 286; A. Stanchinskii, "Sotsial-demokraticheskoe podpol'e v Saratove i zhurnal 'Saratovskii rabochii' v 1899 g.," *PR,* no. 2(14) (1923): 106.

13 V. G. Arkhangel'skii, *Katerina Breshkovskaia* (Prague, 1938), pp. 99–103; Shirokova, *Ocherkin istorii,* p. 72; Saar, "Vozniknovenie," pp. 280–81; V. M. Chernov, *Zapiski sotsialista-revoliutsionera* (Berlin-Petrograd-Moscow; 1922), pp. 332–33; Maureen Perrie, *The Agrarian Policy of the Russian Socialist-Revolutionary Party from Its Origins through the Revolution of 1905–1907* (Cambridge, Eng., and New York, 1976), p. 24.

14 E. K. Breshko-Breshkovskaia, *Hidden Springs of the Russian Revolution* (Stanford, Calif., 1931), p. 207; Chernov, p. 333; Perrie, p. 24.

15 Rakitnikova, pp. 164–65.

16 "V. S. Aref'ev (Nekrolog)," *Vestnik russkoi revoliutsii,* no. 2 (February 1902), sec. 3, pp. 115–16; Thomas Fallows, "Forging the Zemstvo Movement: Liberalism and Radicalism on the Volga, 1890–1905," (Ph.D. diss., Harvard University, 1981), pp. 621–23; Rakitnikova, pp. 164–65; Sletov, pp. 56–57; Shirokova, *Ocherki istorii,* pp. 64, 66; *LL,* no. 41 (December 9, 1897), and no. 42 (July 7, 1898). Members of the large Aref'ev family played key roles in the peasant movement before, during, and after the 1905 revolution.

17 A. A. Bogdanov, "Puti proletarskogo pisatelia," *Krasnaia nov',* no. 2 (1927): 227; Saar, "Vozniknovenie," p. 279; Fallows, "Zemstvo Movement," pp. 624–29.

18 G. Saar, "Saratovskaia organizatsiia RSDRP v nachale 900-kh gg.," *PR,* nos. 11–12 (82–83) (1928): 122; and his "Pervye popytki sots.-demokraticheskoi raboty sredi saratovskikh rabochikh," *PR,* no. 4 (75) (1928): 128–53. Claims that P. Rumiantsev, P. Maslov, A. Sanin, N. Bauman, and A. Bogdanov carried out Marxist work in Saratov between 1890 and 1895 lack credence: Sanin later specifically denied that he did so; Bogdanov was not a Marxist at the time; Maslov and Rumiantsev left no trace during the 1890s. For claims and counterevidence, see D. M. Konovalov, *Saratovskii agent "Iskry"* (Saratov, 1969), p. 25; L. Frug, "Nikolai Bauman," *Bor'ba klassov,* nos. 7–8 (1934): 119; A. Sanin, " 'Samarskii vestnik' v rukakh marksistov (1896–1897 gg.)," *PR,* no. 12 (35) (1924): 276–77. Assertions that Lenin's Petersburg *Soiuz za osvobozhdenie rabochego klassa* founded a circle in Saratov are improbable; P. S. Gusiatnikov, *Nazrevanie revoliutsionnogo krizisa v Rossii v nachale XX veka* (Moscow, 1959), p. 37. Locals K. M. Takhtarev, N. Plaksin, E. Golubeva, M. Z. Semenov all became Marxists but did so late in the decade. For claims and counterevidence about these individuals, see Saar, "Pervye popytki," pp. 128–53; his "Vozniknovenie," pp. 275–76; Malinin, pp. 11, 23; Stanchinskii, p. 90; Konovalov, pp. 15–37. Shirokova, *Ocherki istorii,* (pp. 72–78) subjects to stringent criticism all claims of early SD work in Saratov.

19 Malinin, p. 23; M. M. Essen, *Pervyi shturm* (Moscow, 1957), pp. 27–28; Stanchinskii, p. 90.

20 Lushnikov (pp. 169–70) lists titles of publications read in the circles: (*Istoricheskie pis'ma* (Lavrov), *Morozovskaia stachka, Rabochii den', Kak ministr zabotitsia o rabochikh,* and the especially popular *Khitraia mekhanika*—all of Populist origin. See also Malinin, pp. 26, 33; G. F. Khodakov, pp. 25–29; Saar, "Vozniknovenie," p. 286; Stanchinskii, pp. 91–92. Early worker SDs in Saratov were Dubrovinskii, Bochkov, Shepelev, Tokarev, Lialov, Voronin, Gromov, Ivanov, and Kanatchikov; the first local student SD

contingent included Ksandrov, Malinin, L'vov, Arkhangel'skii, Arkhangel'skaia, Lebedev, and Feofanov.

21 Lushnikov, pp. 174–76; Malinin, pp. 27–28; Shirokova, *Ocherki istorii,* pp. 80–81.

22 Lushnikov, p. 178–82. By 1905, Lushnikov had become a prominent worker-SR and was an SR deputy to the soviet; Zelenskii, too, apparently later became an SR.

23 V. A. Sushitskii, "Saratovskaia sotsial-demokraticheskaia rabochaia gruppa (1898–1899 gg.)," *Saratovskii Gosudarstvennyi Oblastnoi Muzei,* no. 14 (1928), pp. 3–4; G. Saar, "Istoriia i vospominaniia o Saratovskoi organizatsii R.S.D.R.P.(bol'.)," *Vestnik Sar. Gubk. RKP(b),* no. 3 (1923): 39; Stanchinskii, pp. 92–96; Saar, "Vozniknovenie," p. 286; "Iz istorii rabochego dvizheniia kontsa 90-kh godov," *Krasnyi arkhiv,* no. 93 (1939): 171; *Nakanune,* nos. 9–10 (Sept.–Oct. 1899): 115; G. F. Khodakov, p. 31; Malinin, p. 24.

24 Saar, "Saratovskaia organizatsiia," p. 122; and his "Pervye popytki," pp. 128–53.

25 Malinin, pp. 11–14, 30; *Nakanune,* no. 19 (July 1900): 227; D. M. Konovalov, pp. 40–41; Stanchinskii, pp. 89, 92, 105.

26 Argunov, "Iz proshlogo," p. 108; Ostrovskii, ed., *Lenin i Saratovskii,* p. 250.

27 Lushnikov, p. 173; P. Lebedev, "K istorii Saratovskoi organizatsii RSDRP (1901–1902 gg.)," *PR,* no. 3(15) (1923): 232–33; Stanchinskii, p. 105. See also S. Kanatchikov, *Istoriia moego byta* (Moscow, 1934), pp. 18–23 (R. Zelnik's translation of this memoir has recently been issued by Stanford University Press).

28 Lebedev, "K istorii," pp. 230–35, 240; Stanchinskii, p. 87–106.

29 Malinin, pp. 27, 33; Kanatchikov, pp. 139–49.

30 See various issues of *Russkii rabochii, Nakanune,* and *Letuchie listki.* See also Sletov, p. 47.

31 Akimova and Arkhangel'skaia, pp. 92–97, 132–43; Essen, pp. 27–28; *Perepiska V. I. Lenina i redaktsii gazety 'Iskry' s sotsial-dem. organizatsiiami v Rossii, 1900–1903 gg.,* 3 vols. (Moscow, 1969–70) 1:284. Early widely used songs were "Stand, Rise Up Working People," "Show Me a Dwelling Place," *"Vpered"* (Forward), *"Tkachi"* (Weavers), and *"Dubunuski"* (Little Oak[?]). Songs widely used by both parties after 1903 were *"Varshavianka"* (Little Warsaw), *"Krasnoe znamia"* (Red Banner), and "You Have Fallen, a Victim." Memoirists, contemporary newspapers, and court indictments all suggest the great importance of songs in the revolutionary movement.

32 Malinin, pp. 26, 31, 38; A. Egorov (Martov), "Zarozhdenie politicheskikh partii i ikh deiatel'nost'," in *Obshchestvennoe dvizhenie v Rossii v nachale*

XX-go veka, L. Martov, P. Maslov, A. Potresov, eds., 4 vols. (St. Petersburg, 1909–14), 1:385; "Iz istorii," *KA,* p. 171. Both parties had problems initiating any sort of mass movement; during the May Day demonstration of 1901 and the June 1901 strikes, individual SRs and SDs provided leadership, while the SR and SD organizations played no role. The May Day affair was something of a minor coup: a group of student and worker SRs and SDs commandeered all the boats and rowed along the entire Saratov riverbank singing revolutionary songs as the police ran along the shore shouting imprecations.

33 Lebedev, "K istorii," pp. 236–38, 243–44; G. F. Khodakov, pp. 33, 48–49; Konovalov, pp. 40–41, 47; Saar, "Saratovskaia organizatsiia, pp. 125–27; Malinin, p. 42

34 Kanatchikov, pp. 40–41; G. F. Khodakov, pp. 32, 38–40, 52; Saar, "Sar. org.," pp. 112–24; Konovalov, p. 47; *Leninskaia Iskra i mestnye organizatsii v Rossii (1900–1903 gg.),* 3 vols. (Perm, 1971) 1:284; Lebedev, "K istorii," pp. 242, 249; *Bor'ba za sozdanie marksistskoi partii v Rossii. Obrazovanie RSDRP. Vozniknovenie bol'shevizma (1894–1904 gody). Dok. i mat.* (Moscow, 1961), p. 365; Malinin, pp. 42, 49; *Iskra,* no. 7 (August 1901): 5, 17, no. 9 (October 1901): 6, and no. 11 (November 20, 1901): 12; *Revoliutsionnaia Rossiia* [hereafter *RR*], no. 3 (1902): 13; and G. L. Shidlovskii, "Vekhi zhizni K. S. Eremeeva," *Krasnaia letopis',* no. 3 (1931): 157–65.

35 Sletov, p. 67; *Nakanune,* nos. 31–32; *Iskra,* no. 7; Lebedev, "K istorii," p. 244. The SR brochure calling for unity on the basis of a "political" program had the title *Neprimirimyi* (Irreconcilable).

36 *Iskra,* no. 34, in reprint edition, L. Lepeshinskii, ed. (Leningrad, 1925–29), vols. 1–7, p. 76; *Perepiska Lenina,* 2: 549–50; Hildermeier, p. 110; Malinin, pp. 51–53; Konovalov, p. 47; G. F. Khodakov, p. 54; Saar, "Sar. org.," p. 127. The Artisanal Union's paper was called *Remeslennyi listok* (Artisans' Sheet).

37 Lebedev, "K istorii," p. 244; Kanatchikov, pp. 37, 124; Ostrovskii, ed., *Lenin i sar. krai,* p. 248: "even the SRs have come out behind *Iskra*"; Malinin, pp. 51–52; A. I. Spiridovich, *Istoriia bol'shevizma v Rossii ot vozniknoveniia do zakhvatoi vlasti, 1883–1903–1917* (Paris, 1922), p. 45; *Perepiska Lenina,* 1: 284, 454, and 2: 338; *RR,* no. 30 (August 20, 1903): 23; Hildermeier, p. 110, n. 4, and p. 244, n. 140; *Iskra,* no. 21 (June 1, 1902): 8. Soviet historians accuse the joint groups of "economism" and "terrorism," an oxymoron. Oppenheim misses the point when he suggests that Rykov's moderation in the 1920s found its origin in his earlier cooperation with SRs; Samuel A. Oppenheim, "The Making of a Right Communist—A. I. Rykov to 1917," *Slavic Review* 36, no. 3 (1977): 420–40.

38 During its existence, the SRs channeled all their worker-oriented agita-

tion through the *Ob"edinnenka;* even a year or more after its breakup, prominent SDs still advocated reviving the joint committee. *RR,* no. 33 (October 1, 1903): 22; Lebedev, "K istorii," pp. 245–48; *Demonstranty pered sudom* (n.p., 1902); Saar, "Sar. org.," pp. 129–30; G. F. Khodakov, pp. 42–44; P. Voevodin, "Dvadtsat' let raboty v bol'shevistskikh organizatsiiakh i vstrechy s tov. Leninym," *PR,* no. 3 (1922): 183; *RR,* no. 9 (July 1902): 9–10; *Narodnoe delo,* no. 2 (September 1902): 89–91; no. 3 (January 1903): 104–11; *Iskra,* no. 22 (May 5, 1902): 6–7. The *Ob"edinnenka's* paper had the title *Golos truda* (Voice of Labor).

39   Lebedev recalled that just as he ran toward the prostrate and bleeding Rykov shouting, "They've killed him!" the police dragged the hapless young activist to his feet and marched him off. Rykov, D'iakova, and others were released without charges. *Iskra,* no. 22, pp. 6–7; no. 29 (December 1, 1902): 5; *RR,* no. 25 (June 1, 1903); no. 33, p. 21; Lebedev, "K istorii," p. 242. See also Jonathan Sanders, "Lessons from the Periphery: Saratov, January 1905," *Slavic Review* 46, no. 2 (Summer 1987): 232–33.

40   Lebedev, "K istorii," p. 247; Malinin, pp. 34, 56–57; *Iskra,* no. 34, pp. 4–5; G. F. Khodakov, pp. 54–55.

41   *Lenin i sar. krai,* pp. 257–59; *Iskra,* no. 21 (June 1902); and no. 24 (August 1902). The offending articles were entitled "Why the Social Democrats Must Declare Decisive and Unconditional War on the Socialist Revolutionaries" and "Revolutionary Adventurism."

42   *RR,* no. 11 (September 1902): 25; no. 33, pp. 21–22; *Iskra,* no. 23 (August 1902); G. F. Khodakov, pp. 54–55; *Bor'ba za sozdanie,* pp. 421–22. The joint letter protested against *Iskra's* "polemics" and the aspersions it cast upon Balmashev.

43   *Iskra,* no. 43 (July 1, 1903); no. 44 (July 15, 1903); no. 48 (September 15, 1903).

44   Lebedev, "K istorii," p. 245. According to Liadov, Lenin replied that "it was necessary to tell everything to the workers"; see Ostrovskii, ed., *Lenin i sar. krai,* pp. 257–59; and M. Liadov, "Moi vstrechi," Ostrovskii, ed., *Lenin i sar. krai,* p. 199.

45   "V stenograficheskii otchet sarat. gub. P. Stolypina za 1904 god," *Krasnyi arkhiv,* no. 17 (1926): 85; N. Cherevanin, "Dvizhenie intelligentsii," in *Obshchestvennoe dvizhenie,* 1: 279–82 (see n. 32 above); *RR,* no. 13 (November 1902): 14–15; no. 17 (February 1, 1903); no. 32 (September 15, 1903); and no. 41 (February 15, 1904); *Iskra,* no. 77 (November 5, 1904); *Narodnoe delo,* no. 5 (June 1904).

46   Sletov, p. 104; Hildermeier, pp. 114–15, 410; Konovalov, pp. 52–53; Spiridovich, *Partiia,* p. 128; B. Nikolaevskii, *Istoriia odnogo predatelia*

(Berlin, 1932), pp. 49–53, 63; Breshko-Breshkovskaia, *Hidden Springs,* pp. 287–88; A. Argunov, "Azev v partii S-R," *Na chuzhoi storone,* no. 6 (1924): 168; *RR,* no. 50 (August 1, 1904): 22–24.

47 Saar, "Sar. org.," p. 39; Kanatchikov, p. 21.

48 Members of the SR workers' circle were P. Gorelin, P. Vlasov, A. Evseev, M. Shkoda, V. Shpurin, and Mal'tsev. *RR,* no. 14 (December 1902): 23; no. 19 (March 1, 1903): 20; no. 20 (March 15, 1903); no. 28 (July 15, 1903): 21–23; no. 36 (November 15, 1903): 22; no. 28 (July 15, 1903); no. 40 (January 15, 1904); no. 44 (April 1, 1904); no. 49 (July 1, 1904): 7–10.

49 *RR,* no. 31 (September 1, 1903): 22; no. 33, p. 24; no. 35 (November 1, 1903); no. 39 (January 1, 1904): 14–15, 22; no. 40 (January 15, 1904); no. 41 (February 15, 1904); no. 44 (April 1, 1904); no. 46 (May 5, 1904): 27; Spiridovich, *Partiia,* p. 130.

50 E. Breshko-Breshkovskaia, "Vospominaniia i dumy," *Sotsialist-Revoliut- sioner,* no. 4 (1912): 103–29; and her "Pis'mo starogo druga (Pis'mo piatoe)," *RR,* no. 67 (May 15, 1905): 5–7; I. Rakitnikova, "Revoliutsion- naia rabota v krest'ianstve v Saratovskoi gubernii v 1900–1902 gg.," *Katorga i ssylka,* no. 10(47) (1928): 7–17. See also M. I. Leonov, "Deiatel'nost' eserov v derevne na rubezhe XIX–XX vv.," *Krest'ianskoe dvizhenie v trekh russkikh revoliutsiiakh. Mezhvuzovskii sbornik* (Kuibyshev, 1982), pp. 29–37; and Perrie, pp. 29–37.

51 Breshko-Breshkovskaia, "Vospominaniia," pp. 102–8, 124–27, and her "Pis'mo," p. 6; Rakitnikova, "Rev. rabota," pp. 9–10; Perrie, pp. 36–41.

52 Breshko-Breshkovskaia, "Vospominaniia," p. 104; Rakitnikova, "Rev. rabota," pp. 9, 13, 16; *Iskra,* no. 7, p. 5; Fallows, pp. 630–36; Perrie, pp. 40–41; *RR,* no. 17, p. 17; no. 29 (August 5, 1903): 8–9. Among the peasant activists were I. Kogin from Spasko-Aleksandrovskoe and Grishin from Malygina, both in Petrovsk District. In 1897 police interro- gated Kogin for receiving Populist literature from A. A. Bogdanov, who had gotten it from the Evreinov-Gorelin circle. For examples of the Saratov SR Committee's proclamations to peasants, see *RR,* no. 17, p. 19; and no. 23 (May 1, 1903): 19. Numerous titles printed abroad also appeared in the villages. Balashov District villages with persistent unrest were Botsmanovo (home of the Aref'evs), Chirikova, Makarovo, Glebova, Kliuchi, and Trubetskoe.

53 Fallows assigns the beginning of rural troubles in Balashov to fall and early winter of 1901. News first reached Saratov shortly after Christmas. The Chenykaev propagandists displayed the greatest activity precisely in these months. The Aref'evs, evidently preparing for a spring 1902 "assault," agitated for the overthrow of the government "from village policeman to the tsar" and for "rebellion" (see Fallows, pp. 638–39). On

the arrest and trial of Chernykaev, Obukhova, several Aref'evs, and the Avdeevs, see Rakitnikova, "Rev. rabota," pp. 11–12; *RR,* no. 5 (March 1902): 18; and no. 17, p. 20.

54 Breshko-Breshkovskaia, "Pis'mo," p. 6; her "Vospominaniia," pp. 104, 126–29; Leonov, "Deiatel'nost' eserov v derevne na rubezhe XIX–XX vv.," p. 34; Rakitnikova, "Rev. rabota," pp. 13–15; *RR,* no. 5, p. 18; no. 10 (August 1902): 21–22; no. 17, p. 19; no. 29, p. 9; no. 39, p. 16; Spiridovich, *Partiia,* pp. 89–91; *Narodnoe delo,* no. 5 (June 1904): 113, 119–20; V. Gorn, *Krest'ianskoe dvizhenie za poltora veka* (Moscow, 1909), pp. 82–83.

55 *RR,* no. 8 (June 1902): 22; no. 11, pp. 19–20; no. 13, pp. 17–18; no. 19, p. 14; no. 30, p. 17; no. 58, pp. 17–18; *Narodnoe delo,* no. 2 (September 1902): 91–92; *Osvobozhdenie,* no. 7 (September 1902): 109–10; *Iskra,* no. 7, p. 5; V. Gorn, "Krest'ianskoe dvizhenie do 1905 g.," in *Obshchestvennoe dvizhenie,* I: 244, 250. In 1903 the peasant-oriented SR journal *Narodnoe delo* remarked that peasants arrested the previous year in Saratov Province were socialists, "as opposed to previous years when no such claim could be made" (no. 4, June 1903: 169). Similarly, *Revoliutsionnaia Rossiia* noted that "experience with propaganda in Saratov Province shows that peasants, just like the more conscious workers, were beginning to relate critically toward the existing order and were accepting the ideals of socialism" (no. 17, p. 18). Peasants of all ages and of both sexes became involved.

56 *Narodnoe delo,* no. 2, pp. 95–96; *RR,* no. 15 (January 1903): 18; *Osvobozhdenie,* no. 4 (1902): 63–64. Arrests were reported in *Osvobozhdenie,* no. 15 (January 19, 1903): 257–58; and *RR,* no. 10, pp. 21–22.

57 *RR,* no. 25, p. 19; no. 26 (June 15, 1903): 16–18; no. 39 (January 1, 1904); no. 49 (July 1, 1904); *Iskra,* no. 52 (November 7, 1903); Gorn, *Krest'ianskoe,* pp. 91–92; and his "Krest'ianskoe dvizhenie," pp. 253–57.

58 Perrie, pp. 58–62; "Obzor revoliutsionnago dvizheniia v Saratovskoi gubernii, 1902–1906," TsGAOR, fond 102,00, d. 1800, ch. 29, l. 66 ob. (from notes made by Scott Seregny in Soviet archives; archival references below are also from this source); *RR,* no. 25, p. 19; no. 29, pp. 8–10; no. 30, pp. 17–18; no. 39 (January 1, 1904); no. 44, pp. 20–21; *Narodnoe delo,* no. 4, p. 119. In June–July 1903, peasants from Turki burned one gentryman's entire reserve of grain; Stolypin quickly arrived with a hundred cossacks. The governor blamed revolutionary propaganda and, when threats failed to induce villagers to reveal the guilty parties, arrested individuals according to predrawn lists.

59 Malinin, p. 89; Lebedev, "K istorii," p. 249.

60 Malinin, pp. 43–46, 49–50; Konovalov, pp. 40–41; *Perepiska Lenina,* I: 97, 117, 221–22; G. F. Khodakov, pp. 47, 50–51; Allan K. Wildman, "Lenin's

Battle with Kustarnichestvo: The *Iskra* Organization in Russia," *Slavic Review* 23, no. 3 (1963): 481–82; Lebedev, "K istorii," pp. 243–44.

61   G. F. Khodakov, pp. 53–55; *Slavnye bol'sheviki* (Moscow, 1958), p. 127; *Lenin i sar. krai*, pp. 255, 265; *Perepiska V. I. Lenina i rukovodimykh im uchrezhdenii RSDRP s partiinimi organizatsiiami 1903–1905 gg.: sbornik dok.*, 3 vols. (Moscow, 1974–77), 2: 516–17; M. Liadov, *O vtorom s"ezde partii: vosp. uchastnikov* (Moscow, 1933), pp. 15–16; and his "Moi vstrechi," *Vospominaniia o II s"ezde RSDRP* (Moscow, 1959), pp. 52–53; *Iskra*, no. 31 (January 1, 1903): 6; no. 39 (May 1903).

62   *Lenin i sar. krai*, p. 265; *Perepiska Lenina i redaktsii Iskry*, 2: 357–58; *1905 god v Tsaritsyne* (Volgograd, 1960), pp. 119–21; Soviet historian Malinin found the phenomenon of Saratov being out of touch with SD centers characteristic enough that he named his book *Sviazhite nam s Vavilonom!* (Connect us with Babylon!). The severity of the isolation is shown by the fact that during spring and summer of 1903 the SDs, having no press and receiving nothing from abroad, were forced to distribute SR literature with title pages torn out. See *Listovki saratovskikh bol'shevikov, 1902–1917 gg.* (Saratov, 1979), p. 7; Breshko-Breshkovskaia, "Vospominaniia," p. 105.

63   *Perepiska Lenina i redaktsii Iskry*, 3: 447–48, 473; *Iskra*, no. 43, pp. 9–10.

64   As noted, the SRs complained of the SD Committee's lack of militance during the Bering strike. See Malinin, pp. 66–72; Lebedev, "K istorii," pp. 248–49; Konovalov, pp. 65–66; and *Perepiska i ruk.*, (n. 61 above), 2: 93–94.

65   *Perepiska i ruk.*, 3: 69–71, 92, 116–17, 138–39; G. F. Khodakov, pp. 69–71; Saar, "Sar. org.," p. 131.

66   M. Semenov, "1905 god v Saratovskoi gubernii," *PR*, no. 3 (1926): 198.

67   *Iskra*, no. 80 (December 15, 1904): 5.

68   Ibid., p. 5; I. L-ii, "Banketnaia kampaniia v Saratove (1904–1905)," *Minuvshie gody*, no. 12 (1908): 37–39 (the author of this article was I. M. Liakhovetskii, who later achieved fame as the Soviet diplomat Maiskii); G. F. Khodakov, pp. 72–73; Malinin, pp. 80–86; Sanders, pp. 233–34.

69   T. Emmons, "Russia's Banquet Campaign," *California Slavic Studies*, 10 (1977): 49, 62–63; Semenov, pp. 200–1; L-ii [I. M. Liakhovetskii], pp. 51–52; Semenov, p. 201. Liakhovetskii recalled that the SRs' position coincided with that of the radical SDs (Leninists), both of which groups considered as treasonous the use of noncontroversial terminology at the liberal (zemstvo) banquets (L-ii, pp. 50–51). Meanwhile, the SD Committee circulated a resolution requesting signatures for a basically liberal (nonsocialist) reform; L-ii, pp. 51–52; *RR*, no. 61 (March 15, 1905): 10. But as *Revoliutsionnaia Rossiia* conceded a few months later, SRs, in opposing this and other liberal-Menshevik measures, failed to offer alternatives.

70 *RR,* no. 61, pp. 10–11; V. Nevskii, "Ianvarskie dni 1905 g. v provintsii," *Krasnaia letopis',* no. 4 (1922): 120–23; Sanders, "Lessons from the Periphery," p. 236. The SR I. I. Drugov, a railroad employee, stated, "I invite Saratov workers to go out on strike at once, and to ask the other classes of the population to support them." The SD Vasil'ev asked the public to attend a meeting the next day to discuss a strike (Nevskii, p. 122, n. 2).

71 SD leaflets are cited and/or quoted in G. F. Khodakov, pp. 79–80; Nevskii, pp. 121–22; full texts can be found in *Krasnaia letopis',* no. 1 (1922): 216–33. SR leaflets are cited in Nevskii, p. 124, and are quoted in *RR,* no. 59 (February 10, 1905): 22; no. 61, p. 11; no. 64 (April 15, 1905): 13. Sanders (p. 238) notes the similarity of the two parties' leaflets.

72 G. M. Derenkovskii, I. M. Raschetnova, M. S. Simonova, "1905 god v Saratove," *Istoricheskie zapiski* 54 (1955): 75–77, 80; *Tretii s"ezd RSDRP. Aprel'–Mai 1905 goda. Protokoly* (Moscow, 1959), pp. 136–37; Nevskii, pp. 120, 125, 129–30; G. F. Khodakov, pp. 84, 87; Sanders, "Lessons from the Periphery."

73 Nevskii, p. 122; Hildermeier, p. 219; *RR,* no. 58, p. 19; no. 61, pp. 11–12; no. 64, pp. 12–13.

74 *RR,* no. 61, pp. 11–12; no. 64, pp. 12–13; Sanders, pp. 237–41; Nevskii, pp. 123–24. According to Sanders, at some meetings, when speakers began to read lists of demands, workers shouted, "Begin with the fourth point!" (that is, the economic points).

75 Nevskii, pp. 125–30; *Iskra,* no. 86 (February 3, 1905): 4–5; *RR,* no. 59, p. 15; no. 61, pp. 11–12; Derenkovskii, et al., p. 78.

76 I. M. Pushkareva, *Zheleznodorozhniki Rossii v burzhuazno-demokraticheskikh revoliutsiiakh* (Moscow, 1975), p. 92. The railroad administration granted eleven of fourteen economic demands. For the SR outlook on this matter, see *RR,* no. 64, pp. 12–14. Without mentioning the actions or motivations of the SD Committee or of the strike committee, Nevskii states that "a decision was made to call off the strike on the 19th" (p. 130).

77 "Chemu uchit Saratovskaia zabastovka," in *RR,* no. 64, pp. 12–14.

78 Sanders, pp. 238, 241–44. Reichman also notes the role of the Saratov strike as a model for later 1905 actions; see Henry Reichman, *Railwaymen and Revolution, Russia 1905* (Berkeley, 1987).

79 I. S. Sokolov, *1905-i god na Riazano-Ural'skoi zheleznoi doroge* (Saratov, 1925), p. 22; G. F. Khodakov, pp. 83–84; Derenkovskii, pp. 80–81; *Krasnaia letopis',* no. 1 (1922): 223–26; *RR,* no. 60 (March 5, 1905): 23. On February 13, the SDs issued a leaflet urging workers to "stand together and continue the strike. Armed struggle lies ahead when the whole working class unites" (Khodakov, p. 84). But Saratov workers in this case had no such intent.

80 G. F. Khodakov, p. 85. For SR leaflets, see *RR,* no. 59, p. 15; no. 60, p. 23; no. 63 (April 5, 1905): 25; no. 67, p. 23; no. 68 (June 1, 1905): 22–23; no. 73 (August 15, 1905): 28; no. 74 (September 1, 1905); for SD leaflets, see *Krasnaia letopis',* no. 1 (1922), pp. 223–30.

81 N. M. Druzhinin, "V Saratove 1905 g. (Vospominaniia)," *Voprosy istorii KPSS,* no. 10 (1979), pp. 100–101; Derenkovskii, p. 84–86; G. F. Khodakov, pp. 90–94; Lenin, *Polnoe sobranie,* 10: 162. While supporting the Bolshevik Third Congress, the Saratov SDs continued their contacts with the Menshevik OK, openly supported the OK's call for a Fourth Congress, and only six months later lined up behind the new agrarian program outlined by Lenin at the Third Congress.

82 Derenkovskii, p. 81; *RR,* no. 68, pp. 22–24; G. F. Khodakov, p. 87; *Ist. sar. kraia,* pp. 107–8.

83 *RR,* no. 68, pp. 22–23; Derenkovskii, pp. 81–82; G. F. Khodakov, pp. 87–88; Malinin, p. 105; *RR,* no. 68, pp. 22–23; *Ist. sar. kraia,* pp. 170–72; *Proletariat,* no. 17(4) (July 1905).

84 Sokolov, p. 29; Pushkareva, p. 132; G. F. Khodakov, pp. 94–95; Druzhinin, p. 103. Among others, the SRs organized a printers' union. See *Ist. sar. krai,* pp. 175–76; *Proletariat,* no. 29 (16) (August 1905); no. 11 (1905).

85 L. Kamenev, "Iosif Petrovich Gol'denburg," *PR,* no. 5 (1922): 9–11; Druzhinin, p. 101; Malinin, p. 104; G. F. Khodakov, 98–101.

86 Hildermeier (pp. 218–19) claims that the SR Workers' Union dates from 1906, whereas *Revoliutsionnaia Rossiia* and other sources show that the union was formed in 1903, after which it repeatedly issued leaflets under its own signature. Hildermeier notes that in 1906 the SR Union had nearly two hundred factory and artisanal workers, and in 1907 three hundred, suggesting an SR workers' organization in Saratov of quite respectable size. *RR,* no. 67 (May 5, 1905); no. 73 (August 15, 1905); *Ist. sar. kraia,* pp. 172–73, 176–77; "Obzor," fond 102,00, d. 1800, ch. 29, l. 68 ob.

87 This analysis of the October events in Saratov represents a reading of the following (sometimes conflicting) sources: *Ist. sar. kraia,* pp. 171–76; P. Argunov, "Iz vospominanii o pervoi russkoi revoliutsii," *Katorga i ssylka,* no. 1(74) (1931), pp. 154–62; Druzhinin, pp. 105–8; "Nachal'nik Sar. Okh. ot 24 Okt. 1905. G. Saratov," in Sokolov, pp. 69–76; G. F. Khodakov, pp. 101–12; and Z. S. Petrov, "Oktiabr' 1905 goda," in *1905 god v Saratovskoi gubernii (Po materialam zhandarmskogo upravleniia)* (Saratov, 1925), pp. 57–70.

88 The following sources provide data on the 1905 Saratov soviet: N. D. Demochkin, "Partiia i sovety v 1905 g. Dok. i mat.," *Voprosy istorii KPSS,* no. 2 (1965): 89; G. F. Khodakov, pp. 119–27; Druzhinin, pp. 108–10; *Ist.*

sar. kraia, pp. 192–201; Z. S. Petrov, "Partiia i Sovet rab. dep.," *1905,* pp. 71–102.

89 Soviet authors Gokhlerner and Kharlamova feel that the main centers of the peasant movement in fall of 1905 were Nikolaevskii Gorodok and other places where "the energy, planning, and organization of activities of the revolutionary [peasant] committees were provided by Bolshevik leadership"; V. M. Gokhlerner and K. P. Kharlamova, "Iz istorii krest'ianskikh revoliutsionnykh komitetov v Saratovskoi gubernii v 1905 g.," *Povolzhskii krai,* no. 5 (1977): 119. These and other Soviet authors tend to portray the SDs as supplanting the SRs in the minds of many peasants; G. F. Khodakov claims "significant success . . . of Saratov Bolsheviks in the villages" after which "a sizable portion of the peasants (mainly the poor) began to leave the SRs in favor of the SD-Bolsheviks" (p. 118).

90 N. Maksimov (Rakitnikov), "Iz vospominanii ob Azeve," *Znamia truda,* nos. 21–22 (September 1909): 3.

91 N. Karpov, ed., *krest'ianskoe dvizhenie v revoliutsii 1905 goda v dokumentakh* (Leningrad, 1926), pp. 143–46, 161–62.

92 See V. G. Tan-Bogoraz, "Po gubernii bespokoinoi," in his *Novoe krest'ianstvo* (Moscow, 1905); "Obzor," fond 102,00, op. 5, d. 80, ch. 5 (1905), l. 4; d. 80, ch. 5, l. 17; d. 1800, ch. 29, l. 63.

93 The SR circle in Balashov consisted of Feologov, Gubaev, Raksin, M. Aref'ev, Belynskii, and Taraksin; members of the SD group were Basner, Tverin, Bredin, Il'in, and Veselovskii. See "Obzor," d. 1800, ch. 29, ll. 5–6, 10–11, 52–53, 66–67.

94 Spiridovich, *Partiia,* pp. 220–21; "Obzor," d. 1800, ch. 29, ll. 51, 64, 67; d. 80, ch. 5, 25–27; S. Mazurenko, "S"ezd krest'ian 18 dekabria 1905 g.," *Byloe,* no. 8 (1908): 35–36; and his "Eshche po povodu s"ezda saratovskikh krest'ian 18-go dekabria 1905 g.," *Byloe,* no. 8 (1908): 149–52; E. A. Morokhovets, *Krest'ianskoe dvizhenie i Sotsial-Demokratiia v epokhu pervoi russkoi revoliutsii* (Leningrad and Moscow, 1926), pp. 63–69.

95 *Ist. sar. kraia,* pp. 173–75; G. F. Khodakov, pp. 116–17.

96 Gokhlerner and Kharlamova, p. 89–120; Druzhinin, p. 108; I. Belokurov, *Iz zapisok agrarnika* (Moscow, 1926), pp. 26–80; N. Bazhenov [I. Belokurov], "Kak u nas proizoshlo agrarnoe dvizhenie," *Russkoe bogatstvo,* no. 4 (April 1909): 97–120; no. 5 (March 1909): 92–111; I. Illarionov et al., "Selo Nikolaevskii Gorodok Saratovskoi gubernii v 1905 g.," *PR,* no. 12(47) (1925): 194–203; Aleksandr Studentsov, *Saratovskoe krest'ianskoe vosstanie 1905 goda. Iz vospominanii raz"ezdnogo agitatora* (Penza, 1926).

97 *Ist. sar. kraia,* pp. 164–65, 195–97; Morokhovets, p. 65; Druzhinin, p. 108;

Mazurenko, "Eshche po povodu," p. 151; Gokhlerner and Kharlamova, pp. 117–18; G. F. Khodakov, pp. 100–101, 112, 118–19; Studentsov, pp. 46–47; *KPSS v rezoliutsiiakh i resheniiakh s"ezdov, konferentsii, i plenumov TsK*, pt. 1 (Moscow, 1953), p. 109.

98 Druzhinin, p. 136; Studentsov, p. 1; Derenkovskii, pp. 106, 118; Sokolov, pp. 69–76.

CHAPTER 6

1 Much of this material is summarized in L. N. Blinov, "Narodnyi uchitel' v Rossii," in kn. D. I. Shakhovskoi, ed., *Vseobshchee obrazovanie v Rossii* (Moscow, 1902), pp. 63–84, and V. R. Leikina-Svirskaia, *Intelligentsiia v Rossii vo vtoroi polovine XIX veka* (Moscow, 1971), pp. 158–71. For a recent study, see Ben Eklof, *Russian Peasant Schools: Officialdom, Village Culture and Popular Pedagogy, 1861–1914* (Berkeley, Calif., 1986), chaps. 7 and 8.

2 E. G. Kornilov, "Zemskie uchitelia v revoliutsionnom dvizhenii 70-kh gg. XIX v.," *Uchenye zapiski Moskovskogo gosudarstvennogo pedagogicheskogo instituta im. V. I. Lenina 439* (Moscow, 1971): 132; *Osvobozhdenie*, no. 11 (35), Nov. 12/25, 1903, 194–95; N. M. Pirumova, *Zemskaia intelligentsiia i ee rol' v obshchestvennoi bor'be do nachala XX v.* (Moscow, 1986), chap. 2.

3 See Allen Sinel, "The Campaign for Universal Primary Education in Russia, 1890–1904," *Jahrbücher für Geschichte Osteuropas* 30, no. 4 (1982): 481–507, and B. B. Veselovskii, *Istoriia zemstva za sorok let*, 4 vols. (St. Petersburg, 1909–11), vol. 1.

4 *Trudy mestnykh komitetov o nuzhdakh sel'skokhoziaistvennoi promyshlennosti*, 58 vols. (St. Petersburg, 1903), vol. 37 (Saratov Province), pp. 608, 413–14, 398–99.

5 N. Rakitnikov, "Ocherk istorii narodnago obrazovaniia v Balashovskom u.," *Saratovskaia zemskaia nedelia* [hereafter *SZN*], no. 8, sec. 2 (1902): 25; Veselovskii, *Istoriia*, 4:384–86.

6 K—v, "K voprosu o deiatel'nosti Saratovskago gubernskago zemstva v oblasti narodnago obrazovaniia," *SZN*, no. 10, sec. 2 (1904): 10–12; D., "Nachal'noe narodnoe obrazovanie v Saratovskoi gubernii v 1902 godu," *SZN*, no. 9, sec. 2 (1903): 2–3; Veselovskii, *Istoriia*, 1:569; F. Sviridov, "Vneshkol'noe obrazovanie v Saratovskoi gubernii," *Obrazovanie*, nos. 5–6, sec. 2 (1901): 75–80.

7 *Trudy mestnykh komitetov*, 37:601.

8 Rakitnikov, "Ocherk," p. 37; "Narodnoe obrazovanie na uezdnykh zemskikh sobraniiakh XXXVI sessii 1901 goda," *SZN*, no. 1, sec. 2 (1902): 33–43. By 1903, although there were considerable variations among

districts, Saratov ranked twelfth among zemstvo provinces, with an average salary of 293 rubles: S. Anikin, "Vystavka v Iaroslavle," *SZN,* no. 8, sec. 3 [1903]: 103. Still, the Serdobsk zemstvo in 1903 urged that teachers' salaries at least be brought up to the level of wages of a metalworker. *Russkiia vedomosti,* no. 287, October 19, 1903, p. 2.

9   A. V. Panov, "Voprosy narodnago obrazovaniia na gubernskom zemskom sobranii (pis'mo iz Saratova)," *Obrazovanie,* no. 2, sec. 3 (1902): 34; K—v, "K voprosu," p. 21.

10 *SZN,* nos. 1–16, sec. 3 (1901): 184–85. On the teachers' societies, see V. Ia. Murinov, "Obshchestva vzaimnago vspomoshchestvovaniia uchashchim i uchivshim," in Shakhovskoi, ed., *Vseobshchee obrazovanie,* pp. 85–98.

11 *Saratovskii listok,* no. 112, May 10, 1903, p. 2; *Spravochnaia kniga uchitel'skikh obshchestv vzaimopomoshchi* (Moscow, 1905), pp. 53–54.

12 On the 1897 courses, see appendices to *SZN* (1897), nos. 27–28, pp. 1–13; no. 29, pp. 15–25; no. 32, pp. 27–41. The numbers of teachers attending, many at their own expense, are as follows: 150 in 1897; 250 in 1898; 302 in 1899; 274 in 1900; 248 in 1901: A. S., "Neskol'ko slov o Saratovskikh pedagogicheskikh kursakh gubernskago zemstva," *SZN,* nos. 26–29, sec. 3 (1901): 99–100. Appendix to *SZN,* no. 29 (1897): 1–3; Rakitnikov, "Ocherk," p. 38.

13 Veselovskii, *Istoriia,* 1:506; *SZN,* no. 4, sec. 2 (1901): 103–108; P. Grigor'ev, "Zemskie pedagogicheskie kursy i pravila 1875 goda," *Russkaia shkola,* no. 3 (1903): 135–36.

14 Panov, "Voprosy," pp. 31–33.

15 Val. Denisov, "Znachenie uchitel'skikh kursov po otzyvam zemskikh uchitelei," *Obrazovanie,* no. 7, sec. 2 (1904): 42–47; V. Vakhterov, "Zaprosy narodnykh uchitelei i obshcheobrazovatel'nye kursy," in *Zemskie obshcheobrazovatel'nye kursy dlia uchitelei: sbornik statei* (St. Petersburg, 1906), pp. 37–52. By contrast, in Saratov in 1901, at courses for teachers in church-run schools, there was a heavy emphasis on applied subjects such as agriculture; of a total of 130 lessons, 66 were devoted to singing: F. Ch., "Otgoloski uchitel'skikh s"ezdov, kursov i soveshchanii," *Vestnik vospitaniia,* no. 9, sec. 2 (1901): 88–89.

16 "S"ezd uchitelei Kamyshinskago uezda (Doklad Gub. Zem. Uprave z. m. Predsedatelia Upravy A. D. Iumatova)," *SZN,* nos. 38–41, sec. 2 (1901): 16–28; "S"ezd uchitelei Balashovskago uezda," *SZN,* no. 4, sec. 2 (1903): 1–2, 21–23.

17 A. V. Panov, "Shag vpered: zasedanie uchilishchnoi komissii Saratovskago uezdnago zemstva pri uchastii uchitelei," *Obrazovanie,* no. 12, sec. 2 (1901): 31–42; G. S., "Soveshchanie shkol'noi komissii Saratovskago

uezdnago zemstva s uchiteliami zemskikh shkol," *Vestnik Vladimirskago gub. zemstva*, no. 19 (1901): 15–19.

18 *Zhurnaly uchilishchnoi komissii Saratovskago uezdnago zemstva pri uchastii gg. uchashchikh zemsko-obshchestvennykh uchilishch Saratovskago uezda* (Saratov, 1901); *Spravochnaia kniga po nizshemu obrazovaniiu, God tret'ii (svedeniia za 1905 god)*, comp. S. I. Antsyferov (St. Petersburg, 1908), pt. 2, pp. 261–62; *Dlia narodnago uchitelia*, no. 4 (1909): 29.

19 A. A. Loktin, "Uchitel'skie kursy i s"ezdy," *Vestnik vospitaniia*, no. 6, sec. 2 (1904): 77–78; *Russkiia vedomosti*, no. 183, July 3, 1904, p. 2.

20 Reports of the Saratov delegates can be found in *Trudy I-go vserossiiskago s"ezda predstavitelei obshchestv vspomoshchestvovaniia litsam uchitel'skago zvaniia*, ed. V. M. Evteev, 2 vols. (Moscow, 1907), 1:255–65, 270–73, and 2:665–69, 779–80.

21 TsGIA, f. 733, op. 195, d. 623, l. 124–25; *Saratovskii listok*, no. 111, May 29, 1903, pp. 2–3; no. 112, May 30, 1903, p. 2.

22 Ul'ianov, Anikin, A. A. Bogdanov (a zemstvo employee, former teacher, and SD), and Z. A. Serebriakova (zemstvo employee): TsGAOR, f. 102,00, op. 233 (1905), d. 1800, ch. 29, l. 50b-6, 70b-8, 190b-20.

23 TsGAOR, f. 102,00, op, 233 (1905), d. 1800, ch. 29, l. 48; *Svod vysochaishikh otmetok po vsepoddaneishim otchetam za 1902 g. general-gubernatorov, gubernatorov, voennykh gubernatorov i gradonachal'nikov* (St. Petersburg, 1905), pp. 42–43.

24 "K voprosu o roli narodnykh uchitelei v sotsial'norevoliutsionnom dvizhenii," *Revoliutsionnaia Rossiia*, no. 40, January 15, 1904, p. 7. On the party union, see Scott J. Seregny, "Revolutionary Strategies in the Russian Countryside: Rural Teachers and the Socialist Revolutionary Party on the Eve of 1905," *Russian Review* 44, no. 3 (1985): 221–38.

25 "S"ezd uchitelei Balashovskago uezda," p. 21. In general, see Ben Eklof, "The Village and the Outsider: The Rural Teacher in Russia, 1864–1914," *Slavic and European Education Review*, no. 1 (1979): 1–19.

26 *Obzor nachal'nago narodnago obrazovaniia v Saratovskoi gubernii za 1900–1901 uchebnyi god* (Saratov, 1901), p. 43; *Obzor nachal'nago . . . za 1915–16 uchebnyi god* (Saratov, 1917), p. 54; V. Shcherba, "K voprosu o podgotovke uchitel'skago personala," *SZN*, nos. 6–7, sec. 3 (1903): 2 (includes comparable figures for other provinces).

27 Anikin, "Vystavka," pp. 102–3; D., "Nachal'noe narodnoe obrazovanie," p. 5; *Obzor*, pp. 38–41.

28 N. Lozanov, "Ob otkrytii uchitel'skoi seminarii v gor. Saratove," *SZN*, no. 2, sec. 3 (1903): 53–54; Vas. Golubev, "Polozhenie narodnago obrazovaniia v Saratovskoi gubernii (po otzyvam mestnykh zhitelei)," *SZN*, no. 2, sec. 3 (1902): 167.

29 S. Anikin, "O material'noi i iuridicheskoi neobezpechennosti russkago narodnago uchitelia," in *Trudy I-go vserossiiskago s"ezda,* 1:257; I. P. Belokonskii, "Obzor deiatel'nosti zemstv po narodnomu obrazovaniiu za 1902 g.," *Russkaia shkola,* no. 2 (1903): 163. N. V. Tulupov, "Kurskaia vystavka po narodnomu obrazovaniiu," *Russkaia mysl',* no. 8, sec. 2 (1902): 117; *Obzor,* p. 56.

30 A. Bagil'dinskii, "Iz Atkarska," *SZN,* nos. 6–7, sec. 2 (1905): 33–38; A. Ivashkin, "Iz vospominanii o narodnykh uchiteliakh," *SZN,* no. 2, sec. 3 (1905): 42; A. L., "Vnutrennaia khronika," *Zhurnal dlia vsekh,* no. 5 (1904): 317.

31 TsGIA, f. 733, op. 173, d. 127, l. 130b–14.

32 *Obzor,* p. 57.

33 V. Serebriakov, "Sovremennoe sostoianie russkoi derevni i eia nuzhdy po otzyvam sel'skikh zhitelei," *SZN,* nos. 10–12, sec. 3 (1905): 6; "S"ezd uchitelei Balashovskago uezda," p. 16; *Saratovskii dnevnik,* no. 112, June 4, 1905, p. 2; *Saratovskii listok,* no. 189, September 17, 1905, p. 3.

34 *Saratovskii listok,* no. 184, September 10, 1905, p. 3; no. 194, September 23, 1905, p. 3; at least one-third of zemstvo schools in Saratov in 1901 turned children away: A. V. Panov, "Nachal'noe narodnoe obrazovanie v Saratovskoi gubernii, "*Obrazovanie,* nos. 7–8, sec. 2 (1901): 111. Another problem was late scheduling of exams by members of the school board, without consulting teachers, after most pupils had been pulled out of school for field work. *Saratovskii listok,* no. 120, June 18, 1905, p. 3.

35 Ivashkin, "Iz vospominanii," p. 44; Serebriakov, "Sovremennoe sostoianie," p. 7.

36 Compare the success of French teachers in acquiring such status: Barnett Singer, "The Teacher as Notable in Brittany, 1880–1914," *French Historical Studies* 9 (1976): 635–59, and Eugen Weber, *Peasants into Frenchmen* (Stanford, 1976), pp. 317–18.

37 Golubev, "Polozhenie narodnago obrazovaniia," pp. 168–73.

38 Serebriakov, "Sovremennoe sostoianie," pp. 5, 27–30; Teodor Shanin, *The Awkward Class: Political Sociology of Peasantry in a Developing Society: Russia, 1910–1925* (Oxford, 1972), p. 178.

39 Veselovskii, *Istoriia,* 4:385; "Voprosy narodnago obrazovaniia na XXXVI ocherednom Gubernskom Zemskom Sobranii," *SZN,* no. 2, sec. 2 (1902): 11–18.

40 *Privolzhskii krai,* no. 31, February 13, 1905, p. 2; no. 187, September 19, 1905, p. 2; *Volzhskii vestnik,* no. 13, November 23, 1905, p. 4; no. 35, December 20, 1905, p. 4.

41 Pirumova, *Zemskaia intelligentsiia,* pp. 190–93.

42 Serebriakov, "Sovremennoe sostoianie," p. 7.

43 *Russkiia vedomosti,* no. 287, October 19, 1903, p. 2; *Saratovskii dnevnik,* no. 217 (1904), cited in Ivashkin, "Iz vospominanii," pp. 52–53; Prokhozhii, "Ustranenie zemskago rabotnika, Saratov," *Osvobozhdenie,* no. 24 (48), May 21/June 3, 1904, pp. 439–40; *Revoliutsionnaia Rossiia,* no. 43, March 15, pp. 22, 24; no. 44, April 1, pp. 20–21; no. 45, April 15, 1904, p. 14.

44 TsGIA, f. 733, op. 201, d. 43, 1. 41; TsGAOR, f. 102,00, p. 233 (1905), d. 1800, ch. 29, 1. 70b-8 and f. 63, op. 12, d. 1304 (1903), 1. 1140b; *Russkoe bogatstvo,* no. 11, sec. 2 (1904): 174–78. The district zemstvo voted to continue issuing salaries and petitioned Governor Stolypin for their reinstatement. On Anikin, see Scott J. Seregny, "Politics and the Rural Intelligentsia in Russia: A Biographical Sketch of Stepan Anikin, 1869–1919," *Russian History* 7, pts. 1–2 (1980): 176–77.

45 See *Obzor,* pp. 6–7; *Osvobozhdenie,* no. 24 (48), May 21/June 3, 1904, p. 439.

46 Peasant expectations about the war may have played a role. Anikin notes that among peasants in Saratov Province was widespread the notion that victory over Japan would result in a favorable solution to the land question; thus peasants may have been receptive to simple explanations for Russia's military reversals which provided targets for their frustration. S. Anikin, "Za 'pravednoi zemlei' (pamiati I. M. Igoshina)," *Vestnik Evropy,* no. 3 (1910), p. 96.

47 *Pravo,* no. 11, March 20, 1905, cols. 824–25, and especially the zemstvo's report on these events in "Polozhenie zemstva Saratovskoi gubernii," *Russkiia vedomosti,* no. 91, April 4, 1905, p. 3; see also Voskresenskii, "Narodnoe obrazovanie na uezdnykh zemskikh sobraniiakh sessii 1905 goda," *SZN,* nos. 10–12, sec. 2 (1905): 41–42; *Pravo,* no. 12, March 27, 1905, cols. 946–47; no. 14, April 12, 1905, col. 1144; Ivashkin, "Iz vospominanii," p. 53; *Privolzhskii krai,* no. 35, February 15, 1905, p. 2.

48 I. Nikolaev, "Povtoritel'nye zaniatiia so vzroslymi," *SZN,* nos. 6–7, sec. 2 (1904): 35–67; Panov, "Voprosy," pp. 35–37; K—v, "K voprosu," pp. 13, 21–22; "Polozhenie zemstva Saratovskoi gubernii," p. 3; "Iz khroniki zemskikh shkol v Saratovskoi gub.," *SZN,* no. 2, sec. 2 (1905): 23–26.

49 *Pravo,* no. 28, July 17, 1905, cols. 2329–30; *Zhurnaly ekstrennago Saratovskago Gubernskago Zemskago sobraniia 15–20 marta 1905 goda* (Saratov, 1905), pp. 114–18; "Polozhenie zemstva Saratovskoi gubernii," p. 3.

50 "Iz khroniki zemskikh shkol," pp. 24–25; *Russkiia vedomosti,* no. 76, March 20, 1905, p. 3; *Pravo,* no. 12, March 27, 1905, col. 946.

51 *Pravo,* no. 11, March 20, 1905, cols. 852–53; *Russkiia vedomosti,* no. 63, March 7, 1905, p. 2. School officials sent a similar warning at the start of the new school year: *Saratovskii listok,* no. 194, September 23, 1905, p. 2.

52 On the Banquet Campaign, see Seregny,"Politics and the Rural Intel-

ligentsia," p. 177–78; *Russkiia vedomosti,* no. 278, October 23, 1905, p. 4, and the chapters by Thomas Fallows and Michael Melancon in this volume. On literacy, see Anikin, "Vystavka," pp. 99, 101; V. Golubev, "Narodnoe obrazovanie v Saratovskoi gubernii," appendix to *SZN,* nos. 11–12 (1902): 5–6; Panov, "Nachal'noe narodnoe obrazovanie," pp. 107–108.

53 *Iskra,* no. 94, March 25, 1905, p. 4; N. Sokolov, "Kratkii ocherk istorii Vserossiiskago soiuza uchitelei i deiatelei po narodnomu obrazovaniiu," *Vestnik soiuza uchitelei i deiatelei po narodnomu obrazovaniiu,* no. 2 (1905): 3.

54 TsGAOR, f. 102,00, op. 5, d. 80, l. 4–5; *Saratovskii dnevnik,* no. 80, April 16, 1906, p. 2.

55 TsGIA; f. 733, op. 173, d. 56, l. 205–205ob.

56 TsGAOR, f. 102,00 (1905), d. 999, ch. 1, tom I, l. 214–214ob; *Saratovskii dnevnik,* no. 108, May 31, 1905, p. 2; no. 110, June 2, 1905, p. 2; *Saratovskii listok,* no. 107, June 2, 1905, p. 2; TsGIA, f. 733, op. 173, d. 56, l. 206.

57 Anikin had attended a conference in April (Moscow) where he was delegated to organize a section of the union in Saratov: TsGAOR, f. 63, op. 14, d. 787, l. 33–34. For a complete account of the union, see Scott J. Seregny, *Russian Teachers and Peasant Revolution: The Politics of Education in 1905* (Bloomington, Ind., 1989).

58 TsGIA, f. 733, op. 173, d. 56, l. 1980b–2020b.

59 *Russkiia vedomosti,* no. 259, September 23, 1905, p. 3; *Pravo,* no. 29, July 24, 1905, col. 2400; TsGIA, f. 733, op. 173, d. 56, l. 2020b.

60 TsGAOR, f. 102,00 (1905), d. 999, ch. 1. tom I, l. 1570b.

61 *Russkiia vedomosti,* no. 278, October 23, 1905, p. 4; TsGAOR, f. 6862, op. 1, d. 54, l. 125–280b.

62 TsGIA, f. 733, op. 173, d. 56, l. 208–2080b. The Balashov teachers decided to join the Teachers' Union.

63 *Spravochnaia kniga po nizshemu obrazovaniiu,* pp. 261–62, 282–82; *Privolzhskii krai,* no. 187, September 16, 1905, p. 2; *Saratovskii listok,* no. 189, September 17, 1905, p. 3.

64 *Saratovskii listok,* no. 187, September 14, 1905, pp. 2–3; Saratovskoe uezdnoe zemstvo, *Zhurnaly ocherednogo chrezvychainago Saratovskago uezdnago zemskago sobraniia v 1907 godu* (Saratov, 1908), pp. 19–25.

65 M. N., "Derevenskiia zametki," *Saratovskii listok,* no. 176, August 31, 1905, p. 2; *Saratovskii dnevnik,* no. 42, February 23, 1906, p. 2; *Russkiia vedomosti,* no. 33, February 7, 1905, p. 2.

66 E. D. Chermenskii, *Burzhuaziia i tsarizm v pervoi russkoi revoliutsii,* 2d ed. (Moscow, 1970), pp. 57, 60–61; K. V. Sivkov, "Krest'ianskie prigovory 1905 goda," *Russkaia mysl',* no. 4, sec. 2 (1907): pp. 24–48.

67 *Russkiia vedomosti,* no. 76, March 21, 1905, p. 3; M. A. Vodolagin, *Ocherki istorii Volgograda, 1589–1967* (Moscow, 1968), pp. 145–46.

68 *Russkiia vedomosti,* no. 190, July 16, 1905, p. 2; no. 202, July 28, 1905, p. 3. A Ministry of Interior circular of April 15, 1905, specifically ruled out participation by persons not legally members of the commune.

69 TsGAOR, f. 102,00, op. 5, d. 80, l. 1–30b; *Agrarnoe dvizhenie v Rossii v 1905–1906 gg. (Trudy Imperatorskago Vol'nago Ekonomicheskago Obshchestva),* 2 vols. (St. Petersburg, 1908), 1:131; TsGAOR, f. 518, op. 1, d. 76, l. 299–2990b; d. 77, l. 48–490b; *Pravo,* no. 21, May 29, 1905, col. 1766; *Severnyi krai,* no. 133, May 25, 1905, p. 1. Twenty-two peasants were also arrested in this affair.

70 The best general treatment is E. I. Kiriukhina, "Vserossiiskii Krest'-ianskii Soiuz v 1905 g.," *Istoricheskie zapiski* 50 (1955): 95–141, and "Mestnye organizatsii Vserossiiskogo Krest'ianskogo Soiuza v 1905 godu," *Uchenye zapiski Kirovskogo pedagogicheskogo instituta* 10 (1956): 83–157.

71 *Protokoly vtorogo delegatskago s"ezda Vserossiiskago soiuza uchitelei i deiatelei po narodnomu obrazovaniiu, 26–29 dekabria, 1905 goda* (St. Petersburg, 1906), p.34. On the union movement in Saratov, see Seregny, "Politics and the Rural Intelligentsia," pp. 180–85, and Timothy Mixter's chapter.

72 *Saratovskii dnevnik,* no. 41, February 22, 1906, p. 4; M. I. Semenov, "1905 god v Saratovskoi gubernii: vospominaniia," *Proletarskaia revoliutsiia,* no. 3 (1926): 210–12, 216–17; *Russkiia vedomosti,* no. 248, October 25, 1908, p. 5, and no. 250, October 28, 1908, p. 6 (trial of Saratov peasant union); *Saratovskii dnevnik,* no. 48, March 2, 1906, p. 4; *Severnye otkliki,* no. 17, May 20, 1906, p. 4. The peasant union was also endorsed by the Saratov Union of Medical Personnel (*Russkii vrach,* no. 49 [1905]: 1553).

73 *Saratovskii dnevnik,* no. 14, January 19, 1906, p. 3.

74 Ibid., no. 70, March 29, 1906, p. 3.

75 Ibid., no. 61, March 17, 1906, p. 3; no. 74, April 4, 1906, p. 2; no. 44, February 25, 1906, p. 3 (Balashov); *Russkiia vedomosti,* no. 271, October 15, 1905, p. 2 (Atkarsk). The third teacher-deputy was P. V. Kalianov, who was from Kamyshin and active in the peasant union: *Saratovskii dnevnik,* no. 80, April 16, 1906, p. 2.

76 *Saratovskii dnevnik,* no. 230, November 16, 1905, p. 3; no. 23, January 29, 1906, p. 4; no. 32, February 10, 1906, p. 3; no. 70, March 29, 1906, p. 2; *Russkiia vedomosti,* no. 308, November 23, 1905, p. 2; N. Karpov, ed., *Krest'ianskoe dvizhenie v revoliutsii 1905 goda v dokumentakh* (Leningrad, 1926), pp. 258–59; I. P. Shmygin, *Bol'shevistskie organizatsii Srednego Povolzh'ia v bor'be za krest'ianskie massy v revoliutsii 1905–1907 gg.* (Ul'ianovsk, 1962), pp. 173–75.

77 TsGIA, f. 733, op. 201, d. 43, l. 41, 43–44, 51–510b, 58; see also *Kalendar'-*

spravochnik 1908/9 uchebnyi god, "Narodnyi uchitel'," comp. O. N. Smirnov
(Kiev, 1908), p. 206. Some estimates place the total number of repressed
teachers in the empire at twenty thousand.

78 *Saratovskii dnevnik*, no. 36, February 15, 1906, pp. 3–4; no. 69, March 28,
1906, p. 3 (communal petition on behalf of I. Nesudimov, also chosen
from his volost in Petrovsk as a Duma elector); on Plan, see *Saratovskii
dnevnik*, no. 41, February 22, 1906, p. 4, and *Privolzhskii krai*, no. 178,
August 22, 1906, p. 2 (thanks to Tim Mixter for this last citation).

79 *Kliazma*, no. 96, April 17, 1906, p. 3 (Atkarsk); *Russkii vrach*, no. 10, 1906,
p. 314: *Saratovskii dnevnik*, no. 70, March 29, 1906, p. 2 (Saratov provincial
zemstvo assembly resolution against employee participation in political
unions); no. 4, January 5, 1906, p. 3; no. 21, January 23, 1906, p. 3. On
teachers' associations after 1905, see P. Zhulev, "Uchitel'skie obshchestva
vzaimopomoshchi," *Russkaia shkola*, no. 1 (1912): 1–20; *Russkaia shkola*, nos.
7–8, sec. 2 (1911): 126; E. Zviagintsev, "Letnye uchitel'skie kursy," *Vestnik
vospitaniia*, no. 1 (1912): 115–17.

80 J. A. Jackson, "Professions and Professionalization—Editorial Introduction," in Jackson, ed., *Professions and Professionalization* (Cambridge, 1970),
p. 14.

CHAPTER 7

1 Ministerstvo gosudarstvennykh imushchestv, *Statisticheskii obzor gosudarstvennykh imushchestv za 1858 god* (St. Petersburg, 1861), pp. 646–47. For
more details on the early life of the settlers, see chapter 2 above (Hart).

2 Tsentral'nyi statisticheskii komitet, *Pervaia vseobshchaia perepis' naseleniia
Rossiiskoi Imperii, 1897 g.* (St. Petersburg, 1904), 38:225.

3 Flegont V. Dukhovnikov, "Nemtsy, drugie inostrantsy i prishlye liudi v
Saratove," *Saratovskii krai*, no. 1 (1893), 239–39. Tsentral'nyi statisticheskii
komitet, *Spiski naselennykh mest Rossiiskoi Imperii* (St. Petersburg, 1862),
38:XI. Winfred Kohls, "Beitrag zur Geschichte der deutschen Kolonisten
in Russland, eine Untersuchung russische Pressepolemik und der
deutschen diplomatischen Berichte aus der St. Petersburger Amtszeit des
Botschafters von Schweinitz," in *Archivalische Fundstücke zu den russisch-
deutschen Beziehungen*, ed. Erich Amburger (Berlin, 1973), pp. 152–57.

4 *Saratovskiia gubernskiia vedomosti*, November 16, 1895, p. 1.

5 For a detailed account of the zemstvo reform and its impact on the Volga
Germans, see James W. Long, "The Volga Germans and the Zemstvos,
1865–1917," *Jahrbücher für Geschichte Osteuropas* 30, no. 3 (1982): 336–61.

6 A. Klaus, "O zaniatiiakh komissii," *Pravitel'stvennyi vestnik*, January 20,
1870, pp. 1–4.

7   The law of June 4, 1871, is found in *Polnoe sobranie zakonov Rossiiskoi Imperii,* Sobranie vtoroe, 46, art. 49705.

8   Two former colonists gave the Saratov Office high praise for its able leadership of the colonies. A. A. Klaus, "Obshchina-sobstvennik i eia iuridicheskaia organizatsiia," *Vestnik Evropy,* no. 2 (March 1870): 82. Also, Gerhard Bonwetsch, *Geschichte der deutschen Kolonien an der Wolga* (Stuttgart, 1919), p. 49.

9   Konstantin I. Popov, "Zapiski o Saratove K. I. Popova," *Saratovskii krai,* no. 1 (1893): 168. In 1845 the provincial governor, A. M. Fadeev, wrote, "In short, then, it was very difficult to find a capable but honest bureaucrat." "Vospominaniia A. M. Fadeeva," *Russkii arkhiv,* no. 5 (1891): 49.

10 The best work on the reform and the state peasants is Nikolai M. Druzhinin, *Gosudarstvennye krest'iane i reforma P. D. Kiseleva,* 2 vols. (Moscow-Leningrad, 1946, 1958).

11 Saratovskii gubernskii statisticheskii komitet, *Pamiatnaia knizhka Saratovskoi Gubernii na 1872 god* (Saratov, 1873), vol. 2, pt. 2, pp. 154–55.

12 Ibid.

13 Thomas S. Pearson, "The Origins of Alexander III's Land Captains: A Reinterpretation," *Slavic Review* 40, no. 3 (Fall 1981): 384–403. George L. Yaney, *The Systematization of Russian Government* (Urbana, Ill., 1973), pp. 368–71. The traditional view of the land captains as a gentry-initiated reactionary measure is ably presented in P. A. Zaionchkovskii, *Rossiiskoe samoderzhavie v kontse XIX stoletiia* (Moscow, 1970), pp. 398–405.

14 *Privolzhskii krai,* March 15, 1906, p. 2.

15 Max Praetorius, *Galka eine deutsche Ansiedlung an der Wolga* (Leipzig, 1912), pp. 44–61.

16 *Saratovskii dnevnik,* September 23, 1905, p. 3; *Privolzhskaia gazeta,* June 3, 1906, p. 3; and *Saratovskii vestnik,* May 21, 1917, p. 5.

17 *Privolzhskii krai,* October 12, 1904, p. 2.

18 *Saratovskii dnevnik,* December 21, 1906, p. 4.

19 Ia. Ditts, "Putevyia zametki," *Privolzhskaia gazeta,* February 25, 1906, p. 2.

20 Jacob Wagele, "Feuilleton," *Saratowsche deutsche Zeitung,* February 19, 1865, pp. 257–58.

21 For details of this interesting development, see James W. Long, *From Privileged to Dispossessed: The Volga Germans, 1860–1917* (Lincoln, Neb., 1988).

22 P. Luppov, *Nemetskiia nachal'nyia shkoly v Rossii* (Petrograd, 1916), pp. 10–33; A. Gorodetskii, "Nemetskiia shkoly," *Kamyshinskii ezhenedel'nik,* February 5, 1906, p. 2; and G. U., *Nemetskiia tserkovno-prikhodskiia uchilishcha v Kamyshinskom Uezde* (Saratov, n.d.), pp. 2–4. The struggle between the supporters of secular and those of religious educa-

tion was not confined to the colonies, but, as indicated in Scott Seregny's chapter, became acute throughout Russia during the last two decades of the nineteenth century.

23 Provisions of this law can be found in *Svod zakonov Rossiiskoi Imperii (izdaniia 1902),* vol. 9, "Osoboe prilozhenie k zakonam o sostoianiikh, polozheniia o sel'skom sostoianii," p. 1326. The government enforced mandatory Russian-language instruction on the Volga Germans later than on other poeples; in 1875, Russian-language instruction was introduced in the Lutheran parish schools in the Baltic provinces; the government imposed it on the Armenians in 1884, the Poles in 1885, and the Baltic peoples in 1887.

24 Peter Sinner, *Nemtsy nizhnego povolzh'ia* (Saratov, 1925), p.12.

25 G. U., *Nemetskiia tserkovno-prikhodskiia uchilishcha,* p. 1.

26 A. Leopol'dov, "O saratovskikh i samarskikh kolonistakh," *Severnaia pchela,* March 7, 1860, p. 212. In 1863 Leopol'dov expressed essentially the same ideas in "Neskol'ko slov o kolonistakh," *Volga,* December 18, 1863, p. 554. Aleksandr Leongard, "Golos iz Saksonii za saratovskikh i samarskikh kolonistvo,' *Severnaia pchela,* May 2, 1860, p. 395.

27 *Saratovskiia gubernskiia vedomosti,* November 17, 1874, p. 2.

28 Ibid., December 8, 1874, pp. 2–3, and December 14, 1874, p. 2.

29 N. A., "K voprosu o nemetskikh shkolakh," *Privolzhskaia zhizn',* October 14, 1910, p. 1. A colonist in his memoirs stated that military conscription was the greatest stimulus to learn Russian. Peter K. Haller, *Vospominaniia P. K. Gallera* (Saratov, 1927), p. 65.

30 Transcript of oral history interview of Gus Lebsack, p. 1. This oral history, as well as many others, is available in the Special Collections of Morgan Library at Colorado State University. Oral history interviews were conducted by the staff of the CSU Germans from Russia in Colorado Project. Eduard Seib, "Der Wolgadeutsche im Spiegel seines Brauchtums," *Heimatbuch der Deutschen aus Russland* (1967/68), p. 153.

31 Georg Lobsack, *Einsam Kampft das Wolgaland* (Leipzig, 1936), p. 116.

32 Saratovskoe gubernskoe zemstvo, *Sbornik statisticheskikh svedenii po Saratovskoi gubernii* (Saratov, 1891), II:57–58.

33 Francis S. Laing, "German-Russian Settlements in Ellis County, Kansas," *Collections of the Kansas State Historical Society, 1909–1910* 11 (1910): 502. Other reports that the initial glowing reports of America in the Volga German settlements had been replaced by more realistic accounts of hard times and rough frontier life in an alien land can be found in Saratovskoe gubernskoe zemstvo, *Sbornik statisticheskikh svedenii,* II:58.

34 A. N. Pavlov, "Pochemu nashi nemtsy pereseliaiutsia v Ameriku," *Saratovskii spravochnyi listok,* December 23, 1877, p. 2.

35 Data on Volga German military service has been drawn from many diverse sources, but the following two published annual statistics were most useful. Ministerstvo vnutrennikh del, *Sbornik pravitel'stvennykh rasporiazhenii po voinskoi povinnosti*, vols. 3–6 (1874–77), p. 52, in the appendix of each volume. Saratovskii gubernskii statisticheskii komitet, *Statisticheskii obzor Saratovskoi Gubernii za* [1895–1911], list 10 on pp. 7–8 of each volume.

36 Although we have no reliable statistics of this emigration, oral history interviewees repeatedly mentioned the fear of mobilization, not conscription, as the main reason for leaving Russia. (See, for example, transcript of oral interview of Philip Legler, p. 5.) For a more general discussion of the inequities and social impact of the mobilization during the Russo-Japanese War, see Allan Wildman, *The End of the Russian Imperial Army* (Princeton, N.J., 1980), pp. 27–45.

37 Saratovskoe gubernskoe zemstvo, *Sbornik svedenii po Saratovskoi gubernii za 1905 god* (Saratov, 1905), vol. 2, pt. 2, pp. 75–110; *Privolzhskii krai*, July 29, 1905, p. 2.

38 Transcript of oral history interview of Amalie Klein, p. 33.

39 Transcript of oral history interview of Fred Ostwald, p. 8.

40 Saratovskoe gubernskoe zemstvo, *Sbornik statisticheskikh svedenii po Saratovskoi Gubernii* (Saratov, 1891), 11:116; Saratovskoe gubernskoe zemstvo, *Materialy dlia otsenki zemel' Saratovskoi Gubernii* (Saratov, 1905), 1:131; Tsentral'nyi statisticheskii komitet M.V.D., *Statistika zemlevladeniia 1905 g.* (St. Petersburg, 1906), 2:46–47.

41 Kamyshinskoe uezdnoe zemskoe sobranie, "Doklad A. M. Loginova," *Postanovleniia Kamyshinskogo Uezdnogo Zemskogo Sobraniia*, February 28, 1903, p. 2.

42 *Saratovskii dnevnik*, May 9, 1905, p. 2.

43 Saratovskoe gubernskoe zemstvo, *Sbornik svedenii po Saratovskoi gubernii za 1905 god* (Saratov, 1905), 2:41–42.

44 Ia. Ditts, "Otnoshenii nashikh nemtsev k Gosudarstvennoi Dume," *Privolzhskaia gazeta*, March 14, 1906, p. 2.

45 Ia. Ditts, "Putevyia zametki," *Kamyshinskii vestnik*, January 1, 1906, p. 3.

46 Kamyshinskoe uezdnoe zemstvo, *Postanovleniia Kamyshinskago Uezdnago Ocherednago Zemskago Sobraniia* 4 (1907): 2–3; and K. Dumler, "O nemetskikh shkolakh," *Saratovskii listok*, August 13, 1905, p. 3. The complexity and divisiveness of the school issue in the colonies was cogently expressed by Pastor Seib in two lead newspaper articles. See *Unsere Zeit*, March 16, 1906, p. 1, and March 22, 1906, p. 2.

47 *Agrarnoe dvizhenie v Rossii v 1905–06 gg. (Trudy Imperatorskago Vol'nago Obshchestva)*, 2 vols. (St. Petersburg, 1908), 1:162.

48 Post-1905 Volga German developments are examined in Long, *From Privileged to Dispossessed.*

CHAPTER 8

1 Although there are many works on Stolypin's activities as prime minister, including books by Conroy, Manning, Diakin, Hosking, Avrekh, and others, there is little on his provincial experience. Besides the one source specifically on this topic (Maria Bock, "Stolypin in Saratov," *Russian Review* 12, no. 3 [July 1953]: 187–93), the only available accounts of Stolypin's provincial experience are the relevant chapters in the memoir by Maria Bok, *Vospominaniia o moem ottse P. A. Stolypine* (New York, 1953) and the biography by Mary Schaeffer Conroy, *Petr Arkad'evich Stolypin: Practical Politics in Late Tsarist Russia* (Boulder, Colo., 1976), pp. 7–17.

2 TsGAOR, f. 102, op. 5, ed. 2587, ll. 1, 3–5; ibid., op. 5, ed. kh. 1587, l. 21; TsGIA, f. 1405, op. 15, ed. 8019, l. 5; and Thomas Fallows, "Forging the Zemstvo Movement: Liberalism and Radicalism on the Volga, 1890–1905" (Ph.D. diss., Harvard University, 1981), p. 764–74.

3 Bok, *Vospominaniia o moem ottse,* p. 137.

4 Ibid., pp. 139–40.

5 Stolypin must have departed from Saratov no later than late August 1905, for he was already in Kolnoberzhe when news arrived of the Portsmouth peace in early September (ibid., p. 145). Along with his family ties to Kolnoberzhe, Stolypin also had close ties with landed Saratov society. In the words of his daughter, "we, too, belonged to the gentry of Saratov" (ibid., p. 118). The governor owned land in both Volsk and Saratov districts (he sold his Saratov land in 1901), and he had an older brother, Dmitrii A. Stolypin, who from 1881 to 1893 served as a zemstvo deputy in both the Volsk district and the Saratov provincial zemstvo assembly. (This information comes from the property lists of the first and second curia citizens entitled to vote in Saratov zemstvo elections, *Saratovskiia gubernskiia vedomosti,* 1880–1906.)

6 Saratovskoe gubernskoe zemstvo, *Sbornik svedenii po Saratovskoi gubernii za 1904 god,* 2 vols. (Saratov, 1905), 1:128–31. A list of the soldiers from Saratov who were wounded or killed during the war shows that the greatest military recruiting was done among peasants in Serdobsk, Balashov, and Atkarsk districts, which also proved to be the centers of rural unrest in 1905–06. *Saratovskiia gubernskiia vedomosti,* January 5, 1906, pp. 1–2, and January 26, 1906, p. 3.

7 Saratovskoe gubernskoe zemstvo, *Zhurnaly . . . sessii 28–29 maia 1904 goda*

(Saratov, 1904), pp. 19–20, 57–64; and ibid., *Zhurnaly ekstrennago . . . 26 avgusta 1904 goda* (Saratov, 1904), pp. 1–14.

8 Bok, *Vospominaniia o moem ottse,* pp. 140–43.

9 Institut Russkoi literatury (Pushkinskii Dom), f. 334, n. 651, l. 41; Gosudarstvennyi Istoricheskii Muzei [hereafter GIM], f. 31, ed. 142, ll. 170, 173, 228, 234, 238, 253. Nikolai L'vov played a major part in tying together the national and local constitutionalist movements, for he was among the first to speak out openly in the province against the regime (in his public criticism of Sviatopolk-Mirskii at the Balashov District Zemstvo Assembly in October); yet he was also Saratov's leading representative in organizing the nationwide Zemstvo Conference of November 6–7 in St. Petersburg and helped draft (in November 1904) the text of the "Fundamental Law" that served as the liberals' primary document on political reform throughout 1905. See Balashovskoe uezdnoe zemstvo, *Zhurnaly XXXIX ocherednogo . . . 1904 goda* (Balashov, 1905), pp. 17–24; TsGAOR, f. 102, IV DP, op. 5, ed. kh. 1350, chast' 20, 1905 g., ll. 1–2.; ibid., f. 63, op. 13, ed. 741, 1904 g., l. 169; ibid., f. 102, DP. OO, op. 1904, ed. kh. 1000, chast' 1, ll. 44–46, 78–80, 162, and chast' 2, ll. 1–7; F. Kokoshkin, "Raboty zemskikh s"ezdov i 'Russkiia vedomosti,'" *Russkiia Vedomosti 1863–1913. Sbornik statei* (St. Petersburg, 1914), p. 91; and *Chastnoe soveshchanie zemskikh deiatelei proiskhodivshee 6, 7, 8 i 9 noiabria 1904 goda v S-Peterburge* (Moscow, 1905), pp. 69–71, 78–79.

10 Terence Emmons, "Russia's Banquet Campaign," *California Slavic Studies* 10 (1977): 84.

11 TsGAOR, f. 102, no. 1250, 1905 g. ll. 56–57, 66–67, 9, 213–14; idem, f. 102, IV DP., op. 5, ed. kh. 1350, chast' 20, 1905 g., ll. 7–11, 69–80; G. M. Derenkovskii, I. M. Raschetnova, and M. S. Simonova, "1905 god v Saratove," *Istoricheskie zapiski* 54 (1955): 82; N. M. Druzhinin, "V Saratove v 1905 g. (Vospominaniia)," *Povolzhskii krai,* no. 5 (1977): 72; and Jonathan Sanders, "Lessons from the Periphery: Saratov, January 1905," *Slavic Review* 46, no. 2 (Summer 1987): 232–33.

12 On the Banquet Campaign in Saratov see TsGAOR, f. 102, op. 1904, ed. 1000, t. 1, ll. 65–66, 71–72, 90, 93–96, 213–14, 281–85; ibid., no. 1250, chast' 2, ll. 52–53, 91, 171–73; L-ii [I. M. Liakhovetskii] "Banketnaia kampaniia v Saratove (1904–1905)," *Minuvshie gody* 12 (December 1908): 29–62; Emmons, "Russia's Banquet Campaign," p. 62; Scott J. Seregny, "Politics and the Rural Intelligentsia in Russia: A Biographical Sketch of Stepan Anikin," *Russian History* 7, pts. 1–2 (1980): 169–200; and Reginald E. Zelnik, "Russian Bebels: An Introduction to the Memoirs of Semen Kanatchikov and Matvei Fisher," *Russian Review* 25, no. 3 (July 1976): 249–89, and 25, no. 4 (October 1976): 436–37.

13 D. I. Shakhovskoi, "Soiuz osvobozhdeniia," *Zarnitsy,* no. 2 (1909): 142; and Roberta T. Manning, *The Crisis of the Old Order in Russia: Gentry and Government* (Princeton, N. J., 1982), pp. 83, 427.

14 The petitions were (1) "from the workers of Saratov" (appealing for civil liberties, political amnesty, and a constituent assembly elected on the basis of four-tail suffrage), signed by 975 people; (2) an address from "the taxpayers of zemstvo duties and other residents of the city of Saratov and Saratov Province" (expressing solidarity with the zemstvo and exhorting it to live up to its great national destiny, for "a hundred thousand eyes are upon you and the fate of millions depends on your decisive voice"), signed by 2,393 people; (3) an appeal from the Pedagogical society (for educational reform), signed by 592 teachers; and (4) an address by a group of Saratov women (endorsing the St. Petersburg All-Zemstvo Congress and calling on the Saratov zemstvo to uphold its moral duty), signed by 600 women. See Saratovskoe gubernskoe zemstvo, *Protokol ot 9, 10 i 11-go ianvaria 1905 g. komissii, izbrannoi Gubernskim Zemskim Sobraniem po povodu tekushchikh sobytii politicheskago kharaktera* (Saratov, 1905), pp. 1–4 passim; and TsGAOR, f. 102, IV DP., op. 5, ed. kh. 1350, 1905 g., chast' 20, l. 14.

15 TsGAOR, f. 102, chast' 3, l. 52; and ibid., f. 102, IV DP., op. 5, ed. kh. 1350, chast' 20, 1905 g., l. 14.

16 *Protokol,* pp. 32, 39–40, 44.

17 TsGAOR, f. 102, chast' 2, ll. 89–90, 171–73, 212, 223; and chast' 3, ll. 50–57.

18 TsGAOR, f. 102, IV DP., ed. kh. 1350. chast' 20. 1905 g., ll. 7–18; L. K. Erman, *Intelligentsiia v pervoi russkoi revoliutsii* (Moscow, 1966), pp. 62–63, 66; Derenkovskii, Raschetnova, and Simonova, "1905 god v Saratove," pp. 74–80; and I. M. Pushkareva, *Zheleznodorozhniki Rossii v burzhuazno-demokraticheskikh revoliutsiiakh* (Moscow, 1975) pp. 92–93, 105. An incisive analysis of the railway strike is presented in Sanders, "Lessons from the Periphery," pp. 229–44.

19 TsGAOR, f. 102, no. 1250, chast' 2, ll. 286–87.

20 Ibid., IV DP., no. 2425, chast' 5, 1905 g., ll. 15–16.

21 Ibid., op. 5, ed. kh. 1350, chast' 20, 1905 g., ll. 7–9.

22 Ibid., ll. 3–4, 7, 13, 14; ibid., no. 2425, chast' 5, 1905 g., ll. 17, 22; ibid., no. 1250, chast' 1, l. 18, 97; chast' 2, l. 9.

23 In the meantime, Nessel'rode had fled to Paris to escape further prosecution for his role in the zemstvo assembly meeting of mid-January and did not return until the summer of 1905. TsGAOR, f. 102, IV DP., ed. kh. 1350, chast' 20, 1905 g., ll. 17, 28, 35–36.

24 TsGAOR, f. 102, DP. OO, op. 1904, ed. kh. 1000, chast' 1, l. 91; and Seregny, "Politics and the Rural Intelligentsia," p. 179.

25 TsGAOR, f. 102, DP. OO, no. 1250, chast' 2, ll. 18–21.

26 Once, while criticizing railway administrator Kandaurov for his quick concessions during the January strike, Stolypin himself said, "As a representative of state authority I cannot speak out against the workers" (ibid., IV DP., ed. kh. 1350, chast' 20, 1905, l. 11). For more on *popechitel'stvo,* see Thomas Fallows, "The Zemstvo and the Bureaucracy, 1890–1904," in Terence Emmons and Wayne S. Vucinich, eds., *The Zemstvo in Russia: An Experiment in Local Self-Government* (Cambridge, Eng., 1982), pp. 184–92.

27 TsGAOR, f. 102, IV DP., ed. kh. 1350, chast' 20, 1905 g., l. 15.

28 Ibid., ll. 15–16.

29 For more on the national significance of the Balashov doctors' strike, see TsGAOR, f. 102, DP. OO, ed. kh. 999, chast' 42, 1905 g., l. 135; ibid., op. 5, ed. kh. 1325, 1905 g., ll. 121–23, 141–45, 158–59; G. S. Kuz'mina, "Iz istorii uchastiia meditsinskoi intelligentsii v pervoi russkoi revoliutsii (Balashovskaia zabastovka vrachei v iiule 1905 g.)," *Sovetskoe zdravookhranenie,* no. 8 (1973): 67–71; idem, "Iz istorii uchastiia meditsinskoi intelligentsii v pervoi russkoi revoliutsii," *Povolzhskii krai,* no.5 (1977): 145–62; Nancy Frieden, *Russian Physicians in an Era of Reform and Revolution, 1856–1905* (Princeton, N.J., 1981), pp. 310–11, 320, and Erman, pp. 116–17.

30 *Vrachebno-sanitarnaia khronika Saratovskoi gubernii,* March–April 1905, pp. 364–65; (July 1905), p. 765; TsGIA, f. 1288, op. 3, no. 17, 1904 g., ll. 1–4; and Kh. I. Idel'chuk, *N. I. Teziakov i ego rol' v razvitii zemskoi meditsiny i stroitel'stve sovetskogo zdravookhraneniia* (Moscow, 1960), pp. 115–19.

31 TsGAOR, f. 102, DP. OO, no. 999, chast' 1, tom 1, 1905 g., ll. 155–59, 174–75, 210–11. A similar event took place in Balashov on May 18, when K. B. Veselovskii chaired a radical gathering of seventy teachers. Ibid., op. 5, no. 1325, 1905 g., l. 56.

32 Ibid., no. 1325, ll. 4–5.

33 *Vrachebno-sanitarnaia khronika Saratovskoi gubernii,* February 1905, pp. 178–85; April 1905, p. 252; May 1905, pp. 535–43; and Petrovskoe uezdnoe zemstvo, *Deloproizvodstvo . . . sessii 6 i 7 marta 1905 g.* (Petrovsk, 1905), p. 54.

34 Saratovskoe gubernskoe zemstvo, *Doklad o vyrabotke vidov i predpolozhenii Saratovskago Gub. Zem. Sobraniia po voprosam, kasaiushchimsia usovershenstvovaniia Gos. blagoustroistva i uluchsheniia narodnago blagosostoianiia dlia predstavleniia na Vysochaishee Imia, soglasno Vysochaishego Ukaza ot 18-go fevralia sego goda* (Saratov, 1905), pp. 8–9; and Saratovskoe gubernskoe zemstvo, *Zhurnaly ekstrennago . . . 15–20 marta 1905 goda* (Saratov, 1905).

35 TsGAOR, f. 102, DP. OO, op. 5, no. 1325, 1905 g., ll. 3, 7, 8; and ibid., no. 999, chast' 42, 1905 g., ll. 49, 58.

36 Ibid., no. 1325, ll. 2, 6.

37   Ibid., ll. 3–5, 10, 12, 77; ibid., IV DP., no. 1000, chast' 1, tom 2, 1905 g., l. 299; *Vrachebno-sanitarnaia khronika Saratovskoi gubernii,* July 1905, pp. 763–64; N. Rossov, "Saratovskoe Gubernskoe Zemstvo v 1905 godu," *Saratovskaia zemskaia nedelia,* nos. 10–12 (1905): 10–24, 30–31; and letter of S. A. Kotliarevskii to M. M. Kovalevskii, written in Saratov on June 5, 1905 (Bakhmeteff Archives, Columbia University).

38   TsGAOR, f. 102, DP. OO, op. 5, no. 1325, 1905 g., ll. 11, 14.

39   Ibid., ll. 20–21, 24, 27–28, 67, 117–20; and "Balashovskoe sobytie 21-go iiulia," *Saratovskaia zemskaia nedelia,* no. 8, (August 1905): 31–33. Stolypin wrote his own version of the incident in *Pravo,* no. 30 (August 2, 1905): 2448–49, to which L'vov replied with his own account, "Soobshchenie o Balashovskikh sobytiiakh'," printed in *Russkiia vedomosti,* August 6, 1905, pp. 2–3, and *Pravo,* no. 32 (August 14, 1905): 2605–2607.

40   TsGAOR, f. 102, DP. OO, op. 5, no. 1325, 1905 g., ll. 15–17, 42, 63–76, 83–85; and "Balashovskoe sobytie," pp. 33–36, 40.

41   TsGAOR, f. 102, DP. OO, op. 5, no. 1325, 1905 g., ll. 31–62, 75–82, 88–90, 94–108, 134–44; *Vrachebno-sanitarnaia khronika Saratovskoi gubernii,* August–September 1905, pp. 900–908; October–November 1905, pp. 1066–1068; and "Balashovskoe sobytie," pp. 40–51.

42   TsGAOR, f. 102, DP. OO, op. 5, no. 1325, 1905 g., l. 105.

43   Petrovskoe uezdnoe zemstvo, *Deloproizvodstvo . . . sessii 6 i 7 marta 1905 g.* (Petrovsk, 1905), pp. 4–49, 64–83.

44   TsGAOR. f. 102, DP. OO, OOO, chast' 45, 1905 g. ll. 20–23; TsGAOR, f. 102, IV DP., op. 5, ed. kh. 2425, chast' 48, 1905 g., ll. 3–6; and Seregny, "Politics and the Rural Intelligentsia," pp. 181–82.

45   TsGAOR, f. 102, DP. OO, 1905 g., ed. kh. 999, chast' 45, ll. 20–23; and ibid., ed. kh. 2425, ll. 3–6.

46   Ibid., ed. kh. 999, chast' 45, l. 17; and ibid., ed. kh. 2425, ll. 7–9.

47   Petrovskoe uezdnoe zemstvo, *Protokoly . . . 4–12 avgusta 1905 goda* (Petrovsk, 1905), pp. 1–39; and *Vrachebno-sanitarnaia khronika Saratovskoi gubernii,* August–September 1905, pp. 894–98.

48   TsGAOR, f. 102, DP. OO, op. 5, no. 1325, 1905 g., ll. 4–5.

49   Ibid., ll. 61–62.

50   Ibid., op. 1905, ed. kh. 999, chast' 45, ll. 16–18.

51   Ibid., l. 18.

52   This quotation is taken from a report written by Stolypin in July of 1905; see Baron A. Meyendorff, "A Brief Appreciation of P. Stolypin's Tenure of Office" (unpublished MS, Bakhmeteff Archive, Columbia University), p. 16. See also TsGAOR, f. 102, DP. OO, op. 5, no. 1325, 1905 g., l. 43.

53   TsGAOR, f. 102, IV DP., op. 5, 1325, 1905 g., l. 144; ibid., op. 1905, ed. kh. 999, chast' 45, ll. 19, 32; D. N. Liubimov, "Russkaia smuta nachale

deviatisotykh godov 1902–1906 po vospominaniiam i lichnym zapiskam i dokumentam" (unpublished MS, Bakhmeteff Archive, Columbia University), pp. 243–44; and I.V. Gessen, "V dvukh vekakh," *Arkhiv russkoi revoliutsii* 22 (1937), p. 246.

54 The main orators at the October 12 gathering were also the prominent leaders in the Saratov strike in October, in general: the "Strike Committee" of the union of railway workers included SR leaders from the railway union (G. Sushkin and I. Ia. Drugov), N. D. Rachinskii, from the provincial zemstvo staff, and the SD journalist A. A. Gerasimov, TsGAOR, f. 102, IV DP., op. 5, ed. kh. 1350, chast' 20, 1905 g., ll. 41–47, 50–51, 69–70.

55 Ibid., ll. 58, 72–73, 101–102.

56 Ibid., ll. 37–38, 54–56, 61, 74.

57 Ibid., ll. 40–41, 43, 60.

58 TsGAOR, f. 102, IV DP., ed. kh. 1350, ll. 44, 79–80, 115–18, 125; and Bok, *Vospominaniia o moem ottse*, p. 149.

59 Fallows, "Forging the Zemstvo Movement," pp. 562–644.

60 A Ministry of Justice study on the peasant movement in Saratov noted 191 disturbances in Balashov, 46 each in Atkarsk and Petrovsk, 36 in Serdobsk, 22 in Saratov, and 15 in Kuznetsk; it recorded no instance of unrest in Volsk and Kamyshin. The raw data from the Free Economic Society's survey of peasant unrest in 1905 records only three disturbances in Kamyshin and none in Volsk (TsGIA, f. 91, op. 2, ed. kh. 786, ll. 235–344). See also V. M. Gokhlerner,"Iz istorii krest'ianskogo dvizheniia v Saratovskoi gubernii v gody pervoi russkoi revoliutsii (1905–07 gg.)," *Uchenye zapiski Saratovskogo gosudarstvennogo universiteta* 55 (1956): 244; and Fallows, "Forging the Zemstvo Movement," pp. 115–44.

61 TsGIA, f. 1405, I DP., op. 194, ed. kh. 81, 1905 g., ll. 55–150; and Timothy Mixter, "Of Grandfather-Beaters and Fat-Heeled Pacifists: Perceptions of Agricultural Labor and Hiring Market Disturbances in Saratov, 1872–1905," *Russian History* 7, pts. 1–2 (1980): 167–68.

62 *Saratovskii listok,* April 29, 1906, p. 3.

63 TsGAOR, f. 102, IV DP., no. 2425, chast' 5, 1905 g., ll. 44–45; and *Istoriia Saratovskogo kraia, 1590–1917,* ed. V. A. Osipov et al. (Saratov, 1964), pp. 153–55.

64 TsGAOR, f. 102, IV DP., op. 5, ed. kh. 1350, chast' 20, 1905 g., ll. 142–46.

65 The list of arrested reveals some of the leaders of the Soviet: V. D. Obukhov (a nobleman and a Marxist zemstvo statistician), P. V. Polianskii, A. P. Gerasimov (the editor of *Saratovskii Dnevnik*), N. N. Samsonov, G. M. Galperin (a city duma employee), and G. K. Ul'ianov (a former teacher).

66 Semen Mazurenko, "S"ezd krest'ian 18 dekabria 1905 g.," *Byloe,* no. 8 (1908): 35–38.

67 See the comments on the disarray of the SD party organization in Saratov in mid-1906 in a letter by a teacher of medical assistants, V. I. Firsov, in TsGAOR, f. 102, op. 6, ed. kh. 2, chast' 9, 1906 g., ll. 39–40; ibid., VII DP., no. 7244, chast' 26, 1905 g., l. 2; ibid., VII DP., no. 5, chast' 52, 1906 g., ll. 1–3.; and M. I. Semenov, "1905 god v Saratovskoi gubernii (Vospominaniia)," *Proletarskaia revoliutsiia,* no. 3 (50) (1926): 208.

68 *Saratovskii listok* issues of 1906, February 28 (p. 2), March 2–5 (p. 2), and March 17 (p. 2); and TsGAOR, f. 102, op. 6, no. 2, chast' 9, 1906 g., ll. 62–63.

69 The clearest example of this was the preelectoral meeting in Saratov of March 13, where over a thousand people heard speeches by SR, SD, Kadet, Octobrist, and "nonparty" spokesmen. That same week, Count Uvarov and Prince Kuropatkin journeyed into Balashov villages to campaign against the Kadet candidates in the volost elections (*Saratovskii listok,* March 14, 1906, p. 2). A correspondent from *Saratovskii listok* was impressed by a new phenomenon in Saratov life: "the political parties that have arisen just now" (January 22, 1906, p. 3).

70 *Saratovskii listok,* March 5, 1906, p. 3. The Kadet Maslennikov made the same observation: ". . . everyone can be divided into two parties. One group is trying to keep everything in the old way, the other wants to reform Russian life in a new fashion." *Saratovskii listok,* February 22, 1906, p. 2, and March 5, 1906, p. 3.

71 TsGAOR, f. 102, IV DP., no. 2425, chast' 5, 1905 g., l. 42.

72 Ibid., op. 5, ed. kh. 1350, chast' 20, 1905 g., l. 67.

73 E. Zviagintsev, "K zakrytiiu 'Saratovskoi zemskoi nedeli,'" *Saratovskaia zemskaia nedelia,* nos. 10–12 (1905): i–xi; *Saratovskii listok,* January 6, 1906, p. 2; January 15, 1906, p. 2; February 2, 1906, p. 2; February 5, 1906, p. 2; February 18, 1906, p. 2; March 8, 1906, p. 2; March 9, 1906, p. 2; March 15, 1906, p. 2; March 23, 1906, p. 2; and Bok, *Vospominaniia o moem ottse,* pp. 149–50.

74 Saratovskoe gubernskoe zemstvo, *Zhurnaly ocherednogo . . . 1905 goda* (Saratov, 1906), passim, but especially pp. 458–92; *Saratovskii listok:* January 6, 1906, p. 2; January 15,1906, p. 2; January 25, 1906, p. 3; January 29, 1906, pp. 2–3; February 7, 1906, p. 3; February 10, 1906, pp. 1–3; February 20, 1906, p. 3; February 26, 1906, p. 2; A. V. Zenkovskii, "Moi Vospominaniia" (unpublished MS, Bakhmeteff Archive, Columbia University), pp. 52–87; Kamyshinskoe uezdnoe zemstvo, *Doklady i zhurnaly . . . 1905 goda* (Kamyshin, 1906), pp. 2–11, 57–58; Idel'chuk, p. 37; and Z. Solov'ev, "Pamiati Nikolaia Ivanovicha Teziakova," *Izvestiia Narodnogo Komissariata zdravookhraneniia RSFSR,* no. 1 (1925): 119.

75 *Saratovskii listok,* March 1, 1906, p. 2.

76   Ibid., February 14, February 16, February 18, March 23, March 25, March 29, March 30, April 6, April 9, April 11, April 13, April 15, 1906; Semenov, "1905 god v Saratovskoi gubernii," pp. 201–2; Tan [V. G. Bogoraz], *Muzhiki v Gosudarstvennoi dume. Ocherki* (Moscow, 1907), pp. 57–58; Terence Emmons, *The Formation of Political Parties and the First National Elections in Russia* (Cambridge, Mass., 1983), pp. 283–84, 321–22; Seregny, "Politics and the Rural Intelligentsia," pp. 187–88; and D. A. Kolesnichenko, "Vozniknovenie i deiatel'nost' 'Trudovoi gruppy,' " *Istoriia SSSR*, no. 4 (1967): 77–79.

77   Bok, *Vospominaniia o moem ottse,* pp. 145–46; Semenov, "1905 god v Saratovskoi gubernii," p. 212; and Liubimov, "Russkaia smuta," p. 243.

78   For examples of Stolypin's personal intervention in village disturbances, see *Revoliutsionnaia Rossiia,* June 15, 1905, p. 21, and September 15, 1905, pp. 18–19; A. A. Argunov, "Iz vospominanii o pervoi russkoi revoliutsii," *Katorga i ssylka,* no. 1 (74) (1931): 145 (thanks to Timothy Mixter for these sources); and I. I. Babikov, "Krest'ianskoe dvizhenie v Saratovskoi gubernii nakanune pervoi russkoi revoliutsii," *Uchenye zapiski Saratovskogo gosudarstvennogo universiteta* 55 (1956): 210–11.

79   TsGIA, f. 1284, op. 194, 1906 g., ed. kh. 20, ll. 22–23; "Vsepoddaneishii otchet Saratovskogo gubernatora P. Stolypina za 1904 god," *Krasnyi arkhiv,* no. 4 (17) (1926): 83–87; and A. Stolypin, *P. A. Stolypin, 1862–1911* (Paris, 1927), pp. 13–14.

80   *Gosudarstvennaia deiatel'nost' predsedatelia Soveta stats-sekretaria Petra Arkad'evicha Stolypina,* 2 vols. (St. Petersburg, 1911), 1: 4–8.

81   Bok, *Vospominaniia o moem ottse,* pp. 150–51.

82   TsGAOR, f. 102, op. 6, ed. kh. 2, chast' 9, 1906 g., ll. 62–63.

CHAPTER 9

1   Tan [V. G. Bogoraz], *Muzhiki v Gosudarstvennoi dume* (Moscow, 1907), p. 56. I would like to thank Rex Wade and Scott Seregny for their patience and assistance in recasting this chapter and Tom Fallows for many mutually beneficial conversations about Saratov society.

2   M. M. Gran, "Prishlye sel'skokhoziaistvennye rabochie Samarskoi gubernii v sanitarnom otnoshenii (K voprosu o znachenii prodovol'stvennykh punktov)," *Saratovskaia zemskaia nedelia,* nos. 42–45 (December 1901): 41.

3   Roberta T. Manning, *The Crisis of the Old Order in Russia: Gentry and Government* (Princeton, N.J., 1982), p. 143; B. B. Veselovskii, *Krest'ianskii vopros i krest'ianskoe dvizhenie v Rossi, 1902–1906 gg.* (St. Petersburg, 1907), pp. 86–87.

4   Robert S. Edelman, "Rural Proletarians and Peasant Disturbances: The

Right Bank Ukraine in the Revolution of 1905," *Journal of Modern History* 57, no. 2 (June 1985): 263–64.

5   S. B. Okun', ed., *Krest'ianskoe dvizhenie v Rossii v 1850–1856 gg. Sbornik dokumentov* (Moscow, 1962), pp. 76–87; V. A. Fedorov, "Krest'ianskoe trezvennoe dvizhenie 1858–1860 gg.," in *Revoliutsionnaia situatsiia v Rossii v 1859–1861 gg.* (Moscow, 1962), pp. 114, 120–21, 123; S. B. Okun' and K. V. Sivkov, eds., *Krest'ianskoe dvizhenie v Rossii v 1857–mae 1861 gg.: Sbornik dokumentov* (Moscow, 1963), pp. 185–89, 208–211, 620; Thomas S. Fallows, "Forging the Zemstvo Movement: Liberalism and Radicalism on the Volga, 1890–1905," Ph.D. diss., Harvard University, 1981, p. 45.

6   Petr Serafimovich Kabytov, *Agrarnye otnosheniia v Povolzh'e v period imperializma, 1900–1917 gg.* (Saratov, 1982), pp. 11–15; N. I. Teziakov, "Otkhozhie promysly i rynki naima sel'skokhoziaistvennykh rabochikh v Saratovskoi gubernii," *Saratovskaia zemskaia nedelia,* no. 1, sec. 3 (1905): 11; Timothy Mixter, "Of Grandfather-Beaters," p. 141.

7   Orlando Figes, "The Russian Land Commune and the Agrarian Question, 1905–1930," *Peasant Studies,* 11, no. 2 (Winter 1984): 121; N. P. Oganovskii, ed., *Sel'skoe khoziaistvo Rossii v XX veke* (Moscow, 1923), pp. 12, 18 (calculations from); I. Zhilkin, "Iz golodnago kraia: Pis'mo v redaktsiiu," *Vestnik Evropy,* 47, no. 2 (1912): 273, 293–94; *Protokoly pervoi obshchepartiinoi konferentsii P. S.-R.: August 1908* (Paris, 1908), p. 187.

8   On the role of large villages, see: N. Karpov, ed., *Krest'ianskoe dvizhenie v revoliutsii 1905 goda v dokumentakh* (Leningrad, 1926), p. 144 (Stolypin's opinion); *Privolzhskii krai* [hereafter *PK*], no. 60, March 18, 1906, p. 2; Tan [V. G. Bogaraz], "Po gubernii bezpokoinoi," in Tan, ed., *Novoe krest'ianstvo: Ocherki derevenskikh nastroenii* (Moscow, 1905), p. 80. The thirty-nine restive large villages included: Ivanovka 2, Makarovo, Mikhailovka, Sestrenki, Trubetskoe (Trubetchino), Samoilovka (Tri Ostrova), Shepelevka, and Glebovka, Balashov District; Balanda, Berezovka, Danilovka, Bolshaia and Malaia Dmitrievka, Shirokii Karamysh, Malye Kopeny, and Medvedevka, Atkarsk District; Annenkovo and Plan, Kuznetsk District; Salamatino and Nizhnaia Dobrinka, Kamyshin District; Kamaevka, Kliuchi, Urleika, Spasko-Aleksandrovskoe, and Lopatino, Petrovsk District; Novye Burasy, Irinovka, Lesnaia Neelovka, Sinenkie, Sukhoi Karbulak, Usovka, Nikolaevskii Gorodok, Teplovka, and Lipovka, Saratov District; Bekovo, Khovanshchina, and Borki, Serdobsk District; Kamennyi Brod and Ol'khovka, Tsaritsyn District. Population figures for these villages and rural Saratov settlements as a whole are calculated from: Oganovskii, *Sel'skoe khoziaistvo,* pp. 12, 18; N. A. Troinitskii, comp., *Naselennyia mesta Rossiiskoi imperii v 500 i bolee zhitelei s ukazaniem vsego nalichnago v nikh*

naseleniia i chisla zhitelei preobladaiushchikh veroispovedanii, po dannym pervoi vseobshchei perepisi naseleniia 1897 g. (St. Petersburg, 1907), pp. 197–207. The reportage of disturbances was likely to be somewhat biased toward large villages, as newspaper correspondents and police were more apt to be present there.

9 L. N. Liubomirova, "Vnenadel'naia arenda i ee vliianie na polozhenie krest'ian Saratovskoi gubernii (60 g. XIX v.–nach. XX v.)," *Povolzhskii krai,* no. 5 (1977): 164–69; V Serebriakov, "Sovremennoe sostoianie russkoi derevni i eia nuzhdy po otzyvam sel'skikh zhitelei," *Saratovskaia zemskaia nedelia,* nos. 10–12, sec. 3, (1905): 10, 12, 14–15; *PK,* no. 103, May 20, 1906, p. 3; Fallows, "Forging the Zemstvo Movement," pp. 120–23, 125, 141, 173–74 n. 124; *Izvestiia Krest'ianskikh Deputatov* [hereafter *IKD*], no. 10, May 30, 1906, p. 2; *Vest',* no. 6, April 8, 1906, p. 30; *Revoliutsionnaia Rossiia* [hereafter *RR*], no. 7, June 1902, p. 20, Kabytov, *Agrarnye otnosheniia,* p. 54; A. Lopukhovskii, "Stachka v Arkadake," *Saratovskii dnevnik,* [hereafter *SD*], no. 140, July 2, 1906, p.2

10 Liubomirova, "Vnenadel'naia arenda," p. 166 and n. 31; I. I. Babikov, "Krest'ianskoe dvizhenie v Saratovskoi gubernii nakanune pervoi russkoi revoliutsii," *Uchenye zapiski Saratovskogo gosudarstvennogo universiteta,* no. 55 (1956): 179.

11 L. N. Liubomirova, "Krest'iane-darstvenniki Saratovskoi gubernii v poreformennyi period (80–90-e gody XIX veka)," *Povolzhskii krai,* no. 4 (1975): 89–105; I. V. Chernyshev, *Agrarnyi vopros v Rossii* (Kursk, 1927), p. 35; Tsentral'nyi statisticheskii komitet M.V.D., *Ezhegodnik Rossii 1908 g.* (St. Petersburg, 1909), p. 236; Fallows, "Forging the Zemstvo Movement," pp. 44, 642–43.

12 A. M. Anfimov, *Krest'ianskoe khoziaistvo Evropeiskoi Rossii, 1881–1904* (Moscow, 1980), p. 42: I. Belokurov, *Iz zapisok agrarnika* (Moscow, 1926), pp. 7–11, 15; N. Bazhenov [I. Belokurov], "Kak u nas proizoshlo agrarnoe dvizhenie: Zapiski krest'ianina," *Russkoe bogatstvo,* no. 4 (1909): 97–99; *PK,* no. 44, March 1, 1906, p. 3; no. 127, June 20, 1906, p. 2; no. 135, June 29, 1906, p. 2; no. 153, July 21, 1906, p. 2; no. 163, August 3, 1906, p. 2; Mixter, "Of Grandfather-Beaters," p. 141; "Biudzhet krest'ianina Saratovskoi gub.," *Mir bozhii,* no. 4 (1903): 45–46.

13 Tsentral'nyi statisticheskii komietet M.V.D., *Ezhegodnik Rossii 1907 g.* (St. Petersburg, 1908), pp. 178–79; Liubomirova,"Vnenadel'naia arenda," pp. 170–71; V. F. Meien, comp., *Rossiia v dorozhnom otnoshenii,* vol. 2 (St. Petersburg, 1902), pp. 429 (map), 438–40.

14 Saratovskoe gubernskoe zemstvo, *Sbornik svedenii po Saratovskoi gubernii za 1905 god,* 3 vols. (Saratov, 1905–06), 2, sec. 2, pp. 75, 77, 91, 93, 106–07, 109, 111–12; I. V. Chernyshev, "Saratovskaia guberniia," in *Agrarnoe*

dvizhenie v Rossii v 1905–1906 gg., pt. 1, *Trudy Imperatorskago Vol'nago Ekonomicheskago Obshchestva*, no. 3 (May–June 1908): 134, 135, 138; *PK*, no. 92, May 4, 1906, p. 2; *SD*, no. 126, July 28, 1904, p. 3; *Nasha zhizn'*, no. 137, June 30, 1905, p. 4; V. M. Gokhlerner, "Krest'ianskoe dvizhenie v Saratovskoi gubernii v gody pervoi russkoi revoliutsii," *Istoricheskie zapiski*, 52 (1955): 189, 196, and 196 n. 38; Tan,"Po gubernii," pp. 98–99.

15 Fallows, "Forging the Zemstvo Movement," pp. 570–71, 573, 596–644; V. N. Katin-Iartsev, "Konstantin Mikhailovich Takhtarev, 1871–1925: (Pamiati druga)," *Katorga i ssylka*, no. 19 (1925): 233; I. I. Rakitnikova, "Revoliutsionnaia molodezh' 90-kh godov na rabote v derevne," *Narodovol'tsy 80-kh i 90-kh godov*, 2: 164–77; Scott J. Seregny, "Politics and the Rural Intelligentsia in Russia: A Biographical Sketch of Stepan Anikin, 1869–1919," *Russian History* 7, pts. 1–2 (1980): 175–76; M. I. Semenov, "1905 god v Saratovskoi gubernii," *Proletarskaia revoliutsiia*, no. 3 (50) (1926): 212.

16 Timothy R. Mixter, "Migrant Agricultural Laborers in the Hiring Markets of the European Russian Steppe, 1894–1914," paper presented at the Seminar on the History of Russian Society in the Twentieth Century: Colloquium on Rural Society, 1905–30, Philadelphia, January 1982, pp. 26–27; E. Diubiuk, "Ekonomicheskaia zapashka i spol'nyi posev," *Saratovskaia zemskaia nedelia*, nos. 10–12 (1905), sec. 5, pp. 1–6.

17 Fallows, "Forging the Zemstvo Movement," pp. 12–33, 89–150 (especially tables on pp. 26, 30, and 148–49); Tsentral'nyi statisticheskii komitet, *Statistika zemlevladeniia 1905 g.* (St. Petersburg: 1906), vol. 2, *Saratovskaia guberniia*, p. 10, and *Svod dannykh*, p. 12; Oganovskii, *Sel'skoe khoziaistvo*, pp. 118–23; Diubiuk, "Ekonomicheskaia," pp. 1–6; Mixter, "Of Grandfather-Beaters," pp. 141 n. 4, 143, 149–68; Timothy Mixter, "Migrant Agricultural Laborers in the Steppe Grainbelt of European Russia, 1830–1913," Ph.D. diss., University of Michigan, 1989; Saratovskoe gubernskoe zemstvo, *Sbornik svedenii po Saratovskoi gubernii za 1905 god* (Saratov, 1906), 3: 78–79; Chernyshev, *Agrarnyi vopros*, pp. 79–80; Tan [V. G. Bogoraz], "Deputaty vtoroi Dumy: Ocherki i nabroski," *Russkoe bogatstvo*, no. 5 sec. 2 (1907): 90–96; esp. 94–95.

18 Mixter, "Of Grandfather-Beaters," p. 141 n. 4; Fallows, "Forging the Zemstvo Movement," p. 118–22; V. Obukhov, "Izmenenie v chastnovladel'cheskom khoziaistve v Saratovskoi gubernii," *Saratovskaia zemskaia nedelia*, no. 8, sec. 3 (1902): 133; Serebriakov, "Sovremennoe," pp. 9–10, 12–15, esp. 13; Chernyshev, *Agrarnyi vopros*, pp. 79–82.

19 Saratovskoe gubernskoe zemstvo, *Materialy dlia otsenki zemel' Saratovskoi gubernii*, vol. 2, *Ekspluatatsiia pashin v chastnovladel'cheskikh khoziaistvakh i krest'ianskiia vnenadel'nyia arendy* (Saratov, 1905), pp. 17, 89, 117–31; Fall-

ows, "Forging the Zemstvo Movement," pp. 121–34, 137–44, 145–46, 148; Mixter, "Of Grandfather-Beaters," pp. 141–42, 149 n. 34, 164; Chernyshev, "Saratovskaia guberniia," p. 135.

20   K. Kocharovskii, "Krest'ianskaia obshchina v Saratovskoi gubernii," *Russkoe bogatstvo*, no. 11 (1901), sec. 2, pp. 124–26, 132–35, 137; Stephen Frank, "Cultural Conflict and Criminality in Rural Russia, 1861–1900," Ph.D. diss., Brown University, 1986, passim; Belokurov, *Iz zapisok*, 14, 17–19, 25–28, 32, 40, 42–45; Tan, "Po gubernii," pp. 85–88, 94, 98–99; "The Russian Peasantry in 1907–1908: A Survey by the Socialist Revolutionary Party," Maureen Perrie, trans., *History Workshop* 4 (Autumn 1977): 181, 182, 185; *Zemlia i volia*, no. 1, August 1905, pp. 13–14; *PK*, no. 166, August 6, 1906, p. 3. For reports that poor or middle peasants were the most apt to protest, see Chernyshev, "Saratovskaia guberniia," pp. 132, 133–34, 135, 137, 138, 140, 141, 147, 148. For reports that all strata in the village participated, see: Chernyshev, ibid., pp. 131, 134, 138, 140, 141, 142, 148; *Russkiia vedomosti* [hereafter *RV*], no. 294, November 8, 1905, p. 3; Perrie, trans., "The Russian Peasantry," pp. 182–83. Often the form of protest determined who participated.

21   The term "conscious" was commonly used at the time to denote peasants who had some leftist sympathies and some knowledge of political and economic relationships, however murky. It is used in that spirit here and does not necessarily entail peasant class-consciousness. Similarly, the term "blackhundred" was commonly used at the time to denote people holding conservative, right-leaning views, and sometimes carried a sense that the person was uneducated. I use the term this way unless it is capitalized, in which case I am referring to the specific organization, the Blackhundreds.

22   *Zemlia i volia*, no. 1 (August 1905): 13; Tan, "Po gubernii," pp. 19, 61; Fallows, "Forging the Zemstvo Movement," p. 841.

23   As paraphrased in Seregny, "Politics and the Rural Intelligentsia," p. 181.

24   Chernyshev, "Saratovskaia guberniia," p. 131.

25   Anfimov, *Krest'ianskoe khoziaistvo*, pp. 80, 85.

26   *RR*, no. 11, September 1902, pp. 19–20; no. 75, September 15, 1905, p. 19; *Iskra*, no. 23, August 1, 1902, p. 4; *Istoriia Saratovskogo kraia 1590–1917*, V. A. Osipov et al., eds., (Saratov, 1964), pp. 139–40; Petr Maslov, *Agrarnyi vopros v Rossii* (St. Petersburg, 1908), 2:120. On proactive and defensive forms of collective action, see Charles Tilly, *From Mobilization to Revolution* (Reading, Mass., 1978), passim. For later cases of protest due to conflicts over landownership, see: *PK*, no. 126, June 18, 1906, p. 2; *Vest'*, no. 6, April 8, 1906, pp. 30–31; and n. 46 below.

27   *R.R.*, no. 11, September 1902, p. 19; no. 13, November 1902, p. 17; no. 19, March 1903, p. 15.

28 *Iskra*, no. 23, August 1, 1902, pp. 3–4; *R.R.*, no. 11, September 1902, pp. 19–20; *PK*, no. 53, March 9, 1906, p. 3; Fallows, "Forging the Zemstvo Movement," pp. 132–34, 141; *IKD*, no. 10, May 30, 1906, p. 2; Serebriakov, "Sovremennoe," pp. 9, 10, 11, 13; Chernyshev, "Saratovskaia guberniia," pp. 144–45, Belokurov, *Iz zapisok*, pp. 7–11; *Vest'*, no. 6, April 8, 1906, p. 30; V. V. Khizhniakov, "O shtrafakh v sel'skom khoziaistve," *Pravo*, no. 18, April 30, 1900, col. 896; E. P. Thompson, "The Moral Economy of the English Crowd in the Eighteenth Century," *Past & Present*, no. 50 (February 1971): 128–32, 136.

29 Obukhov, "Izmenenie," p. 133; Fallows, "Forging the Zemstvo Movement," pp. 122, 173. According to Fallows, there had been relatively few changes in the amount of land rented out before 1899. Thus peasants may have felt it was their customary right to rent the land.

30 Mixter, "Of Grandfather-Beaters," p. 164 n. 93; TsGIA, f. 1405, op. 107, ed. khr. 6661, listy 173, 187, 193, 197, 204; Fallows, "Forging the Zemstvo Movement," pp. 140–45, 175 n. 155; Chernyshev, "Saratovskaia guberniia," pp. 144–45; Tan, "Po gubernii," pp. 93–94; *PK*, no. 145, July 12, 1906, p. 2.

31 *RR*, no. 7, June 1902, p. 20; no. 19, March 1903, p. 15.

32 Mixter, "Of Grandfather-Beaters," pp. 152–68; Timothy Mixter, "The Hiring Market as Workers' Turf: Migrant Agricultural Laborers and the Mobilization of Collective Action in the Steppe Grainbelt of European Russia, 1853–1913," in Esther Kingston-Mann and Timothy Mixter, eds., *Peasant Economy, Culture, and Politics in European Russia, 1800–1921* (forthcoming); *RR*, no. 10, August 1902, pp. 21–22; no. 11, September 1902, p. 20; no. 55, November 20, 1904, p. 20; TsGAOR, f. 102, 3-e d-vo, g. 1904, ed. khr. 1, ch. 43 L. V., listy 2–200b; TsGIA, f. 1405, op. 101, ed. khr. 7995.

33 Harvey J. Kaye, "Another Way of Seeing Peasants: The Work of John Berger," *Peasant Studies* 9, no. 2 (Winter 1982): 85–105; Tan, "Po gubernii," pp. 7, 31–32; E. P. Thompson, "Eighteenth-Century English Society: Class Struggle Without Class?" *Social History 3*, no. 2 (May 1978): 150–51; Frank, "Cultural Conflict," passim.

34 *PK*, no. 101, May 18, 1906, p. 3; *Iuzhnoe obozrenie*, no. 3120, June 10, 1906, p. 2; S. A-n [Stepan Anikin], "Po rodnym mestam," *Russkoe bogatstvo*, no. 1 (January 1907), sec. 2, pp. 53–54; *PK*, no. 111, June 1, 1906, p. 2.

35 Tan, "Po gubernii," pp. 14, 82, 92; Fallows, "Forging the Zemstvo Movement," pp. 599–600; A. A. Argunov, "Iz proshlago partii Sotsialistov-Revoliutsionerov," *Byloe*, no. 10(22) (1907): 103; Belokurov, *Iz zapisok*, pp. 19, 20–23, 34; *Iskra*, no. 42, June 15, 1903, p. 6. As the first and

last citations indicate, peasants also elected and even paid people to distribute books and read them aloud.

36 On progressive urban areas influencing their hinterlands, see Ted W. Margadant, "French Rural Society in the Nineteenth Century: A Review," *Agricultural History* 53, no. 3 (July 1979): 648–49. On Anikin's newspaper, see Seregny, "Politics and the Rural Intelligentsia," pp. 185–86. On newspapers in the village, see Belokurov, *Iz zapisok,* pp. 12–14; Karpov, *Krest'ianskoe dvizhenie,* p. 259.

37 S. Anikin, "Za 'pravednoi zemlei' (pamiati I. M. Igoshina)," *Vestnik Evropy* 45, no. 3 (1910): 97–98; Aleksandr Studentsov, *Saratovskoe krest'ianskoe vosstanie 1905 goda* (Penza, 1926), pp. 1 n, 16; Maslov, *Agrarnyi vopros,* 2:216, 243.

38 Fallows, "Forging the Zemstvo Movement," pp. 628–44; I. Rakitnikova, "Revoliutsionnaia rabota v krest'ianstve v Saratovskoi gubernii v 1900–1902 gg.," *Katorga i ssylka,* no. 10 (47) (1928): 10–11 n. 15; *RR,* no. 19, March 1903, pp. 14–15; Gokhlerner, "Krest'ianskoe," pp. 200–1, 203, 206 n. 93, 226–27; Studentsov, *Saratovskoe,* passim; Chernyshev, "Saratovskaia," pp. 135, 138; V. P. Antonov-Saratovskii, *Krasnyi god* (Moscow-Leningrad, 1927), p. 168; Belokurov, *Iz zapisok,* pp. 13–23, 30, 60–62, 69, passim; V. M. Gokhlerner and K. P. Kharlamova, "Iz istorii krest'ianskikh revoliutsionnykh komitetov v Saratovskoi gubernii v 1905 g.," *Povolzhskii krai,* no. 5 (1977): 89–120; *PK,* no. 112, June 2, 1906, p. 2; Tan, "Po gubernii," pp. 9, 12.

39 Anikin, "Za 'pravednoi zemlei,' " pp. 97, 98, 104.

40 John Bushnell, *Mutiny amid Repression: Russian Soldiers in the Revolution of 1905–1906* (Bloomington, Ind., 1985), pp. 34, 226, and passim; John Bushnell, "Peasant Economy and Peasant Revolution at the Turn of the Century: Neither Immiseration nor Autonomy," *Russian Review,* 47, no. 1 (January 1988): 83–86.

41 On the liberals and conservatives in Saratov Province and their contention, see Fallows, "Forging the Zemstvo Movement," passim, and Mixter, "Migrant Agricultural Laborers in the Steppe Grainbelt of European Russia, 1830–1913," passim.

42 For examples of independent social spaces, see Tan, "Po gubernii," pp. 18–22, 41, 72, 78, 79–80, 85, 89–93; *PK,* no. 57, July 27, 1906, p. 2; Belokurov, *Iz zapisok,* pp. 11–14, 36–37; Karpov, ed., *Krest'ianskoe dvizhenie,* pp. 47–54; *Iskra,* no. 52, November 7, 1903, p. 5; Seregny, "Politics and the Rural Intelligentsia," p. 176; Anikin, "Za 'pravednoi zemlei,' " pp. 90–91; *Rech',* no. 101, June 16, 1906, Prilozhenie, p. 1; Gokhlerner and Kharlamova, "Iz istorii," p. 97 and n. 34.

43 Tan, "Po gubernii," pp. 13, 19, 20, 22, 71, 72, 82–83, 85, 90; Seregny,

"Politics and the Rural Intelligentsia," pp. 172, 176; Anikin, "Za 'pravednoi zemlei,'" pp. 89, 102; Belokurov, *Iz zapisok,* pp. 11–12; I. Belokurov, "Vstrechi s N. E. Baumanom," *Katorga i ssylka,* no. 4 (77) (1931): 198; Chernyshev, "Saratovskaia guberniia," p. 141; *PK,* no. 99, May 16, 1906, p. 1; *Protokoly pervoi obshchepartiinoi konferentsii,* p. 187.

44 Tan, "Po gubernii," pp. 79–80, 88–89, 92–93.

45 Ibid., pp. 22, 26, 39, 71, 72, 80, 85, 89–93; *PK,* no. 145, July 12, 1906, p. 2; *Protokoly pervoi obshchepartiinoi konferentsii,* p. 44; Seregny, "Politics and the Rural Intelligentsia," pp. 172, 176; *Zemlia i volia,* no. 1 (August 1905): 13–14; S. A-n [Anikin], "Po rodnym mestam (Iz nabliudenii byvshago deputata)," *Russkoe bogatstvo,* no. 11 (1906), sec. 2, pp. 14–15; Chernyshev, "Saratovskaia guberniia," pp. 134, 137, 139, 146; *Iskra,* no. 52, November 7, 1903, p. 5. As Anikin indicates, while elders in one village knelt before a local noble begging him to rescind a rent increase, youth, angry at such degrading tactics, chose instead to send him a threatening letter and engage in arson.

46 V. M. Gokhlerner, "Iz istorii krest'ianskogo dvizheniia v Saratovskoi gubernii v gody pervoi russkoi revoliutsii (1905–07 gg.)," *Uchenye zapiski Saratovskogo gosudarstvennogo universiteta,* 55 (1956): 226, 228, 244; K. F. Shatsillo, "The Pinkening of the Liberals at the Beginning of the First Russian Revolution," *Soviet Studies in History* 20, no. 3 (Winter 1981–82): 60–61; Fallows, "Forging the Zemstvo Movement," p. 713; A. Argunov, "Iz vospominanii o pervoi russkoi revoliutsii," *Katorga i ssylka,* no. 1 (74) (1931): 144; *Iskra,* no. 93, March 17, 1905, p. 6; *Nasha zhizn',* no. 129, June 22, 1905, p. 4; *Zemlia i volia,* no. 1, August 1905, pp. 13–14; Babikov, "Krest'ianskoe," p. 191.

47 Chernyshev, "Saratovskaia guberniia," p. 131; Tan, "Po gubernii," pp. 65, 72, 78–79, 90; Gokhlerner, "Krest'ianskoe," pp. 190–91.

48 On the declaration and Bychenkov, see *RR,* no. 67, May 15, 1905, p. 13; *Istoriia,* p. 149; Tan, "Po gubernii," p. 84; *Rech',* no. 101, June 16, 1906, "Prilozhenie k no. 101—Gosudarstvennaia Duma," p. 1; Gokhlerner, "Krest'ianskoe," p. 189.

49 Karpov, ed., *Krest'ianskoe dvizhenie,* p. 144; Tan, "Po gubernii," pp. 84–89; Vill'iam E. Uolling [William E. Walling], *Poslanie Rossii (Istinnoe znachenie Russkoi Revoliutsii)* (Berlin, 1910), pp. 266–68; *RR,* no. 69, June 15, 1905, p. 21.

50 Tan, "Po gubernii," pp. 81, 83, 87–99; *Zemlia i volia,* no. 1, August 1905, p. 13; Uolling, *Poslanie Rossii,* pp. 268–69; *Polveka nazad: Vospominaniia uchastnikov revoliutsionnykh sobytii 1905 goda v Saratovskoi gubernii* (Saratov, 1955), pp. 133, 138, Karpov, ed., *Krest'ianskoe dvizhenie,* p. 144; Cherny-

shev, "Saratovskaia guberniia," p. 131; *RR,* no. 75, September 15, 1905, p. 19.

51 Tan, "Po gubernii," pp. 12–14, 39, 65–66, 76, 84–85, 87–95, 102. For another case in which a socialist culture appeared to be emerging in Nikolaevskii Gorodok, see *PK,* no. 102, May 19, 1906, p. 2.

52 Chernyshev, "Saratovskaia guberniia," p. 131; Karpov, ed., *Krest'ianskoe,* p. 144; Tan, "Po gubernii," p. 85; Veselovskii, *Krest'ianskii,* pp. 65–66. For the Petrovka declaration, see *RR,* no. 73, August 15, 1905, p. 26. See also *Pravo,* no. 27, July 10, 1905, cols. 2245–2246; *RR,* no. 69, June 15, 1905, p. 22; Maslov, *Agrarnyi vopros,* 2:179–80, 244.

53 V. P. Antonov-Saratovskii, *Krasnyi god,* pp. 151–53; Maslov, *Agrarnyi vopros,* 2:198–202, 244–45; Tan, "Po gubernii," pp. 38–49, Karpov, ed., *Krest'ianskoe,* pp. 47–48, 51–54; Fallows, "Forging the Zemstvo Movement," pp. 822–24; *Severnyi kavkaz,* no. 90, August 6, 1905, pp. 2–3; Veselovskii, *Krest'ianskii,* pp. 34, 47; *RV,* no. 294, November 8, 1905, p. 3; *Pravo,* no. 30, August 2, 1905, cols. 2466–2467, 2497; Gokhlerner, "Krest'ianskoe," pp. 195, 197.

54 Antonov-Saratovskii, *Krasnyi god,* pp. 148–49, 153; *Nasha zhizn',* no. 127, June 20, 1905, p. 4; *Severnyi kavkaz,* no. 87, July 30, 1905, p. 4; Gokhlerner, "Krest'ianskoe," p. 198; *RR,* no. 75, September 15, 1906, p. 19; *Pravo,* no. 32, August 14, 1905, col. 2582; *PK,* no. 53, March 9, 1906, p. 3.

55 Gokhlerner, "Iz istorii," pp. 228, 244.

56 Belokurov, *Iz zapisok,* pp. 15–18; Bazhenov, "Kak," *Russkoe bogatstvo,* no. 4, (April 1909): 102–3.

57 *Bez zaglaviia,* no. 7, March 5, 1905, p. 257; *Polveka,* pp. 132–33, 138, 142; *PK,* no. 103, May 20, 1906, p. 3; *Nasha zhizn',* no. 137, June 30, 1905, p. 4; *PK,* no. 52, March 8, 1906, p. 3; *Pravo,* no. 38, September 25, 1905, col. 3214; *Istoriia,* pp. 173–74; Antonov-Saratovskii, *Krasnyi god,* p. 149; *RR,* no. 75, September 15, 1905, p. 19; Tan,"Po gubernii," pp. 26, 51–52, 55, 98–99, 102.

58 *Polveka,* p. 133; *Severnyi kavkaz,* no. 87, July 30, 1905, p. 4; *Pravo,* no. 32, August 14, 1905, col. 2583; no. 34, August 28, 1905, cols. 2815–2816; *Saratovskii listok* [hereafter *SL*] no. 128, June 20, 1906, p. 2; no. 129, June 21, 1906, p. 2; *RR,* no. 75, September 15, 1905, p. 19; *RV,* no. 294, November 8, 1905, p. 3.

59 Veselovskii, *Krest'ianskii,* pp. 86–87; Gokhlerner, "Iz istorii," pp. 242–44; Gokhlerner, "Krest'ianskoe," pp. 196 n. 38, 200–210. Gokhlerner put the figure at about 200 estates "destroyed" in the fall of 1905; 293 for the entire year (ibid., pp. 200, 216). For attacks against liberals and conservatives, see TsGAOR, f. 102, 4-e d-vo, 1908 g., d. 62, ch. 1, list 21; Tan, "Deputaty," pp. 90–96; *Vserossiiskaia politicheskaia stachka v oktiabre 1905*

goda, pt. 2, L. M. Ivanov et al., eds., in series *Revoliutsiia 1905–1907 gg. v Rossii: Dokumenty i materialy* A. M. Pankratova et al., eds. (Moscow-Leningrad, 1955), p. 429; TsGIA, f. 1405, op. 194, 1908 g., ed. khr. 81, listy 62, 64, 740b., 780b.; *Istoriia,* p. 189; Chernyshev, "Saratovskaia guber-niia," pp. 133–35, 148; I. Larskii,"Po povodu (Iz zhizni v provintsii): Revoliutsiia v derevne," *Mir bozhii,* no. 12 (December 1905), sec. 2, p. 27; Mary Stolypin Bock, "Stolypin in Saratov," *Russian Review* 12, no. 3 (July 1953): 192 (This citation probably refers to N. N. L'vov); Fallows, "Forg-ing the Zemstvo Movement," pp. 82–88, 91–94, 140–44; 324–25, 641, 824–27; Manning, *Crisis of the Old Order,* pp. 156–57, 162, 163, 177, 178, 451 n. 52; Karpov, ed., *Krest'ianskoe,* p. 260; *Vysshii pod"em revoliutsii 1905–1907 gg.: Vooruzhennye vosstaniia noiabr'-dekabr' 1905 goda* [hereafter *RVR (Novem-ber–December 1905)*], pt. 2, A. L. Sidorov et al., eds. (Moscow-Leningrad, 1955), p. 761; Studentsov, *Saratovskoe,* p. 44; *RV,* no. 294, November 8, 1905, p. 3; I. Konovalov, "V derevne: (Iz Saratovskoi gub.)," *Sovremennyi mir* 16, no. 2 (1909), sec. 2, pp. 20–21.

60 Belokurov, *Iz zapisok,* pp. 26–27, 36–46, 49, 54, 57, and passim; Stu-dentsov, *Saratovskoe,* pp. 1 n, 16, 27, 30, 31, 31n, 32, 35, 37, 38, 43, 44, 45; *Protokoly delegatskago soveshchaniia Vserossiiskago Krest'ianskago Soiuza 6–10 noiabria 1905 v Moskve* (Moscow, 1906), pp. 19, 24–25; *RV,* no. 294, November 8, 1905, p. 3; Tan, "Po gubernii," p. 54; *Vserossiiskaia,* pp. 426–28, 430; S. A-n [Stepan Anikin], "Po rodnym mestma," *Russkoe bogatstvo,* no. 12 (January 1907), sec. 2, p. 52; Maslov, *Agrarnyi vopros,* 2:243, 245–46; Gokhlerner, "Krest'ianskoe," pp. 209, 210, 215; Chernyshev, "Saratovskaia guberniia," pp. 140, 141, 144, 147; *RVR (November–December 1905),* pp. 762, 766; S. Prokopovich, "Formy i rezul'taty agrarnago dvizheniia v 1906 godu," *Byloe* 2, no. 1(13) (1907): 155–56.

61 Belokurov, *Iz zapisok,* pp. 27, 38–39, 55, 56–57 (quote), 66–67; *Vserossiiskaia,* pp. 425–27; Chernyshev, "Saratovskaia guberniia," pp. 133–34, esp. 135 and 139; Studentsov, *Saratovskoe,* pp. 35–36, 45; Prokopovich, "Formy," p. 156. *RV,* no. 292, November 6, 1906, p. 3; Bock, "Stolypin," pp. 190–91; Larskii, "Po povodu," sec. 2, p. 26; A. S., "Vnutrennoe obozrenié," *Russkaia mysl'* 26, no. 12 (1905), sec. 2, p. 205.

62 Larskii, "Po povodu," sec. 2, p. 27; *RV,* no. 294, November 8, 1905, p. 3; Chernyshev, "Saratovskaia guberniia," pp. 142, 146; Prokopovich, "Formy," 156; Maslov, *Agrarnyi vopros,* 2: 243; Manning, *Crisis of the Old Order,* p. 154; Studentsov, *Saratovskoe,* p. 27; *Protokoly delegatskago sov-eshchaniia,* p. 24.

63 Studentsov, *Saratovskoe,* pp. 1–16; Gokhlerner, "Krest'ianskoe," pp. 200–201, 203, 206 n 93; *Bez zaglaviia,* no. 7, March 5, 1906, pp.

258–59; *Vserossiiskaia,* pp. 425, 427; *Istoriia,* p. 190; Chernyshev, "Saratovskaia guberniia," pp. 134, 138, 140, 148: Viktor Obninskii, *Polgoda russkoi revoliutsii: Sbornik materialov k istorii russkoi revoliutsii (oktiabr' 1905–aprel' 1906 gg.)* (Moscow, 1906), p. 55.

64 A. V. Shapkarin, ed., *Krest'ianskoe dvizhenie v Rossii v 1890–1900 gody: Sbornik dokumentov,* (Moscow, 1959), pp. 67–87; *Vserossiiskaia,* pp. 429–30; Belokurov, *Iz zapisok,* pp. 20–25 (esp. 20, 23–24), 28, 29, 30, 31, 38, 39–40, 41–42, 45, 51, 58, 60–62, 63; Maslov, *Agrarnyi vopros,* 2:243, 247–48; Argunov, "Iz vospominaniia," pp. 143–44; I. Illarionov, et al., "Selo Nikolaevskii Gorodok Saratovskoi gubernii v 1905 g., " *Proletarskaia revoliutsiia,* no. 12 (47) (1925): 194–203; Gokhlerner and Kharlamova, "Iz istorii," pp. 89–120; V. V. Lozhkin, "K izucheniiu istochnikov po istorii 'Nikolaevskoi respubliki' (1905)," in V. I. Buganov et al., *Istochnikovedenie otechestvennoi istorii: Sbornik statei 1981* (Moscow, 1982), pp. 145–66; *Pravo,* no. 43, November 8, 1905, col. 3559; Tan, "Deputaty," sec. 2, pp. 90–96; Studentsov, *Saratovskoe,* pp. 16, 33, 37; Gokhlerner, "Krest'ianskoe," pp. 206, 215–16; *RVR (November–December 1905),* pp. 758, 762; *Narodnaia zhizn',* no. 1, April 16, 1906, p. 43.

65 I. S-v, "Stranichka iz istorii nashei smuty: ('Malinovskoe delo')," *Istoricheskii vestnik 29* (May 1908): 550–57 (quotation, p. 550); K., "Na krest'ianskoi Golgofe," *Soznatel'naia Rossiia,* no. 1 (1906): 72–83; no. 4 (1906): 100–106; " 'Istinno-russkoe' predstavitel'stvo pred tsarem," *Soznatel'naia Rossiia,* no. 2 (1906): 95; Antonov-Saratovskii, *Krasnyi god,* p. 168; Babikov, "Krest'ianskoe," p. 209; Prokopovich, "Formy," p. 169; *PK,* no. 115, June 6, 1906, p. 2; no. 140, July 6, 1906, p. 2; "Milost' poddannym," *Soznatel'naia Rossiia,* no. 3 (1906): 96.

66 *Protokoly delegatskago soveshchaniia,* pp. 75–76, 77–79, 91 (quotation, p. 78); *Materialy k krest'ianskomu voprosu: Otchet o zasedaniiakh delegatskago s''ezda Vserossiiskago Krest'ianskago Soiuza 6–10 noiabria 1906 g.* (Rostov-on-Don, 1905): 45–46, 70–71; Studentsov, *Saratovskoe,* pp. 42–46; V. I. Nevskii, ed., *Revoliutsiia 1905 goda: Materialy i ofitsial'nye dokumenty* (Moscow, 1925), p. 205. For examples of the initial horrifying, and to some extent misleading, newspaper reports, see Obninskii, *Polgoda,* pp. 55, 56; *RV,* no. 292, November 6, 1905, p. 3.

67 *RV,* no. 248, October 25, 1908, p. 5; no. 250, October 28, 1908, p. 6; Semen Mazurenko, "S''ezd krest'ian 18 dekabria 1905 g.," *Byloe,* no. 8 (1908): 35–39; Semen Mazurenko, "Eshche po povodu s''ezda Saratovskikh krest'ian 18-go dekabria 1905 g.," *Byloe,* no. 8 (1908): 149–52.

68 *RVR (November–December 1905),* pp. 759–61, 767; Maslov, *Agrarnyi vopros,* 2:257–59, 261; Manning, *Crisis of the Old Order,* p. 148; Veselovskii, *Krest'ianskii,* pp. 89, 99–100; Antonov-Saratovskii, *Krasnyi god,*

pp. 170–72; N. Chuzhak, "Ocherki provintsial'noi zhizni: Derevenskiia kartinki," *Nasha mysl'*, January 21, 1906, pp. 21–22; S. A-n, "Po rodnym mestam," *Russkoe bogatstvo* (January 1907), sec. 2, pp. 41, 59; Uolling, *Poslanie Rossii*, pp. 264–66; *Novaia mysl'*, no. 3 (1906): 72; *Istoriia*, pp. 189n, 190–92; Karpov, ed., *Krest'ianskoe*, pp. 260, 264; Belokurov, *Iz zapisok*, pp. 69–70; *PK*, no. 140, July 6, 1906, p. 2; Ia. L. Teitel, "Sudy po agrarnym delam v gody reaktsii (Iz zapisok chlena okruzhn, suda), "*Letopis revoliutsii*, no. 1 (1923): 134–37.

69 Antonov-Saratovskii, *Krasnyi god*, pp. 164, 173–74; Bock, "Stolypin," pp. 188–89, 193.

70 V. Golubev, "Zemskaia reaktsiia," *Bez zaglaviia*, no. 4, February 12, 1906, pp. 136–38; Manning, *Crisis of the Old Order*, pp. 177, 195–97, 222, 231, 235, 237, 238, 474 n. 42; Veselovskii, *Krest'ianskii*, pp. 101, 126, 129; Tan, "Po gubernii," pp. 18–20; V. Levitskii, "Pravyia partii," *Obshchestvennoe dvizhenie v Rossii v nachale XX-go veka*, vol. 3, no. 5, L. Martov, P. Maslov, and A. Potresov, eds. (St. Petersburg, 1914), pp. 371, 375, 386–87; Bock, "Stolypin," pp. 191–92; *RR*, no. 75, September 15, 1905, pp. 17, 19; Studentsov, *Saratovskoe*, pp. 38n, 41nn; Chernyshev, "Saratovskaia guber-niia," pp. 132, 136, 139, 140, 149; Semenov, "1905," pp. 214–15; *Trudy vtorogo s'ezda Upolnomochennykh Dvorianskikh Obshchestv 31 gubernii 14–18 noiabria 1906 g.* (St. Petersburg, 1906), pp. 186–87; S. A-n, "Po rodnym mestam," *Russkoe bogatstvo*, no. 11 (November 1906), sec. 2, pp. 18–20; Tan, "Deputaty," sec. 2, p. 93; *Mirskiia vest'*, no. 1, April 29, 1906, pp. 22, 24; *PK:* no. 61, March 19, 1906, p. 3; no. 81, April 19, 1906, p. 2; no. 84, April 22, 1906, p. 4; no. 98, May 14, 1906, p. 2; no. 111, June 1, 1906, p. 2; nos. 112–13, June 3, 1906, p. 2; no. 115, June 6, 1906, p. 2; no. 116, June 7, 1906, p. 3; no. 117, June 8, 1906, p. 3; no. 126, June 18, 1906, p. 2; no. 127, June 20, 1906, p. 2; no. 130, June 23, 1906, p. 3; no. 132, June 25, 1906, p. 2; no. 135, June 29, 1906, p. 2; no. 140, July 6, 1906, p. 2 (2 articles); no. 141, July 7, 1906, p. 3; no. 151, July 19, 1906, pp. 2–3; no. 158, July 28, 1906, p. 2; no. 170, August 11, 1906, p. 2; no. 174, August 17, 1906, p. 2; no. 192, September 8, 1906, p. 3; *SL*, no. 137, July 1, 1906, p. 2; no. 146, July 12, 1906, p. 3; "Krest'ianskoe dvizhenie: Pravitel'stvennaia vlast' v derevne," *Trudovoi Narod: Narodno-Sotsialisticheskoe Obozrenie*, no. 1 (1906): 65–66.

71 *PK*, no. 49, March 4, 1906, p. 2; no. 50, March 5, 1906, p. 2; no. 51, March 7, 1906, p. 2; no. 54, March 10, 1906, p. 2; no. 63, March 21, 1906, p. 2; *SL*, no. 78, April 14, 1906, p. 2; *PK*, no. 76, April 13, 1906, p. 3.

72 The data on professions was culled from *Privolzhskii krai* and *Saratovskii listok* issues between March 1, 1906, and April 19, 1906. See also Leopold H. Haimson, "Conclusion" in Leopold H. Haimson, ed., *The Politics of Rural Russia, 1905–1914* (Bloomington, Ind., 1979), pp. 283, 286–87;

Terence Emmons, *The Formation of Political Parties and the First National Elections in Russia* (Cambridge, Mass., 1983), pp. 244, 246, 248. On past and present prison experience, see *PK,* no. 74, April 4, 1906, p. 2.

73   *PK,* no. 56, March 12, 1906, p. 2; no. 73, April 9, 1906, p. 2; no. 74, April 11, 1906, p. 2. The only possible exception to the list of left-leaning delegations may have been Balashov District (see *PK,* no. 74, April 11, 1906, p. 2). On the Union of Laboring People, see: *PK,* no. 59, March 16, 1906, pp. 1–2; no. 60, March 18, 1906, pp. 1–2; Seregny, "Politics," pp. 185–88. Tan, *Muzhiki,* pp. 57–58; L. M. Bramson, *K istorii Trudovoi partii: Trudovaia gruppa Pervoi Gosudarstvennoi Dumy* (Petrograd, 1917), pp. 10–11. It would seem that though an election coalition was formed between peasants and workers, the city and peasant Unions of Laboring People never merged. It is not clear if the latter was ever more than a temporary phenomenon of the election process. (*PK,* no. 76, April 13, 1906, p. 2; no. 78, April 15, 1906, pp. 1, 3.) On the election process and results, see: *PK,* no. 75, April 12, 1906, p. 2; no. 76, April 13, 1906, pp. 2–3; no. 77, April 14, 1906, pp. 2–3; no. 78, April 15, 1906, p. 3; no. 79, April 16, 1906, p. 3.

74   *IKD,* no. 10, May 30, 1906, p. 2; Maslov, *Agrarnyi vopros,* 2:282–83.

75   Maslov, *Agrarnyi vopros,* 2:282–83; *IKD,* no. 10, May 30, 1906, p. 2; *PK,* no. 74, April 11, 1906, pp. 2–3; no. 75, April 12, 1906, p. 3; no. 115, June 6, 1906, p. 2; no. 132, June 25, 1906, p. 2.

76   *Rech',* May 25, 1906, p. 4; *Narodnaia zhizn',* no. 3, April 30, 1906, p. 20.

77   V. A. Maklakov, *The First State Duma,* trans. Mary Belkin, (Bloomington, Ind., 1964), pp. 90–113, esp. 90–91, 108–13; Manning, *Crisis of the Old Order,* pp. 213–14, 251–54; *Iuzhnoe obozrenie,* no. 3120, June 10, 1906, p. 2. The quotation is from *PK,* no. 126, June 18, 1906, p. 2. See also *Istoriia,* p. 207; *PK,* no. 110, May 31, 1906, p. 2; *Vtoroi period revoliutsii 1906–1907 gody,* pt. 2, *Mai–Sentiabr' 1906 goda,* no. 2, M. S. Simonova et al., eds., in *Revoliutsiia 1905–1907 gg. v Rossii: Dokumenty i materialy,* A. L. Sidorov et al., eds., [hereafter *RVR (1906)*] (Moscow, 1962), p. 313.

78   P. N. Pershin, *Agrarnaia revoliutsiia v Rossii,* book 1: *Ot reformy k revoliutsii* (Moscow, 1966), p. 49.

79   Gokhlerner and Kharlamova, "Iz istorii," pp. 238–41, 244–45; Gokhlerner, "Krest'ianskoe," pp. 221–24. The figure Gokhlerner lists for strikes (66) quite likely underestimates their number, if the number of villages participating is counted. Prokopovich, "Formy," p. 163; *PK,* no. 119, June 10, 1906, p. 2; no. 123, June 15, 1906, p. 2; no. 126, June 18, 1906, p. 2; no. 129, June 22, 1906, p. 3.

80   M. Beliakov, "Tseny na rabochiia ruki po Saratovskoi gubernii za vremia s maia po dekabr' mesiats 1906 goda," Saratovskoe gubernskoe zemstvo *Sbornik svedenii po Saratovskoi gubernii za 1906 god* 2 (Saratov, 1906): 111–16;

Prokopovich, "Formy," p. 169; *PK,* no. 136, July 1, 1906, p. 3; no. 140, July 6, 1906, p. 2; *SD,* no. 140, July 2, 1906, p. 2; TsGIA, f. 91, op. 2, ed. khr, 786, list 294ob.; N. I. Teziakov, "Iz vospominanii zemskikh vrachei: N. I. Teziakov," in *Ocherki istorii russkoi obshchestvennoi meditsiny,* ed., P. I. Kal'iu (Moscow, 1965), p. 247; *Protokoly delegatskago soveshchaniia,* pp. 90–91; *PK,* no. 112, June 2, 1906, p. 2; no. 123, June 15, 1906, p. 2; no. 126, June 18, 1906, p. 2; no. 145, July 12, 1906, p. 2; *RVR (1906),* pp. 315–17; Edelman, "Rural Proletarians," passim. Strikes in the steppe grain belt did not have to be as long as those in industry, because employers were faced with the pressure of completing the harvest before wheat, rye, and oats spilled out.

81 Beliakov, "Tseny," pp. 112–16; *SD,* no. 140, July 2, 1906, p. 2; *PK,* no. 109, May 30, 1906, p. 2; no. 112, June 2, 1906, p. 2; nos. 112–13, June 3, 1906, p. 2; no. 119, June 10, 1906, p. 2; no. 126, June 18, 1906, p. 3; no. 129, June 22, 1906, p. 3; no. 134, June 28, 1906, p. 2; no. 145, July 12, 1906, p. 2; Chernyshev, "Saratovskaia guberniia," pp. 135, 141, 147; Prokopovich, "Formy," p. 170; Teziakov, "Iz vospominanii," p. 247; *PK,* no. 72, April 6, 1906, p. 2; no. 136, July 1, 1906, p. 3.

82 *PK,* no. 132, June 25, 1906, p. 2; no. 134, June 28, 1906, p. 2; no. 135, June 29, 1906, p. 3; no. 140, July 6, 1906, p. 2; no. 145, July 12, 1906, p. 2 (two articles); no. 150, July 18, 1906, p. 2; no. 156, July 26, 1906, p. 2; *SD,* no. 140, July 2, 1906, p. 2; Chernyshev, "Saratovskaia guberniia," p. 132; Beliakov, "Tseny," pp. 112–13, 115–16; *Tovarishch,* no. 41, August 22, 1906, p. 2; Prokopovich, "Formy," pp. 166, 169; *SL,* no. 147, July 13, 1906, p. 3; no. 166, August 5, 1906, p. 3; *Istoriia,* p. 210.

83 *SD,* no. 140, July 2, 1906, p. 2; Beliakov, "Tseny," pp. 112–16; *PK,* no. 72, April 6, 1906, p. 2; no. 112, June 2, 1906, p. 2; nos. 112–13, June 3, 1906, p. 2; no. 118, June 9, 1906, p. 2; no. 123, June 15, 1906, p. 2; no. 124, June 16, 1906, p. 2; no. 125, June 17, 1906, p. 2; no. 126, June 18, 1906, p. 3; no. 127, June 20, 1906, p. 2; no. 132, June 25, 1906, p. 2; no. 134, June 28, 1906, p. 2; Chernyshev, "Saratovskaia guberniia," p. 142; *SL,* no. 147, July 13, 1906, p. 3. For strike demands or actions that amounted to a call for changes in the political order at the national or local level, see: Beliakov, "Tseny," p. 115; *SL,* no. 147, July 13, 1906, p. 3; *PK,* no. 134, June 28, 1906, p. 2; no. 170, August 11, 1906, p. 2; Chernyshev, "Saratovskaia guberniia," p. 132. See also the Arkadak strike noted below.

84 Mixter, "Of Grandfather-Beaters," pp. 153–66; *SD,* no. 140, July 2, 1906, p. 2; *SL,* no. 181, August 24, 1906, p. 2; Fallows, "Forging the Zemstvo Movement," p. 627; TsGIA, f. 1162, op. 6, ed. khr. 100 (Viazemskii's service record); *Al'manakh sovremennykh russkikh gosudarstvennykh deiatelei* (St. Petersburg, 1897), p. 1116; *PK,* no. 103, May 20, 1906, p. 3; S., "Iz praktiki russkikh khoziaistv: Organizatsii arendy v im. 'Arkadak,'

Saratovskoi gub.," *Vestnik sel'skago khoziaistva,* nos. 6 and 8 (1906): A. M. Anfimov, *Krupnoe pomeshchich'e khoziaistvo Evropeiskoi Rossii* (Moscow, 1969), pp. 86, 144–47,353, 382–86; *SD,* no. 142, July 5, 1906, p. 2; L. P. Vasitskii, "Otchet o deiatel'nosti Arkadakskago lechebno-prodovol'stvennago punkta," in *Lechebno-prodovol'stvennye punkty na rynkakh naima sel'sko-kho-ziaistvennykh rabochikh v Saratovskoi gubernii v 1906 g.* (Saratov, 1906), p. 17.

85 Vasitskii, "Otchet," p. 17; *PK,* no. 136, July 1, 1906, p. 3; Teziakov, "Iz vospominanii," p. 247; Prokopovich, "Formy," p. 169; *Istoriia,* pp. 207–8; *SD,* no. 140, July 2, 1906, p. 2; Gokhlerner, "Krest'ianskoe," p. 226. For an examination of the reasons why cobblers often led rural protest, see: E. J. Hobsbawm and Joan Wallach Scott, "Political Shoemakers," *Past & President,* no. 89 (November 1980): 86–114.

86 *PK,* no. 98, May 14, 1906, p. 2; no. 104, May 21, 1906, p. 2; *SD,* no. 140, July 2, 1906, p. 2; A. V. Shestakov, *Naemnyi trud v sel'skom khoziaistve* (Moscow-Leningrad, 1924), p. 162; *Samarskii kur'er,* no. 567 (138), July 4, 1906, p. 2; Teziakov,"Iz vospominanii," p. 247; TsGIA, f. 91, op. 2, ed. khr. 786, list 294ob.; Prokopovich, "Formy," p. 169; *PK,* no. 136, July 1, 1906, p. 3, and no. 140, July 6, 1906, p. 2. These sources suggest that at least 100 rubles was raised, and perhaps as much as 1,000 rubles.

87 Beliakov, "Tseny," pp. 114–16; Chernyshev, "Saratovskaia gubernii," p. 131; Gokhlerner, "Krest'ianskoe," p. 226; *SD,* no. 140, July 2, 1906, p. 2; no. 141, July 4, 1906, p. 3; no. 142, July 5, 1906, p. 2; *PK,* no. 103, May 20, 1906, p. 3; no. 128, June 21, 1906, p. 2; no. 129, June 22, 1906, p. 3; no. 132, June 25, 1906, p. 2; Tan, "Po gubernii," pp. 19, 61; *Zemlia i volia,* no. 1, August 1905, p. 13; *SL,* no. 134, June 27, 1906, p. 3. Teziakov gives a figure of 44–45 communes joining the strike. See Teziakov, "Iz vospominanii," p. 247.

88 Prokopovich, "Formy," pp. 166 and 169; Beliakov, "Tseny," pp. 115–16; *Istoriia,* p. 210; *PK,* no. 140, July 6, 1906, p. 2; Chernyshev, "Saratovskaia guberniia," p. 132; *Tovarishch,* no. 41, August 22, 1906, p. 2; *SD,* no. 140, July 2, 1906, p. 2. Some newspaper reports even claim that the peasants and agricultural workers were not looking for a compromise and never hoped to win, viewing the confrontation rather as a test of strength wherein, through their organization, they could show that a new era had come, promising a new, equal division of power. See *PK,* no. 129, June 22, 1906, p. 3.

89 *PK,* no. 132, June 25, 1906, p. 2.

90 *SD,* no. 140, July 2, 1906, p. 2; no. 143, July 6, 1906, pp. 2–3; Beliakov, "Tseny," pp. 115–16; Teziakov, "Iz vospominanii," pp. 247–48; Chernyshev, "Saratovskaia guberniia," p. 132.

91 Besides Gerasimenko's figures, see Veselovskii, *Krest'ianskii,* pp. 155–56,

156n 3. See also Chernyshev, "Saratovskaia guberniia," pp. 138, 140, 144; *RVR (1906),* p. 320; *PK,* no. 192, September 8, 1906, p. 3; Gokhlerner, "Krest'ianskoe," pp. 204, 209–10, 214–15, 224; *PK,* no. 49, March 4, 1906, p. 2; no. 109, May 30, 1906, p. 2; *SL,* no. 164, August 3, 1906, p. 3; no. 180, August 23, 1906, p. 2; Golubev, "Zemskaia reaktsiia," p. 137; "Milost' krest'ianam," *Soznatel'naia Rossiia,* no. 2 (1906), p. 91; A. L-ch. "Spokoinyi nabor," *Narodnyi trud: Narodno-sotsialisticheskoe obozrenie,* 2 (1906): 65; Maslov, *Agrarnyi vopros,* 2:320; *SL,* no. 203, September 23, 1906, p. 2. One source suggests that Saratov was one of the three provinces where peasants frequently told the authorities they would not submit recuits willingly. See K. P-v. "Pered rekrutskim naborom," *Trudovoi narod* 2 (1906): 56.

92 Tan, "Po gubernii," pp. 20–22, 47, 55, 56, 79–81, 83–84 (especially), 92–93; *Narodnyi trud: Narodno-sotsialisticheskoe obozrenie* 9 (1907?): 63; *Iskra,* no. 93, March 17, 1905, p. 6; Obninskii, *Polgoda,* p. 54; Anikin, "Za 'pravednoi zemlei,'" p. 102; *RVR (November–December 1905),* p. 762; Gokhlerner, "Krest'ianskoe," p. 225; *PK,* no. 110, May 31, 1906, p. 2; no. 123, June 15, 1906, p. 2; no. 138, July 4, 1906, p. 3; no. 145, July 12, 1906, p. 2; no. 153, July 21, 1906, p. 2; no. 163, August 3, 1906, p. 2; no. 166, August 6, 1906, p. 3; no. 168, August 8, 1906, p.3; Chernyshev, "Saratovskaia guberniia," pp. 136–37, 143–44, 149; *SL,* no. 164, August 3, 1906, p. 3; *RVR* (1906), pp. 321–22; *PK,* no. 191, September 7, 1906, p. 2; *PK,* no. 125, June 17, 1906, p. 2; no. 126, June 18, 1906, p. 3; no. 134, June 28, 1906, p. 2; *Narodno-sotsialisticheskoe obozrenie,* no. 2 (1906), p. 64. For cases of peasants protecting members of the rural intelligentsia or new social institutions from priests or police, see: Tan, "Po gubernii," pp. 20–22, 79–81, 92–93, 99–102; *PK,* no. 72, April 6, 1906, p. 2; no. 98, May 14, 1906, p. 2; no. 118, June 9, 1906, p. 2; no. 178, August 22, 1906, p. 2; *RV,* no. 292, November 6, 1905, p. 3; *SL,* no. 168, August 8, 1906, p. 3. There is some indication that more than a few members of the lower clergy came out in support of the peasantry by 1906, particularly in Balashov District, and that these new allies to some extent offset the loss of support from zemstvo deputies. See *Pravo,* January 15, 1906, col. 123.

93 Maslov, *Agrarnyi vopros,* 2:445; *PK,* no. 120, June 11, 1906, p. 3; no. 125, June 17, 1906, p. 2. Atkarsk and Serdobsk district gentry led the way in sales.

94 Konovalov, "V derevne," sec. 2, pp. 19–20.

95 Maslov, *Agrarnyi vopros,* 2:446, 448; Beliakov, "Tseny," pp. 108–20 (esp. p. 112).

96 On the disgruntlement, see: Konovalov, "V derevne," pp. 18–21; "The

Russian Peasantry," pp. 180–90; S. A-n, "Po rodnym mestam," *Russkoe bogatstvo*, no. 11 (1906), sec. 2, pp. 1–20, and no. 1 (1907), sec. 2, pp. 36–65.

CHAPTER 10

1 See, for example, D. A. Baturinskii, *Agrarnaia politika tsarskogo pravitel'stva i krest'ianskii pozemel'nyi bank* (Moscow, 1925); N. Karpov, *Agrarnaia politika Stolypina* (Leningrad, 1925); I. Litvinov, *Stolypinshchina* (Kharkov, 1931); P. N. Efremov, *Stolypinskaia agrarnaia politika* (Moscow, 1941); P. V. Meshcheriakov, *Pereselentsy* (Cheliabinsk, 1941); L. B. Beliavskaia, "K voprosy o pereselencheskoi politike tsarizma v period stolypinskoi agrarnoi reformy," *Uchenye zapiski Tomskogo politekhnicheskogo instituta* (Tomsk, 1958); S. M. Dubrovskii, *Stolypinskaia zemel'naia reforma* (Moscow, 1963); P. N. Pershin, *Agrarnaia revoliutsiia v Rossii*, bk. 1 (Moscow, 1966); S. M. Sidel'nikov, *Agrarnaia politika samoderzhaviia v period imperializma* (Moscow, 1980), and so on.

2 See P. I. Shul'pin, "Stolypinskaia reforma v Nizhegorodskoi gubernii," in *Gor'kovskaia oblast'*, no. 11 (1940); V. N. Liubimov, *Chuvashiia v gody stolypinskoi agrarnoi politiki* (Cheboksary, 1948); I. N. Tregubov, "Stolypinskaia reforma i razlozhenie krest'ianstva v Simbirskoi gubernii," *Uchenye zapiski Ul'ianovskogo pedinstituta*, no. 4 (1950); Kh. F. Usmanov, *Stolypinskaia agrarnaia reforma v Bashkirii* (Ufa, 1958); A. M. Grebnev, *Agrarnye otnosheniia v Penzenskoi gubernii mezhdu pervoi i vtoroi burzhuazno-demokraticheskimi revoliutsiiami v Rossii* (Penza, 1959); I. V. Grishkunaite, "Agrarnaia politika Solypina v Litve," in *Ezhegodnik po agrarnoi istorii Vostochnoi Evropy* (Kiev, 1962); L. P. Bakatova, "Stolypinskaia agrarnaia reforma v Permskoi gubernii," *Uchenye zapiski Permskogo universiteta*, no. 108 (1964); N. V. Volkov, "Krest'ianskoe dvizhenie v Iaroslavskoi, Kostromskoi i Vladimirskoi guberniiakh v period stolypinskoi agrarnoi reformy," in *Uchenye zapiski Moskovskogo pedinstituta*, no. 439 (1971); L. P. Lipinskii, *Stolypinskaia agrarnaia reforma v Belorussii* (Minsk, 1978); S. K. Kivimiae, *Stolypinskaia agrarnaia reforma v Pribaltike* (Tallin, 1981); P. S. Kabytov, *Agrarnye otnosheniia v Povolzh'e v period imperializma* (Saratov, 1982).

3 M. Ia. Kosenko, "Agrarnaia reforma Stolypina v Saratovskoi gubernii," Candidate diss., Saratov, 1950; and idem., "Iz istorii provedeniia stolypinskoi agrarnoi reformy v Saratovskoi gubernii," *Uchenye zapiski Saratovskogo gosudarstvennogo pedinstituta*, no. 22 (1956).

4 V. I. Lenin, *Collected Works* (Moscow, 1962), 13: 277. (I have provided citations from the official English-language edition of Lenin's works—Trans.)

5   Ibid., p. 443.
6   *Polnoe sobranie zakonov Rossiiskoi imperii,* 30: 747–48.
7   *Sbornik rechei Stolypina* (St. Petersburg, 1912), pp. 45–46.
8   Lenin, *Collected Works* (Moscow, 1963), 16: 360.
9   *Birzhevye vedomosti,* October 8, 1906.
10 Kosenko, "Iz istorii," p. 175.
11 *Gosarkhiv Saratovskoi oblasti,* f. 4, d. 13, l. 83.
12 Kosenko, "Iz istorii," p. 176.
13 *Obzor deiatel'nosti zemleustroitel'nykh komissii za pervyi god ikh sushchestvovaniia* (St. Petersburg, 1908), p. 1.
14 Kosenko, "Iz istorii," p. 178.
15 *Obzor deiatel'nosti zemleustroitel'nykh komissii,* p. 1.
16 TsGIA, f. 408, op. 1, d. 4, l. 32.
17 *Privolzhskii krai,* no. 244, 1906.
18 Kosenko, "Iz istorii," p. 176.
19 TsGIA, f. 408, op. 1, d. 83, l. 48–49.
20 *Gosarkhiv Saratovskoi oblasti,* f. 400, d. 1, l. 10.
21 Kosenko, "Iz istorii," p. 178.
22 S. M. Sidel'nikov, *Agrarnaia reforma Stolypina: Uchebnoe posobie* (Moscow, 1973), p. 131.
23 *Golos pravdy,* February 14, 1910; *Sankt-Peterburgskie vedomosti,* March 5, 1910; *Permskie vedomosti,* March 6, 1911.
24 *Sankt-Peterburgskie vedomosti,* September 17, 1911.
25 Ibid., January 30, 1913.
26 *Ustroistvo pokazatel'nykh krest'ianskikh khoziaistv na khutorakh i otrubakh v Saratovskoi gubernii* (Saratov, 1909), p. 28.
27 Ibid., p. 1.
28 Cited in Dubrovskii, *Stolypinskaia zemel'naia reforma,* p. 11.
29 I. V. Chernyshev, *Agrarno-krest'ianskaia politika Rossii za 150 let* (St. Petersburg, 1918), p. 381.
30 *Staryi Vladimirets,* October 14, 1908.
31 *Volzhskoe slovo,* July 5, 1908.
32 Ibid., July 13, 1908.
33 *Novoe vremia,* February 27, 1908.
34 *Gosarkhiv Saratovskoi oblasti,* f. 1, op. 1, d. 162, l. 12.
35 *Ukreplenie nadelov v lichnuiu sobstvennost' v Kazanskoi gubernii* (Kazan, 1911), p. 67.
36 *Volzhskii krai,* February 18, 1907.
37 Ibid.
38 *Gosarkhiv Saratovskoi oblasti,* f. 449, d. 254, l. 9.

39 I have compiled the above statistics based on information found in Kosenko, "Iz istorii," p. 181.

40 Ibid.

41 *Rus'*, October 23, 1908.

42 I. V. Mozzhukhin, *Zemleustroistvo v Bogorodskom uezde Tul'skoi gubernii* (Moscow, 1917), pp. 160, 171.

43 *Rus'*, October 23, 1908.

44 *Ural'skaia zhizn'*, February 21, 1909; *Volgar'*, March 24, 1910; N. N. Gul'tsev, *Stolypinskaia agrarnaia reforma v Voronezhskoi gubernii i ee krakh* (Leningrad, 1953), p. 8; S. Arkhangel'skii, "Krest'ianstvo i krest'ianskoe dvizhenie v Nizhegorodskom krae v period 1906–1917 gg.," in *Nizhegorodskii krai*, pt. 3 (Nizhnii Novgorod, 1926), p. 79.

45 Kosenko, "Iz istorii," p. 181.

46 Ibid., p. 180.

47 Ibid.

48 *Gosarkhiv Saratovskoi oblasti*, f. 1, op. 1, d. 162, l. 1; d. 7490, l. 62; d. 7502, l. 116; d. 7647, l. 3; d. 7662, l. 4; d. 7748, l. 19; d. 8175, l. 34; d. 8456, l. 47; d. 8464, l. 26; d. 8502, l. 56–59; d. 8533, l. 94, d. 8746, l. 58; d. 9052, l. 28, d. 9333, l. 4; d. 9447, ll. 16; f. 53, kn. 1, d. 24, l. 6; f. 400, d. 122, l. 61; *Gosarkhiv Volgogradskoi oblasti*, f. 6, op. 1, d. 50, l. 8; A. V. Shapkarin, ed., *Krest'ianskoe dvizhenie v Rossii, iiun' 1907–iiul' 1914: Sbornik dokumentov* (Moscow and Leningrad, 1966), pp. 179–81, and elsewhere.

49 Shapkarin, *Krest'ianskoe dvizhenie v Rossii*, pp. 179–81.

50 TsGIA, f. 1291, op. 120, d. 1, l. 228.

51 *Gosarkhiv Saratovskoi oblasti*, f. 1, op. 1, d. 8175, l. 25; d. 8533, l. 1; d. 8761, l. 28; d. 9052, l. 27; d. 9060, l. 29; d. 9169, l. 17; d. 9194, ll. 11; d. 9333, l. 46; d. 9447, ll. 16, 65; d. 9460, l. 41; f. 53, op. 1, d. 57, l. 1–2; d. 61, l. 12; f. 400, op. 1, d. 122, l. 62, and others.

52 TsGIA, f. 1291, op. 120, d. 17, l. 40.

53 *Gosarkhiv Saratovskoi oblasti*, f. 1, op. 1, d. 9196, l. 1.

54 Shapkarin, *Krest'ianskoe dvizhenie v Rossii*, p. 290.

55 *Novoe vremia*, June 11, 1911.

56 TsGIA, f. 1405, op. 253, d. 387, ll. 11–12.

57 Shapkarin, *Krest'ianskoe dvizhenie v Rossii*, pp. 291–93.

58 TsGIA, f. 408, op. 1, d. 149, l. 125.

59 Ibid., d. 956, l. 19.

60 Lenin, *Collected Works*, 17: 252–53.

61 Kosenko, "Iz istorii," p. 180.

62 Ibid.

63 I. V. Chernyshev, *Obshchina posle 9 noiabria g.* (Petrograd, 1917), pt. 1, p. xiii.

64 *Russkoe znamia*, February 22, 1909.

65 Ibid.
66 TsGIA, f. 408, op. 1, d. 1551, l. 11; d. 128, ll. 33–34. *Rech'*, October 14, 1910; *Svet*, December 9, 1910; *Nizhegorodskii listok*, July 18, 1911; *Odesskie novosti*, September 11, 1912; and others.
67 *Gosarkhiv Saratovskoi oblasti*, f. 1, op. 1, d. 9169, l. 1.
68 TsGAOR, f. 102, fourth record keeping, 1914, d. 62, ch. 1, l. 1; d. 13, ch. 1, l. 1; d. 83, ch. 1, l. 2–4; d. 53, ch. 1, l. 3; and others.
69 TsGIA, f. 408, op. 1, d. 293, l. 12.
70 Chernyshev, *Obshchina*, p. xiii; Dubrovskii, *Stolypinskaia zemel'naia reforma*, p. 199.
71 Kosenko, "Iz istórii," p. 179.
72 Kosenko, "Agrarnaia reforma Stolypina," p. 227.
73 A. I. Tiumenev, *Ot revoliutsii k revoliutsii* (Leningrad, 1925), p. 29.
74 Kosenko, "Iz istorii," p. 184.
75 Dubrovskii, *Stolypinskaia zemel'naia reforma*, p. 554.
76 Ibid., p. 559.
77 Ibid., p. 554.
78 *Gosarkhiv Saratovskoi oblasti*, f. 1, op. 1, d. 9052, l. 28.
79 Ibid., d. 8465, l. 47; d. 8175, l. 34.
80 Ibid., d. 8464, l. 26; d. 9333, l. 4.
81 Ibid., d. 7490, l. 62.
82 Ibid., d. 8746, l. 58.
83 Ibid., d. 7502, l. 116.
84 Ibid., d. 135, l. 12.
85 *Saratovskii listok*, July 1, 1917.
86 *Saratovskii vestnik*, May 11, 1917.
87 *Saratovskii listok*, June 26, 1917.
88 Ibid., July 16, 1917.
89 *Zemlia i volia* (Saratov), June 29, 1917.
90 *Saratovskii vestnik*, May 21, 1917.
91 Ibid., July 25, 1917.
92 *Zemlia i volia* (Saratov), June 8, 1917.
93 *Krasnyi arkhiv*, no. 2 (15) (1926), p. 42.

CHAPTER 11

1 Gyorki, Jeno, comp. *Vengerskie internatsionalisty v Velikoi Oktiabr'skoi sotsialisticheskoi revoliutsii* (Moscow, 1959), p. 26.
2 Walentyna Najdus, *Polacy w Rewolucji 1917 roku* (Warsaw, 1967), pp. 6, 8, 17, 50, 52; L. I. Lubny-Gertsyk, *Dvizhenie naseleniia na territorii SSSR za vremia mirovoi voiny i revoliutsii* (Moscow, 1926), p. 23; V. G. Khodakov,

"Bor'ba rabochikh Saratovskoi gubernii pod rukovodstvom Kommunisticheskoi organizatsii za rabochii kontrol' nad proizvodstvom v 1917–18 gg." (Candidate diss., Saratov Pedagogical Institute, 1953), p. 4; "Professional'nye soiuzy Saratovskoi gubernii za 10 let," *Nizhnee Povolzh'e*, no. 10 (1927): 152; V. Ts. Urlanik, "Dinamika naseleniia Rossii nakanune oktiabria," *Uchenye zapiski Vsesoiuznogo zaochno-ekonomicheskogo instituta*, no. 2 (1957): 124; A. G. Kovalevskii, *Ocherki po demografii Saratova (rozhdaemost' i smertnost' za 1914–1927 gg.)* (Saratov, 1928), p. 11.

3   I. N. Kokshaiskii, *Predvaritel'nye dannye perepisi naseleniia goroda Saratova i ego prigorodov* (Saratov, 1916), pp. 9, 13.

4   Gaston V. Rimlinger, "The Management of Labor Protest in Tsarist Russia, 1870–1905," *The International Review of Social History* 5 (1961): 230.

5   N. L. Klein, "Ob osobennostiakh polozheniia i urovne ekspluatatsii promyshlennykh rabochikh Srednego Povolzh'ia v period kapitalizma," *Nash krai* (Kuibyshev), no. 1 (1974): 22–23; A. Kh. Kliachko, "Materialy o polozhenii promyshlennykh rabochikh Saratovskoi gubernii," *Trudy Saratovskogo ekonomicheskogo instituta* 2 (1949): 63–67.

6   Inspectors examined ninety-eight Saratov factories representing twenty-seven industries. See *Fabriki i zavody g. Saratova v sanitarnom otnoshenii* (Saratov, 1911).

7   E. N. Burdzhalov, *Vtoraia russkaia revoliutsiia: Moskva, front, periferiia* (Moscow, 1971), p. 202.

8   E. E. Diakevich, *Ocherk o deiatel'nosti Saratovskoi 'Birzhi truda' za god sushchestvovaniia (27 noiabria 1914 g. po 1 ianvaria 1916 g.)* (Saratov, 1916), p. 7.

9   Kokshaiskii, *Predvaritel'nye dannye perepisi*, pp. 30–32.

10 Stanislas Kohn and Alexander F. Meyendorff, *The Cost of the War to Russia* (New Haven, Conn., 1932), pp. 24, 27. See also Tsentral'noe statisticheskoe upravlenie, *Rossiia v mirovoi voine, 1914–1918 goda (v tsifrakh)* (Moscow, 1925), p. 21. A comprehensive account of the food supply problem can be found in T. M. Kitanina, *Voina, khleb i revoliutsiia (Prodovol'stvennyi vopros v Rossii, 1914–oktiabr' 1917 g.)* (Leningrad, 1985).

11 A. F. Milovzorov, *Krest'ianskoe chastnovladel'cheskoe khoziaistvo Saratovskoi gubernii posle goda voiny* (Saratov, 1916), pp. 9, 12.

12 V. P. Miliutin, *Sel'sko-khoziaistvennye rabochie i voina* (Petrograd, 1917), pp. 71, 118.

13 Ibid., p. 124.

14 A. M. Anfimov, *Rossiiskaia derevnia v gody pervoi mirovoi voiny (1914–fevral' 1917 g.)* (Moscow, 1962), p. 189.

15 Victoria E. Bonnell, "Trade Unions, Parties, and the State in Tsarist Russia: A Study of Labor Politics in St. Petersburg and Moscow," *Politics and Society* 9 (1980): 299–322.

16 "Professional'nye soiuzy," p. 150; V. Sviatlovskii, "Professional'noe dvizhenie rabochikh v 1905 g.," *Krasnaia letopis'*, nos. 2–3 (1922): 181–82. Tailors and clerical workers appear to have retained the strongest union organizations. See A. Ezhov, "V Saratove (1907–1917 gg.)," *Kommunisticheskii put'*, no. 10 (1923): 189.

17 In 1906, 61.2 percent of the total number of workers in Saratov were on strike; by 1908 the number had dropped to 6.5 percent. See V. R. Varzar, *Statistika stachek rabochikh na fabrikakh i zavodakh za trekhletie 1906–1908* (St. Petersburg, 1910), pp. 4, 17, 62, 80, 134, 140, 179, 186. Some Soviet historians have criticized Varzar's statistics for excluding certain categories of workers, but until more evidence is produced, his statistics, whatever their shortcomings, remain the best available. See A. S. Amal'rik, "K voprosu o chislennosti i geograficheskom razmeshchenii stachechnikov v Evropeiskoi Rossii v 1905 godu," *Istoricheskie zapiski* 52 (1955): 142; Kliachko, "Materialy o polozhenii rabochikh," p. 74.

18 After the Fifth Party Conference in 1908, Lenin denounced the "new revisionists," such as the right-wing Menshevik "liquidators" (*likvidatory*), for shunning illegal conspiratorial work, which they thought would compromise possible gains through legal activities in trade unions, cooperatives, and the dumas. Arguing that party work at the local level should develop organically, the liquidators believed that the SD Central Committee should function as a coordinating organ but should not set policy for all party groups. Plekhanov and the so-called Party Mensheviks now sided with Lenin against the liquidators, while a third group of Mensheviks fought to preserve party unity. Lenin, likewise, battled against left-wing and conciliationist elements within his own faction. The Bolshevik "boycotters" and "recallists" (*otzovisti*) and ultimatists—"upside-down" liquidators, as Lenin called them—insisted that all legal activities were illusory, especially after the change in the electoral law in June 1907. As a consequence, they demanded the recall of SD delegates elected to the Duma. In addition, some left-wing Bolshevik intellectuals, such as A. A. Bogdanov, A. Lunacharsky, the writer Maxim Gorky, and Saratov's Liadov, not only rejected Duma activities but also espoused a variety of quasi-religious philosophical ideals referred to as "God-building" (*bogostroitel'stvo*). By 1909 the left Bolsheviks had launched their own paper, *Vpered!* (Foward!) with the goal of challenging Lenin's hold on the party paper, *Proletarii,* and opened their own party school in Italy. Moreover, a group of "Party Bolsheviks," led by Saratov-born Rykov, tried to reconcile the various factions. Trotsky headed yet another nonfactional SD center.

19 Saratov Province sent ten leftist deputies to the Second Duma, including four SDs, among whom was the Bolshevik V. M. Serov. No conservative

candidates or even Kadets were elected. See G. F. Khodakov, "Bor'ba Saratovskikh rabochikh pod rukovodstvom bol'shevikov v period revoliutsii 1905–1907 gg.," *Uchenye zapiski Saratovskogo gosudarstvennogo universiteta* 55 (1956): 116.

20 V. N. Pozoiskaia, "Saratovskaia partiinaia organizatsiia v gody tsarskoi reaktsii (1907–1910 gg.)," *Povolzhskii krai,* no. 4 (1975): 46–56 passim.

21 Ezhov, "V Saratove," pp. 186–87. Ezhov finally linked up with a group of like-minded students he had met at a public cafeteria subsidized by local liberals. The students attended the technical high school and could well have been prototypes for Konstantin Fedin's hero, Kirill Izvekov, in *Early Joys.*

22 Pozoiskaia, "Saratovskaia partiinaia organizatsiia," p. 43; idem, "Bor'ba bol'shevikov pod rukovodstvom V. I. Lenina protiv otzovistov i ul'timatistov po voprosu dumskoi taktiki (1907–1910 gg.)," *Uchenye zapiski Saratovskogo gosudarstvennogo universiteta* 59 (1958): 161; V. I. Tomarev, "Tsaritsynskaia gruppa RSDRP mezhdu dvumia revoliutsiiami (1907–1917 gg.)," *Istoriko-kraevedcheskie zapiski,* no. 5 (1977): 45. For elsewhere in Russia, see R. C. Elwood, *Russian Social Democracy in the Underground: A Study of the RSDRP in the Ukraine, 1907–1914* (Assen, Netherlands, 1974), pp. 64–65.

23 Ch., "Saratovskaia organizatsiia s 1909 po 1917," *Vestnik Saratovskogo Gubkoma RKP,* no. 3(28) (1923): 50. A handful of workers led by a young tobacco worker, I. A. Galaktionov, managed to issue a leaflet criticizing the Duma and calling for the unification of the proletariat into a single workers' party. (See Pozoiskaia, "Saratovskaia partiinaia organizatsiia," pp. 59–60.) The most comprehensive coverage of SD activities along the Volga at this time can be found in R. A. Garafutdinov, *Leninskoe rukovodstvo stanovleniem i razvitiem partiinykh organizatsii Povolzh'ia (1900–1910 gg.)* (Kazan, 1983). Like all Soviet authors, however, he grossly exaggerates Bolshevik activities and ignores the role of local populists.

24 P. Kudelli, "Svetloi pamiati Anny Il'inichny Ul'ianovoi Elizarovoi," *Proletarskaia revoliutsiia,* no. 6 (1935): 134. The police report is found in V. I. Tomarev, "Pod"em rabochego dvizheniia v Povolzh'e v 1910–1914 gg.," *Povolzhskii krai,* no. 1 (1972): 88.

25 See Robert A. Maguire, *Red Virgin Soil: Soviet Literature in the 1920s* (Princeton, N.J., 1968).

26 A. Voronsky, *Waters of Life and Death,* trans. L. Zarine (Westport, Conn., 1936), p. 270.

27 G. Rubashkina, "Vol'skaia organizatsiia SDRP (bol'shevikov)," *Vestnik Saratovskogo Gubkoma RKP,* no. 5(30) (1923): 80; Tomarev, "Tsaritsynskaia gruppa," p. 46.

28 Khodakov, *Ocherki istorii,* p. 215. In neighboring Samara, united SD groups agitated in factories and workshops and published a nonfactional newspaper that printed articles written by all of the émigré leaders. See O. Piatnitsky, *Memoirs of a Bolshevik* (New York, n.d.), pp. 191–95.

29 G. A. Malinin, *Sviazhite nas s "Vavilonom"! (Iz istorii rasprostraneniia pro-izvedenii V. I. Lenina v Saratovskoi gubernii)* (Saratov, 1973), p. 155; Tomarev, "Pod"em," p. 92. M. Korbut, "Strakhovaia kampaniia 1912–1914 gg.," *Proletarskaia revoliutsiia,* no. 2(73) (1928): 107. A. Ezhov, "Moi vospominaniia o Maiake," *Vestnik Saratovskogo Gubkoma RKP,* no. 6(31) (1923): 69.

30 See Michael S. Melancon, "The Socialist Revolutionaries from 1902 to February 1917: A Party of the Workers, Peasants, and Soldiers" (Ph.D. diss., Indiana University, 1985). The police documents can be found in F. Bulkin, "Soiuz metallistov i departament politsii," *Krasnaia letopis',* no. 5 (1923): 252–67.

31 Cited in Michael F. Hamm, "Kharkov's Progressive Duma, 1910–1914: A Study in Russian Municipal Reform," *Slavic Review* 40 (1981): 20, 26, 33, 36.

32 P. A. Bugaenko et al., *Saratovskii universitet, 1909–1959* (Saratov, 1959), pp. 12–13.

33 E. D. Chermenskii, "Vybory v IV gosudarstvennuiu dumu," *Voprosy istorii,* no. 4 (1947): 23.

34 Elwood, *Russian Social Democracy in the Underground,* p. 273.

35 Lenin's thesis on the war first became known in Petrograd in September 1914, and no. 33 of the Bolshevik newspaper *Sotsial-Demokrat,* with the antiwar manifesto of the Central Committee, in November 1914. S. V. Tiutiukhin admits that the tactical stance of the Bolshevik Central Committee remained unknown in some localities until early 1915 and that "in these conditions many complex questions had to be resolved independently in the provinces, without ruling directives from the party center." (See his *Voina, mir, revoliutsiia: Ideinaia bor'ba v rabochem dvizhenii Rossii, 1914–1917 gg.,* Moscow, 1972, p. 13.) For a description of the situation in Saratov when war broke out, see V. I. Tomarev, *Bol'sheviki Povolzh'ia vo glave bor'by proletariev protiv tsarizma* (Volgograd, 1977), pp. 244–45; and V. Podsumkov, "Bol'shevistskaia gazeta v Saratov 25 let tomu nazad," in the newspaper *Kommunist* (Saratov), June 7, 1941, p. 2.

36 Antonov's claims can be found in V. P. Antonov-Saratovskii, *Pod stiagom proletarskoi bor'by: Otryvki iz vospominanii o rabote v Saratove za vremia s 1915 g. do 1918* (Moscow and Leningrad, 1925), p. 8. Also see M. G., "Iz istorii Saratovskoi bol'shevistskoi organizatsii (1916–1918)," *Kommunisticheskii put',* no. 17(80) (1927): 34. G. I. Lomov endorsed Antonov's statement

years later. (See G. I. Lomov et al., eds., *Nasha gazeta, No. 1–9, 1915,* Saratov, 1935, p. vii.) However, the year after Antonov's memoir appeared serialized in *Proletarskaia revoliutsiia* (1926), several prominent Bolsheviks—including Lomov—wrote letters to the editors insisting that even Antonov had supported the Menshevik position until mid-1915: see G. Lomov et al., "Pis'ma v redaktsiiu zh. 'Proletarskaia revoliutsiia,'" *Proletarskaia revoliutsiia,* no. 2(49) (1926): 276. Even earlier, in 1922, Ol'minskii wrote that during his exile in 1916, Lomov was the first advocate of the inevitability of revolution and Antonov was his main opponent. See "Tri pis'ma," *Proletarskaia revoliutsiia,* no. 4 (1922): 276.

37 Tomarev, *Bol'sheviki Povolzh'ia,* pp. 257–62.

38 *Kommunist,* January 7, 1941, p. 2. These personal bonds forged in the underground may well have weighed heavily in later factional developments within the party. For instance, in November 1917, Nogin and Miliutin resigned from the Soviet government because they opposed single-party rule. Ol'minskii and Nogin worked together within the Moscow Bolshevik organization in 1917.

39 Antonov-Saratovskii, *Pod stiagom,* p. 35.

40 Tomarev, *Bol'sheviki Povolzh'ia,* pp. 247–48.

41 Tiutiukhin, *Voina, mir, revoliutsiia,* p. 82.

42 Khodakov, *Ocherki istorii,* pp. 227–28.

43 Antonov-Saratovskii, *Pod stiagom,* pp. 129–33; S. Poltavskii, "O Saratovskom Maiake," *Otkliki,* no. 12 (1913): 13. See V. V. Babushkin, "Maiak," in *Fevral': Sbornik vospominanii o 1917 g. Kniga pervaia* (Saratov, 1922), pp. 13–15; and Ezhov, "Moi vospominaniia o Maiake," p. 69.

44 A Soviet treatment of *Nasha gazeta* can be found in I. Bas, *Bol'shevistskaia pechat' v gody imperialisticheskoi voiny* (Moscow, 1939), pp. 121–53; see also Antonov-Saratovskii, *Pod stiagom,* pp. 19–43. At first the editorial board was made up of Lebedev, Lomov, and Antonov. "But almost immediately," wrote Lomov, "our party men of letters considered Antonov and me too undiplomatic, people who under the repressive conditions of tsarism would be unable to hold out even for a few issues . . . the editorial board now coopted Ol'minskii into its makeup." See Lomov, *Nasha gazeta,* pp. vii–viii.

45 Sh. Levin, "Sotsialisticheskaia pechat' vo vremia imperialisticheskoi voiny," *Krasnyi arkhiv,* no. 2 (1922): 220; Antonov-Saratovskii, *Pod stiagom,* p. 24. See *Nasha gazeta,* no. 6, September 18, 1915.

46 For additional evidence of this, see A. Martsinovskii, *Zapiski rabochego-bol'shevika* (Saratov, 1923), p. 70.

47 Quoted in Levin, "Sotsialisticheskaia pechat'," pp. 222–23; see also *Kommunist,* no. 49, Feburary 27, 1959, p. 2.

48   S. I. Mitskevich, "Vospominaniia o revoliutsii v Saratove," *Rabotnik pros-veshcheniia*, no. 8 (1922): 26. The editors themselves expressed surprise that they were able to publish ten issues before being shut down. Antonov mentioned that rumors had circulated that the paper had held out as long as it had because a new police chief had been appointed, who had not yet arrived from Astrakhan. See Antonov-Saratovskii, *Pod stiagom*, p. 25.

49   "Professional'nye soiuzy," p. 15. For events in Petrograd, see Tsuyoshi Hasegawa, *The February Revolution: Petrograd, 1917* (Seattle, Wash., 1981), pp. 73–103, and S. A. Smith, *Red Petrograd: Revolution in the Factories, 1917–18* (Cambridge, Eng., 1983), pp. 48–53.

50   Antonov-Saratovskii, *Pod stiagom*, p. 34; Bas, *Bol'shevistskaia pechat'*, pp. 139–40.

51   M. G. Fleer, ed., *Rabochee dvizhenie v gody voiny (Materialy po istorii rabochego dvizheniia v Rossii)* (Moscow, 1925), pp. 98, 101.

52   Ch., "Saratovskaia organizatsiia," p. 51.

53   Antonov-Saratovskii, *Pod stiagom*, p. 41.

54   Iu. K. Milonov, "Nakanune velikikh sobytii," in *Za vlast' sovetov (Sbornik vospominanii starykh bol'shevikov)*, ed. A. V. Babushkin et al. (Saratov, 1968), p. 12.

55   Ibid., pp. 10–11; Institut marksizma-leninizma pri TsK KPSS, *Bol'sheviki v gody imperialisticheskoi voiny, 1914-fevral' 1917 gg.: Sbornik dokumentov mestnykh bol'shevistskikh organizatsii* (Moscow, 1939), p. 97; Antonov-Saratovskii, *Pod stiagom*, p. 58.

56   V. V. Babushkin, "Razgrom organizatsii," in *Pervoe maia: Sbornik vospominanii*, bk. 2 (Saratov, 1922): 53–57.

57   Martsinovskii, *Zapiski*, p. 71.

58   T. V. Sapronov, "Tri mesiatsa na Volge (1916)," *Proletarskaia revoliutsiia*, no. 8(43) (1925): 216–17.

59   V. P. Antonov-Saratovskii, "Saratov s fevralia po oktiabr' 1917," *Proletarskaia revoliutsiia*, no. 2(25) (1924): 154–55; K. I. Plaksin, "Nakanune," *Fevral': Sbornik vospominanii*, p. 9; Martsinovskii, *Zapiski*, pp. 73–74.

60   Plaksin, "Nakanune," pp. 9–11.

61   *Vestnik soiuza gorodov*, no. 38, November 1916, p. 330.

62   See reports in *Pochta*, no. 1, January 1, 1917, p. 3; no. 13, January 17, 1917, p. 3; and no. 19, January 25, 1917, p. 3; in *Saratovskii golos*, no. 63, January 12, 1917, p. 3; no. 64, January 13, 1917, p. 3; no. 69, January 19, 1917, p. 4; no. 92, February 18, 1917, p. 4; and no. 94, February 21, 1917, p. 4; *Saratovskii vestnik*, no. 24, January 29, 1917, p. 6.

63   See issues of *Vestnik soiuza gorodov* for 1916.

64   *Saratovskii golos*, no. 63, January 12, 1917, p. 4; no. 64, January 13, 1917, p. 3; *Pochta*, no. 4, January 4, 1917, p. 3; no. 15, January 19, 1917, p. 3;

no. 35, February 17, 1917, p. 3; *Saratovskii vestnik,* no. 24, January 29, 1917, p. 2.

65   E. N. Burdzhalov, *Vtoraia russkaia revoliutsiia: Vosstanie v Petrograde* (Moscow, 1967), p. 83.

CHAPTER 12

1   For further bibliographical references on 1917 in Saratov, see Donald J. Raleigh, *Revolution on the Volga: 1917 in Saratov* (Ithaca, N.Y., 1986). The most valuable sources for the February Revolution in Saratov are: *Izvestiia Saratovskoi gorodskoi dumy* (Saratov, 1917), pp. 64–78; *Saratovskii vestnik,* no. 49, March 2, 1917, and no. 51, March 5, 1917; *Saratovskii listok,* no. 49, March 2, 1917, no. 50, March 3, 1917, and no. 51, March 5, 1917; *Izvestiia Saratovskogo Soveta rabochikh i soldatskikh deputatov* [hereafter *Izvestiia Saratovskogo Soveta*], no. 6, March 14, 1917, and no. 16, March 29, 1917. Also of value are memoirs found in *Fevral': Sbornik vospominanii o 1917 g. Kniga pervaia* (Saratov, 1922) and G. Sukharev et al., eds., *Za vlast' Sovetov: Vospominaniia uchastnikov revoliutsionnykh sobytii 1917 god v Saratovskoi gubernii* (Saratov, 1957).

2   This survey of events in the district towns is based on Saratov newspapers as well as on V. V. Vas'kin and G. A. Gerasimenko, *Fevral'skaia revoliutsiia v Nizhnem Povolzh'e (1917-pervaia polovina 1918 gg.)* (Saratov, 1966); V. V. Vas'kin, "Soldaty Nizhnego Povolzh'ia v Fevral'sko-martovskie dni 1917 goda," in *Iz istorii Saratovskogo Povolzh'ia* (Saratov, 1968), pp. 92–110; M. A. Vodolagin, *Krasnyi Tsaritsyn* (Volgograd, 1967); I. Presniakov, "Iz podpol'ia na prostor," *Partiinyi sputnik,* nos. 9–10 (1923): 68–72; S. Manturov, *Iz revoliutsionnogo proshlogo Kamyshina (1905–1920)* (Volgograd, 1963); I. I. Ponomarchuk, *Kuznetskii uezd posle Fevral'skoi revoliutsii* (Kuznetsk, 1958); N. P. Bul'in et al., *Stranitsy zhizni (Iz istorii Serdobskoi organizatsii KPSS)* (Penza, 1961); G. Rubashkina, "Vol'skaia organizatsiia SDRP (bol'shevikov)," *Vestnik Sartatovskogo Gubkoma RKP,* no. 5 (30) (1923): 80–81.

3   For a discussion of the February Revolution in the Saratov countryside, see G. A. Gerasimenko, "Vozniknovenie volostnykh obshchestvennykh ispolnitel'nykh komitetov v Nizhnem Povolzh'e (mart–mai 1917 goda)," *Povolzhskii krai,* no. 2 (1973): 50–80; and idem, *Nizovye krest'ianskie organizatsii v 1917–pervoi polovine 1918 godov (Na materialakh Nizhnego Povolzh'ia)* (Saratov, 1974).

4   See *Protokoly zasedaniia Saratovskogo Voennogo Komiteta* (Saratov, 1917); Vas'kin and Gerasimenko, *Fevral'skaia revoliutsiia,* pp. 113–15; and I. M. Ionenko, *Soldaty tylovykh garnizonov v bor'be za vlast' Sovetov (Po materialam Povolzh'ia i Urala)* (Kazan, 1976), p. 113.

5 *Izvestiia Saratovskogo Soveta,* no. 18, April 2, 1917. The regional conference of soviets, the first of its kind in the country held after February, is analyzed in A. I. Razgon, "O sostave sovetov Nizhnego Povolzh'ia v marte–aprele 1917 g.," in *Sovety i soiuz rabochego klassa i krest'ianstva v Oktiabr'skoi revoliutsii* (Moscow, 1964), pp. 83–122.

6 *Saratovskii vestnik,* no. 127, June 11, 1917, and no. 138, June 28, 1917. See also *Sotsial-Demokrat,* no. 25, June 9, 1917; and I. I. Mints et al., *Oktiabr' v Povolzh'e* (Saratov, 1967), p. 102.

7 See Russell Snow, *The Bolsheviks in Siberia, 1917–1918* (Rutherford, Ohio, 1977), pp. 69–70, 87, 106, 108; Andrew Ezergailis, *The 1917 Revolution in Latvia* (Boulder, Colo., 1974), pp. 16–18; Ronald G. Suny, "Nationalism and Social Class in the Russian Revolution: The Cases of Baku and Tiflis," in *Transcaucasia, Nationalism and Social Change: Essays in the History of Armenia, Azerbaijan, and Georgia,* ed. Ronald G. Suny (Ann Arbor, Mich., 1983), pp. 246, 250; A. I. Lepeshkin, *Mestnye organy vlasti Sovetskogo gosudarstva (1917–1920 gg.)* (Moscow, 1957), pp. 89, 99–100; G. A. Trukan, *Oktiabr' v Tsentral'noi Rossii* (Moscow, 1967), p. 53.

8 For a discussion of the activities of party organizations at this time, see Raleigh, *Revolution on the Volga,* pp. 128–36.

9 The Saratov Bolshevik organization's response to Lenin's April Theses is discussed in *Sotsial-Demokrat,* no. 5, April 12, 1917; no. 6, April 16, 1917; no. 7, April 22, 1917; and no. 8, April 25, 1917.

10 *Saratovskii vestnik,* no. 103, May 13, 1917, and *Proletarii Povolzh'ia,* no. 11, May 13, 1917.

11 G. A. Gerasimenko, *Sovety Nizhnego Povolzh'ia v Oktiabr'skoi revoliutsii* (Saratov, 1972), p. 51.

12 See, for example, the various accounts found in *Sotsial-Demokrat,* no. 26, June 10, 1917; *Proletarii Povolzh'ia,* no. 22, June 22, 1917; and *Saratovskii listok,* no. 144, July 5, 1917.

13 This section on workers' attitudes is based on Raleigh, *Revolution on the Volga,* pp. 150–62.

14 My analysis of soldiers' attitudes is based on reports in the local press and on the protocols of the Saratov Military Committee. Also useful are I. M. Ionenko and R. S. Tseitlin, "Kazanskii Voenno-okruzhnoi komitet (aprel'–oktiabr' 1917 goda)," in *Ocherki istorii narodov Povolzh'ia i Priural'ia,* no. 4: *Obshchestvenno-politicheskoe dvizhenie i klassovaia bor'ba na Srednei Volge (konets XIX–nachale XX veka)* (Kazan, 1972), pp. 89–110; M. A. Golubov, "Saratov v 1917 g.: Vospominaniia pomoshchika Kursovogo ofitsera Saratovskoi shkoly praporshchikov," unpublished manuscript dated Innsbruck, Austria, 1955 (Columbia University, Butler Library); V. V. Vas'kin, "Kontrrevoliutsiia v bor'be za armiiu v 1917 g.," in *Revoliutsionnoe*

dvizhenie v russkoi armii v 1917 godu: Sbornik statei, ed. I. I. Mints et al. (Moscow, 1981), pp. 147–53.

15   Apart from the local press, the most valuable sources are the works of G. A. Gerasimenko already cited and his "Organizatsiia volostnykh zemel'nykh komitetov v Nizhnem Povolzh'e," *Povolzhskii krai,* no. 3 (1975): 54–84; "Vozniknovenie Sovetskoi vlasti v volostiakh Saratovskoi gubernii," *Povolzhskii krai,* no. 1 (1972): 60–81; and M. Ia. Kosenko,"Iz istorii bor'by krest'ian Saratovskoi gubernii letom i osen'iu 1917 g.," *Uchenye zapiski Saratovskogo unviersiteta* 68 (1960): 55–69. See also A. V. Shestakov, eds., *Sovety krest'ianskikh deputatov i drugie krest'ianskie organizatsii,* vol. 2: *1917 god v derevene: Vospominaniia krest'ian* (Moscow and Leningrad, 1929); V. P. Miliutin, ed., *Agrarnaia revoliutsiia,* vol. 2: *Krest'ianskoe dvizhenie v 1917 godu* (Moscow, 1928); K. G. Kotel'nikov and V. L. Meller, eds., *Krest'ianskoe dvizhenie v 1917 godu* (Moscow and Leningrad, 1927).

16   For information on Khvalynsk, see *Saratovskii listok,* no. 136, June 24, 1917; the situation in Nikolaevsk is discussed in Mints, *Oktiabr' v Povolzh'e,* p. 126.

17   F. Bobylev, "Kuznetskaia respublika," in *Fevral': Sbornik vospominanii,* pp. 37–39.

18   *Proletarii Povolzh'ia,* no. 27, July 6, 1917.

19   P. A. Lebedev, "Fevral'–oktiabr' v Saratove (vospominaniia)," *Proletarskaia revoliutsiia,* no. 10 (1922): 245–46. See also V. P. Antonov-Saratovskii, "Saratov s fevralia po oktiabr' 1917," *Proletarskaia revoliutsiia,* no. 2 (25) (1924): 187.

20   Even though Russian socialism was seriously divided, the fact that the socialist parties dominating the Soviet won 82.3 percent of the votes cast in the city demonstrates how strong a socialist political culture was in provincial Russia. See *Saratovskii listok,* no. 152, July 12, 1917, and no. 159, July 20, 1917.

21   See, for example, *Proletarii Povolzh'ia,* no. 44, July 26, 1917; *Saratovskii vestnik,* no. 162, July 23, 1917; *Sotsial-Demokrat,* no. 63, September 3, 1917; and Lebedev, "Fevral'–oktiabr'," p. 246.

22   This summary is based on reports in *Izvestiia Saratovskogo Soveta, Sotsial-Demokrat, Proletarii Povolzh'ia,* and the protocols of the Saratov Soviet (V. P. Antonov-Saratovskii, ed., *Saratovskii Sovet rabochikh deputatov, 1917–1918: Sbornik dokumentov* [Moscow-Leningrad, 1931], and V. G. Khodakov, "Rabochii kontrol' v Saratovskoi gubernii v period podgotovki Velikoi Oktiabr'skoi sotsialisticheskoi revoliutsii (mart–oktiabr' 1917 goda)," *Uchenye zapiski Saratovskogo universiteta* 47 (1956): 49–76.

23   The most valuable sources on soldiers' behavior at this time are the protocols of the Saratov Soviet, *Izvestiia Kazanskogo Voenno-okruzhnogo*

Komiteta (the official organ of the Kazan Military District), *Saratovskii vestnik,* and S. Sh. Ovrutskaia, "Proval politiki kontrrevoliutsionnoi voenshchiny v iiule–avguste 1917 g.," *Istoricheskie zapiski* 87 (1971): 351–82.

24 See Donald J. Raleigh, "Revolutionary Politics in Provincial Russia: The Tsaritsyn 'Republic' in 1917," *Slavic Review* 40, no. 2 (1981): 194–209.

25 Antonov-Saratovskii, *Saratovskii Sovet,* pp. 184–89; *Saratovskii vestnik,* no. 193, September 1, 1917; *Sotsial-Demokrat,* no. 63, September 3, 1917; and V. K. Medvedev, "Saratovskii Sovet ot fevralia k oktiabriu 1917 g.," *Uchenye zapiski Saratovskoi oblastnoi partiinoi shkoly,* no. 1 (1948): 76–77.

26 Antonov-Saratovskii, *Saratovskii Sovet,* pp. 191–92; *Proletarii Povolzh'ia,* no. 81, September 3, 1917, p. 4; and V. A. Osipov, ed., *1917 god v Saratovskoi gubernii: Sbornik dokumentov, fevral' 1917-dekabr' 1918 gg.* (Saratov, 1957), pp. 136–37.

27 V. P. Antonov-Saratovskii, *Pod stiagom proletarskoi bor'by: Otryvki iz vospominanii o rabote v Saratove za vremia s 1915 g. do 1918* (Moscow and Leningrad, 1925), p. 145.

28 See Raleigh, *Revolution on the Volga,* pp. 245–46.

29 Robert F. Browder and Alexander F. Kerensky, eds., *The Russian Provisional Government, 1917: Documents* (Stanford, Calif., 1961), 3:1644–45; *Izvestiia Kazanskogo Voenno-okruzhnogo Komiteta,* no. 93, September 16, 1917; no. 94, September 17, 1917; no. 102, September 30, 1917.

30 Raleigh, "Revolutionary Politics in Provincial Russia," pp. 206–7; Rubashkina, "Vol'skaia organizatsiia," p. 81; G. A. Gerasimenko et al., eds., *Khronika revoliutsionnykh sobytii v Saratovskom Povolzh'e, 1917–1918* (Saratov, 1968), pp. 103–5, 116; G. A. Gerasimenko and D. S. Tochenyi, *Sovety Povolzh'ia v 1917 godu: Bor'ba partii, bol'shevizatsiia sovetov, Oktiabr'skie dni* (Saratov, 1977), pp. 154–56; Shchegol'kov,"Na zare: Sovetskaia vlast' v Serdobske (Vospominaniia ob Oktiabre)," *Kommunisticheskii put',* no. 9 (34) (1923): 52–55; *Sbornik ves' Kuznetsk* (Kuznetsk, 1927), p. 75.

31 *Proletarii Povolzh'ia,* no. 88, September 13, 1917, no. 90, September 16, 1917; *Saratovskii vestnik,* no. 202, September 13, 1917; and M. Levinson, "Krest'ianskoe dvizhenie v Saratovskoi gubernii v 1917 g.," in *1917 god v Saratove* (Saratov, 1927), pp. 80–81.

32 *Saratovskii vestnik,* no. 222, October 8, 1917.

33 *Proletarii Povolzh'ia,* no. 115, October 17, 1917, pp. 3–4; no. 116, October 18, 1917; P. S., comp., "Khronika Oktiabr'skoi revoliutsii v Saratov," *Kommunisticheskii put',* no. 20 (1927): 116.

34 V. P. Antonov-Saratovskii, "Oktiabr'skie dni v Saratove," in *Rasskazyvaiut uchastniki velikogo Oktiabria* (Moscow, 1957), p. 291.

35 Medvedev, "Saratovskii Sovet," p. 82.

36 See *Saratovskii vestnik,* no. 238, October 27, 1917; *Proletarii Povolzh'ia,* no.

124, October 27, 1917; V. P. Antonov-Saratovskii, ed., *Godovshchina sotsial'noi revoliutsii v Saratove* (Saratov, 1918), pp. 2–3; M. I. Vasil'ev-Iuzhin, "Proletarskaia revoliutsiia v Saratove," *Sovetskoe stroitel'stvo,* nos. 10–11 (1927): 121–22.

37 Antonov-Saratovskii, *Godovshchina,* pp. 4–6.

38 Ibid., pp. 7–8.

39 Vasil'ev-Iuzhin,"Proletarskaia revoliutsiia v Saratove," p. 139. Some of the most vocal opponents of the Bolsheviks later joined the party during the Civil War. See E. P., "Iz zhizni Saratovskoi organizatsii," *Vestnik Saratovskogo Gubkoma RKP,* no. 24 (1922): 12.

40 Golubov, "Saratov v 1917 g.," pp. 47–48.

41 See, for example, *Izvestiia Saratovskogo gubernskogo Soveta krest'ianskikh deputatov* (no number) November 4, 1917; *Saratovskii listok,* no. 238, November 5, 1917; Donald J. Raleigh, ed., *A Russian Civil War Diary: Alexis Babine in Saratov, 1917–1922* (Durham, N.C., 1988), pp. 22–40.

42 *Saratovskii vestnik,* no. 251, November 23, 1917; no. 247, November 17, 1917.

43 Ibid., no. 248, November 18, 1917. See also S. Sh. Ovrutskaia, "Politicheskoe bankrotstvo eserov na vyborakh v Uchreditel'noe sobranie (Po materialam Saratovskoi gubernii," in *Nekotorye voprosy otechestvennoi i vseobshchei istorii* (Saratov, 1971), pp. 42–59.

44 For a discussion of the recognition of Soviet power in the rest of the province, see Raleigh, *Revolution on the Volga,* pp. 302–11.

45 F. A. Rashitov, "Osnovye etapy Sovetskogo stroitel'stva v Saratovskoi gubernii v pervoi polovine 1918 goda," *Materialy k nauchnoi konferentsii aspirantov i molodykh nauchnyk sotrudnikov,* no. 1 (Saratov, 1965): 9.

46 *Saratovskii vestnik,* no. 252, November 24, 1917.

47 Z. Petrov, "Saratovskii proletariat v bor'be za vlast'," in *1917 god v Saratove* (Saratov, 1927), pp. 26–27. G. A. Gerasimenko, "Ustanovlenie Sovetskoi vlasti v uezdakh Nizhnego Povolzh'ia," in *Iz istorii Saratovskogo Povolzh'ia* (Saratov, 1968), p. 81; and G. A. Gerasimenko and V. P. Sem'ianinov, *Sovetskaia vlast' v derevne na pervom etape Oktiabria* (Saratov, 1980), p. 45.

48 Gerasimenko and Tochenyi, *Sovety Povolzh'ia,* pp. 291–94.

49 Antonov-Saratovskii, *Saratovskii Sovet,* p. 286.

CHAPTER 13

1 See the preceding chapters by Melancon, Fallows, and Mixter (5, 8, and 9) for references to armed detachments in 1905, especially during the October strike.

2 See *Izvestiia Saratovskogo Soveta rabochikh i soldatskikh deputatov* [hereafter *Izvestiia Saratovskogo Soveta*], no. 6, March 14, 1917; F. Morozov,

"Fevral'skaia revoliutsiia v Saratove," in *Fevral': Sbornik vospominanii o 1917 g.* (Saratov, 1922), pp. 25–26; M. I. Vasil'ev-Iuzhin, "1917 god v Saratove," in G. Sukharev et al., eds., *Za vlast' Sovetov: Vospominaniia uchastnikov revoliutsionnykh sobytii 1917 god v Saratovskoi gubernii* (Saratov, 1957), pp. 9–17; V. P. Antonov-Saratovskii, "Saratov s fevralia po oktiabr' 1917," *Proletarskaia revoliutsiia,* no. 2 (1924): 156–61. Throughout this chapter I shall devote only limited space to the general history of events in Saratov in 1917, covered in chapter 12, except when necessary to understand the development and role of the Red Guard.

3 Morozov, pp. 28–29; Vasil'ev-Iuzhin, "1917 god v Saratove," pp. 18–20; V. I. Chepenko, "Bol'sheviki zavoda Beringa," in *Za vlast' Sovetov,* p. 132; E. D. Rumiantsev, "Rabochaia militsiia i Krasnaia gvardiia Povolzh'ia v bor'be za vlast' sovetov" (dissertation, Kazan University, 1971), pp. 44–48.

4 *Izvestiia Saratovskogo Soveta,* March 15, no. 7 and March 17, no. 8; Rumiantsev, "Rabochaia militsiia," pp. 46–47, 51–52; V. P. Antonov-Saratovskii, ed., *Saratovskii Sovet rabochikh deputatov (1917–1918). Sbornik dokumentov,* (Moscow-Leningrad, 1931), p. 9.

5 P. Lebedev, "Fevral'–oktiabr' v Saratove (vospominaniia)," *Proletarskaia revoliutsiia,* no. 10 (1922): 237; Rumiantsev, "Rabochaia militsiia," p. 52.

6 *Izvestiia Saratovskogo Soveta,* no. 6, March 14, 1917; V. V. Vas'kin, "Iz istorii bor'by za bol'shevizatsiiu Saratovskogo garnizona v 1917 godu," in *Materialy k nauchnoi konferentsii aspirantov i molodykh nauchnykh sotrudnikov* (Saratov, 1965), pp. 101–103.

7 Antonov-Saratovskii, *Saratovskii Sovet,* pp. 7–9; Rumiantsev," Rabochaia militsiia," pp. 52–53.

8 *Saratovskii listok,* no. 60, March 17, 1917; Rumiantsev, "Rabochaia militsiia," pp. 59–64.

9 *Izvestiia Saratovskogo Soveta,* no. 12, March 22, 1917; Antonov-Saratovskii, *Saratovskii sovet,* pp. 4, 67; Rumiantsev, "Rabochaia militsiia," p. 67; E. D. Rumiantsev, "Fabrichno-zavodskaia militsiia i ee deiatel'nost' v Povolzh'e (mart–leto 1917 g.)," in *Ocherki istorii narodov Povolzh'ia i Priural'ia,* no. 4 (Kazan, 1972): 79.

10 Rumiantsev, "Rabochaia militsiia," pp. 65, 68.

11 For the Soviet and duma elections, see Rex A. Wade, *Red Guards and Workers' Militias in the Russian Revolution* (Stanford, Calif., 1984), pp. 217–19. There also exists an erroneous set of figures for the Soviet elections, first used by Antonov-Saratovskii and repeated by some later writers.

12 Rumiantsev, "Rabochaia militsiia,", pp. 77–109 passim.

13 *Sotsial-Demokrat* (Saratov), no. 13, May 7, 1917; *1917 god v Saratovskoi gubernii: Sbornik dokumentov, fevral' 1917–dekabr' 1918 gg.* (Saratov, 1957), p. 100; G. F.

Khodakov, *Ocherki istorii Saratovskoi organizatsii KPSS; Chast' pervaia, 1898–1918*, 2d ed. (Saratov, 1968), pp. 273–74.

14 *Proletarii Povolzh'ia*, no. 38, July 19, 1917.

15 As quoted in Rumiantsev, "Rabochaia militsiia," p. 94.

16 *1917 god v Saratovskoi gubernii*, p. 137; *Proletarii Povolzh'ia*, no. 76, September 1, 1917.

17 *Sotsial-Demokrat* (Saratov), no. 63, September 3, 1917.

18 *Sotsial-Demokrat* (Saratov), no. 65, September 10, 1917; *1917 god v Saratovskoi gubernii*, pp. 147–48; Chepenko, pp. 134–35; A. V. Afanas'ev, "Iz istorii organizatsii Krasnoi gvardii v g. Saratove (sentiabr'–oktiabr' 1917 g.), *Povolzhskii krai* (Saratov), no. 2 (1975): 141–42.

19 Z. Petrov, "Saratovskii proletariat v bor'be za vlast'," in *1917 god v Saratove* (Saratov, 1927), p. 13; *Proletarii Povolzh'ia*, no. 97, September 24, 1917, and no. 106, October 6, 1917; A. A. Fedorov, "Sorok let tomu nazad," T. K. Chugunov, "Za vlast' sovetov," and V. N. Krasichkov, "V Saratovskikh zheleznodorozhnykh masterskikh"—all in *Za vlast' Sovetov*, pp. 112, 130, and 120, respectively.

20 Rumiantsev, "Rabochaia militsiia," pp. 188 and 224; V. K. Medvedev, "Saratovskii Sovet ot fevralia k oktiabriu 1917 g.," in *Uchenye zapiski Saratovskoi oblastnoi partiinoi shkoly*, no. 1 (1948): 81.

21 Antonov-Saratovskii, *Saratovskii Sovet*, pp. 196–97; *Izvestiia Saratovskogo Soveta*, no. 81, September 12, 1917; Rumiantsev, "Rabochaia militsiia," p. 170, citing the account in *Saratovskii vestnik*.

22 Petrov, p. 11; G. A. Gerasimenko and F. A. Rashitov, *Sovety Nizhnego Povolzh'ia v Oktiabr'skoi revoliutsii* (Sartov, 1972), p. 85.

23 Lebedev, "Fevral'–oktiabr'," p. 250; Petrov, p. 6.

24 Medvedev, p. 81.

25 P. S., comp., "Khronika Oktiabr'skoi revoliutsii v Saratove," *Kommunisticheskii put'*, no. 19 (Saratov, 1927): 33, 35; Rumiantsev, "Rabochaia militsiia," p. 170.

26 *1917 god v Saratovskoi gubernii*, pp. 164, 168, 265; Gerasimenko and Rashitov, p. 93; Rumiantsev, "Rabochaia militsiia," p. 248.

27 Krasichkov, pp. 120–21; Medvedev, p. 81.

28 The following account of the October revolution, unless otherwise noted, is from the following sources: Lebedev, "Fevral'–oktiabr'," pp. 250–61; Vasil'ev–Iuzhin, "1917 god v Saratove," pp. 23–45; *Godovshchina sotsial'noi revoliutsii v Saratove* (Saratov, 1918), pp. 3–8; V. P. Antonov-Saratovskii, "Oktiabr'skie dni v Saratove," *Proletarskaia revoliutsiia*, no. 10 (1922): 279–92; G. A. Gerasimenko et al., eds., *Khronika revoliutsionnykh sobytii v Saratovskom Povolzh'e, 1917–1918* (Saratov, 1968), pp. 134–51; Gerasimenko and Rashitov, pp. 101–14.

29 N. Nedostupov, "Oktiabr' v Saratove," in *V boiakh za diktaturu pro-letariata. Sbornik vospominanii* (Saratov, 1933), pp. 7–8.

30 P.S., comp., "Khronika Oktiabr'skoi revoliutsii v Saratove," *Kommunisticheskii put'*, no. 20 (Saratov, 1927): 120.

31 See the accounts of Chugunov, p. 130; Chepenko, p. 135; Krasichkov, p. 121; Fedorov, p. 112; and P. D. Shcherbakov, "Dni velikikh svershenii," in *Za vlast' Sovetov*, p. 97.

32 Lebedev, "Fevral'–oktiabr'," pp. 258–59.

33 Shcherbakov, p. 97.

Glossary of Russian Terms

chinovnik(i): state official(s) holding one of fourteen ranks (*chiny*) within the bureaucracy

darstvennik(i): peasants who at the time of the Emancipation opted to receive the one-quarter, so-called beggar's, allotment unencumbered by redemption payments

desiatina (*desiatiny*): land measure, equals 2.7 acres

druzhina (*druzhiny*): armed workers' detachment or militia active in the revolutions of 1905 and 1917

duma: elected municipal government, established in 1870 as part of the Great Reforms

Duma (State Duma): elected national assembly, granted by Nicholas II in 1905, which first met in April 1906

intelligenty: members of the intelligentsia

narod: the "people," or masses, often used by educated Russians to refer to the peasantry

nizy: the lower classes or strata of society, unprivileged and disenfranchised, as opposed to the privileged orders, or *verkhi*

odnodvortsy: free settlers or homesteaders granted land on the frontiers by the Muscovite state in the sixteenth and seventeenth centuries; at the time of the Emancipation they merged with the general peasant population

obshchestvo: educated society or "public" in the nineteenth and early twentieth centuries, as distinct from the state bureaucracy, toward which it was often critically disposed, and from the *narod*

obshchestvennost': public-mindedness, or social autonomy from the state

otrabotka: peasant leasing of private land in exchange for labor

otrezki: lands "cut off" from peasant allotments in the Emancipation process and hence a source of tension between peasants and gentry in succeeding decades

obshchina: Russian village commune, generally with repartitional tenure

otrub and *khutor:* forms of separation from the commune and consolidation of land under the terms of the Stolypin land reform

posad: trading and commercial settlement adjacent to the central administrative quarter of early Russian towns

pomeshchik(i): gentry landowner(s)

raznochintsy: literally, "people of mixed ranks," or the democratic intelligentsia of the 1860s reform era drawn from various social groups

skhod: village communal assembly of household heads

Saratovtsy (singular: *Saratovets*): natives or residents of Saratov Province

soslovie (sosloviia): legal estates in prerevolutionary Russia

uezd (uezdy): district(s), a subdivision of a Russian province (*guberniia*) before 1917

volost: a subdivision of the district (*uezd*), usually consisting of ten to fifteen villages, which possessed its own administration and served as the lowest unit in the Ministry of Interior's bureaucracy in the countryside

Zemlia i volia: Land and Liberty, name of Populist revolutionary organizations operating from the 1860s through the 1880s

zemlevol'tsy: adherents of Land and Liberty

zemstvo: local elected organs of self-government, established in 1864 at the district and provincial levels; responsible for education, health, and general welfare in the countryside until 1917

zemtsy: zemstvo men; elected deputies and officers of zemstvos

Bibliography

ARCHIVAL SOURCES AND MANUSCRIPTS

Tsentral'nyi Gosudarstvennyi Istoricheskii Arkhiv SSSR (Leningrad): TsGIA
    Fond 91   Imperatorskoe Vol'noe Ekonomicheskoe Obshchestvo
    Fond 92   Komitet gramotnosti
    Fond 408   Komitet po zemleustroitel'nym delam
    Fond 733   Ministerstvo narodnogo prosveshcheniia, Departament narodnogo prosveshcheniia
    Fond 1275   Sovet ministrov
    Fond 1284   Ministerstvo vnutrennykh del, Departament obshchikh del
    Fond 1288   Ministerstvo vnutrennykh del, Glavnoe upravlenie po delam mestnogo khoziaistva
    Fond 1291   Ministerstvo vnutrennykh del, Zemskii otdel
    Fond 1405   Ministerstvo iustitsii
Tsentral'nyi Gosudarstvennyi Arkhiv Oktiabr'skoi Revoliutsii SSSR (Moscow): TsGAOR
    Fond 95   Sledstvennaia komissiia 1862 g. po delam o rasprostranenii revoliutsionnykh vozzvanii i propagande
    Fond 102   Departament politsii
        Fond 102,OO Departament politsii, Osobyi otdel
        Fond 102 3-e deloproizvodstvo
        Fond 102 4-e deloproizvodstvo
    Fond 109   Tret'e otdelenie sobstvennoi ego imperatorskogo velichestva Kantseliarii
    Fond 518   Soiuz soiuzov
Otdel Rukopisei: Gosudarstvennaia Publichnaia Biblioteka (Leningrad): ORGPB
    Fond 438   Obshchestvo dlia posobiia nuzhdaiushchimsia literatoram i uchenym
Institut Russkoi Literatury (Pushkinskii Dom)
    Fond 334   D. I. Shakhovskoi

Gosudarstvennyi Istoricheskii Muzei (Moscow): GIM
 Fond 31 V. A. Maklakov
Gosudarstvennyi arkhiv Saratovskoi oblasti (Saratov) ·
 Fond 1   Kantseliariia Saratovskogo gubernatora
 Fond 4   Saratovskaia gubernskaia zemskaia uprava
 Fond 53 Saratovskoe zhandarmskoe upravlenie
 Fond 400 Saratovskaia gubernskaia zemleustroitel'naia komissiia
 Fond 449 Saratovskaia uezdnaia zemleustroitel'naia komissiia
Bakhmeteff Archive of Russian and East European History and Culture, Columbia University
 Golubov, M. A. "Saratov v 1917 g.: Vospominaniia pomoshchika Kursovogo ofitsera Saratovskoi shkoly praporshchikov." Unpublished manuscript dated Innsbruck, Austria, 1955.
 Liubimov, D. N. "Russkaia smuta nachala deviatisotykh godov 1902–1906 po vospominaniiam i lichnym zapiskam i dokumentam."
 Meyendorff, Baron A. "A Brief Appreciation of P. Stolypin's Tenure of Office."
 Zenkovskii, A. V. "Moi vospominaniia."
Morgan Library, Colorado State University. Special Collections
 Oral history interview of Gus Lebsack

NEWSPAPERS AND PERIODICALS

Iskra. Munich, Geneva, etc., 1900–05. Social Democratic émigré organ.
Izvestiia Kazanskogo Voenno-okruzhnogo Komiteta. Kazan, 1917.
Izvestiia Krest'ianskikh Deputatov. St. Petersburg, 1906. Organ of Trudovik Group during the First Duma.
Izvestiia Saratovskogo Soveta rabochikh i soldatskikh deputatov. Saratov, 1917. Organ of the Saratov Soviet.
Izvestiia Saratovskoi gorodskoi dumy. Saratov, 1907–16. Monthly published by city duma.
Kamyshinskii ezhnedel'nik. Kamyshin, 1906.
Kamyshinskii vestnik. Kamyshin, 1906.
Letuchie listki izdavaemye fondom vol'noi russkoi pressy v Londone. London, 1893–99.
Narodnoe delo. Paris, 1902–04. Socialist Revolutionary occasional booklet.
Nasha zhizn'. St. Petersburg, 1904–06.
Osvobozhdenie. Paris-Stuttgart, 1902–05. Liberal émigré organ of Union of Liberation.
Pochta. Saratov, 1915–17.
Pravo. St. Petersburg, 1898–1917.
Privolzhskaia gazeta. Kamyshin, 1906.

Bibliography

Privolzhskaia zhizn'. Kamyshin, 1910–12.

Privolzhskii krai. Saratov, 1903–07. Menshevik-leaning daily.

Proletarii Povolzh'ia. Saratov, 1917. Menshevik newspaper.

Rech'. St. Petersburg, 1906–17. Kadet party central organ.

Revoliutsionnaia Rossiia. Geneva-Paris, 1902–05. Socialist Revolutionary émigré organ.

Russkiia vedomosti. Moscow, 1863–1918. Moderately liberal daily.

Saratovskaia zemskaia nedelia. Saratov, 1896–1905. Periodical published by the Saratov provincial zemstvo.

Saratovskiia gubernskiia vedomosti. Saratov, 1838–1917. Official organ of the Saratov provincial administration.

Saratovskii dnevnik. Saratov, 1877–1907. Moderate liberal daily; during 1905 close to SRs.

Saratovskii golos. Saratov, 1916–17. Conservative daily.

Saratovskii listok. Saratov, 1880–1917. Liberal daily later associated with the Kadet party.

Saratovskii spravochnyi listok. Saratov, 1865–79.

Saratovskii vestnik. Saratov, 1907–17. Liberal daily that replaced *Saratovskii dnevnik*; moderate socialist newspaper in 1917.

Saratowsche deutsche Zeitung. Saratov, 1906.

Severnaia pchela. St. Petersburg, 1825–64.

Sotsial-Demokrat. Saratov, 1917. Bolshevik newspaper.

Unsere Zeit. Saratov, 1906.

Vestnik russkoi revoliutsii. Geneva, 1901–05. Socialist Revolutionary journal.

Volga. Saratov, 1906–16.

Volzhskii vestnik. Kazan, 1883–1906.

Zemlia i volia. Saratov, 1917–18. Organ of Saratov Committee of the Socialist Revolutionary party.

BIBLIOGRAPHIES

Khovanskii, N. F. "K bibliografii Saratovskago kraia." *Trudy Saratovskoi uchenoi arkhivnoi komissii* 20 (1895): 88–108.

Serdiuk, I. I. *Revoliutsionnoe dvizhenie i bor'ba za Sovetskuiu vlast' v Saratovskoi gubernii, 1861–1920: Ukazatel' literatury.* Saratov, 1963.

Sineskov, N. A., comp. *Ukazatel' materialov po istorii revoliutsionnogo dvizheniia Stalingradskogo kraia 1905–1922 gg.* Stalingrad, 1930.

Sokolov, S. D. "Istochniki i posobiia dlia izucheniia Saratovskago kraia: Ukazatel' knig, broshiur, zhurnal'nykh i gazetnykh statei i zametok napechatennykh vne Saratovskago kraia." *Trudy Saratovskoi uchenoi arkhivnoi komissii* 26 (1910): i–vi, 145–229.

————. "Saratovtsy pisateli i uchenye." *Trudy Saratovskoi uchenoi arkhivnoi komissii* 30 (1913): 257–336 (letters A–K); 32 (1915): 221–84.

Sokolov, S. D., and V. A. Sushitskii. *Materialy dlia ukazatelia po revoliutsionnomy dvizheniiu v Saratovskom krae, 1861–1921.* Saratov, 1928.

Sushitskii, V. A. *Materialy dlia ukazatelia po revoliutsionnomu dvizheniiu v Saratovskom krae, vyshedshei v 1928 godu, 1861–1921.* Saratov, 1930.

————. "Materialy dlia ukazatelia po revoliutsionnomu dvizheniiu v Saratovskom krae, 1861–1921 (I-e dopolnenie)." *Izvestiia Saratovskogo Nizhne-Volzhskogo instituta kraevedeniia im. M. Gor'kogo* 5 (1932): 50–63.

————. "Saratovskie tiurmy: Opyt annotirovannoi bibliografii po istorii Saratovskikh tiurem, kak mest zakliucheniia politicheskikh 'prestupnikov.'" *Izvestiia Saratovskogo Nizhne-Volzhskogo instituta im. M. Gor'kogo* 6 (1933): 157–97.

BOOKS AND ARTICLES

A. S. "Neskol'ko slov o Saratovskikh pedagogicheskikh kursakh gubernskago zemstva." *Saratovskaia zemskaia nedelia,* nos. 26–29, sec. 3 (1901): 99–104.

Afanas'ev, A. V. "Iz istorii organizatsii Krasnoi gvardii v g. Saratove (sentiabr'–oktiabr' 1917 g." *Povolzhskii krai,* no. 2 (1975): 135–48.

Agrarnoe dvizhenie v Rossii v 1905–1906 gg. (Trudy Imperatorskago Vol'nago Ekonomicheskago Obshchestva). 2 vols. St. Petersburg, 1908.

Akimova, T., and V. K. Arkhangel'skaia. *Revoliutsionnye pesni v Saratovskom Povolzh'e.* Saratov, 1967.

Akimova, T. M., and A. M. Ardabatskaia. *Ocherki istorii Saratova, XVII–XVIII vv.* Saratov, 1940.

Alexander, John T. *Emperor of the Cossacks: Pugachev and the Frontier Jacquerie of 1773–75.* Lawrence, Kans., 1973.

Amal'rik, A. S. "K voprosu o chislennosti i geograficheskom razmeshchenii stachechnikov v Evropeiskoi Rossii v 1905 godu." *Istoricheskie zapiski* 52 (1955): 142–85.

Anfimov, A. M. *Krest'ianskoe khoziaistvo Evropeiskoi Rossii, 1881–1904.* Moscow, 1980.

————. *Krupnoe pomeshchich'e khoziaistvo Evropeiskoi Rossii.* Moscow, 1969.

————. *Rossiiskaia derevnia v gody pervoi mirovoi voiny (1914–fevral' 1917 g.).* Moscow, 1962.

A-n, S. [Stepan Anikin]. "Po rodnym mestam (Iz nabliudenii byvshago deputata)." *Russkoe bogatstvo,* no. 11, sec. 2 (1906): 1–20; no. 1, sec. 2 (1907): 36–65.

Anikin, S. "O material'noi i iuridicheskoi neobezpechennosti russkago narodnago uchitelia." In *Trudy I-go vserossiiskago s"ezda,* 1:255–65.

————. "Vystavka v Iaroslavle." *Saratovskaia zemskaia nedelia,* no. 8, sec. 3 (1903): 93–112.

Bibliography

———. "Za 'pravednoi zemlei' (pamiati I. M. Igoshina)." *Vestnik Evropy*, no. 3 (1910): 86–108.

Annenkov, P. V. *Literaturnye vospominaniia*. Moscow, 1983.

Antonov-Saratovskii, V. P. *Krasnyi god*. Moscow-Leningrad, 1927.

———. "Oktiabr'skie dni v Saratove." *Proletarskaia revoliutsiia*, no. 10 (1922): 278–98.

———. "Oktiabr'skie dni v Saratove." In *Rasskazyvaiut uchastniki velikogo Oktiabria*. Moscow, 1957.

———. *Pod stiagom proletarskoi bor'by: Otryvki iz vospominanii o rabote v Saratove za vremia s 1915 g. do 1918*. Moscow and Leningrad, 1925.

———. "Saratov s fevralia po oktiabr' 1917." *Proletarskaia revoliutsiia*, no. 2 (25) (1924): 144–71; no. 4 (27) (1924): 178–210.

Antonov-Saratovskii, V. P., ed., *Godovshchina sotsial'noi revoliutsii v Saratove*. Saratov, 1918.

———, ed. *Saratovskii Sovet rabochikh deputatov, 1917–1918: Sbornik dokumentov*. Moscow-Leningrad, 1931.

Aptekman, O. V. "Dmitrii Rogachev; 'Ispoved' k druz'iam' i pis'ma k rodnym." *Byloe*, no. 26 (1924): 71–101.

———. *Obshchestvo "Zemlia i Volia" v 1870-kh godakh*. Moscow, 1924.

———. "Partiia Narodnogo prava." *Byloe*, no. 7 (1907): 177–206.

Argunov, A. A. "Azev v partii S-R." *Na chuzhoi storone*, no. 5 (1924): 157–200.

———. "Iz proshlogo partii Sotsialistov-Revoliutsionerov." *Byloe*, no. 10 (22) (1907): 94–112.

———. "Iz vospominanii o pervoi russkoi revoliutsii." *Katorga i ssylka*, no. 1 (74) (1931): 142–62.

Arkhangel'skii, V. G. *Katerina Breshkovskaia*. Prague, 1938.

Avrich, Paul. *Russian Rebels, 1600–1800*. New York, 1972; 1975.

Babikov, I. I. "Krest'ianskoe dvizhenie v Saratovskoi gubernii nakanune pervoi russkoi revoliutsii." *Uchenye zapiski Saratovskogo gosudarstvennogo universiteta* 55 (1956): 172–218.

Babushkin, A. V., et al., eds. *Za vlast' Sovetov (Sbornik vospominanii starykh bol'shevikov)*. Saratov, 1968.

Bagil'dinskii, A. "Iz Atkarska." *Saratovskaia zemskaia nedelia*, nos. 6–7, sec. 2 (1905): 33–40.

"Balashovskoe sobytie 21-go iiulia," *Saratovskaia zemskaia nedelia*, no. 8 (1905): 31–51.

Balashovskoe uezdnoe zemstvo. *Zhurnaly XXXIX ocherednogo Balashovskago uezdnago zemskago sobraniia 1904 goda*. Balashov, 1905.

Baron, Samuel H., ed. and trans. *The Travels of Olearius in Seventeenth Century Russia*. Stanford, Calif., 1967.

Bartlett, Roger P. *Human Capital: The Settlement of Foreigners in Russia, 1762–1804.* Cambridge, Eng., 1979.

Bas, I. *Bol'shevistskaia pechat' v gody imperialisticheskoi voiny.* Moscow, 1939.

Bazhenov, N. [I. Belokurov]. "Kak u nas proizoshlo agrarnoe dvizhenie: Zapiski krest'ianina." *Russkoe bogatstvo,* no. 4 (April 1909): 97–120; no. 5 (March 1909): 92–III.

Bazilevskii, B. [V. Ia. Vasilev], ed. *Gosudarstvennyia prestupleniia v Rossii v XIX veke.* 3 vols. Paris, 1903–05.

Belokurov, I. *Iz zapisok agrarnika.* Moscow, 1926.

——. "Vstrechi s N. E. Baumanom." *Katorga i ssylka,* no. 4 (77) (1931): 197–201.

Berezov, F. A. "Iz byta krest'ian Saratovskoi gub." *Russkoe bogatstvo,* no. 8 (1908): 55–68.

"Biudzhet krest'ianina Saratovskoi gub." *Mir bozhii,* no. 4 (1903): 45–46.

Blinov, L. N. "Narodnyi uchitel' v Rossii." In *Vseobshchee obrazovanie v Rossii: sbornik statei,* ed. kn. D. I. Shakhovskoi, pp. 63–84, Moscow, 1902.

Bock, Maria Stolypin. "Stolypin in Saratov." *Russian Review* 12, no. 3 (July 1953): 187–93.

Bok, Maria. *Vospominaniia o moem ottse P. A. Stolypine.* New York, 1953.

Bonnell, Victoria E. "Trade Unions, Parties, and the State in Tsarist Russia: A Study of Labor Politics in St. Petersburg and Moscow." *Politics and Society* 9 (1980): 299–322.

Bonwetsch, Gerhard. *Geschichte der deutschen Kolonien an der Wolga.* Stuttgart, 1919.

Bor'ba za sozdanie marksistskoi partii v Rossii. Obrazovanie RSDRP. Vozniknovenie bol'shevizma (1894–1904 gody). Dokumenty i materialy. Moscow, 1961.

Bramson, L. M. *K istorii Trudovoi partii: Trudovaia gruppa Pervoi Gosudarstvennoi Dumy.* Petrograd, 1917.

Breshko-Breshkovskaia, E. K. *Hidden Springs of the Russian Revolution.* Stanford, Calif., 1931.

——. "Vospominaniia i dumy." *Sotsialist-Revoliutsioner,* no. 4 (1912): 103–129.

Brooks, Jeffrey. *When Russia Learned to Read: Literacy and Popular Literature, 1861–1917.* Princeton, N.J., 1985.

Browder, Robert F., and Alexander F. Kerensky, eds. *The Russian Provisional Government, 1917: Documents.* 3 vols. Stanford, Calif., 1961.

Bugaenko, P. A., et al. *Saratovskii universitet, 1909–1959.* Saratov, 1959.

Bul'in, N. P., et al. *Stranitsy zhizni (Iz istorii Serdobskoi organizatsii KPSS.* Penza, 1961.

Burdzhalov, E. N. *Vtoraia russkaia revoliutsiia: Moskva, front, periferiia.* Moscow, 1971.

——. *Vtoraia russkaia revoliutsiia: Vosstanie v Petrograde.* Moscow, 1967.

Bushkanets, E. G. *Ucheniki N. G. Chernyshevskogo po gimnazii v osvoboditel'nom dvizhenii vtoroi poloviny 1850-kh—nachala 1860-kh gg.* Kazan, 1963.

Bibliography

Bushnell, John. *Mutiny amid Repression: Russian Soldiers in the Revolution of 1905–1906.* Bloomington, Ind., 1985.

Carstensen, Fred V. *American Enterprise in Foreign Markets: Studies of Singer and International Harvester in Imperial Russia.* Chapel Hill, N.C., 1984.

Ch. "Saratovskaia organizatsiia s 1909 po 1917." *Vestnik Saratovskogo Gubkoma RKP,* no. 3 (28) (1923): 50–51.

Chastnoe soveshchanie zemskikh deiatelei proiskhodivshee 6, 7, 8 i 9 noiabria 1904 goda v S-Peterburge. Moscow, 1905.

Chermenskii, E. D. *Burzhuaziia i tsarizm v pervoi russkoi revoliutsii.* 2d ed. Moscow, 1970.

———. "Vybory v IV gosudarstvennuiu dumu." *Voprosy istorii,* no. 4 (1947): 21–40.

Chernov, V. M. *Zapiski sotsialista-revoliutsionera.* Berlin-Petrograd-Moscow, 1922.

Chernykh, V. A. "Pis'mo A. A. Sleptsova A. S. Korsakovu ot 21 maia 1861 g." *Revoliutsionnaia situatsiia v Rossii v 1859–1861 gg.* 4 (Moscow, 1965): 420–25.

———. "Zemlevolets Aleksandr Mordvinov (Iz arkhivnykh razyskanii)." In *Osvoboditel'noe dvizhenie v Rossii* (Saratov) 3 (1973): 37–56.

Chernyshev, I. V. *Agrarno-krest'ianskaia politika Rossii za 150 let.* St. Petersburg, 1918.

———. *Agrarnyi vopros v Rossii.* Kursk, 1927.

———. *Obshchina posle 9 noiabria g.* Petrograd, 1917.

Chernyshevskii, N. G. *Polnoe sobranie sochinenii.* 16 vols. Moscow, 1939–53.

Conroy, Mary Schaeffer. *Petr Arkad'evich Stolypin: Practical Politics in Late Tsarist Russia.* Boulder, Colo., 1976.

D. "Nachal'noe narodnoe obrazovanie v Saratovskoi gubernii v 1902 godu." *Saratovskaia zemskaia nedelia,* no. 9, sec. 2 (1903): 1–8.

Demchenko, Adol'f. *N. G. Chernyshevskii: nauchnaia biografiia.* Saratov, 1978.

Denisvo, Val. "Znachenie uchitel'skikh kursov po otzyvam zemskikh uchitelei." *Obrazovanie,* no. 7, sec. 2 (1904): 39–67.

Derenkovskii, G. M., I. M. Raschetnova, and M. S. Simonova. "1905 god v Saratove." *Istoricheskie zapiski* 54 (1955): 74–104.

Diakevich, E. E. *Ocherk o deiatel'nosti Saratovskoi 'Birzhi truda' za god sushchestvovaniia (27 noiabria 1914 g. po 1 ianvaria 1916 g.).* Saratov, 1916.

D'iakov, V. A., D. V. Koroliuk, and I. S. Miller, eds. *Russko-pol'skie revoliutsionnye sviazi 60-kh godov i vosstanie 1863 goda: Sbornik statei i materialov.* Moscow, 1962.

Diubiuk, E. "Ekonomicheskaia zapashka i spol'nyi posev." *Saratovskaia zemskaia nedelia,* no. 10, sec. 5 (1905): pp. 1–6.

D'ova. *Revoliutsionnye kruzhki v Saratove.* Saratov, 1906.

Druzhinin, N. M. "V Saratove v 1905 g. (Vospominaniia)." *Povolzhskii krai,* no. 5 (1977): 69–88.

————. "V Saratove v 1905 g. (Vospominaniia)." *Voprosy istorii KPSS,* no. 10 (1979): 99–110.

Druzhinin, Nikolai M. *Gosudarstvennye krest'iane i reforma P. D. Kiseleva.* 2 vols. Moscow-Leningrad, 1946–1958.

Dubrovskii, S. M. *Stolypinskaia zemel'naia reforma.* Moscow, 1963.

Dukhovnikov, Flegont V. "Nemtsy, drugie inostrantsy i prishlye liudi v Saratove." *Saratovskii krai,* no. 1 (1893): 237–64.

"Dva pis'ma S. G. Shiriaeva k redaktoru 'Vpered.'" *Byloe,* no. 4 (1903): 21–29.

E. P. "Iz zhizni Saratovskoi organizatsii." *Vestnik Saratovskogo Gubkoma RKP,* no. 24 (1922): 10–12.

Edelman, Robert S. "Rural Proletarians and Peasant Disturbances: The Right Bank Ukraine in the Revolution of 1905." *Journal of Modern History* 57, no. 2 (June 1985): 248–77.

Eklof, Ben. *Russian Peasant Schools: Officialdom, Village Culture, and Popular Pedagogy, 1861–1914.* Berkeley, Calif., 1986.

Elwood, R. C. *Russian Social Democracy in the Underground: A Study of the RSDRP in the Ukraine, 1907–1914.* Assen, Netherlands, 1974.

Emmons, Terence. *The Formation of Political Parties and the First National Elections in Russia.* Cambridge, Mass., 1983.

————. *The Russian Landed Gentry and the Peasant Emancipation of 1861.* Cambridge, Eng., 1968.

————. "Russia's Banquet Campaign." *California Slavic Studies* 10 (1977): 45–86.

Erman, L. K. *Intelligentsiia v pervoi russkoi revoliutsii.* Moscow, 1966.

Ershov, A. "Kazanskii zagovor 1863 g." *Golos minuvshago,* no. 6 (1913): 199–232; no. 7 (1913): 199–228.

Esper, Thomas. "The Odnodvortsy and the Russian Nobility." *Slavonic and East European Review* 45, no. 1 (January 1967): 124–34.

Essen, M. M. *Pervyi shturm.* Moscow, 1957.

Ezhov, A. "Moi vospominaniia o Maiake." *Vestnik Saratovskogo Gubkoma RKP,* no. 6 (31) (1923): 69–70.

————. "V Saratove (1907–1917 gg.)." *Kommunisticheskii put',* no. 10 (1923): 189.

F. Ch. "Otgoloski uchitel'skikh s"ezdov, kursov i soveshchanii." *Vestnik vospitaniia,* no. 9, sec. 2 (1901): 88–109.

Fabriki i zavody g. Saratova v sanitarnom otnoshenii. Saratov, 1911.

Fadeev, A. M. "Vospominaniia A. M. Fadeeva." *Russkii arkhiv,* no. 4 (1891): 465–94; no. 5 (1891): 14–60.

Fallows, Thomas. "Forging the Zemstvo Movement: Liberalism and Radicalism on the Volga, 1890–1905." Ph.D. diss., Harvard University, 1981.

————. "Saratov as Local History." Unpublished paper.

————. "The Zemstvo and the Bureaucracy, 1890–1904." In Terence Emmons and Wayne S. Vucinich, eds., *The Zemstvo in Russia: An Experiment in Local Self-Government,* pp. 177–241, Cambridge, Eng., 1982.

Fedorov, V. A. "Krest'ianskoe trezvennoe dvizhenie 1858–1860 gg." In *Revoliutsionnaia situatsiia v Rossii v 1859–1861 gg.* 2 (Moscow, 1962): 107–126.

Fevral': Sbornik vospominanii o 1917 g. Kniga pervaia. Saratov, 1922.

Field, Daniel. *Rebels in the Name of the Tsar.* Boston, 1976.

Figes, Orlando. "The Russian Land Commune and the Agrarian Question, 1905–1930." *Peasant Studies* 11, no. 2 (Winter 1984): 119–30.

Figner, Vera N. *Vospominaniia.* 2 vols. Moscow, 1964.

Fleer, M. G., ed. *Rabochee dvizhenie v gody voiny (Materialy po istorii rabochego dvizheniia v Rossii).* Moscow, 1925.

Frank, Stephen. "Cultural Conflict and Criminality in Rural Russia, 1861–1900." Ph.D. diss., Brown University, 1986.

Freeze, Gregory L., ed. *From Supplication to Revolution: A Documentary Social History of Imperial Russia.* Oxford, 1988.

Frieden, Nancy. *Russian Physicians in an Era of Reform and Revolution, 1856–1905.* Princeton, N.J., 1981.

Frolenko, M. F. *Sobranie sochinenii.* Moscow, 1930.

G. S. "Soveshchanie shkol'noi komissii Saratovskago uezdnago zemstva s uchiteliami zemskikh shkol." *Vestnik Vladimirskago gub. zemstva,* no. 19 (1901): 15–19.

G. U. *Nemetskiia tserkovno-prikhodskiia uchilishcha v Kamyshinskom Uezde.* Saratov, n.d.

Gan, P. A. *O nastoiashchem byte meshchan Saratovskoi gubernii.* St. Petersburg, 1860.

Garafutdinov, R. A. *Leninskoe rukovodstvo stanovleniem i razvitiem partiinykh organizatsii Povolzh'ia (1900–1910 gg.).* Kazan, 1983.

Geraklitov, A. A. *Istoriia Saratovskogo kraia v XVI–XVIII vv.* Saratov, 1923.

———. "Melochi iz proshlogo Saratovskogo kraia: k istorii Saratovskikh pozharov 1754 i 1757 gg." *Trudy Saratovskoi uchenoi arkhivnoi komissii* 28 (1911): 1–19.

———. "Ocherki iz zhizni i byta Eltonskikh solianykh lomshchikov i vozchikov poloviny XVIII v." *Trudy Saratovskoi uchenoi arkhivnoi komissii* 26 (1910): 59–82.

———. "Uchrezhdenie v Saratove solianogo komissarstva (1747 g.)." *Trudy Saratovskoi uchenoi arkhivnoi komissii* 28 (1911): 1–37.

Gerasimenko, G. A. *Nizovye krest'ianskie organizatsii v 1917–pervoi polovine 1918 godov (Na materialakh Nizhnego Povolzh'ia).* Saratov, 1974.

———. "Organizatsiia volostnykh zemel'nykh komitetov v Nizhnem Povolzh'e." *Povolzhskii krai,* no. 3 (1975): 54–84.

———. "Ustanovlenie Sovetskoi vlasti v uezdakh Nizhnego Povolzh'ia." In *Iz istorii Saratovskogo Povolzh'ia,* ed. V. A. Osipov, pp. 71–91, Saratov, 1968.

―――. "Vozniknovenie Sovetskoi vlasti v volostiakh Saratovskoi gubernii." *Povolzhskii krai,* no. 1 (1972): 60–81.

―――. "Vozniknovenie volostnykh obshchestvennykh ispolnitel'nykh komitetov v Nizhnem Povolzh'e (mart–mai 1917 goda)," *Povolzhskii krai,* no. 2 (1973): 50–80.

Gerasimenko, G. A., and F. A. Rashitov. *Sovety Nizhnego Povolzh'ia v Oktiabr'skoi revoliutsii.* Saratov, 1972.

Gerasimenko, G. A., and V. P. Sem'ianinov. *Sovetskaia vlast' v derevne na pervom etape Oktiabria.* Saratov, 1980.

Gerasimenko, G. A., and D. S. Tochenyi. *Sovety Povolzh'ia v 1917 godu: Bor'ba partii, bol'shevizatsiia sovetov, Oktiabr'skie dni.* Saratov, 1977.

Gerasimenko, G. A., et al., eds. *Khronika revoliutsionnykh sobytii v Saratovskom Povolzh'e, 1917–1918.* Saratov, 1968.

Gessen, I. V. "V dvukh vekakh." *Arkhiv russkoi revoliutsii* 22 (1937): 3–424.

Ginev, V. N. *Narodnicheskoe dvizhenie v srednem povolzh'e.* Moscow-Leningrad, 1966.

Godovshchina sotsial'noi revoliutsii v Saratove. Saratov, 1918.

Gokhlerner, V. M. "Iz istorii krest'ianskogo dvizheniia v Saratovskoi gubernii v gody pervoi russkoi revoliutsii (1905–07 gg.)." *Uchenye zapiski Saratovskogo gosudarstvennogo universiteta* 55 (1956): 219–45.

―――. "Krest'ianskoe dvizhenie v Saratovskoi gubernii v gody pervoi russkoi revoliutsii," *Istoricheskie zapisiki* 52 (1955): 186–234.

Gokhlerner, V. M., and K. P. Kharlamova. "Iz istorii krest'ianskikh revoliutsionnykh komitetov v Saratovskoi gubernii v 1905 g." *Povolzhskii krai,* no. 5 (1977): 89–119.

Golubev, V. "Narodnoe obrazovanie v Saratovskoi gubernii." Appendix to *Saratovskaia zemskaia nedelia,* nos. 11–12 (1902): 1–26.

―――. "Polozhenie narodnago obrazovaniia v Saratovskoi gubernii (po otzyvam mestnykh zhitelei)." *Saratovskaia zemskaia nedelia,* no. 2, sec. 3 (1902): 153–73.

―――. "Zemskaia reaktsiia." *Bez zaglaviia,* no. 4 (1906): 136–38.

Gorn, V. *Krest'ianskoe dvizhenie za poltora veka.* Moscow, 1909.

Gosudarstvennaia deiatel'nost' predsedatelia Soveta stats-sekretaria Petra Arkad'evicha Stolypina. 2 vols. St. Petersburg, 1911.

Gran, M. M. "Prishlye sel'skokhoziaistvennye rabochie Samarskoi gubernii v sanitarnom otnoshenii (K voprosu o znachenii prodovol'stvennykh punktov)." *Saratovskaia zemskaia nedelia,* nos. 42–45 (1901): 32–51.

Gray, Camilla. *The Great Experiment: Russian Art, 1863–1922.* New York, 1962.

Grigor'ev, P. "Zemskie pedagogicheskie kursy i pravila 1875 goda." *Russkaia shkola,* no. 3 (1903): 129–39.

Bibliography

Grot, Ia. K. "Epizod iz Pugachevshchiny," *Drevnaia i novaia Rossiia* (Moscow) 3, no. 1 (1877): 229–48.

Gusiatnikov, P. S. *Nazrevanie revoliutsionnogo krizisa v Rossii v nachale XX veka.* Moscow, 1959.

Gyorki, Jeno, comp. *Vengerskie internatsionalisty v Velikoi Oktiabr'skoi sotsialisticheskoi revoliutsii.* Moscow, 1959.

Haimson, Leopold H., ed. *The Politics of Rural Russia, 1905–1914.* Bloomington, Ind., 1979.

Haller, Peter K. *Vospominaniia P. K. Gallera.* Saratov, 1927.

Hamm, Michael F. "Kharkov's Progressive Duma, 1910–1914: A Study in Russian Municipal Reform." *Slavic Review* 40, no. 1 (1981): 17–36.

Hasegawa, Tsuyoshi. *The February Revolution: Petrograd, 1917.* Seattle, Wash., 1981.

Hildermeier, Manfred. *Die Sozialrevolutionare Partei Russlands: Agrarsozializmus und Modernisierung im Zarenreich (1900–1914).* Cologne and Vienna, 1978.

Idel'chuk, Kh. I. N. I. *Teziakov i ego rol' v razvitii zemskoi meditsiny i stroitel'stve sovetskogo zdravookhraneniia.* Moscow, 1960.

Illarionov, I., et al."Selo Nikolaevskii Gorodok Saratovskoi gubernii v 1905 g." *Proletarskaia revoliutsiia,* no. 12 (47) (1925): 194–203.

Institut marksizma-leninizma pri TsK KPSS. *Bol'sheviki v gody imperialisticheskoi voiny, 1914–fevral' 1917 gg.: Sbornik dokumentov mestnykh bol'shevistskikh organizatsii.* Moscow, 1939.

Ionenko, I. M. *Soldaty tylovykh garnizonov v bor'be za vlast' sovetov (Po materialam Povolzh'ia i Urala).* Kazan, 1976.

Ionenko, I. M., and R. S. Tseitlin. "Kazanskii Voenno-okruzhnoi komitet (aprel'–oktiabr' 1917 goda)." In *Ocherki istorii narodov Povolzh'ia ia Priural'ia.* No. 4 *Obshchestvenno-politicheskoe dvizhenie i klassovaia bor-ba na Srednei Volge (konets XIX–nachale XX veka),* pp. 89–110, Kazan, 1972.

Ionova, G. I. "Revoliutsionnaia agitatsiia sredi rabochikh v nachale 1860-kh godov." *Revoliutsionnaia situatsiia v Rossii v 1859–1861 gg.* 1 (Moscow, 1960): 360–79.

Istoriia Saratovskogo kraia, 1590–1917, ed. V. A. Osipov et al. Saratov, 1964.

Itenberg, B. S., and S. S. Volk, eds. *Revoliutsionnoe narodnichestvo semidesiatykh godov XIX veka: Sbornik dokumentov.* 2 vols. Moscow, 1964–65.

Iurovskii, L. N. *Saratovskie votchiny: statistiko-ekonomicheskie ocherki i materialy iz istorii krupnogo zemlevladeniia i krepostnogo khoziaistva v kontse XVIII i v nachale XIX stoletiia.* Saratov, 1923.

Ivanchin-Pisarev, A. I. *Khozhdenie v narod.* Moscow-Leningrad, 1929.

Ivashkin, A. "Iz vospominanii o narodnykh uchiteliakh." *Saratovskaia zemskaia nedelia,* no. 2, sec. 3 (1905): 41–54.

"Iz khroniki zemskikh shkol v Saratovskoi gub." *Saratovskaia zemskaia nedelia,* no. 2, sec. 2 (1905): 21–26.

Jones, Robert E. *The Emancipation of the Russian Nobility, 1762–1785.* Princeton, N.J., 1973.

———. "Urban Planning and the Development of Provincial Towns in Russia, 1762–1796." In *The Eighteenth Century in Russia,* ed. J. G. Garrard, pp. 321–44, Oxford, 1973.

K—v. "K voprosu o deiatel'nosti Saratovskago gubernskago zemstva v oblasti narodnago obrazovaniia." *Saratovskaia zemskaia nedelia,* no. 10, sec. 2 (1904): 10–22.

Kabytov, Petr Serafimovich. *Agrarnye otnosheniia v Povolzh'e v period imperializma, 1900–1917 gg.* Saratov, 1982.

Kalendar'-spravochnik 1908/9 uchebnyi god, "Narodnyi uchitel'". Comp. O. N. Smirnov. Kiev, 1908.

Kamyshinskoe uezdnoe zemstvo. *Doklady i zhurnaly Kamyshinskago uezdnago zemskago sobraniia 1905 goda.* Kamyshin, 1906.

Kamyshinskoe uezdnoe zemstvo. *Postanovleniia Kamyshinskago Uezdnago Zemskago Sobraniia.* Kamyshin, 1903, 1907.

Karpov, N., ed. *Krest'ianskoe dvizhenie v revoliutsii 1905 goda v dokumentakh.* Leningrad, 1926.

Kedrov, S. I. "Bibliografiia." *Izvestiia obshchestva arkheologii, istorii, i etnografii pri Kazanskom universitete,* 11, no. 3 (1893): 300–14.

Khodakov, G. F. "Bor'ba saratovskikh rabochikh pod rukovodstvom bol'shevikov v period revoliutsii 1905–1907 gg." *Uchenye zapiski Saratovskogo gosudarstvennogo universiteta* 55 (1956): 85–123.

———. *Ocherki istorii Saratovskoi organizatsii KPSS: Chast' pervaia, 1898–1918.* Saratov, 1957. 2d ed. 1968.

Khodakov, V. G. "Bor'ba rabochikh Saratovskoi gubernii pod rukovodstvom Kommunisticheskoi organizatsii za rabochii kontrol' nad proizvodstvom v 1917–18 gg." Candidate diss., Saratov Pedagogical Institute, 1953.

———. "Rabochii kontrol' v Saratovskoi gubernii v period podgotovki Velikoi Oktiabr'skoi sotsialisticheskoi revoliutsii (mart–oktiabr' 1917 goda)." *Uchenye zapiski Saratovskogo gosudarstvennogo universiteta* 47 (1956): 49–76.

Khovanskii, N. F. "Pugachev i pugachevshchina v selakh i derevniakh Saratovskoi gubernii." *Trudy Saratovskoi uchenoi arkhivnoi komissii* 29 (1912): 149–55.

Kimball, Alan. "Student Interests and Student Politics: Kazan University before the Crisis of 1862." *Acta Slavica Iaponica* 4 (Sapporo, Japan, 1988): 1–15.

———. "Who Were the Petrashevtsy?" *Mentalities/Mentalités* 5, no. 2 (1988): 1–12.

Kiriukhina, E. I. "Mestnye organizatsii Vserossiiskogo Krest'ianskogo Soiuza v 1905 godu." *Uchenye zapiski Kirovskogo pedagogicheskogo instituta* 10 (1956): 83–157.

Bibliography

――――. "Vserossiiskii Krest'ianskii Soiuz v 1905 g." *Istoricheskie zapiski* 50 (1955): 95–141.

Kitanina, T. M. *Voina, khleb i revoliutsiia (Prodovol'stvennyi vopros v Rossii, 1914–oktiabr' 1917 g.).* Leningrad, 1985.

Klaus, A. A. "Obshchina-sobstvennik i eia iuridicheskaia organizatsiia." *Vestnik Evropy,* no. 2 (1870): 573–628; no. 3 (1870): 72–118.

Klein, N. L. "Ob osobennostiakh polozheniia i urovne ekspluatatsii promyshlennykh rabochikh Srednego Povolzh'ia v period kapitalizma." *Nash krai* (Kuibyshev), no. 1 (1974): 19–27.

Kliachko, A. Kh. "Materialy o polozhenii promyshlennykh rabochikh Saratovskoi gubernii." *Trudy Saratovskogo ekonomicheskogo instituta* 2 (1949): 61–74.

Klokman, Iu. R. *Sotsial'no-ekonomicheskaia istoriia russkogo goroda: vtoraia polovina XVIII veka.* Moscow, 1967.

Koch, Fred C. *The Volga Germans in Russia and the Americas from 1763 to the Present.* University Park, Pa., 1977.

Kocharovskii, K. "Krest'ianskaia obshchina v Saratovskoi gubernii." *Russkoe bogatstvo,* no. 11, sec. 2 (1901): 113–41.

Kohls, Winfred. "Beitrag zur Geschichte der deutschen Kolonisten in Russland, eine Untersuchung russische Pressepolemik und der deutschen diplomatischen Berichte aus der St. Petersburger Amtszeit des Botschafters von Schweinitz." In *Archivalische Fundstücke zu den russisch deutschen Beziehungen,* ed. Erich Amburger, pp. 152–57, Berlin, 1973.

Kohn, Stanislas, and Alexander F. Meyendorff. *The Cost of the War to Russia.* New Haven, Conn., 1932.

Kokoshkin, F. "Raboty zemskikh s"ezdov i 'Russkiia vedomosti.'" *Russkiia Vedomosti 1863–1913. Sbornik statei.* St. Petersburg, 1914.

Kokshaiskii, I. N. *Predvaritel'nye dannye perepisi naseleniia goroda Saratova i ego prigorodov.* Saratov, 1916.

Kolesnichenko, D. A. "Vozniknovenie i deiatel'nost' 'Trudovoi gruppy.'" *Istoriia SSSR,* no. 4 (1967): 76–89.

Konovalov, D. M. *Saratovskii agent "Iskry."* Saratov, 1969.

Konovalov, I. "V derevne (Iz Saratovskoi gubernii)." *Sovremennyi mir,* no. 2, sec. 2 (1909): 14–33.

Korbut, M. "Strakhovaia kampaniia 1912–1914 gg." *Proletarskaia revoliutsiia,* no. 2 (73) (1928): 107–8.

Kornilov, E. G. "Zemskie uchitelia v revoliutsionnom dvizhenii 70-kh gg. XIX v." *Uchenye zapiski Moskovskogo gosudarstvennogo pedagogicheskogo instituta im. V. I. Lenina* 439 (1971): 116–35.

Koroleva, S. A. *Povolzh'e.* vol. 2 of *Velikaia Rossiia: geograficheskie, etnograficheskie i kul'turno-bytovye ocherki sovremennoi Rossii,* ed. A. N. Anuchin. Moscow, n.d.

Korotkov, Iu. N. "U istokov pervoi 'Zemli i Voli' (neopublikovannaia stranitsa iz tetradi A. A. Sleptsova)." *Istoricheskie zapiski* 79 (1966): 176–209.

Kosenko, M. Ia. "Agrarnaia reforma Stolypina v Saratovskoi gubernii." Candidate diss., Moscow State Historical-Archival Institute, 1951.

————. "Iz istorii bor'by krest'ian Saratovskoi gubernii letom i osen'iu 1917 g." *Uchenye zapiski Saratovskogo universiteta* 68 (1960): 55–69.

————. "Iz istorii provedeniia stolypinskoi agrarnoi reformy v Saratovskoi gubernii." *Uchenye zapiski Saratovskogo pedinstituta* 22 (1956): 171–97.

Kotel'nikov, K. G., and V. L. Meller, eds. *Krest'ianskoe dvizhenie v 1917 godu.* Moscow and Leningrad, 1927.

Kovalevskii, A. G. *Ocherki po demografii Saratova (rozhdaemost' i smertnost' za 1914–1927 gg.).* Saratov, 1928.

Krest'ianskoe dvizhenie v Rossii v 1857–mae 1861 gg.: Sbornik dokumentov, ed. S. B. Okun' and K. V. Sivkov. Moscow, 1963.

Kusheva, E. N. "Saratov v pervoi polovine XVIII v." In *Problemy sotsial'no-ekonomicheskoi istorii russkogo goroda: vtoraia polovina XVIII veka,* pp. 40–51, Moscow, 1967.

Kuz'mina, G. S. "Iz istorii uchastiia meditsinskoi intelligentsii v pervoi russkoi revoliutsii (Balashovskaia zabastovka vrachei v iiule 1905 g.)." *Sovetskoe zdravookhranenie,* no. 8 (1973): 67–81.

————. "Iz istorii uchastiia meditsinskoi intelligentsii v pervoi russkoi revoliutsii." *Povolzhskii krai,* no. 5 (1977): 142–62.

Larskii, I. "Po povodu (Iz zhizni v provintsii): Revoliutsiia v derevne." *Mir bozhii,* no. 12 (1905): 26–31.

Lebedev, P. A. "Fevral'–oktiabr' v Saratove (vospominaniia)." *Proletarskaia revoliutsiia,* no. 10 (1922): 238–56.

————. "K istorii Saratovskoi organizatsii RSDRP (1901–1902 gg.)." *Proletarskaia revoliutsiia,* no. 3 (15) (1923): 227–51.

Lechebno-prodovol'stvennye punkty na rynkakh naima sel'sko-khoziaistvennykyh rabochikh v Saratovskoi gubernii v 1906 g. Saratov, 1906.

Leikina-Svirskaia, V. R. *Intelligentsiia v Rossii vo vtoroi polovine XIX veka.* Moscow, 1971.

————.. "'Kazanskii zagovor' 1863 g." *Revoliutsionnaia situatsiia v Rossii v 1859–1861 gg.* 1 (Moscow, 1960): 423–49.

Lemke, M. K. *Ocherki osvoboditel'nago dvizheniia "shestidesiatykh godov" po neizdannym dokumentam s portretami.* St. Petersburg, 1908.

Leninskaia Iskra i mestnye organizatsii v Rossii (1900–1903 gg.). 3 vols. Perm, 1971.

Leonov, M. I. "Deiatel'nost' eserov v derevne na rubezhe XIX-XX vv." In *Krest'ianskoe dvizhenie v trekh revoliutsiiakh. Mezhvuzovskii sbornik,* pp. 29–37, Kuibyshev, 1982.

Leopol'dov, A. F. "Letopis': Saratovskaia guberniia so vremeni prisoedineniia k

Rossiiu do 1821 g." *Zhurnal ministerstva vnutrennykh del* 39 (1841), no. 2, pp. 223–78; no. 3, pp. 411–42; no. 4, pp. 27–100.

Levinson, M. "Krest'ianskoe dvizhenie v Saratovskoi gubernii v 1917 g." In *1917 god v Saratove.* Saratov, 1927, pp. 78–81.

L—ii [I. M. Liakhovetskii]. "Banketnaia kampaniia v Saratove (1904–1905)." *Minuvshie gody,* no. 12 (December 1908): 29–62.

Linkov, Ia. I. "Voskresnye shkoly i russkoe revoliutsionnoe dvizhenie 1860-kh godov." *Istoricheskii arkhiv,* no. 6 (November–December, 1956): 176–79.

Listovki saratovskikh bol'shevikov, 1902–1917 gg. Saratov, 1979.

Liubomirova, L. N. "Krest'iane-darstvenniki Saratovskoi gubernii v poreformennyi period (80–90-e gody XIX veka)." *Povolzhskii krai,* no. 4 (1975): 89–105.

———. "Vnenadel'naia arenda i ee vliianie na polozhenie krest'ian Saratovskoi gubernii (60 g. XIX v.–nach. XX v.)." *Povolzhskii krai,* no. 5 (1977): 162–79.

Lobsack, Georg. *Einsam Kampft das Wolgaland.* Leipzig, 1936.

Loktin, A. A. "Uchitel'skie kursy i s"ezdy." *Vestnik vospitaniia,* no. 6, sec. 2 (1904): 77–78.

Lomov, G. I., et al. "Pis'ma v redaktsiiu zh. 'Proletarskaia revoliutsiia.'" *Proletarskaia revoliutsiia,* no. 2 (49) (1926): 276–79.

Lomov, G. I., et al., eds. *Nasha gazeta, No. 1–9, 1915.* Saratov, 1935.

Long, James W. *From Privileged to Dispossessed: The Volga Germans, 1860–1917.* Lincoln, Nebr., 1988.

———. "The Volga Germans and the Zemstvos, 1865–1917." *Jahrbücher für Geschichte Osteuropas* 30, no. 3 (1982): 336–61.

Lozanov, N."Ob otkrytii uchitel'skoi seminarii v gor. Saratove." *Saratovskaia zemskaia nedelia,* no. 2, sec. 3 (1903): 50–74.

Lozhkin, V. V. "K izucheniiu istochnikov po istorii 'Nikolaevskoi respubliki' (1905)." In V. I. Buganov et al., *Istochnikovedenie otechestvennoi istorii: Sbornik statei 1981,* pp. 145–66. Moscow, 1982.

Lubny-Gertsyk, L. I. *Dvizhenie naseleniia na territorii SSSR za vremia mirovoi voiny i revoliutsii.* Moscow, 1926.

Luppov, P. *Nemetskiia nachal'nyia shkoly v Rossii.* Petrograd, 1916.

Lushnikov, G. "Vospominaniia o vozniknovenii v Saratove sots.-demokraticheskoi rabochei gruppy, 1896–1899 gg." *Kommunisticheskii put',* no. 10 (35) (1923): 169–85.

M. G. "Iz istorii Saratovskoi bol'shevistskoi organizatsii (1916–1918)." *Kommunisticheskii put',* no. 17 (80) (1927): 34–36.

McKinsey, Pamela Sears. "From City Workers to Peasantry: The Beginning of the Russian Movement 'To the People.'" *Slavic Review* 38, no. 4 (December 1979): 629–49.

————. "The Kazan Square Demonstration and the Conflict between Russian Workers and *Intelligenty.*" *Slavic Review* 44, no. 1 (Spring 1985): 83–103.

Maklakov, V. A. *The First State Duma.* Trans. Mary Belkin. Bloomington, Ind., 1964.

Malinin, G. A. *Sviazhite nas s "Vavilonom"! (Iz istorii rasprostraneniia proizvedenii V. I. Lenina v Saratovskoi gubernii).* Saratov, 1973.

Manning, Roberta T. *The Crisis of the Old Order in Russia: Gentry and Government.* Princeton, N.J., 1982.

Manturov, S. *Iz revoliutsionnogo proshlogo Kamyshina (1905–1920).* Volgograd, 1963.

Martsinovskii, A. *Zapiski rabochego-bol'shevika.* Saratov, 1923.

Maslov, Petr. *Agrarnyi vopros v Rossii.* 2 vols. St. Petersburg, 1908.

Materialy k krest'ianskomu voprosu: Otchet o zasedaniiakh delegatskago s"ezda Vserossiiskago Krest'ianskago Soiuza 6–10 noiabria 1905 g. Rostov-on-Don, 1905.

Mavrodin, V. V., et al., eds. *Krest'ianskaia voina v Rossii v 1773–75 gg.* 3 vols. Moscow-Leningrad, 1961–70.

Mazurenko, Semen. "Eshche po povodu s"ezda Saratovskikh krest'ian 18-go dekabria 1905 g." *Byloe,* no. 8 (1908): 149–52.

————. "S"ezd krest'ian 18 dekabria 1905 g." *Byloe,* no. 8 (1908): 35–39.

Medvedev, V. K. "Saratovskii Sovet ot fevralia k oktiabriu 1917 g." *Uchenye zapiski Saratovskoi oblastnoi partiinoi shkoly,* no. 1 (1948): 47–87.

Melancon, Michael S. "The Socialist Revolutionaries from 1902 to February 1917: A Party of the Workers, Peasants, and Soldiers." Ph.D. diss., Indiana University, 1985.

Miliutin, V. P. *Sel'sko-khoziaistvennye rabochie i voina.* Petrograd, 1917.

Miliutin, V. P., ed. *Agrarnaia revoliutsiia.* Vol. 2, *Krest'ianskoe dvizhenie v 1917 godu.* Moscow, 1928.

Milovzorov, A. F. *Krest'ianskoe chastnovladel'cheskoe khoziaistvo Saratovskoi gubernii posle goda voiny.* Saratov, 1916.

Minarik, L. P. *Ekonomicheskaia kharakteristika krupneishikh zemel'nykh sobstvennikov Rossii kontsa XIX–nachala XX vv.* Moscow, 1971.

Ministerstvo gosudarstvennykh imushchestv. *Statisticheskii obzor gosudarstvennykh imushchestv za 1858 god.* St. Petersburg, 1861.

Ministerstvo vnutrennykh del. *Sbornik pravitel'stvennykh rasporiazhenii po voinskoi povinnosti.* Vols. 3–6. St. Petersburg, 1874–77.

Minkh, A. N. *Iz zapisok mirovago posrednika: 1861–1866.* Saratov, 1911.

Mints, I. I., et al. *Oktiabr' v Povolzh'e.* Saratov, 1967.

Mitskevich, S. I. "Vospominaniia o revoliutsii v Saratove." *Rabotnik prosveshcheniia,* no. 8 (1922): 26–30.

Mixter, Timothy. "Of Grandfather-Beaters and Fat-Heeled Pacifists: Perceptions of Agricultural Labor and Hiring Market Disturbances in Saratov, 1872–1905." *Russian History* 7, pts. 1–2 (1980): 139–68.

Bibliography

Morokhovets, E. A. *Krest'ianskoe dvizhenie i Sotsial-Demokratiia v epokhu pervoi russkoi revoliutsii.* Leningrad and Moscow, 1926.

Mosse, W. E. "Revolution in Saratov (October–November 1917)." *Slavonic and East European Review* 49, no. 117 (1971): 586–602.

Murinov, V. Ia. "Obshchestva vzaimnago vspomoshchestvovaniia uchashchim i uchivshim." In *Vseobshchee obrazovanie v Rossii,* ed. D. I. Shakhovskoi, pp. 85–98. Moscow, 1902.

Najdus, Walentyna. *Polacy w Rewolucji 1917 roku.* Warsaw, 1967.

"Narodnoe obrazovanie na uezdnykh zemskikh sobraniiakh XXXVI sessii 1901 goda." *Saratovskaia zemskaia nedelia,* no. 1, sec. 2 (1902): 33–34.

Nechetnyi, St. [Stepan Sletov]. "Ocherki po istorii P.S.-R." *Sotsialist-Revoliutsioner,* no. 4 (1912): 1–102.

Nechkina, M. V. *Vstrecha dvukh pokolenii (Iz istorii russkogo revoliutsionnogo dvizheniia kontsa 50-kh—nachala 60-kh godov XIX veka.) Sbornik statei.* Moscow, 1980.

Nemetskiia tserkovno-prikhodskiia uchilishcha v Kamyshinskom Uezde. Saratov, n.d.

Nevskii, V. "Ianvarskie dni 1905 g. v provintsii." *Krasnaia letopis',* no. 4 (1922): 52–132.

Nevskii, V. I., ed. *Revoliutsiia 1905 goda: Materialy i ofitsial'nye dokumenty.* Moscow, 1925.

Nikolaev, I. "Povtoritel'nye zaniatiia so vzroslymi." *Saratovskaia zemskaia nedelia,* nos. 6–7, sec. 2 (1904): 33–67.

1905 god v Saratovskoi gubernii (Po materialam zhandarmskogo upravleniia): Sbornik statei. Saratov, 1925.

1905 god v Tsaritsyne. Volgograd, 1960.

1917 god v Saratove. Saratov, 1927.

1917 god v Saratovskoi gubernii: Sbornik dokumentov (fevral' 1917–dekabr' 1918 gg.). Saratov, 1957.

Norman, Henry. *All the Russias.* London, 1902.

Novikova, N. N. *Revoliutsionery 1861 g. ("Velikoruss" i ego komitet v revoliutsionnoi bor'be 1861 g.).* Moscow, 1968.

Obninskii, Viktor. *Polgoda russkoi revoliutsii: Sbornik materialov k istorii russkoi revoliutsii (oktiabr' 1905–aprel' 1906 gg.).* Moscow, 1906.

Obshchestvennoe dvizhenie v Rossii v nachale XX-go veka. Ed. L. Martov, P. Maslov, and A. Potresov. 4 vols. St. Petersburg, 1909–14.

Obukhov, V. "Izmenenie v chastno-vladel'cheskom khoziaistve v Saratovskoi gubernii." *Saratovskaia zemskaia nedelia,* no. 8, sec. 3 (1902): 131–37.

Obzor deiatel'nosti zemleustroitel'nykh komissii za pervyi god ikh sushchestvovaniia. St. Petersburg, 1908.

Obzor nachal'nago narodnago obrazovaniia v Saratovskoi gubernii za 1900–1901 uchebnyi god. Saratov, 1901.

Obzor nachal'nago narodnago obrazovaniia v Saratovskoi gubernii za 1915–16 uchebnyi god. Saratov, 1917.

Ocherki istorii narodov Povolzh'ia i Priuralia, vol., 2/3. Kazan, 1969.

Oganovskii, N. P., ed. *Sel'skoe khoziaistvo Rossii v XX veke.* Moscow, 1923.

Okun', S. B., ed. *Krest'ianskoe dvizhenie v Rossii v 1850–1856 gg.: Sbornik dokumentov.* Moscow, 1962.

Oppenheim, Samuel A. "The Making of a Right Communist—A. I. Rykov to 1917," *Slavic Review* 36, no. 3 (September 1977): 420–40.

Osipov, V. A., ed. *1917 god v Saratovskoi gubernii: Sbornik dokumentov, fevral' 1917–dekabr' 1918 gg.* Saratov, 1957.

Ostrovskii, V. B., ed. *Lenin i Saratovskii krai: sbornik dokumentov i materialov.* Saratov, 1975.

Ovrutskaia, S. Sh. "Politicheskoe bankrotstvo eserov na vyborakh v Uchreditel'noe sobranie (Po materialam Saratovskoi gubernii." In *Nekotorye voprosy otechestvennoi i vseobshchei istorii,* pp. 42–59, Saratov, 1971.

————. "Proval politiki kontrrevoliutsionnoi voenshchiny v iiule–avguste 1917 g." *Istoricheskie zapiski* 87 (1971): 351–82.

P. S., comp. "Khronika Oktiabr'skoi revoliutsii v Saratove." *Kommunisticheskii put',* no. 19, pt. 1 (1927): 29–36; no. 20, pt. 2 (1927): 111–25.

Panov, A. V. "Nachal'noe narodnoe obrazovanie v Saratovskoi gubernii." *Obrazovanie,* nos. 7–8, sec. 2 (1901): 103–28.

————. "Shag vpered: zasedanie uchilishchnoi komissii Saratovskago uezdnago zemstvo pri uchastii uchitelei." *Obrazovanie,* no. 12, sec. 2 (1901): 31–42.

————. "Voprosy narodnago obrazovaniia na gubernskom zemskom sobranii (pis'mo iz Saratova)." *Obrazovanie,* no. 2, sec. 3 (1902): 30–38.

Panteleev, L. F. *Vospominaniia.* Moscow, 1958.

Pearson, Thomas S. "The Origins of Alexander III's Land Captains: A Reinterpretation." *Slavic Review* 40, no. 3 (Fall 1981): 384–403.

Perepiska V. I. Lenina i redaktsii gazety "Iskra" s sotsial-demokraticheskimi organizatsiiami v Rossii, 1900–1903 gg. 3 vols. Moscow, 1969–70.

Perepiska V. I. Lenina i rukovodimykh im uchrezhdenii RSDRP s partiinimi organizatsiiami 1903–1905 gg.: Sbornik dokumentov. 3 vols. Moscow, 1974–77.

Perrie, Maureen. *The Agrarian Policy of the Russian Socialist-Revolutionary Party from Its Origins through the Revolution of 1905–1907.* Cambridge, Eng., and New York, 1976.

Pershin, P. N. *Agrarnaia revoliutsiia v Rossii.* 2 vols. Moscow, 1966.

Pervoe maia: Sbornik vospominanii. Bk. 2. Saratov, 1922.

Petrov, Z. "Saratovskii proletariat v bor'be za vlast'." In *1917 god v Saratove,* pp. 5–30, Saratov, 1927.

Bibliography

Petrovskoe uezdnoe zemstvo. *Deloproizvodstvo ekstrennogo Petrovskago uezdnago zemskago sobraniia sessii 6 i 7 marta 1905 g.* Petrovsk, 1905.

Petrovskoe uezdnoe zemstvo. *Protokoly Petrovskago uezdnago zemskago sobraniia 4–12 avgusta 1905 goda.* Petrovsk, 1905.

Piatnitsky, O. *Memoirs of a Bolshevik.* New York, n.d.

Pirumova, N. M. *Zemskaia intelligentsiia i ee rol' v obshchestvennoi bor'be do nachala XX v.* Moscow, 1986.

Pisarevskii, G. G. "Iz istorii inostrannoi kolonizatsii v Rossii v XVIII v." *Zapiski Moskovskogo arkheologicheskogo instituta* 5 (1909): 182–204.

Piskanov, N. K., and O. V. Tsekhnovitser, eds. *Shestidesiatie gody: Materialy po istorii literatury i obshchestvennomu dvizheniiu.* Moscow and Leningrad, 1940.

Plekhanov, G. V. "Russkii rabochii v revoliutsionnom dvizhenii (po lichnym vospominaniiam)." In his *Sochineniia*, 3:122–207. 24 vols. Moscow, 1923–28.

Poltavskii, S. "O Saratovskom Maiake." *Otkliki*, no. 12 (1913): 13–14.

Polveka nazad: Vospominaniia uchastnikov revoliutsionnykh sobytii 1905 goda v Saratovskoi gubernii. Saratov, 1955.

Ponomarchuk, I. I. *Kuznetskii uezd posle Fevral'skoi revoliutsii.* Kuznetsk, 1958.

Popov, Konstantin I. "Zapiski o Saratove K. I. Popova." *Saratovskii krai*, no. 1 (1893): 168.

Porokh, I. V. *Istoriia v cheloveke: N. A. Mordvinov—deiatel' obshchestvennogo dvizheniia v Rossii 40–80 godov XIX v.* Saratov, 1971.

Poteten'kin, P. M. *Krest'ianskie volneniia v Saratovskoi gubernii v 1861–1863 gg.* Saratov, 1940.

Pozoiskaia, V. N. "Bor'ba bol'shevikov pod rukovodstvom V. I. Lenina protiv otzovistov i ul'timatistov po voprosu dumskoi taktiki (1907–1910 gg.)." *Uchenye zapiski Saratovskogo gosudarstvennogo universiteta* 59 (1958): 159–80.

———. "Saratovskaia partiinaia organizatsiia v gody tsarskoi reaktsii (1907–1910 gg.)." *Povolzhskii krai*, no. 4 (1975): 39–62.

Praetorius, Max. *Galka eine deutsche Ansiedlung an der Wolga.* Leipzig, 1912.

Presniakov, I."Iz podpol'ia na prostor." *Partiinyi sputnik*, nos. 9–10 (1923): 68–72.

Pribyleva-Korba, Anna. *Aleksandr D. Mikhailov.* Leningrad-Moscow, 1925.

"Professional'nye soiuzy Saratovskoi gubernii za 10 let." *Nizhnee Povolzh'e*, no. 10 (1927): 151–76.

Prokopovich, S. "Formy i rezul'taty agrarnago dvizheniia v 1906 godu." *Byloe* 2, no. 1 (13) (1907): 155–77.

Pronshtein, A. P., ed. *Don i Nizhnoe Povolzh'e v period krest'ianskoi voiny 1773–75 gg.* Rostov-on-Don, 1961.

Protokoly delegatskago soveshchaniia Vserossiiskago Krest'ianskago Soiuza 6–10 noiabria 1905 v Moskve. Moscow, 1906.

Protokoly pervoi obshchepartiinoi konferentsii P.S.-R.: Avgust 1908. Paris, 1908.

Protokoly vtorogo delegatskago s"ezda Vserossiiskago soiuza uchitelei i deiatelei po narod-nomu obrazovaniiu, 26–29 dekabria, 1905 goda. St. Petersburg, 1906.

Protokoly zasedaniia Saratovskogo Voennogo Komiteta. Saratov, 1917.

Protopopov, D. D. *Istoriia Sankt-Peterburgskago Komiteta gramotnosti, sostoiavshago pri Imperatorskom Vol'nom Ekonomicheskom obshchestve (1861–1895).* St. Petersburg, 1898.

Pushkareva, I. M. *Zheleznodorozhniki Rossii v burzhuazno-demokraticheskikh revoliut-siiaky.* Moscow, 1975.

Pushkin, A. S. *The History of Pugachev.* Trans. Earl Sampson. Ann Arbor, Mich., 1983.

Rakitnikova, N. "Ocherk istorii narodnago obrazovaniia v Balashovskom u." *Saratovskaia zemskaia nedelia,* no. 8, sec. 2 (1902): 25–46.

Rakitnikova, I. "Revoliutsionnaia molodezh' 90-kh godov na rabote v derevne." In *Narodovol'tsy 80-kh i 90-kh godov,* 2: 157–77. 2 vols. Moscow, 1929.

————. "Revoliutsionnaia rabota v krest'ianstve v Saratovskoi gubernii v 1900–1902 gg." *Katorga i ssylka,* no. 10 (47) (1928): 7–17.

Raleigh, Donald J. "Revolutionary Politics in Provincial Russia: The Tsaritsyn 'Republic' in 1917." *Slavic Review* 40, no. 2 (1981): 194–209.

————. *Revolution on the Volga: 1917 in Saratov.* Ithaca, N.Y., 1986.

Raleigh, Donald J., ed. *A Russian Civil War Diary: Alexis Babine in Saratov, 1917–1922.* Durham, N.C., 1988.

Rashitov, F. A. "Osnovnye etapy Sovetskogo stroitel'stva v Saratovskoi gubernii v pervoi polovine 1918 goda." In *Materialy k nauchnoi konferentsii aspirantov i molodykh nauchnykh sotrudnikov,* no. 1 (Saratov, 1965): 1–48.

Razgon, A. I. "O sostave sovetov Nizhnego Povolzh'ia v marte–aprele 1917 g." In *Sovety i soiuz rabochego klassa i krest'ianstva v Oktiabr'skoi revoliutsii,* pp. 83–122, Moscow, 1964.

Reichman, Henry. *Railwaymen and Revolution: Russia, 1905.* Berkeley, Calif., 1987.

Revoliutsiia 1905–1907 gg. v Rossii: Dokumenty i materialy. 15 vols. Moscow, 1955–63.

Revoliutsionnaia situatsiia v Rossii v seredine XIX veka: Kollektivnaia monografiia. Moscow, 1978.

Revoliutsionnaia situatsiia v Rossii v 1859–1861 gg. 9 vols. Moscow, 1960–86.

Rimlinger, Gaston V. "The Management of Labor Protest in Tsarist Russia, 1870–1905." *The International Review of Social History* 5 (1961): 226–48.

Rossiia: polnoe geograficheskoe opisanie nashego otechestva. Ed. V. P. Semenov-Tian'-Shanskii. 19 vols. St. Petersburg, 1899–1913. Vol. 6 includes Saratov Province.

Rossov, N. "Saratovskoe Gubernskoe Zemstvo v 1905 godu." *Saratovskaia zemskaia nedelia,* no. 9 (1905): 1–29; nos. 10–12 (1905): 1–40.

Rubashkina, G. "Vol'skaia organizatsiia SDRP (bol'shevikov)." *Vestnik Sara-tovskogo Gubkoma RKP,* no. 5 (30) (1923): 80–81.

Rumiantsev, E. D. "Fabrichno-zavodskaia militsiia i ee deiatel'nost' v Povolzh'e (mart–leto 1917 g.)." In *Ocherki istorii narodov Povolzh'ia i Priural'ia,* no. 4, pp. 78–88, Kazan, 1972.

————. "Rabochaia militsiia i Krasnaia gvardiia Povolzh'ia v bor'be za vlast' Sovetov." Dissertation, Kazan University, 1971.

"The Russian Peasantry in 1907–1908: A Survey by the Socialist Revolutionary Party." Trans. Maureen Perrie. *History Workshop* 4 (Autumn 1977): 17–191.

S—v, I. "Stranichka iz istorii nashei smuty: ('Malinovskoe delo')." *Istoricheskii vestnik* 29 (May 1908): 550–57.

Saar, G. P. "Pervye popytki sotsial-demokraticheskoi raboty sredi Saratovskikh rabochikh." *Proletarskaia revoliutsiia,* no. 4 (75) (1928): 128–53.

————. "Saratovskaia organizatsiia RSDRP do 1907 g." *Vestnik Saratovskogo Gubkoma RKP(b),* no. 3 (1923): 38–42.

————. "Saratovskaia organizatsiia RSDRP v nachale 900-kh gg." *Proletarskaia revoliutsiia,* nos. 11–12 (82–83) (1928): 112–32.

————. "Vozniknovenie Saratovskoi organizatsii RSDRP." *Proletarskaia revoliutsiia,* nos. 6–7 (77–78) (1928): 265–92.

Sanders, Jonathan. "Lessons from the Periphery: Saratov, January 1905." *Slavic Review* 46, no. 2 (Summer 1987): 229–44.

Sanin, A. "'Samarskii vestnik' v rukakh marksistov (1896–1897 gg.)." *Proletarskaia revoliutsiia,* no. 12 (35) (1924): 248–82.

Sapir, Boris, ed. *Vpered! 1873–1877: Materialy iz arkhiva V. N. Smirnova.* 2 vols. Dordrecht, Netherlands, 1970.

Sapronov, T. V. "Tri mesiatsa na Volge (1916)." *Proletarskaia revoliutsiia,* no. 8 (43) (1925): 216–37.

Saratovets [I. I. Mainov]. "Saratovskii semidesiatnik: Iz vospominanii." *Minuvshie gody,* no. 1 (1908): 244–76; no. 3 (1908): 171–208; no. 4 (1908): 252–82.

"Saratovskaia guberniia." *Entsiklopedicheskii slovar'.* Ed. F. A. Brokgauz and I. A. Efron, 28: 403–11. 82 vols. St. Petersburg, 1890–1904.

Saratovskii gubernskii statisticheskii komitet. *Pamiatnaia knizhka Saratovskoi Gubernii na 1872 god.* Saratov, 1873.

Saratovskii gubernskii statisticheskii komitet. *Statisticheskii obzor Saratovskoi Gubernii za 1895–1911.* Saratov, 1895–1912.

Saratovskii gubernskii statisticheskii komitet. *Saratovskii sbornik: Materialy dlia izucheniia Saratovskoi gubernii.* Saratov, 1881.

Saratovskoe gubernskoe zemstvo. *Materialy dlia otsenki zemel' Saratovskoi gubernii.* 3 vols. Saratov, 1905–10.

Saratovskoe gubernskoe zemstvo. *Protokol ot 9, 10 i 11-go ianvaria 1905 g. komissii, izbrannoi Gubernskim Zemskim Sobraniem po povodu tekushchikh sobytii politicheskago kharaktera.* Saratov, 1905.

Saratovskoe gubernskoe zemstvo. *Sbornik statisticheskikh svedenii po Saratovskoi gubernii.* 12 vols. Saratov, 1883–97.

Saratovskoe gubernskoe zemstvo. *Sbornik svedenii po Saratovskoi gubernii za 1904 god.* 2 vols. Saratov, 1905.

Saratovskoe gubernskoe zemstvo. *Sbornik svedenii po Saratovskoi gubernii za 1905 god.* 3 vols. Saratov, 1905–06.

Saratovskoe gubernskoe zemstvo. *Sbornik svedenii po Saratovskoi gubernii za 1906 god.* 2 vols. Saratov, 1906.

Saratovskoe gubernskoe zemstvo. *Zhurnaly ekstrennago Saratovskago Gubernskago Zemskago sobraniia 26 avgusta 1904 goda. Saratov, 1904.*

Saratovskoe gubernskoe zemstvo. *Zhurnaly ekstrennago Saratovskago Gubernskago Zemskago sobraniia 15–20 marta 1905 goda.* Saratov, 1905.

Saratovskoe gubernskoe zemstvo. *Zhurnaly ocherednogo Saratovskago Gubernskago Zemskago sobraniia 1905 goda.* Saratov, 1906.

Saratovskoe gubernskoe zemstvo. *Zhurnaly Saratovskago Gubernskago zemskago sobraniia sessii 28–29 maia 1904 goda.* Saratov, 1904.

Saratovskoe uezdnoe zemstvo. *Zhurnaly ocherednogo chrezvychainago Saratovskago uezdnago zemskago sobraniia v 1907 godu.* Saratov, 1908.

Sazhin, V N. "Literaturnyi fond v gody revoliutsionnoi situatsii." In *Epokha Chernyshevskogo: Revoliutsionnaia situatsiia v Rossii v 1859–1861 gg.*, pp. 138–57, Moscow, 1978.

Sbornik ves' Kuznetsk. Kuznetsk, 1927.

Semenov, M. I. "1905 god v Saratovskoi gubernii (Vospominaniia)." *Proletarskaia revoliutsiia,* no. 3 (50) (1926): 197–217.

Serebriakov, V. "Sovremennoe sostoianie russkoi derevni i eia nuzhdy po otzyvam sel'skikh zhitelei." *Saratovskaia zemskaia nedelia,* no. 5, sec. 3 (1905): 90–110; nos. 10–12, sec. 3 (1905): 1–32.

Seregny, Scott J. "Politics and the Rural Intelligentsia in Russia: A Biographical Sketch of Stepan Anikin, 1869–1919." *Russian History* 7, pts. 1–2 (1980): 169–200.

———. "Revolutionary Strategies in the Russian Countryside: Rural Teachers and the Socialist Revolutionary Party on the Eve of 1905." *Russian Review* 44, no. 3 (1985): 221–38.

———. *Russian Teachers and Peasant Revolution: The Politics of Education in 1905.* Bloomington, Ind., 1989.

"S"ezd uchitelei Balashovskago uezda." *Saratovskaia zemskaia nedelia,* no. 4, sec. 2 (1903): 1–45.

"S"ezd uchitelei Kamyshinskago uezda (Doklad gub. Zem. Uprave z.m. Predsedatelia Upravy A. D. Iumatova)." *Saratovskaia zemskaia nedelia,* nos. 38–41, sec. 2 (1901): 16–23.

Shablin, V. N. "Iz istorii obshchestvennogo dvizheniia v Saratove v nachale 60-kh godov XIX v. (Gimnazicheskie volneniia v Saratove v 1862–1863 gg.)."

In *Nekotorye voprosy otechestvennoi i vseobshchei istorii,* ed. V. M. Gokhlerner, pp. 60–70. Saratov, 1971.

Shakhmatov, A. I., comp. *Istoricheskie ocherki goroda Saratova i ego okrugi.* Saratov, 1891.

Shakhovskoi, D. I."Soiuz osvobozhdeniia." *Zarnitsy,* no. 2 (1909).

Shanin, Teodor. *The Awkward Class: Political Sociology of Peasantry in a Developing Society: Russia, 1910–1925.* Oxford, 1972.

Shapkarin, A. V., ed. *Krest'ianskoe dvizhenie v Rossii v 1890–1900 gg.: Sbornik dokumentov.* Moscow, 1959.

———. *Krest'ianskoe dvizhenie v Rossii, iiun' 1907–iiul' 1914: Sbornik dokumentov.* Moscow and Leningrad, 1966.

Shatsillo, K. F. "The Pinkening of the Liberals at the Beginning of the First Russian Revolution." *Soviet Studies in History* 20, no. 3 (Winter 1981–82): 45–73.

Shchapov, A. P. *Sochineniia.* 3 vols. St. Petersburg, 1906–08.

Shchegol'kov. "Na zare: Sovetskaia vlast' v Serdobske (Vospominaniia ob Oktiabre)." *Kommunisticheskii put',* no. 9 (34) (1923): 51–62.

Shcherba, V. "K voprosu o podgotovke uchitel'skago personala." *Saratovskaia zemskaia nedelia,* nos. 6–7, sec. 3 (1903): 1–13.

Shestakov, A. V. *Naemnyi trud v sel'skom khoziaistve.* Moscow-Leningrad, 1924.

Shestakov, A. V., ed. *Sovety krest'ianskikh deputatov i drugie krest'ianskie organizatsii.* Vol. 2, *1917 god v derevne: Vospominanniia krest'ian.* Moscow and Leningrad, 1929.

Shidlovskii, G. L. "Vekhi zhizni K. S. Eremeeva." *Krasnaia letopis',* no. 3 (1931): 157–65.

Shirokova, V. V. *Ocherki istorii obshchestvennogo dvizheniia v Saratovskoi gubernii v poreformennyi period: material k kursu kraevedeniia.* Saratov, 1976.

———. *Partiia "Narodnogo prava".* Saratov, 1972.

Shishko, Leonid E. "K kharakteristike dvizheniia nachala 70-kh godov (Iz lichnykh vospominanii)." *Russkoe bogatstvo,* no. 10 (1906): 51–85.

Shmygin, I. P. *Bol'shevistskie organizatsii Srednego Povolzh'ia v bor'be za krest'ianskie massy v revoliutsii 1905–1907 gg.* Ul'ianovsk, 1962.

Shvetsova, E. A., comp. *Krest'ianskaia voina pod predvoditel'stvom Stepana Razina: sbornik dokumentov.* 4 vols. Moscow, 1954–76.

Sinel, Allen. "The Campaign for Universal Primary Education in Russia, 1890–1904." *Jahrbücher für Geschichte Osteuropas* 30, no. 4 (1982): 481–507.

Sinner, Peter. *Nemtsy nizhnego povolzh'ia.* Saratov, 1925.

Sleptsov, A. A. "Vospominaniia A. A. Sleptsova," ed. S. A. Reiser. In *N. G. Chernyshevskii: stat'i, issledovaniia i materialy,* ed. E. I. Pokusaev, et al., 3:249–82. 8 vols. Saratov, 1958–78.

Sletov, S. N. *K istorii vozniknoveniia partii sotsialistov-revoliutsionerov.* Petrograd, 1917.

Smirnov, Pavel. "Okladnaia rospis' piatiny po gorodu Saratovu 1634 g." *Trudy Saratovskoi uchenoi arkhivnoi komissii* 33 (1916): i–xxiii.

Smith, S. A. *Red Petrograd: Revolution in the Factories, 1917–18.* Cambridge, Eng., 1983.

Snytko, T. G. "Studencheskoe dvizhenie v russkikh universitetakh v nachale 60-kh godov i vosstanie 1863 g." In *Vosstanie 1863 g. i russko-pol'skie revoliutsionnye sviazi 60-kh godov: Sbornik statei i materialov,* ed. V. D. Koroliuka and I. S. Miller, pp. 176–322, Moscow, 1960.

Sokolov, I. S. *1905 god na Riazano-Ural'skoi zheleznoi doroge: Po vospominaniiam uchastnikov i materialam Saratovskogo gubernskogo arkhiva.* Saratov, 1925.

Sokolov, N. "Kratkii ocherk istorii Vserossiiskago soiuza uchitelei i deiatelei po narodnomu obrazovaniiu." *Vestnik soiuza uchitelei i deiatelei po narodnomu obrazovaniiu,* no. 2 (1905): 3–14.

Sokolov, N. S. *Raskol v Saratovskom krae.* Saratov, 1888.

Spiridovich, A. I. *Istoriia bol'shevizma v Rossii ot vozniknoveniia do zakhvatoi vlasti, 1883–1903–1917.* Paris, 1922.

———. *Partiia sotsialistov-revoliutsionerov i eia predshestvenniki, 1886–1916.* Moscow, 1918.

Spravochnaia kniga po nizshemu obrazovaniiu, God tret'ii (svedeniia za 1905 god). Comp. S. I. Antsyferov. St. Petersburg, 1908.

Spravochnaia kniga uchitel'skikh obshchestv vzaimopomoshchi. Moscow, 1905.

Stanchinskii, A. "Sotsial-demokraticheskoe podpol'e v Saratove i zhurnal 'Saratovskii rabochii' v 1899 g." *Proletarskaia revoliutsiia,* no. 2 (14) (1923): 87–108.

Starik [S. F. Kovalik]. "Dvizhenie revoliutsionnogo narodnichestva po bol'shemu protsessu (193-kh)." *Byloe,* no. 10 (1906): 1–30; no. 11 (1906): 30–72; no. 12 (1906): 56–81.

Stasov, Vladimir V. *Nadezhda Vasil'evna Stasova: vospominaniia i ocherki.* St. Petersburg, 1899.

Stolypin, A. P. *A. Stolypin, 1862–1911.* Paris, 1927.

Studentsov, Aleksandr. *Saratovskoe krest'ianskoe vosstanie 1905 goda. Iz vospominanii raz"ezdnogo agitatora.* Penza, 1926.

Sushitskii, V. A. "Iz istorii revoliutsionnoi deiatel'nosti A. Kh. Khristoforova v Saratove (organizatsiia rabochikh tovarishchestv)." *Katorga i ssylka,* no. 6 (13) (1924): 84–94.

———. "Saratovskaia sotsial-demokraticheskaia rabochaia gruppa (1898–1899 gg.)." *Saratovskii Gosudarstvennyi Oblastnoi Muzei,* no. 14 (1928): 1–5.

Sviatlovskii, V. "Professional'noe dvizhenie rabochikh v 1905 g." *Krasnaia letopis',* nos. 2–3 (1922): 165–96.

Sviridov, F. "Vneshkol'noe obrazovanie v Saratovskoi gubernii." *Obrazovanie,* nos. 5–6, sec. 2 (1901): 75–80.

Bibliography

Svod vysochaishikh otmetok po vsepoddaneishim otchetam za 1902 g. general-gubernatorov, gubernatorov, voennykh gubernatorov i gradonachal'nikov. St. Petersburg, 1905.

Tan [V. G. Bogoraz]. "Deputaty vtoroi Dumy: Ocherki i nabroski." *Russkoe bogatstvo,* no. 5, sec. 2 (1907): 90–108.

————. *Krasnoe i chernoe. Ocherki.* Moscow, 1907.

————. *Muzhiki v Gosudarstvennoi dume. Ocherki.* Moscow, 1907.

————. "Po gubernii bezpokoinoi." In his *Novoe krest'ianstvo: Ocherki derevenskikh nastroenii,* pp. 5–109. Moscow, 1905.

Teitel, Ia. L. "Sudy po agrarnym delam v gody reaktsii (Iz zapisok chlena okruzhn. suda)." *Letopis revoliutsii,* bk. 1 (1923), pp. 134–37.

Teziakov, N. I. "Iz vospominanii zemskikh vrachei: N. I. Teziakov." In *Ocherki istorii russkoi obshchestvennoi meditsiny,* ed. P. I. Kal'iu, pp. 239–62. Moscow, 1965.

————. "Otkhozhie promysly i rynki naima sel'skokhoziaistvennykh rabochikh v Saratovskoi gubernii." *Saratovskaia zemskaia nedelia,* no. 1, sec. 3 (1903): 1–39.

Tiumenev, A. I. *Ot revoliutsii k revoliutsii.* Leningrad, 1925.

Tiutiukhin, S. V. *Voina, mir, revoliutsiia: Ideinaia bor'ba v rabochem dvizhenii Rossii, 1914–1917 gg.* Moscow, 1972.

Tkacheva, N. K. "Iz istorii odnodvortsev v XVIII v." *Ezhegodnik po agrarnoi istorii vostochnoi evropy 1968 g.,* pp. 133–41. Leningrad, 1972.

Tomarev, V. I. *Bol'sheviki Povolzh'ia vo glave bor'by proletariev protiv tsarizma.* Volgograd, 1977.

————. "Pod"em rabochego dvizheniia v Povolzh'e v 1910–1914 gg." *Povolzhskii krai,* no. 1 (1972): 82–97.

————. "Tsaritsynskaia gruppa RSDRP mezhdu dvumia revoliutsiiami (1907–1917 gg.)." *Istoriko-kraevedcheskie zapiski,* no. 5 (1977): 4–53.

Troinitskii, N. A., comp. *Naselennyia mesta Rossiiskoi imperii v 500 i bolee zhitelei s ukazaniem vsego nalichnago v nikh naseleniia i chisla zhitelei preobladaiushchikh veroispovedanii, po dannym pervoi vseobshchei perepisi naseleniia 1897 g.* St. Petersburg, 1907.

Trudy mestnykh komitetov o nuzhdakh sel'skokhoziaistvennoi promyshlennosti. Vol. 37 (Saratov Province). 58 vols. St. Petersburg, 1903.

Trudy I-go vserossiiskago s"ezda predstavitelei obshchestv vspomoshchestvovaniia litsam uchitel'skago zvaniia. Ed. V. M. Evteev. 2 vols. Moscow, 1907.

Trudy vtorogo s"ezda Upolnomochennykh Dvorianskikh Obshchestv 31 gubernii 14–18 noiabria 1906 g. St. Petersburg, 1906.

Tsentral'noe statisticheskoe upravlenie. *Rossiia v mirovoi voine, 1914–1918 goda (v tsifrakh).* Moscow, 1925.

Tsentral'nyi statisticheskii komitet. *Pervaia vseobshchaia perepis' naseleniia Rossiiskoi Imperii, 1897 g.* Ed. N. A. Troinitskii. Vol 38 (Saratov). 89 vols. in 24. St. Petersburg, 1899–1905.

Tsentral'nyi statisticheskii komitet. *Spiski naselennykh mest Rossiiskoi Imperii.* Vol. 38 (Saratov). 47 vols. in 42. St. Petersburg, 1861–85.

Tsentral'nyi statisticheskii komitet M.V.D. *Ezhegodnik Rossii 1908 g.* St. Petersburg, 1909.

Tsentral'nyi statisticheskii komitet M.V.D. *Statistika zemlevladeniia 1905 g.* St. Petersburg, 1906.

Tulupov, N. V. "Kurskaia vystavka po narodnomu obrazovaniiu." *Russkaia mysl',* no. 8, sec. 2 (1902): 108–26.

Ukreplenie nadelov v lichnuiu sobstvennost' v Kazanskoi gubernii. Kazan, 1911.

Ul'ianov, G. "Vospominaniia o M. A. Natansone." *Katorga i ssylka,* no. 4 (89) (1932): 62–76.

Uolling, Vill'iam E. [William E. Walling]. *Poslanie Rossii (Istinnoe znachenie Russkoi Revoliutsii).* Berlin, 1910.

Urlanik, V. Ts. "Dinamika naselaniia Rossii nakanune oktiabria." *Uchenye zapiski Vsesoiuznogo zaochno-ekonomicheskogo instituta,* no. 2 (1957): 113–34.

Ustroistvo pokazatel'nykh krest'ianskikh khoziaistv na khutorakh i otrubakh v Saratovskoi gubernii. Saratov, 1909.

Vakhterov, V. "Zaprosy narodnykh uchitelei i obshcheobrazovatel'nye kursy." In *Zemskie obshcheobrazovatel'nye kursy dlia uchitelei: sbornik statei.* St. Petersburg, 1906.

Varzar, V R. *Statistika stachek rabochikh na fabrikakh i zavodakh za trekhletie 1906–1908.* St. Petersburg, 1910.

Vasil'ev-Iuzhin, M. I. "Proletarskaia revoliutsiia v Saratove." *Sovetskoe stroitel'stvo,* nos. 10–11 (1927): 119–41.

Vas'kin, V. V. "Iz istorii bor'by za bol'shevizatsiiu Saratovskogo garnizona v 1917 godu." In *Materialy k nauchnoi konferentsii aspirantov i molodykh nauchnykh sotrudnikov.* Saratov, 1965.

———. "Kontrrevoliutsiia v bor'be za armiiu v 1917 g." In *Revoliutsionnoe dvizhenie v russkoi armii v 1917 godu: Sbornik statei,* ed. I. I. Mints et al., pp. 147–53. Moscow, 1981.

———. "Soldaty Nizhnego Povolzh'ia v Fevral'sko–martovskie dni 1917 goda." In *Iz istorii Saratovskogo Povolzh'ia,* ed. V. A. Osipov, pp. 92–110. Saratov, 1968.

Vas'kin, V. V., and G. A. Gerasimenko. *Fevral'skaia revoliutsiia v Nizhnem Povolzh'e (1917–pervaia polovnia 1918 gg.).* Saratov, 1966.

V boiakh za diktaturu proletariata: Sbornik vospominanii uchastnikov Oktiabria i grazhdanskoi voiny v Nizhnem Povolzh'e. Saratov, 1933.

Veselovskii, B. B. *Istoriia zemstva za sorok let.* 4 vols. St. Petersburg, 1909–11.

———. *Krest'ianskii vopros i krest'ianskoe dvizhenie v Rossii, 1902–1906 gg.* St. Petersburg, 1907.

Vodolagin, M. A. *Krasnyi Tsaritsyn.* Volgograd, 1967.

———. *Ocherki istorii Volgograda, 1589–1967.* Moscow, 1968.

Bibliography

Volga ot Tveri do Astrakhani. St. Petersburg, 1862.

Volkov, N. [I. I. Mainov]. "Iz zhizni saratovskikh kruzhkov." *Byloe,* no. 4 (May 1903): 3–21.

"Voprosy narodnago obrazovaniia na XXXVI ocherednom Gubernskom Zemskom Sobranii." *Saratovskaia zemskaia nedelia,* no. 2, sec. 2 (1902): 7–27.

Voskresenskii. "Narodnoe obrazovanie na uezdnykh zemskikh sobraniiakh sessii 1905 goda." *Saratovskaia zemskaia nedelia,* nos. 10–12, sec. 2 (1905): 40–52.

Vosstanie 1863 goda: Materialy i dokumenty; russko-pol'skie revoliutsionnye sviazi. 2 vols. Moscow, 1963.

Vrachebno-sanitarnaia khronika Saratovskoi gubernii. Saratov, 1905.

Vul'fson, G. N. *Raznochinno-demokraticheskoe dvizhenie v Povolzh'e i na Urale v gody pervoi revoliutsionnoi situatsii.* Kazan, 1974.

———. "Soratnik N. G. Chernyshevskogo P. A. Rovinskii i Kazanskoe otdelenie 'Zemli i Voli.'" *Revoliutsionnaia situatsiia v Rossii v 1859–1861 gg.,* 8:134–47. Moscow, 1979.

Wade, Rex A. *Red Guards and Workers' Militias in the Russian Revolution.* Stanford, Calif., 1984.

Wildman, Allan K. *The End of the Russian Imperial Army: The Old Army and the Soldiers' Revolt, March–April 1917.* Princeton, N.J., 1980.

———. "Lenin's Battle with Kustarnichestvo: The *Iskra* Organization in Russia." *Slavic Review* 23, no. 3 (1963): 479–503.

Williams, Hattie P. *The Czar's Germans, With Particular Reference to the Volga Germans.* Denver, 1975.

Woehrlin, William F. *Chernyshevsky: The Man and the Journalist.* Cambridge, Mass., 1971.

Yaney, George L. *The Systematization of Russian Government.* Urbana, Ill., 1973.

Zaionchkovskii, P. A. *Krizis samoderzhaviia na rubezhe 1870–1880 godov.* Moscow, 1964.

———. *Provedenie v zhizn' krest'ianskoi reformy 1861 g.* Moscow, 1958.

———. *Rossiiskoe samoderzhavie v kontse XIX stoletiia.* Moscow, 1970.

"Zakliuchenie prokurora Peterburgskoi sudebnoi palaty, Fuksa, po delu 'Obshchestvo druzei' ot 10 dekabria 1877." *Istoriko-revoliutsionnyi sbornik* 3 (1926): 63–106.

Za vlast' Sovetov. Vospominaniia uchastnikov revoliutsionnykh sobytii 1917 goda v Saratovskoi gubernii. Ed. G. Sukharev et al. Saratov, 1957.

Zelnik, Reginald E. *Labor and Society in Tsarist Russia: The Factory Workers of St. Petersburg, 1855–1870.* Stanford, Calif., 1971.

———. "Russian Bebels: An Introduction to the Memoirs of Semen Kanatchikov and Matvei Fisher." *Russian Review* 25, no. 3 (July 1976): 249–89; no. 4 (October 1976): 417–47.

Zelnik, Reginald E., ed. and trans. *A Radical Worker in Tsarist Russia: The Autobiography of Semen Ivanovich Kanatchikov.* Stanford, Calif., 1986.

Zhelvakova, I. A. "Saratovskii pomeshchik o khode reformy 19 fevralia 1861 g." *Revoliutsionnaia situatsiia v Rossii v 1859–1861 gg.* 4 (Moscow, 1965): 450–53.

Zhilkin, I. "Iz golodnago kraia: Pis'mo v redaktsiiu." *Vestnik Evropy* 47, no. 2 (1912): 261–96.

Zhulev, P. "Uchitel'skie obshchestva vzaimopomoshchi." *Russkaia shkola,* no. 1 (1912): 1–20.

Zhurnaly uchilishchnoi komissii Saratovskago uezdnago zemstva pri uchastii gg. uchashchikh zemsko-obshchestvennykh uchilishch Saratovskago uezda. Saratov, 1901.

Zven'ia: Sbornik materialov i dokumentov po istorii literatury, iskusstva i obshchestvennoi mysli XIX veka. 8 vols. Moscow-Leningrad, 1932–36, 1950.

Zviagintsev, E. "K zakrytiiu 'Saratovskoi zemskoi nedeli.'" *Saratovskaia zemskaia nedelia,* nos. 10–12 (1905): 12–20.

———. "Letnye uchitel'skie kursy." *Vestnik vospitaniia,* no. 1 (1912): 115–55: no. 2 (1912): 71–92.

Contributors

THOMAS FALLOWS earned his Ph.D. in history at Harvard University in 1981. He has published a number of articles and book reviews on zemstvo and gentry politics in Russia at the turn of the century. Since 1981 he has worked in international banking and is currently a vice president in corporate finance at Citibank in Milan, Italy.

GRIGORII ALEKSEEVICH GERASIMENKO studied and taught at Saratov University, where he wrote a number of monographs on peasant organizations, the soviets, and other aspects of the 1917 revolution in Saratov and the Volga region. He has since taught at the Higher Komsomol School and is currently chairman of the Department of the History of the USSR in the Academy of Social Sciences attached to the Central Committee of the Communist Party. His most recent book is *Bor'ba krest'ian protiv stolypinskoi argrarnoi politiki* [The Peasants' Struggle against the Stolypin Agrarian Policy] (Saratov, 1985).

JAMES G. HART received a Ph.D. in history from the University of Virginia in 1981 and has taught Russian and Soviet history for the past eight years at the University of the South in Sewanee, Tennessee. He is currently Director of Research and Records in the Office of University Relations at Sewanee. Hart has published articles on seventeenth- and eighteenth-century Russian frontier history and is writing a book on the rebellion led by "the Robin Hood of the Volga," Stepan Razin.

ALAN KIMBALL has recently been a visiting research scholar at the Slavic Research Center of Hokkaido University, a fellow at the Kennan Institute for Advanced Russian Studies, and Visiting Honors Professor at the United States Naval Academy. He teaches regularly at the University of Oregon and is currently finishing a book on the mobilization of political opposition in the Russian Empire in the middle of the nineteenth century. Kimball received his Ph.D. from the University of Washington in 1967.

JAMES W. LONG earned a Ph.D. in history from the University of Wisconsin in

1968 and is currently Professor of History at Colorado State University. He is the author of *The German-Russians* (ABC-Clio Press, 1978) and *From Privileged to Dispossessed: The Volga Germans, 1860–1917* (University of Nebraska Press, 1988), and has written several articles on French-Russian economic and political relations.

PAMELA SEARS MCKINSEY received her Ph.D. in modern Russian history in 1974 from the University of Missouri. She has published articles on early worker organization in Russia, Populism, and Russian cottage industry. She is currently a research associate of the Center for Russian and East European Studies at the University of Michigan, Ann Arbor.

MICHAEL MELANCON received his Ph.D. from Indiana University in 1985 and currently teaches Russian and Soviet history at Auburn University. He has published several articles on the Socialist Revolutionaries and related topics, and his book on the Socialist Revolutionaries during World War I and the February revolution is forthcoming.

TIMOTHY R. MIXTER is Assistant Professor of History at Temple University. He has published several articles on the peasantry and is coeditor of the forthcoming *Peasant Economy, Culture, and Politics of European Russia, 1800–1921*.

DONALD J. RALEIGH received his Ph.D. in history from Indiana University in 1978, and is currently Professor of Soviet History at the University of North Carolina, Chapel Hill. He is the author of *Revolution on the Volga: 1917 in Saratov* (Cornell University Press, 1986). Raleigh translated and edited E. N. Burdzhalov's *Russia's Second Revolution: The February 1917 Uprising in Petrograd* (Indiana University Press, 1987) and also edited and annotated *A Russian Civil War Diary: Alexis Babine in Saratov, 1917–1922* (Duke University Press, 1988).

SCOTT J. SEREGNY received a Ph.D. in history from the University of Michigan in 1982 and is currently Associate Professor of History at Indiana University at Indianapolis. He has written articles on the rural intelligentsia and peasant politics in late Imperial Russia and is the author of *Russian Teachers and Peasant Revolution: The Politics of Education in 1905* (Indiana University Press, 1989).

REX A. WADE is Professor of Russian History at George Mason University. He is the author of *The Russian Search for Peace, February–October 1917* (Stanford University Press, 1969) and of *Red Guards and Workers' Militias in the Russian Revolution* (Stanford University Press, 1984), as well as numerous articles on the Russian Revolution and revolutionary movement. He received his Ph.D. from the University of Nebraska in 1963.

ALLAN K. WILDMAN received his Ph.D. from the University of Chicago in 1961 and is Professor of History at the Ohio State University. He is the author of *The Making of a Workers' Revolution: Russian Social Democracy, 1891–1903* (University of Chicago Press, 1967); *The End of the Russian Imperial Army: The Old Army and the Soldiers' Revolt, March–April 1917* (Princeton University Press, 1980); and *The End of the Russian Imperial Army: The Road to Power and Peace* (Princeton University Press, 1987). He is currently editor of *The Russian Review.*

Index

238–43; market factors and, 196–98, 200, 243, 262–63; Populism and, 52–56, 59–62, 63–64, 78–80, 90–91; rent and labor strikes in 1906, 229, 231, 236–37; response to emancipation, 37–40, 50, 193–94, 351n. 37, 355n. 14; Revolution of 1905, 106–11, 180–81, 191–232 passim, 371n. 89, 388n. 60; Revolution of 1917, 286–88, 294, 302–3, 337–38; and revolutionary parties, 90–93, 107–12, 205–6, 216–17, 231–32; and rural teachers, 121–38; Russo-Japanese War, 195–96, 376n. 46; and State Duma, 220–24, 231; Stolypin's agrarian reform, 233–54; temperance movements, 36–37, 227; and Third Element, 204–5, 212; village cohesion, 198–200. *See also* Agrarian reform; Peasant Union; Volga Germans

Pel'konen, Iogan (Johan), 53–54
Penza Province, 51–52, 191
People's Will, 70–71, 74, 77, 83
People's Will, New, 78
Perovskaia, Sof'ia, 196
Peshekhonov, A. V., 77
Petersburg. *See* St. Petersburg
Petition campaign, 133, 209–11, 385n. 14
Petrograd. *See* St. Petersburg
Petrov, A. A., 105
Petrovsk District: early history, 15, 18, 22, 25, 26; twentieth century, 181, 197–98, 201–2, 205, 224, 287
Petrovsk Zemstvo Economic Council, 169, 174–76, 212
Plehve, V. K., 89, 113, 114, 125
Plekhanov, Georgii V., 57, 60; in Saratov, 6, 51, 62–64, 65–68, 71–72, 358n. 63
Pleshcheev, Aleksei, 30, 31
Plotnikov cast-iron foundry, 55, 67
Podgornov, N. M., 136
Pokrovskaia Sloboda (Samara Province), 90, 97
Poles, 256–57, 270, 283, 286
Poliak, V. N., 165, 179, 184
Polivanov, P. S., 55, 64–65, 69, 70

Poltava Province. *See* Kharkov and Poltava provinces
Pontriagin, Lieutenant, 319
Popov, Konstantin, 142
Population: character, 2, 74–75, 256–57; impact of World War I on, 255–63; size, 4, 5, 17, 193, 256–58, 263, 346n. 26
Populism (Populists), 6, 7, 49, 333–34, 339; efforts to organize peasants, 52, 61–62, 78–80, 90–93; efforts to organize workers, 50–51, 64–68, 68–70, 83; neo-populists, 74, 75–78; Saratov city organization, 52–55, 64–69; use of workers among peasants, 55–56, 59–62, 63–64. *See also* Black Repartition; Chaikovskii Circle; Land and Liberty; Lavrov, Peter; People's Will; Socialist Revolutionary Party
Potapov, General Alexander, 28, 34, 40, 45
Privolzhskaia gazeta (The Volga-Region Newspaper), 266
Proletarii Povolzh'ia (The Proletariat of the Volga Region), 283
Provincial capital, establishment of, 10, 21, 25, 27, 345n. 21
Provisional Government, 279, 282, 283, 284, 296, 312, 337
Public Executive Committee (PEC, *Obshchestvennyi ispolnitel'nyi komitet*), 278–79, 280, 281–82, 285, 290, 308, 309, 310–13
Public opinion, 29–33, 40–44, 331–32, 276, 340. *See also* Social Organizations; Social Reform
Pugachev, Emelian, 3, 8, 10, 34, 53, 329; folk memories of, 50, 192–93; rebellion led by, 20–25, 26

Rabochaia gazeta (Workers' Gazette), 85
Radishchev, Alexander, 5, 35
Radishchev Museum, 5, 116
Radus-Zenkovich, V. A., 269
Railroads, 4, 6; and agrarian relations, 195, 197, 203
Railroad Union, All-Russian, 102
Railroad workers, 267, 307; in Revolu-